STYLE IN RHETORIC
AND COMPOSITION

STYLE IN RHETORIC AND COMPOSITION

A Critical Sourcebook

Paul Butler
University of Houston

BEDFORD / ST. MARTIN'S   Boston   •   New York

For Bedford/St. Martin's

Executive Editor: Leasa Burton
Editorial Assistant: Sarah Guariglia
Production Supervisor: Sarah Ulicny
Marketing Manager: Molly Parke
Project Management: DeMasi Design and Publishing Services
Text Design: Anna Palchik
Cover Design: Donna Lee Dennison
Composition: Jeff Miller Book Design
Printing and Binding: RR Donnelley & Sons Company

President: Joan E. Feinberg
Editorial Director: Denise B. Wydra
Editor in Chief: Karen S. Henry
Director of Marketing: Karen R. Soeltz
Director of Editing, Design, and Production: Marcia Cohen
Assistant Director of Editing, Design, and Production: Elise S. Kaiser

Library of Congress Control Number: 2009920855

Manufactured in the United States of America.

4 3 2 1 0 9
f e d c b a

For information, write: Bedford / St. Martin's, 75 Arlington Street, Boston, MA 02116 (617-399-4000)

ISBN-10: 0-312-54733-1
ISBN-13: 978-0-312-54733-2

ACKNOWLEDGMENTS
Acknowledgments and copyrights appear at the back of the book on pages 458–59, which constitute an extension of the copyright page.

Dedicated to Joseph M. Williams (1933–2008)

With gratitude for his many contributions to the field.

CONTENTS

INTRODUCTION
The Stylistic (Re)Turn in Rhetoric and Composition   *1*

**Part One   THE RISE AND FALL OF THE
STUDY OF STYLE**   *11*

Introduction   *13*

The Rise   *18*

1 On Prose Style   *18*
ARISTOTLE

2 From *Orator*   *37*
CICERO

3 Book X, Chapter 2   *54*
QUINTILIAN

The Fall   *59*

4 Apologies and Accommodations: Imitation and the
Writing Process   *59*
FRANK M. FARMER AND PHILLIP K. ARRINGTON

5 The Erasure of the Sentence   *82*
ROBERT J. CONNORS

6 Whatever Happened to the Paragraph?   *108*
MIKE DUNCAN

Part Two **STYLISTIC INFLUENCES AND DEBATES**   *133*

Introduction   *135*

7 Theories of Style and Their Implications for the
Teaching of Composition   *140*
LOUIS T. MILIC

8 A Generative Rhetoric of the Sentence   *146*
FRANCIS CHRISTENSEN

9 The Relation of Grammar to Style   *155*
VIRGINIA TUFTE

10 Closing the Books on Alchemy   *165*
MARTHA KOLLN

11 Use Definite, Specific, Concrete Language   *177*
RICHARD OHMANN

12 Defining Complexity   *186*
JOSEPH M. WILLIAMS

Part Three **STYLE AND PEDAGOGY**   *203*

Introduction   *205*

13 Teaching Style   *209*
EDWARD P. J. CORBETT

14 Grammars of Style: New Options in
Composition   *219*
WINSTON WEATHERS

15 Revitalizing Style: Toward a New Theory and
Pedagogy   *239*
ELIZABETH D. RANKIN

16 Making a Case for Rhetorical Grammar   *250*
    LAURA R. MICCICHE

17 Down from the Haymow: One Hundred Years of
    Sentence-Combining   *267*
    SHIRLEY K. ROSE

Part Four STYLE AND CULTURE *277*

    Introduction   *279*

18 "How I Got Ovuh": African World View and
    Afro-American Oral Tradition   *283*
    GENEVA SMITHERMAN

19 Professing Multiculturalism: The Politics of Style
    in the Contact Zone   *303*
    MIN-ZHAN LU

20 The Feminine Style: Theory and Fact   *318*
    MARY P. HIATT

21 The Cultures of Literature and Composition:
    What Could Each Learn from the Other?   *324*
    PETER ELBOW

Part Five STYLE AND THE FUTURE   *337*

    Introduction   *339*

22 Ancient and Contemporary Compositions
    That "Come Alive": Clarity as Pleasure,
    Sound as Magic   *343*
    T. R. JOHNSON

23 The National Prose Problem   *369*
    KATHRYN FLANNERY

24 Style and the Public Intellectual: Rethinking
    Composition in the Public Sphere   *389*
    PAUL BUTLER

25 Sounding the Other Who Speaks in Me: Toward a
   Dialogic Understanding of Imitation   *410*
   FRANK FARMER

26 Style/Substance Matrix   *428*
   RICHARD A. LANHAM

   ADDITIONAL READINGS   *449*

   ABOUT THE EDITOR   *457*

   INDEX   *461*

STYLE IN RHETORIC
AND COMPOSITION

INTRODUCTION

The Stylistic (Re)Turn in Rhetoric and Composition

Decades ago, in his presidential inaugural address, John F. Kennedy rallied Americans to dedicate themselves to public service with a sentence that has become a part of our national lexicon: "Ask not what your country can do for you; ask what you can do for your country." The phrase, whose call to volunteerism ultimately resulted in the start of the Peace Corps and similar initiatives, endures today not only because of its laudable purpose but also because of its *style*—that is, in two short clauses Kennedy reverses the order of repeated words, using a figure of speech known as *antimetabole* (sometimes also called *chiasmus*). The stylistic effect, achieved through the parallel rhythm and syntax of the words, is to make the sentence moving and memorable.

Regardless of whether students know the term *style*, they can easily recognize writing that has a powerful impact on them. The study of style, which is concerned with analyzing readers' responses to texts and how writers achieve those effects, can, in turn, give students knowledge of how to deploy similar techniques in their own writing.

Composition and literary scholar Richard Ohmann has defined style as "a way of writing," and his short definition, though just one of many, indicates what is really at stake with style: Given all the possible ways of conveying our meaning, how do we choose which ones to use? Style, then, involves a series of both conscious and unconscious choices that writers make about everything from the words we use (diction) and their arrangement in sentences (syntax) to the tone with which we express our point of view (e.g., ironic, formal, or colloquial) and the way we achieve emphasis in a sentence (e.g., by placing the most important information at the end). The figure of speech in Kennedy's address, another stylistic choice, is just one of hundreds of similar devices—like parallelism, alliteration, and metaphor—that writers use for specific effects. Style can thus be seen as a rich array of resources for writers, borrowing, for instance, from the fields of grammar, linguistics, psycholinguistics, and literature to achieve their aims. In composition, however, style, one of the five canons of rhetoric (along with invention, arrangement, delivery, and memory), is, above all, a *rhetorical* concept, meaning that it is connected to a writer's purpose, subject matter, audience, and context.

1

If style offers such a rich array of resources for readers and writers, then why is it relatively invisible today in the field of composition and rhetoric—and often in composition classrooms as well? The short answer is that style fell out of disciplinary favor among practitioners in the 1980s when it became associated with formalism and current-traditional rhetoric, and thus focused on the textual product and static language practices (e.g., mechanical correctness). Ironically, at the same time it was acquiring these pejorative affiliations—a period that paralleled composition's process era—some scholars were devising innovative techniques like sentence combining and generative rhetoric to connect style to invention and other forms of language production. Yet, style's decline also resulted from larger forces inside and outside the field. It got lost, for instance, amid the advent of new ideas from literary and rhetorical theory that caused an unprecedented bouleversement in disciplinary thinking about language and culture. Thus the study of style, competing in a climate of tremendous change, waned.

Despite its sometime disappearance from composition theory and pedagogy, however, style has reemerged in the twenty-first century as an area of significant interest in the field. Indeed, amid composition's various disciplinary reincarnations—the rhetorical turn, the public turn, the visual turn, and the digital turn, for example—another shift is now occurring: the *stylistic turn* in rhetoric and composition. What accounts for the renewed interest in style at this point in history, and why does its recent recuperation matter to composition students and instructors?

The answer, stated succinctly, is that style's recovery is an indispensable part of persuasive discourse, reinvigorated by such dynamic forces as culture, identity, dialect, oral discourse, genre, multimodal forms, and global influence. These areas, it has been suggested, constitute a "diaspora" of rhetoric and composition, areas where the study of style has migrated in the field (Butler 2007). Style, then, offers a way for composition to embrace the cacophony of difference that defines our field; stylistic pedagogy, the difference that defines our students. Stylistic difference is inherent in language variation, which allows the constantly changing influences—in words and phrases, new cultures and new media, for example—to hold sway.

If style thus stands at a pivotal moment in composition studies, then how is its 2,500-year history important in today's composition classroom? The answer is that throughout its history (which is too extensive to enumerate here), style has faced many of the same concerns important to current writing instructors and students. For example, does style simply mean the use of ornate words? Students are often taught not to use "flowery language," which contravenes our ideas of decorum and our preference for a plain (or "scientific") style. In ancient Greece, this very debate manifested itself in the development of two contrasting styles—the Attic, which embraced unadorned prose, and the Asiatic, which favored plentiful figures of speech. These opposing viewpoints eventually resulted in three "levels of style"—plain, middle, and grand—associated with proof, pleasure, and persuasion, respectively. Yet even the Roman orator Cicero, who favored the simpler Attic style, never considered these divisions rigid, thinking of them instead as "symphonic," according to Michael Halloran and Merrill Whitburn (1982), and necessary for the ideal orator. All writers today—from composition classrooms to professional writing contexts—face the same issues: Given the audience, is it more effective to use a formal style or a plain (even colloquial) one? If we want to reach more than one audience at the same time, how might we integrate different stylistic levels persuasively?

A second relevant debate follows closely from the first: Is style separate from meaning and thus simply added on as the "dress of thought"? Or do style and meaning form an organic whole? These questions are evident today, for instance, in different approaches to revision: Is it simply a process of "cleaning up" an essay at the end of the process, or does it involve a more comprehensive look at how our meaning is achieved through the essay's structure, paragraphs, and words? The problem goes as far back as Plato, who discussed style as excessive adornment, always added on to meaning, which alone could be "true" (see Neel 1988). In the sixteenth century, French philosopher Peter Ramus went even further, separating the canons of invention and arrangement from rhetoric and placing them instead under "dialectic," a category he considered more prestigious. Ramistic "rhetoric" thus became exclusively the province of delivery and style, whose concern with eloquent language deepened the meaning-style schism as well as style's negative reputation. Even today, style is often associated with "fluff," to use Richard Lanham's (2006) word. As a field, composition has not been able to escape these pejorative connotations, which may be another reason for style's disappearance from writing classrooms.

While the view of style as a degraded form of rhetoric, unconnected to content, may seem difficult to dislodge, a group of composition scholars working in the 1970s and 1980s, in a series of language experiments, did just that. In fact, these scholars emphasized the conjunction of style and meaning in devising a plethora of innovative pedagogies, including generative rhetoric, sentence-combining exercises using both cued and open formats, imitation exercises, and the ideas of tagmemic rhetoric, developed in Young, Becker, and Pike's (1970) textbook *Rhetoric: Discovery and Change*. All of these techniques were considered a part of invention and were designed to help students add details, complicate their ideas, and write more sophisticated sentences (to achieve "syntactic maturity"). With a few early exceptions, the pedagogies did not rely on extensive grammatical knowledge. They did, however, depend in large part on repeated practice in a series of textbook exercises for students. While evidence suggests that the exercises *worked*, their prosaic subject matter did not always coincide with the increasingly rhetorical nature of composition classrooms.

In fact, of the many reasons already cited for style's sudden vanishing from composition, one of the most significant is the disjuncture between stylistic exercises and the changing needs of composition classrooms. How can sentence-combining exercises, or any exercises, despite their effectiveness in improving writing fluency, respond to the unique needs of different classrooms and instructors seeking specific outcomes? In other words, how can style be integrated into the rhetorical situation of composition classes?

Some recent, edited collections in the field have tried to answer that question, either directly or indirectly, including *The Elements of Alternate Style*, *Alt Dis*, and *Refiguring Prose Style*. In addition, textbooks such as Joseph Williams's (2005) *Style: Ten Lessons in Clarity and Grace*, Martha Kolln's (2007) *Rhetorical Grammar*, and Richard Lanham's (2007) *Revising Prose* offer explanations with accompanying exercises for students. In *A Rhetoric of Pleasure: Prose Style and Today's Composition Classroom*, T. R. Johnson (2003) includes an appendix of exercises he uses with students, and in Part Three of this volume, the articles discuss various connections between style and pedagogical approaches in writing classrooms, some describing the stylistic assignments used with students. While instructors have understandably objected to the use of exercises unconnected to rhetorical purpose, many teachers interested in style attest to the usefulness of practice exercises in developing stylistic knowledge and acumen in student writers. Inevitably, then, we come back to the same central question: How can instructors use style pedagogy productively to help the students in our classrooms? Ideally, all instructors would design stylistic practice around their own students' work to help students learn. But how would one systematically approach such a task? Would it be effective? Who decides?

If the articles in this critical sourcebook raise these questions, they also provide potential answers. On a practical level, much of the recent work in style begins with analyzing some of the stylistic techniques used by writers—including student writers—and practicing ways to incorporate them into the process of writing essays. Imitation is advocated by several authors in this volume. However, unlike former examples, it is often taught today as a conversation that students can enter on the same level as established writers, whose work students appropriate and transform (see Lu and Farmer in this book). Another area is Johnson's idea of a sound- and voice-directed rhetoric of pleasure that captures the rhythms of oral speech and incorporates them into written discourse. A different strategy is to borrow more from the oral tradition and discourses that go beyond Standard English. In this collection, the work of Geneva Smitherman shows, for example, how the use of indirection in African languages, frequently adapted in the informal oral discourse of the African American community, can make writing more effective—and interesting. This use of oral discourse finds parallels in several other techniques that have already influenced new pedagogy—for instance, Winston Weathers's nontraditional array of stylistic options, known as Grammar B (see Part Three), as well as the idea of hybrid, mixed, or alternative discourses in the collection *Alt Dis*. These ideas suggest the future of teaching style in the field—not as a replacement for composition's rich stylistic tradition, but, on the contrary, as a complement.[1]

Why is such a stylistic reinvention important? The example from John F. Kennedy that begins this introduction gives some idea of style's significance. Even though Kennedy uttered his phrase approximately fifty years ago, it still resonates as a part of our cultural heritage. Why do we recall it vividly today along with the words of Martin Luther King Jr., Abraham Lincoln, Gloria Anzaldúa, or Virginia Woolf? We remember them because of their style. Kennedy's use of antimetabole (or chiasmus) creates a repeated parallel structure that is difficult to forget. Style, in other words, makes writing memorable. It is never divorced from content, of course, since we rarely recall nonsensical words, no matter how clever they may be. But it is essential to see style for what it is: a key way to separate what is memorable from forgettable in history. On a narrower level, style is part of what makes writing persuasive, one of the goals we seek in our composition classrooms. The persuasive ability that stylistic study can develop, tied to emotional elements in writing, is never far from the broader reach of memory. If style has this impact on readers and writers, one might ask, then how can it have the same influence on the field? In the five parts of the collection that follow, various writers approach that question from different perspectives.

Part One, "The Rise and Fall of the Study of Style," which begins with a title alluding to the work of Robert Connors (1981, 2000), examines some of the rich possibilities that style provides for language and writing before moving to its disappearance, specifically from the field of composition. In classical rhetoric, the discussion of style goes hand in hand with the development of the ideal orator. Quintilian, for example, outlines this ethical dimension in other parts of his work when he discusses the idea of "the good man speaking well." While the qualities of style enumerated by the classical rhetors represent many of the same stylistic ideals we espouse today, the differences are also important. Besides showing that the way we think about style is culturally and historically determined, the articles suggest that values not only change but stay the same over time. The writers emphasize the view of style as a way of developing eloquence through a variety of stylistic means, including imitation. Even though we may not place the same value on eloquence today, its cultural power and importance in writing have not been abandoned, even if its definition has changed to accommodate a print-based society. Some have argued, of course, that the advent of a new orality in our technologized and globalized world has made their observations more relevant now than ever. Although the articles depicting the various ways style was valued in ancient Greece and Rome constitute the rise of the canon, the articles that comprise its fall also value style while asking what might have accounted for its untimely demise from composition. One of the common threads running through the fall is the failure to find a smoking gun, that is, a single event or reason that clearly explains style's disappearance or justifies its exorcism from the field. The articles about the fall also provide useful historical evidence of the importance of various practices in the field, indicate ongoing pockets of current activity, and propose possible avenues for style's revival.

Part Two, "Stylistic Influences and Debates," explores the possibilities and limitations of style in the discipline, particularly during a two-decade period (from the 1960s through the mid-1980s) that constitutes what some have called the "Golden Age" of style in the field. One universal theme in these readings is the belief that style has many pedagogical and theoretical possibilities that often work together in ways the authors investigate by inventive means. In a period of almost unparalleled optimism about the linguistic possibilities in the field, the study of style figured prominently. At the same time, these influences were not without their share of debate. These readings, often through various types of research conducted by the authors, attempt to refute some of the prevailing ideas about style present both inside and outside the field. Thus despite the enthusiasm with which the articles approach the possibilities of stylistic invention, they also signal a cautionary tale, asking readers to look behind the conventional wisdom that so often supported stylistic knowledge and practice at the time. In fact, one theme of these readings is that we should not always accept the way ideas have been taken up or accepted in the field. There is a tendency, they warn, not to question certain established beliefs, as though they are the final word on the subject. Given this warning, the readings here should be viewed not only in the context of the time in which they were written but also the intervening years during which ideas have changed. How have stylistic influences and debates evolved over the years? What remains in our belief systems about style, and what has fallen away? Are some ideas worth revisiting, given the changes in our disciplinary knowledge and the different needs of our students and of composition classrooms?

Part Three, "Style and Pedagogy," makes a number of overtures to innovative pedagogies of style, either opening up new territory altogether or rethinking some of the pedagogies that have been used since the time of classical rhetoric. Indeed, in a field with models that begin with the *progymnasmata*, a set of "elementary exercises" in ancient Greece and Rome (see Crowley and Hawhee 2009), the inventory of pedagogical possibilities available to those with an interest in style is impressive. One theme that runs throughout this set of readings is style's close connection to grammar, not in the sense that style requires explicit grammatical knowledge but, rather, in the ways style and grammar work together to produce writing achievement. The authors also demonstrate how pedagogy works closely with its theoretical underpinnings, with theory sometimes serving as the very basis of new stylistic teaching. What's more, influences from outside rhetoric and composition are evident in the readings, illustrating the way in which the field has been inculcated in the various critical theories circulating within the humanities. One of the main ideas throughout the readings is that style is constantly reinventing itself pedagogically, opening up new ways of writing to students in composition courses and encouraging, at the same time, a new way of thinking. Hence, in many respects, style serves as the catalyst for pedagogical invention, renewing the field in significant ways through teaching. As part of that process, the authors focus on making old pedagogies new, exploring applications to philosophical and ideological debates in the field, and thinking about where the study of style needs to go, why, and how its innovative uses are possible in a constantly changing field not always open to stylistic study.

Part Four, "Style and Culture," reflects the movement in composition and rhetoric to find connections between style and the enormous cultural changes that have affected the discipline. Far from being just incidental or superfluous, the cultural influences on style have been responsible for far-reaching developments reflecting, for example, new language policies in the field. In addition, culture suggests the important links, for instance, between style and identity, affirming the increasingly important nature of gender, race, social class, sexuality, and other identity markers in the field. Clearly, composition studies also has been drawn to the contestation of cultures, indicated best, perhaps, by Mary Louise Pratt's (1991) idea of the contact zone, and many of the readings are indebted to this concept as a productive force in the field. One of the questions surrounding style's future in the discipline concerns whether it functions as more than a conduit for the influence of outside cultures. The writers in this part begin to answer that question, looking at style as a force of negotiation and, even more importantly, as a force of change. In that regard, the readings take up one of the traditional definitions of style as deviation from a norm and, for all practical purposes, they embrace that view. Certainly the cultural currents in constant flux in society include influences on language that appear, like a maelstrom, to change with opposing linguistic and cultural forces. In the midst of this upheaval, no one is left unchanged or unaffected, including the discipline of composition and its relationship to style. The authors suggest, in fact, that those impacts emanate both from without and within the culture of composition studies. Thus the readings set the stage not only for the future of style but also for the future of the field itself as it stands buffeted constantly by outside forces, trying to withstand the crosscurrents that define and refine its disciplinary identity.

Part Five, "Style and the Future," contemplates the way in which style, as the inheritor of a number of changes and influences already, stands poised to move itself—and the discipline—into the twenty-first century. In that regard, the readings explore the new developments in stylistic study in the field, following its movements, for instance, into multimedia, visual rhetoric, the public sphere, and new theories or interpretations of stylistic theories. In these readings, the authors do not hesitate to articulate new visions of style for composition and rhetoric or to redeploy it in new, often creative, ways. Considered collectively, the readings represent a snapshot of the reemergence of style in the field over the past decade. They make an argument, simply by their compilation here, for the end of style's elision, at least from the standpoint of disciplinary identity. While the writers respond in unusual ways to established ideas from stylistic history, theory, and pedagogy, they also begin important new conversations with each other, anticipating, as it were, the potential of disciplinary change catalyzed through the study of style. The actual adoption and implementation of the ideas offered by these authors will take more time of course. These new approaches to stylistic study suggest, in fact, that the field, without forgetting its past affiliations with stylistic study, must leave behind some of its past conceptions and reimagine style in different ways in the future. At the same time, the readings represent a strong affirmation that style figures importantly in a growing, ever-evolving discipline. They suggest in no uncertain terms that the renaissance of stylistic study in the field is under way and will continue unabated in the years ahead.

Illustrating the importance of style in composition and rhetoric is the structuring principle of the different parts in this collection. While the study of style has broad historical reach and works across many disciplines, the intent with these essays is to show how stylistic study has been especially important in rhetoric and composition. Some other significant influences on style, for example, those from the fields of literature and linguistics, are listed in the Additional Readings section at the back of this book. That section also features the work of other rhetors who wrote on style in classical rhetoric. While this volume includes work by Aristotle, Cicero, and Quintilian, contributions from the Sophists and Plato, among others, are also listed in Additional Readings. In literature, two symposia at Indiana University in the 1960s, one of which produced Roman Jakobson's (1960) highly influential essay "Concluding Statement: Linguistics and Poetics," are listed, as is the work of Sister Miriam Joseph (2005), whose eloquent book on style in the Renaissance has recently enjoyed a second printing. In linguistics, influences like corpus analysis (see Enkvist, Spencer, and Gregory 1964), sociolinguistics (see Labov 1972), and the more recent work of the New London Group (2000) would, if space permitted, complement the collection nicely. Furthermore, an article on the plain language movement, a major force in government and business several years ago, could round out the articles, along with additional attention to language diversity—for example, the impact of World Englishes (see Cliett 2003).

While these five parts work successfully as independent representations of the collection's overall ideas, they also work together to present a new view of style in the discipline. Indeed, the sections, taken together, offer a rich, historical overview of style in rhetoric and composition, including its interdisciplinary influences. They also suggest a complicated notion of stylistic study as it has encountered the disciplinary forces that have shaped it and, at least for a short time, rendered it invisible. The canon of style, though seemingly inactive for some time, is moving forward at a rate that defies the perception that it ever disappeared from rhetoric and composition. Clearly, style has evolved into a flexible and definitive canon of rhetoric, forged in the past and future movements of the field. In that sense, it stands positioned to become one of the most important tools in the future of rhetoric and composition and one of the most valuable resources available to writing students and teachers.

Although the essays in this collection are representative of outstanding work on style, they necessarily cannot encompass the full breadth of material available on this far-reaching topic. However, the range of articles—not to mention the structure of the book—is far richer today because of the help of five outstanding reviewers. Their comments, questions, and suggestions were instrumental in shaping this volume, which has changed significantly from its original conception. I therefore owe a debt of gratitude to Stephen A. Bernhardt, University of Delaware, Deborah Rossen-Knill, University of Rochester, and three anonymous reviewers. I also am extremely grateful to Bedford/ St. Martin's for supporting the idea of this collection and for recognizing its importance to the field. I am particularly indebted to executive editor Leasa Burton, whose steadfast support for the volume has been instrumental in seeing it through all phases of its development, and editorial assistant Sarah Guariglia, who has offered highly insightful suggestions for revision. Both Leasa and Sarah have helped improve the collection in ways too numerous to mention. I also would like to thank other members of Bedford/St. Martin's for their support, including president Joan Feinberg, editorial director Denise Wydra, editor in chief Karen Henry, publishing services manager Emily Berleth, and assistant managing editor John Amburg. I am grateful as well to Frank Farmer, who generously suggested several articles that might be useful to include in this collection and also offered enormously helpful comments on the book's editorial content. My gratitude extends to Louise Wetherbee Phelps, whose thoughtful question a few years ago helped me formulate my initial vision for this book. Finally, I thank Lindal Buchanan and Jim Zebroski, two professional colleagues and friends, who read various drafts and offered invaluable feedback and support.

NOTE

1. Other recent ideas in line with the discipline's stylistic tradition include Sharon Myers's (2003) pedagogical uses of templates, collocations, and concordances in "ReMembering the Sentence" and Susan Peck MacDonald's (2007) proposal for the recuperation of a broader concept of language in "The Erasure of Language."

WORKS CITED

Bishop, Wendy, ed. 1997. *Elements of Alternate Style: Essays on Writing and Revision.* Portsmouth, NH: Heinemann-Boynton/Cook.

Butler, Paul. 2007. "Style in the Diaspora of Composition Studies." *Rhetoric Review* 26: 5–24.

Cliett, Victoria. 2003. "The Expanding Frontier of World Englishes: A New Perspective for Teachers of English." In *Language Diversity in the Classroom: From Intention to Practice,* ed. Geneva Smitherman and Victor Villanueva, 67–75. Carbondale: Southern Illinois University Press.

Connors, Robert J. 1981. "The Rise and Fall of the Modes of Discourse." *College Composition and Communication* 32: 444–55.

———. 2000. "The Erasure of the Sentence." *College Composition and Communication* 52: 96–128.

Crowley, Sharon, and Debra Hawhee. 2009. *Ancient Rhetorics for Contemporary Students.* 4th ed. New York: Pearson/Longman.

Enkvist, Nils Erik, John Spencer, and Michael J. Gregory, eds. 1964. *Linguistics and Style.* London: Oxford University Press.

Halloran, S. Michael, and Merrill D. Whitburn. 1982. "Ciceronian Rhetoric and the Rise of Science: The Plain Style Reconsidered." In *The Rhetorical Tradition and Modern Writing,* ed. James J. Murphy, 58–72. New York: MLA.

Jakobson, Roman. 1960. "Concluding Statement: Linguistics and Poetics." In *Style in Language,* ed. Thomas Sebeok, 350–77. Cambridge, MA: MIT Press.

Johnson, T. R. 2003. *A Rhetoric of Pleasure: Prose Style and Today's Composition Classroom.* Portsmouth, NH: Heinemann-Boynton/Cook.

Johnson, T. R., and Tom Pace, eds. 2005. *Refiguring Prose Style: Possibilities for Writing Pedagogy.* Logan: Utah State University Press.

Joseph, Sister Miriam. 2005. *Shakespeare's Use of the Arts of Language.* Philadelphia: Paul Dry.

Kennedy, John F. 1961. "Inaugural Address of President John F. Kennedy," Washington, D.C., January 20, 1961. John F. Kennedy Presidential Library and Museum. Historical Resources. http://www.jfklibrary.org/Historical+Resources/Archives/Reference+Desk/Speeches/JFK/003POF03Inaugural01201961.htm (accessed August 7, 2008).

Kolln, Martha. 2007. *Rhetorical Grammar: Grammatical Choices, Rhetorical Effects.* 5th ed. New York: Longman.

Labov, William. 1972. *Language in the Inner City.* Philadelphia: University of Pennsylvania Press.

Lanham, Richard A. 2006. *The Economics of Attention: Style and Substance in the Age of Information.* Chicago: University of Chicago Press.

———. 2007. *Revising Prose.* 5th ed. New York: Pearson/Longman.

MacDonald, Susan Peck. 2007. "The Erasure of Language." *College Composition and Communication* 58: 585–625.

Myers, Sharon. 2003. "ReMembering the Sentence." *College Composition and Communication* 54: 610–28.

Neel, Jasper. 1988. *Plato, Derrida, and Writing.* Carbondale: Southern Illinois University Press.

New London Group. 2000. "A Pedagogy of Multiliteracies: Designing Social Futures." In *Multiliteracies: Literacy Learning and the Design of Social Futures,* ed. Bill Cope and Mary Kalantzis, 3–37. London: Routledge/Taylor & Francis.

Pratt, Mary Louise. 1991. "Arts of the Contact Zone." *Profession* 91: 33–40.

Ramus, Peter. 1986. "Arguments in Rhetoric against Quintilian." In *Arguments in Rhetoric against Quintilian: Translation and Text of Peter Ramus's* Rhetoricae Distinctiones in Quintilianum, ed. James J. Murphy, 77–160, trans. Carole Newlands. Carbondale: Southern Illinois University Press.

Schroeder, Christopher, Helen Fox, and Patricia Bizzell. 2006. *Alt Dis: Alternative Discourses and the Academy.* Portsmouth, NH: Heinemann-Boynton/Cook.

Williams, Joseph M. 2005. *Style: Ten Lessons in Clarity and Grace.* 8th ed. New York: Pearson.

Young, Richard E., Alton L. Becker, and Kenneth L. Pike. 1970. *Rhetoric: Discovery and Change.* New York: Harcourt.

PART ONE

The Rise and Fall of the Study of Style

Introduction to Part One

While the canon of style has been an important part of rhetorical history for more than 2,500 years—and of literary and linguistic history for centuries—its affiliation with composition studies is far more recent, dating back roughly to the discipline's beginning in the 1960s. Yet, despite its influence on rhetoric and composition, including the role it played in composition teaching before 1960, stylistic study has been largely absent from discussions in the field in the past few decades. What accounts for this widespread invisibility? Given composition's rich multidisciplinary history, how is it possible that the study of style could have suddenly—and precipitously—fallen off the radar screen of a developing field?

Several rhetoric and composition scholars have recently tried to answer that question, and their answers, while varied, suggest a common denominator: style's eclipse within composition studies stems from its affiliation with current-traditional rhetoric, a formalist approach to writing that emphasizes the written product (rather than its process), prescriptive rules that often conflate style with grammar and usage, and static language practices. However, as composition scholars have been asking with increasing frequency, how is it possible that the formal aspects of style alone (grammatical correctness, for example), which ancient rhetoricians like Aristotle and Cicero treated as *virtues* of style, could now be the linchpin in the canon's disciplinary demise? Why has style's arguably overstated connection to certain formal, and often narrow, aspects of language erased a wide variety of stylistic work in the field?

For example, the study of style in composition has traditionally included the notion of developing maturity in writing, as evidenced in the practices of generative rhetoric, sentence combining, and imitation. While students may be adept at identifying metaphors or similes in their reading, they can also learn to achieve varying effects on audiences by using rhetorical schemes such as asyndeton (omission of conjunctions), anaphora (initial repetition), or ellipsis (deliberate omission). As social debates over Ebonics or African American Vernacular English (AAVE), gender, rap lyrics, and "politically correct" usage regularly become the latest *cause célèbre*, stylistic analysis can help the public understand aspects of language and culture often overlooked by the media and politicians.

The way composition scholars address stylistic study today has antecedents in classical rhetoricians' approach to style and suggests important connections across the centuries. Aristotle, in the piece excerpted here from Book 3 of his *Rhetoric*, includes among the virtues of style several elements that scholars regularly discuss today, namely, clarity, propriety, which for Aristotle suggests achieving a "mean" between ordinary speech and poetic language and composing in a natural rather than an artificial way, and ornamentation, by which Aristotle means "to deviate [from accepted usage]" and make language unfamiliar. These stylistic virtues, adapted in various ways throughout history, suggest a profound interest in the canon of style by classical rhetors. While these elements remain important in our thinking about style today, one virtue enumerated by Aristotle—grammatical correctness— is arguably, in contrast, now one of the main sources of style's declining fortunes. Instead of making assumptions about Aristotle's meaning, however, it is useful to ask, especially given the recent fate of style, what, precisely, Aristotle means by "correctness" and how it is related to his idea of clarity. Although Aristotle arguably thinks of correctness as an aspect of writing clarity, the term has acquired different connotations over the years, associated now with a far more rigid view of adherence to mechanical rules and prescribed formulas in writing.

While Aristotle's view of correctness may be nuanced, his discussion of stylistic "frigidities," or faults, which occur when someone violates the virtues of clarity or appropriateness, is less flexible. Aristotle defines faults as style that deviates too far from standard usage. As George Kennedy explains, Aristotelian frigidities often result from "the use of ponderous compounds . . . from unfamiliar words, from inappropriate epithets, and from far-fetched metaphors." Even though Aristotle's notion of frigidities as stylistic flaws— which many other ancient rhetors like Longinus, author of *On the Sublime*, also discussed—may seem unusual today, think about the way those in public contexts respond to language that deviates from the norm. The idea of frigidities and its current analogue of classifying deviations from accepted usage as "errors" in writing raise important questions about how style can be used to subvert—and possibly change—our conventional uses of language.

Aristotle, of course, is not the only one to talk about propriety as a critical stylistic virtue. The Roman orator Cicero, in his treatise *Orator*, values appropriate "levels" of style, which he labels plain (for proof), middle (for pleasure), and vigorous or grand (for persuasion). Cicero argues that the ideal orator—embodied, he says, by the Greek Demosthenes—controls and combines not only the three levels of style but also aspects of voice, rhythm, tone, delivery, arrangement, and invention, always underscored, according to Cicero, by a skilled use of propriety. (He does not mention a fourth level, the "forceful" style, discussed by Greek orator Demetrius as an "exchange of blows" that often expresses strong emotion.) In this excerpt, Cicero's discussion of plain style is largely based on notions of the Attic Orators in Greece, celebrated for a style that is concise, refined, and generally without ornament. For Cicero, eloquence seems vested primarily in the plain style, embellished, he says, with some figures of speech normally associated with the grand style. In contrast, the grand style regularly includes ornate figures and expressions and is sometimes associated with Atticism's counterpart—Asiatic style.

It is significant that Cicero describes orators of the grand style as "much to be despised" if they do not temper their words with the other two styles, and he compares the grand orator without this type of balance to "a raving madman among the sane." As a general rule, in thinking about style, Cicero, like Aristotle, says that "too much is more offensive than too little," a point of view that anticipates negative perceptions of an ornate style as flowery or pompous. Yet all of the levels of style, taken together, constitute a complete Ciceronian view of an eloquent speaker who, he says, "can discuss common-place matters simply, lofty subjects impressively, and topics ranging between in a tempered style." Cicero's insistence that different levels of style are appropriate for different audiences and purposes anticipates important discussions in composition scholarship about how colloquial language, dialect, and variations in genre and register can be used in different rhetorical situations. Cicero also prefigures current debates in the field about whether style and meaning are separate entities or an organic whole. He embraces a unity of style and content but makes an important practical distinction about style's effects on audiences when he says that "the same thing is often either approved or rejected according as it is expressed in one way or another."

The emphasis on achieving rhetorically effective expression is at the heart of imitation, a practice advocated by another Roman orator, Quintilian, who, in the excerpt here from his *Institutio oratoria*, contends that "a great portion of art consists in imitation." While acknowledging the overall importance of the canon of invention, Quintilian says it is "nevertheless advantageous to copy what has been invented with success." Yet Quintilian's general approval of imitation does not suggest a blind adherence to its precepts. Addressing what has since become a frequent criticism of imitation in composition pedagogy, Quintilian argues that the goal is not simply to equal the achievements of those we imitate—the equivalent today of what is often called slavish or rote imitation—but rather to exceed their original limits. In doing so, Quintilian suggests, we emulate the best of different writers, specifically, "the energy of Cæsar, the asperity of Cælius, the accuracy of Pollio, the judgment of Calvus." Quintilian also asserts that imitating various styles is a highly rhetorical undertaking, requiring different models for different subject matters. The idea of combining the imitated features of others with a person's excellent individual style forms the complete orator—or the ideal writer. The same concept, in fact, becomes the leitmotif of several recent articles on imitation surveyed by Frank Farmer and Phillip Arrington in the pages that follow.

While Quintilian's review of imitation in antiquity assumes its rightful place in writing and speaking, Farmer and Arrington's survey of articles on imitation since the early 1960s suggests, by contrast, that imitation has been ignored by composition, hidden in the discipline's dark closet out of indifference and disdain. They claim that many formal aspects of composition instruction have disappeared because they are associated with the product approach to writing, the cornerstone of a current-traditional rhetoric locked away when process approaches began to dominate the field. Why has imitation suffered this undeserved fate, the authors ask, in light of the many process-oriented justifications for its use? As a pedagogical practice, Farmer and Arrington argue, imitation has traditionally been used in the field based on a common assumption: by imitating a variety of linguistic and rhetorical devices as well as organizational and discourse structures, students can internalize the same features in their own writing. Defining imitation as "the approximation, whether conscious or unconscious, of exemplary models, whether textual, behavioral, or human, for the expressed goal of improved student writing," the authors show how compositionists first offer apologies for imitation and then justify its use by attempting to link it to process approaches. In the end, the authors tie the future of imitation's fortunes—which they view as clearly on the wane—to the social theories of Lev Vygotsky and Mikhail Bakhtin, whom they see as offering a new rationale for imitation in the field. Following Bakhtin's lead, Farmer and Arrington ask us to rethink imitation's relationship not to the sentence, but to the utterance. In his use of a dialogic nature of utterance, Bakhtin allows us to understand, for example, how our words are always derived from another person's words. In articulating an optimistic view of imitation's future in the field, the authors claim, as Bakhtin does, that *"the ultimate word . . . has not yet been spoken"* (qtd. in Farmer and Arrington).

If Farmer and Arrington lead the way in asking why the rhetorical practice of imitation has been out of style, then Robert Connors asks a broader question about the fall from grace of what he calls "sentence rhetorics": Francis Christensen's generative rhetoric, sentence combining, and rhetorical imitation. In examining the sudden demise in the mid-1980s of these much-used "sentence pedagogies," Connors asks, "What iceberg did this *Titanic* meet?" In posing that question, Connors examines a conundrum in the field: Why did three widely accepted pedagogies, at the height of their popularity within composition studies, vanish like the seventeen-year cicada after receiving what Connors deems minor criticisms at best? After all, as Connors points out, practice in the manipulation of sentences, the so-called "school of syntactic methods," was a central part of composition pedagogy for years. Devices such as T-units (sentence combining), cumulative sentences (Christensen's generative rhetoric), and pattern practice and modeling (imitation) helped students achieve growth in writing maturity, clarity, unity, and coherence. Given the apparent success of these pedagogies, then, it is difficult to understand why they disappeared. Connors hypothesizes three principal reasons: antiformalism, which was suspicious of any pedagogy emphasizing form over content; antibehaviorism, which saw style exercises as arhetorical and as an erosion of the individual; and antiempiricism, related to other cognitive developments in the field, which questioned the scientific experimentalism of these sentence pedagogies. Connors ends with a crucial question: What reduced the sentence "from a vital, if unfinished, inquiry into why a popular stylistic method worked so well to a half-hidden and seldom-discussed classroom practice on the level of, say, vocabulary quizzes?" In trying to answer that question, Connors's article helps us think about the general evolution of English departments and their shifting emphasis on theory, texts, and status-based divisions, resulting in diminishing focus on the sentence — in essence, an erasure of style.

One other erasure Connors mentions is that of the paragraph, and Mike Duncan investigates that particular elision in a *College English* article in which he argues for reclaiming a unified paragraph theory in composition studies. In an inquiry similar to Connors's, the author wonders why the field suddenly dropped its studies of the paragraph in the mid-1980s. Duncan examines a prescriptive position, based on ideas of explicit paragraph structure, including first-position topic sentences and an ideal arrangement that can be "described, measured, and emulated" pedagogically; a more inductive descriptive position; and a related functionalist approach that sees sentences as "free-form entities." He also acknowledges the influence of a cognitive approach, derived from studies in psychology and computational linguistics on readability. In attempting to rehabilitate the paragraph, Duncan asks what is responsible for its erasure and, like Connors and Farmer and Arrington, he attributes the cause to the field's attitude toward current-traditional rhetoric and its movement toward "fresher, more progressive topics." But he argues that the value of paragraph theory has never been disproved, and that "robust paragraph formation is essential to effective writing." In an unusual move, Duncan does not locate the paragraph's revival exclusively within composition and rhetoric but proposes instead an interdisciplinary approach, incorporating collaborative insights from psychology, linguistics, and other fields. He suggests that in composition and elsewhere, the paragraph can be revitalized by "paragraph rebels," who, eschewing ignorance of the important developments in other fields, together develop new terminology to describe the paragraph, renew attention to "flow," and do research on the most effective pedagogies for teaching the paragraph.

WORKS CITED

Demetrius. 1961. *A Greek Critic: Demetrius on Style*, trans. G. M. A. Grube. Toronto: University of Toronto Press.
Longinus. 1991. *On Great Writing (On the Sublime)*, trans. G. M. A. Grube. Indianapolis: Hackett.

1   *On Prose Style*

ARISTOTLE

CHAPTERS 2–9: *LEXIS*, OR STYLE

Chapters 2–4 are primarily concerned with *lexis* in the sense of diction, or choice of words, chapters 5–9 with the composition of words into sentences, which came to be known as *synthesis*, "putting together." Aristotle's discussion applies both to oral speech and to written prose.

Chapter 2: The *Aretē*, or Virtue, of Good Prose Style; Word Choice and Metaphors

This chapter begins with a definition of the virtue or excellence (*aretē*) of prose style and civic oratory as *clarity*, but with the accompanying requirement that a writer or speaker seek a mean between ordinary speech and poetic language as appropriate to the subject. In chapter 5, Aristotle will add a requirement of grammatical correctness and in subsequent chapters will discuss various forms of ornamentation. These concepts were reformulated by his student Theophrastus in a treatise, now lost, *On Lexis*, as "correctness, clarity, propriety, and ornamentation" and appear in some form in most subsequent Greek and Roman treatments of rhetoric. See *Rhetoric for Herennius* 4.17; Cicero, *On the Orator* 3.37 and *Orator* 79; Quintilian 8.1–2; etc.

[1404b] 1. Let the matters just discussed be regarded as understood, and let the virtue of style [*lexeōs aretē*] be defined as "to be clear" (speech is a kind of sign, so if it does not make clear it will not perform its function)—and neither flat nor above the dignity of the subject, but appropriate [*prepon*].[1] The poetic style is hardly flat, but it is not appropriate for speech. 2. The use of nouns and verbs in their prevailing [*kyrios*][2] meaning makes for clarity; other kinds of words, as discussed in the *Poetics*,[3] make the style ornamented rather than flat. To deviate [from prevailing usage] makes language seem more elevated;

From *The Rhetoric*, Book 3, in Aristotle, *On Rhetoric: A Theory of Civic Discourse*, ed. George A. Kennedy (New York: Oxford University Press), 220–43.

for people feel the same in regard to *lexis* as they do in regard to strangers compared with citizens. 3. As a result, one should make the language unfamiliar,[4] for people are admirers of what is far off, and what is marvelous is sweet. Many [kinds of words] accomplish this in verse and are appropriate there; for what is said [in poetry] about subjects and characters is more out of the ordinary, but in prose[5] much less so; for the subject matter is less remarkable, since even in poetry it would be rather inappropriate if a slave used fine language or if a man were too young for his words, or if the subject were too trivial, but in these cases, too, propriety is a matter of contraction or expansion. 4. As a result, authors should compose without being noticed and should seem to speak not artificially but naturally.[6] (The latter is persuasive, the former the opposite; for [if artifice is obvious] people become resentful, as at someone plotting against them, just as they are at those adulterating wines.) An example is the success of Theodorus' voice when contrasted with that of other actors; for his seems the voice of the actual character, but the others' those of somebody else.[7] 5. The "theft"[8] is well done if one composes by choosing words from ordinary language. Euripides does this and first showed the way.

Since speech is made up of nouns and verbs,[9] and the species of nouns are those examined in the *Poetics*, from among these one should use glosses[10] and double words and coinages rarely and in a limited number of situations. (We shall later[11] explain where; the reason has already been given: the usage departs from the appropriate in the direction of excess.) 6. A word in its prevailing and native meaning and metaphor[12] are along useful in the *lexis* of prose. A sign of this is that these are the only kinds of words everybody uses; for all people carry on their conversations with metaphors[13] and words in their native and prevailing meanings. Thus, it is clear that if one composes well, there will be an unfamiliar quality and it escapes notice and will be clear. This, we said, was the virtue of rhetorical language. 7. The kind of words useful to a sophist are homonyms[14] (by means of these he does his dirty work), to a poet synonyms. **[1405a]** By words that are both in their prevailing meaning and synonymous I mean, for example, *go* and *walk*; for when used in their prevailing sense, these are synonymous with each other.

Now what each kind of word is and how many species of metaphor there are and that metaphor has very great effect both in poetry and speeches has been said, as noted above, in the *Poetics*.[15] 8. In speech it is necessary to take special pains to the extent that speech has fewer resources than verse. Metaphor especially has clarity and sweetness and strangeness, and its use cannot be learned from someone else.[16] 9. One should speak both epithets and metaphors that are appropriate, and this will be from an analogy. If not, the expression seems inappropriate because opposites are most evident when side-by-side each other. But one should consider what suits an old man just as a scarlet cloak is right for a young one; for the same clothes are not right [for both]. 10. And if you wish to adorn, borrow the metaphor from something better in the same genus, if to denigrate, from something worse. I mean, for example, since they are opposites in the same genus, saying of a person who begs that he "prays" or that a person praying "begs," because both are forms of asking. That is composing in the way described, as also when Iphicrates called Callias a "begging priest" rather than a "torchbearer" and the latter replied that Iphicrates was not initiated into the Mysteries or he would not have called him a begging priest but a torchbearer;[17] for both are religious epithets, but one is honorable, one dishonorable. Then there are the "parasites of Dionysius," but the persons in question call themselves "artistes." These are both metaphors, the former one that sullies the profession, the latter the contrary. Pirates now call themselves "businessmen." Thus, one can say that a criminal "has made a mistake" or that someone making a mistake "has committed a crime" or that a thief either took or "plundered." A phrase like that of Euripides' Telephos, "lording the oar and landed in Mysia," is inappropriate [in prose], since *lording* is too elevated; there is no "theft" [if the metaphor is too flagrant].

11. There is a fault in the syllables if the indications of sound are unpleasant; for example, Dionysius the Brazen[18] in his *Elegies* calls poetry "Calliope's screech" because both are sounds; but the metaphor is bad because it implies meaningless sounds. 12. Further, in naming something that does not have a proper name of its own, metaphor should be used,[19] and [should] not be far-fetched but taken from things that are related and of similar species, so that it is clear the term is related; for example, in the popular riddle [*ainigma*], [1405b] "I saw a man gluing bronze on another with fire,"[20] the process has no [technical] name, but both are a kind of application; the application of the cupping instrument is thus called "gluing." From good riddling it is generally possible to derive appropriate metaphors; for metaphors are made like riddles; thus, clearly, [a metaphor from a good riddle] is an apt transference of words.

13. And the source of the metaphor should be something beautiful; verbal beauty, as Licymnius says,[21] is in the sound or in the sense, and ugliness the same; and thirdly there is what refutes the sophistic argument: for it is not as Bryson[22] said that nothing is in itself ugly, since it signifies the same thing if one word is used rather than another and more like the object signified and more adapted to making the thing appear "before the eyes."[23] Moreover, one word does not signify in the same way as another, so in this sense also we should posit one as more beautiful or more ugly than another; for both signify the beautiful or the ugly, but not solely as beauty or ugliness.[24] Or if they do, [it is] only in degree. These are the sources from which metaphors should be taken: from the beautiful either in sound or in effect or in visualization or in some other form of sense perception. It makes a difference whether the dawn is called "rosy-fingered"[25] or "purple-fingered." 14. In the use of epithets the transference is also sometimes from the bad or ugly, for example *mother-slayer*, sometimes from the better, for example *avenger of his father*.[26] When the winner in a mule race offered Simonides a paltry sum [for an ode in honor of the victory], he declined the commission as though annoyed at composing about "half-asses"; but when the winner paid enough he wrote, "Hail, daughters of storm-footed mares!"[27] Nevertheless, they *were* daughters of asses. 15. The same effect can be achieved by diminution. A diminutive [*hypokorismos*] makes both bad and good less so, as Aristophanes does sarcastically in the *Baby-*

Ionians[28] when he substitutes *goldlet* for *gold*, *cloaklet* for *cloak*, *insultlet* for *insult*, and *diseaselet* [for *disease*]. But one should be careful and observe moderation in both [epithets and diminutives].

Chapter 3: *Ta Psykhra*, or Frigidities

Having discussed virtues of style. Aristotle now turns briefly to their opposites, the faults that come from violating the principles of clarity and appropriateness in choice of words and that make the language "frigid." Longinus follows the same approach in chapters 3–4 of *On Sublimity*. Frigidity, Aristotle says, may result from the use of ponderous compounds—often coined by the speaker—from unfamiliar words, from inappropriate epithets, and from far-fetched metaphors.

1. Frigidities in [prose] *lexis* come about in four ways: [first] in double words,[29] as in Lycophron's phrase "the many-faced heaven of the great-summited earth" and "the narrow-passaged shore" and as Gorgias spoke of "beggar-mused flatterers, forsworn and right solemnly sworn" **[1406a]** and as in Alcidamas' expression "his soul full of anger and his face becoming fire-colored" and "end-fulfilling deemed he their zeal would be" and "end-fulfilling he made the persuasion of his words," and the foam of the sea was "copper-blue."[30] All these seem poetic because of the doubling.

2. This is one cause of frigidity, and another is the use of glosses,[31] as when Lycophron called Xerxes "a *monster* man"[32] and Sciron "a *sinis* man"[33] and Alcidamas spoke of "[bringing no such] *toys* to poetry" and "the *wretchedlessness* of his nature" and one who was "*whetted* with the unmixed anger of his thought."

3. Third is use of epithets that are long or untimely or crowded.[34] In poetry it is appropriate to speak of "white milk,"[35] but in speech such things are not only rather unsuitable, but if used immoderately they convict [the writer of artificality] and make it clear that this is "poetry." Though there is some need to use them (for they change what is ordinary and make the *lexis* unfamiliar), nevertheless one should aim at the mean, for it does less harm than speaking carelessly; carelessness lacks merit, moderation lacks fault. As a result, Alcidamas' phrases seem frigid; for he uses epithets not as seasonings but as the main course, so frequent, extended, and conspicuous are they: for instance, not "sweat" but "wet sweat"; not "to the Isthmian games" but "to the convocation of the Isthmian games"; not "laws" but "the royal laws of cities"; not "in a race" but "in a racing impulse of the soul"; not "museion"[36] but adding "Nature's museion"[37]; and "sullen-visaged the thought of his soul"; and the artificer not of *favor* but of "pandemic favor," and "steward of the pleasure of the listeners," and hidden not by *boughs*, but "boughs of the wood," and not "he covered his body" but "he covered his body's shame," and "anti-mimicking was the desire of his soul" (this is at one and the same time both a compound and an epithet, so the result is poetry), and "so extravagant an excess of wickedness." Thus, by speaking poetically in an inappropriate way [Alcidamas and other sophists] impart absurdity and frigidity, and

also lack of clarity because of the verbiage, for when a speaker throws more words at someone who already understands, he destroys the clarity of the darkness. People coin double words when something has no name of its own and the word is easily formed, as is *pastime* [*to khronotribein*]. But if there is much of this, [the diction] becomes completely poetical. **[1406b]** Thus, *lexis* using double words is most useful to dithyrambic poets, for they are sensitive to sound,[38] but glosses to epic poets, for they are stately and self-assured.[39]

4. The fourth kind of frigidity occurs in metaphors; for there are inappropriate metaphors, some because they are laughable (comic poets, too, use metaphor), some because too lofty and tragic. And they are inappropriate if far-fetched, for example Gorgias's phrase about "pale and bloodless doings"[40] or "You have sown shamefully and have reaped badly." These are too poetic. And as Alcidamas calls philosophy "a fortress against the laws" and the *Odyssey* "a fair mirror of human life" and "bringing no such toys to poetry." All these are unpersuasive for the reasons given.[41] Yet Gorgias's exclamation to the swallow when she flew down and let go her droppings on him is in the best tragic manner: he said, "Shame on you, Philomela"; for if a bird did it there was no shame, but [it would have been] shameful for a maiden. He thus rebuked the bird well by calling it what it once had been rather than what it now was.[42]

Chapter 4: *Eikōn,* or Simile

An *eikōn* is a "likeness" (English *icon*). Though Aristotle views the simile as a characteristic poetic device, seen especially in the extended similes of epic poetry, simile is not discussed in the *Poetics*. In this chapter of the *Rhetoric* it is treated as an expanded form of the metaphor: a metaphor, that is, with an explicit comparison, whether provided by a verb, adjective, or adverb. Later rhetoricians often reverse this concept, taking a metaphor to be an abbreviated simile or regarding a simile as a figure, involving several words, while metaphor is a trope, the "turning" of the meaning of a single word. This distinction between tropes and figures is not explicit in Aristotle's work and is a development of his successors in the Hellenistic period. Aristotle has discussed *parabolē,* or comparison, as a topic of invention in 2.20.2–7; but neither there nor here does he relate it to simile, which he regards as a device of style; see McCall 1969.

1. A simile is also a metaphor; for there is little difference: when the poet says, "He rushed as a lion," it is a simile, but "The lion rushed" [with *lion* referring to a man] would be a metaphor; since both are brave, he used a metaphor [i.e., a simile] and spoke of Achilles as a lion.[43] 2. The simile is useful also in speech, but only occasionally; for it is poetic. [Similes] should be brought in like metaphors; for they *are* metaphors, differing in the form of expression. 3. Examples of similes are what Androtion said to Idreus, that he was "like puppies that have been chained"; for they jump to bite, and Idreus, freed from prison, was vicious.[44] And [another example is] the way Theodamus likened Archidamus to "a Euxenus that does not know geometry";

this is from analogy, for Euxenus will then be an Archidamus who knows geometry.[45] And [another example is] the one in the *Republic* of Plato, that those who strip the dead [on a battle field] are like ours that snap at stones but do not bite the throwers; and the one applied to the citizen body, that it is like a ship's captain who is strong but deaf; and the one about the verses of poets, that they are like youths without beauty (for when they latter have lost the bloom of youth and the former their meter, they do not seem the same).[46] [1407a] And [another example is] Pericles' simile for the Samians, that they are like children who accept the candy but keep crying, and his remark about the Boeotians, that they are like oaks, (for oaks are felled by oaks,[47] and the Boeotians by fighting each other). And [another example is] Demosthenes' about the citizen body, that it is like those sick on board ship.[48] And [another] the way Democritus likened orators to nannies who, after swallowing the pabulum, moisten the baby's lips with their spit. And [another is] the way Antisthenes compared skinny Cephisodotus to incense, because "He gives pleasure by wasting away." All these can be spoken both as similes and as metaphors, so whichever are approved when spoken as metaphors clearly will make similes too, and similes are metaphors needing[49] an explanatory word. 4. Metaphor from analogy should always have a correspondence between the two species of the same genus: thus, if the wine cup is the "shield" of Dionysus, the shield can fittingly be called the "cup" of Ares.[50] Speech, then, is composed from these things.[51]

Chapter 5: *To Hellenizein*, or Grammatical Correctness

> In chapters 5–9 attention turns to style as influenced by a variety of considerations of composition in the combination of words. The first of these considerations is what Aristotle calls "speaking Greek," by which he means observance of the rules of grammar and the conventions of idiom of the language; but much of what he says really relates more to clarity than to correctness. Perhaps the chapter is a survival of some earlier thoughts on clarity, placed here because it deals with composition of sentences rather than with choice of words. Although Protagoras and other sophists had made a start at the study of grammar, it was in Aristotle's time still a relatively undeveloped field of study. Systematic grammars of the Greek language did not appear until the second century B.C., when they reflect the research of Stoic philosophers.

1. The first principle [*arkhē*] of *lexis* is to speak [good] Greek [*to helleni-zein*]. This is done in five ways,[52] 2. [of which the] first is in the [correct] use of connectives, when a speaker preserves the natural responsion between those that are prior and those that are posterior to each other, as some require. Thus, *ho men* and *ho ego* require [in a subsequent clause] *de* and *ho de*, respectively.[53] The correlatives should occur while the first expression is still in the mind and not be widely separated, nor should another connective be substituted for the one needed; for it is rarely appropriate: "But I, when he spoke to me (for there came Cleon both begging and demanding), went, taking them along." In

these words many connectives are thrown in, in place of what is expected; and if the interval is long, the result is unclear.[54]

3. On the other hand, then, one merit is found in the use of connectives, a second, on the other hand, in calling things by their specific names and not by circumlocutions.[55] 4. Third is not to use amphibolies[56]—unless the opposite effect [obscurity] is being sought. People do this when they have nothing to say but are pretending to say something. Such are those [philosophers] who speak in poetry, Empedocles, for example. When there is much going around in a circle, it cheats the listeners and they feel the way many do about oracles: whenever the latter speak amphibolies most people nod in assent: "Croesus, by crossing the Halys [river], will destroy a great kingdom."[57] **[1407b]** Since there is generally less chance of a mistake, oracles speak of any matter in generalities. In the game of knucklebones one can win more often by calling odd or even than by specifying a particular number of counters, and the same is true about *what* will be in contrast to *when* it will happen, which is why soothsayers do not specify the time. All these things are alike, so they should be avoided except for the reason mentioned.

5. The fourth [rule is to observe] Protagoras' classification of the gender of nouns: masculine, feminine, and neuter. There should be correct grammatical agreement: "Having come and having spoken, she departed."[58] 6. Fifth is the correct naming of plural and singular: "Having come, they beat me." What is written should generally be easy to read and easy to speak—which is the same thing. Use of many connectives[59] does not have this quality; nor do phrases not easily punctuated,[60] for example, the writings of Heraclitus. To punctuate the writings of Heraclitus is a difficult task because it is unclear what goes with what, whether with what follows or with what precedes. For example, in the beginning of his treatise he says, "Of the Logos that exists always ignorant are men." It is unclear whether *always* goes with what proceeds [or what follows]. 7. Further, the lack of correspondence creates a solecism (*to soloikizein*)[61] if you do not join words with what fits both: for example, if you are speaking of sound and color, seeing is not common to them, but perceiving is. And it is unclear if you do not first set forth what you are talking about when you are going to throw in much in the middle: for example, "I intended, after talking with that man about this and that and in this way, to go," instead of "I intended, after talking with that man, to go" and then "This and that transpired and in this way."

Chapter 6: *Onkos,* or Expansiveness, and *Syntomia,* or Conciseness

Onkos literally means "bulk, mass, swelling"; here it implies "elevation, dignity," though in other writers it is often a pejorative term. As Aristotle implies in section 7, *onkos* can be regarded as a stylistic form of *auxēsis,* amplification, of which some inventional aspects were discussed in 2.18.4, 2.19.26, and 2.26. Note the prescriptive tone of this chapter with its practical advice on how to amplify. As in the case of arguments in books 1–2, Aristotle is setting out "available" techniques. Although it appears several times in Demetrius' treatise *On Style* (a work showing strong Aristotelian influence), *onkos* did not gain acceptance among later rhetoricians as a technical term.

1. The following things contribute to expansiveness [*onkos*] in *lexis:* to use a definition instead of a word, for example, not *circle* but "a plane figure equidistant from the center." For conciseness [*syntomia*], [one should make use of] the opposite: the word for the definition. 2. And if something is shameful or inappropriate, if the shame is in the definition, use the word, and if in the word, use the definition. 3. And make something clear by metaphor and epithets, while guarding against the poetic. 4. And make the singular plural, as poets do: though there is a single harbor, they say "to Achaean harbors," and "the tablet's many-leaved folds."[62] 5. And do not join [words with a single definite article] but use one with each: *tēs gynaikos tēs hēmeteras*; but for conciseness the opposite: *tēs hēmeteras gynaikos.*[63] 6. And speak [expansively] with a conjunction but if concisely, without a conjunction, yet not without grammatical connection: for example, "having gone and having conversed" compared with "having gone, I conversed." **[1408a]** 7. Antimachus'[64] technique of describing something on the basis of properties it does not have is also useful; he applies it to Teumessos [in the passage beginning], "There is a windy little hill . . ." Amplification of this sort can go on indefinitely.[65] What it is not can be said of things good and bad, whichever is useful. This is the source of words the poets introduce such as *stringless* or *lyreless* music, for they apply privatives. This is popular when expressed in metaphors by analogy; for example, the trumpet is "lyreless music."

Chapter 7: *To Prepon*, or Appropriateness, Propriety

The beginning of chapter 2 identified appropriateness of style to subject as a necessary quality of good speaking or writing. In this chapter, Aristotle explains the concept more fully.

1. The *lexis* will be appropriate if it expresses emotion and character and is proportional to the subject matter. 2. Proportion exists if there is neither discussion of weighty matters[66] in a casual way nor shoddy things solemnly and if ornament is not attached to a shoddy word. Otherwise, the result seems comedy, like the [tragic] poetry Cleophon composes. Some of what he used to say is like calling a fig "Madame." 3. Emotion is expressed if the style, in the case of insolence (*hybris*), is that of an angry man; in the case of impious and shameful things, if it is that of one who is indignant and reluctant even to say the words; in the case of admirable things, [if they are spoken] respectfully; but if [the things] are pitiable, [if they are spoken] in a submissive manner; and similarly in other cases. 4. The proper *lexis* also makes the matter credible: the mind [of the listener] draws a false inference of the truth of what a speaker says because they [in the audience] feel the same about such things, so they think the facts to be so, even if they are not as the speaker represents them; 5. and the hearer suffers along with the pathetic speaker, even if what he says

amounts to nothing. As a result, many overwhelm their hearers by making noise.

6. Proof from signs is expressive of character, because there is an appropriate style for each genus and moral state. By *genus* I mean things like age—boy, man, old man—or woman and man or Spartan and Thessalian and by *moral state* [*hexis*] the principles by which someone is the kind of person he is in life; 7. for lives do not have the same character in accordance with [each and] every moral state.[67] If, then, a person speaks words appropriate to his moral state, he will create a sense of character. A rustic and an educated person would not say the same thing nor [say it] in the same way. Listeners react also to expressions speechwriters[68] use to excess: "Who does not know?" "Everybody knows . . ." The listener agrees out of embarrassment in order to share in the [alleged] feelings of all others.

8. Opportune or inopportune usage is a factor common to all [three] species [of rhetoric]. **[1408b]** 9. There is a commonly used defense for every hyperbole: the speaker should preempt criticism[69] for something seems true when the speaker does not conceal what he is doing. 10. Further, do not use all analogous effects [of sound and sense] together; for thus the hearer is tricked. I mean, for example, if the words are harsh, do not deliver them with a harsh voice and countenance. Otherwise, what you are doing is evident. But if sometimes one feature is present, sometimes not, you accomplish the same thing without being noticed. But if, as a result, gentle things are said harshly and harsh things gently, the result is unpersuasive.

11. Double words and frequent epithets and especially unfamiliar words suit one speaking passionately; for it is excusable that an angry person calls a wrong "heaven-high" or "monstrous." And [this can be done] when a speaker holds the audience in his control and causes them to be stirred either by praise or blame or hate or love, as Isocrates does at the end of the *Panegyricus*: "[How great the] fame and name . . ." and [earlier] "who endured . . . [to see the city made desolate"].[70] Those who are empassioned mouth such utterances, and audiences clearly accept them because they are in a similar mood. That is why [this emotional style] is suited to poetry, too, for poetry is inspired. It should be used as described—or in mockery,[71] as Gorgias did and as in the *Phaedrus*.[72]

Chapter 8: Rhythm in Prose

A sense of rhythm begins to be evident in some Greek prose of the late fifth century, but real feeling for it is first seen in the writings of Plato, Isocrates, and Demosthenes in the fourth. Demosthenes in particular (though ignored by Aristotle) avoids a succession of short syllables. The reader needs to keep in mind that Greek (and Latin) meter was quantitative, based on long and short syllables, not on stress accent.

1. The form of the language[73] should be neither metrical nor unrhythmical. The former is unpersuasive (for it seems to have been shaped) and at the same time also diverts attention; for it causes [the listener] to pay attention to when the same foot will come again—as when children anticipate the call

of heralds (in the law courts): "Whom does the freedman choose as his sponsor?" [The children call out] "Cleon!" 2. But what is unrhythmical is unlimited; and there should be a limit, but not by use of meter, for the unlimited is unpleasant and unknowable.[74] And all things are limited by number. In the case of the form of language, number is rhythm, of which meters are segments. 3. Thus, speech should have rhythm but not meter; for the latter will be a poem. The rhythm should not be exact; this will be achieved if it is [regular] only up to a point.[75]

4. Of rhythms, the heroic [dactylic hexameter] is solemn and not conversational and needs musical intonation;[76] the iambic by itself is the language of the many; thus, all people most often speak in iambics. But [formal speech] should be dignified and moving. The trochaic meter is rather too much of a comic dance, as is clear from trochaic tetrameters; for they are a tripping rhythm. **[1409a]** What remains is the *paian*, it came into use beginning with Thrasymachus, though at the time people did not recognize what it was. The paean is a third kind of rhythm, related to those under discussion; for it has the ratio of three to two [three short syllables and one long, the latter equal in time to two beats], whereas the others are one to one [the heroic, with one long syllable and two shorts] or two to one [iambic and trochaic, a long and a short or a short and a long, respectively]. And one-and-a-half [i.e., the proportion of three to two] is the mean ratio and this is what a paean is. 5. The other rhythms should be avoided for the reasons given and because they are [poetic] meters; and the paean should be adopted, for it alone of the rhythms mentioned is not a meter, and thus its presence most escapes notice. As it is, only the opening paean is in use, but it is necessary to distinguish the opening from the closing. 6. There are two species of paean opposite to each other, of which one [called a first paean] is suitable for an opening, as it is now used.[77] This is the one that begins with a long syllable and ends with three shorts: *Dālŏgĕnĕs eite Lukian* and *khrȳsĕŏkŏma Hekate pai Dios;* the other [called a fourth paean] is the opposite, where three shorts begin and a long ends: *mĕtă dĕ găn hŭdătă ōkĕŏnŏn ēphănĭsĕ nūx.* This makes an ending, for a short syllable [at the end] makes the expression seem cut short.[78] It should instead be cut off with a long syllable and be a clear termination, not through the action of a scribe or the presence of a marginal mark[79] but through the rhythm. 7. That *lexis* should, therefore, be rhythmical and not unrhythmical and what rhythms make it well rhythmed and what they are like has been said.

Chapter 9: Periodic Style

This chapter is somewhat difficult. One problem is the extent to which Aristotle thinks of a period as essentially a rhythmical unit; he says it has magnitude, is limited, and has number, he equates it with a line of verse in section 4, and the need for rhythm might be assumed from the previous chapter; but he does not here specifically speak of rhythms. See Fowler 1982, which denies that rhythm is involved, and, on the other side of the question, Adamik 1984. The most conspicuous features of a period and of its subdivision called a *kōlon* seem to be some syntactical completion (at least a complete phrase), unitary thought, and length that is a mean between "too short" and "too long," in order for the hearer to grasp the thought easily. Aristotle does not use the word *period* to mean one of the long complex sentences of Isocrates (or later Cicero) but quotes *parts* of Isocrates' complex sentences as good examples of periods. Thus, he would apparently view a long Isocratean sentence as made up of several periods.

1. The *lexis* [of formal speech and artistic prose] is necessarily either *strung-on*[80] and given unity by connection, like the preludes in dithyrambs, or *turned-down*[81] and like the antistrophes of the ancient poets. 2. The strung-on style is the ancient one;[82] for in the past all used it, but now not many do. I call that strung-on which has no end in itself except in so far as the thought is completed. It is unpleasant because it is unlimited, for all wish to foresee the end.[83] Thus, as they complete the course [runners] pant and are exhausted; for they do not tire while the goal is in sight ahead. 3. This, then, is the strung-on style of *lexis*, but the turned-down style is that in periods. I call a period [*periodos*] an expression [*lexus*] having a beginning and end in itself and a magnitude easily taken in at a glance.[84] **[1409b]** This is pleasant and easily understood, pleasant because opposed to the unlimited and because the hearer always thinks he has hold of something, in that it is always limited by itself, whereas to have nothing to foresee or attain is unpleasant. And it is easily understood because easily retained in the mind. This is because utterance in periods has number, which is the most easily retained thing. Thus, all people remember verses better than prose;[85] for it has number by which it is measured. 4. And a period should also be complete in thought and not cut off, as it is in the iambic line:

Calydon [is] this land, of Pelops' soil . . .[86]

Because of the line division it is possible to misunderstand the meaning, as though in this quotation Calydon were in the Peloponnesus.

5. A period is either divided into cola[87] or simple. *Lexis* in cola is completed and divided and easily uttered by the breath, not in its division but in the whole. A colon is one of the two parts of a period. I call a period simple when it has only one colon. 6. The cola and the periods should be neither stubby nor long. A short one often causes the hearer a bump; for when [his mind] is rushing toward what is to come and its measure, of which he has his own definition, if he is pulled up short by the speaker's pausing, he necessarily trips, as it were, at the abrupt close. Long ones cause him to be left behind, as do those walkers who go past the [expected] turning point; for they, too, leave behind their fellow strollers. Similarly, long periods turn into a *logos*[88] and are like a prelude. This is the source of the parody [of Hesiod, *Works and Days* 265–66] by Democritus of Chios, attacking Melanippides on the ground that he was composing preludes rather than antistrophes:

A man does wrong to himself when he does it to another,
And a long prelude is the worst thing for a composer.

Much the same applies to those who speak long cola, while those that are too short do not constitute a period. Thus, they drag the hearer headlong.

7. *Lexis* in cola is either divided or contrasted. It is divided in this example: "Often have I admired those organizing panegyric festivals and those instituting athletic contests." It is contrasted when in each colon opposite lies with opposite or the same is yoked with its opposites, **[1410a]** for example, "They helped both, both those who stayed and those who followed; to the latter they provided more than they had had at home and for the former they left enough behind." *Staying* and *following* are opposites, as are *enough* and *more*. [Another examples is] "And so both to those needing money and those wishing to enjoy it . . . ," where *enjoy* is opposed to acquisition. And again, [other examples are] "It happens often in these circumstances that the wise fail and the foolish succeed" [and] "Straightway they were thought worthy of meeds of valor and not much later they took command of the sea" [and] "To sail through the land, and to march through the sea, yoking the Hellespont and digging through Athos . . ." [and] "And though citizens by nature, by law deprived of their city . . ." [and] "Some of them miserably perished, and others were shamefully saved." And [another is] Privately to use barbarian servants, and collectively to overlook the many who were enslaved . . ." [and] ". . . either while living to hold it or when dead to loose it."[89] And [another is] what someone said to Pitholaus and Lycophron[90] in the lawcourt: "When these men were at home, they sold you, but coming to you now, they have been bought." All these examples do what has been said. 8. Such a *lexis* is pleasing because opposites are most knowable and more knowable when put beside each other and because they are like a syllogism, for refutation [*elenkos*] is a bringing together of contraries.[91]

> Up to this point in the chapter Aristotle has not used the word *antithesis* (some other translations paraphrastically insert it) even though some of the examples are clearly antithetical, but now he speaks of antithesis as the sort of thing he is discussing. For his readers it was hardly a technical term, since the meaning was clear from its two roots, as in *opposition*. It was, however, one of the characteristics of the prose style of Gorgias, though that sophist is not here mentioned; and Aristotle procedes to discuss other examples of what have come to be known as the Gorgianic figures. Note that Aristotle has no term for "figure of speech."

9. *Antithesis*, then, is one such thing, as is *parisōsis* if the cola are equal [in the number of syllables], and *paromoiōsis* if each colon has similar extremities [in sound]. This can occur either at the beginning or at the end [of the colon]. At the beginning it always takes the form of [similar] complete words,[92] but at the end it may consist of [the same] final syllables or [the same] grammatical form or the same word. At a beginning [of a colon] are found such things as *Agron gar elaben argon par'autou* and *Doretoi t'epelonto pararretoi t'epeesin*,[93] at an end *Oiēthes an auton ou paidion* tetokenai, *all'auton paidion* gegonenai or *en plaistais de* phrontisi *kai en elakhistais* elpisin[94] and inflexion of the same word: (*Axios de stathēnai* khalkous, *oukh axios ōn* khalkou?)[95] and recurrence of the same word ("You spoke of him in life meanly and now you write of him

meanly"). [One also finds] use of the same [concluding] syllable: "What would you have suffered so striking if you had seen the man shirking?" It is possible for one example to have all these features—for the same [colon] to be an antithesis and *parison* and *homoeoteleuton*.[96] **[1410b]** 10. The beginnings of periods have mostly been enumerated in the *Theodectea*.[97] There are also false antitheses, for example, the one [the comic poet] Epicharmus wrote:

> Sometimes I was in their house, sometimes I was with them.

NOTES

1. Aristotle applies to word choice the concept of virtue as a mean between two extremes that is fundamental to his ethical philosophy. His emphasis on clarity as the most important requirement of good oratorical style is consistent with his stress on logical proof in the earlier books and his dislike of the style of sophists. For some possible implications, see Consigny 1987. Artistic prose in Greek, though influenced by Gorgianic mannerism derived from poetry, was largely a matter of the purification of diction and regularization of syntax into an efficient, elegant tool of expression. The great models of Attic prose are Plato, Lysias, Isocrates, and Demosthenes.

2. *Kyrios* refers to the prevailing meaning in current usage and may also be translated "proper" in the sense found in dictionary definitions; it is not necessarily the semantic, etymological, or essential meaning of the word. Modern literary critics, however, have called the concept into serious question, emphasizing the context as the determinant of meaning; cf. especially Richards 1936, 37–41.

3. *Poetics* 21–22.

4. The view of literary language as "defamiliarization" has been greatly extended in modern times by the Russian Formalist School, leading to Roman Jakobson's famous definition of poetry as "organized violence committed on ordinary speech"; see Erlich 1981, 219.

5. Lit. "in bare words"; Aristotle has no technical term for prose.

6. Perhaps the earliest statement in criticism that the greatest art is to disguise art.

7. The statement sounds as though Theodorus was still acting when Aristotle first wrote this passage; that would date it to the mid-350s B.C.; see Burkert 1975.

8. The concealment of the art involved in choosing words; see 3.2.10.

9. *Onomata*, "name words" (including adjectives) and *rhēmata*, "sayings, verbs, predicates," are the two major parts of speech recognized by Aristotle. In 3.5.2 he adds *syndesmoi*, "connectives." See also introduction to Appendix I.E. Full categorization of parts of speech is largely a development of the study of grammar in the third to the first century B.C.

10. Strange or rare words; see 3.3.2.

11. In chap. 3, 7.

12. *Metaphor* is itself a metaphor and literally means "carrying something from one place to another, transference." In *Poetics* 21.7 it is defined as "a movement [*epiphora*] of an alien [*allotrios*] name either from genus or species or from species to genus or from species to species or by analogy"; see Appendix I.E. On Aristotle's concept of the metaphor and the difference between its function in poetics and rhetoric, see Ricoeur 1977, 7–43. Ricoeur says (p. 20) that the Aristotelian idea of *allotrios* tends to assimilate three distinct ideas: *deviation* from ordinary usage *borrowing* from an original usage, and *substitution* for an absent word by an available ordinary word.

13. Ordinary language contains many metaphorical expressions that have often lost their force, e.g., "It's raining cats and dogs," "The sun is smiling," etc.

14. By *homonym* Aristotle means a word that is "equivocal"; see 2.24.2, *Categories* 1.1, and *Sophistical Refutations*, 1.7.

15. See Appendix I.E.

16. Cf. *Poetics* 22.17, where it is also said that an ability to use metaphor is a "sign of natural ability."

17. The incident probably took place about 390 B.C., when both served in a war between Athens and Sparta; see Xenophon, *Hellenica* 6.3.3. Callias was a heredity torchbearer in the Mysteries and apparently thought Iphicrates was just ignorant. Though a prominent Athenian general, he came from humble origins and had family connections with the barbarous Thracians.

18. So called because he first proposed (early fifth century) the use of bronze rather than silver money at Athens.

19. This is known as *katakhrēsis* or *abusio*, but to regard it as metaphor is sometimes thought inconsistent with a rigorous "substitution" theory; cf. Genette 1982, 50–52.

20. The answer to the riddle is "cupping" or "bleeding," done by a physician with a hot bronze cup (in modern times a glass) that draws out blood as it cools.

21. The rhetorician mentioned in Plato's *Phaedrus* (267c2) as having written a discussion of beautiful words.

22. Sophist and mathematician, contemporary with Aristotle. The view here expressed was taken up later by the Stoics; see Cicero, *Letters to His Friends* 9.22.

23. To be discussed in 3.10–11.

24. Each word, though signifying one category of object and interchangeable in some contexts, carries its own connotations of beauty or virtue; cf. the difference between *vase, jar, pot,* and *jug.*

25. As frequently in the Homeric poems.

26. Either epithet could be applied to Orestes, as in Euripides, *Orestes* 1587–88.

27. Simonides of Ceos (c. 556–468 B.C.), fr. 10 ed. page.

28. Produced 426 B.C., now lost; fr. 90 ed. Kock.

29. Or compounds, which Aristotle thinks of as poetic. Greek, like German, forms compounds easily; and though the result is intelligible, it can also be pompous. Elaborate compounds were especially characteristic of the tragic style of Aeschylus and are ridiculed in Aristophanes' *Frogs* 830–94.

30. Lycophron and Alcidamas, like Gorgias, were sophists of the late fifth and early fourth centuries who used poetic language in prose.

31. Lit., "tongues." The term *gloss* comes to be used chiefly of archaic or rare words, but Aristotle means anything that sounds strange and might puzzle an audience; cf. 3.10.2. Some of his examples are really strained metaphors. In *Poetics* 21.6 (see Appendix I.E) a gloss is defined as a word "other people use," thus words borrowed from another dialect or language.

32. *Pelōron* ("monster"), the reading of Parinius 1741, was a "gloss" (strange word) because archaic.

33. *Sinis* means "ravager"; both Sciron and Sinis were famous robbers.

34. By *epithet* (what is "added on") is meant a descriptive adjective or phrase.

35. Colloquial in the United States today, but Aristotle did not know about chocolate milk.

36. "Place, or haunt, of the Muses," Eng. museum.

37. The text is in doubt here.

38. A dithyramb was originally a hymn to Bacchus, thus somewhat wild and metrically varied; in the late fifth century it was a lyric vehicle for virtuoso performers, of whom Timotheus is the best known.

39. The manuscripts continue, ". . . metaphor to iambic poets, for they now use these, as has been said." But this was probably a marginal comment by some later reader, than copied into the text. The cross-reference is to the end of chap. 1.

40. On the basis of Demetrius *On Style* 116, Friedrich Solmsen (1979, 69) reconstructed Gorgias's original statement as "Trembling and wan are the writings, pale and bloodless the doings."

41. Some of the expressions Aristotle finds affected in Greek may be acceptable in English. The context of their use of course determines their suitability, but two thousand and more years of literature have dulled the ear for metaphor.

42. In Greek mythology Philomela (in some versions her sister Procne) was transformed into a swallow by the gods. On this passage see Rosenmeyer 1955.

43. The simile comparing Achilles to a lion occurs in *Iliad* 20.164. "The lion rushed," meaning Achilles, does not occur in the Homeric poems; thus, Aristotle says *would be.* The Homeric poems and early Greek literature generally make very little use of metaphor but much of simile. Their personification of abstract forces or things represents a genuine view that these had life. Historically, at least in Greece, the use of metaphor seems to have developed out of the compression of simile, rather than the other way around, as Aristotle would have it; see Stanford 1936.

44. Androtion was a fourth-century Athenian politician, best known from Demosthenes' speech against him in 346 B.C.; Idreus succeeded Mausolus as king of Caria in 351.

45. I.e., they are equally stupid except that Euxenus knows some geometry.

46. The passages in the *Republic* are 5.469e, 6.488a, and 10.601b, respectively.

47. Perhaps from thrashing in a storm, perhaps from being cut down by oak-handled axes or oak wedges.

48. Probably not Demosthenes the famous orator, whom Aristotle seems to avoid quoting, presumably because of his hostility to Macedon; perhaps the fifth-century general of the same name.

49. When the metaphor would be obscure or too violent, it "needs" to be recast as a simile.

50. On metaphor from analogy, see *Poetics* 21.11–14 in Appendix I.E, where the same example is given.

51. That is, from the different kinds of words discussed above; *kyria,* glosses, compounds, coined words, and metaphors, which include epithets and similes.

52. Others could easily be added, and the chapter is one of the least successful sections of the *Rhetoric*.

53. As in English, "on the one hand" implies a following "on the other."

54. Though the sentence has a number of words that Aristotle would regard as connectives ("but," "when," "for," "both," "and") its faults come from the cumbersome syntax, not from separating connectives or failing to use the expected responses. As the notes have indicated, Aristotle himself is capable of writing awkward sentences even worse than this one, with parentheses that may lead the reader to forget the beginning of the sentence; but the *Rhetoric* is neither a speech nor a literary work. In his *published* dialogues, his language was regarded as elegant and correct; see, e.g., Quintilian 10.1.83.

55. Though the point is probably clear without any illustrations, their absence is another sign of the sketchy nature of this chapter. Note that Aristotle's sentence illustrates the use of connectives he has just discussed.

56. An amphiboly (lit. what "shoots both ways") in dialectic is an equivocation based on a word or phrase with an ambiguous meaning, often creating a fallacious argument.

57. A famous and ambiguous response by the Delphic oracle to Croesus, king of Lydia. He interpreted it as encouragement, but the kingdom destroyed was his own.

58. In Greek, participles have distinct feminine forms. In the next example, the participle is in the masculine plural to agree with *they*.

59. *Polloi syndesmoi*, or *polysyndeton*, regarded by later rhetoricians as a figure of speech involving a surfeit of conjunctions, i.e., A and B and C, etc., rather than A, B, C, etc.

60. Classical Greek was generally written without punctuation and even without spacing between the words and thus had to be "punctuated" by the reader.

61. A mistake in usage; in later rhetorical theory contrasted to a "barbarism," or mistake in the form of a word.

62. Of a tablet made up of only two pieces of thin wood, jointed together loosely.

63. Cope captures the difference in English by *that wife of ours* as contrasted with *our wife*.

64. Greek poet of about 400 B.C., author of an epic on the Theban cycle.

65. Cf. Christian amplification of the glory of God or Christ: without beginning or end, ineffable, unbegotten, etc.

66. Lit., those with "good *onkos*."

67. Aristotle here employs terminology also seen in his later ethical writings, esp. *Nicomachean Ethics* 2.1. *Hexis* is an acquired moral principle that has become a permanent habit of character. Note its connection with education in the example given.

68. Logographers, i.e., professional writers (like Lysias) of speeches for clients to deliver in the law courts.

69. The better manuscripts give *should add a censure;* but ancient rhetoricians (e.g., Quintilian 8.3.37) advised anticipation ("You may not want to believe what I am going to say, but. . . ."); some scribe may have wrongly inserted the single letter that makes the difference in meaning.

70. Reference to Isocrates' *Panegyricus* 186 and 96, respectively (c. 380 B.C.). But Aristotle perhaps misquoted from memory: manuscripts of the *Rhetoric* read *phēmē de kai gnōmē* (fame and reputation), whereas Isocrates' text has *phēmēn de kai mnēmēn* (fame and memory); rhyme (*homoeoteleuton*) contributes to the effect in both cases.

71. *Eirōneia;* see book 2, n. 22.

72. Cf. Gorgias's mockery of the swallow, cited above in 3.3.4; Plato, *Phaedrus* 231d, 241e.

73. *To schēma tēs lexeōs*, the term adopted by later rhetoricians for "figure of speech," but here the language's metrical configuration.

74. A basic Aristotelian principle in metaphysics, physics, and other sciences; cf. *Metaphysics* 2.4.999a27.

75. Prose rhythm, like other aspects of style, should be a mean between the inartistic and the poetic.

76. That is, it is chanted. In Aristotle's time rhapsodes no longer used a lyre.

77. Aristotle speaks as though the paean was frequently found in formal prose in the fourth century, but in fact it is rather rare. He does not consider the cretic (long–short–long) which has the same proportions and is the commonest ancient prose rhythm. The examples of paeans cited in the next sentence are from poetry, probably from Simonides of Ceos. Note that the third example consists of three paeans.

78. Some later rhetoricians, however, regard the last syllable of a sentence as automatically lengthened by position, as is the last syllable of a verse; cf. Cicero, *Orator* 217 and Quintilian's comment, 9.4.93.

79. *Paragraphē*. Though written punctuation was undeveloped, a mark was often made in the margin to indicate the change of speaker in a dramatic text.

80. Or "running" (*eiromenē*); strung together with connectives. Though this is seen in what is called *paratactic* sentence structure, such as "We met, and we went for a walk, and we then had a drink," Aristotle is probably thinking of smaller units, as in polysyndeton; for otherwise it is not the opposite of his description of period style.

81. *Katestrammenē*, the periodic style.

82. The manuscripts insert here the opening of Herodotus' *Histories:* "Of Herodotus of Thurii this is the account of the investigation." Kassel double-brackets the quotation as something added by Aristotle to the otherwise completed text. Though Herodotus' work in general is an example of the strung-on style, the opening sentence does not illustrate the use of connectives.

83. Compare what is said about unrhythmical prose in the previous chapter.

84. Compare the concept of unity of plot in *Poetics* 7; but note that a period, unlike a plot, lacks a "middle." *Periodos*, from *peri* (around) and *hodos* (road), another of Aristotle's visual metaphors, suggests a circular motion; but, as the examples cited show, the technique is more one of antithesis and balance than circularity. Aristotle may not have originated the usage of *periodos* as a stylistic term; the Byzantine encyclopedia *Suda* attributes it to Thrasymachus. Note that an Aristotelian period is not a long sentence with subordinate clauses but a single clause or phrase, often within a longer sentence.

85. Lit. "what is heaped up, indiscriminate."

86. Attributed by the manuscripts to Sophocles, but actually the first line of Euripides' *Meleager*. Aristotle thinks of a period, or its members, as equivalent to a line of verse; the line is metrically complete, but incomplete in thought because of the slight pause at the end. The next line, however, continues without grammatical break, making the geography clear: "Alas, across the straits facing pleasant plains, woe, woe!" (Demetrius, *On Style* 58).

87. A colon (the visual image is that of the limbs of the body) is either a clause or a phrase that has some grammatical independence. A period may be made up of either one or two cola; as sec. 7 will explain, if there are two they may be parallel or contrasted.

88. *Logos* can mean anything from a word to a sentence to a speech but here seems roughly equivalent to "introductory remarks." Cf. its use to refer to the prooemium and narration in Gorgias's *Helen* 5 in Appendix I.A.

89. The quotations in this section are all from Isocrates' *Panegyricus* (1, 35, 41, 48, 72, 89, 105, 149, 181, and 186, respectively) but apparently from memory, since they are not very accurate. The most famous is the reference to Xerxes' invasion of Greece in 480 B.C., when he built a bridge of rafts across the Hellespont and dug a canal for his ships through the isthmus of Athos.

90. Assassins of Alexander of Pherai in 358 B.C. The text is uncertain, but the antithesis clear.

91. Cf. what is said about the refutative enthymeme in 2.23.30.

92. This resembles what is later known as the figure anaphora, but Aristotle's example (*Agron*, etc.) is a play on similar words rather than repetition of the same word: "*Land* they took, *unworked*, from him." It probably comes from a lost play of Aristophanes.

93. *Iliad* 9.526.

94. *Dōretoi* etc. = "Ready for *gifts* they were and ready for *persuasion* by words," from *Iliad* 9.526; *oiēthēs* etc. = "You would have thought him not to have *begotten* a child but himself to have *become* one"; *en plaistias* etc. = "in the greatest *cares* and the smallest *hopes*." Sources of the last two examples are unknown.

95. "Worthy of being set up *in bronze* but not worth a coin *of bronze*." Source unknown.

96. *Parison* is another name for *parisōsis* (sec. 9). *Homoioteleuton* is *paramoiōsis* at the end of cola.

97. Probably Aristotle's own lost survey of the rhetoric of Theodectes, who was repeatedly quoted in 2.23.

BIBLIOGRAPHY

Modern Editions of the Greek Text of the *Rhetoric*

Dufour, Médéric, and Andre Wartelle. 1960–73. *Aristote, "Rhétorique."* With French translation. 3 vols. Paris: Les Belles Lettres.

Kassel, Rudolf. 1976. *Aristotelis "Ars Rhetorica."* Berlin: De Gruyter.

Ross, W. David. 1959. *Aristotelis "Ars Rhetorica."* Oxford: Clarendon.

Translations of the *Rhetoric*

Cooper, Lane, trans. [1932] 1960. *The Rhetoric of Aristotle*. New York: Appleton-Century-Crofts.

Freese, John H., trans. 1926. *Aristotle, "The 'Art' of Rhetoric."* With Greek text. Cambridge: Loeb Classical Library. Harvard University Press.

Roberts, W. Rhys, trans. 1924. *Rhetorica = The Works of Aristotle*. Vol. 11. Oxford: Clarendon. Rpt. 1954 in *Aristotle, "Rhetoric" and "Poetics."* Trans. W. Rhys Roberts and Ingram Bywater. New York: Modern Library. Also rpt., with corrections, 1984 in *The Works of Aristotle*. Ed. Jonathan Barnes, 2.2 152–2269. Princeton: Princeton University Press.

Books and Articles Referred to in the Notes, with Additional Works Useful for Study of the *Rhetoric*

Adamik, Tomás. 1984. "Aristotle's Theory of the Period." *Philologus* 128:184–201.

Arnauld, Antoine. 1858. *La Logique, ou l'art de penser*. Paris: Jules Delalain.

Arnhart, Larry. 1981. *Aristotle on Political Reasoning*. DeKalb: Northern Illinois University Press.

Barnes, Jonathan, Malcolm Schofield, and Richard Sorabji, eds. 1979. *Articles on Aristotle: Psychology and Aesthetics*. London: Duckworth.

Benoit, W. L. 1980. "Aristotle's Example: The Rhetorical Induction," *Quarterly Journal of Speech* 66: 182–92.

Blettner, Elizabeth. 1983. "One Made Many and Many Made One: The Role of Asyndeton in Aristotle's *Rhetoric*." *Philosophy and Rhetoric* 16: 49–54.

Brandes, Paul D. 1989. *A History of Aristotle's "Rhetoric."* Metuchen, N.J.: Scarecrow.

Burkert, Walter. 1975. "Aristoteles im Theater: Zur Datierung des 3. Buch der *Rhetorik* und der *Poetik*." *Museum Helveticum* 32.67–72.

Carawan, E. M. 1983. "*Erotēsis*: Interrogation in the Courts of Fourth-Century Athens." *Greek, Roman, and Byzantine Studies* 24:209–26.

Chroust, Anton-Hermann. 1964. "Aristotle's Earliest Court of Lectures on Rhetoric." *L'Antiquité Classique* 33.58–72. Rpt. in Erickson 1974: 22–36.

Conley, Thomas. 1982. "*Pathē* and *Pisteis*: Aristotle, *Rhet*. II 2–11." *Hermes* 110:300–315.

———. 1984. "The Enthymeme in Perspective," *Quarterly Journal of Speech* 70:168–87.

———. 1990a. *Rhetoric in the European Tradition*. New York: Longman.

———. 1990b. "Aristotle's *Rhetoric* in Byzantium." *Rhetorica* 8:29–44.

Consigny, Scott. 1987. "Transparency and Displacement: Aristotle's Concept of Rhetorical Clarity." *Rhetoric Society Quarterly* 17:413–19.

Cope, Edward M. [1867] 1970. *An Introduction to Aristotle's "Rhetoric."* Reprint. Hildesheim: Olms.

———. [1877] 1970. *The "Rhetoric" of Aristotle, with a Commentary*. 3 vols. Ed. J. E. Sandys. Reprint. Hildesheim: Olms.

Corbett, Edward P. J. 1990. *Classical Rhetoric for the Modern Student*. 3d. ed. New York: Oxford University Press.

Demetrius. 1961. *A Greek Critic: Demetrius on Style*, trans. G. M. A. Grube. Toronto: University of Toronto Press.

Donadi, Francesco. 1983. *Gorgiae Leontini in Helenam laudatio*. Rome: Bretschneider.

Douglas, Alan E. 1955. "The Aristotelian *Synagōgē Technōn* after Cicero, *Brutus*, 46–48." *Latomus* 14:536–39.

Dover, Kenneth J. 1974. *Greek Popular Morality in the Time of Plato and Aristotle*. Berkeley: University of California Press.

———. 1978. *Greek Homosexuality*. Cambridge: Harvard University Press.

Düring, Ingmar. 1957. *Aristotle in the Ancient Biographical Tradition*. Göteborg: Göteborg University.

———. 1966. *Aristoteles: Darstellung und Interpretation seinen Denken*. Heidelberg: Carl Winter Verlag.

Edel, Abraham. 1982. *Aristotle and His Philosophy*. Chapel Hill: University of North Carolina Press.

Eden, Kathy. 1986. *Poetic and Legal Fiction in the Aristotelian Tradition*. Princeton: Princeton University Press.

Eggs, Ekkhard. 1984. *Die "Rhetorik" des Aristoteles: Ein Beitrag zur Theorie der Alltagsargumentation und zur Syntax von Komplexen Sätzen*. Frankfurt: Lang.

Enos, Richard Lee, ed. 1982. "The Most Significant Passage in Aristotle's *Rhetoric*: Five Nominations," *Rhetoric Society Quarterly* 12:2–20.

Erickson, Keith, ed. 1974. *Aristotle: The Classical Heritage of Rhetoric*. Metuchen, N.J.: Scarecrow.

———. 1975. *Aristotle's "Rhetoric": Five Centuries of Philological Research*. Metuchen, N.J.: Scarecrow.

Erlich, Victor. 1981. *Russian Formalism: History–Doctrine*. New Haven: Yale University Press.

Fortenbaugh, William W. 1970. "Aristotle's *Rhetoric* on Emotion." *Archiv für Geschichte der Philosophie* 52:40–70. Rpt. in Erickson 1974: 205–34, and in Barnes et al. 1979: 133–53.

———. 1975. *Aristotle on Emotion: A Contribution to Philosophical Psychology, Rhetoric, Poetics, Politics, and Ethics*. New York: Barnes & Noble.

———. 1985. "Theophrastus on Delivery." *Rutgers University Studies* 2:269–88.

———. 1986. "Aristotle's Platonic Attitude toward Delivery." *Philosophy and Rhetoric* 19:242–54.

Fowler, R. L. 1982. "Aristotle on the Period." *Classical Quarterly* 32:89–99.

Fuhrmann, Manfred. 1960. *Das Systematische Lehrbuch.* Göttingen: Vandenhoeck & Ruprecht.

Gabin, Rosalind J. 1987. "Aristotle and the New Rhetoric: Grimaldi and Valesio." *Philosophy and Rhetoric* 20:170–82.

Gaines, Robert N. 1986. "Aristotle's Rhetorical Rhetoric." *Philosophy and Rhetoric* 19:194–200.

Garver, Eugene. 1986. "Aristotle's *Rhetoric* as a Work of Philosophy." *Philosophy and Rhetoric* 19: 1–22.

———. 1988. "Aristotle's *Rhetoric* on Unintentionally Hitting the Principles of the Sciences." *Rhetorica* 6:381–93.

Genette, Gérard. 1982. *Figures of Literary Discourse.* Trans. Alan Sheridan. New York: Columbia University Press.

Green, Lawrence D. 1990. "Aristotelian Rhetoric, Dialectic, and the Traditions of *Antistrophos.*" *Rhetorica* 8:5–27.

Grimaldi, William M. A. 1975. *Studies in the Philosophy of Aristotle's "Rhetoric."* Wiesbaden: Steiner.

———. 1980–88. *Aristotle, "Rhetoric": A Commentary.* 2 vols. New York: Fordham University Press.

Hamilton, William [1866] 1969. *Lectures on Logic.* Reprint. Stuttgart: Frommann Verlag.

Hauser, Gerald A. 1968. "The Example in Aristotle's *Rhetoric*: Bifurcation or Contradiction?" *Philosophy and Rhetoric* 1:78–90.

———. 1985. "Aristotle's Example Revisited." *Philosophy and Rhetoric* 18:171–79.

Havelock, Eric A. 1982. *The Literate Revolution in Greece and Its Cultural Consequences.* Princeton: Princeton University Press.

Heidegger, Martin. 1962. *Being and Time.* Trans. John Macquarries and Edward Robinson. New York: Harper & Row.

Hellwig, Antje. 1973. *Untersuchungen zur Theorie der Beredsamkeit bei Platon und Aristoteles.* Göttingen: Vandenhoeck & Ruprecht.

Hesiod. 2006. *Works and Days.* Ed. and trans. Glenn W. Most, 86–153. Cambridge, MA: Harvard University Press.

Hill, Forbes, 1981. "The Amorality of Aristotle's *Rhetoric.*" *Greek, Roman, and Byzantine Studies* 22:133–47.

Johnstone, C. L. 1980. "An Aristotelian Trilogy: Ethics, Rhetoric, and the Search for Moral Truth." *Philosophy and Rhetoric* 13:1–24.

Kassel, Rudolf. 1971. *Der Text der Aristotelischen "Rhetorik."* Berlin: De Gruyter.

Kennedy, George A. 1963. *The Art of Persuasion in Greece.* Princeton: Princeton University Press.

———. 1980. *Classical Rhetoric and Its Christian and Secular Tradition from Ancient to Modern Times.* Chapel Hill: University of North Carolina Press.

———, ed. 1989. *The Cambridge History of Literary Criticism.* Vol. 1: *Classical Criticism.* Cambridge: Cambridge University Press.

Killeen, J. F. 1971. "Aristotle, *Rhet.* 1413a." *Classical Philology* 76:186–87.

Kinneavy, James. 1987. "William Grimaldi—Reinterpreting Aristotle." *Philosophy and Rhetoric* 20:183–200.

Leighton, Stephen R. 1982. "Aristotle and the Emotions." *Phronesis* 27:144–74.

Levin, Samuel R. 1982. "Aristotle's Theory of Metaphor." *Philosophy and Rhetoric* 15:24–46.

Lienhard, Joseph T. 1966. "A Note on the Meaning of *Pistis* in Aristotle's *Rhetoric.*" *American Journal of Philology* 87:446–54.

Lord, Carnes. 1981. "The Intention of Aristotle's *Rhetoric.*" *Hermes* 109:326–39.

———. 1986. "On the Early History of the Aristotelian Corpus." *American Journal of Philology* 107:137–61.

Lossau, Manfred. 1974. "Der Aristotelische *Gryllos* antilogisch." *Philologus* 11:12–21.

McCall, Marsh. 1969. *Ancient Rhetorical Theories of Simile and Metaphor.* Cambridge: Harvard University Press.

MacKay, L. A. 1953. "Aristotle, *Rhetoric*, III, 16, 11 (1417b12–20)." *American Journal of Philology* 74:281–86.

Matson, Patrician P., Philip Rollinson, and Marion Sousa, eds. 1990. *Readings from Classical Rhetoric.* Edwardsville: Southern Illinois University Press.

May, James A. 1988. *Trials of Character: The Eloquence of Ciceronian Ethos.* Chapel Hill: University of North Carolina Press.

Merlan, Philip. 1954. "Isocrates, Aristotle, and Alexander the Great." *Historia* 3:68–69.

Miller, Carolyn R. 1987. "Aristotle's 'Special Topics' in Rhetorical Practice and Methodology." *Rhetoric Society Quarterly* 17:61–70.

Mills, Michael J. 1985. "*Phthonos* and Its Related *Pathē* in Plato and Aristotle." *Phronesis* 30:1–12.

Mirhady, David. 1991. "Non-Technical *Pisteis* in Aristotle and Anaximenes." *American Journal of Philology* 112:5–28.

Murphy, James J. 1974. *Rhetoric in the Middle Ages*. Berkeley: University of California Press.

Natali, Carlo. 1989. *"Paradeigma:* The Problems of Human Acting and the Use of Examples in Some Greek Authors of the Fourth Century B.C." *Rhetoric Society Quarterly* 19:141–52.

Nikolaides, A. G. 1982. "Aristotle's Treatment of the Concept of *Proatēs.*" *Hermes* 110:414–22.

Nussbaum, Martha C. 1986. *The Fragility of Goodness*. Cambridge: Cambridge University Press.

Ober, Josiah. 1989. *Mass and Elite in Democratic Athens: Rhetoric, Ideology and the Power of the People*. Princeton: Princeton University Press.

Ong, Walter J. 1982. *Orality and Literacy: The Technologizing of the Word*. New York: Methuen.

Palmer, Georgiana P. 1934. *The Topoi of Aristotle's "Rhetoric" as Exemplified in the Orators*. Chicago: University of Chicago Press.

Pearson, Lionel. 1962. *Popular Ethics in Ancient Greece*. Stanford: Stanford University Press.

Pease, A. S. 1926. "Things without Honor." *Classical Philology* 21:27–42.

Perelman, Chaim, and L. Obrechts-Tyteca. 1969. *The New Rhetoric: A Treatise on Argumentation*. Trans. John Wilkinson and Purcell Weaver. Notre Dame: University of Notre Dame Press.

Rabe, Hugo, ed. 1896. *Commentaria in Aristotelem Graeca*. Vol. 15. Berlin: Reimer.

Radermacher, Ludwig. 1951. *Artium scriptores*. Vienna: Oesterreichische Akademie der Wissenschaften.

Radt, Stefan L. 1979. "Zu Aristoteles *Rhetorik.*" *Mnemosyne* 32:284–306.

Richards, I. A. 1936. *Philosophy of Rhetoric*. Oxford: Oxford University Press.

Ricoeur, Paul. 1977. *The Rule of Metaphor*. Trans. Robert Czerny, Kathleen McLaughlin, and John Costello. Toronto: University of Toronto Press.

Rist, John M. 1989. *The Mind of Aristotle: A Study in Philosophical Growth*. Toronto: University of Toronto Press.

Rorty, A. O. 1984. "Aristotle on the Metaphysical Status of *Pathē.*" *Review of Metaphysics* 37:521–46.

Rosenmeyer, Thomas G. 1955. "Gorgias, Aeschylus, and *Apatē.*" *American Journal of Philology* 76:225–60.

Ryan, Eugene E. 1984. *Aristotle's Theory of Rhetorical Argumentation*. Montreal: Bellarmin.

Schiappa, Edward. 1990. "Did Plato Coin *Rhētorikē?*" *American Journal of Philology* 111:457–70.

Schröder, Joachim. 1985. "Ar. *Rhet*. A2. 1356a35–b10, 1357a22–b1." *Hermes* 113:172–82.

Solmsen, Friedrich. 1929. *Die Entwicklung der Aristotelischen Logik und Rhetorik*. Berlin: Weidmann.

———. 1938. "Aristotle and Cicero on the Orator's Playing Upon the Feelings." *Classical Philology* 33:390–404.

———. 1941. "The Aristotelian Tradition in Ancient Rhetoric." *American Journal of Philology* 62:35–50 and 169–90. Rpt. in Erickson 1974:278–309.

———. 1979. Review of Kassel, *Aristoteles "Ars rhetorica."* *Classical Philology* 74:68–72.

Sprague, Rosamond Kent, ed. 1972 *The Older Sophists*. Columbia: University of South Carolina Press.

Sprute, Jürgen. 1982. *Die Enthymemtheorie der Aristotelischen Rhetorik*. Göttingen: Vandenhoeck & Ruprecht.

Stanford, William B. 1936. *Greek Metaphor*. Oxford: Blackwell.

Thür, Gerhard. 1977. *Beweisführung vor den Schwurgerichthöfen Athens*. Vienna: Oesterreichische Akademie der Wissenschaften.

Toulmin, Stephen. 1958. *Uses of Argument*. Cambridge: Cambridge University Press.

Wartelle, André. 1981. *Lexique de la "Rhétorique" d'Aristote*. Paris: Les Belles Lettres.

Wieland, Wolfgang. 1968. "Aristoteles als Rhetoriker und die Exoterischen Schriften." *Hermes* 86:323–46.

Wikramanayake, George H. 1961. "A Note on the *Pisteis* in Aristotle's *Rhetoric.*" *American Journal of Philology* 82:193–96.

Wisse, Jakob. 1989. *Ethos and Pathos from Aristotle to Cicero*. Amsterdam: Hakkert.

Wooten, Cecil W. 1973. "The Ambassador's Speech: A Particularly Hellenistic Genre of Oratory." *Quarterly Journal of Speech* 59:209–12.

2   *From* Orator

CICERO

There are in all three oratorical styles, in each of which certain men have been successful, but very few have attained our ideal of being equally successful in all. The orators of the grandiloquent style, if I may use an old word, showed splendid power of thought and majesty of diction; they were forceful, versatile, copious, and grave, trained and equipped to arouse and sway the emotions; some attained their effect by a rough, severe, harsh style, without regular construction or rounded periods; others used a smooth, ordered sentence-structure with a periodic cadence. At the other extreme were the orators who were plain, to the point, explaining everything and making every point clear rather than impressive, using a refined, concise style stripped of ornament. Within this class some were adroit but unpolished and intentionally resembled untrained and unskillful speakers; others had the same dryness of style, but were neater, elegant, even brilliant and to a slight degree ornate. Between these two there is a mean and I may say tempered style, which uses neither the intellectual appeal of the latter class nor the fiery force of the former; akin to both, excelling in neither, sharing in both, or, to tell the truth, sharing in neither, this style keeps the proverbial "even tenor of its way," bringing nothing except ease and uniformity, or at most adding a few posies[1] as in a garland, and diversifying the whole speech with simple ornaments of thought and diction. Those who have gained power in one or another of these three styles have had a great name as orators, but it is open to question whether they have attained the result which we desire. We see, to be sure, that there have been some whose speech was ornate and weighty, and also shrewd and plain. Would that we could find an example of such an orator among the Romans! It would be fine not to seek our models among foreigners, but to be content with our own. But I recall that in that dialogue which I published under the title of *Brutus*, though I paid high tribute to Romans, both to encourage others and because I loved my own people, still I placed Demosthenes far above all others,[2] as one whom I might consent to

From *Orator*, trans. H. M. Hubbell (Cambridge, MA: Harvard University Press, 1952), 319–79.

37

identify with that ideal eloquence, not with that which I had myself found in anyone. No one has ever excelled him either in the powerful, the adroit, or the tempered style. For this reason we must advise those whose misguided views have been spread abroad, who desire to be called "Atticists" or insist that they speak in the Attic style, — we must advise them to admire that man above all who, I am sure, was as Attic as Athens itself. Let them learn what is Attic, and measure eloquence by his strength, not by their own weakness. At the present time one praises only what one hopes to be able to imitate. However, as these are men of high ambition but poor judgement, I think it not out of place to explain to them the true glory of Atticism.

The eloquence of orators has always been controlled by the good sense of the audience, since all who desire to win approval have regard to the good-will of their auditors, and shape and adapt themselves completely according to this and to their opinion and approval. Accordingly, Caria, Phrygia, and Mysia, where there is the least refinement and taste, have adopted a rich and unctuous diction which appeals to their ears. But their neighbors, the Rhodians, though separated only by a narrow strait, never approved this style, Greece showed it even less favor, and the Athenians utterly repudiated it, holding with sound and discerning judgement that they could listen to nothing that was not pure and well chosen. The orator who complied with their scruples dared not use a word that was unusual or offensive. As an illustration, Demosthenes, who, I said, excels all others, in his masterpiece, the famous oration *In Defence of Ctesiphon*,[3] began calmly, then in his discussion of the laws he continued without adornment; after that he gradually aroused the jury, and when he saw them on fire, throughout the rest of the oration he boldly overleaped all bounds; yet, careful as he was to weigh every word, Aeschines criticizes and attacks some points, and in mockery calls his language harsh, offensive, and intolerable,[4] even asking him, while denouncing him as a brute, whether these are words or monstrosities. Aeschines, then, thought that not even Demosthenes was "Attic." It is easy, indeed, to criticize some flaming word, if I may use this expression, and to laugh at it when the passion of the moment has cooled. That is why Demosthenes in excusing himself jestingly says that the fortunes of Greece did not depend on his using this word or that, or extending his hand in this direction or in that.[5] What reception would a Mysian or Phyrigian have had at Athens, when even Demosthenes was censured as affected? If he had ever begun to sing in the Asiatic manner, in a whining voice with violent modulations, who would have put up with him? Rather I might say, who would not have cried "Put him out"?

Those speakers, then, who conform to the refined and scrupulous Attic taste, must be considered to speak in Attic style. There are many kinds of Atticists: but these of our day[6] apprehend the nature of one kind only. They think that the only one who attains the Attic norm is he who speaks in rough and unpolished style, provided only that he is precise and discriminating in thought. Their mistake is in assuming him to be the only one; they are quite right in calling him Attic. If this is the only Attic style, then, according to their principles, even Pericles did not speak in the Attic manner, yet every one granted his pre-eminence. If he had used the plain style, Aristophanes[7] would never have said that he "lightened, and thundered, and embroiled all Greece." Let us agree, then, that the Attic manner of speech belonged to Lysias, that most charming and exquisite writer (who could deny it?), provided that we understand that the Attic quality in Lysias is not that he is plain and un-adorned, but that he has nothing strange or wanting in taste. On the other hand, we must concede that ornate, vehement, and eloquent language is found in the Attic orators, or else deny that Aeschines and Demosthenes are Attic. And here come some who take the title "Thucydideans"—a new and unheard-of group of ignoramuses. Those who follow Lysias at least follow a pleader of sorts, not indeed grand and stately, but for all that refined and pre-cise, and able to hold his own famously in the law-court. Thucydides, on the other hand, gives us history, wars and battles—fine and dignified, I grant, but nothing in him can be applied to the court or to public life. Those famous speeches contain so many dark and obscure sentences as to be scarcely intelli-gible, which is a prime fault in a public oration. Are men so perverse as to live on acorns after grain has been discovered? Are we, then, to suppose that the diet of men could be improved by the assistance of the Athenians,[8] but that their oratory could not? Furthermore, what Greek rhetorician[9] ever took any examples from Thucydides? Every one praises him, I grant, but as an intelli-gent, serious, and dignified commentator on events—one to describe wars in history, not to handle cases in law-courts. Consequently he has never been classed as an orator, nor, to tell the truth, would his name be known unless he had written his history, although he was of noble birth and had been honored with public office.[10] No one, however, succeeds in imitating his dignity of thought and diction, but when they have spoken a few choppy, disconnected phrases, which they could have formed well enough without a teacher, each one thinks himself a regular Thucydides. I have even seen a man who wished to resemble Xenophon, whose style is indeed sweeter than honey, but far re-moved from the wrangling of the forum.

Let us return, then, to our task of delineating that ideal orator and mold-ing him in that eloquence which Antonius had discovered in no one. This is doubtless a great and arduous task, Brutus, but nothing, I think, is hard for a lover. And I do love and always have loved your talents, your interests, and your character. As time goes on my heart grows warmer day by day, not only with a consuming desire to be with you, to talk to you, to listen to your learned discourse, but also because of your wonderful reputation for amazing virtues, which, though apparently incompatible, are harmonized by your wis-dom. For example, is there any difference so great as that between kindliness and severity? Yet, who was ever considered more upright or more genial than you? What is so hard as to please everybody in settling a multitude of dis-putes? You are able, however, to send away even the unsuccessful litigants with friendly and contented feelings. The result is that, though you do noth-ing to gain favor, everything you do is favorably received. Consequently Gaul is the only country in the world which is not ablaze in the general conflagra-tion.[11] There you reap the reward of your merit, gaining fame in the full light of Italy, and associating with the best of citizens[12] both in the flower of youth and in the strength of manhood. Most important of all—even in your busiest days you never neglect the pursuit of learning, but are always either writing something yourself or arousing me to write. I began this work, then, as soon as I had finished *Cato*,[13] which I would never have undertaken through fear of this age so unfriendly to virtue, had I not considered it base not to yield when you urged so strongly and kindled the memory of one so dear to me.[14] I call you to witness that it was because you asked me that I dared, albeit reluctantly, to write this book. For I wish that you should share the reproach with me, so that if I cannot defend myself against so weighty a charge, you may take the blame for imposing an excessive task on me, as I take the blame for accepting it. However, any error in my judgement will be counterbalanced by the glory of dedicating the work to you.

It is always difficult to describe the "form" or "pattern" of the "best" (for which the Greek word is χαρακτήρ[15]) because different people have different notions of what is best. "I like Ennius," says one, "because his diction does not depart from common usage." "I like Pacuvius," says another, "for all his lines are embellished and carefully elaborated; in Ennius there is much careless work." Suppose that another likes Accius. There is a difference of opinion, as there is in the case of Greek authors, and it is not easy to explain which type is the most excellent. In the case of painting, some like pictures rough, rude, and sombre, others on the contrary prefer them bright, cheerful, and brilliantly colored. How can you draw up a rule or formula, when each is supreme in its own class, and there are many classes? This misgiving, however, did not deter me from my undertaking; I held that in all things there is a certain "best," even if it is not apparent, and that this can be recognized by one who is expert in that subject.

There are several[16] kinds of speeches differing one from the other, and impossible to reduce to one type; so I shall not include at this time that class to which the Greeks give the name *epideictic* because they were produced as show-pieces, as it were, for the pleasure they will give,[17] a class comprising eulogies, descriptions,[18] histories,[19] and exhortations like the *Panegyric*[20] of Isocrates, and similar orations by many of the Sophists, as they are called, and all other speeches unconnected with battles of public life. Not that their style is negligible; for it may be called the nurse of that orator whom we wish to delineate and about whom we design to speak more particularly. This style increases one's vocabulary and allows the use of a somewhat greater freedom in rhythm and sentence structure. It likewise indulges in a neatness and symmetry of sentences, and is allowed to use well-defined and rounded periods; the ornamentation is done of set purpose, with no attempt at concealment, but openly and avowedly, so that words correspond to words as if measured of in equal phrases, frequently things inconsistent are placed side by side, and things contrasted are paired[21]; clauses are made to end in the same way and with similar sound. But in actual legal practice we do this less frequently and certainly less obviously. In the *Panathenaicus* Isocrates confesses that he strove eagerly for these effects,[22] for he had written, not for a trial in court, but to entertain the audience. Thrasymachus of Calchedon and Gorgias of Leontini are said to have been the first to practice this and, after them, Theodorus of Byzantium and many others called "cunning artificers of speech" by Socrates in the *Phaedrus*.[23] They show many clever phrases but these are like a new and immature product, choppy, resembling verselets, and sometimes over-ornamented. Therefore Herodotus and Thucydides are the more admirable because, though contemporary with those whom I have just mentioned, they are far removed from such tricks, or I might better say, from such folly.[24] Herodotus flows along like a peaceful stream without any rough water; Thucydides moves with greater vigor, and in his description of war, sounds, as it were, the trumpet of war. These were the first, as Theophrastus says, to rouse history to speak in a fuller and more ornate style than their predecessors had used. In the next generation came Isocrates, who is always praised by me more than the others of this group, not without an occasional quiet and scholarly objection from you, Brutus; but you may, perhaps, grant my point if I tell you what I praise in him. For inasmuch as Thrasymachus and Gorgias— the first according to tradition to attempt an artificial arrangement of words— seemed to him to be cut up into short rhythmical phrases, and Theodorus on the other hand seemed too rugged and not "round" enough, as one may say, Isocrates was the first to undertake to expand his phrases and round out the sentences with softer rhythms. Through his teaching of this to his pupils, who attained eminence, some as speakers and some as writers, his home came to be regarded as the laboratory of eloquence. Consequently, just as when Cato praised me I could easily endure even to be censured by all others, so Isocrates should, I think, make light of the criticisms of others in comparison with the judgement of Plato. For as you know, on almost the last page of the *Phaedrus*[25] Socrates is represented as speaking these words: "Isocrates is a young man now, my dear Phaedrus, but I should like to tell you my prophecy about him." "What is it?" said he. "He seems to me to possess too great talent to be judged by the standard of Lysias's speeches, and, furthermore, he has a greater capacity for achievement. It would not at all surprise me if, as he grows older, he will excel all who have ever engaged in oratory in this style which he now affects, as much as a man surpasses a boy; or if he is not content with this, by some divine impulse he will aspire to greater things; for nature has implanted a real philosophy in the man's mind." Socrates made this prophecy about the youth, but Plato wrote it when Isocrates was in middle life, and writing as a contemporary, and as a critic too of all rhetoricians, he admires him only. As for me, those who dislike Isocrates must let me err with Socrates and Plato. The epideictic oration, then, has a sweet, fluent, and copious style, with bright conceits and sounding phrases. It is the proper field for sophists, as we said, and is fitter for the parade than for the battle; set apart for the gymnasium and the palaestra, it is spurned and rejected in the forum. But because eloquence receives nourishment from this until it later takes on color and strength by itself, it as not amiss to speak of what we may call the cradle of the orator. So much for the school and the parade; let us now enter the thick of the fray.

The orator must consider three things, what to say,[26] in what order, and in what manner and style to say it. It will therefore be our task to explain what is best in each division, but in a way somewhat different from that which is usually followed in a textbook. We shall lay down no rules—that was not our undertaking—but we shall outline the form and likeness of surpassing eloquence: nor shall we explain how this is to be produced, but how it looks to us. The first two topics I shall treat briefly, for they are not specially marked out for the highest praise, but are rather fundamental, and apart from that are shared in common with many other pursuits. For to discover and decide what to say is important, to be sure, and is to eloquence what the mind is to the body; but it is a matter of ordinary intelligence rather than of eloquence. For that matter is there any cause in which intelligence is superfluous? Our perfect orator, then, should be acquainted with the topics of reasoning and argument. For in all matters under controversy and debate the questions which are asked are: (1) Was it done? (2) What was done? (3) What was the nature of the act?[27] The question, Was it done? is answered by evidence; the question, What was done? by definition; the question, What was the nature of the act? by the principles of right and wrong. To be able to use these the orator—not an ordinary one, but this outstanding orator—always removes the discussion, if he can, from particular times and persons, because the discussion can be made broader about a class than about an individual, so that whatever is proved about the class must necessarily be true of the individual. Such an inquiry, removed from particular times and persons to a discussion of a general topic, is called θέσις or "thesis." Aristotle trained young men in this, not for the philosophical manner of subtle discussion, but for the fluent style of the rhetorician, so that they might be able to uphold either side of the question in copious and elegant language. He also taught the "Topics"—that was his name for them—a kind of sign or indication of the arguments from which a whole speech can be formed on either side of the question. Therefore our orator—it is not a mere declaimer in a school that we seek, or a ranter in the forum, but a scholarly and finished speaker—our orator, finding certain definite "topics" enumerated, will run rapidly over them all, select those which fit the subject, and then speak in general terms. This is the source of the commonplaces, as they are called.[28] But he will not use this stock unintelligently, but weigh everything and select. For the decisive arguments are not always to be found [in the same categories]. Therefore he will exercise judgement, and will not only discover something to say, but will estimate its value. Nothing is more fruitful than the human mind, particularly one which has had the discipline of education. But just as fruitful and fertile fields produce not only crops but harmful weeds, so sometimes from these categories arguments are derived which are inconsequential, immaterial, or useless. And unless the orator's judgement exercises a rigid selection among these, how can he linger and dwell on his strong points, or make the difficulties seem slight, or conceal what cannot be explained away, and even suppress it entirely, if feasible, or distract the attention of the audience, or bring up some other point which if brought forward can be established more easily than the one which he feels will stand in his way?

The results of his invention he will set in order with great care. (Arrangement, it will be remembered, was the second of the three points to discuss.) The orator will certainly make fair "porches"[29] and gorgeous approaches to his oration. And when he has gained attention by the introduction, he will establish his own case, refute and parry the opponents' argument, choosing the strongest points for the opening and closing, and inserting the weaker points in between.

So far we have sketched briefly and summarily the qualifications of our orator in relation to the first two parts of oratory. These divisions are weighty and important, but, as has been said before, they require less art and labor. When, however, the speaker has discovered what to say and how to arrange his subject-matter, then comes the all-important question of the manner of presentation. It was a shrewd remark that our Carneades[30] used to make, that Clitomachus repeated the substance of his teaching, but Charmadas reproduced the style also. If style, then, makes so much difference in philosophy, where the attention is concentrated on the meaning, and words as such are not weighed, what must we think of the importance of style in suits at law which are wholly swayed by oratorical skill? On this point I judged from your letter, Brutus, that you did not seek my opinion or oratorical perfection in invention and disposition, but I thought you wished to know what I considered the best oratorical style. A hard task, I swear; indeed the hardest of all. For not only is language soft, pliant, and so flexible that it follows wherever you turn it, but also the varieties in ability and taste have produced styles widely different. Fluency and volubility please those who make eloquence depend on swiftness of speech; others like clearly marked pauses and breathing spells. Could two things be more different? Yet there is something good in each. Some spend their labor on smoothness and uniformity, and on what we may call a pure and clear style; others affect a harshness and severity of language and an almost gloomy style. And so, according to our previous division of orators into three classes,[31] those who aim to be impressive, or plain, or moderate, there are found to be as many kinds of orators as we said there were styles of oratory.

Since I have begun to carry out my task somewhat more fully than you requested—you asked only about the use of language, but I included a brief treatment of invention and arrangement in my answer—so now I shall speak not merely about the method of expression, but also about the manner of delivery. Consequently no essential topic will be omitted,[32] for there is no need of discussing memory in this connection; it is common to many arts.

Manner of speech falls into two sections, delivery and use of language. For delivery is a sort of language of the body, since it consists of movement or gesture as well as of voice or speech. There are as many variations in the tones of the voice as there are in feelings, which are especially aroused by the voice. Accordingly the perfect orator, whom we have been delineating for some time, will use certain tones according as he wishes to seem himself to be moved and to sway the minds of his audience. I should be more explicit on this point if this were the occasion for instruction, or if you desired it. I might also speak about gestures, which include facial expression. The way in which the orator uses these makes a difference which can scarcely be described. For many poor speakers have often reaped the rewards of eloquence because of a dignified delivery, and many eloquent men have been considered poor speakers because of an awkward delivery. Demosthenes was right, therefore, in considering delivery to be the first, second, and third in importance.[33] If, then, there can be no eloquence without this, and this without eloquence is so important, certainly its rôle in oratory is very large. Therefore the one who seeks supremacy in eloquence will strive to speak intensely with a vehement tone, and gently with lowered voice, and to show dignity in a deep voice, and wretchedness by a plaintive tone. For the voice possesses a marvellous quality, so that from merely three registers, high, low, and intermediate, it produces such a rich and pleasing variety in song. There is, moreover, even in speech, a sort of singing—I do not mean this "epilogue"[34] practiced by Phrygian and Carian rhetoricians which is almost like a *canticum*[35] in a play—but the thing which Demosthenes[36] and Aeschines mean when they accuse each other of vocal modulations. (Demosthenes goes still farther and says that Aeschines had a clear and pleasant voice.) Here I ought to emphasize a point which is of importance in attaining an agreeable voice: nature herself, as if to modulate human speech, has placed an accent, and only one, on every word, and never farther from the end of the word than the third syllable. Therefore let art follow the leadership of nature in pleasing the ear. Certainly natural excellence of voice is to be desired; this is not in our power, but the use and management of the voice is in our power. The superior orator will therefore vary and modulate his voice; now raising and now lowering it, he will run through the whole scale of tones. He will also use gestures in such a way as to avoid excess: he will maintain an erect and lofty carriage, with but little pacing to and fro, and never for a long distance. As for darting forward, he will keep it under control and employ it but seldom. There should be no effeminate bending of the neck, no twiddling of the fingers, no marking the rhythm with the finger-joint. He will control himself by the pose of his whole frame, and the vigorous and manly attitude of the body, extending the arm in moments of passion, and dropping it in calmer moods. Furthermore, what dignity and charm is contributed by the countenance, which has a role second only to the voice. After assuring that the expression shall not be silly or grimacing, the next point is the careful control of the eyes. For as the face is the image of the soul, so are the eyes its interpreters, in respect of which the subjects under discussion will provide the proper limits for the expression of joy or grief.

We must now turn to the task of portraying the perfect orator and the highest eloquence. The very word "eloquent" shows that he excels because of this one quality, that is, in the use of language, and that the other qualities are overshadowed by this.[37] For the all-inclusive word is not "discoverer," or "arranger," or "actor,"[38] but in Greek he is called ῥήτωρ[39] from the word "to speak," and in Latin he is said to be "eloquent." For everyone claims for himself some part of the other qualities that go to make up an orator, but the supreme power in speaking, that is eloquence, is granted to him alone.

Certain philosophers, to be sure, had an ornate style—for example Theophrastus received his name from his divinely beautiful language,[40] and Aristotle challenged even Isocrates, and the Muses were said to speak with the voice of Xenophon, and Plato was, in dignity and grace, easily the first of all writers or speakers—yet their style lacks the vigor and sting necessary for oratorical efforts in public life. They converse with scholars, whose minds they prefer to soothe rather than arouse; they converse in this way about un-exciting and noncontroversial subjects, for the purpose of instructing rather than captivating; and some think they exceed due bounds in aiming to give some little pleasure by their style.[41] It is therefore easy to distinguish the elo-quence which we are treating in this work from the style of the philosophers. The latter is gentle and academic; it has no equipment of words or phrases that catch the popular fancy; it is not arranged in rhythmical periods, but is loose in structure; there is no anger in it, no hatred, no ferocity, no pathos, no shrewdness; it might be called a chaste, pure, and modest virgin. Conse-quently it is called conversation rather than oratory. While all speaking is oratory, yet it is the speech of the orator alone which is marked by this special name.

More care must be taken to distinguish the oratorical style from the simi-lar style of the Sophists mentioned above,[42] who desire to use all the orna-ments which the orator uses in forensic practice. But there is this difference, that, whereas their object is not to arouse the audience but to soothe it, not so much to persuade as to delight, they do it more openly than we and more fre-quently; they are on the look-out for ideas that are neatly put rather than rea-sonable; they frequently wander from the subject, they introduce mythology, they use far-fetched metaphors and arrange them as painters do color com-binations; they make their clauses balanced and of equal length, frequently ending with similar sounds.[43] History is nearly related to this style. It involves a narrative in an ornate style, with here and there a description of a country or a battle. It has also occasional harangues and speeches of exhortation. But the aim is a smooth and flowing style, not the terse and vigorous language of the orator. The eloquence which we are seeking must be distinguished from this no less than from the poetic style. For the poets have given rise to the in-quiry as to the difference between them and the orators. It once seemed to be a matter of rhythm and verse, but now rhythm has become common in ora-tory. For everything which can be measured by the ear, even if it does not make a complete verse—that is certainly a fault in prose—is called rhythm, in Greek ῥυθμός. For that reason some, I know, have held that the language of Plato and Democritus, which, though not in verse, has a vigorous movement and uses striking stylistic ornaments, has more right to be considered poetry than has comedy, which differs from ordinary conversation only by being in some sort of verse. However, this is not the chief mark of a poet, although he deserves more credit for seeking the virtues of the orator, limited as he is by the form of the verse. As for my own opinion, although some poets use grand and figurative language, I recognize that they have a greater freedom in the formation and arrangement of words than we orators have, and also that, with the approval of some critics, they pay more attention to sound than to sense. And indeed if they have one point in common—this is discernment in selection of subject matter and choice of words—we cannot for that reason pass over their dissimilarity in other things. But there is no doubt a difference between poetry and oratory, and if there is any dispute about it, the investigation is not necessary for our present purpose. Distinguishing the orator, then, in point of style from the philosopher, the sophist, the historian, and the poet, we must set forth what he is to be.

The man of eloquence whom we seek, following the suggestion of Antonius, will be one who is able to speak in court or in deliberative bodies so as to prove, to please, and to sway or persuade. To prove is the first necessity, to please is charm, to sway is victory; for it is the one thing of all that avails most in winning verdicts. For these three functions of the orator there are three styles, the plain style for proof, the middle style for pleasure, the vigorous style for persuasion; and in this last is summed up the entire virtue of the orator. Now the man who controls and combines these three varied styles needs rare judgement and great endowment; for he will decide what is needed at any point and will be able to speak in any way which the case requires. For after all the foundation of eloquence, as of everything else, is wisdom. In an oration, as in life, nothing is harder than to determine what is appropriate. The Greeks call it πρέπον; let us call it *decorum* or "propriety." Much brilliant work has been done in laying down rules about this; the subject is in fact worth mastering. From ignorance of this mistakes are made not only in life but very frequently in writing, both in poetry and in prose. Moreover the orator must have an eye to propriety not only in thought but in language. For the same style and the same thoughts must not be used in portraying every condition in life, or every rank, position, or age, and in fact a similar distinction must be made in respect of place, time, and audience. The universal rule, in oratory as in life, is to consider propriety. This depends on the subject under discussion, and on the character of both the speaker and the audience. The philosophers are accustomed to consider this extensive subject under the head of duties—not when they discuss absolute perfection, for that is one and unchanging; the literary critics consider it in connection with poetry; orators in dealing with every kind of speech, and in every part thereof. How inappropriate it would be to employ general topics and the grand style when discussing cases of stillicide[44] before a single referee, or to use mean and meagre language when referring to the majesty of the Roman people. This would be wrong in every respect; but others err in regard to character—either their own or that of the jury, or of their opponents; and not merely in the statement of facts, but often in the use of words. Although a word has no force apart from the thing, yet the same thing is often either approved or rejected according as it is expressed in one way or another. Moreover, in all cases the question must be, "How far?" For although the limits of propriety differ for each subject, yet in general too much is more offensive than too little. Apelles said that those painters also make this error, who do not know when they have done enough. This is an important topic, Brutus, as you well know, and requires another large volume; but for our present discussion the following will be enough: Since we say "This is appropriate"—a word we use in connection with everything we do or say, great or small—since, I repeat, we say "This is appropriate" and "That is not appropriate," and it appears how important propriety is everywhere (and that it depends upon something else and is wholly another question whether you should say "appropriate" or "right";—for by "right" we indicate the perfect line of duty which every one must follow everywhere, but "propriety" is what is fitting and agreeable to an occasion or person; it is important often in actions as well as in words, in the expression of the face, in gesture and in gait, and impropriety has the opposite effect); the poet avoids impropriety as the greatest fault which he can commit; he errs also if he puts the speech of a good man in the mouth of a villain, or that of a wise man in the mouth of a fool; so also the painter[45] in portraying the sacrifice of Iphigenia, after representing Calchas as sad, Ulysses as still more so, Menelaus as in grief, felt that Agamemnon's head must be veiled, because the supreme sorrow could not be portrayed by his brush; even the actor seeks for propriety; what, then, think you, should the orator do?[46] Since this is so important, let the orator consider what to do in the speech and its different divisions: it is certainly obvious that totally different styles must be used, not only in the different parts of the speech, but also that whole speeches must be now in one style, now in another.

It follows that we must seek the type and pattern of each kind—a great and arduous task, as we have often said; but we should have considered what to do when we were embarking; now we must certainly spread our sails to the wind, no matter where it may carry us. First, then, we must delineate the one whom some deem to be the only true "Attic" orator. He is restrained and plain, he follows the ordinary usage, really differing more than is supposed from those who are not eloquent at all. Consequently the audience, even if they are no speakers themselves, are sure they can speak in that fashion. For that plainness of style seems easy to imitate at first thought, but when attempted nothing is more difficulty. For although it is not full-blooded, it should nevertheless have some of the sap of life, so that, though it lack great strength, it may still be, so to speak, in sound health. First, then, let us release him from, let us say, the bonds of rhythm. Yes, the orator uses certain rhythms, as you know, and these we shall discuss shortly; they have to be employed with a definite plan, but in a different style of speech; in this style they are to be wholly eschewed. It should be loose but not rambling; so that it may seem to move freely but now to wander without restraint. He should also avoid, so to speak, cementing[47] his words together too smoothly, for the hiatus and clash of vowels has something agreeable about it and shows a not unpleasant carelessness on the part of a man who is paying more attention to thought than to words. But his very freedom from periodic structure and cementing his words together will make it necessary for him to look to the other requisites. For the short and concise clauses must not be handled carelessly, but there is such a thing even as a careful negligence. Just as some women are said to be handsomer when unadorned—this very lack of ornament becomes them—so this plain style gives pleasure even when unembellished: there is something in both cases which lends greater charm, but without showing itself. Also all noticeable ornament, pearls as it were, will be excluded; not even curling-irons will be used; all cosmetics, artificial white and red, will be rejected; only elegance and neatness will remain. The language will be pure Latin, plain and clear; propriety will always be the chief aim. Only one quality will be lacking, which Theophrastus mentions fourth among the qualities of style—the charm and richness of figurative ornament. He will employ an abundance of apposite maxims dug out from every conceivable hiding place; this will be the dominant feature in this orator. He will be modest in his use of what may be called the orator's stock-in-trade. For we do have after a fashion a stock-in-trade, in the stylistic embellishments, partly in thought and partly in words. The embellishment given by words is twofold, from single words and from words as they are connected together. In the case of "proper" and ordinary words, that individual word wins approval which has the best sound, or best expresses the idea; in the case of variations from the common idiom we approve the metaphor, or a borrowing from some source, or a new formation or the archaic and obsolete (yet even obsolete and archaic words are to be classed as "proper" except that we rarely use them). Words when connected together embellish a style if they produce a certain symmetry which disappears when the words are changed, though the thought remains the same; for the figures of thought which remain even if the words are changed are, to be sure, numerous, but relatively few are noticeable. Consequently the orator of the plain style, providing he is elegant and finished, will not be bold in coining words, and in metaphor will be modest, sparing in the use of archaisms, and somewhat subdued in using the other embellishments of language and of thought. Metaphor he may possibly employ more frequently because it is of the commonest occurrence in the language of townsman and rustic alike. The rustics, for example, say that the vines are "bejewelled,"[48] the fields "thirsty," the crops "happy," the grain "luxuriant." Any of these metaphors is bold enough, but there is a similarity to the source from which the word is borrowed, or if a thing has no proper term the borrowing seems to be done in order to make the meaning clear, and not for entertainment. The restrained speaker may use this figure a little more freely than others, but not so boldly as if he were speaking in the grandest style. Consequently, impropriety—the nature of which should be plain from what has been said about propriety—appears here too, when a metaphor is farfetched, and one is used in the plain style which would be appropriate in another. This unaffected orator whom certain people call "Attic," and rightly so, except that he is not the only "Attic"—this orator will also use the symmetry that enlivens a group of words with the embellishments that the Greeks call σχήματα, figures as it were, of speech. (They apply the same word also to figures of thought.) He will, however, be somewhat sparing in using these. For as in the appointments of a banquet he will avoid extravagant display, and desire to appear thrifty, but also in good taste, and will choose what he is going to use. There are, as a matter of fact, a good many ornaments suited to the frugality of this very orator I am describing. For this shrewd orator must avoid all the figures that I described above, such as clauses of equal length, with similar endings, or identical cadences, and the studied charm produced by the change of a letter,[49] lest the elaborate symmetry and a certain grasping after a pleasant effect be too obvious. Likewise if repetition of words requires some emphasis and a raising of the voice, it will be foreign to this plain style of oratory. Other figures of speech he will be able to use freely, provided only he breaks up and divides the periodic structure and uses the commonest words and the mildest of metaphors. He may also brighten his style with such figures of thought as will not be exceedingly glaring. He will not represent the State as speaking[50] or call the dead from the lower world,[51] nor will he crowd a long series of iterations into a single period. This requires stronger lungs, and is not to be expected of him whom we are describing or demanded from him. For he will be rather subdued in voice as in style. But many of these figures of thought will be appropriate to this plain style, although he will use them somewhat harshly: such is the man we are portraying. His delivery is not that of tragedy nor of the stage; he will employ only slight movements of the body, but will trust a great deal to his expression. This must not be what people call pulling a wry face, but must reveal in a well-bred manner the feeling with which each thought is uttered.

A speech of this kind should also be sprinkled with the salt of pleasantry, which plays a rare great part in speaking. There are two kinds, humor and wit. He will use both; the former in a graceful and charming narrative, the latter in hurling the shafts of ridicule. Of this latter there are several kinds,[52] but now we are discussing another subject. We here merely suggest that the orator should use ridicule with a care not to let it be too frequent lest it become buffoonery; nor ridicule of a smutty nature, lest it be that of low farce; nor pert, lest it be impudent; nor aimed at misfortune, lest it be brutal, nor at crime, lest laughter take the place of loathing; nor should the wit be inappropriate to his own character, to that of the jury, or to the occasion; for all these points come under the head of impropriety. He will also avoid far-fetched jests, and those not made up at the moment but brought from home; for these are generally frigid. He will spare friends and dignitaries, will avoid rankling insult; he will merely prod his opponents, nor will he do it constantly, nor to all of them nor in every manner. With these exceptions he will use wit and humor in a way in which none of these modern "Attics" do, so far as I know, though this is certainly an outstanding mark of Attic style. For my part, I judge this to be the pattern of the plain orator—plain but great and truly Attic; since whatever is witty and wholesome in speech is peculiar to the Athenian orators. Not all of them, however, are humorous. Lysias is adequate and so is Hyperides; Demades is said to have excelled them all, Demosthenes is considered inferior. Yet it seems to me that none is cleverer than he; still he is not witty so much as humorous; the former requires a bolder talent, the latter a greater art.[53]

The second style is fuller and somewhat more robust than the simple style just described, but plainer than the grandest style which we shall presently discuss. In this style there is perhaps a minimum of vigor and a maximum of charm. For it is richer than the unadorned style, but plainer than the ornate and opulent style. All the ornaments are appropriate to this type of oration, and it possesses charm to a high degree. There have been many conspicuous examples of this style in Greece, but in my judgement Demetrius of Phalerum led them all. His oratory not only proceeds in calm and peaceful flow, but is lighted up by what might be called the stars of "transferred" words (or metaphor) and borrowed words. By "transferred" I now mean, as often before, words transferred by resemblance from another thing in order to produce a pleasing effect, or because of lack of a "proper" word; by "borrowed"[54] I mean the cases in which there is substituted for a "proper" word another with the same meaning drawn from some other suitable sphere. It is, to be sure, a "transfer" when Ennius says

I am bereft of citadel and town,[55]

but a "transfer" of quite a different kind than when he says

Dread Africa trembled with terrible tumult.[56]

The latter is called ὑπαλλαγή or "hypallage" by the rhetoricians, because as it were words are exchanged[57] for words; the grammarians call it μετωνυμία or "metonymy" because nouns[58] are transferred. Aristotle, however, classifies them all under metaphor and includes also the misuse of terms, which they call κατάχρησις or "catachresis," for example, when we say a "minute" mind instead of "small"; and we misuse related words on occasion either because this gives pleasure or because it is appropriate. When there is a continuous stream of metaphors, a wholly different style of speech is produced; consequently the Greeks call it ἀλληγορία or "allegory."[59] They are right as to the name, but from the point of view of classification Aristotle does better in calling them all metaphors. The Phalerian uses these very frequently, and they are attractive to a degree; and although he has many metaphors, yet the cases of metonymy are more numerous than in any other orator. To the same oratorical style—I am discussing the mean and tempered style—belong all figures of language, and many of thought. This speaker will likewise develop his arguments with breadth and erudition, and use commonplaces without undue emphasis. But why speak at length? It is commonly the philosophic schools which produce such orators[60]: and unless he be brought face to face with the more robust speaker, the orator whom I am describing will find approval on his own merits. It is, as a matter of fact, a brilliant and florid, highly colored and polished style in which all the charms of language and thought are intertwined. The Sophists are the source from which all this has flowed into the forum, but scorned by the simple and rejected by the grand, it found a resting-place in this middle class of which I am speaking.

The orator of the third style is magnificent, opulent, stately, and ornate; he undoubtedly has the greatest power. This is the man whose brilliance and fluency have caused admiring nations to let eloquence attain the highest power in the state; I mean the kind of eloquence which rushes along with the roar of a mighty stream, which all look up to and admire, and which they despair of attaining. This eloquence has power to sway men's minds and move them in every possible way. Now it storms the feelings, now it creeps in; it implants new ideas and uproots the old. But there is a great difference between this and the other styles. One who has studied the plain and pointed style so as to be able to speak adroitly and neatly, and has not conceived of anything higher, if he has attained perfection in this style, is a great orator, if not the greatest. He is far from standing on slippery ground, and, when once he gets a foothold, he will never fall. The orator of the middle style, whom I call moderate and tempered, once he has drawn up his forces, will not dread the doubtful and uncertain pitfalls of speaking. Even if not completely successful, as often happens, he will not run a great risk; he has not far to fall. But this orator of ours whom we consider the chief—grand, impetuous, and fiery, if he has natural ability for this alone, or trains himself solely in this, or devotes his energies to this only, and does not temper his abundance with the other two styles, he is much to be despised. For the plain orator is esteemed wise because he speaks clearly and adroitly; the one who employs the middle style is charming; but the copious speaker, if he has nothing else, seems to be scarcely sane. For a man who can say nothing calmly and mildly, who pays no attention to arrangement, precision, clarity, or pleasantry—especially when some cases have to be handled entirely in this latter style, and others largely so—if without first preparing the ears of his audience he begins trying to work them up to a fiery passion, he seems to be a raving madman among the sane, like a drunken reveller in the midst of sober men.

We have him now, Brutus, the man whom we are seeking, but in imagination, not in actual possession. If I had once laid my hands on him, not even he with his mighty eloquence would have persuaded me to let him go. But we have certainly discovered that eloquent orator whom Antonius never saw. Who is he, then? I will describe him briefly, and then expand the description at greater length. He in fact is eloquent who can discuss commonplace matters simply, lofty subjects impressively, and topics ranging between in a tempered style. You will say, "There never was such a man." I grant it; for I am arguing for my ideal, not what I have actually seen, and I return to that Platonic Idea of which I had spoken; though we do not see it, still it is possible to grasp it with the mind. For it is not an eloquent *person* whom I seek, nor anything subject to death and decay, but that absolute quality, the possession of which makes a man eloquent. And this is nothing but abstract eloquence, which we can behold only with the mind's eye. He, then, will be an eloquent speaker—to repeat my former definition—who can discuss trivial matters in a plain style, matters of moderate significance in the tempered style, and weighty affairs in the grand manner.

NOTES

1. The *tori*, "posies," seem to have been small bouquets set into a garland of leaves.
2. *Brutus* 35.
3. Generally known as the oration *On the Crown*.

4. Aeschines, *In Ctes.* 166 ff.

5. Dem. *De Cor.* 232.

6. The self-styled "Attici" whom Cicero is criticizing.

7. *Acharnians* 530–531.

8. The allusion is to the legend that the human race lived on acorns until Triptolemus, the favorite of Demeter, sowed grain in Attica.

9. *i.e.* teacher of oratory.

10. Thucydides was elected a general in the Peloponnesian War.

11. He refers to the civil war between Caesar and the Pompeian party. Brutus had been appointed governor of Cisalpine Gaul in 46 B.C.

12. Cicero emphasizes the fact that the inhabitants of Brutus's province (Cisalpine Gaul, *i.e.* North Italy) have the high dignity of Roman citizenship.

13. The work in praise of Cato, the opponent of Caesar, who committed suicide at Utica.

14. Cicero, afraid that his encomium of Cato will be unfavorably received by Caesar, is trying to shift the blame to Brutus. Cicero was, however, mistaken; Caesar was not offended.

15. *i.e.* "distinctive mark" or "character," "stamp on a coin."

16. The deliberative (address to legislative bodies), the forensic (address to judicial bodies), the epideictic (including all other speeches, eulogies, patriotic addresses, etc.).

17. Aristotle, *Rhet.* 1. 3, 2, says that the audience at such an oration act as spectators rather than as judges.

18. *e.g.* the *Euboicus* of Dio of Prusa.

19. History was regularly regarded in antiquity as a branch of rhetoric, much to the disadvantage of history.

20. In the form of an exhortation to the Greeks to unite against Persia, but largely devoted to the praise of Athens.

21. Cicero's roundabout way of translating the Greek "antithesis."

22. Isocrates, *Panathenaicus* 1. 2.

23. Plato, *Phaedrus* 266 E.

24. This is true of Herodotus, but Thucydides was certainly influenced by the Gorgianic style, as other ancient critics were aware.

25. Plato, *Phaedrus* 279 A.

26. To use the technical rhetorical terms, (1) *inventio*, discussed in §§ 44–49; (2) *dispositio* (50); (3) *actio* (55–60); and *elocutio* (61–236).

27. Literally, Is it? What is it? Of what sort is it?

28. *i.e.* general arguments.

29. *Cf.* a similar comparison in Pindar, *Ol.* 6. 1: χρυσέας ὑποστάσαντες εὐτυχεῖ προθύρῳ θαλάμου κίονας, ὡς ὅτε θαητὸν μέγαρον πάξομεν ἀρχομένου δ᾽ ἔργου πρόσωπον χρὴ θέμεν τηλαυγές.

30. Carneades (214/3–129/8 B.C.), head of the New Academy at Athens. He is referred to as "our" because both Cicero and Brutus adhered to this school of philosophy. Carneades was famous for eloquence as well as philosophy. Clitomachus and Charmadas were two pupils of Carneades; Clitomachus, a foreigner, grasped the philosophical teachings of his master, but failed to attain his eminence in oratory.

31. *Cf.* §§ 20, 21.

32. There were normally five chapters in a treatise on rhetoric: invention, arrangement, expression, memory, delivery.

33. This saying of Demosthenes is reported by several ancient authors, *e.g.* Philodemus, περὶ ῥητορικῆς 1. 196. 3 (Sudhaus): Δημοσθένης καὶ πρῶτον καὶ δεύτερον καὶ τρίτον εἶναι τὴν ὑπόκρισιν ἐν τῇ ῥητορικῇ. *Cf.* also Pseudo-Plutarch, *Vita X Orat.* 845 B, and Cicero, *Brutus* 142.

34. Epilogue was the technical term for the concluding appeal to the emotions of the audience. Longinus (*Rhet. Graeci* 1. 197, 4. Sp.) says that in such appeals the tone is between speech and song.

35. The lyrical and recitative passages of a Roman comedy.

36. Demosthenes (*De Corona* 259, 291) accuses Aeschines of shouting, howling and bellowing. Aeschines in turn (*In Ctesiphontem* 209, 210) comments on the pitch of Demosthenes' voice— ὁ τόνος τῆς φωνῆς. It is this last phrase which Cicero translates by *vocis inflexiones*.

37. That is, the Latin word for eloquence (*eloquentia*) is obviously derived from *eloquor*, "speak."

38. That is, the orator is not named from any of the minor functions of the orator which have just been discussed: *inventio*, invention or discovery of arguments, *dispositio*, disposition or arrangement, *actio*, action or delivery.

39. Connected with the verb ἐρῶ, "speak."

40. His name, originally Tyrtamus, was changed by Aristotle (Diog. Laert. 5. 38). Theophrastus is compounded from θεός, "god," and θράζω, "speak."

41. The Stoics deprecated any attention to elegance of style.

42. § 37.

43. He refers to the Gorgianic figures; see Volkmann, *Rhetorik der Griechen und Römer*, pp. 465–488.

44. The legal technicalities about water dripping from a roof on adjoining property.

45. Timanthes of Cythnos, fl. circa 400 B.C.

46. The translation alters the structure of this rambling and incoherent sentence without, I hope, doing violence to the thought.

47. For this figurative use of *coagmentare* cf. *Brutus* 68.

48. The buds are compared with jewels.

49. *Cf. De Oratore* 2. 256, quoting from Cato, *nobiliorem, mobiliorem*.

50. *e.g. In Cat.* 1 18 *(patria) tecum, Catilina, sic agit et quodam modo tacita loquitur*.

51. *e.g. Pro Caelio* 33: Cicero calls Appius Claudius Caecus from the dead to witness the shame of his descendants.

52. Cicero had discussed this at length in *De Oratore* 2. 253–289.

53. The discussion of the plain style is extended by Cicero out of all proportion to the space allotted to the middle and grand styles, because this was the chief point of debate between him and the Atticists.

54. Literally "changed."

55. Ennius, *Andromache*, Frag. 88 V.² *Remains of Old Latin*, L.C.L., i. p. 250.

56. Ennius, *Annales* Frag. 310 V.² Ennius wrote: "Africa *terribili tremit horrida terra tumultu*," *Remains*, i. p. 114. *Cf.* Cic. *De Oratore* 3, 167.

57. Latin *summutatur* = Greek ὑπαλλάττονται.

58. Aeolic ὤνυμα is the basis of μετωνυμία for the word metonymy.

59. Cicero intends *alia oratio* to be a literal translation of ἀλληγορία.

60. Demetrius of Phalerum, whom Cicero regards as the outstanding orator in this style, was a Peripatetic.

WORKS CITED

Aeschines. 1979. *Against Ctesiphon (On the Crown)*, ed. Rufus B. Richardson. New York: Arno.

Aristophanes. 2002. *Acharnians*, ed. S. Douglas Olson. Oxford: Oxford University Press.

Aristotle. 1991. *The Rhetoric*, Book 3. In *On Rhetoric: A Theory of Civic Discourse*, ed. George A. Kennedy, 220–43. New York: Oxford University Press.

Cicero. 1988. *Cato: Major de Senectute.* Cambridge: Cambridge University Press.

Demosthenes. 1970. *On the Crown.* Ed. William Watson Goodwin. London: Cambridge University Press.

Isocrates. 1929. *Panathenaicus. Isocrates Vol. 2*, trans. George Norlin. Cambridge, MA: Harvard University Press.

Isocrates. 1929. *Panegyricus. Isocrates Vol. 1*, trans. George Norlin. Cambridge, MA: Harvard University Press.

Pindar. 2004. *Olympian Odes: English and Greek*, trans. William H. Race. Athens: Greek Font Society.

Plato. 1914. *Phaedrus. Plato. Vol. 1*, trans. Harold North Fowler, 412–579. Cambridge, MA: Harvard University Press.

Volkmann, Richard von. 1872. *Die Rhetorik der Griechen und Römer, in systematischer Übersicht dargestellt.* Berlin: Ebeling.

3

Book X, Chapter 2

QUINTILIAN

From these authors, and others worthy to be read, must be acquired a stock of words, a variety of figures, and the art of composition. Our minds must be directed to the imitation of all their excellences, for it cannot be doubted that a great portion of art consists in imitation—for even though to invent was first in order of time and holds the first place in merit, it is nevertheless advantageous to copy what has been invented with success. Indeed, the whole conduct of life is based on the desire of doing ourselves that which we approve in others. Thus boys follow the traces of letters in order to acquire skill in writing; thus musicians follow the voice of their teachers, painters look for models to the works of preceding painters, and farmers adopt the system of culture approved by experience. We see, in short, that the beginnings of every kind of study are formed in accordance with some prescribed rule. We must indeed, be like or unlike those who excel; and nature rarely forms one *like*, though imitation does so frequently. But the very circumstance that renders the study of all subjects so much more easy to us than it was to those who had nothing to imitate, will prove a disadvantage to us unless it be turned to account with caution and judgment.

Undoubtedly, then, imitation is not sufficient of itself, if for no other reason than that it is the mark of an indolent nature to rest satisfied with what has been invented by others. For what would have been the case, if, in those times which were without any models, mankind had thought that they were not to execute or imagine anything but what they already knew? Assuredly nothing would have been invented. Why then is it unlawful for anything to be devised by us which did exist before? Were our rude forefathers led, by the mere natural force of intellect, to the discovery of so many things, and shall not we be roused to inquiry by the certain knowledge that those who inquired did find new things? When those who had no master in any subject have transmitted so many discoveries to posterity, shall not the experience which

From *On the Teaching of Speaking and Writing: Translations from Books One, Two, and Ten of* Institutio oratoria, ed. James J. Murphy (Carbondale: Southern Illinois University Press, 1987), 132–38.

we have in some things assist us to bring to light others, or shall we have nothing but what we derive from other men's bounty, as some painters aim at nothing more than to know how to copy a picture by means of compasses and lines?

It is dishonorable even to rest satisfied with simply equaling what we imitate. For what would have been the case, again, if no one had accomplished more than he whom he copied? We should have nothing in poetry superior to Livius Andronicus, nothing in history better than the Annals of the Pontiffs; we should still sail on rafts; there would be no painting but that of tracing the outlines of the shadow which bodies cast in the sunshine. If we take a view of all arts, no one can be found exactly as it was when it was invented; no one that has confined itself within its original limits; unless, indeed, we have to convict our own times, beyond all others, of this unhappy deficiency, and to consider that now at last nothing improves; for certainly nothing does improve by imitation only. But if it is not allowable to add to what has preceded us, how can we ever hope to see a complete orator, when among those whom we have hitherto recognized as the greatest no one has been found in whom there is not something defective or censurable? Even those who do not aim at the highest excellence should rather try to excel, than merely follow, their predecessors; for he who makes it his object to get before another, will possibly, if he does not go by him, at least, get abreast of him. But assuredly no one will come up with him in whose steps he thinks that he must tread, for he who follows another must of necessity always be behind him. Besides, it is generally easier to do more, than to do precisely the same; exact likeness is attended with such difficulty that not even nature herself has succeeded in contriving that the simplest objects, and such as may be thought most alike, shall not be distinguished by some perceptible difference. Moreover, everything that is the resemblance of something else must necessarily be inferior to that of which it is a copy, as the shadow to the substance, the portrait to the natural face, and the acting of the player to the real feeling. The same is the case with regard to oratorical composition; for in the originals, which we take for our models, there is nature and real power, while every imitation, on the contrary, is something counterfeit, and seems adapted to an object not its own. Hence it happens that declamations have less spirit and force than actual pleadings, because in one the subject is real, in the other fictitious. In addition to all this, whatever excellences are most remarkable in an orator are inimitable— natural talent, invention, energy, easiness of manner, and whatever cannot be taught by art. In consequence, many students, when they have selected certain words or acquired a certain rhythm of composition from any orator's speeches, think that what they have read is admirably represented in their own sentences. However, words fall into desuetude, or come into use, according to the fashion of the day, so that the most certain rule for their use is found in custom. They are not in their own nature either good or bad (for in themselves they are only sounds), but only as they are suitable and properly applied, or otherwise; and when our composition is best adapted to our subject, it becomes most pleasing from its variety.

Everything, therefore, relating to this department of study, is to be considered with the nicest judgment. First of all, we must be cautious as to the authors whom we would imitate, for many have been desirous to resemble the worst and most faulty originals. In the next place, we must examine what there is, in the authors whom we have chosen for models, that we should set ourselves to attain, for even in great writers there occur faulty passages and blemishes which have been censured by the learned in their remarks on one another. I wish that our youth would improve in their oratory by imitating what is good, as much as they are deteriorated in it by copying what is bad.

Nor let those who have sufficient judgment for avoiding faults, be satisfied with forming a semblance, a mere cuticle, if I may so express myself, of excellence, or rather one of those images of Epicurus, which he says are perpetually flying off from the surfaces of bodies. This, however, is the fate of those who, having no thorough insight into the merits of a style, adapt their manner, as it were, to the first aspect of it; and even when their imitation proves most successful, and when they differ but little from their original author in language and harmony, they yet never fully attain to his force or fertility of language, but commonly degenerate into something worse, lay hold on such defects as border on excellences, and become tumid instead of great, weak instead of concise, rash instead of bold, licentious instead of exuberant, tripping instead of dignified, careless instead of simple. Accordingly, those who have produced something dry and inane, in a rough and inelegant dress, fancy themselves equal to the ancients; those who reject embellishment of language or thought, compare themselves, forsooth, to the Attic writers; those who become obscure by curtailing their periods, excel Sallust and Thucydides; the dry and jejune rival Pollio; and the dull and languid, if they but express themselves in a long period, declare that Cicero would have spoken just like themselves. I have known some, indeed, who thought that they had admirably represented the divine orator's manner in their speeches, when they had put at the end of a period *esse videatur*.[1] The first consideration, therefore, for the student, is, that he should understand *what he proposes to imitate*, and have a thorough conception [of] *why it is excellent*.

Next, in entering on his task, let him consult his own powers — for some things are inimitable by those whose natural weakness is not sufficient for attaining them, or whose natural inclination is repugnant to them — lest he who has but a feeble capacity, should attempt only what is arduous and rough, or lest he who has great but rude talent should waste his strength in the study of refinement, and fail of attaining the elegance of which he is desirous; for nothing is more ungraceful than to treat of delicate subjects with harshness. I did not suppose, indeed, that by the master whom I instructed in my second book,[2] those things only were to be taught to which he might see his pupils severally adapted by nature; he ought to improve whatever good qualities he finds in them; to supply, as far as he can, what is deficient; to correct some things and to alter others; for he is the director and regulator of the minds of others; to mold his own nature may be more difficult. But not even such a teacher, however he may wish everything that is right to be found in the highest excellence in his pupils, will labor to any purpose in that to which he shall see that nature is opposed.

There is another thing also to be avoided, a matter in which many err; we must not suppose that poets and historians are to be the objects of our imitation in oratorical composition, or orators and declaimers in poetry or history. Every species of writing has its own prescribed law, each its own appropriate dress; for comedy does not strut in tragic buskins, nor does tragedy step along in the slipper of comedy—yet all eloquence has something in common, and let us look on that which is common as what we must imitate. On those who have devoted themselves to one particular kind of style, there generally attends this inconvenience, that if, for example, the roughness of some writer has taken their fancy, they cannot divest themselves of it in pleading those causes which are of a quiet and subdued nature; or if a simple and pleasing manner has attracted them, they become unequal to the weight of their subject in complex and difficult causes; when not only the nature of one cause is different from that of another, but the nature of one part of a cause differs from that of another part, and some portions are to be delivered gently, others roughly, some in a vehement, others in an easy tone, some for the purpose of informing the hearer, others with a view to excite his feelings—all which require a different and distinct style. I should not, therefore, advise a student to devote himself entirely to any particular author, so as to imitate him in all respects. Of all the Greek orators Demosthenes is by far the most excellent, yet others on some occasions may have expressed themselves better; and he himself has expressed many things better on some occasions than on others. But he who deserves to be imitated most, is not therefore the only author to be imitated. "What then?" the reader may ask, "is it not sufficient to speak on every subject as Cicero spoke?" To me, assuredly, it would be sufficient if I could attain all his excellences. Yet what disadvantage would it be to assume, on some occasions, the energy of Cæsar, the asperity of Cælius, the accuracy of Pollio, the judgment of Calvus? For besides that it is the part of a judicious student to make, if he can, whatever is excellent in each author his own, it is also to be considered, that if, in a matter of such difficulty as imitation, we fix our attention only on one author, scarcely any one portion of his excellence will allow us to become masters of it. Accordingly, since it is almost denied to human ability to copy fully the pattern which we have chosen, let us set before our eyes the excellences of several, that different qualities from different writers may fix themselves in our minds, and that we may adopt, for any subject, the style which is most suitable to it.

But let imitation (for I must frequently repeat the same precept) not be confined merely to words. We ought to contemplate what propriety was observed by those great men with regard to things and persons; what judgment, what arrangement, and how everything—even what seems intended only to please—was directed to the attainment of success in their cause. Let us notice what is done in their exordium; how skillful and varied is their statement of facts; how great is their ability in proving and refuting; how consummate was their skill in exciting every species of emotion; and how even the applause which they gained from the public was turned to the advantage of their cause; applause which is most honorable when it follows unsolicited, not when it is anxiously courted. If we gain a thorough conception of all these matters, we shall then be such imitators as we ought to be. But he who shall add to these borrowed qualities excellences of his own, so as to supply what is deficient in his models and to trim off what is redundant, will be the complete orator whom we desire to see; and such an orator ought now surely to be formed, when so many more examples of eloquence exist than fell to the lot of those who have hitherto been considered the best orators: for to them will belong the praise, not only of surpassing those who preceded them but of instructing those who followed.

NOTES

1. That is, by using an admired Ciceronian phrase. See Quintilian's citation of this term (from Cicero's *Pro Ligario*) in *Institutio* IX.iv.73.

2. That is, Chapter Eight of Book II.

WORKS CITED

Quintilian. 1953. *Institutio Oratoria*, trans. H. E. Butler, vol. 3, bk 7–9. Cambridge, MA: Harvard University Press.

4

Apologies and Accommodations: Imitation and the Writing Process

FRANK M. FARMER AND
PHILLIP K. ARRINGTON

There is neither a first nor a last word.
> —MIKHAIL BAKHTIN, *SPEECH GENRES AND OTHER LATE ESSAYS*

Imitation has long been a method and theoretical basis for rhetorical instruction. It has also enjoyed a complex, if not always glorious, history—a lineage which extends from the apprenticeship of sophists in Plato's Greece to the moral education of orators in Quintilian's Rome; from the nurturing of abundant expression in a Renaissance text by Erasmus to the cultivation of taste in an Enlightenment text by Hugh Blair. In the last few decades, however, we have witnessed dramatic changes in how we look upon imitation—changes largely influenced, we think, by the "process movement," with its various emphases on invention and revision, expression and discovery, cognition and collaboration. In the wake of shifting so much of our attention to writing processes, we might well expect imitation to have been pronounced as dead as Nietzsche's God was a century ago.

But if the literature reviewed here is any indication, rumors of imitation's death have been greatly exaggerated. Most of the studies in our survey are favorably—and surprisingly—disposed to imitation's continued practice. Such studies typically call for a revised understanding of imitation, a "novel" approach which reveals the proponent's understanding of the need to somehow demonstrate imitation's acceptability to a community which presumably resists its use. Why? Most likely because imitation turns on assumptions about writing and learning which many find discomforting, if not altogether objectionable. There are, of course, fairly complex historical, cultural, and theoretical reasons for our current aversion to imitation, many of which we explore later in our review. But the important point for us is that those who argue for imitation—however much they may differ in their various arguments—

From *Rhetoric Society Quarterly* 23 (1993): 12–34.

share an awareness that its use must be justified *in answer to, and anticipation of, its critical refusal by the community at large*. What we infer from this awareness is the community's largely *tacit* rejection of imitation.

That's not to say, of course, that explicit criticism of imitation is wholly absent from the literature.[1] But in a context where many readily assent to the idea that "almost any form of direct imitation leads to a distortion of the writing process," there is little urgency to speak against its use in the writing classroom (Judy and Judy 127). Indeed, only those who desire a reevaluation of imitation need speak at all, and they must do so in a manner circumscribed by an understanding of how their various arguments are likely to be received. Our purpose, then, is not to critique the arguments offered by imitation's champions, but rather to situate those arguments within the larger context of the process movement in composition.

UNDERSTANDING ARGUMENTS FOR IMITATION

In the pages to follow, we will discuss the ways imitation has been justified during the last three decades. As a convenient strategy for understanding the many and various arguments we encountered, we have identified four categories into which the majority of justifications generally fall: namely, *stylistic, inventional, interventional,* and *social*. We will examine representative studies from each category and discuss their importance in the present context of composition studies. After reviewing these many arguments, we will attempt to understand their larger significance from the perspective of Mikhail Bakhtin's concepts of answerability and authoritative discourse.

Though our review is by no means exhaustive, we do believe the scholarship cited here is indicative of the published literature on imitation since Braddock, Lloyd-Jones, and Schoer's 1963 landmark study.[2] Because imitation is an elusive term at best, we have sought to isolate a working definition that would help us keep a certain focus, yet allow us to accommodate the kinds of justifications we will chronicle in the pages to follow. For our purposes, then, imitation is *the approximation, whether conscious or unconscious, of exemplary models, whether textual, behavioral, or human, for the expressed goal of improved student writing*.[3] We would also point out that despite our efforts to understand something of the current moment in imitation's long history, this is *not* an historical study as such. We may, on occasion, allude to certain periods and figures relevant to our discussion; and, as a necessary part of our review, we will later report on the historical observations of several other scholars in the field. But tracing, constructing, or otherwise investigating the long history of imitation is beyond the scope and purpose of our study.[4]

Within the boundaries of our present moment, however, we do incorporate widely recognized trends, as is evident in our arrangement of the categories below. Generally, our groupings move from text-centered rhetorics to subsequent models of composing offered by expressivist and cognitive rhetorics, then to more recent conceptions derived from social and communal rhetorics. Admittedly, our categories—like all categories—are tenuous but useful impositions, fictions of a sort. As such, they are not meant to be regarded as hermetic or indisputable. Rather, they are intended to enable a degree of understanding previously unrealized or unnamed.

Stylistic Justifications

To the extent that process approaches to writing instruction define themselves in opposition to what Daniel Fogarty, Richard Young, Maxine Hairston, and others have called "current-traditional" rhetoric, these approaches will likely oppose, as well, the formalism implied by that rhetoric. When Richard Young tells us that current-traditional rhetoric usually stresses "the composed product . . . the analysis of discourse into words, sentences, and paragraphs . . . a strong concern with usage . . . and with style," we understand at once that Young is describing a rhetoric devoted to the teaching of discursive forms ("Paradigms" 31). It is hardly surprising, then, that many advocates of process approaches view current-traditional rhetoric—and the formalism implied by it—as a lamentable inheritance from our recent past.

Richard Coe, for example, has argued that "what the past two decades saw was a conflict between a (traditional) *formal* approach and a (renewed) *process* approach" (14). Aware that a concern with form often seems antithetical to process approaches, Coe argues that the kind of form he advocates teaching is "worlds . . . away from traditional static formalism." His method is to teach form "in the context of various processes: creative, communicative, mental, social, and learning." Thus, for Coe, "formalism is not rejected, but subordinated to process" (26). Despite Coe's defense of form, more common are the kinds of reservations voiced by critics like John Gage. Skeptical of the value of teaching forms, Gage questions "the assumption that adequate choice of such forms is determined by the mere knowledge of the availability of those options, rather than by the prior existence of some real intention." For Gage—and several others—the important question is "whether knowing the forms is the same as knowing how to use them" (3).

Nonetheless, a concern with form seems inevitable in pedagogies that seek to improve the stylistic quality of student writing, a fact which may partially explain Elizabeth Rankin's observation that, among composition scholars anyway, style is no longer in style (12). Since imitation's fortunes have traditionally been wedded to style, a good case can be made that a diminished respect for style as an intellectual concern is likewise a narrowing of the possible uses of imitation in the classroom. Indeed, the most common justifications for imitation are stylistic ones, and usually can be paraphrased thus: By imitating a variety of linguistic features, organizational structures, rhetorical devices, etc., students will internalize these and gradually develop a wide repertoire of available forms, which can later be drawn upon when needed to enhance the stylistic virtuosity of the student's own writing. In simpler terms, and as one observer put it: "standing behind imitation as a teaching method is the simple assumption that an inability to write is an inability to design" (Gruber 493–94).

Obviously, those who argue for the value of imitation based on its supposed contributions to a writer's style must believe that style can, in fact, be taught. Louis Milic argues that of the three prevalent theories of style, only one allows for this possibility, namely, what Milic calls "rhetorical dualism." Unlike "psychological monism" (i.e., Buffon's "Style is the man"), which sees style as the inevitable expression of self, or "Crocean aesthetic monism," which posits style as an organic whole, "with no seam between meaning and style" (paradoxically rendering the idea of style meaningless), rhetorical dualism unabashedly upholds the form-content dichotomy and, by so doing, allows for a stylistic subject matter which can be taught (67). For Milic, to be able to teach style at all necessitates a return to the "practices of the old rhetoric," which, among other things, "justify certain classroom procedures," such as imitation (68).

But precisely what is being imitated when students attempt to master the stylistic forms evident in other texts? Which forms? Whose styles? What structures? The answers to these questions encompass a daunting range of possibilities, including sentence type and length; figures, schemes, tropes; parts of speech; additions and substitutions; kinds of modifications; rhetorical devices; levels of generality and texture; word choices; subordination and co-ordination; syntactical patterns; phrasings, common locutions, idiomatic expressions; and even macro-categories of styles, from Cicero's Plain, Middle, and Grand to Walker Gibson's Tough, Sweet, and Stuffy. The choice of which formal categories to use depends, of course, on the teacher's inclinations and the specific pedagogical focus. The important point, according to Winston Weathers, is that "we must identify some *set of categories* . . . to serve as a framework in which various styles can be achieved" (147). This necessity, we think, echoes the form-content split which Milic posits as a condition for the teaching of style.

Other studies affirm this split—especially those which advocate the practice of what is called "close" imitation, a method where students imitate and analyze in detail a model sentence or passage for its identifiable, formal characteristics. Richard Graves, for example, presents his students with classically inspired sentence models based on such various figures and tropes as isocolon, antithesis, epistrophe, anaphora, and so on. Students are expected not only to practice and learn these forms, but also to be able to locate examples of each in other texts. In much the same spirit, Malcolm Kiniry and Ellen Strenski encourage their students to become "active explorers of forms" through the "imitation of [expository] models." Their organizational "schema"—listing, definition, seriation, classification, summary, comparison/contrast, analysis, and argument—constitute a basis for sequencing assignments which introduce students to "a small repertory of expository forms" that can be applied "flexibly in a variety of academic situations." For the authors, the value in teaching such forms is providing students with "the opportunity to practice various rhetorical strategies in a variety of contexts" (191–92).

Besides patterns of organization, entire styles and genres can also be presented as imitable forms. Jacqueline Spencer has her students imitate examples of "business letters, friendly letters, formal essays, arguments, short stories, poems," and so on (43). Likewise, Miles Myers uses "three alternative forms of imitation: *genre models, dictation,* and *paraphrasing*" (15). The "commonsense assumption" of the genre model, claims Myers, "is that students learn to write by reading" (15)—an assumption, Sheila Ryan points out, shared by "numerous landmark studies [which] suggest that exposure to models of different genres should enhance students' ability to write in those forms" (284). Ryan advocates letting students develop "genre-specific principles in the context of writing to communicate effectively" (287).

Both genre and style are traditionally linked with classifications of literary forms and therefore share a legacy of belletristic associations. When reclaimed from the positivist arena (e.g., as "deviation from linguistic norm"), style is defined largely in expressive or aesthetic terms. It should not be too surprising, then, that one of the many uses of literature in the composition classroom is to model exemplary stylistic qualities in prose. Ann Loux, for example, holds that "writing imitations helps students become engaged with theme and structure in literature which they might otherwise find irrelevant or impenetrable" (466). Phyllis Brooks has her students write what she calls "persona paraphrases" to effect the quality of voice found in the modeled language. Since voice is here assumed to be comprised of stylistic nuances, patterns, characteristics, etc., Brooks has her students imitate, for example, the device of "parenthetical modification" as found in the writing of James Baldwin (163).

A number of stylistic justifications for imitation are developmental in nature, often intent on addressing the special problems of basic or "remedial" writers. Donna Gorrell argues that "imitation offers a way for unskilled writers to learn form and structure while generating and finding expression for their own ideas" (54). Echoing this observation, Donald Larmouth notes that "the problem for most inexperienced writers is finding some way to organize their ideas, and models provide at least one way [to do so] (17). Eric Walborn has argued that "the classical triad of *ars, imitatio,* and *exercitatio* (theory, imitation, and practice) [can be] employed to speed natural language acquisition and to encourage language competence and control" (2).

Julia Falk is also concerned with developmental problems of language acquisition. Falk, however, argues that the forms of written discourse are best learned without formal instruction, that is to say, unconsciously. Falk notes that "students may be able to utilize their natural language capacities to internalize the basic principles, structures, and organization of style prior to any overt teaching on the part of the instructor" (438). This is possible because students master language through "hypothesis formation and testing" within a linguistic environment, not through drills and exercises (441). She recommends that students be encouraged to do "extensive reading in the particular form of writing they will later be expected to produce themselves" (438). In that way, students absorb models of desirable style by intellectually engaging the sort of texts they themselves might be asked to write.

Inventional Justifications

One of the salient characteristics of the process movement in composition has been the revived interest in rhetorical invention. For Richard Young and others, invention is "the distinctive feature of the new rhetoric" ("Arts" 54). It is no mere coincidence, according to Young, that

> the shift in attention from composed product to composing process is occurring at the same time as the reemergence of invention as a rhetorical discipline. Invention requires a process view of rhetoric; and if the composing process is to be taught, rather than left to the student to be learned, arts associated with the various stages of the process are necessary. ("Paradigms" 35)

This alliance of process and invention is not only reasonable but useful too, especially for those who see in this relationship further evidence that composition studies are in the midst of a paradigm shift. In any case, such a yoking seems to be widely acknowledged as a matter of crucial importance to the emergence of composition studies as an organized field of inquiry.

Understandably, many advocates of imitation justify its use by pointing to imitation's heuristic or inventional capabilities. Such arguments assert that rather than imitate the textual features of written products, students are far better served if they imitate the discovery procedures of experienced writers, or perhaps certain heuristic methods designed expressly for the purpose of generating ideas. Even in the very earliest days of the process "revolution," D. Gordon Rohman asked teachers "to devise ways that students could imitate the principle of Pre-writing through journal-keeping, meditation, and the use of analogical thinking" (109).

But more developed and substantial studies have since followed. Perhaps most notable among these is Kenneth Roemer's "Inventive Modeling: *Rainy Mountain*'s Way to Composition." Using N. Scott Momaday's *The Way to Rainy Mountain* as an example of inventive technique, Roemer asks his students to imitate Momaday's heuristic strategy of writing about personal experience from different perspectives. As Roemer points out, Momaday's method was to assume three distinct voices—a storytelling, an "objective," and a personal voice—through which Momaday hoped to glimpse some understanding of his Kiowan heritage. Momaday juxtaposed these voices in such a way as to imply a running dialogue of sorts, with "the storytelling voice on the verso page and the two answering voices on the recto." But as Momaday's narrative proceeds, Roemer observes, "the three voices tend to merge," and each distinct voice begins to appropriate characteristics of the other two. "This movement," writes Roemer, "gives the book a dynamic quality, a sense of discovery: a feeling of rich but fragmented pasts coalescing into a rich, meaningful, and personalized present" (771).

In applying Momaday's heuristic to the writing classroom, Roemer first asks his students to choose their own "significant landscape" of personal experience, encouraging them to collect materials from a time or place in their lives which they regard as especially meaningful (773). After organizing these materials, students are asked to write about their personal "landscapes" by "trying on" the three voices suggested by Momaday. According to Roemer, doing so enables students

> to discover and write about new insights, about relationships that link their identities to communities of relatives, friends, stories, and physical and cultural environments. Thus they come to realize, in a very intimate way, how the process of writing can transcend the functions of communication and persuasion to achieve the power of agents that shape how they perceive reality. (774)

Roemer warns, however, that modeling a heuristic procedure, like modeling a finished product, can result in an "abstract" or "artificial" understanding on the student's part, unless the "good" instructor is especially careful to "discourage mechanical and stale thinking" (776).

Taking a somewhat less personal tack, Victoria Winkler differentiates between what she calls "structural" and "inventional" models, the former aligned with product approaches, the latter with process. Borrowing a distinction from W. H. Leatherdale, Winkler argues that a structural model is a "manifest analogy," that is, a direct, proportional analogy which identifies and explains the formal (structural) and functional similarities between the model and the thing modeled" (115). An inventional model, on the other hand, represents what Leatherdale (via Winkler) would call an "imported analogy." The Bohr-Rutherford model of atomic structure, to use Leatherdale's example, was "imported" from perceived similarities "between planetary systems and atomic structure" (116). Winkler points out that rhetoric, too, has its imported analogies, especially in the form of Young, Becker, and Pike's tagmemic system, as well as Kenneth Burke's Pentad. Both systems demand a shifting of perspectives, a "looking at the subject *as if* it were something else" (119). Inventional models are important, then, because they have the potential to "guide and direct the writer's cognitive processes in generating the substance of discourse," while structural models, at their best, "assist the writer in giving form to that substance." Inventional models, for Winkler, can provide "cognitive maps to an unknown territory" (120).[5]

Frank D'Angelo offers what is likely the most philosophical argument for imitation's heuristic value. For D'Angelo, imitation is considered to be "the process whereby the writer participates in archetypal forms and ideas" ("Imitation" 283). These archetypal forms—or "paradigms"—are the "structural counterparts of the topics of invention" which should not be thought of merely as "static, conventional forms," but rather as "*dynamic organizational processes and patterns of thought*" ("Paradigms" 42). Underlying the formal structure of any model text, then, are the "elements that model the writer's cognitive processes" ("Teaching" 173). Thus, by imitating the structures of a model text, students "can internalize the formal principles which are necessary for subsequent invention" ("Imitation" 290).

The notion that form generates content, that language structures are necessarily prior to the ideas they beget, is a quite common justification among those who argue for imitation's generative possibilities. W. Ross Winterowd, for example, believes that not only do structures convey meaning, they also "force meaning" (163). For this reason, teachers should encourage the internalization of these structures, not by formal instruction in grammar but "through the age-old practice of imitation" (166). It is at the level of the sentence, according to Winterowd, "that the real generative capacity of language lies" (167). Francis Christensen would agree, of course, noting that the "mere form" of his "cumulative sentence" results in an inevitable teasing out of ideas. The cumulative sentence possesses heuristic value because "the additions stay with the same idea, probing its bearing and implications, exemplifying it or seeking an analogy or metaphor for it, or reducing it to details" (156). And, most important, this form can be taught. James Gray, for example, asks students to examine "variations of the cumulative sentence in scores of sentences written by professional writers and imitate these methods of modification in sentences of their own" (186).

Finally, one of the more unusual explanations for how imitation helps generate ideas and insights comes from Barrett Mandel. Believing that the *conscious* mind inhibits or even precludes the kind of "fresh thinking" necessary for good writing, Mandel argues that activities such as copying, imitating, and parodying can elicit discoveries much in the same way as freewriting is thought to do—through bypassing the conscious mind. Rote copying, for example, allows the "whole organism to have the experience of producing mature prose *without conceptualizing* consciously at all." When used with freewriting, parody, and other forms of imitation, rote copying is able to "create a climate in which nonconscious illumination can occur" (376–77).

Interventional Justifications

Another important way to justify imitation is to think of it as a kind of interventional strategy, a tool for modeling solutions to the inevitable problems that arise at different stages in the writing process. This group of arguments understands imitation to be something that best occurs *within* the student's writing process, not as an abstracted exercise occurring somewhere outside of any real purpose for writing.

Such is the justification offered by Michael Flanigan, for example, who advocates the use of "dynamic" as opposed to "static" models. Flanigan notes that "the central problem" in modeling is not with the models themselves, but with "how and when they are used" (214). According to Flanigan, "if models are used as problems surface in students' writing and are directly related to problems students are attempting to solve, then it makes sense to show how others have dealt with such problems" (214). Here, then, the model is not presented as a problem to be solved, but rather as "a solution to a real, in process problem" (215). Paul Eschholz likewise holds that the best use of models is in their problem-solving capabilities. For Eschholz, the individual conference is an especially good time to model how other writers solve many of the same kinds of problems faced by his students. Eschholz keeps files of models that highlight certain features of good writing—an exemplary lead, reasoning by analogy, and so on (29–30). "The number of ways that prose models can be used," Eschholz notes, "is endless" (35).

While that may be true, it is far more instructive to examine a concrete illustration of how modeling can be used to solve a particular writing problem. In "Modeling: A Process Method of Teaching," Muriel Harris provides an account of how modeling an alternative writing behavior proved to be especially beneficial to "Mike," a student sent to her writing lab for help in overcoming "choppy sentences" (77). Using a talking-aloud protocol to help diagnose Mike's particular problems, Harris concluded that Mike's inability to "move forward" in his writing resulted from interruptions brought about by "constant editing," as well as from plans and goals "so ineffective that they sent him into unproductive spirals" (77–78). After having Mike make an initial (and unsuccessful) attempt at freewriting, Harris decided to model the specific behaviors which she felt could help Mike solve his writing problems. In each of the four one-hour sessions to follow, Mike began by suggesting a topic for Harris to write on. Harris would then model her own talking-aloud protocol by "thinking about the rhetorical situation . . . plus a few operators to achieve my goal" (78). After a few minutes of initial planning, Harris records that she "would start writing and keep writing. In particular I stressed that I would plunge ahead and try to finish each sentence I wrote without planning the whole sentence beforehand" (78). When she was finished, Harris suggested a topic to Mike and he, in turn, "would try to copy the behavior he had observed" (78).

After completing these sessions, Harris reports that data collected on Mike's writing processes indicate a number of significant improvements, including a more efficient use of planning strategies. While Harris cautions against basing any absolute claims on one case study, she does maintain that "we need to think long and hard about showing, not telling, students about composing processes" (79).

One obvious way to "show" individual writing processes in action is for students and teachers alike to model their own drafting of actual works in progress. Here the focus shifts back to the text itself, not so much as a completed product but as its own narrative of becoming. In promoting teacher writing in the classroom, Richard Larson believes that teachers can become "guides, meticulous Virgils leading a writing class . . . along, paragraph by paragraph, sentence by sentence, even word by word" (292). Larson encourages students to imitate "my method, not my words" (293). Judith Langer and Arthur Applebee stress the rhetorical benefits of these demonstrations, arguing that teachers "model the drafting process . . . to heighten the sense of what is appropriate to a particular purpose for writing" (11). Elaine Maimon likewise argues that "English instructors who share their own work in progress with students teach these novices a great deal about academic development and the interdependence of the scholarly community" (125).[6]

The modeling of students' drafts may also have significant value in the writing classroom. Erika Lindemann, for example, opts for the use of "good" student writing because it "teaches writers of similar age and experience how to plan their work, how to anticipate problems of organization and language, and how to frame their notions of audience, purpose, subject, and persona" (90). Bernard McCabe also reinforces the positive value of student writing by using student essays to generalize the very qualities which make for a good composition. The composite model arrived at through this inductive approach then serves as a model for all students to emulate (43).

A kind of "delayed" modeling of the writing process can be seen in the retrospective accounts offered by writers in explaining how their finished products came to be. While the reliability of such accounts has been challenged, some find considerable value in this form of process modeling.[7] Jack Selzer, for example, asks his students to read "descriptions or accounts of how different writers have responded to different exigencies" (282). He suggests that the *Paris Review Interviews* is an especially good source for such accounts and recommends that students likewise "log their own writing processes" and share these with their classmates. Selzer also sees value in asking students "to observe or interview other writers (both peers and professional people) as they adapt their composing activities to different circumstances for writing" (282). Similarly, John Ruszkiewicz recommends that "teachers use what they have written in the past, both distant and recent, as the subject matter for studies of writing development and the composing process" ("Back" 222). He also advises student writers to do likewise, "for what it reveals to them about writing as a process" ("Back" 223).

Social Justifications

Several proponents of imitation argue that it is the quality of *relationship*—to a teacher, a style, an author, a work, an audience, a community, and so on—that most greatly benefits the apprentice writers in our classrooms. After all, Julia Falk points out, "established professional writers rarely recount and proclaim the influence of writing courses they may have taken in high school and college. Instead, they cite the influence of other writers" (439). We place all such arguments—from the personal relationship between student and teacher to the more abstract reifications of "community,"—under the general heading of *social* justifications, though we recognize a considerable range of meanings associated with that term.

Most important among this group of studies, we believe, is Robert Brooke's "Modeling a Writer's Identity: Reading and Imitation in the Writing Classroom." Brooke claims that "when a student (or any writer) successfully learns something about writing by imitation, it is by imitating another *person* and not a text or process" (23). Drawing upon the work of Goffman, Erikson, and Laing, Brooke sees the imitation of a teacher or writer as one very important way—indeed, *the* most important way—by which students learn to negotiate an identity for themselves through language. This "process of identity formation," according to Brooke, "involves a complex interrelationship of model, past experience, and interpretation, much of which cannot take place at a conscious level" (38). As he demonstrates from interviews with students, the modeled identity can be accepted, transformed, or rejected outright. Regardless of how students respond, "the teacher . . . just isn't in control of the identity the student will develop. Students are not as tractable as that" (38). Most important, Brooke argues, is the fact that assuming, developing, or realizing an identity necessarily implies "a way of being a certain person in the social world." Therefore, composition courses should work to engender "a writer's identity" in students, because "it is in a writer's *stance* towards experience that written language, both writing and reading, moves from being just a 'skill' to being a way of acting in the world" (38). Later, in *Writing and Sense of Self*, Brooke provides more elaboration of how the modeling of "writerly behavior" takes place in the classroom (152).

The importance of social role-playing in the development of identity also finds expression in the work of Richard Lanham. Privileging the "social, dramatic, role-playing self" over the more traditional conception of the inviolate soul, Lanham attacks the stylistic "dogma" of sincerity, arguing that "the adolescent stylist should be encouraged to impersonate other people, not 'be himself'" (115–16). As Lanham sees the matter,

> If the central self is established through a pattern of experimentation with social or dramatic selves—with roles—then sincerity in prose will have to follow a similar pattern and find a central style by playing at, and with, a great many styles. And the two processes will influence one another. To play with styles is to play with roles, with ways of thinking, and, thus, with ways of being. (124)

Though Lanham emphasizes linguistic "play" and formal technique more so than Brooke, both proceed from the assumption that selfhood is a process negotiated through experimentation with other selves. From this vantage, the student writer who has imitated or "tried on" many selves is sooner able to lay claim to one of her own than the student writer who is constantly implored to "be yourself" or "be original." The command to be uniquely expressive may, in fact, inhibit the apprentice writer not yet sure of the self she is supposed to express.

One durable form of sociolinguistic role-playing is parody, an imitative practice that, according to some, has special benefits for novice writers. Hans Guth, for example, sees in parodic imitation "an exploring of possibilities, a delightful discovery and acting out of new patterns and new powers" (127). But parody, by definition, is *critical* role-playing: it not only approximates the parodied language, but comments on that language while doing so. By its very nature, parody demonstrates that not all relationships to a model need be deferential, affirming, or idealizing.[8] Indeed, many champions of imitation point to the value of writers having to "work against" what is or what came before—another writer, a form, an influence, a tradition, and so on.

D. G. Kehl, for example, has collected testimonials from accomplished writers on the significance of imitation to their own development. On balance, such testimonials serve to remind that any existing model is always, to some extent, an invitation to revise. In order to make a verbal stand among predecessors, the student writer—like any other writer—must often confront the necessity of having to wrestle with the overwhelming influence of a master or, say, a favorite teacher or author.

This "agonistic" conception of imitation finds its best expression in the work of David Bartholomae. Paraphrasing Harold Bloom's notion of the "anxiety of influence," Bartholomae argues that by engaging in such requisite struggles, we invent our discursive, historical selves. In the unavoidable confrontation of writer and writer, student and teacher, apprentice and master, a momentous drama occurs. As Bartholomae puts it: "a writer learns . . . to write within and against the writing that precedes him, that haunts him, and that threatens to engulf him" ("Against" 27).[9]

Elsewhere, Bartholomae suggests that imitation may play a key part in how students learn the conventions of academic discourse communities. He thus argues that mastering academic discourse is "more a matter of imitation or parody than a matter of invention or discovery" ("Inventing" 143). Bartholomae observes that in his students' efforts to acquire the specialized languages of the academy, "there are two gestures present . . . one imitative and one critical. The writer continually audits and pushes against a language that would render him "like everyone else" and mimics the language and interpretive systems of the privileged community" (157). Much in the same vein, David Hamilton advocates "serious parodies" of the methods of science (788), and James Porter suggests that recent discussions concerning intertextuality demand that "we rethink our ideas about plagiarism" and that *imitatio* should be understood as "an important stage in the linguistic development of the writer" (42). Alan C. and William C. Purves hold that different communities offer "various models of texts . . . based on the quantity and type of information, on the structure of that information, on linguistic or stylistic forms, and on the visual format of texts, and they ask their members to learn these common models and become loyal to them" (193–94).

What is pervasive in all the arguments discussed here is an abiding consciousness that imitation must somehow be made to "fit" a paradigmatic standard which endorses process approaches to the teaching of writing. Thus, in *stylistic* justifications, proponents hold that the formalism implied by their arguments can be subordinated to the writing process, or that the internalization of linguistic forms can enhance the range of options at a writer's disposal when she is *later* engaged in her writing process. In *inventional* and *interventional* arguments, champions of imitation make a direct attempt to subsume imitation within *the writing process itself*, thereby accommodating it to the current paradigm. Finally, in the *social* justifications group, advocates shift the locus of thinking about process away from expressive, textual, and cognitive perspectives to communally or interpersonally modeled behaviors and attitudes, some of which can only be acquired by or through the imitative gesture. In all of these arguments, though, what remains constant is a shared understanding that if imitation is to be found acceptable, *it must be justified according to the prevailing norms and values corresponding to process approaches and sanctioned by the disciplinary community at large.* The need to justify imitation at all occurs precisely because, as Chaim Perelman might point out, it "fails to respect certain rules or values,"—standards, in other words, in danger of being "infringed upon or violated." For Perelman, justification is a decidedly social act that "always occurs within a social context; it is always "situated" (1099).

Arguments for imitation, we believe, reveal a tacit awareness that imitation is thought to be a settled matter, a practice deemed incompatible with process approaches to the teaching of writing. If, in fact, this were not the case, if imitation enjoyed the blessings of the community at large, there would be little need for any justification at all. If imitation were sanctioned as a pedagogical norm, discussions would center upon further refinements and explorations of its uses in the classroom, and (paradoxically?) we would witness more arguments against imitation than for it.

Others, of course, have commented upon the waning fortunes of imitation. Writing in the early 1970s, Edward P. J. Corbett observed that our aversion to imitation derives from "the suspicion . . . that imitation stultifies and inhibits the writer rather than empowers and liberates him" (249). This view was echoed by Leonard Tourney, who also noticed that "imitation [had] fallen on hard times." According to Tourney, "We prize creativity, originality, sincerity, and to these a dependence on 'models' seems as antithetical as the terrestrial poles." "Nothing," Tourney adds, "suggests our disesteem for an imitation than the bad verbal company it keeps. Imitations are variously cheap, facile, bad, and mere. They cost less" (3).

As these comments suggest, many observers trace imitation's fall to attitudes inherited from our not too distant Romantic past. Maurice Hunt explains the "virtual disappearance of *imitatio* . . . for the teaching of writing" as a phenomenon originating in "cultural Romanticism or Post-Romanticism" (16). Penelope Starkey points out that "only since the Romantic concern with originality has imitation fallen into disrepute" (435). Dale Sullivan likewise acknowledges the influence of Romanticism on imitation's current status, but sees other explanations as well.

Sullivan identifies three "aspects of the modern temper" which make it difficult, if not impossible, for us to "appreciate imitation" in the same way our predecessors could (15). Besides "the Romantic emphasis on genius," Sullivan also isolates "the myth of progress," and "the technological mind-set" as reasons for imitation's fall (16). The first, according to Sullivan, "militates against" teachers looking for "examples of excellence in the past," especially in "a culture [that] believes that future works will be superior" (16). The second follows from "the application of science to the writing process," one premise being that the writing process is knowable through scientific analysis and ultimately reducible to a set of perfectible techniques (17–18). Sullivan touches upon only two of the many problems suggested by a wholly scientific approach to the teaching of writing:

> For a teacher to recommend that her students imitate another writer
> is tantamount to admitting that she does not know every aspect of the
> writing process. Furthermore, the teacher of pure technique, or process,
> could be, at least in theory, a nonwriting scientist, but imitation requires
> the teacher to be a practitioner, for true imitation is an apprenticeship be-
> tween the teacher and the student. (17–18)

Sullivan apprehends correctly that neither Romanticism nor scientism
alone is especially hospitable to further examinations of imitation's uses in the
writing classroom (though Sullivan believes that imitation still holds considerable promise for "bridging the gap" between "the new Romantics and the
new classicists") (18). In any case, and significantly, both of these broad epistemological traditions—Romanticism and scientism—find expression in two
familiar (and widely challenged) theories of process offered by James Berlin
and Lester Faigley. In separate discussions, Berlin and Faigley argue that *expressivist* theories of process are derived historically from Romanticism, and
that *cognitive* theories of process are derived from the same positivist epistemology which informs problem-solving traditions in cognitive psychology.
While we can dangerously oversimplify these relationships, it would be hard
to deny the influence of Romanticism on expressivist theories, or the influence
of a "science consciousness" on cognitive ones.[10]

It is likewise hard to deny the influence of expressivist and cognitive
theories on our present understanding of the writing process. Though some
of the earliest conceptions of this process emerged from those committed to
writing as self-expression, "the strongest proponent" of process approaches
has been cognitive rhetoric (Berlin 480). It has certainly provided the discipline with some of its most sophisticated models of what that process
may involve. And yet, given the epistemological traditions out of which these
two schools arose—and apart from the profound differences between them—
we should not be too surprised that they share a less than enthusiastic stance
toward the practice of imitation. Put otherwise, it is not mere happen-
stance that both Donald Murray and Linda Flower are able to find their own
"good reasons" for rejecting imitation—though, to be sure, these reasons
proceed from very different assumptions about knowledge, selfhood, and
reality.[11]

An Atmosphere of the Already Spoken

As we have seen, there exists no shortage of ways that apologists for imitation
seek to accommodate their individual positions to a less than welcome reception from the community at large. For this reason, and despite our groupings
above, no single argument in our review can properly be regarded as a cate-
gorical statement. In fact, no argument here should be considered as a *statement* at all—if, by using that word, we are taken to mean a consummate
declaration of one's final say on the issue at hand. We think it better to regard
the many arguments above as *utterances*—situated instances of address and
rejoinder within a dialogic context.

The utterance, of course, figures prominently in the language theory of Mikhail Bakhtin. In his efforts to understand the "metalinguistic" nature of the utterance, Bakhtin identifies a number of qualities which distinguish it from purely linguistic phenomena, such as the sentence. For example, Bakhtin observes, the utterance is not limited to expressions of everyday, practical speech. Rather, it subsumes both oral and written discourse and can, in fact, take the form of something as fleeting as clearing one's throat to something as imposing as, say, *Remembrance of Things Past*.[12] Moreover, and because of its thoroughly contextual nature, the utterance is neither repeatable—able to replicate its meaning absolutely—nor neutral—able to abstract itself from the "speaker's evaluative attitude" (*Speech* 84). For our purposes here, though, the most compelling feature of the utterance is its relationship to other utterances.

Bakhtin points out that the utterance always presupposes "*other* . . . participants in speech communication" (*Speech* 72). The change of speaking subjects, the back-and-forth movement of conversational rejoinders, is how we typically perceive actual dialogue. But as Michael Holquist suggests, we miss something very important if we believe that "speaking and listening [are] mutually opposed, unitary activities: [that] a person *did either* one or the other." Holquist reminds us that, for Bakhtin, this seeming "*duality* of roles" falls apart, that dialogue does not proceed sequentially. "Rather, we speak and listen "simultaneously," not as machines, but as "consciousnesses engaged in active understanding" ("Answering" 63). Bakhtin's model of communication, in other words, is far more complex than the familiar "talking-head" diagrams so often encountered in linguistic representations.

Part of this complexity results from the fact that "every word is directed toward an *answer* and cannot escape the profound influence of the answering word that it anticipates" (*Dialogic* 280). Every utterance bears within its voicing an awareness of that which it answers and an expectation of how it might be answered itself. As Bakhtin explains,

> The word in living conversation is directly, blatantly, oriented toward a future answer-word: it provokes an answer, anticipates it and structures itself in the answer's direction. Forming itself in an atmosphere of the already spoken, the word is at the same time determined by that which has not yet been said but which is needed and in fact anticipated by the answering word. (280)

Bakhtin thus cautions that no utterance can be fully understood apart from all those *other* utterances to which it is responding, and from which it is anticipating a response. Utterances, as Bakhtin puts it, are not self-sufficient; they cannot be understood as isolated statements, indifferent or unaware of what else has been—or might be—said. Not only, then, must we pay attention to what the utterance is "about," its semantic reference or "theme," but we must try to understand the utterance in relationship to "others' utterances on the same topic to which we are responding or with which we are polemicizing" (*Speech* 92). Taken together, such utterances form a dialogic context, whose influence no "new" utterance can entirely escape. Bakhtin explains why this is so:

> When speaking, I always take into account the apperceptive background of the addressee's perception of my speech: the extent to which he is familiar with the situation; whether he has special knowledge of the given cultural area of communication, his views and convictions (from my viewpoint), his sympathies and antipathies—because all this will determine his active responsive understanding of my utterance. These considerations also determine my choice of genre . . . compositional devices . . . [and] language vehicles. (*Speech* 95–96)

What Bakhtin has in mind is clearly beyond the univocality of traditional audience analysis. In Bakhtin's scheme of things, the anticipated reply has, as it were, a shaping influence on the author's utterance, even to the extent of determining compositional choices—both *strategic* and *stylized*, as Kenneth Burke might point out (3).

The importance of this insight is that it enables us to situate the arguments of those who try to make imitation acceptable to a paradigmatic standard which has, for the most part, found the practice to be obsolete or misguided. This is why none of the arguments above is about imitation per se; each is, as well, about *the present moment of imitation*, whether this is acknowledged or not. Thus, against a rather hostile "atmosphere of the already spoken," imitation's advocates must stake their claims, must try to provoke the "not yet spoken" word in order to sustain a dialogue that many in our community have quit altogether. The silence of imitation's critics, as we noted earlier, implies a tacit rejection of imitation. But more than that, it implies that judgments about imitation embody, in some measure, what Bakhtin calls authoritative discourse.

The "authoritative word," Bakhtin tells us, aspires to be indisputable and thus seeks out no answering other. Wishing itself to be the last word, "it demands our unconditional allegiance" (*Dialogic* 343). It can assume a number of varied forms, from the hieratic to the pedestrian (Bakhtin mentions in passing "religious dogma . . . acknowledged scientific truth . . . a currently fashionable book") (343), and the warrants for its authority can stem from "authority as such, or the authoritativeness of tradition, of generally acknowledged truths, of the official line," and so on (344). Much academic writing can be included here as well. David Lodge has argued that "scholarly discourse aspires to the condition of monologue inasmuch as it tries to say the last word on a given subject, to affirm its mastery over all previous words on that subject." For Lodge, such discursive posing cannot avoid a measure of "bad faith" on the part of that scholar who, seemingly, would prefer silent admiration to voiced engagement (94).

Not surprisingly, then, authoritative discourse is of necessity "located in a distanced zone" and, in fact, requires distance from other discourses if it is to maintain its privileged status (342). This distance serves the function of insulating the authoritative word from the necessity of having to engage another's word in dialogue. Even though authoritative discourse is capable of provoking abundant, and often vehement, response (we think here of scriptural exegesis, published court decisions, etc.), it balks at responding to the very answers it provokes. However, the authoritative word is sometimes able to be dialogized by bringing it into a "zone of familiar contact." According to Bakhtin, "there is a struggle constantly being waged to overcome the official line with its tendency to distance itself from the zone of contact, a struggle against various kinds and degrees of authority" (345).

Composition's "official line"—that imitation is incompatible with process approaches to the teaching of writing—has been vigorously assailed by many, the majority of whom offer thoughtful, compelling arguments for its use. But whether or not these arguments provoke an answering word, whether or not they have succeeded in bringing imitation back into the "conversation," remains highly doubtful. True, we have seen how imitation's advocates "parry objections . . . make all kinds of provisos, and so forth" in anticipation of less than friendly responses from those to whom their utterances are addressed (*Speech* 95). But defenders of imitation are quite aware— often painfully so—that their words will be greeted not so much with criticism, but with indifference, with the silence of the authoritative word. The review above, we think, is a chronicle of attempts made by imitation's advocates to break that silence, to return imitation to a zone of dialogic contact.

Anticipating our own readers' objections, we allow that much of our narrative will be for some, too speculative or dramatic to capture, fully and accurately, imitation's present moment. And yet, our starting premise remains: those who argue for imitation cannot help cast "a sideward glance at someone else's hostile word"; that such words are mostly unspoken and that such glances—however manifested in, or implied by, individual utterances—tell us much about the present consensus on imitation (Bakhtin "Problems" 196). What we surmise is that, despite the many justifications for imitation chronicled above, none has yet provoked a communal response, none has been able to engender an authentic dialogue about how imitation might be seriously rethought.

The Future of Imitation in Composition Studies

Might we say, then, that imitation belongs properly on the shelf, its usefulness a reminder of just how far we have come in our understanding of how to teach writing? Have we packed imitation away, relegating it forever to our attic of obsolete methods, snug there among other curiosities of a past best left undisturbed?

No, for to say that imitation is no longer regarded as a matter worthy of our attention is not to say that it shall always remain so. To entertain such finalities, we would have to ignore the sheer number of those who continue to argue for imitation's virtues. We would have to ignore, too, the strategies by which proponents of imitation seek to be heard and understood, as well as the possibility of seeing arguments for imitation as *answers*—situationally provoked answers—to a paradigmatic standard which resists its use.

Supporters of imitation, whatever arguments they have marshalled on its behalf, may well find encouragement in Bakhtin's claim that *"the ultimate word . . . has not yet been spoken"* (*"Problems"* 166). Bakhtin contends that "[e]ven *past* meanings . . . can never be stable (finalized, ended once and for all)—they will always change (be renewed) in the process of subsequent, future development of the dialogue" (*Speech* 170). Predicting the course of that development, though, is a different matter entirely, and a tricky one at that. Still, we regard one study to be especially suggestive in mapping some promising directions for reconsidering imitation in writing pedagogy.

In "Originality and Imitation in the Work and Consciousness of an Adolescent Writer," Louise Wetherbee Phelps and Sandra Mano report on the results of a case-study of one subject, "Simon," age twelve, "an articulate young man interested in becoming a professional writer" (290). Through interviews and textual data, Phelps and Mano concluded that imitation played "a central role" in Simon's writing development (290). Yet Simon's expressed preference for models over rules, as well as his ability to "point out the sources of specific lexical, syntactic, and generic selections," demonstrated a consciously imposed apprenticeship that Simon was not always at ease with. Phelps and Mano report that "he alternated between taking pleasure in his own creative impulses and criticizing them as imitative" (291). They interpret this ambivalence to signify "one moment in the process by which an individual, most acutely in adolescence, simultaneously assimilates his culture and separates himself from it in order to contribute new ideas and make critical judgements" (292). To better understand Simon's predicament, the authors suggest that imitation needs to be rethought specifically in terms of "social learning theory . . . Soviet psychology . . . and classical rhetoric" (292). In particular, Phelps and Mano mention the work of L. S. Vygotsky as a source for "fresh perspectives" on imitation (292).

Here, we think, is an especially rich line of inquiry to explore. Vygotsky's research, coupled with the theoretical investigations of his contemporary, Bakhtin, might allow us to see how our own words originally—and, to some extent, always—derive from *someone else's words*, might enable us to chart the subtle and complex ways we assimilate, rework, and deploy other people's words for our own purposes. Imitation, so figured, might come to be understood as a dialogue with, not a parroting of, *the language of the other*, without whom no such thing as "a language of one's own" would be possible.[13]

Taking a broader view, we might do well to remind ourselves that Simon's doubts about imitation are ones we share. Like Simon, we must honestly confront our traditions while, at the same time, establish our identity within and against those traditions. To understand Simon's predicament is, quite simply, to understand something of our own. This very recognition may mark a more genuine dialogue with our past. We might find ourselves having come full circle to understand that we are both a part of—and apart from—a past we will never repeat, but whose resonant and distorting echo we will always sound.

NOTES

1. See, for example, Boyd, Judy and Judy, Moffett, Murray, and Rohman. Murray designates the idea that "students learn best by imitating models of great writing" (107) as one of his "myths" about writing. More recently, Richard Boyd criticizes Bartholomae, Brooke, et al. for not attending to the ideological consequences of "master-apprentice" relationships in the writing classroom. For an overview of earlier objections to the use of imitation in the writing classroom, see Eschholz.

2. This starting point is not an arbitrary one. Among those questions in need of future research, Braddock, et al. identified the following: "How is writing affected by extensive study and imitation or parody of models?" Twenty-three years later, George Hillocks concluded that "the available research into process would not lead us to expect the study of models to have much impact on improvement in writing," particularly if teachers merely lecture about the qualities of the chosen models (*Research* 228). Hillocks, though, does concede that models are "significantly more useful than the study of grammar" ("What Works" 160–61) and calls for more investigation of the use of models in the presentational, individualized, or environmental modes of instruction ("What Works" 163). Steve Graham generally confirms the view that models are of questionable value, reporting that "empirical research, albeit limited, does not support the efficacy of the overall modeling approach" (4), a position noted earlier, and with some qualification, by Hanigan. Since the publication of Hillocks' meta-analysis, however, recent empirical studies indicate somewhat more favorable assessments of imitation's value. For survey data on writers in transition to non-academic settings, see Winsor; for experimental data on student writing, see Shimabukuro, Simmons, and Stolarek; see Purves and Purves for a review of interdisciplinary perspectives on modeling, and their implications for writing research.

3. Richard McKeon has identified at least five different meanings of the word prevalent in antiquity, including the familiar ones bequeathed to us by Plato and Aristotle. In our own time, the term has become even more elusive, if for no other reason than the proliferation of contexts in which it is now used. What imitation means, say, to a specialist in early childhood development is quite different from what it means to a literary critic, music historian, speech therapist, and so on. At the risk of belaboring the obvious, imitation has sundry meanings which result from its many uses in a variety of rhetorical genres and communities of inquiry. While no definition is without problems, we believe ours to be appropriate to our community and consistent with our stated purposes.

4. For a sampling of historical scholarship on imitation (broadly conceived), see Auerbach, Brower, Clark, Corbett, Crowley, Dickinson, Flanigan, Hunt, McDonald, McKeon, Ong, Rodd, Sullivan, and Todorov.

5. In addition to Winkler's borrowing from Leatherdale, modeling theory has also found its way into other pedagogical and methodological discussions. Warren Werner, for example, uses Gordon Laing's classification of models to elaborate a distinction between model and example — a necessary distinction to make, Werner argues, if writing students are to benefit from the use of models. More recently, Michael Pemberton has borrowed Rom Harre's distinction between a model's *subject* and its *source* to demonstrate the inescapable limitations of critiques which seek to argue the epistemological inadequacy of existing models of the writing process. Every model, Pemberton argues, will entail its own limitations, and cannot avoid doing otherwise.

6. For a useful, though somewhat dated, annotated bibliography on teacher modeling, see Robert C. Wess.

7. See, for example, Flower and Hayes ("Uncovering") and Barbara Tomlinson.

8. For other studies on parodic forms of imitation, see Brower, Klancher, Ruszkiewicz ("Parody"), and Sommers. Parody, in its broadest sense, is crucial to Bakhtin's characterization of the novel as a carnivalesque, travestying genre.

9. Not all observers, though are enthusiastic about agonistic relationships to models. James Moffett (208) and Mina Shaughnessy (223) both allude to the inhibiting, debilitating effects novice writers may experience when presented with models of exemplary prose.

10. One quite common oversimplification is to conflate the many approaches to scientific inquiry under the disparaging rubric of positivism, which, in turn, is believed to possess a simplistic uniformity of approach. For a necessary and important corrective to this view, see Berkenkotter.

11. Flower and Hayes are critical of providing students with examples of good and bad writing, not merely because of the difficulties involved in making that determination, but because, in either case, such writing is usually someone else's finished product. See "Problem-Solving Strategies and the Writing Process."

12. Our comparison is intended to dramatize the nature of the utterance, not to suggest any equivalence of value between these two types. Our example does, however, illustrate Bakhtin's distinction between primary and secondary speech genres. "Clearing one's throat" is primary to the extent that doing so signifies an "immediate relation . . . to the real utterances of others." As a secondary speech genre, Proust's novel mediates "speech communion" by its ability to "absorb and digest various primary (simple) genres" (*Speech* 62). Bakhtin's fullest discussion of the utterance is found in the essay "The Problem of Speech Genres" in *Speech Genres and Other Late Essays*.

13. Though seldom acknowledged in the literature, Vygotsky was an explicit advocate of imitation in human learning (187–88). Bakhtin, as far as we know, never "endorsed" imitation, but his favorable remarks on parody and paraphrase, as well as his sophisticated understanding of the subtleties of double-voiced discourse, suggest that the problem of imitation was of some importance to his theory of language. Others, too, have alluded to the possibility that the work of Vygotsky and Bakhtin might require us to rethink the importance of imitation in language learning. See, for example, Flanigan, Schuster, and Klancher.

WORKS CITED

Auerbach, Erich. *Mimesis: The Representation of Reality in Western Literature*. Trans. Willard R. Trask. Princeton, NJ: Princeton UP, 1953.

Bakhtin, M. M. *The Dialogic Imagination: Four Essays*. Ed. Michael Holquist. Trans. Michael Holquist and Caryl Emerson. U of Texas P Slavic Series 1. Austin: U of Texas P, 1981.

———. "Problems of Dostoevsky's Poetics." Ed. and trans. Caryl Emerson. *Theory and History of Literature* 8. Minneapolis: U of Minnesota P, 1984.

———. *Speech Genres and Other Late Essays*. Trans. Vern W. McGee. Ed. Caryl Emerson and Michael Holquist. U of Texas P Slavic Series 8. Austin: U of Texas P, 1986.

Bartholomae, David. "Against the Grain." *Writers on Writing*. Ed. Tom Waldrep. New York: Random House, 1985. 19–29.

———. "Inventing the University." *When a Writer Can't Write*. Ed. Mike Rose. New York: Guilford, 1985. 134–65.

Berkenkotter, Carol. "The Legacy of Positivism in Empirical Composition Research." *Journal of Advanced Composition* 9 (1989): 69–82.

Berlin, James. "Rhetoric and Ideology in the Writing Class." *College English* 50 (September 1988): 477–94.

Boyd, Richard. "Imitate Me; Don't Imitate Me: Mimeticism in David Bartholomae's 'Inventing the University.'" *Journal of Advanced Composition* 11 (1991): 335–45.

Braddock, Richard, Richard Lloyd-Jones, and Lowell Schoer. *Research in Written Composition*. Champaign: NCTE, 1963.

Brooke, Robert. "Modeling a Writer's Identity: Reading and Imitation in the Writing Classroom." *College Composition and Communication* 39 (February 1988): 23–41.

———. *Writing and Sense of Self*. Urbana: NCTE, 1991.

Brooks, Phyllis. "Mimesis: Grammar and the Echoing Voice." *College English* 35 (November 1973): 161–68.

Brower, Reuben. *Mirror on Mirror: Translation, Imitation, Parody*. Cambridge: Harvard UP, 1974.

Burke, Kenneth. *The Philosophy of Literary Form: Studies in Symbolic Action*. Rev. ed. New York: Vintage, 1957.

Christensen, Francis. "A Generative Rhetoric of the Sentence." *College Composition and Communication* 14 (October 1963): 155–61.

Clark, Donald Lemen. "Imitation: Theory and Practice in Roman Rhetoric." *Quarterly Journal of Speech* 37 (1951): 11–22.

Coe, Richard M. "An Apology for Form; or, Who Took the Form Out of the Process?" *College English* 49 (January 1987): 13–28.

Corbett, Edward P. J. "The Theory and Practice of Imitation in Classical Rhetoric." *College Composition and Communication* 22 (October 1971): 243–50.

Crowley, Sharon. "Rhetoric, Literature, and the Dissociation of Invention." *Journal of Advanced Composition* 6 (1985–86): 17–31.

D'Angelo, Frank. "Imitation and Style." *College Composition and Communication* 24 (October 1973): 283–90.

———. "Imitation and the Teaching of Style." *Forum: Essays on Theory and Practice in the Teaching of Writing*. Ed. Patricia Stock. Portsmouth, NH: Boynton/Cook, 1983. 173–88.

———. "Paradigms as the Structural Counterparts of Topoi." *Linguistics, Stylistics, and the Teaching of Writing.* Ed. Donald McQuade. New York: City U of New York, Queens College, 1979. 41–51.

Dickinson, Barbara Ann. "Imitation in the Writing Process: Origins, Implications, Applications." *DAI* 49 (1988): 1081–A.

Eschholz, Paul A. "The Prose Models Approach: Using Products in the Process." *Eight Approaches to Teaching Composition.* Ed. Timothy R. Donovan and Ben W. McClelland. Urbana: NCTE, 1980. 21–36.

Faigley, Lester. "Competing Theories of Process: A Critique and a Proposal." *College English* 48 (October 1986): 527–42.

Falk, Julia S. "Language Acquisition and the Teaching and Learning of Writing." *College English* 41 (December 1979): 436–47.

Flanigan, Michael C. "Composition Models: Dynamic and Static Imitations." *Theory into Practice* 19 (Summer 1980): 211–19.

Flower, Linda, and John R. Hayes. "Problem-Solving Strategies and the Writing Process." *College English* 39 (December 1977): 449–61.

———. "Uncovering Cognitive Processes in Writing: An Introduction to Protocol Analysis." *Research on Writing: Principles and Methods.* Ed. Peter Mosenthal, Lynne Tamor, and Sean A. Walmsely. New York: Longman, 1983. 207–20.

Fogarty, Daniel. *Roots for a New Rhetoric.* New York: Russell and Russell, 1959.

Gage, John T. "Towards an Epistemology of Composition." 2 (1981): 1–9.

Gibson, Walker. *Tough, Sweet and Stuffy.* Bloomington: Indiana UP, 1966.

Gorrell, Donna. "Freedom to Write through Imitation." *Journal of Basic Writing* 6 (Fall 1987): 53–59.

Graham, Steve. "Composition Research and Practice: A Unified Approach." *Focus on Exceptional Children* 14 (April 1982): 1–16.

Graves, Richard L. "A Primer for Teaching Style." *College Composition and Communication* 25 (May 1974): 186–90.

Gray, James. "Sentence Modeling." *Theory and Practice in the Teaching of Composition: Processing, Distancing, Modeling.* Ed. Miles Myers and James Gray. Urbana: NCTE, 1983. 185–202.

Gruber, William E. "'Servile Copying' and the Teaching of English Composition." *College English* 39 (December 1977): 491–97.

Guth, Hans P. "How I Write: Five Ways of Looking at the Blackbird." *Writers on Writing.* Ed. Tom Waldrep. New York: Random House, 1985. 117–31.

Hairston, Maxine. "The Winds of Change: Thomas Kuhn and the Revolution in the Teaching of Writing." *College Composition and Communication* 33 (February 1982): 76–88.

Hamilton, David. "Interdisciplinary Writing." *College English* 41 (March 1980): 780–90.

Harris, Muriel. "Modeling: A Process Method of Teaching." *College English* 45 (January 1983): 74–84.

Hillocks, George. *Research on Written Composition: New Directions for Teaching.* Urbana: NCTE, 1986.

———. "What Works in Teaching Composition: A Meta-Analysis of Experimental Treatment Studies." *American Journal of Education* 93 (November 1984): 133–70.

Holquist, Michael. "Answering as Authoring: Mikhail Bakhtin's Translinguistics." *Bakhtin: Essays and Dialogues on His Work.* Ed. Gary Saul Morson. Chicago: U of Chicago P, 1986. 59–71.

Hunt, Maurice. "*Imitatio* Revisited: A Curriculum Based upon Mimesis." *Freshman English News* 7 (Fall 1988): 16–19.

Judy, Stephen, and Susan J. Judy. *An Introduction to the Teaching of Writing.* New York: John Wiley & Sons, 1981.

Kehl, D. G. "Composition in the Mimetic Mode: *Imitatio* and *Exercitatio.*" *The Territory of Language: Linguistics, Stylistics, and the Teaching of Composition.* Ed. Donald McQuade. Rev. ed. Carbondale: Southern Illinois UP, 1986. 284–91.

Kiniry, Malcolm, and Ellen Strenski. "Sequencing Expository Writing: A Recursive Approach." *College Composition and Communication* 36 (May 1985): 191–202.

Klancher, Jon. "Bakhtin's Rhetoric." *Reclaiming Pedagogy: The Rhetoric of the Classroom.* Ed. Patricia Donahue and Ellen Quandahl. Carbondale: Southern Illinois UP, 1989. 83–96.

Langer, Judith, and Arthur Applebee. "Learning to Manage the Writing Process: Tasks and Strategies." *ERIC* ED 234 420.

Lanham, Richard. *Style: An Anti-Textbook.* New Haven: Yale UP, 1974.

Larmouth, Donald. "Models in Remedial English: An Interim Report." *Minnesota English Journal* 6 (Spring 1970): 14–24.

Larson, Richard. "Back to the Board." *College Composition and Communication* 29 (October 1978): 292–94.

Lindemann, Erika. *A Rhetoric for Writing Teachers.* 2nd ed. New York: Oxford UP, 1987.

Lodge, David. *After Bakhtin: Essays on Fiction and Criticism.* London: Routledge, 1990.

Loux, Ann. "Using Imitation in Literature Classes." *College Composition and Communication* 38 (December 1987): 466–72.

Maimon, Elaine P. "Maps and Genres: Exploring Connections in the Arts and Sciences." *Composition and Literature: Bridging the Gap.* Ed. Winifred Bryan Homer. Chicago: U of Chicago P, 1983. 110–25.

Mandel, Barrett. "The Writer Writing Is Not at Home." *College Composition and Communication* 31 (December 1980): 370–77.

McCabe, Bernard J. "A Program for Teaching Composition to Pupils of Limited Academic Ability." *Classroom Practices in Teaching English, 1965–66.* Co-Chairs Michael F. Shugrue and George Hillocks. Champaign: NCTE, 1965. 39–46.

McDonald, James C. "Imitation of Models in the History of Rhetoric: Classical, Belletristic, and Current-Traditional." *DAI* 48 (1988): 2613–A.

McKeon, Richard. "Literary Criticism and the Concept of Imitation in Antiquity." *Modern Philology* 34 (August 1936): 1–35.

Milic, Louis. "Theories of Style and Their Implications for the Teaching of Composition." *College Composition and Communication* 16 (May 1965): 66–69, 126. Rpt. in *Teaching Freshman Composition.* Ed. Gary Tate and Edward P. J. Corbett. New York: Oxford UP, 1967. 255–60.

Moffett, James. *Teaching the Universe of Discourse.* Portsmouth, NH: Boynton/Cook, 1983.

Murray, Donald. *A Writer Teaches Writing.* Boston: Houghton Mifflin Co., 1968.

Myers, Miles. "Modeling: Writing as the Approximation of Texts." *Theory and Practice in the Teaching of Composition: Processing, Distancing, Modeling.* Ed. Miles Myers and James Gray. Urbana: NCTE, 1983. 4–18.

Ong, Walter. "From Mimesis to Irony: The Distancing of Voice." *The Horizon of Literature.* Ed. Paul Hernadi. Lincoln: U of Nebraska P, 1982. 11–42.

Pemberton, Michael A. "Modeling Theory and Composing Process Models." *College Composition and Communication* 44 (February 1993): 40–58.

Perelman, Chaim. "The New Rhetoric: A Theory of Practical Reasoning." Trans. E. Griffin-Collart and Otto Bird. *The Rhetorical Tradition: Readings from Classical Times to the Present.* Ed. Patricia Bizzell and Bruce Herzberg. Boston: St. Martin's Press, 1990. 1077–1103.

Phelps, Louise Wetherbee, and Sandra Mano. "Originality and Imitation in the Work and Consciousness of an Adolescent Writer." *Solving Problems in Literacy: Learners, Teachers, and Researchers.* Ed. Jerome Niles. Rochester, NY: National Reading Conference, Inc., 1986. 290–93. Yearbook of the National Reading Conference, vol. 35.

Porter, James. "Intertextuality and the Discourse Community." *Rhetoric Review* 5 (Fall 1988): 34–47.

Purves, Alan C., and William C. Purves. "Viewpoints: Cultures, Text Models, and the Activity of Writing." *Research in the Teaching of English* 20 (May 1986): 174–97.

Rankin, Elizabeth. "Revitalizing Style: Toward a New Theory and Pedagogy." *Freshman English News* 14 (Spring 1985): 8–13.

Rodd, Thomas. "Before the Flood: Composition Teaching in America 1637–1900." *English Journal* 72 (February 1983): 62–69.

Roemer, Kenneth M. "Inventive Modeling: *Rainy Mountain*'s Way to Composition." *College English* 46 (December 1984): 767–82.

Rohman, D. Gordon. "Pre-Writing: The Stage of Discovery in the Writing Process." *College Composition and Communication* 16 (May 1965): 106–12.

Ruszkiewicz, John J. "Back to the Source: Personal Research in Writing." *College Composition and Communication* 30 (May 1979): 222–23.

———. "Parody and Pedagogy: Explorations in Imitative Literature." *College English* 40 (February 1979): 693–701.

Ryan, Sheila M. N. "Do Prose Models Really Teach Writing?" *Language Arts* 63 (March 1986): 284–90.

Schuster, Charles. "Mikhail Bakhtin as Rhetorical Theorist." *College English* 47 (October 1985): 594–607.

Selzer, Jack. "Exploring Options in Composing." *College Composition and Communication* 35 (October 1984): 276–84.

Shaughnessy, Mina. *Errors and Expectations: A Guide for the Teacher of Basic Writing.* New York: Oxford UP, 1977.

Shimabukuro, James N. "The Effect of Alternate Instructional Sequences on Student Imitation of Model Essay Subjects." *DAI* 47 (1987): 4282–A.

Simmons, Kathryn A. "An Experimental Study of the Effects of Stylistic Imitation on the Writing Quality of High School Seniors." *DAI* 47 (1986): 168–A.

Sommers, Jeffrey. "Developing a Written Voice through the Use of Written Models." *Kentucky English Bulletin* 34 (Fall 1984): 36–43.

Spencer, Jacqueline. "Learning to Write through Imitation." *English Quarterly* 15 (Winter 1982): 42–45.

Starkey, Penelope. "*Imitatio* Redux." *College Composition and Communication* 25 (December 1974): 435–37.

Stolarek, Elizabeth Ann. "Prose Modeling: Role of Model Description and Explication in Learning Form by Expert and Novice Writers." *DAI* 52 (1992): 2911–A.

Sullivan, Dale L. "Attitudes toward Imitation: Classical Culture and the Modern Temper." *Rhetoric Review* 8 (Fall 1989): 5–21.

Todorov, Tzvetan. *Theories of the Symbol.* Trans. Catherine Porter. Ithaca, NY: Cornell UP, 1982. 111–46.

Tomlinson, Barbara. "Talking about the Composing Process: The Limitations of Retrospective Accounts." *Written Communication* 1 (October 1984): 429–45.

Tourney, Leonard. "Imitation: Creative Possibilities of an Unfashionable Doctrine." *ERIC* ED 105 519.

Vygotsky, L. S. *Thought and Language.* Trans. and ed. Alex Kozulin. Rev. ed. Cambridge, MA: MIT Press, 1986.

Walborn, Eric D. "*Imitatio* Revisited: Its Theoretical and Practical Implications into the Twenty-First Century." *ERIC* ED 281 202.

Weathers, Winston. "Teaching Style: A Possible Anatomy." *College Composition and Communication* 21 (May 1970): 144–49.

Werner, Warren W. "Models and the Teaching of Technical Writing." *Journal of Technical Writing and Communication* 19 (1989): 69–81.

Wess, Robert C. "Imitation Theory and Teacher Writing: An Annotated Bibliography." *Rhetoric Society Quarterly* 11 (Fall 1981): 243–52.

Winkler, Victoria. "The Role of Models in Technical and Scientific Writing." *New Essays in Technical and Scientific Communication: Research, Theory, Practice.* Ed. Paul V. Andersen, R. John Brockman, and Carolyn Miller. Farmingdale, NY: Baywood Publishing Co., 1983. 111–22.

Winsor, Dorothy A. "Joining the Engineering Community: How Do Novices Learn to Write Like Engineers?" *Technical Communication* 37.2 (1990): 171–72.

Winterowd, W. Ross. "Style: A Matter of Manner." *Quarterly Journal of Speech* 56 (April 1970): 161–67.

Young, Richard. "Arts, Crafts, Gifts, and Knacks: Some Disharmonies in the New Rhetoric." *Reinventing the Rhetorical Tradition.* Ed. Aviva Freedman and Ian Pringle. Ottawa: Canadian Council of Teachers of English, 1980. 53–60.

———. "Paradigms and Problems: Needed Research in Rhetorical Invention." *Research on Composing: Points of Departure.* Ed. Charles R. Cooper and Lee Odell. Urbana: NCTE, 1978. 29–47.

5   *The Erasure of the Sentence*

ROBERT J. CONNORS

In the 1980s, as composition studies matured, theoretical and critical interrogation of much of the field's received wisdom began in earnest. The field of composition studies, increasingly in the hands of the new generation of trained specialist PhDs, began to do more and more effectively what intellectual fields have always done: define, subdivide, and judge the efforts of members. Some elements of the older field of composition teaching became approved and burgeoned, while others were tacitly declared dead ends: lore-based and therefore uninteresting, scientistic and therefore suspect, mechanistic and therefore destructive. Little attention has been paid to these preterite elements in the older field of composition; they have been dropped like vestigial limbs, and most of those who once practiced or promoted those elements have retired or moved to more acceptable venues, maintaining a circumspect silence about their earlier flings with now-unpopular ideas such as paragraph theory, or structural linguistics, or stage-model developmental psychology. Of all of the inhabitants of this limbo of discarded approaches, there is no more dramatic and striking exemplar than what was called the school of syntactic methods. These sentence-based pedagogies rose from older syntax-oriented teaching methods to an extraordinary moment in the sun during the 1970s bidding fair to become methodologically hegemonic. But like the mayfly, their day was brief though intense, and these pedagogies are hardly mentioned now in mainstream composition studies except as of faint historical interest. The sentence itself as an element of composition pedagogy is hardly mentioned today outside of textbooks. But we can learn as much from watching the working out of Darwinian intellectual failures as from participating in the self-congratulatory normal science of the current winners, and so I offer this history of syntactic methods since 1960 in the spirit of the old New England gravestone: "As you are now, so once was I; as I am now, so you shall be."

From the earliest point in American composition-rhetoric, the sentence was a central component of what students were asked to study, practice, and

From *College Composition and Communication* 52 (2000): 96–128.

become conversant with. From the 1890s onward, chapters on The Sentence in most textbooks were fairly predictable. Western rhetorical theories about the sentence date back to classical antiquity, with roots in Latin grammar and in the oral rhetorical theories of the classical period, and they came to their nineteenth-century form by a long process of accretion. Traditional sentence pedagogy assumed grammatical knowledge of the sort inculcated by Reed and Kellogg diagrams, but the prime elements in these textbook chapters were taxonomic, all this time focused on their place in sentence construction. Along with the breakdown of sentences by grammatical types—simple, compound, complex, and compound-complex—which was usually taken up in the grammar chapters of textbooks, the traditional classification of sentences is by function: declarative, imperative, interrogative, and exclamatory sentences. The traditional rhetorical classifications of sentences were also covered: long and short, loose and periodic, and balanced. In addition, sentence pedagogy nearly always included coverage of the old abstractions that informed modern composition-rhetoric from 1890 through the present: those of Adams Sherman Hill (clearness, energy, force), Barrett Wendell, (unity, coherence, emphasis), or C. S. Baldwin (clearness and interest).[1]

All of these traditional sentence pedagogies included many exercises and much practice, and we fail to understand them if we think of them only as defined by their abstractions and classifications. Most sentence chapters in textbooks asked students to create many sentences, and indeed, sentence-level pedagogy was an important part of traditional writing courses. It became even more central during the 1950s, a period when composition teachers were looking to structural linguistics with expectation and sentence-writing was much discussed. But as I have discussed in more detail elsewhere (*Composition-Rhetoric* 162–70), it was just as structural linguistics was gaining a serious foothold in composition pedagogy that its theoretical bases came under sustained and successful attack from Noam Chomsky and the theory of transformational-generative grammar.

Here we enter a more familiar modern territory, the post-1960 era of composition and composition studies. And it is here that we find the beginnings of the three most important of the sentence-based rhetorics that were to seem so promising to writing teachers of the New Rhetoric era: the generative rhetoric of Francis Christensen, imitation exercises, and sentence-combining. I want to take up these three more modern syntactic methods in roughly chronological order, beginning with the ideas of Francis Christensen.

CHRISTENSEN RHETORIC

Francis Christensen, a professor of English at the University of Southern California, began to publish essays in the early 1960s complaining that traditional theories of the sentence widely taught throughout the first sixty years of this century were primarily taxonomic rather than generative or productive. Except in providing examples, they were not of much real help to teachers in showing students how to write good sentences. In 1963, Christensen published what is arguably his most important article, "A Generative Rhetoric of the Sentence." In this article and in other works published up to his death in 1970, Christensen described a new way of viewing sentences and a pedagogical method that could be used to teach students how to write longer, more mature, more varied, and interesting sentences.

In the opening sentence of "A Generative Rhetoric of the Sentence," he announced his intentions: "If a new grammar is to be brought to bear on composition, it must be brought to bear on the rhetoric of the sentence" (155). Christensen was certain that the sentence is the most important element in rhetoric because it is "a natural and isolable unit" ("Course" 168). Complaining that the traditional conceptions of the sentence were merely descriptive, Christensen argued that traditional sentence pedagogy simply did not help students learn to write. "We do not really teach our captive charges to write better—we merely expect them to" ("Generative" 155). Christensen indicated that both the grammatical and rhetorical classifications of sentences are equally barren in the amount of real assistance they give to students. "We need a rhetoric of the sentence that will do more than combine the ideas of primer sentences. We need one that will generate ideas" ("Generative" 155).

Christensen rhetoric did not follow the traditional canons of rhetoric, which begin with conceptualization or invention; instead it opted for a view that all other skills in language follow syntactic skills naturally. According to Christensen, you could be a good writer if you could learn to write a good sentence. His pedagogy consisted of short, base-level sentences to which students were asked to attach increasingly sophisticated systems of initial and final modifying clauses and phrases—what he called "free modifiers." Effective use of free modifiers would result in effective "cumulative sentences," and Christensen's most famous observation about teaching the cumulative sentence was that he wanted to push his students "to level after level, not just two or three, but four, five, or six, even more, as far as the students' powers of observation will take them. I want them to become sentence acrobats, to dazzle by their syntactic dexterity" ("Generative" 160).

For some years after 1963, Christensen's syntactic rhetoric was widely discussed, praised, and damned. His few short articles—and all of them were contained in *Notes toward a New Rhetoric*, a book of 110 pages—created an intense interest in syntactic experimentation and innovation. Several experiments confirmed the effectiveness of using generative rhetoric with students. During the early 1970s, two published reports appeared on the use of the *Christensen Rhetoric Program* (an expensive boxed set of overhead transparencies and workbooks that had appeared in 1968). Charles A. Bond, after a rather loosely controlled experiment, reported that there was a "statistically significant difference" between the grades of a group of students taught using Christensen methods and those of a control group taught by conventional methods; he also mentioned that his students were enthusiastic about cumulative sentences. R. D. Walshe, teaching a group of adult night-class students in Australia (it is hard to imagine two groups of native-speaking English students as far removed from one another as Bond's American first-year students and Walshe's Australian working people), found that although some of Christensen's claims for his system were inflated, the *Christensen Rhetoric Program* generally worked well and was liked by his students.

These tests of Christensen's program were unscientific and anecdotal, and it was not until 1978 that a full-scale empirical research test was done on the Christensen system. The experiment's creator, Lester Faigley, began with two hypotheses: First, that the Christensen sentence method would increase syntactic maturity in those who used it, and second, that the *Christensen Rhetoric Program* as a whole would produce a measurable qualitative increase in writing skill. Faigley tested four experimental sections and four control sections in his experiment. The experimental sections used Christensen's *A New Rhetoric*, and the control sections used a well-known content-oriented rhetoric textbook, McCrimmon's *Writing with a Purpose*. Faigley proved both of his hypotheses; he found that the writing produced by the Christensen program not only was measurably more mature but also received better average ratings (.63 on a six-point scale; statistically significant) from blind holistic readings ("Generative" 179). Faigley's experiment showed that the Christensen method does produce measurable classroom results.

IMITATION

The argument about Christensen rhetoric was in full swing during the middle 1960s when another syntactic method was first popularized: imitation exercises. Unlike Christensen rhetoric, imitation was part of the rediscovered trove of classical rhetorical theory that was coming to light in English departments. From the time of Isocrates and Aristotle, exercises in direct imitation and in the copying of structures had been recommended by theorists and teachers of rhetoric, and after Edward P. J. Corbett published his essay "The Uses of Classical Rhetoric" in 1963 and his *Classical Rhetoric for the Modern Student* in 1965, the use of imitation exercises in composition classes enjoyed a renaissance of popularity. There are, of course, different meanings for the term *imitation*, but in rhetoric it has always meant one thing: the emulation of the syntax of good prose models by students wishing to improve their writing or speaking styles. The recurring word used by the ancients concerning imitation, according to Corbett, was *similis*; the objective of imitation exercises was to make the student's writing similar to that of a superior writer ("Theory" 244). This similarity does not imply that the student's writing will be identical to the writing she imitates; the similarity that imitation promotes is not of content, but of form. Corbett recommends several different sorts of exercises, the first and simplest of which involves "copying passages, word for word from admired authors" ("Theory" 247). For students who have spent some time copying passages, Corbett recommends a second kind of imitation exercise: pattern practice. In this exercise, the student chooses or is given single sentences to use as patterns after which he or she is to design sentences of his or her own. "The aim of this exercise," says Corbett, "is not to achieve a word-for-word correspondence with the model but rather to achieve an awareness of the variety of sentence structure of which the English language is capable" ("Theory" 249). The model sentences need not be followed slavishly, but Corbett suggests that the student observe at least the same kind, number, and order of phrases and clauses.

After Corbett's initial arguments for imitation, other scholars took the method up as an important technique. As Winston Weathers and Otis Winchester put it in their 1969 textbook on imitation, *Copy and Compose*, writing "is a civilized art that is rooted in tradition" (2). The assumption that imitation makes about contemporary student writing is that it is often stylistically barren because of lack of familiarity with good models of prose style and that this barrenness can be remedied by an intensive course in good prose models. Weathers and Winchester—whose *Copy and Compose* and *The New Strategy of Style*, as well as Weathers's *An Alternate Style: Options in Composition*, recommended imitation as a primary exercise—became the most notable proponents of imitation. Weathers and Winchester used a slightly more complex model of imitation than did Corbett: They asked their students first to copy a passage, then to read a provided analysis of the model's structure, and finally to compose an imitation. During the 1970s, Frank D'Angelo, William Gruber, Penelope Starkey, S. Michael Halloran, and other writers all supported classically based imitation exercises as effective methods for attaining improved student sentence skills. A second set of imitation exercises proposed during the late 1960s and early 1970s were called "controlled composition exercises," and were actually a hybrid, melding some aspects of imitation and some aspects of sentence-combining. Controlled composition, according to Edmund Miller, is "the technique of having students copy a passage as they introduce some systematic change" (ii).

From the middle 1960s onward, a small but significant number of voices kept reproposing the value of imitation. Frank D'Angelo noted that imitation connoted counterfeiting and stereotyping in most people's minds, when it should connote originality and creativity. A student who practices imitation, he suggests, "may be spared at least some of the fumblings of the novice writer" for forms in which to express his thoughts (283). A "student will become more original as he engages in creative imitation," claimed D'Angelo (283). Weathers and Winchester took the argument further: "Originality and individuality are outgrowths of a familiarity with originality in the work of others, and they emerge from a knowledge of words, patterns, constructions, and procedures that all writers use" (*Copy and Compose* 2).

Like Christensen rhetoric, imitation was put to the test, in this case by Rosemary Hake and Joseph Williams, who performed an experiment in 1977 that compared sentence-combining pedagogy with an imitation pedagogy that they evolved under the term "sentence expansion." Hake and Williams found that the students in their imitation group learned to write better expository prose with fewer flaws and errors than students using sentence-combining pedagogies ("Sentence" 143). Since sentence-combining was known by the late seventies to produce better syntactic results than non-sentence methods, this finding was important. Imitation, proponents claimed, provided students with practice in the "ability to design" that is the basis of a mature prose style. The different imitation techniques, whether they consist of direct copying of passages, composition of passages using models, or controlled mutation of sentence structures, all have this in common: They cause students to internalize the structures of the piece being imitated; as Corbett points out, internalization is the key term in imitation. With those structures internalized, a student is free to engage in the informed processes of choice, which are the wellspring of real creativity. William Gruber, writing in 1977, argued that imitation assists in design: "Standing behind imitation as a teaching method is the simple assumption that an inability to write is an inability to design—an inability to shape effectively the thought of a sentence, a paragraph, or an essay" (493–94). Gruber argued that imitation liberates students' personalities by freeing them of enervating design decisions, at least temporarily. Without knowledge of what has been done by others, claimed proponents of imitation exercises, there can be no profound originality.

THE SENTENCE-COMBINING JUGGERNAUT

Sentence-combining in its simplest form is the process of joining two or more short, simple sentences to make one longer sentence, using embedding, deletion, subordination, and coordination. In all probability sentence-combining was taught by the grammaticus of classical Rome, but such exercises have tended to be ephemera, and none has come down to us. Shirley Rose's article of 1983, "Down from the Haymow: One Hundred Years of Sentence-Combining," traced the use of similar techniques back to the nineteenth century and argued that teachers asking students to combine short sentences into long ones was a pedagogy growing out of schoolbook grammar and structural grammar as well as more modern grammatical ideas (483).

While combining exercises can be found in the 1890s, it was not until 1957, when Noam Chomsky revolutionized grammatical theory with his book *Syntactic Structures*, that the theoretical base was established upon which modern sentence-combining pedagogies would be founded. This base was, of course, Chomskian transformational-generative (TG) grammar, which for a while caused tremendous excitement in the field of composition. TG grammar, which quickly swept both traditional and structural grammar aside in linguistics between 1957 and 1965, seemed at that time to present to composition the possibility of a new writing pedagogy based on the study of linguistic transformations. In 1963, Donald Bateman and Frank Zidonis of Ohio State University conducted an experiment to determine whether teaching high-school students TG grammar would reduce the incidence of errors in their writing. They found that students taught TG grammar both reduced errors and developed the ability to write more complex sentence structures. Despite some questionable features in the Bateman and Zidonis study, it did suggest that learning TG grammar had an effect on student writing.

The Bateman and Zidonis study was published in 1964, and . . . [then in 1965] a study was published that was to have far more importance for sentence-combining: Kellogg Hunt's *Grammatical Structures Written at Three Grade Levels*. Francis Christensen had been using the term "syntactic fluency" since 1963, but Christensen's use of it was essentially qualitative and impressionistic. Hunt's work would become the basis for most measurements of "syntactic maturity," a quantitative term that came to be an important goal of sentence-combining. To recap Hunt's study quickly: He wished to find out what elements of writing changed as people matured and which linguistic structures seemed to be representative of mature writing. To this end he studied the writings of average students in the fourth, eighth, and twelfth grades and expository articles in *Harper's* and *The Atlantic*. At first Hunt studied sentence length, but he quickly became aware that the tendency of younger writers to string together many short clauses with "and" meant that sentence length was not a good indicator of maturity in writing. He studied clause length, and as he says, he "became more and more interested in what I will describe as one main clause plus whatever subordinate clauses happen to be attached to or embedded within it" ("Synopsis" 111). This is Hunt's most famous concept, the "minimal terminable unit" or "T-unit." "Each T-unit," says Hunt, is "minimal in length and each could be terminated grammatically between a capital and a period" (112).

The T-unit, Hunt found, was a much more reliable index of stylistic maturity than sentence length. Eventually he determined the three best indices of stylistic maturity: the average number of words per T-unit, the average number of clauses per T-unit, and the average number of words per clause. When applied to writing at different grade levels, he found that these numbers increased at a steady increment. Below (Table 5-1) is a chart that Frank O'Hare adapted from Hunt's work and from similar work by Roy O'Donnell, William Griffin, and Raymond Norris:

TABLE 5-1   Words per T-unit, clauses per T-unit, words per clause

	Grade Level						Superior Adults
	3	4	5	7	8	12	
Words/T-unit	7.67	8.51	9.34	9.99	11.34	14.4	20.3
Clauses/T-unit	1.18	1.29	1.27	1.30	1.42	1.68	1.74
Words/Clause	6.5	6.6	7.4	7.7	8.1	8.6	11.5

O'Hare (22).

As you can see, the rise in these three indices over time is obvious. Although these preliminary studies of Bateman and Zidonis and of Hunt used no sentence-combining at all, they did represent the bases from which high-modern sentence-combining sprang: the methodological linguistic base of TG grammar and the empirical quantitative base of Hunt's studies of syntactic maturity.

These two bases were brought together in the first important experiment involving sentence-combining exercises, that of John Mellon in 1965. Mellon called the 1969 report of his experiment *Transformational Sentence-Combining: A Method for Enhancing the Development of Syntactic Fluency in English Composition*, and his was the first study actually asking students to practice combining kernel sentences rather than merely to learn grammar. "Research," wrote Mellon, ". . . clearly shows that memorized principles of grammar, whether conventional or modern, clearly play a negligible role in helping students achieve 'correctness' in their written expression" (15). What *could* help students do this, reasoned Mellon, was instruction in TG grammar plus practice exercises in combining short "kernel sentences" into longer, more complex sentences.

With Mellon's initial publication of his work in 1967 and then with the national publication by NCTE in 1969, sentence-combining was established as an important tool in helping students write more mature sentences. But the grammar question still remained open. Since Mellon had to spend so much time teaching the principles of TG grammar in order to allow his students to work on his complex exercises, there was doubt as to which activity — learning the grammar or doing the exercises — had gotten the results. After all, Bateman and Zidonis had gotten error reduction — though admittedly not scientifically measured growth — from mere TG grammar instruction alone. How much importance did the sentence-combining exercises really have?

These questions were put to rest once again and for all in 1973 with the publication of Frank O'Hare's research monograph *Sentence Combining: Improving Student Writing without Formal Grammar Instruction*. This study, which was the spark that ignited the sentence-combining boom of the late 1970s, showed beyond a doubt that sentence-combining exercises, without any grammar instruction at all, could achieve important gains in syntactic maturity for students who used them. Testing seventh graders, O'Hare used sentence-combining exercises with his experimental group over a period of eight months without ever mentioning any of the formal rules of TG grammar. The control group was not exposed to sentence-combining at all.

O'Hare's test measured six factors of syntactic maturity and found that "highly significant growth had taken place on all six factors" (55). His experimental group of seventh graders, after eight months of sentence-combining, now wrote an average of 15.75 words per T-unit, which was 9 percent higher than the 14.4 words per T-unit Hunt had reported as the average of twelfth graders. The other factors were similarly impressive. Just as important as the maturity factors, though, were the results of a second hypothesis O'Hare was testing: whether the sentence-combining group would write compositions that would be judged better in overall quality than those of the control group. Eight experienced English teachers rated 240 experimental and control essays written after the eight-month test period, and when asked to choose between matched pairs of essays, chose an experimental-group essay 70 percent of the time. The results suggested that sentence-combining exercises not only improved syntactic maturity but also affected perceived quality of writing in general.

The O'Hare study focused interest in sentence-combining, which had been associated with Mellon's complex directions, as a pedagogic tool. A follow-up study by Warren E. Combs found that the gains in writing quality that were produced by O'Hare's methods persisted over time and were still notable as long as two months after the sentence-combining practice had been discontinued. Textbooks began to appear using sentence-combining exercises, notably, William Strong's *Sentence-Combining: A Composing Book* in 1973, which used "open" exercises, and O'Hare's own *Sentencecraft* of 1975. There remained now only one important question about sentence-combining: Was it useful for first-year students in college, or were they too old to be helped by the practice it gave? There was no doubt that it worked at the secondary-school level, but an article by James Ney in 1976 describing his attempts to use sentence-combining in a first-year class cast doubt on the technique's usefulness for eighteen year olds. Some teachers who had tried small doses of sentence-combining in first-year classes anecdotally reported no noticeable change in student writing.

Were college students too old for syntactic methods? This last question was answered in 1978 by the publication of the first results of a large and impressively rigorous study conducted under an Exxon grant at Miami University of Ohio by Donald Daiker, Andrew Kerek, and Max Morenberg. This college-level study used ninety of William Strong's "open" exercises and others created by the Miami researchers. These "open" exercises, some of which were lengthy and gave considerable stylistic and creative leeway to students, gave no directions on how best to complete them, and thus there was no "correct" answer or combination. Morenberg, Daiker, and Kerek's experimental and control groups each consisted of six sections of first-year college students, and their experiment was conducted over a fifteen-week semester (245–48). The Miami researchers found that their experimental group, like O'Hare's, evidenced both statistically meaningful gains in syntactic maturity and a gain in overall quality of the writing they produced. Daiker, Kerek, and Morenberg's sentence-combining group moved during the experiment from a high-twelfth-grade-level of syntactic maturity to a level approximating high-sophomore- or junior-level college writing skills. In addition, their experimental group showed statistically significant gains in three qualitative measures of general essay quality: holistic, forced-choice, and analytic (Morenberg, Daiker, and Kerek 250–52).

The late 1970s, just after the Miami experiment, were the high-water mark for sentence-combining. The literature grew so fast it was difficult to keep up with it; Daiker and his colleagues hosted an entire large conference devoted to sentence-combining at Miami in 1978 and another in 1983; scores of normal-science experiments were conducted using it in classrooms across the nation during the early 1980s. The lesson of sentence-combining was simple but compelling; as O'Hare said, "writing behavior can be changed fairly rapidly and with relative ease" (68). The result: Sentence-combining was a land-rush for a time. Between 1976 and 1983, there were no fewer than 49 articles in major journals about sentence-combining and hundreds of papers and conference presentations.[2] The success of the method provoked nasty quarrels about who "owned" it or had a moral right to profit from it. Revisionist narratives about development of the technique were published. Everyone, it seemed, wanted a piece of the pie now that it had been proven so tasty.

With the potency during the early 1980s of the movement toward empirical research—a movement that had been materially strengthened by the popularity of some of the sentence-combining research—we might expect that sentence-combining would have continued as a potent force in the developing field of composition studies. The research was there; the pedagogy was usable by almost any teacher and provided results that could be seen impressionistically as well as measured; the method had powerful champions. It had been long assumed that sentence-combining could be a useful part of a complete rhetoric program, but by the late 1970s, the venerable Kellogg Hunt was suggesting that sentence-combining was so useful that it should take up all class time in a first-year course, that "in every sense, sentence-combining can be [a] comprehensive writing program in and of itself, for at least one semester" ("Anybody" 156).

Look upon my works, ye mighty, and despair.

THE COUNTERFORCES

In an astonishing reversal of fortune for sentence rhetorics, the triumphalism, the quarrels, and the debates of the early 1980s—now mostly forgotten—died away after 1983 or so. The articles on sentence issues fell away radically, and those that were written were more and more about applications to learning disabilities, or English as a second language, or special education. Erstwhile syntactic rhetoricians turned to other issues. The devaluation of sentence-based rhetorics is a complex phenomenon, and we need to approach it with circumspection. Let me first try to establish the reality of what I'm calling the "erasure of the sentence" in clearly numerical terms. Table 5-2 lists raw numbers of books and articles appearing in general-composition journals about the three sentence rhetorics discussed in this essay.

TABLE 5-2 Books and composition journal articles about sentence rhetorics, 1960–1998

	Christensen	Imitation	Sentence-combining
1960–1965	4	1	1
1966–1970	13	2	2
1971–1975	12	5	3
1976–1980	6	4	31
1981–1985	2	3	23
1986–1990	2	5	3
1991–1998	1	2	2

While I can't claim that this chart, which I derived from a combination of ERIC searching and my own research, is exhaustive or even directly replicable, the numbers themselves are less important than the trends they show. And these numerical trends strongly match our intuitive sense of what has been going on. We see, starting with Christensen's first articles in the early 1960s, a strong interest in sentence-writing that was mostly taken up with generative rhetoric and imitation during the early period of the New Rhetoric, say, 1963–1975. After 1976, the interest in Christensen begins to peter out as sentence-combining gathers momentum; a truly extraordinary burst of activity occurred in the late 1970s and early 1980s. But after 1984, general articles on sentence-combining died out, and more and more of the essays published had to do with use of sentence-combining in classes in English as a second language or with behaviorally disordered or autistic students; an ERIC search shows only three essays published on general-composition sentence-combining after 1986. The few general articles that were published after 1986 came more and more to be critical, but even the criticisms died away. After the mid-1980s, the sentence rhetorics of the 1960s and 1970s were gone, at least from books and journals.[3] Shirley Rose's 1983 article on the history of sentence-combining, which probably felt when she wrote it like a historical background to a vital part of the field, now looks more like the *ave atque vale* of the field to sentence-combining.

What iceberg did this *Titanic* meet? It was not a sudden ending, certainly; there had been criticisms of sentence rhetorics going back to the 1960s. There had been some sentence-combining studies reporting equivocal results. There had been arguments over the differences between Christensen's "syntactic fluency" and Hunt's "syntactic maturity." And there had been ongoing questions about the meaning and validity of T-units and the relationship between syntactic maturity and holistically rated writing quality. But all of these had been essentially in-house issues, methodological or pragmatic, mostly waged in the pages of *Research in the Teaching of English*. By the early 1980s, sentence rhetorics had been criticized by some theorists for over fifteen years—but finally the criticisms were coming to bite.

That this devaluation of sentence rhetorics took place slowly meant that it was not noticeable as such by most people in the field. But once noted, it stands out as quite an extraordinary phenomenon. The story of sentence rhetorics is analogous, perhaps, to that of the U.S. space exploration effort of the 1960s. John F. Kennedy determined in 1961 that we would beat the Russians to the moon, and as a result of amazing effort, technological breakthrough, heart-rending sacrifice, and incalculable spondulix, Apollo landed on the Mare Tranquilitatis in 1969. We went back a few more times, put up flags, drove about in dune-buggies, collected dusty gray rocks, and came home. We had seen what it had to offer. And after a while, we did not go back any more.

Similarly, in the early 1960s, a few scholars in composition determined to update the ages-old notion that students needed to be able to write good sentences before they could write good essays. Through new discovery, imaginative application of literary ideas, grammatical theory, and empirical research breakthroughs, methods and measurements were evolved that could determine whether student writers were writing better sentences. Teaching methods relating to the measurements were tested, and they succeeded, repeatedly and incontrovertibly, in producing better sentence writers. In addition, researchers determined that there was indeed a correlation between sentence skill and general perceived writing skill, discovering repeatedly that experimental sentence-writing groups were also holistically rated better writers. The techniques were honed and refined for different levels, and they finally appeared in easily usable textbooks available to all. We had said we wanted newer and better teaching techniques, and the sentence rhetorics of the 1960s and 1970s provided them. And, as a discipline, we then peered quizzically at what we had wrought, frowned, and declared that no, this was not what we had really wanted. We had seen what it had to offer. And after a while, we did not go back any more.

To understand the reasons for the erasure of sentence rhetorics, we need to look at the kinds of criticisms that were leveled at them almost as soon as they demonstrated any success. It will become apparent, doing this, that sentence rhetorics were not dragged under by any sudden radical uprising in the early 1980s, but rather finally succumbed to an entire line of criticism that had been ongoing for at least fifteen years. The reasons for the erasure of the sentence are multiple and complex, but as we look back over the varied critiques of syntactic rhetorics that were leveled beginning with Johnson, I think we can induce some general themes—themes that I would argue represent an important, if sometimes tacit, set of underlife definitions for composition studies in the past two decades.

The first and most obvious of the lines of criticism that would engulf sentence rhetorics was what we might call anti-formalism—the idea that any pedagogy based in form rather than in content was automatically suspect. Some part of this anti-formalist position is a result of distrust of traditional textbook pedagogies, what we might call the reaction against rhetorical atomism. For much of rhetorical history, and certainly for all of the history of composition, the pedagogical method of taking discourse apart into its constituent components and working on those components separately had been accepted almost absolutely. In American composition-rhetoric, this meant the familiar textbook breakdown of the "levels" of discourse—the word, the sentence, the paragraph, the essay. The great difference between the early New Rhetoric of the 1960s and 1970s and the work that came after it is largely found in the New-Rhetoric acceptance of atomistic formal levels up until the late 1970s and the later rejection of them. The first exposition of this point was by James Moffett in his classic 1968 book *Teaching the Universe of Discourse*, in which Moffett surveyed sentence rhetorics (including Christensen and early [Mellon] sentence-combining) and concluded that teachers must "leave the sentence within its broader discursive context" (186). Teachers can help students relate to syntactic options only in the context of a whole discourse, Moffett believed, and thus a teacher can only help a student "if the units of learning are units larger than the hindsight sentence." He criticized traditional writing pedagogy for moving from "little particle to big particle" toward the whole composition. "For the learner," Moffett wrote, "basics are not the small-focus technical things but broad things like meaning and motivation, purpose and point, which are precisely what are missing from exercises" (205). This was a line of attack that came to be heard more and more often.

We first see it in responses to Francis Christensen's work, which began to draw criticism almost as soon as it was formulated. The ink was hardly dry on the large and ambitious *Christensen Rhetoric Program*, Christensen's expensive boxed set of workbooks and projector overlays, when the first serious critique of his theory was published in 1969. Sabina Thorne Johnson, in an article called "Some Tentative Strictures on Generative Rhetoric," admitted that Christensen offered "a revolution in our assessment of style and in our approach to the teaching of composition" (159), but she also had some important reservations about the *generative* nature of the cumulative sentence. Johnson's critique was essential: "Christensen seems to believe that form can generate content (*Program*, p. vi). I don't believe it can, especially if the content is of an analytical or critical nature" (159). Johnson went on to criticize Christensen's reliance upon narrative and descriptive writing for his examples and as the basis for his theory, complaining that narrative and descriptive skills seldom carry over to exposition. She initiated a line of argument against syntactic methods that later came to seem conclusive: that students need training in higher-level skills such as invention and organization more than they need to know how to be "sentence acrobats."

Christensen himself died (of natural causes) shortly after Johnson's article appeared, and the attack on his theory led to a colorful exchange between Johnson and Christensen's widow Bonniejean that can be surveyed in back issues of *College English*. This debate was joined by A. M. Tibbetts, who made several telling points. Although Christensen is useful in the classroom, said Tibbetts, the claims he made for his system are simply "not empirically true as stated" (142). It is true that pattern practice with cumulative sentences can help students learn to use free modifiers, Tibbetts continued, but that is only one of the skills writers need. While he admitted that Christensen's method produced clever sentences from students, Tibbetts complained that that was part of the problem. "What we are generally after in expository writing," Tibbetts warned, "is accuracy rather than cleverness" (144). He rearticulated Johnson's reservations about the formal generativity of the *Christensen Rhetoric Program*. Christensen's theory, argued Tibbetts, is not designed to teach young people how to do the most valuable things any grammar-rhetoric should be designed to teach—how to think; how to separate and define issues; how to isolate fallacies; how to make generalizations and value judgments—in brief, how to express the truths and realities of our time and how to argue for improvements. He criticizes, as did Johnson, Christensen's "fiction fallacy," as he calls it: the idea that students should learn to write like Welty and Faulkner. Narrative and descriptive writing, Tibbetts claims, require no logical analysis and lead to "arty, false descriptions of adolescent mental states" (143). If you want nothing but "sentence acrobats," Tibbetts

warned, "you are likely to get what you deserve—dexterous rhetorical acrobats who dexterously tell untruths" (143).

W. Ross Winterowd, no enemy to linguistic issues in composition, also
questioned Christensen's work in 1975, when he pointed out that Christensen
rhetoric exercises "take sentences out of the living content of the rhetorical situation and make them into largely meaningless dry runs" (338). Although he
was himself trained in linguistics, Winterowd had deep reservations about
large claims made for formalist "technologies":

> I can envision no "technology" of composition, no effective program-
> ming of students for efficiency in learning to write—nor would most
> composition teachers want such efficiency. From my point of view, "effi-
> cient" exercises in sentence-building, for instance, are downright morbid
> because they miss the point concerning the creative act of producing
> meaningful language in a rhetorical situation. (90)

And when James Moffett reacted to the formalist orientation of early sentence-
combining, his Parthian shot—"It's about time the sentence was put in its
place" (187)—could have been the watchword on syntactic rhetorics for a
whole group of theorists whose work was gaining power.

The two *loci classici* of this anti-formalist position were the papers given at
the second Miami sentence-combining conference in 1983 by Donald Murray
and by Peter Elbow (their invitation by the Miami group seems in retrospect
not unlike Brutus's decision to allow Antony to speak at Caesar's funeral).[4]
Murray's essay is one of the wildest and most subtle he ever wrote, an almost
unreadable melange of brainstorming lists, poem drafts, and endless badly
combined sentences that commit formal mayhem on sentence-combining
while never mentioning the technique, inviting students to write as badly as
he does here in order to learn to write well. Elbow was much more open in his
challenges to the formalist assumptions of sentence-combining, and he deserves to be quoted at length:

> I think sentence-combining is vulnerable to attack for being so a-rhet-
> orical—so distant from the essential process of writing. In sentence-
> combining the student is not engaged in figuring out what she wants to
> say or saying what is on her mind. And because it provides prepackaged
> words and ready-made thoughts, sentence-combining reinforces the
> push-button, fast-food expectations in our culture. As a result the stu-
> dent is not saying anything to anyone: The results of her work are more
> often "answers" given to a teacher for correction—not "writing" given
> to readers for reactions. (233)

Though Elbow followed up this frontal barrage with a quick statement that
these were his misgivings in their most extreme form, the remainder of his
essay is a careful assessment of the dangers of making sentence-based work a
very important part of writing instruction. Believing that "every one of our
students at every moment is *capable* of generating a perfectly intelligible,
lively sentence." Elbow says that the way to bring student skills out most usefully is "by leaving syntax more alone—that is, by learning to do a better job

of writing down words in the order in which they come to mind" (241). Indeed, the whole thesis of Elbow's essay is that students do better and are truer to their own language when they leave their syntax alone. Elbow's final word on form-based work is that it is not, cannot be, genuinely generative. "[Sentence-combining] gives the wrong model for generating by implying that when we produce a sentence we are making a package for an already completed mental act" (245).[5]

The second strand of criticism leveled against syntactic rhetorics is related to anti-formalism; we might call it anti-automatism or anti-behaviorism. This set of critiques was based in the idea that pedagogies that meant to tap into non-conscious behavioral structures and to manipulate them for a specific end were inherently demeaning to students. The debate on behaviorism had been raging since the 1950s, of course, but it was given new impetus in composition in 1969 with the notorious publication of Robert Zoellner's "Talk-Write: A Behavioral Pedagogy for Composition" in *College English*. Zoellner's open plea for consideration of behavioral aspects to writing pedagogy struck a powerful nerve; *College English* printed no fewer than eight passionate rejoinders to Zoellner in 1969 and 1970. Behaviorism in psychology was the subject of deep distrust on the part of most humanists, and any proposal for pedagogical uses of it was bound to be regarded with suspicion. It was here that syntactic pedagogies were problematical, because they all used exercises to build "skills" in a way that was not meant to be completely conscious. These skills would then be on tap for all conscious student-writing purposes. What most syntactic theorists wanted from their pedagogies was a systematic and intense exposure of student writers to models and activities that would not only teach them "correct structure," but would rather, as W. Ross Winterowd suggests, "activate their competence" in language so that it "spills over into the area of performance" (253). Effective generation, imitation, or combination would be praised, and incorrect syntactic manipulation could be corrected and criticized. But for many critics, the behaviorist, exercise-based formats of these pedagogies were deeply troubling. They were perceived as a-rhetorical, uncreative, and in some senses destructive of individuality.

Imitation exercises in particular were perceived as actively insulting to the creativity of student writers. Probably the most controversial of the syntactic methods in the 1970s, imitation exercises seemed to ask their team to play defense from the beginning. Objections to imitation were made on several grounds, and most theorists who discussed imitation even in the 1970s felt compelled to defend their interest in it. Frank D'Angelo claimed in 1973 that popular feeling against imitation existed because it was perceived as drudgery, "dull, heavy, and stultifying" (283), and spent his essay explicating how imitation was actually close to invention. But the complaint about drudgework was only a part of the reason that imitation was a pedagogy besieged from its inception. The main reason for the unpopularity of imitation was that it was perceived as "mere servile copying," destructive of student individuality and contributory to a mechanized, dehumanizing, Skinnerian view of writing. The romanticism of the age, seen clearly in much of the anti-Zoellner criticism, would grow more and more potent as the 1970s segued into the 1980s. Teachers and theorists reacted against any form of practice that seemed to compromise originality and the expression of personal feelings, and imitation exercises were among the most obvious indoctrinations to "tradition" and "the system." As a result of this fear of loss of individuality and originality in student writing, those who recommended imitation were fighting a battle that they were the first to join and, ultimately, the first to lose.

Although imitation's defenders sought to clear it of the charges of automatism leveled against it by the age, arguments against imitation never disappeared, even during its heyday, since it was the most overtly anti-romantic of the sentence-based writing pedagogies. D'Angelo noted in 1973 that imitation connotes counterfeiting and stereotyping in most people's minds, when it should connote originality and creativity. William Gruber, whose essay is titled " 'Servile Copying' and the Teaching of English Composition," knew that imitation was distrusted by many teachers when he argued that imitation does not affect creativity. Gruber argued that imitation exercises liberate students' personalities by freeing them of enervating design decisions, at least temporarily. Without knowledge of what has been done by others, he claimed, there can be no profound originality: "Self-expression is possible only when the self has a defined area to work in" (497). But Gruber admitted that imitation "seems, I suppose, an 'inorganic' way of teaching writing" (495) and that his students initially seemed suspicious of it. "The greater part of students' mistrust of imitation . . . seems to derive more from emotional factors than from intellectual ones: for they grew up during the sixties, and they seem either to balk at any extreme formalization of the process of education, or to want one instant set of rules for all writing" (496). Gruber was indeed up against the powerful psychological backwash of the 1960s, as were, eventually, all proponents of sentence rhetorics.

The problem was in the exercises. Critics pointed out that sentence-combining exercises were quintessentially *exercises*, context-stripped from what students really wanted to say themselves. James Britton and his colleagues called such exercises "dummy runs," a term Britton's group evolved to describe tasks unrelated to the larger issues of creative composing in which a student is "called upon to perform a writing task in order (a) to exercise his capacity to perform that kind of task, and/or (b) to demonstrate to the teacher his proficiency in performing it" (104–05). And, as early as 1968, James Moffett was defining exercises as the central definition of old and discredited pedagogy:

> An exercise, by my definition, is any piece of writing practiced only in schools—that is, an assignment that stipulates arbitrary limits that leave the writer with no real relationships between him and a subject and an audience. I would not ask a student to write anything other than an authentic discourse, because the learning process proceeds from intent and content down to the contemplation of technical points, not the other way. (205)

Moffett was primarily attacking the old workbook "drill and kill" exercises that had stultified students since the 1920s, but he reports here on a keen resentment that had been building against all pedagogies based in the older ideas of exercises as "mental discipline." The wholesale (and heartfelt) assault on the teaching of grammar in composition that had been set off by Richard Braddock, Richard Lloyd-Jones, and Lowell Schoer's *Research in Written Composition* in 1963 was a related phenomenon. Many teachers had simply come to disbelieve in the efficacy of any exercise-based teaching. By 1980, this attack on the "from parts to the whole" tradition associated with exercises and textbooks had become much more general. Despite the flashy research claims to the contrary, many people felt that syntactic rhetorics were really not that much different from the old-time "grammar workbook" exercises whose usefulness had been aggressively challenged.

The final line in the congeries of criticisms that brought down syntactic rhetorics was anti-empiricism. Now we are in complex territory, and I must be careful to limit my claims. The empirical-research strand in English studies had existed since the 1920s, when educational psychometricians first began to try testing classroom pedagogies against one another. Modern empirical research in composition, however, was much newer, dating back primarily to the potent critiques of Braddock, Lloyd-Jones, and Schoer in *Research in Written Composition*, which had pointed to serious methodological problems in most extant English research and laid the ground for defensible studies. In 1966, Braddock had founded the journal *Research in the Teaching of English* to publish the newer and better work he envisioned, and most compositionists cheered. For the next two decades the empirical strand in composition waxed powerful, with syntactic methods as its first great success and with the cognitive psychology-based research associated mainly with Carnegie-Mellon as its second. In the Big Tent atmosphere of the New Rhetoric era of the 1960s and early 1970s, there was a general air of good feeling produced by the vision, widely shared, that all—rhetoricians, process-based teachers, linguists, stylisticians, experimenters, psychologists—could work together to reform and improve the teaching of writing; workers in different vineyards need not be enemies. Once sentence rhetorics began to get serious ink in the late 1970s, however, a number of teachers looked at them more closely and began to feel some discomfort, especially with their pre- and post-test scientism, their quantifications, their whole atmosphere of horse race experimentalism. This discomfort was not eased by the huge success of sentence-combining, with its Huntian movement toward a possible pedagogical hegemony. So in the late 1970s, we see the first serious signals of an open anti-empiricism movement within the coalescing field of composition studies.

Anti-scientism and anti-empiricism were not completely novel in the field, of course. We saw a sort of prequel to the movement in the point-counterpoint debate about psychology and invention heuristics in 1971 and 1972 between Janice Lauer and Ann Berthoff.[6] In its modern form, however, the movement probably begins with Susan Wells's and Patricia Bizzell's work in the late 1970s. Wells looked carefully at Christensen's work, arguing that it was empiricist in both method and epistemology, with an asocial contemplation of static phenomena at its center. The natural attitude for a student doing Christensen exercises, said Wells, is

> minute and unquestioning attention to his or her own perceptions, passive receptivity to the messages of sensation, and the desire to work in isolation. . . . These characteristics amount to a sort of contemplation. . . . Contemplation is not distinguished by its objects, but by the relation of thinker to thought, and Christensen's rhetoric enforces a contemplative relation. (472)

And, in an important essay in 1979, Pat Bizzell made the point, which she and others would sharpen over the next decade, that cultural and community traditions would be "as important—if not more important—in shaping the outcome of our debate, as any empirical evidence adduced and interpreted by the competing schools of thought" (768).

This humanist- and theory-based criticism found its first voice in the late 1970s and early 1980s in attacks on the most obvious and successful empirical research going: syntactic pedagogical research.[7] We can see echoes of the antiempirical position in some of the arguments I've mentioned against generative rhetoric and imitation, but the real edge of this criticism was directed at sentence-combining, whose basis in quantitative methods was almost total. One criticism resulting from this reliance on empiricism was that sentence-combining was a practice without a theory, a method without a principle, an *ars* without an *exercitatio*. As Winterowd complained in 1975, "in our self-made ghetto, compositionists have neglected theory, opting to concern ourselves with the pragmatics of everyday teaching" (90–91). James Kinneavy brought this complaint down to specifics in 1979, noting that ". . . few efforts have been made to place sentence-combining into a larger curricular framework," and that it still awaited a philosophic rationale (60, 76). This lack of a general theory was not seen at first as a particular problem, since the new research strand of sentence-combining was so novel and powerful that it submerged other questions.[8] But by 1983, when Miami held its second sentence-combining conference, the problem of theory had become obvious to many participants. The book that emerged from that conference, *Sentence-Combining: A Rhetorical Perspective*, is a fascinating collection, the last major statement made by the discipline about sentence rhetorics, and as a collection it shows clear awareness of the changing weather around sentence rhetorics.

By 1983, it was no longer enough to report that sentence-combining "worked" if no one could specify *why* it worked. Stars of the 1978 Miami conference Rosemary Hake and Joseph Williams were back, this time with more questions than answers. "Sentence-combining is at this moment operating at a very crude level of sophistication," they claimed, ". . . interesting theoretical speculation about sentence-combining has been very infrequent" ("Some" 100–01). Kenneth Dowst, in his essay "An Epistemic View of Sentence-Combining: Practice and Theories," takes on directly the popular perception that sentence-combining was "a practice devoid of a theory" (333).

After examining the relation of sentence-combining to epistemic rhetoric, Dowst comes to the conclusion that sentence-combining *has* a theory, but that it is "a theory that many teachers are finding problematic and many students inadequately relevant. To wit: formalism" (333). The connection with formalism is not the only one possible, says Dowst, but other connections, to rhetoric or epistemic theory, "remain only to be enacted" (333). Despite the hopes expressed at the 1983 conference, they never were. And in the increasingly theoretical world of composition studies post-1985, practice without theory was increasingly associated with the lore-world of earlier composition and condemned.

Another criticism was that sentence-combining represented methodological hegemony of a kind destructive to a truly humanistic epistemology. Michael Holzman, in his "Scientism and Sentence Combining" in 1983, dry-gulches sentence-combining with such energy that he almost appears paranoid about its possibilities. After slashing and burning all the research findings down to the affirmation that "sentence-combining exercises do appear to help students learn how to combine sentences (although this skill deteriorates rapidly)" (77), Holzman makes his central claim for an end to "scientistic" research. "The humanities are the sciences of man," he writes, ". . . It would be a serious mistake to allow the fascination of methodologies for social scientific research to bring us to doubt that literacy is primarily a humanistic attainment" (78–79). Holzman's fear — that the clear-cut successes of the sentence-combining research might slant the whole evolving discipline of composition studies away from traditional humanistic/rhetorical lines and into the camp of social sciences and psychology — was beginning to be widely shared in the early 1980s and came to its real fruition four years later, with the wholesale reaction against cognitive approaches and empiricism in general that marked the beginning of the Social-Construction Era.[9] The best-known example of this methodological critique was Stephen North's famous chapter on the experimentalists in his *The Making of Knowledge in Composition* in 1987, which calls out the Miami researchers in particular for criticism (although not as harshly as it does some other experimentalists).

The result of all of these lines of criticism of syntactic methods was that they were stopped almost dead in their tracks as a research program and ceased being a popular teaching project just a little later. The degree to which the attacks succeeded can be seen in the curious growth of the truly lore-oriented conception that "research has shown that sentence-combining doesn't work." When preparing to write this essay, I asked a number of friends and colleagues in composition studies what had ever happened to sentence-combining. At least half of them replied that it had lost currency because it had been shown not to work, not to help students write better. So far as I can determine, this is simply not true. Outside of a few essays, including Marzano's and Holzman's, that really did take a slash-and-burn attitude toward reporting balanced opinions of the research, I can find no work that genuinely "disproved" the gains created for students through sentence practice. It is true that Lester Faigley showed, in two essays in 1979 and 1980, that Hunt's concept of syntactic maturity did not correlate with generally perceived writing quality ("Problems"; "Names"). But Faigley himself did not question the holistic quality gains of the sentence-combining students, stating that the answer must be that sentence combining and generative rhetoric "affect some part of the writing process more fundamental than the enhancement of syntactic maturity" ("Problems" 99).[10]

Warren Combs and William Smith published an essay in 1980 that reported that students would write demonstrably longer sentences if simply told to do so by the teacher ("Overt and Covert Cues"), but their experiment was short-term, and they specifically stated that their "findings in no way call the efficacy of SC [sentence-combining] instruction into question" (35).[11] It is true that the Miami group's last report, which appeared in the non-mainstream *Perceptual and Motor Skills*, found that absent other writing work, the gains made by the sentence-combiners were self-sustaining, but that the advantage that the experimental group had shown over the control group disappeared after two years. The control group, in other words, caught up to the sentence-combiners after twenty-eight months. This shows, as the Miami researchers comment, that the sentence-combining practice "simply accelerated the positive changes that would have occurred after a longer period of normal maturation and experience" (Kerek, Daiker, and Morenberg 1151). In other words, syntactic gains, if not practiced, only persisted for two years. But by this criterion, if our methods in any given first-year composition course don't measurably put our students ahead of other students *forever*, they don't work and are not worth doing. That's a high hurdle for any pedagogy to clear. There were, finally, a few articles published with "Questions" in their titles: Mary Rosner's "Putting 'This and That Together' to Question Sentence-Combining Research" in 1984 and Aviva Freedman's "Sentence Combining: Some Questions" in 1985, but these essays were concerned with specific queries about technical style and abstracting ability. Neither questioned the general writing success of students using the technique.

It really does seem that the current perception that somehow sentence rhetorics "don't work" exists as a massive piece of wish-fulfillment. Leaving aside the question of syntactic fluency or maturity entirely, the data from holistic and analytic general essay readings are unequivocal. George Hillocks, reviewing the research in 1986, looked closely into all the major sentence-combining research and found many lines of inquiry that needed to be followed up. But after his careful dissection, he still concluded his section on sentence rhetorics with a quote that recognized the value of the technique: "Even with so many questions left unanswered, one is tempted to agree with Charles Cooper (1975c) that 'no other single teaching approach has ever consistently been shown to have a beneficial effect on syntactic maturity and writing quality' (p. 72)" (151). In other words, if people believe that research has shown that sentence rhetorics don't work, their belief exists not because the record bears it out but because it is what people want to believe.

Why we want to believe it is the interesting part.

So what was it that erased the sentence, wiped what had been the "fore-front in composition research today . . . at the cutting edge of research design" in 1980[12] off the radar screen of composition studies? What reduced it from a vital, if unfinished, inquiry into why a popular stylistic method worked so well to a half-hidden and seldom-discussed classroom practice on the level of, say, vocabulary quizzes? It was not, as we have seen, that sentence rhetorics were proved useless. Neither was this erasure the simple playing out of a vein of material before the onslaughts of the normal scientists who followed the major researchers of sentence rhetorics. If the last important work in sentence-combining, Daiker, Kerek, and Morenberg's *Rhetorical Perspective*, shows any-thing, it is that many of the most interesting questions about sentence rhetorics were still being raised and not answered.[13]

I think that we have, to a large extent, already seen what it was. The sen-tence was erased by the gradual but inevitable hardening into disciplinary form of the field of composition studies as a subfield of English studies. The anti-formalism, anti-behaviorism, and anti-empiricism that marked the criti-cism of sentence rhetorics can be found in some earlier writers and thinkers in the older field of composition, but not with the hegemony they gradually achieved as disciplinary structures were formed after 1975. These three attitu-dinal strands are hallmarks of English studies and not of works in the other fields—speech, psychology, education—from which composition grew after 1950. Departmental structures are lasting and durable, and as it became ap-parent that composition studies as a field would almost universally find its departmental home in the same place its primary course identity—first-year composition—resided, cross-disciplinary elements in the older composition-rhetoric world were likely to fade. The graduate students after 1975 who would make up the core of composition studies were, for better or worse, En-glish graduate students, and they would go on to become English professors.

On a sheer demographic basis, it is not strange to see many default atti-tudes based around English departments—textuality, holism, stratification by status, theory-desire, distrust of scientism—gradually come to define composition studies. However complex the feelings composition people had and have about English departments, such departments are usually our na-tive lands. Even if we reject much of the culture, we still speak the language. And one result of the increasing English-identification of composition studies has been a gradual movement away from connections that had helped define an earlier, looser version of composition that arose in the 1950s. We have dropped much of our relationship with non-English elements—with educa-tion and with high school teachers, with speech and communications and with oral rhetoric, with psychology and with quantitative research.

This is not the place for a complete discussion of the changing demo-graphics of composition studies as it became a clear subfield of English. In this article I wanted to show, in a very delimited instance, evidence of the movement's power and potency by examining one part of its effects. When a phenomenon is hard to see or define, looking at what it has done may point to important realities about it. In this case, as in a tornado documentary, the effects exist as a trail of destruction. There was indeed much destruction in the wake of the disciplinary formation of composition studies, but since most of it was destruction of things few people after 1980 had ever believed in or fought for, the destruction was not noticed by many. Who remembers a vital NCTE College Section? Who mourns for the Four Communications Skills or the modes of discourse? But we should remember that swept away with the modes and the five types of paragraphs were other, newer, and potentially more valuable things. The loss of all defense of formalism has left some curious vacuums in the middle of our teaching. Rejection of all behaviorist ideas has left us with uncertainties about any methodology not completely rationalistic or any system of pedagogical rewards. Distrust of scientistic empiricism has left us with few proofs or certainties not ideologically based. More has been lost than sentence-combining here, but it seems somehow part of human nature to forget about the preterite. Many people still professionally active today have deep background as generative rhetoricians or imitation adepts or sentence-combining pioneers, but they have lost most of their interest; they do not do that much anymore. They have cut their losses and gone on. We all must.

NOTES

1. C. S. Baldwin's terms, clearness and interest, were not used in his earlier textbook, *A College Manual of Rhetoric*, in 1902, which adopted Hill's version of Whately's terms. They are found in his later text, *Composition: Oral and Written*, from 1909.

2. These numbers do *not* include conference papers at the two Miami sentence-combining conferences, which became 45 separate essays in the two proceeding books.

3. Notice I'm not claiming that sentence rhetorics were gone from teaching. Anecdotal evidence seems to suggest that some teachers have continued to use sentence-combining and Christensen rhetoric even absent any mention of them in books or journals. They have thus become part of what Stephen North calls teacher lore. But isn't it ironic that such techniques, which made strong moves toward grammatical analyses and empirical proofs, have ended up as lore, which North defines (23) as being driven by pragmatic logic and experiential structure?

4. William Strong attempted to respond to Murray and Elbow in a heart-breaking piece with which the 1983 Miami conference (and collection) closes. Strong has read their papers, and his essay is an attempt to explain to them, and to the world at large, that sentence-combining is both more and less than they think and fear. Called "How Sentence Combining Works," Strong's essay admits that sentence-combining is not, cannot be, "real writing," and that it cannot and should never take the place of naturalistic experience. Still, though, Strong will not admit that sentence-combining is a-rhetorical or non-naturalistic, and he believes that "the language in sentence combining often triggers metalinguistic thinking beyond its own discursive content" and "helps students transfer power from oral language performance to writing" (350). Strong's is an extraordinary rhetorical performance, struggling at the end of the Era of Good Feelings for tolerance from a group that was moving inevitably away from him. But finally, his plea for compromise and understanding fell on stony ground. Composition studies after 1980 did not like or trust exercises. Any kind of exercises.

5. Today, more than fifteen years after the first carronades were fired at the various movements associated with the term "process," we are used to thinking of our world as "post-process" and of "expressivism" as a devil term and a dead letter. As an intellectual field, we have managed with considerable success to marginalize that movement, at least insofar as it existed as ongoing intellectual or non-pedagogical discourse. Its greatest champions—Moffett, Britton, Garrison, Emig, Murray, Macrorie, Stewart, Rohmann—have died or retired, leaving Peter Elbow nearly alone to carry the banner. Many people see expressivism today—not unlike sentence-combining, ironically—as a hoary pedagogical survival, *exercitatio* with *ars*, old-time staffroom lore and instructor prejudice, the body still moving after the head has been cut off. It is difficult, on first consideration, to imagine the writing-process movement as a potent destructive force, or to think that

we, in our shining theoretical plumage, are still living in the backwash of its great primary act of pedagogical creation/destruction: the wreck of formalism in all its versions.

But the powerful revolutionary doctrine of the process movement was, finally, terribly simple. It wished to do away with whatever was not authentic in writing and teaching writing. Its great enemy was modern composition-rhetoric, that huge carpetbag of textbook nostrums about modes and forms and methods and sentences and rules and paragraphs and vocabulary and punctuation and exercises and unity and coherence and emphasis. If rhetoric was a fox that knew many small things, process was a hedgehog that knew one great thing: you learn to write by writing and rewriting things important to you with the help of a sympathetic reader/teacher. Everything else is, finally, flummery. Formalism and atomism were huge and inescapable parts of modern composition-rhetoric, and the writing process movement laid down a constant challenge to them from 1960 onward. If, as was the case, formalism or atomism were charges that could be applied even to New Rhetoric ideas such as syntactic rhetorics, then applied they must be. Sadly, regretfully applied, yes, since many sentence-combiners had been friends. But when you build a set of positions based completely on authenticity and anti-formalism, you cannot easily choose some formalism you will be friends with.

Max Morenberg of the Miami sentence-combining group certainly had no doubt who had burnt his topless tower. In two conference presentations, in 1990 and 1992, he surveyed the wreckage and protested against the attitudes that had wrought it. His somewhat bitter titles tell the story: In 1990 he delivered "Process/Schmocess: Why Not Combine a Sentence or Two?" and in 1992 he delivered "'Come Back to the Text Ag'in, Huck Honey!'" Both blamed dichotomizing process/product thinking for the demise of sentence rhetorics. Unfortunately, Morenberg never published either talk outside of ERIC.

6. This whole argument can be seen most easily in Winterowd's *Contemporary Rhetoric* (99–103), along with Winterowd's thoughtful commentary on it.

7. Only a few people saw then that this movement would a few years later in 1987 enlarge the criticism to include the equally powerful cognitive-psychology strand of research; in retrospect it seems clear that the real relation between sentence research and cognitive research lay in their common nemesis. The enlarging reaction against quantitative research would eventually come to include all but the most narrative and humanistic qualitative research as well, and the results would, in the end, be the same: the effective ending of whole lines of research within mainstream composition studies. Of course, much research is still carried on, but it tends to be reported at NCTE and American Educational Research Association, rather than at CCCC. See Charney for the reaction of many researchers to this movement within composition studies.

8. As late as 1981, even such a noted practitioner of theory as the late James Berlin was co-authoring purely practical essays on sentence-combining containing such statements as, "In sum, the 'sentence skills' unit should not be relegated to a few hours devoted to 'style,' but should be seen as central to some of a writer's major concerns" (Broadhead and Berlin 306).

9. In my "Composition Studies and Science," published just a month before Holzman's essay, I made almost the exact plea for the primacy of humanities-based (which I called rhetorical) inquiry over social-science inquiry. Although I made my own howlers in that piece (lumping Pat Bizzell in with all other Kuhn-quoters as an advocate of empirical science!), I was not, I hope, slanting evidence as obviously as Holzman seems to do in his condemnation of sentence-combining, whose whole train of successes he dismisses with a sneer.

10. Faigley's and Holzman's work led to Forrest Houlette's 1984 article on reliability and validity in external criteria and holistic scoring, a piece that seems to suggest that neither criterion can be considered empirically dependable under all conditions without the context of the other. This was the level of epistemological humility syntactic research had reached by 1984: There was no longer any dependable way to determine what writing was actually good.

11. Richard Haswell and his co-authors recently mentioned the study of Combs and Smith as a rare example of replication of research in composition studies (5), and in terms of careful numerical enumeration of syntactic growth, this is true. But Combs and Smith studied their students over a much shorter period (six days) than did O'Hare or the Miami researchers and made no attempt to cover holistic writing-quality issues. (There is also some evidence that the overtly cued students [those told that their teacher would grade long sentences more favorably] simply began to string long sentences together in a few simple ways, since their T-unit numbers went up but their clause numbers did not [see pp. 33–35].)

12. This rather embarrassing quote is from my dissertation, written in 1979 and 1980. It's humbling to watch your own doxa turn into historical grist.

13. Janice Neuleib suggested after hearing an earlier version of this paper that another possible reason for the decline of sentence-combining was not that *all* of the research had been

done, but that all of the impressive and groundbreaking research had been done. No one is much interested in the quotidian mopping-up work of normal science, especially in social science-based fields. The specialized and smaller-scale studies that were called for (but not done) after 1983 were not career-makers. Although I thought at first that this idea might be too cynical, I have been gradually forced to admit its possibility.

WORKS CITED

Baldwin, Charles Sears. *A College Manual of Rhetoric*. New York: Longmans, Green, 1902.
———. *Composition: Oral and Written*. New York: Longmans, Green, 1909.
Bateman, Donald R., and Frank J. Zidonis. *The Effect of a Knowledge of Generative Grammar upon the Growth of Language Complexity*. Columbus: Ohio State UP, 1964.
Bizzell, Patricia. "Thomas Kuhn, Scientism, and English Studies." *College English* 40 (1979): 764–71.
Bond, Charles A. "A New Approach to Freshman Composition: A Trial of the Christensen Method" *College English* 33 (1972): 623–27.
Braddock, Richard, Richard Lloyd-Jones, and Lowell Schoer. *Research in Written Composition*. Urbana: NCTE, 1963.
Britton, James, Tony Burgess, Nancy Martin, Alex McLeod, and Harold Rosen. *The Development of Writing Abilities (11–18)*. Basingstoke: Macmillan. 1975.
Broadhead, Glenn J., and James A. Berlin. "Twelve Steps to Using Generative Sentences and Sentence Combining in the Composition Classroom." *College Composition and Communication* 32 (1981): 295–307.
Charney, Davida. "Empiricism Is Not a Four-Letter Word." *College Composition and Communication* 47 (1996): 567–93.
Chomsky, Noam. *Syntactic Structures*. The Hague: Mouton, 1957.
Christensen, Francis. "A Generative Rhetoric of the Sentence." *College Composition and Communication* 14 (1963): 155–61.
———. *Notes Toward a New Rhetoric: Six Essays for Teachers*. New York: Harper, 1967.
———. "The Course in Advanced Composition for Teachers." *College Composition and Communication* 24 (1973): 163–70.
Christensen, Francis, and Bonniejean Christensen. *A New Rhetoric*. New York: Harper, 1975.
Combs, Warren E. "Sentence-Combining Practice: Do Gains in Judgments of Writing 'Quality' Persist?" *Journal of Educational Research* 70 (1977): 318–21.
Combs, Warren E., and William L. Smith. "The Effects of Overt and Covert Cues on Written Syntax." *Research in the Teaching of English* 14 (1980): 19–38.
Connors, Robert J. "Composition Studies and Science." *College English* 45 (1983): 1–20.
———. *Composition-Rhetoric: Backgrounds, Theory, and Pedagogy*. Pittsburgh: U of Pittsburgh P, 1997.
Cooper, Charles R. "Research Roundup: Oral and Written Composition." *English Journal* 64 (1975): 72–74.
Corbett, Edward P. J. *Classical Rhetoric for the Modern Student*. New York: Oxford UP, 1965.
———. "The Theory and Practice of Imitation in Classical Rhetoric." *College Composition and Communication* 22 (1971): 243–50.
Daiker, Donald A., Andrew Kerek, and Max Morenberg. "Sentence-Combining and Syntactic Maturity in Freshman English," *College Composition and Communication* 29 (1978): 36–41.
———, eds. *Sentence-Combining: A Rhetorical Perspective*. Carbondale: Southern Illinois UP, 1985.
———, eds. *Sentence-Combining and the Teaching of Writing*. Conway, AR: L&S Books, 1979.
———. *The Writers Options: College Sentence-Combining*. New York: Harper and Row, 1979.
D'Angelo, Frank. "Imitation and Style." *College Composition and Communication* 24 (1973): 283–90.
Dowst, Kenneth. "An Epistemic View of Sentence-Combining: Practice and Theories." Daiker et al. *Sentence-Combining: A Rhetorical Perspective*. 321–33.
Elbow, Peter. "The Challenge for Sentence Combining." Daiker et al. *Sentence-Combining: A Rhetorical Perspective*. 232–45.
Faigley, Lester L. "Generative Rhetoric as a Way of Increasing Syntactic Fluency." *College Composition and Communication* 30 (1979): 176–81.
———. "Problems in Analyzing Maturity in College and Adult Writing." Daiker et al. *Sentence-Combining and the Teaching of Writing*. 94–100.
———. "Names in Search of a Concept: Maturity, Fluency, Complexity, and Growth in Written Syntax." *College Composition and Communication* 31 (1980): 291–300.
Freedman, Aviva. "Sentence Combining: Some Questions." *Carleton Papers in Applied Language Studies* 2 (1985): 17–32.

Graves, Richard L., ed. *Rhetoric and Composition: A Sourcebook for Teachers.* Rochelle Park, NJ: Hayden, 1976.

Gruber, William E. "'Servile Copying' and the Teaching of English Composition." *College English* 39 (1977): 491–97.

Hake, Rosemary, and Joseph M. Williams. "Sentence Expanding: Not Can, or How, but When." Daiker et al. *Sentence-Combining and the Teaching of Writing.* 134–46.

———. "Some Cognitive Issues in Sentence Combining: On the Theory That Smaller Is Better." Daiker et al. *Sentence-Combining: A Rhetorical Perspective.* 86–106.

Halloran, S. Michael. "Cicero and English Composition." Conference on College Composition and Communication. Minneapolis. 1978.

Haswell, Richard H., Terri L. Briggs, Jennifer A. Fay, Norman K Gillen, Rob Harrill, Andrew M. Shupala, and Sylvia S. Trevino. Context and Rhetorical Reading Strategies." *Written Communication* 16 (1999): 3–27.

Hill, Adams Sherman. *The Principles of Rhetoric and Their Application.* New York: Harper and Brothers, 1891.

Hillocks, George Jr. *Research on Written Composition: New Directions for Teaching.* Urbana: NCTE, 1986.

Holzman, Michael. "Scientism and Sentence Combining." *College Composition and Communication* 34 (1983): 73–79.

Houlette, Forrest. "Linguistics, Empirical Research, and Evaluating Composition." *Journal of Advanced Composition* 5 (1984): 107–14.

Hunt, Kellogg W. *Grammatical Structures Written at Three Grade Levels.* Urbana: NCTE, 1965.

———. "A Synopsis of Clause-to-Sentence Length Factors." Graves 110–17.

———. "Anybody Can Teach English." Daiker et al. *Sentence-Combining and the Teaching of Writing.* 149–56.

Johnson, Sabina Thorne. "Some Tentative Strictures on Generative Rhetoric." *College English* 31 (1969): 155–65.

Kerek, Andrew, Donald A. Daiker, and Max Morenberg. "Sentence Combining and College Composition." *Perceptual and Motor Skills* 51 (1980): 1059–1157.

Kinneavy, James L. "Sentence Combining in a Comprehensive Language Framework." Daiker et al. *Sentence-Combining and the Teaching of Writing.* 60–76.

Marzano, Robert J. "The Sentence-Combining Myth." *English Journal* 65 (1976): 57–59.

Mellon, John. *Transformational Sentence-Combining: A Method for Enhancing the Development of Syntactic Fluency in English Composition.* Urbana: NCTE, 1969.

———. "Issues in the Theory and Practice of Sentence-Combining: A Twenty-Year Perspective." Daiker et al. *Sentence-Combining and the Teaching of Writing.* 1–38.

Miller, Edmund. *Exercises in Style.* Normal, IL: Illinois SUP, 1980.

Moffett, James. *Teaching the Universe of Discourse.* Boston: Houghton Mifflin, 1968.

Morenberg, Max. "Process/Schmocess: Why Not Combine a Sentence or Two?" Conference on College Composition and Communication. Chicago. March 1990. ERIC ED 319040.

———. "'Come Back to the Text Ag'in, Huck Honey!'" NCTE Convention. Louisville. November 1992. ERIC ED 355557.

Morenberg, Max, Donald Daiker, and Andrew Kerek. "Sentence-Combining at the College Level: An Experimental Study." *Research in the Teaching of English* 12 (1978): 245–56.

Murray, Donald. "Writing Badly to Write Well: Searching for the Instructive Line." Daiker et al. *Sentence Combining: A Rhetorical Perspective.* 187–201.

Ney, James. "The Hazards of the Course: Sentence-Combining in Freshman English." *The English Record* 27 (1976): 70–77.

North, Stephen M. *The Making of Knowledge in Composition.* Upper Montclair, NJ: Heinneman-Boynton/Cook, 1987.

O'Donnell, Roy C., William J. Griffin, and Raymond C. Norris. *Syntax of Kindergarten and Elementary School Children: A Transformational Analysis.* Urbana: NCTE, 1967.

O'Hare, Frank. *Sentence Combining: Improving Student Writing without Formal Grammar Instruction.* Urbana: NCTE, 1973.

———. *Sentencecraft.* Lexington: Ginn, 1975.

Rose, Shirley K. "Down from the Haymow: One Hundred Years of Sentence Combining." *College English* 45 (1983): 483–91.

Rosner, Mary. "Putting 'This and That Together' to Question Sentence-Combining Research." *Technical Writing Teacher* 11 (1984): 221–28.

Starkey, Penelope. "Imitatio Redux." *College Composition and Communication* 25 (1974): 435–37.

Strong, William. "How Sentence Combining Works." *Sentence-Combining: A Rhetorical Perspective.* Ed Daiker et al.: 334–50.

———. *Sentence-Combining: A Composing Book.* New York: Random House, 1973.

Tibbetts, A. M. "On the Practical Uses of a Grammatical System: A Note on Christensen and Johnson." *Rhetoric and Composition: A Sourcebook for Teachers.* Ed. Richard Graves. Rochelle Park, NJ: Hayden Books, 1976. 139–49.

Walshe, R. D. "Report on a Pilot Course on the Christensen Rhetoric Program." *College English* 32 (1971): 783–89.

Weathers, Winston. *An Alternate Style: Options in Composition.* Rochelle Park, NJ: Hayden Books, 1980.

Weathers, Winston, and Otis Winchester. *Copy and Compose.* Englewood Cliffs, NJ: Prentice Hall, 1969.

———. *The New Strategy of Style.* New York: McGraw-Hill, 1978.

Wells, Susan. "Classroom Heuristics and Empiricism." *College English* 39 (1977): 467–76.

Whately, Richard. *Elements of Rhetoric.* New York: Harper and Brothers, 1877.

Winterowd, W. Ross. *Contemporary Rhetoric: A Conceptual Background with Readings.* New York: Harcourt Brace, 1975.

Zoellner, Robert. "Talk-Write: A Behavioral Pedagogy for Composition." *College English* 30 (1969): 267–320.

6

Whatever Happened to the Paragraph?

MIKE DUNCAN

I find discussing paragraphs with my students extraordinarily difficult; I am never sure if I am being too prescriptive or too open-ended when I make my tentative suggestions on their writing. The immense complexities of paragraphs' structures—how they duel with their neighbors, with the whole essay, with ambiguous sections and divisions, and of course with their nebulous, rebellious contents known as sentences—it all feels impossible to explain sometimes. Seeking assistance, I naturally started a hunt for theory concerning the paragraph, and I found a long, unresolved debate about how paragraphs should be taught, as well as about their intrinsic nature.

But there was something odd about the scholarship. In the last fifteen or so years, there has not been any major work on paragraph theory in composition. The last theoretical discussion of the subject in journals appears to be Rick Eden and Ruth Mitchell's largely unanswered "Paragraphing for the Reader" in 1986 and Frank D'Angelo's splendid literature review of the topic sentence from the same *CCC* issue. Save for some scattered empirical work, such as Randall Popken's four studies of topic sentence genres from 1987 to 1991, paragraph theory has all but disappeared from composition research.

In the mid-1960s, and up to even the early 1980s, published work on paragraph theory was common. Scholars such as Francis Christensen and Paul Rodgers wrestled with the nature of the paragraph, and empirical work such as Richard Braddock's 1974 study of topic sentences broke new ground. The debate was not new, of course. Ever since Joseph Angus's 1862 *Handbook of the English Tongue* provided twenty pages of paragraphing tips and Alexander Bain's immensely influential 1866 edition of *English Composition and Rhetoric* set forth formal principles for composing paragraphs, at least two distinct poles of thought on writing paragraphs have existed. I will call these two views "prescriptive" and "descriptive" from this point on. They are loosely analogous to Eden and Mitchell's "formalist" and "functionalist" categories (421), with the functionalists being a branch of the descriptivists.

From *College English* 69 (2007): 470–95.

The "prescriptive" position stands by Bain's ideas of explicit structure and first-position topic sentences as basically sound, and occasionally points to psychological principles concerning the reading process for backing. A paragraph in this view has a definite, ideal structure that can be described, measured, and emulated for instructional purposes; it is an odd marriage of pedagogy for basic writers and readability studies.

The "descriptive" position points to empirical studies that show high use of nontextbook structures and low topic-sentence usage as support for a looser, inductive approach to instruction, with Bain-style rules limited to suggesting a structural ideal that is only rarely seen. The functionalists, a rather loud subset of this group, go even further and claim that Bain-derived theory cruelly locks students into a "deductive cage" (Rodgers, "Alexander Bain" 408) despite the fact that the bars have been "hacksawed by theory and empirical study" (Branson 112). Paragraphs, in this view, should be functionally oriented, free-form entities, with only the vaguest of definitions, as they contain way too many variables in style than any crude, skeletal form can hope to emulate; codifying paragraph structure is seen as being as useless as making lists of rhetorical tropes and figures.

There is also a third, more impersonal stance on paragraphs, which I will call "cognitive." It stems chiefly from studies in psychology and computational linguistics, where the paragraph is examined solely as a cognitive artifact or in the context of readability. This approach focuses on the paragraph writer very little, if at all, but it informs the other two positions. The intersection of these three groups produces what I refer to as paragraph theory.

Current English textbooks tend to follow prescriptive structural models, but real-world practice seems to favor the descriptivists and lean toward the functionalists. The prescriptive approach to teaching paragraphs at its worst leads to such creatures as the five-paragraph essay; the advantages and drawbacks to such a form have been detailed by many (Nichols; Nunnally; Rico; Wesley), so I will only state the obvious: the problem with such structure is not that it is bad, but that it is often presented and understood as an end unto itself, instead of as a stepping-stone to more complex, free-form compositions. In this sense, structural theory entraps the writer, with the five-paragraph "Procrustean bed" (Gopen 196) being the most obvious example.

The problem with descriptivism, on the other hand, is that it is devilishly difficult and perhaps equally cruel to explain to struggling students that they can do anything with a paragraph as long as it works. A teacher can easily end up sounding flippant. So we have something easy to teach, but limiting, or something hard to teach, but expansive. Even with studies from the cognitive camp offering ways to close the gap between them, this dichotomy remains problematic.

But paragraph theory, by and large, is a dead subject in composition, despite a lengthy canon of scholarship. The subject has moved on in recent years to be explored by other fields: psychology conducts readability studies of paragraph use; technical or professional writing looks to formatting, concerns of length, and function; computational linguistics measures cohesion in paragraphs; and literature occasionally examines variations in the drafting process. The demise of paragraph theory appears to be a by-product of a larger shift in composition, away from the content of our teaching "nuts 'n' bolts" issues—writing itself—and toward overly contextual, socioeconomic concerns, as Richard Fulkerson has recently described in *CCC*. While I think such concerns are immensely valuable, I also believe composition cannot afford to fritter away through inattention such a broad area of theory with a large amount of established scholarship, especially one that has taken off in other disciplines. This oversight can be easily alleviated, however, and ideally now rather than later.

Accordingly, I intend to give a chronological overview of how paragraph theory began, flourished, and then declined in composition studies. I will also argue that paragraph theory should be revisited and reclaimed by composition, because the result of that abandoned past scholarship is an uneasy symbiosis of prescriptive and descriptive theory that is far from satisfactory. Even with the welcome addition of advances in cognitive research, there are still questions to be resolved. Furthermore, we as teachers of paragraphs are badly in need of fresh, practical terminology for paragraphs and their ilk, especially in the area of macrostructures and "flow." More empirical study on the teaching of paragraph structure and an increased focus on all approaches to the paragraph in textbooks would not be out of place, also.

When approached vigorously, paragraph theory is very much a study of relativity and context. It is the most obvious and visible evidence of the ebb and flow of our thoughts in writing. Hold a typed page ten feet away— the words fade to smudges, but the indented visual structure remains. The considered construction of paragraphs lies at the very heart of what we do, as the mishandling of such entities is a leading cause of stress for English instructors. Bain's core system of paragraph theory, with all its stress on explicit structure, topic sentences, and uniform rigidity, is so inexorably ingrained into all our textbooks and thought that even today it seems that the last 140 years have just been an extremely long field test for his theories—with the results still up in the air. The goal is how to teach students effective paragraphing, with a secondary aim of delineating structure, but both have proved elusive.

EIGHTEENTH- AND NINETEENTH-CENTURY CONCEPTS OF THE PARAGRAPH: THE RISE OF PRESCRIPTION

Up until Lindley Murray's 1795 edition of *English Grammar*,[1] there is no known theoretical or pedagogical discussion of any length on paragraphs. The great champion of scientific rhetoric in the eighteenth century, George Campbell, does not address them, though he seems to be on the cusp in his 1776 *Philosophy of Rhetoric*.[2] Joseph Priestley likewise veers away in his 1761 *Rudiments of English Grammar* (49–50), going no further than harmony in sentences. Even Hugh Blair, the eminent synthesizer, did not venture beyond the Aristotelian period in any of his lectures published in 1783 (110).

For whatever reason, the terminology to begin a discussion of paragraph structure or function was not yet existent. Discussion of style remained firmly at the sentence level, even though the paragraph had long since become an essential part of English discourse and writers were using paragraphs with skill and aplomb. As Edwin Herbert Lewis comments in 1894, after looking at paragraph use since Shakespeare's time, "the theory of the teachers was [. . .] many years behind the practice of the writers" (20). The paragraph itself, of course, was a familiar term well before this, but mention of it is restricted to punctuation via its proper marking, as that is referred to in Charles Gildon and John Brightland's 1711 *Grammar of the English Tongue* (151). There is a long history of such marks, in dozens of forms, dating back to the Greeks, who only used them to mark changes in speaker (Lewis 9).

Those first comments on the paragraph by Lindley Murray may be brief—a few pages, even in the later editions—but historically, they are a watershed. He lists the modern paragraph mark under the section on "Punctuation," as Gildon and Brightland do (151), and defines it as a separation between two paragraphs, before providing a few pages later four rules for making paragraphs: one, by a change of subject; two, by larger divisions of the subject; three, by intuitive subdivision between facts, premises, and conclusions; and finally, by the consideration of lending "beauty and force to the division" (412–17). This advice is mixed into the rest of his discussion of punctuation; the paragraph receives perhaps three pages combined. While there is hardly a theory here, Murray is still the first to acknowledge in writing that the proper delineation of paragraphs is something worth considering (Shearer 411).The mixing of rhetoric and grammar in Blair and Campbell's work and a movement toward a universal grammar at the time may have influenced the inclusion.[3]

Angus's *Handbook of the English Tongue*, in 1862, goes much further than Murray with the paragraph. Not only does Angus, a teacher at the University of London, devote fourteen pages of his Chapter 9, "Hints on Composition" to a consideration of the paragraph (401–15), but he also possesses a discernible stance on good paragraph usage, couched in the tentative, thoughtful language of an encouraging teacher. He defines the paragraph as "a combination of sentences, intended to explain, illustrate, or prove, or apply some truth; or to give a history of events during any definite portion of time, or in relation to any one subject of thought," and he stresses "unity" as its chief element, as he does earlier with sentences (401).

Angus continues with another historical first: "Properly a paragraph has *one* theme, which may be stated in the margin, or at the beginning, or at the close, or at both beginning and close; or which may be implied only and not stated." This is the origin of the concept that we call today the topic sentence. Angus is surprisingly open as to its placement, though he discourages the implied kind as "defective in clearness" (401). Lengthy examples of all these placements are provided. Angus is loath to make a general statement without reinforcement, and he speaks to situations where one strategy is better than others, such as the theme stated at the close—best for conclusions or introductions.[4] The length of both paragraphs and their sentences within is also considered, and numerous examples of styles of logical paragraph development are provided, with Angus commenting briefly on their validity. But he ends these dissections, along with the rest of his "hints on composition," with an abrupt dismissal, as merely the "mechanical rules" of composition— good for avoiding mistakes, but not enough for good writing (413). The "study of good models" is imperative, and he ends stressing that "*practice* is the grand secret of effectiveness in this as in any other art" (415).

There is nothing ironclad or prescriptive about Angus's advice. He presents a wide variety of models for different situations, all serving the pedagogical role of staving off simple mistakes, and he ends by suggesting that a command of paragraphing comes only with practice. Angus could be considered the founder of the descriptive school of paragraph thought, and in that respect, his ruminations are the antithesis of those of the better-known father of paragraph theory, Alexander Bain.

As the chair of logic at Aberdeen with the responsibility for composition instruction, in 1866 Bain recognized a need for a new pedagogy for a growing influx of new students living through the Industrial Revolution (Lunsford, "Teaching" 220–21). Combining previous rhetorics with the associative psychology of his day (Branson 71), Bain constructed his 1866 *English Composition and Rhetoric* as a list of principles of structure, illustrated with examples, followed by criticism of great works. The book's rigid structure is notable in innumerable ways, but especially in how Bain defines the paragraph as the next division of discourse beyond the sentence, as "a collection of sentences with unity of purpose" (142). In this first edition he states, "[T]here are certain principles that govern the structure of the paragraph," and he provides six: explicit reference; parallel construction; an opening sentence that indicates the subject; consecutive arrangement; unity; and due proportion or marking of subordination (142–52).[5]

The third principle, stated bluntly as, "The opening sentence, unless so constructed as to be obviously preparatory, is expected to indicate with prominence the subject of the paragraph," is a perfect demonstration of Bain's imperative, passive-aggressive writing style (150). According to Branson, this is language steeped entirely in pedagogy and dressed up with "theoretical trappings" (28). While the later editions of Bain's *Rhetoric* are by current standards much more progressive, especially the musing, thoughtful pace of his book *On Teaching English*, the earlier editions were popular and widely taught as prescriptive texts in the United States, despite Bain's view of his work as an analytical tool. However well-intentioned, Bain's *Rhetoric* served not only as a model for instruction in composition for 140 years, but also as a juggernaut-sized target—the "whipping boy" of current-traditionalism—for those bemoaning, rightly or wrongly, the pedagogy of the century to follow (Lunsford, "Alexander Bain's Contributions" 290–93).

It is not without reason that Bain's text is so influential. He offers a simple, algorithmic approach to teaching composition that, at least at first glance, is very tempting even today to overworked teachers with large classes. His treatment of the paragraph rests at the center of this approach; it is his most original advancement, as it presents what Angus does not: a hierarchy, a *system* for paragraphing, rather than mere advice. Later theorists of the nineteenth century were, for the most part, content to rearrange and refine Bain's six principles, with Angus's earlier contributions ignored or glossed over.

John Genung, a professor at Amherst College, and Barrett Wendell, a professor at Harvard during its experimental composition period, were perhaps the greatest advocates of Bain's prescriptive approach. They varied over which hierarchy to use, however, either treating the paragraph as analogous to the sentence, or describing it as an essay "writ small," or granting both analogies validity. Also, the question of whether instruction in the paragraph considered it part of style or part of invention remained (Genung 193–214; Wendell 114–49). These disagreements have an aura of quibbling about them, though; Bain's basic principles unquestionably hold sway. As with Bain, heavily implicit in these systems is a view of the average student as wholly incapable of basic writing tasks. Cookie-cutter concepts, such as Wendell's idea that isolated paragraphs can be simply added together, tend to crop up. This is a rhetoric of writing that speaks from the mountain with an excellent view of the valley.

In his rhetoric text of 1893 (its first edition coming in 1885), Genung inverts Bain's paragraph/sentence analogy, with the paragraph becoming also analogous to an essay. His "subject sentence" must appear at the top of the paragraph for logical purposes, though sometimes it can come at the end (196). Again, this is a pedagogy-focused rhetoric assuming the worst about a student's abilities. Genung has "laws" of paragraph structure, not suggestions.

Wendell's study of paragraphs, fourth in his 1890 lectures, can be summed up best by its table of contents opener, "A paragraph is to a sentence what a sentence is to a word [. . .]" (114), which also serves as his definition of a paragraph, echoing Bain's analogy. He holds that sentences are not planned as paragraphs are, but written and then revised; paragraphs are "prevised," and they are taught best by declared principles. "Good use" of the paragraph is nothing more than a caution against monotonous indentation, and Bain's principles are boiled down to a triad of *unity, mass,* and *coherence.*

Wendell's concept of mass (which later becomes *proportion* and then *emphasis*) is noteworthy as it seems to predict later researchers' conclusions about what parts of a document readers concentrate on: the first part, then the last, then the body (133). These are not "absolute rules" of style, he cautions, but authors who want paragraphs with "firm precision" ought to follow them closely (146). This presentation, like that of Bain's, is two-faced; Wendell is attempting to present his principles as prescriptive and not prescriptive simultaneously. With insidious guidelines like these, it is no wonder that the paragraph was taught via Bain's imperatives.

There was certainly no discussion among these men of the need to back Bain's prescription with empiricism. The many editions of his text apparently stood in lieu of such evidence, and Bain claimed his rhetoric was tested in the field by teachers and revised accordingly (Lunsford, "Alexander Bain's

Contributions" 295). The deductive origins of his paragraph rules remain questionable (Rodgers, "Discourse-Centered" 2), however, and this potential weakness possibly inspired the first attempt to bring paragraph theory together outside of a textbook, Lewis's 1894 dissertation, published as *The History of the English Paragraph*. Lewis takes a broad, historical view that successfully synthesizes nineteenth-century thought on the paragraph. His term *stadia* informs Rodgers's work over seventy years later. Branson views him as the first serious critic of Bain (48) and I would agree.

Lewis states that throughout the nineteenth century, not only was the paragraph the main unit of pedagogy, but all scholarly writings upon it were wholly focused on pedagogy, with theory left vague or absent (20–33). The paragraph was something taught in isolation via principles—either Bain's or a similar version—governing its supposedly correct form. While there were implications that the paragraph must fit somehow into an essay, how this is to be done was rarely stated, though the suggestion was that mastery of the rules will lead naturally to such designs. The topic sentence[6] plus support reigned supreme.

But if topic sentences are mandatory, why are there good paragraphs to be found without them? If the Bain structure of the paragraph is ideal, then why can other, equally appropriate paragraphs exist? Also, are not the relationships between paragraphs important, as well the relationship between a paragraph and the essay as a whole? Lewis tackles these descriptivist questions, stating that the function of the paragraph is chiefly to focus the reader's attention, as its Greek origin of marking a change in speaker strongly implies, and that the paragraph has additional rhetorical and structural powers that Bain's impassive, simplifying pedagogy strips away (1–17).

Sampling 400-odd years of discourse, Lewis shows that paragraph length has remained reasonably constant, though typical sentence length has been cut in half (62). Bain's theories can then be viewed as a response to a perceived thinning out of the written English language—a response posing as necessarily objective and as universal in nature, while obsessed with structure over function in order to form a standard by which masses of lower-class students, instead of the privileged of previous generations, can be readily indoctrinated (Branson 48). Bain had a sizable task. Modern empirical criticisms of Bain have the luxury of favoring the descriptivist view, as they are not concerned with such large-scale sociological enforcement, or even actively oppose it.

Despite the importance of Lewis's sweeping, synthesizing remarks, he remained obscure in his time. But other authors were starting to criticize the ironclad doctrines of Bain.

THE PARAGRAPH REBELS: TOWARD DESCRIPTIVE AND FUNCTIONAL THEORY

Fred Newton Scott and Joseph Denney's 1893 book *Paragraph-Writing* is the first in a series of blows against the Bain tradition. The text acknowledges Bain's influence, in particular his analogy of sentences and paragraphs, but it argues for the paragraph as the center of instruction via nonstructural reasons, a novel concept at the time (Brereton 343–44). As the paragraph is analogous to the essay, it argues, the paragraph allows for more rewriting and practice in less time (it is also easier for teachers to correct errors). Scott and Denney also recommend that the topic sentence be freed from mandatory positional constraints. In their later, secondary school text of 1900, *Elementary English Composition* (and the new edition of 1908), this theme is continued. Discussion of the paragraph is spread out over many chapters and not only divided between "written" and "oral" paragraphs, but between descriptive, narrative, explanatory, and argumentative paragraphs—the four forms of discourse—and through various developmental paradigms such as comparison and contrast, cause and effect, definition, etc.[7] Most striking is the discussion of "topic-sentence" use, which is very prominent (the concept is usually bolded). Scott and Denney advise that the topic sentence be used in a variety of ways and positions, not just in the first position. They are not quite descriptivist or functionalist, as they still have a remarkably dim view of their students' abilities, but this is a new tack.

John Matthews Manly and Edith Rickert, in their 1920 textbook *The Writing of English*, state that the paragraph should not be taught in isolation; it is "related" and "organic" in the sense of being part of a larger whole, instead of "organic" in the sense of its internal structure, à la Bain. After all, an isolated paragraph can be used to support any theory (Lunsford, "Alexander Bain's Contributions" 296). They also speak of concepts that technical writers today find essential: readability, the visual appearance of the page, and the ideal number of paragraphs for a page according to the writer's style and genre. They also talk about "motion": the creation of an expectation, then a fulfillment of that expectation (Manly and Rickert 83–88).

The Writing of English had its opposition, which is not surprising considering how far it steps away from Bain. An aggressive Bain supporter lambasted the text in the same year, speaking of how Bain's work, well grounded in psychology, was needed to "tie down" the "vagrant mind of adolescence" and deal with "fumble-minded" pupils. Giving too much freedom to composition students, he felt, was grounds for disaster, and he took the opportunity to also praise the use of mandatory outlines for essays (Smith 400).

Nonetheless, handbooks appearing in this era also reflect a little anti-Bain sentiment. Garland Greever and Easley S. Jones's 1924 handbook adds paragraph advice to its 1918 edition and is quite reasonable, allowing short paragraphs (although they must not be "scrappy") and flexibility on the usage of topic-sentences. William Strunk's incredibly influential 1918 *Elements of Style* echoes Scott and Denney with "make the paragraph a unit of composition" (Strunk). But it also follows Bain, via "as a rule, begin each paragraph with a topic sentence [. . .]" Strunk does concede that a paragraph needing "rhetorical pause" in "animated narrative" often does not employ one, and transitional one-sentence paragraphs are acceptable (Strunk). E. B. White's edition from 1959, however, adds a preceding "suitable design" section that is much more structural and prescriptive (White 11).

Another paragraph rebel, perhaps the most colorful, is Leon Mones. In the pages of the early *English Journal*, in 1922, he calls Bain "old school" and derides instruction in Bain's formalist "rhetorical sunshine" (456). Eschewing rules, outlines, or restrictions, Mones stressed letting students express themselves, though he still holds to the paragraph as the ideal unit for teaching composition: "The most practical way to teach anyone to write is to have him write numerous paragraphs" (456). Still, he declares that real-world editors know little of rhetorical (paragraph) rules and do not need them; ask one for some, he says, and be astounded at the silence (456–60). Perhaps most important, though, the topic sentence for Mones naturally suggests following patterns of development; therefore, memorizing types of paragraphs is pointless. Prompting questions will elicit development naturally, even in the most unimaginative student (459).

This same thought is echoed by Charles Whitmore in the following year, 1923, in his "A Doctrine of the Paragraph." Whitmore saw too many paragraphs that did not have explicit topic sentences, especially descriptive or narrative paragraphs; some, in fact, had structure only in a spatial or chronological sense (605). He proposes "motive" or "purpose" as a better way to construct paragraphs and states that the first sentence of a paragraph always implies a following commonsensical structure that, as in Mones or Manly and Rickert, need not be taught, though this is only in paragraphs of "an intellectual cast" (609).

Indeed, Whitmore says, if the goal of pedagogy is originality—the ability to eschew form at will, to have options—the question is how slavish dedication to form can produce it. There is the classical idea of imitation, that one must learn the rules before one can break them; but one wonders from where the impetus to break these forms comes. At any rate, Whitmore agrees with Mones: structure is determined by function, or, rather, purpose suggests form (610).

The seeds for a larger descriptivist paragraph theory had been planted at this point, though they were regrettably slow to grow. Cleanth Brooks and Robert Penn Warren's *Modern Rhetoric*, first published in 1949, bears traces of the Mones-Whitmore-Manly-Rickert rebellion, but in the end it still holds firm to Bainish thought (Branson 65). However, there is a stress on levels of generalization in the paragraph in articles of the period that may have influenced Christensen's later work.

A CCCC symposium in 1958, "The Rhetoric of the Paragraph," resurrected the debate; the serious questions originally asked by Lewis in 1894 were asked, and the consensus was that the paragraph must be taught as part of the whole essay and not in isolation, with many of the concerns listed in Manly and Rickert's text also agreed upon (192). There is a general apathy toward a clear definition of the paragraph, however, and a disdain for more than the most general terminology, save for the uses of beginning writers. No new theory was immediately provided, but by the mid-1960s, as composition gained steam as a discipline, a plethora of new theories appeared: three full-bodied rhetorics of the paragraph.

THE 1960S: NEW THEORIES

Christensen's 1965 "A Generative Rhetoric of the Paragraph" appeared first, and is, on close examination, a theory of paragraph structure that does not move very far away from Bain's principles. While it introduces and codifies what will prove to be a useful pedagogical tool in the coming decades—the notion of levels of generality that can be used to diagram and map paragraphs—it is at the same time self-limiting. "Movement" is discussed, but it is different from Mones's "motion," or Whitmore's "motive," for with Christensen, "movement" merely describes a hierarchical movement along X-Y lines of general vs. specific.

Christensen admits that this model is an ideal and that it cannot account for one-sentence paragraphs, introductions, conclusions, transitions, and other unusual strategies; it is easy to make a series of paragraphs that confound the diagrams (Eden and Mitchell 423), which are meant for traditional body paragraphs (Rockas 148). The generative model ends up serving a similar function to Bain's principles, only with a more modern feel. Christensen still works off of the well-seasoned idea that the sentence scales to the paragraph and the paragraph scales to the essay, and while he calls it a "generative" rhetoric, it is hard to defend his approach as being any more generative than Bain's prescriptions, though David Karrafalt tries a few years later (217).

In the same year as Christensen's article appeared, A. L. Becker tried a tagmemic approach that examined expository paragraphs by partitioning them into either three or two grammatical components. He also ends up echoing Bainish hierarchical thought, but in linguistic subject-predicate terminology (237–42) and with the same lack of empirical basis. Christensen's rhetoric overshadows this approach by more directly invoking current-traditionalism in compositional rhetoric. In his contribution to a 1966 *CCC* symposium on the paragraph, Becker admits defeat to a certain extent when, in what is meant as a criticism of Rodgers's stadium at first but later unhappily reflects his own confusion, he says, "paragraphs are the units that a writer, for one reason or another, chooses to mark as paragraphs. This is the only way to describe all paragraphs" (Irmscher et al. 68).

Third, but not last, is Rodgers, with a closely linked set of three articles from 1965 to 1967: "Alexander Bain and the Rise of the Organic Paragraph," "A Discourse-Centered Rhetoric of the Paragraph," and "The Stadium of Discourse." In these, he seconds many of Lewis's assertions, pokes holes in Christensen's rhetoric, and finally introduces what might be called the first full-fledged functionalist theory of paragraphs.

Rodgers begins by spending a great deal of time savaging the deductive origins of Bain's theories, noting how all the principles have easily discerned "but if" clauses that can be attached to them, e.g: "[A] paragraph always has a single topic [. . .] except when it has two or more" ("Discourse" 2); "The paragraph is what the textbook says, except [. . .] it isn't" (3). Likewise, while he thinks that Christensen's levels of generality hold "great promise" (4), he notes that Christensen makes the same kind of "but if" excuses, and that a "discourse-centered" model of the paragraph is needed.

In his second article, Rodgers dissects via close reading a long passage in Walter Pater's "Style" from 1889, in a manner reminiscent of Blair. This approach details how unnervingly complex each paragraph is, and how choice of any one indentation heavily influences previous and future structure in the essay (6–11). Indentation isolates and defines structure, which is just a part of all discourse. With this in mind, it is hard to see how the dictates of Bain's form could ever explain all the possible subtle and minute considerations that Pater weaves his way through, and also—perhaps most important—the accidental constructs and mistakes that restrict motion. Rodgers even discovers, left over from an earlier draft, a hidden conclusion in a deceptively orderly passage. "Tonal fluctuation" and "rhythm," which Rodgers finds "hard to describe," are also mentioned ("Discourse" 9–11), invoking the paragraph rebels with a more aesthetic bent. More than any other composition theorist that I have seen, Rodgers speaks of beauty in a rhetorical sense, thus evoking eighteenth-century rhetoricians.

Rodgers develops this concept to its logical conclusion a year later, in 1967, with "The Stadium of Discourse." Taking Christensen's diagramming approach for a basis, but without measuring levels of generality, he borrows a passage from Charles Darwin, omits paragraph indentations, and outlines the entire "sequence" (a term also borrowed from Christensen) into five "smaller wholes [. . .] each composed of one topic statement, simple or complex [. . .] together with supporting material" ("Stadium" 183–84). These "smaller wholes" he labels stadia. The term comes from Lewis, who speaks of units that do not always have the eminently logical paragraph breaks of Bain's pedagogy. These units may in Darwin's text be one isolated paragraph, or they may encompass many; regardless, they are unified bodies of thought, independent of indentation, and the way they are formed, according to Rodgers, informs a writer's style ("Stadium" 184).

Proposing a new unit of discourse other than the sentence, paragraph, or essay is groundbreaking enough, but Rodgers manages to unite many of the ideas of previous current-traditional opponents under a new functionalist banner with this article. Paragraphs are units of invention again, with no set form or special prescriptions; they are built of and can be stadia, not merely topic sentences and support; the main concern of the writer becomes functional—What do I want to do?—and contextual—What will the intended reader think?

Rodger's approach is a vessel that holds theoretical as well as practical water. Rodgers opines that it is not as pressing to map the internal structure of paragraphs as it is to learn why paragraphs are made—and also, implicitly, to question the concept of a text existing perfectly well without any such indentations. The concept of stadium offers a possible solution, though he does not offer a pedagogical version of his theory, and none seems immediately apparent. Again, the problem Angus faced appears—how does one teach paragraphing in a descriptive fashion; if it has no set form, especially if form is all one is used to teaching? This was Becker's main criticism of the concept of the stadium in *CCC*'s symposium on the paragraph in 1966 (68); what are stadia good for, in terms of teaching? It is a largely unanswered question, though a bit facile to ask.

A coda to the decade comes in 1969 from Willis Pitkin, with the introduction of "discourse blocs," a method of diagramming text that distinguishes "joints"—commas, semicolons, and periods—from "junctures," where thought processes diverge. Decrying the paragraph's being taught as a "self-contained" unit, Pitkin champions the idea of discourse as being "without gaps, a continuum of increasingly complex structures" (139). This at first glance echoes Rodgers's stadium, but his discussion constantly evokes Christensen's generative rhetoric (Pitkin is a former student), as he believes that this "continuum" is also strictly hierarchical in the Bain sense. Indeed, the discourse blocs that Pitkin uses to diagram a sample paragraph appear to be little more than boxes to place clauses and transitions in. While these blocs allow a strange little map of sorts to be constructed from all the blocs placed together in a diagram, that diagram is even more difficult to read than Christensen's sentence diagramming, and it lacks the intuitive nature of stadium. Even Pitkin admits his concept is "sketchy" and he is quite tentative in discussing it, in a manner similar to Becker's (12).

THE 1970S AND 1980S: EMPIRICISM

Descriptivist thought received serious backing from Richard Meade and W. Geiger Ellis's "Paragraph Development in the Modern Age of Rhetoric" in 1970. Noting that writers ignore the current-traditional instruction on paragraph form that they are presented with in favor of looser structures, this study paved the way for further empirical confirmation, which came with Richard Braddock's 1974 "The Frequency and Placement of Topic Sentences in Expository Prose." Braddock tempered his well-known findings—that only 13 percent of popular essay paragraphs have explicit topic sentences—with the disclaimer that many paragraphs in his corpus could have used topic sentences for readability (300–02). Coupled with Rodgers's functional model of the paragraph, though, Braddock's parting words, as careful and wise as they sound on first reading, feel like the ghost of Alexander Bain whispering for caution. Did rigorous prescriptive instruction prepare the writers of Braddock's corpus to be able to write such adrift yet functional paragraphs, even in the face of Meade and Ellis's study showing that less than 50 percent of professional sentences followed those principles, even in the pages of *English Journal* (194–95)? Braddock toes the line, unwilling to make the functionalist leap.

Frank D'Angelo makes a tentative case for Rodgers's approach over Christensen's in 1974 ("Generative" 394), and Arthur Stern praises Rodgers two years later (257), imploring that functionalist, discourse-centered rhetoric be taught somehow instead of Bainish structure or Christensen's rhetoric, the latter of which got a toehold in some textbooks and articles in the early 1970s. However, Stern's call was ignored, at least in textbooks, which remained in Bain's corner as if no competing theory whatsoever had been proposed

(Branson 117). At the same time, no serious criticism of Rodgers's stadium appeared, save an attempt by Robin Markels in 1983 to revive Becker's tagmemic model. A dissertation in the same year by Thomas Utley picked the big three paragraph theories of the 1960s, set them to analyze paragraphs in a corpus, and showed that 32.8 percent could be explained by Becker's tagmemic theory, 30.8 percent fell under the guidelines of Christensen's, and 100 percent fit neatly into Rodgers's stadium.

Rodgers's theory or the descriptive cries of the paragraph rebels were rarely evoked directly. Carol Cohan's brief but illuminating case in 1976 for teaching support sentences before the topic sentence is a practical application of the compromise D'Angelo would take a decade later: that prescriptive models are best used only as stepping-stones to better writing (D'Angelo, "Topic" 438–39). Sentence-combining exercises in the early 1980s also illustrate some of the principles of functional paragraph thought (Steffey 23–26). Lindemann's *A Rhetoric for Writing Teachers* from 2001, still a popular introductory text, discusses Christensen's rhetoric in great detail, but leaves Rodgers to a footnote even in later editions, even though many exercises in the book have a functional bent to them (Lindemann 146–57).

If anything, there is a "muddling" of Bainish prescription with a dash of Christensen and another of Rodgers in the pedagogy. The split is not so much between prescriptivists and descriptivists, but between a number of descriptivists and the functionalist branch; it's not as clear-cut as creationism and evolution, certainly, but there is enough difference in theory that omitting explicit functionalist theory is an easily rationalized move to present a more unified front to the student, and also to teachers.

Much of the difficulty with translating descriptivist thought into pedagogy comes from historical precedent. Textbook writers look to previous textbooks for pointers in paragraph construction, and absorb them along with snippets of current theory that dovetail. Of the post-1960s theorists, most often Christensen gets the call, as his ideas are closest. This conclusion gathers momentum when we take into account Mark Branson's survey of thirty-two textbooks for coverage of the "big three" paragraph theories of the 1960s in his 1988 dissertation on paragraph theory.[8] Ten textbooks followed Christensen's model, five followed Becker's,[9] and two "echoed" Rodgers's functionalist stadium without attribution. The remaining fifteen textbooks followed Bainish prescription. Also, only one text mentioned Braddock's 1974 study, in passing, and not by name (Branson 145). This balance has held, more or less, twenty-two years later, and there seems to be merely a loose familiarity with past or current paragraph theory, which lets the old prescriptive view hold sway by default.[10]

The last two major journal articles on the paragraph in composition appeared in 1986: Eden and Mitchell's "Paragraphing for the Reader" and D'Angelo's "The Topic Sentence Revisited." The first offers a supposedly new, reader-based model of the paragraph, insisting that the reader's experience adds complications to the theories of the 1960s and that paragraphing should be taught as part of editing instead of generation. Backing their statements with research from psychology, Eden and Mitchell claim that readers expect paragraphs to have certain lengths according to genre, to possess a unity of structure, to have a first sentence orienting the reader, to have a punchline in the last sentence, and lastly to possess coherence internally, as well as with the rest of the document (417–18). But it is notable how easily the weighty Bainish principles of the nineteenth century can be extracted from this list: unity, coherence, emphasis via the topic sentence. This reader-based rhetoric feels like Bain's in new clothing.

D'Angelo's piece skillfully assembles the thought of previous decades, as Eden and Mitchell's does, and focuses the debate by concentrating on the topic sentence. But he also calcifies paragraph theory by offering a wholly sensible compromise on topic sentence usage: in a nutshell, he allows that Bain's principles are still a good tool, if only for basic writers. The problem is that this could easily be misconstrued as a way to fully reconcile prescriptive and descriptive paragraph thought. He does not offer the actual goods: how to determine when structural principles should be presented and when introducing a more functional approach is appropriate.

Both these works were a push in the right direction, I think, but not an end to the discussion, which I fear is the way many composition scholars saw them. The synthesis of the past in these two articles was so effective, in fact, that I believe it killed further thought rather than encouraging it. The field saw two decent accommodations with Bain's theories and promptly hitched its wagon to more exciting horses, leaving Eden and Mitchell's plea at the gates and not actually changing pedagogy or textbooks much. With composition becoming increasingly absorbed by the late 1980s with other concerns broader than "nuts 'n' bolts" pedagogy, such as cultural studies (Fulkerson 659), it is not surprising that the paragraph torch passed on to scholars in technical writing, linguistics, and psychology. They were, frankly, more interested in digging deeper empirically into paragraphs, and this attention led to intriguing results that lent ammunition to both prescriptivists and descriptivists.

PARAGRAPH THEORY OUTSIDE COMPOSITION

The shift of paragraph theory to other disciplines is most apparent in the work of Randall Popken, who wrote his dissertation in 1984 on academic paragraph use, and then between 1987 and 1991 further developed this genre-focused approach with a series of four empirical studies approximating Braddock's 1974 methodology in different writing genres: scientific, technical academic, and periodical writing. He found topic sentences most prevalent in the paragraphs of academic and scientific writing (54 percent and 55 percent), and less so in technical writing and familiar essays (32 percent and 30 percent). These results make Branson's textbook survey resonate even more strongly, especially when combined with another study finding 70 percent to 95 percent topic sentence rates in English composition textbooks and sociology textbooks (O'Hear, Ramsey, and Pherson 318).

The concerns of genre are nowhere better illustrated than in technical and professional writing, which has overtly visual concerns for the paragraph. "Macrolevel" structural concerns such as headings (Baker 466), lists, graphics, typography, white space, and text as signs are all huge subjects. As in the field of psychology, there is a focus on short-term memory retention and ideal paragraph length (Markel et al., "Effects" 454–56). With the advent of computers and other technology, the "linear chain" (Rodgers's "sequence") is increasingly being broken and paragraph rules are not absolute (Bush). Concerns have also moved toward finding ways to present text online. Are traditional paragraphs up to speed, especially with longer works? Is it possible, even, to write algorithms that can automatically subdivide texts in at least a workmanlike fashion (Hearst 333)?

Psychology's view of the paragraph[11] is cognitive, focusing on readability issues and the reading process in an effort to further understand how the mind works. If composition has offered a great deal of paragraph theory, psychology has shown how much of that theory is valid. Bain's key historical works in psychology, *The Senses and the Intellect* and *The Emotions and the Will*, predating his *English Composition and Rhetoric* by eleven and six years, respectively, are the logical link between composition and psychology in this area. His structural conclusions on paragraphs spring from these works (Lunsford, "Alexander Bain and the Teaching of Composition" 222), and readability studies in the last twenty years have backed up, at least in general, some of his principles, especially in the realm of the topic sentence.

Heather Stark's 1988 study on paragraph markers is also indicative of the migration of paragraph theory from composition, as she uses such theories to help frame her two empirical studies,[12] which find not only that readability, understanding, and memory retention increase significantly when the author's intentions and the reader's response to the presented cues agree, but also that paragraphs are not just topic markers and sometimes just break up the text to smooth reading (299–301). Elsewhere, topic sentences have been found to minimize memory load and increase recall (Aulls 391) as well as shorten the overall reading time of paragraphs (Kieras 13). Recall and reading time are also affected when new topics reflect preceding topics, when introductory paragraphs are present, and when a shift in topic is major rather than minor (Lorch et al. 350)—and even when the information is simply presented higher in the text (Clements 287). These studies all suggest that explicit structure, à la Bain, is generally good for the reader.

A model of the paragraph is also a concern in linguistics (Zadrozny and Jensen 171) with a multitude of factors to consider aside from coherence, such as recursion (Hwang 461). Most recently, Elizabeth Le has used linguistic models of the paragraph along with coherence theory to reveal differences in French and English academic paragraph construction ("Use" 308–09) as well as problems in translation, with a stated goal being a "grammar of paragraphs" ("Role" 259–60).

The reading process, growing out of van Dijk and Kintsch's concept of macroprocessing (363), was later informed by Morton Gernsbacher's structure-building framework, which involves three steps for how readers build a mental structure of a text: foundation (where the first part of a paragraph is processed first, and recall is strongest), mapping (where further content is added, based on levels of referential, temporal, locational, and casual cohesion), and shifting (when there is not enough cohesion, reading time increases, and a new mental structure is initiated). Poor readers shift too often, and good readers do not (*Language* 880). Coded instructions embedded in the text, called "insight-propositions," can trigger structure-building (Britton 641); the topic sentence is one of these. The reader's skills have also been considered, with explicit structure helping readers with little knowledge of the text's subject (Goldman et al. 273), and less overt structure helping high-knowledge readers via the promotion of inference by "active processing" (McNamara et al. 1).

At first glance, these studies are troubling for the descriptivists. Bain's "old school" rules turn out not to be just the deductively derived nonsense that Rodgers painted them as. Predictable, explicit paragraph structure does help the reader. This observation can be qualified, however, by noting that these studies do not show that structure is a magic cure-all. Sometimes that extra structure can do damage by insulting readers with its simplicity and predictability and by forestalling readers from making their own, perhaps even superior, cognitive connections. Plenty of room for individual style and quirkiness remains. And even so-called "bad" paragraphs can sneak by unnoticed if there is enough global structure or ethos elsewhere, in a manner analogous to the subtle stunt Joseph Williams pulled in his 1981 "Phenomenology of Error."

Unfortunately, the hesitation of descriptivists to embrace Rodgers-style functionalism remains; Braddock's cautious appendix in "The Frequency and Placement of Topic Sentences in Expository Prose" is a model. He points out that even if cognitive research shows that explicit paragraph structure is good for readers, all the paragraphs he found without topic sentences were still getting the job done. Yet for him the possible explanations vary: (1) the paragraphs are adequate but flawed and could use improvement, (2) other structural factors, such as headings or global context, are taking over, (3) our view of paragraph structure is totally inadequate and simplistic, or (4) all of the above.

A functionalist can revel in this confusion with a guilty sort of glee (especially at option 3), and also in the fact that so far no field, including computational linguistics, has modeled the paragraph to the point that it can begin to measure the beauty and aesthetics that Rodgers defended so vigorously forty years ago. From this viewpoint, at least, any attempt to bind the paragraph is bound to fail because of the infinite variables involved. Then again, there are those who think it can be done to a level where it can help assess coherence in student paragraphs.

Whether or not this would intrude upon our roles as teachers, however, is the million-dollar question—quite literally, considering the rise in coherence studies and grants enabling such. Suddenly, Bain's chilly imperatives may become rather warm and comforting. But composition should take heed of this recent research.

AN ARGUMENT FOR PARAGRAPH THEORY

I argue that composition studies should not only reclaim paragraph theory, but also collaborate with the other disciplines examining it. This is not a call for wild theoretical revolution away from the current trends of socioeconomic, cultural, and literature-related pedagogy, but for a timely and happy reunion with past research. I have no objection to current areas of interest, as I find them valuable and fascinating; I am merely taking issue with an important, indeed fundamental, oversight.

While there has been neglect of late, composition has as strong a claim to paragraph theory as any scholarly discipline, as I hope I have adequately demonstrated by my historical overview. Paragraph theory's decline in composition is due to a cyclical trend rather than to any questions about its intrinsic worth, which is quite high—indeed, it provides much of our *raison d'être*. Few would contest that robust paragraph formation is essential to effective writing.

I cannot say this strongly enough. What composition instructor has not been at his or her wit's end, trying to help a student understand why a paragraph or series of paragraphs does or does not work? Indeed, what textbook or style manual[13] can afford not to consider the paragraph at length and to give effective guidance? We have a few terms to bandy about—topic sentence, support, conclusion, types of paragraphs, that elusive concept of "flow"— but while we have literally thousands of years of style discussion to lean on at the sentence level, the paragraph is a relatively new concern, dating only from Murray, and the scant available terminology reflects its still-evolving youth.

I anticipate some resistance to my argument, namely, along the lines that the nature of the paragraph is a decided and even "current-traditional" subject that was discussed unto folly in the past, and that composition has rightly moved onto fresher, more progressive topics. This is a weak counterargument, though, because there are at least two distinct approaches to paragraph theory and, arguably, three that remain to be resolved. One might as well say that the question of ethics in rhetoric has been done in the past and needs no further belaboring. Also, the vigorous activity in psychology and computational linguistics deflates the notion that the nature of paragraphs—bad paragraphs, good paragraphs, average paragraphs, or even just adequate paragraphs—is somehow decided.

I see composition playing a valuable role in synthesis and collaboration. The spread of interest across fields in this area creates an opportunity, however tentative, to combat the problem of linguistics citing only linguistics, psychology citing only psychology, and technical or professional writing citing only technical or professional writing—as well as composition citing only composition. Usually, the overlap is slight. I see hope in composition and psychology scholars, though, as they have a tendency to cite other fields; the usual myopia clears up on occasion.

In a recent collection, *Genetic Criticism*, Daniel Ferrer and Jean-Michel Rabaté discuss "paragraph theory" as if it were what the book's editors praise as a totally new, unexplored "paradiscipline." They fail to cite a single composition scholar, and, indeed, the editors praise them in their introduction to the piece for "brushing aside the commonplaces still offered up in composition manuals" (Deppman, Ferrer, and Groden 133). On one level, this project is practical and desirable for publishing purposes and for the development of a field; on another, it is self-defeating not to use easily available resources, especially in an age of growing cross-disciplinary efforts; and huge online databases. I do not demean any other field's approach to the paragraph; Ferrer and Rabaté's chapter contains a rather thoughtful discussion. I am, however, contending that composition has the most practical application for paragraph theory—helping young writers—and has engaged in the most extensive past deliberation on the issue.[14] I'll go even further, and state that Ferrer and Rabaté are wise to be dismissive of the paragraphing advice in composition manuals, especially since functional and even descriptive thought is often poorly represented. I am not surprised that an observer elsewhere, not familiar with the compositional canon, concludes that we all have little altars on our desks where we burn F papers to appease the topic sentence, among other minor, bloodthirsty grammatical deities.

However, I am pretty confident the future of paragraph theory is not entirely in "semiotics and poststructuralist theory" (Deppman, Ferrer, and Groden 133), given that literary theory, by the authors' admission, does not have any extant theory on the paragraph. Much of the heavy lifting has already been done in composition. Then again, maybe composition does need to be brushed aside, if all we offer are "commonplaces"—a synonym for Aristotle's topics, which the rhetoricians of the eighteenth century dismissed in favor of a more scientific approach. Paragraph theory emerged not long after this shift.

What could composition offer, then? Here are four suggestions, to provoke thought.

New terminology would be a start. Vocabulary constraints may have stalled the thoughts of Blair and Campbell before they could muse on the paragraph. For example, there should be a reasonable standard name for the macrostructure between the paragraph and the essay: a term that teachers can use when describing both difficulties in structures and their functional advantages (how overlapping, nested structures can work together to power effective essays). The concept as described by Rodgers is not extraordinarily difficult or complex, and it is fairly easy to introduce to students with a little forethought. It seems paradoxical, perhaps, to suggest a new term for structure to bolster theory if one is a functionalist, but such a move would be a good step forward that would acknowledge the clear value of both camps. Whether this structure should be called a stadium, bloc, section, unit of thought, or passage is not important as long as a standard takes hold.

Second, I propose that the concept of "motion," "motive," "flow," or "rhythm"—what the ancients called harmony, and what paragraph theorists tend to bump into constantly with all the elegance of a bull in a china shop—should receive more attention in the context of the paragraph, especially from the reader's perspective. We badly need effective language for explaining the temporal movement of ideas at the paragraph and macrostructure levels. Right now, there is little available outside of vague timing phrases. Elements are either placed too early or too late, as in, "Could you place this idea later in your introduction?" or they exist in a form too short or too long for easy reading, creating hazy advice such as, "This historical section of your article is a little too long." Peter Elbow's recent article in *CCC*, "The Music of Form," speaks to the limitations of spatial metaphor (628) and the importance of flow (640), although his aural/visual lens is chiefly focused on the sentence or the whole essay; those pesky paragraphs that lurk in between also need examination. The teaching of prose rhythm, another neglected area of study that has traditionally restricted itself to the sentence,[15] might be a source for inspiration in this area.

Third, I fear that the textbook concerns listed by Branson are still existent, both in composition and in professional writing. Future textbook writers, of both undergraduate and graduate texts, and especially books focused on pedagogy, should take into consideration all approaches to the paragraph, not just the Bain tradition, and not assume that the topic sentence is more than just a useful label. Such additions would not be strenuous.

George Gopen's 2004 *Expectations: Teaching Writing from the Reader's Perspective* contains a thoughtful and quite lengthy discussion of the paragraph; in particular, a strong distinction is made between the "issue/theme" of a paragraph and the "point." A traditional topic sentence supplies both of these in one sentence and position, but quite often the declaration of the subject under discussion (the issue or theme) and the claim being made about that subject (the point) may be found in a number of different and separate sentences and positions within a paragraph, dependent on the rhetorical choices made by the writer. This distinction offers a possible resolution to the descriptivist's dilemma that I outlined previously. When Gopen refuses to "construct a typology of paragraphs" and follows this refusal by saying, "We can note recurring patterns, but we cannot with any hope of success establish unvarying rules concerning their construction" (228), I recall Angus's advice in 1862, and I see prescriptive, descriptive, and cognitive theory not only intersecting but moving in a positive direction.

Last, the elephant in the room also needs consideration. No consistent prescriptive approach, or descriptive approach—or any approach, for that matter—to instruction has been empirically shown to be more effective in producing better paragraphs than any other. Only ambitious, rigorous studies spanning secondary and college instruction can address this issue. I would hazard a guess that an immense amount would be learned about how students learn to write paragraphs. My only specific recommendation would be that paragraphs should be studied in context as much as possible, against nearby paragraphs and within the entire work, rather than in isolation.

The paragraph is still largely thought of, and taught, as a topic sentence with support, with explicit structure making for an easier read. English departments may swing far to the left politically, but most English textbooks remain remarkably conservative and fundamentalist. This is not to say that teachers are demanding only gaslight-era, steam-driven monstrosities of essays, but rather that paragraph theory in journals seems to have petered out, with more progressive theory abandoned pedagogically save for teachers who eschew textbook-based instruction or combat their texts openly. Works such as Gopen's offer hope, but even in the twenty-first century, a largely prescriptive view of the paragraph still reigns, as if Alexander Bain had just issued a 2007 edition of his *English Composition and Rhetoric* with acknowledgments to Francis Christensen.

While the cyclical nature of research in the area might discourage attempts at a unified theory of the paragraph, I think that if such a theory can exist, it will likely be found in the rhetoric of the paragraph rebels—the concept of "flow" or its many synonyms—or via the immense efforts of number-crunching in computational linguistics and psychology, as computers and language models grow exponentially more complex. I think that it would be advantageous for composition to have an important, guiding hand in these matters, given that we have the most potential use of the benefits—additional tools by which to help students learn how to compose effective paragraphs, and, thus, effective essays.[16]

NOTES

1. Murray's text is heavily derivative of Robert Lowth's grammar of 1762, which does not consider the paragraph.

2. As Ned Shearer astutely points out, the end of Campbell's discussion of sentences feels like a transition to a missing consideration of paragraphs (Campbell 415; Shearer 409).

3. The evolution of grammars up to 1800 includes an occasional mix of rhetorical elements, with the most common oddball subsidiary being punctuation. Ian Michael attributes this to the influence of Campbell and Blair (195). While they might not have addressed it explicitly, their work certainly leads toward consideration of the paragraph.

4. A very old, carried-over piece of advice for sentences—Aristotle's discussion of periods in his *Rhetoric* (240–41) contains this.

5. The 1871 edition contains the same six principles and much the same presentation.

6. John McElroy, another Bain adherent, gave the "theme" of a paragraph its modern name in his 1885 textbook, and it seems to have caught on completely ten years later.

7. As Robert Connors ably describes in his overview of discourse taxonomies, these paradigms are still with us and often used to teach paragraph structure. The "taxonomic instinct" he speaks of is immensely strong in paragraph theorizing and instruction (256).

8. Doctoral dissertations concerning paragraphing were fairly popular in the 1980s, and there were at least five on the subject in addition to Utley's in that decade. Mark Branson's from 1988 stands out. He provides the synthesis that Lewis accomplished in 1894, but for the twentieth century; he does not address much post-1980 work, though (Eden and Mitchell and D'Angelo's work from 1986 are absent), or research outside of composition. Suggesting that composition has a choice between Bain, Christensen, and Rodgers for pedagogical paragraph theory, Branson goes a step further (perhaps a little too far) and suggests that paragraphs should not be taught at all at the college level (9–11). Nothing is better than something, he suggests, given that a small study he performs demonstrates that current-traditional topic-sentence instruction makes no difference in writing level. His study is too small to make such a claim, but it serves to rouse attention. He further opines, "As far as those who consider theory today; structure or form of the paragraph is not of significant importance, except how structure of isolated paragraphs informs whole-discourse level decisions" (112), and he declares that the functional rhetoric espoused by Rodgers and others won the theory debate.

9. This fact is likely due to the complexity and linguistic jargon of Becker's text—it's not simple enough for first-year English, whereas Christensen's is—although Branson opines that

Becker's typology is ultimately more helpful than Christensen's vague subordination-coordination language (146).

10. For a current example, in the annotated instructor's edition of Lynn Quitman Troyka and Douglas Hesse's 2005 *Simon and Schuster Handbook for Writers*, a selection of paragraph theory is offered for the curious scholar. Bain's principles get an entire left margin, despite their being 140 years old. Becker and Christensen also get their own pages, but the functionalists (Angus, Lewis, Rodgers, Pitkin, Stern, Eden and Mitchell, the paragraph rebels of the 1920s) are conspicuously absent, though Scott and Denney are mentioned briefly later on. Braddock's oft-cited 1974 study gets discussion, although his results feel glossed over, along with "journalistic" writing. The student does not hear this muted struggle; the presentation of the paragraph in the student's text is Bain once again, with unity, coherence, and the topic sentence all prominent, though filtered through process theory and a few functional options for the topic sentence (80–108). For professional writing, Mike Markel's 2004 *Technical Communication,* which I have used when teaching, is excellent in many respects, but it recommends first-position topic sentences without giving options (224–25), even though headings can easily take their place (Bush), a point with which Markel largely agrees earlier in his text when discussing how to section a document.

11. Any scholar in psychology, I am positive, would give a better rundown; what follows is no more than an interested layperson's perspective, to demonstrate that there is a large, well-established body of work.

12. Stark's methods are good, but not all paragraph studies in this era are as airtight. "Cues People Use to Paragraph Text" by Sandra Bond and John Hayes in 1984 declares paragraphs "psychologically real"—i.e., when readers are presented with a text bereft of paragraphs, they will tend to agree on where paragraph markers should be placed, depending on topic sentences and paragraph length. However, this methodology does not account for semantic cues—a rather big hole, as the authors admit sheepishly, similar to the one in coherence thought (165–66). Branson demonstrates how easily the results of such studies depend heavily on the sample provided, as Christensen's and Becker's shaky models did before them (130–42).

13. Given that our texts define our discipline to at least some extent and "shape teacher and student subjectivities" (Hawhee 504), it is hard simply to dismiss the absence of openly functional approaches as just another case of texts rightly bypassing pie-in-the-sky theory in the interests of practicality.

14. Although psychology comes close, it offers no pedagogy, while composition offers little empirical work.

15. A good overview of prose rhythm theory, ancient and modern, is contained in John Hubert Scott's 1925 *Rhythmic Prose.*

16. I am greatly indebted to this article's reviewers, in particular Joseph Williams, and I would also thank Brad McAdon, Joseph Jones, and Susan Popham for thoughtful comments on early drafts.

WORKS CITED

Angus, Joseph. *Handbook of the English Tongue.* London: Religious Tract Society, 1862.

Aristotle. *On Rhetoric: A Theory of Civic Discourse.* Trans. George A. Kennedy. New York: Oxford UP, 1991.

Aulls, Mark. "Expository Paragraph Properties That Influence Literal Recall." *Journal of Reading Behavior* 7 (1975): 391–400.

Bain, Alexander. *The Emotions and the Will.* New York: Appleton, 1866.

———. *English Composition and Rhetoric (1871).* Delmar, NY: Scholars' Facsimiles & Reprints, 1996.

———. *English Composition and Rhetoric.* New York: Appleton, 1866.

———. *On Teaching English.* New York: Appleton, 1901.

———. *The Senses and the Intellect.* London: Parker, 1855.

Baker, William H. "How to Produce and Communicate Structured Text." *Technical Communication* 41 (1994): 456–66.

Becker, A. L. Contribution to "Symposium on the Paragraph." *CCC* 17 (1966): 67–72.

———. "A Tagmemic Approach to Paragraph Analysis." *CCC* 16 (1965): 237–42.

Blair, Hugh. *Lectures on Rhetoric and Belle Lettres.* 1783. Ed. Linda Ferreira-Buckley and S. Michael Halloran. Carbondale: Southern Illinois UP, 2005.

Bond, Sandra J., and John R. Hayes. "Cues People Use to Paragraph Text." *Research in the Teaching of English* 18 (1984): 147–67.

Braddock, Richard. "The Frequency and Placement of Topic Sentences in Expository Prose." *Research in the Teaching of English* 8 (1974): 287–302.

Branson, Mark K. "What's It Going to Be, Eh? Tracing the English Paragraph into Its Second Century." Diss. U of North Carolina at Greensboro, 1988.

Brereton, John C., ed. *The Origins of Composition Studies in the American College, 1875–1925: A Documentary History.* Pittsburgh: U of Pittsburgh P, 1995.

Britton, B. K. "Understanding Expository Text: Building Mental Structures to Induce Insights." *Handbook of Psycholinguistics.* Ed. Morton Ann Gernsbacher. San Diego: Academic, 1994. 641–74.

Brooks, Cleanth, and Robert Penn Warren. *Modern Rhetoric.* New York: Harcourt, 1949.

Bush, Don. "The Friendly Editor: Paragraphs." *Technical Communication* 42 (1995): 166–68.

Campbell, George. *Philosophy of Rhetoric.* 1776. Ed. Lloyd Bitzer. Carbondale: Southern Illinois UP, 1963.

Christensen, Francis. "Counterstatement: 'Further Comments on the Paragraph' [by Leo Rockas]." *CCC* 18 (1967): 186–88.

———. "A Generative Rhetoric of the Paragraph." *CCC* 16 (1965): 144–56.

Clements, Paul. "The Effects of Staging on Recall from Prose." *New Directions in Discourse Processing.* Ed. R. O. Freedle. Norwood, NJ: Ablex, 1979. 287–330.

Cohan, Carol. "Writing Effective Paragraphs." *CCC* 27 (1976): 363–65.

Connors, Robert. *Composition-Rhetoric: Backgrounds, Theory, and Pedagogy.* Pittsburgh: U of Pittsburgh Press, 1997.

D'Angelo, Frank. "A Generative Rhetoric of the Essay." *CCC* 25 (1974): 388–96.

———. "The Topic Sentence Revisited." *CCC* 37 (1986): 431–41.

Deppman, Jed, Daniel Ferrer, and Michael Groden, eds. *Genetic Criticism: Texts and Avant-Textes.* Philadelphia: U of Pennsylvania P, 2004.

Eden, Rick, and Ruth Mitchell. "Paragraphing for the Reader." *CCC* 37 (1986): 416–30.

Elbow, Peter. "The Music of Form: Rethinking Organization in Writing." *CCC* 57 (2006): 620–66.

Ferrer, Daniel, and Jean-Michel Rabaté. "Paragraphs in Expansion (James Joyce)." Trans. Jed Deppman. Deppman, Ferrer, and Groden 132–51.

Fulkerson, Richard. "Composition at the Turn of the Century." *CCC* 56 (2005): 654–87.

Genung, John F. *The Practical Elements of Rhetoric with Illustrative Examples.* Boston: Ginn, 1893.

Gernsbacher, Morton Ann. *Language Comprehension as Structure Building.* Hillsdale, NJ: Erlbaum, 1990.

Gildon, Charles, and John Brightland. *A Grammar of the English Tongue—1711.* Menston, Eng.: Scolar, 1967.

Goldman, Susan R., Elizabeth U. Saul, and Nathalie Cote. "Paragraphing, Reader, and Task Effects on Discourse Comprehension." *Discourse Processes* 20 (1995): 273–306.

Gopen, George. *Expectations: Teaching Writing from the Reader's Perspective.* New York: Longman, 2004.

Greever, Garland, and Easley S. Jones. *The Century Collegiate Handbook.* New York: Century, 1924.

Hawhee, Debra. "Composition History and the Harbrace College Handbook." *CCC* 50 (1999): 504–23.

Hearst, Marti A. "'Texttiling': Segmenting Text into Multi-paragraph Subtopic Passages." *Computational Linguistics* 23 (1997): 307–43.

Hwang, Shin Ja Joo. "Recursion in the Paragraph as a Unit of Discourse Development." *Discourse Processes* 12 (1989): 461–77.

Irmscher, William, et al. "Symposium on the Paragraph." *CCC* 17 (1966): 60–87.

Karrafalt, David H. "The Generation of Paragraphs and Larger Units." *CCC* 19 (1968): 211–17.

Kieras, David. "Good and Bad Structure in Simple Paragraphs: Effects on Apparent Theme, Reading Time, and Recall." *Journal of Verbal Learning and Verbal Behavior* 17 (1978): 13–28.

Le, Elizabeth. "The Role of Paragraphs in the Construction of Coherence—Text Linguistics and Translation Studies." *IRAL* 24 (2004): 259–75.

———. "The Use of Paragraphs in French and English Academic Writing: Towards a Grammar of Paragraphs." *Text* 19 (1999): 307–43.

Lewis, Edwin Herbert. *The History of the English Paragraph.* Chicago: U of Chicago P, 1894.

Lindemann, Erika. *A Rhetoric for Writing Teachers.* 4th ed. New York: Oxford UP, 2001.

Lorch, Robert F. Jr., et al. "On-Line Processing of the Topic Structure of a Text." *Journal of Memory and Language* 24 (1985): 350–62.

Lowth, Robert. *A Short Introduction to English Grammar (1762).* Delmar, NY: Scholars' Facsimiles & Reprints, 1979.

Lunsford, Andrea A. "Alexander Bain and the Teaching of Composition in North America." *Scottish Rhetoric and Its Influences.* Ed. Lynée Lewis Gaillet. Mahwah, NJ: Erlbaum, 1998. 219–27.

———. "Alexander Bain's Contributions to Discourse Theory." *College English* 44 (1982): 290–300.

Manly, John Matthews, and Edith Rickert. *The Writing of English.* New York: Holt, 1920.

Markel, Mike. *Technical Communication*. 8th ed. Boston: Bedford, 2004.

Markel, Mike, M. Vaccaro, and T. Hewett. "Effects of Paragraph Length on Attitudes toward Technical Writing." *Technical Communication* 39 (1992): 454–56.

Markels, Robin Bell. "Cohesion Paradigms in Paragraphs." *College English* 45 (1983): 450–64.

McElroy, John G. R. *The Structure of English Prose: A Manual of Composition and Rhetoric*. New York: Armstrong, 1885.

McNamara, Danielle S., et al. "Are Good Texts Always Better? Interactions of Text Coherence, Background Knowledge, and Levels of Understanding in Learning from Text." *Cognition and Instruction* 14 (1996): 1–43.

Meade, Richard A., and W. Geiger Ellis. "Paragraph Development in the Modern Age of Rhetoric." *English Journal* 59 (1970): 219–26.

Michael, Ian. *English Grammatical Categories and the Tradition to 1800*. London: Cambridge UP, 1970.

Mones, Leon. "Teaching the Paragraph." *English Journal* 10 (1922): 456–60.

Murray, Lindley, *English Grammar, Adapted to the Different Classes of Learners, 1795*. Menston, Eng.: Scolar, 1968.

Nichols, Duane C. "The Five-Paragraph Essay: An Attempt to Articulate." *English Journal* 55 (1966): 903–08.

Nunnally, Thomas E. "Breaking the Five-Paragraph Theme Barrier." *English Journal* 80 (1991): 67–71.

O'Hear, M., R. Ramsey, and V. Pherson. "Locations of Main Ideas in English Composition Texts." *Research in the Teaching of English* 21 (1987): 318–26.

Pater, Walter. *Appreciations: With an Essay on Style*. London: Macmillan, 1889.

Pitkin, Willis L. "Discourse Blocs." *CCC* 20 (1969): 138–48.

Popken, Randall. "A Study of the Paragraph in Academic Writing." Diss. U of Kansas, 1984.

———. "A Study of Topic Sentence Use in Academic Writing." *Written Communication* 4 (1987): 209–28.

———. "A Study of Topic Sentence Use in the Modern Familiar Essay." *CCTE Studies* 56 (1991): 47–56.

———. "A Study of Topic Sentence Use in Scientific Writing." *Technical Writing and Communication* 18 (1988): 75–86.

———. "A Study of Topic Sentence Use in Technical Writing." *Technical Writing Teacher* 18 (1991): 49–58.

Priestley, Joseph. *The Rudiments of English Grammar*. 1761. Menston, Eng.: Scolar, 1969.

"The Rhetoric of the Paragraph: Principles and Practices." Panel and Workshop Reports. *CCC* 9.3 (1958) 191–92.

Rico, Gabriele L. "Against Formulaic Writing." *English Journal* 77 (1988): 57–58.

Rockas, Leo. "Further Comments on the Paragraph." *CCC* 17 (1966): 148–51.

Rodgers, Paul C. "Alexander Bain and the Rise of the Organic Paragraph." *Quarterly Journal of Speech* 51 (1965): 399–408.

———. "A Discourse-Centered Rhetoric of the Paragraph." *CCC* 17 (1966): 2–11.

———. "The Stadium of Discourse." *CCC* 18 (1967): 178–85.

Scott, Fred Newton, and Joseph V. Denney. *Elementary English Composition*. Chicago: Allyn, 1908.

———. *Paragraph-Writing*. Boston: Allyn, 1893.

Scott, John Hubert. *Rhythmic Prose*. Iowa City: U of Iowa P, 1970.

Shearer, Ned A. "Alexander Bain and the Genesis of Paragraph Theory." *Quarterly Journal of Speech* 58 (1972): 408–17.

Smith, Herbert Winslow. "Concerning Organization in Paragraphs." *English Journal* 9 (1920): 390–400.

Stark, Heather A. "What Do Paragraph Markers Do?" *Discourse Processes* 11 (1988): 275–304.

Steffey, Marda N. "'Paragraph Building' as a Teaching Tool." *ABCA Bulletin* 46 (1983): 23–26.

Stern, Arthur A. "When Is a Paragraph?" *CCC* 27 (1976): 253–57.

Strunk, William. *The Elements of Style*. 1918. *Bartleby.com*. 24 Feb. 2006 http://www.bartleby.com/141/strunk5.html.

———. *The Elements of Style*. Ed. E. B. White. New York: Macmillan, 1959.

Troyka, Lynn Quitman, and Douglas Hesse. *Simon and Schuster Handbook for Writers*. 7th ed., annotated instructor's ed. Upper Saddle River, NJ: Pearson, 2005.

Utley, Thomas Haskell. "Testing Standard Modern Paragraph Theories." Diss. Louisiana State U, 1983.

van Dijk, Teun A., and Walter Kintsch. *Strategies of Discourse Comprehension*. New York: Academic, 1983.

Wendell, Barrett. *English Composition: Eight Lectures Given at the Lowell Institute*. New York: Scribner's, 1895.

Wesley, Kimberly. "The Ill Effects of the Five Paragraph Theme." *English Journal* 90 (2000): 57–60.
Whitmore, Charles. "A Doctrine of the Paragraph." *English Journal* 12 (1923): 605–10.
Williams, Joseph M. "The Phenomenology of Error." *CCC* 32 (1981): 152–68.
Zadrozny, Wlodek, and Karen Jensen. "Semantics of Paragraphs." *Computational Linguistics* 17 (1991): 171–209.

PART TWO

Stylistic Influences and Debates

Introduction to Part Two

The study of style has been important in the history of rhetoric and composition, especially during a three-decade period (beginning in the 1960s) that roughly parallels the discipline's process movement. An active time in the stylistic scholarship of the field, the era is marked by a number of debates directly related to style's theory and pedagogy and its relationships to grammar, usage, and the development of mature writing in composition students. Specifically, this productive period in modern stylistic scholarship focuses on *what style does*, or how it functions, in the context of writers and writing. The articles in this section, then, break ground in significant ways, sometimes because they introduce new concepts of style in action, such as Francis Christensen's idea of free modifiers as a central aspect of generative rhetoric, and sometimes because they challenge conventional wisdom—for example, Richard Ohmann's questioning the shibboleth to "use definite, specific, concrete language"—thereby forcing readers to reevaluate common assumptions about the nature and function of style in the discipline.

While each essay reproduced here stands alone as an expression of style functioning within broader debates in the field, there is also a contrapuntal quality present, as the essays speak collectively to one another either explicitly or implicitly. For example, Virginia Tufte's article on using syntax as style expands upon Christensen's generative rhetoric and also attempts, in its argument, to resolve the apparently conflicting theories of dualistic, organic, and individualist styles illuminated in Louis Milic's article on the topic. Similarly, in his essay on defining complexity, Joseph Williams refers to Christensen's concepts while evaluating the way in which mature styles are influenced by sentence combining, a practice common during the time period (see Shirley Rose's article on this pedagogical practice in Part Three). These essays thus reveal a dynamic interweaving of ideas about how style functions in the field—an agora of intellectual exchange that highlights the controversies about style as it explores its uses for writers.

In "Theories of Style and Their Implications for the Teaching of Composition," Louis Milic reprises a crucial debate about style, originating with Plato, when he asks: Is style simply the dress of thought, added on to meaning for the purpose of saying something differently, depending on the writer's purpose, audience, and context? Or is it inextricably linked to meaning in a way that makes the two an organic whole—inseparable, as it were? For Milic, the distinction makes a crucial difference in teaching style. He argues that only the first theory—which he calls "rhetorical dualism"—allows composition instructors to teach students, for example, to imitate others' writing, to write in high, middle, or low styles, or to use rhetorical schemes like parallelism and ellipsis. The organic theory (or aesthetic monism), on the other hand, erases style altogether, Milic asserts. Although Milic's analysis of stylistic theories is useful in understanding historic debates, it does not allow for an important possibility: that style itself conveys meaning. For example, the title of Martha Kolln's article in this section, "Closing the Books on Alchemy," relies on the pejorative word "alchemy" to suggest an anachronistic belief (for her, that grammar is harmful) and on the accounting phrase "closing the books," an ironic reference to what she thinks has happened to grammar in the field (it is arguably also a veiled allusion to "throwing the book," which is what she obviously wants to do to grammar's detractors). The point is that Kolln conveys much of her meaning *stylistically*, and thus any pedagogy of style is effective only when it illustrates how style and meaning work together (i.e., organically) to achieve a writer's rhetorical purpose. Given the ongoing discussions of Milic's theories of style (see Elizabeth Rankin in Part Three), it is clear that Milic's article sets the stage for important theoretical and pedagogical debates in the field.

While Milic's theories of style and their pedagogical implications are important in structuring the contours of a debate still relevant today, Francis Christensen, in "A Generative Rhetoric of the Sentence," attempts to advance the possibilities of what style can do to help *generate* ideas. Christensen is responding to what he considers a shortcoming in the field: the lack of ways to teach students how to write more mature prose. He searches, then, for a sentence form that can be used to produce content, and his solution, based on syntactic principles, is to add free modifiers (nonrestrictive clauses) in "layers" to a base clause—together constituting what he calls the "cumulative sentence." Christensen suggests that this dynamic process of building one clause upon another is like the mind at work: it moves both forward and backward (toward the main clause), pauses, and prompts new ideas along the way. In this sense, says Christensen, "the mere form of the sentence generates ideas." The principal critique of Christensen's rhetoric, however—one Christensen himself anticipates—is that its generative potential applies primarily to narrative and descriptive sentences and not to the expository or argumentative prose most relevant to composition students. Unlike sentence combining, however, which encourages syntactic fluency in more controlled ways, Christensen's generative rhetoric is notable for encouraging writers to add concrete details in a more open structure as they develop their writing styles. Given the general disappearance of Christensen's ideas from composition theory and pedagogy (see Robert Connors), it is useful to position generative rhetoric as an early attempt to harness style in the service of content, with the goal of increasing sophistication in writing.

Christensen's generative rhetoric serves as an important element in Virginia Tufte's "The Relation of Grammar to Style," a chapter from her book *Grammar as Style*. Tufte's main premise is that grammar (which, for Tufte, specifically means syntax or, as she puts it, the way "words are hooked together and made to work as a unit") can be used to improve a writer's style. According to Tufte, grammar and style essentially merge in the area of syntax, working not in opposition to each other but as complements forged around specific uses and, as Christensen suggests, directions of modification, resulting in what Tufte calls a "more complete marriage." Tufte sees another important role for syntax. Borrowing from Richard Ohmann, and, indirectly at least, from Kenneth Burke's concept of form as the creation and satisfying of a reader's appetite, Tufte suggests that style functions not only as the choices writers make but as "emotional form," meaning that the structure of a sentence raises questions that set up, in turn, "demands for completion." Tufte's exploration of style's role in evoking emotional responses and satisfying readers' expectations is one of the main contributions of this selection—and of her book. She shows how writers can control syntax—or, in other words, a sentence's rhythm or emotional form—as a "series of relationships unfolded over time." Tufte thus adds to the debate about what style can do by proposing its inextricable relationship to grammar through the indispensable crucible of syntax.

While Tufte rehabilitates grammar's relationship to style, Martha Kolln, in "Closing the Books on Alchemy," challenges what she considers composition's untenable position on the teaching of grammar, a disciplinary stance she says rises to the negative level of "alchemy." At its most fundamental level, Kolln's article takes issue with one short statement written forty-five years ago—the conclusion reached by Richard Braddock, Richard Lloyd-Jones, and Lowell Shoer in their 1963 National Council of Teachers of English (NCTE) report, stated in "strong and unqualified terms," that "the teaching of formal grammar has a negligible or, because it usually displaces some instruction and practice in actual composition, even a harmful effect on the improvement of writing." Kolln argues that because of the frequency with which this statement came to be cited in many different circles, it "effectively turned back the clock on grammar research" and was, in 1981, when Kolln's article appeared, "still causing ripples." (Composition's disciplinary position is virtually unchanged today.) Kolln reexamines some of the same research that Braddock, Lloyd-Jones, and Shoer draw upon (and more), and she argues that the conclusion they reach is incorrect, or, at the least, should be far more nuanced than they allow. Kolln's article thus represents an attempt to reevaluate—and refocus—a debate that has recurred regularly in the field for many years. While the nature of the debate about what grammar can do for writers has shifted into the area of rhetorical grammar (see Laura Micciche in Part Three), Kolln's article stands as a counterpoint to the field's long-standing position on teaching formal grammar and represents, in many respects, a lone voice in the wilderness.

In "Use Definite, Specific, Concrete Language," Richard Ohmann, instead of commenting on an existing debate in the field, begins a new one through his counter-reading of a widely repeated rule of usage from Strunk and White's *The Elements of Style*, one that Ohmann asserts has been almost universally endorsed by writing teachers. After complicating the apparent logic in the rule (written verbatim in the article's title), Ohmann argues that the idea of using concrete rather than abstract language is inherently ideological, and that concrete instances often favor a solipsistic approach to reality rather than the socially constructed one he sees as present in abstraction. He cautions that the bromide forces the student writer "toward the language that most nearly reproduces the immediate experience and away from the language that might be used to understand it, transform it, and relate it to everything else." This contention, however, is questioned by John Clifford, who asserts, in a *College English* comment and response, that techniques ranging from prewriting and invention to Aristotle's topics and Ann Berthoff's use of language's symbolic functions "can liberate, not circumscribe, critical thought." Yet in his contention that specificity and concreteness should not be allowed to substitute for abstraction, Ohmann effectively challenges conventional wisdom in the field; for instance, it is generally accepted that specific details and vocabulary contribute to the quality of a writer's prose. Instead of doing more with the surface of writing, however, Ohmann asks us to do less, implying that writing is complicated by playing out abstract concepts and seeing where they lead. Ohmann's view is a valuable counterpart to Richard Lanham's call for an opaque style that looks at the surface of writing, thereby making style visible in what he envisions as a world where words determine thoughts (see Lanham's article in Part Five).

The same concern for complexity in writing advocated by Ohmann is evident in "Defining Complexity," in which Joseph Williams evaluates what constitutes a complex or mature style, looking at such criteria as quantitative measures (e.g., the number of T-units in a text), the way a reader experiences or processes a text (drawing upon the principles of psycholinguistics), the amount of difficulty a writer has in writing complex prose, and the number of times a "base" structure is transformed before it becomes a "surface" structure (here he draws on Chomskyan linguistics). Yet Williams finds, in an important precursor to the ideas he develops in *Style: Ten Lessons in Clarity and Grace*, that readers generally assume that the subject of the sentence is the same as what Williams calls the "agent," or what the sentence's verb refers to. (In his later work, Williams renames the "agent" the "character.") Williams also discovers that nominalizations, or "nouns derived from verbs," are generally more difficult for readers to process but are, paradoxically, often what is considered part of a complex style, even though, as he suggests, "a reader will more easily read a style in which agents and subjects, verbs and what those agents do, coincide, than a style in which they do not." Williams's insights are important in helping determine what makes prose readable or easy to process for readers. While his ideas are important in showing how complexity functions in writing and how nominalizations are often counterintuitive, the essay also adumbrates his larger body of work on what makes prose styles clear.

WORKS CITED

Berthoff, Ann E. 1981. *The Making of Meaning: Metaphors, Models, and Maxims for Teachers.* Portsmouth, NH: Heinemann-Boynton/Cook.

Braddock, Richard, Richard Lloyd-Jones, and Lowell Schoer. 1963. *Research in Written Composition.* Urbana, IL: NCTE.

Burke, Kenneth. 1968. *Counter-Statement*, 2nd ed. Berkeley: University of California Press.

Clifford, John. 1981. "A Comment on 'Use Definite, Specific, Concrete Language.'" *College English* 43, pp. 83–84.

Ohmann, Richard. "Prolegomena to the Analysis of Prose Style." 1958. In *Style in Prose Fiction: English Institute Essays, 1958*, ed. Harold C. Martin, 1–24. New York: Columbia University Press.

Strunk, William Jr., and E. B. White. 2000. *The Elements of Style*, 4th ed. New York: Longman.

7

Theories of Style and Their Implications for the Teaching of Composition

LOUIS T. MILIC

In the teaching of English, the term *style* comes up far too often, I think. The teacher tinkers with the student's style in something like the way an old-fashioned doctor, an empiric, tinkered with his patient's organs, using surgery, bleeding, and drugs, haphazardly and without reference to a general theory of health or illness. The net result is often that ascribed by Lesage to the famous Dr. Sangrado, who reduced many a healthy man to the last extremity. The precise applicability of this analogy I shall not insist on pointing out, but therapy old and new has always required theoretical foundation if it was to be useful to more than one patient.

A theory of style, therefore, would seem to be an important need for any teacher of composition, though this is hardly ever made clear. In fact, a teacher of composition (like any teacher) must also have a theory of learning, but in this too it is unlikely that the beginner at least has much idea of what his theory is or could state it formally. Those who undertake the teaching of composition in college have not usually had courses in educational psychology or learning theory, behaviorist or other. Yet they obviously operate on the basis of some intuitive theory of how learning takes place. The sources of this intuition have a rather unscientific and disorderly appearance. The most potent is surely imitation of one's own learning experience and of one's own teachers. A certain amount of theory is also quarried from commonplaces with the force of received truths: practice makes perfect; if you don't work hard, how do you expect to learn; etc. . . . Information may be picked up from one's colleagues or articles in *Harpers* about the sorry state of American education or in *College English* about the dangers of teaching machines and programmed instruction.

There is no guarantee that this miscellaneous collection of data could profitably be replaced by systematic training in the psychology of learning: teachers required to take such courses are not notably more successful than their untrained colleagues. It is probable that the ingredients of the theory in-

From *College Composition and Communication* 16 (1965): 66–69, 126.

formally held by most teachers, consisting of demonstration, repetition, and examination, are as effective as anything more sophisticated would be, in view of our more or less general ignorance of the factors constituting the process of learning. Since it is not certainly known what would be better than intuition, it is perhaps just as well that time is not wasted on acquiring methods that might prove fallacious. Surely, the main reason why theory is at a discount here is that students, almost regardless of the obstacles interposed by the teacher, cannot be prevented from learning. It is in their natures to learn and this is just as true in composition as in other subjects, as was evidenced in one experiment which showed that students taking physics instead of composition improved as much in composition in their first term in college as students exposed to the regular freshman course. But this should not be taken to imply that students cannot be helped to learn faster or better.

If we are to take the Kitzhaber report seriously, nothing can help; there is no agreement on what good composition is, nor what the subject matter of courses ought to be, nor about the texts, teachers, grades, or anything else, except that the level of writing must be brought up. In view of the seriousness of the situation, I am reluctant to call attention to what seems to me a fundamental deficiency of all the approaches to this problem. No consistent theory of style seems to underlie the several efforts to teach composition. By this I mean that the relationship of thing to idea and idea to word is left unexpressed, to be interpreted according to the fashion of the moment. Whatever interpretation is favored, the consequences are formidable for the related question: to what extent and by what means can the writing behavior of the student be influenced to change. It is obvious that the choice between a stylistic monism and dualism will give vastly different answers and consequently imply vastly different strategies for dealing with our patients.

Though I may be accused of being precipitous in thinking of a college freshman as possessed of a mind and personality in some degree formed, I am speaking advisedly. The problem is clearly different in the earlier formative stages, in grammar school and in high school, when the material is still plastic. But in college we have on our hands a rather intractable entity, chock-full of habits with the force of a dozen years of practice. Thus, in a sense, the problem may be insoluble before we address ourselves to it.

There are only three real theories of style, though there has been much embroidery on the basic fabric. The most familiar is the theory of ornate form, or rhetorical dualism. From the classical rhetoricians who originated it to the rhetoricians of the moment who are still using it, this dualism view has always implied that ideas exist wordlessly and can be dressed in a variety of outfits, depending on the need for the occasion: the grand style, the plain style, the middle style and the low style and the like.

A second theory, the individualist or psychological monism, which finds its most common expression in the aphorism that the style is the man, may have originally sprung from Plato's conception of the *vir bonus*, the good man whose goodness would express itself equally in graceful dancing and graceful expression. The modern version is perhaps descended from Montaigne, who claimed to write in the way that was natural for him, following his own bent, and disdaining affectation. Brought wholly up-to-date, it means that a writer cannot help writing the way he does, for that is the dynamic expression of his personality, illustrated in his handwriting, his walk, and all his activity.

The most modern theory of style, Crocean aesthetic monism, is an organic view which denies the possibility of any separation between content and form. Any discussion of style in Croce's view is useless and irrelevant, for the work of art (the composition) is a unified whole, with no seam between meaning and style. Thus, in the organic view, there is no style at all, only meaning or intuition. It is an elegant solution which has been widely adopted by enthusiasts quite unaware, it seems, that it left them nothing to do. It is so widespread that those who practice it hardly find it necessary even to say that style is not an isolable quality.

Now, how do these recondite theories affect us as teachers of composition? Although the connection between the dabblings of our freshmen and the ideas of Plato and Croce may seem remote, the implications of these theories have important consequences for the teaching of composition. It is in the nature of basic theories to generate implications and for opposed theories to produce contradictory implications. Thus it is evident that eclecticism will not really work and that a choice among these theories must be made by the teacher of composition. He cannot espouse one theory and teach on the basis of another, or, like many a handbook of composition, a conflation of all three.

If the teacher adopts the theory of ornate form, he must be prepared to accept—even to hail enthusiastically—its inevitable implications. The theory is based, as everyone knows, on the belief in the separate existence of content and form. Like any frankly dualistic view, it has attracted the disapproval of those who espouse a hard (or positivist) line. That is, though you can see words, you cannot see ideas or content. If you cannot see (feel, hear, etc.) content, you have no proof that it exists. What you cannot prove the existence of, they say, you have no business theorizing about. Yet, despite its unprovability and perhaps its scientific unsoundness, the dualistic theory has many attractions and advantages. But its implications must be accepted or at least accounted for.

To begin with, the disjunction of content and form permits a belief in a real intended meaning behind every utterance. The writer intends to express something (idea) and he struggles with possibilities until he finds the formulation which best expresses it. Because this seems to many to correspond with every writer's experience, it is readily accepted by everyone, including the critically naive, who proceed to sew it onto one of the monistic theories. Pedagogically, this makes it possible to enjoin the student to clarify his thought (without reference to the possible difficulty that this may be impracticable without the aid of language), to make it logical, before actually embodying it in words. The inelegancies and errors which occur can be treated as correctable by consulting the intended meaning. Correction and revision are done according to some absolute standard of rightness perhaps related to the hierarchy of styles: casual, informal, formal, ceremonial (also known as levels of usage). And if revision and correction are done sufficiently long and diligently, the expression of the intended meaning can become complete. It can reach the point where the reaction of a reader would be "There seems to be no other way to say it."

It should be evident that this theory of style corresponds pretty well with the practices of the old rhetoric. The theory of rhetorical dualism justifies certain classroom procedures. Students can be encouraged to write imitations of Swift, Addison, Johnson, Macaulay, Shaw, or E. B. White. They can be set to write the same paper in a variety of styles, from the low to the grand. They can be taught the mysteries of anaphora, brachylogia, hypallage, and epichireme. Their compositions can be tested for the suitable presence of the seven parts, from exordium to peroration. But, conversely, emphasis on subject and on personality must be excluded. Students should not be told to write naturally, to express their personalities, that is, because such a concept contradicts the fundamental assumptions of the theory of ornate form. Nor should any particular attention be paid to the substance of the writing for the theory explicitly denies any link between substance and form except for logic. The uniformity of the writing of the students which might result must be taken as a vindication of the theory and not as an evil consequence.

If the second theory, the individualist, is espoused, the field of activity is greatly narrowed. In Plato's view, the only route to the improvement of the student's writing (or dancing) is through the general enhancement of his soul. If we wish the writing to be good — Plato believes in an absolute standard — the writer must be a good person. Nothing else will avail. Thus courses in composition would become largely courses in spiritual self-improvement, perhaps with ethics, religion, and psychotherapy as significant components. In the more modern version of this theory, that style is the expression of the student's mind and personality, there is not much more to do. We can exhort him to eschew mannerism and to write naturally, to express himself fully and to be as grammatical as possible while doing it. But what if the student's personality, fully expressed, leads to contortion, gibberish, or paranoia? What is left except to throw up our hands? It is evident that under the influence of this theory we cannot urge the student to adopt another personality or to write more naturally than he does when his natural writing is not bearable. None of the usual tactics used in composition courses have any real bearing here except perhaps finding a subject on which the student can perform competently.

Croce's organic theory of style leaves us even more completely helpless, inasmuch as it explicitly disavows any segmentation between the subject and its form. Croce will have no truck with devices of rhetoric or anything which casts the least shadow on the integrity of expression. The consequences of the disappearance of style which results is that discussion of the student's writing must consist almost exclusively of its philosophy, so to speak. The emphasis which this theory forces on us is the dominance of the subject. For if there is no form, we cannot discuss, much less improve, the student's means of expression. The powerful trend to the study of linguistics and substantive matters in composition courses of late years may find its source in the unconscious adoption of this unitary view. If we cannot teach rhetoric, we must still teach something, but since miscellaneous social and topical subjects have produced no improvement, perhaps the final recourse to the subject matter of the language itself will succeed. Thus the proponents of the linguistic readers have in a way solved the Crocean paradox. Substance cannot be separated from form but if the substance *is the form* we can have the best of both worlds, writing exclusively about form. However ingenious this solution may seem, there is very little evidence that it has succeeded in improving the level of performance in English composition, if a nascent counter-trend to the linguistic approach is any guide, not to mention the shortage of qualified instructors.

It is unfortunately true that composition theory has been going in circles for the last two or three decades and that the level of composition among freshmen has been declining. Those who refer to the good old days are usually rebuffed with sociological facts, such as the greater percentage of students in college now compared to half a century ago. As the base broadens, the average must go down. This is doubtless true, but it is not the entire answer. That, I believe, must be sought in an unhappy confusion in the minds of the teachers of composition. These unfortunates, beginning some three or four decades ago, threw rhetoric into the wastebasket, partly under the stimulus of the new Crocean discovery and partly under the influence of factors which also resulted in the dismissal of Latin from the curriculum, and were left with nothing to teach. Until about 1920, composition texts were rhetorics. After that, they became almost everything else, with results that have horrified all observers. The combination of the individualist theory—Write naturally!—and the organic theory—Content and form are inseparable!—has become a talisman so powerful that only scorn is reserved for those who would profess to doubt its magic power. In fact, it is considered a truth so self-evident that it hardly needs to be stated and thus it underlies the thinking of all or nearly all those who teach composition by any method, even the new rhetoricians.

The welter of theories and panaceas currently ornamenting the composition scene results, I believe, from this fundamental theoretical unsoundness: form cannot be taught by those who do not believe in it and the creative expression of personality cannot be interpreted as a reasonable compromise between form and substance. If we want to teach something in our composition classes, it may be that we must return to some form of rhetoric, which is honestly and unashamedly concerned with form and not with content. It seems to have evaded the scrutiny of interested parties that the decline in composition has not been a feature of educational systems still backwardly tied to old-fashioned rhetorical methods, including Italy, France, Germany, Spain, and England. Perhaps there is a lesson in this.

A distinction may need to be made, also, between the best theory of style for teaching composition and the best theory for analyzing literary works. For teaching, a dualistic theory seems to be essential, at least in the early stages, until the maturing of the literary personality has had an opportunity to influence the student's style. For analysis, the problem is somewhat different. A fusion of expressive and unconscious theories seems to conform to the general practice. Writers, that is, write in a certain way because they select the most effective artifices of expression, but also because they are unconsciously bound to the requirements of individual personality.

The monistic view of style, therefore, cannot be allowed to infect the teaching of our subject, for it vitiates all the available pedagogical resources of rhetoric. In the college composition course, which represents for most students their first formal training in rhetoric, an awareness must be instilled of the existence of alternatives, of different ways of saying the same thing, of the options that the language offers. In this task, the perhaps exhausted vein of the old rhetoric may need a transfusion from the new. To aid instruction in the mechanism of expression, a systematic study of linguistics (rather than a helter-skelter travelogue) may also have a significant place. At the moment, however, only the direction of the journey is clear: the details of the itinerary are waiting to be discovered.

8 A Generative Rhetoric of the Sentence

FRANCIS CHRISTENSEN

If the new grammar is to be brought to bear on composition, it must be brought to bear on the rhetoric of the sentence. We have a workable and teachable, if not a definitive, modern grammar; but we do not have, despite several titles, a modern rhetoric.

In composition courses we do not really teach our captive charges to write better—we merely *expect* them to. And we do not teach them how to write better because we do not know how to teach them to write better. And so we merely go through the motions. Our courses with their tear-out workbooks and four-pound anthologies are elaborate evasions of the real problem. They permit us to put in our time and do almost anything else we'd rather be doing instead of buckling down to the hard work of making a difference in the student's understanding and manipulation of language.

With hundreds of handbooks and rhetorics to draw from, I have never been able to work out a program for teaching the sentence as I find it in the work of contemporary writers. The chapters on the sentence all adduce the traditional rhetorical classification of sentences as loose, balanced, and periodic. But the term *loose* seems to be taken as a pejorative (it sounds immoral); our students, no Bacons or Johnsons, have little occasion for balanced sentences; and some of our worst perversions of style come from the attempt to teach them to write periodic sentences. The traditional grammatical classification of sentences is equally barren. Its use in teaching composition rests on a semantic confusion, equating complexity of structure with complexity of thought and vice versa. But very simple thoughts may call for very complex grammatical constructions. Any moron can say "I don't know who done it." And some of us might be puzzled to work out the grammar of "All I want is all there is," although any chit can think it and say it and act on it.

The chapters on the sentence all appear to assume that we think naturally in primer sentences, progress naturally to compound sentences, and must be taught to combine the primer sentences into complex sentences—and that

From *College Composition and Communication* 14 (1963): 155–67.

complex sentences are the mark of maturity. We need a rhetoric of the sentence that will do more than combine the ideas of primer sentences. We need one that will *generate* ideas.

For the foundation of such a generative or productive rhetoric I take the statement from John Erskine, the originator of the Great Books courses, himself a novelist. In an essay "The Craft of Writing" (*Twentieth Century English*, Philosophical Library, 1946) he discusses a principle of the writer's craft, which though known he says to all practitioners, he has never seen discussed in print. The principle is this: "When you write, you make a point, not by subtracting as though you sharpened a pencil, but by adding." We have all been told that the formula for good writing is the concrete noun and the active verb. Yet Erskine says, "What you say is found not in the noun but in what you add to qualify the noun . . . The noun, the verb, and the main clause serve merely as the base on which meaning will rise . . . The modifier is the essential part of any sentence." The foundation, then, for a generative or productive rhetoric of the sentence is that composition is essentially a process of *addition*.

But speech is linear, moving in time, and writing moves in linear space, which is analogous to time. When you add a modifier, whether to the noun, the verb, or the main clause, you must add it either before the head or after it. If you add it before the head, the direction of modification can be indicated by an arrow pointing forward; if you add it after, by an arrow pointing backward. Thus we have the second principle of a generative rhetoric—the principle of *direction of modification* or *direction of movement*.

Within the clause there is not much scope for operating with this principle. The positions of the various sorts of close, or restrictive, modifiers are generally fixed and the modifiers are often obligatory—"The man who came to dinner remained till midnight." Often the only choice is whether to add modifiers. What I have seen of attempts to bring structural grammar to bear on composition usually boils down to the injunction to "load the patterns." Thus "pattern practice" sets students to accreting sentences like this: "The small boy on the red bicycle who lives with his happy parents on our shady street often coasts down the steep street until he comes to the city park." This will never do. It has no rhythm and hence no life; it is tone-deaf. It is the seed that will burgeon into gobbledygook. One of the hardest things in writing is to keep the noun clusters and verb clusters short.

It is with modifiers added to the clause—that is, with sentence modifiers—that the principle comes into full play. The typical sentence of modern English, the kind we can best spend our efforts trying to teach, is what we may call the *cumulative sentence*. The main clause, which may or may not have a sentence modifier before it, advances the discussion; but the additions move backward, as in this clause, to modify the statement of the main clause or more often to explicate or exemplify it, so that the sentence has a flowing and ebbing movement, advancing to a new position and then pausing to consolidate it, leaping and lingering as the popular ballad does. The first part of the preceding compound sentence has one addition, placed within it; the second part has four words in the main clause and 49 in the five additions placed after it.

The cumulative sentence is the opposite of the periodic sentence. It does not represent the idea as conceived, pondered over, reshaped, packaged, and delivered cold. It is dynamic rather than static, representing the mind thinking. The main clause ("the additions move backward" above) exhausts the mere fact of the idea; logically, there is nothing more to say. The additions stay with the same idea, probing its bearings and implications, exemplifying it or seeking an analogy or metaphor for it, or reducing it to details. Thus the mere form of the sentence generates ideas. It serves the needs of both the writer and the reader, the writer by compelling him to examine his thought, the reader by letting him into the writer's thought.

Addition and direction of movement are structural principles. They involve the grammatical character of the sentence. Before going on to other principles, I must say a word about the best grammar as the foundation for rhetoric. I cannot conceive any useful transactions between teacher and students unless they have in common a language for talking about sentences. The best grammar is the grammar that best displays the layers of structure of the English sentence. The best I have found in a textbook is the combination of immediate constituent and transformation grammar in Paul Roberts's *English Sentences*. Traditional grammar, whether over-simple as in the school tradition or over-complex as in the scholarly tradition, does not reveal the language as it operates; it leaves everything, to borrow a phrase from Wordsworth, "in disconnection dead and spiritless." *English Sentences* is oversimplified and it has gaps, but it displays admirably the structures that rhetoric must work with—primarily sentence modifiers, including relative and subordinate clauses, but, far more important, the array of noun, verb, and adjective clusters. It is paradoxical that Professor Roberts, who has done so much to make the teaching of composition possible, should himself be one of those who think that it cannot be taught. Unlike Ulysses, he doesn't see any work for Telemachus to work.

Layers of structure, as I have said, is a grammatical concept. To bring in the dimension of meaning, we need a third principle—that of *levels of generality* or *levels of abstraction*. The main clause is likely to be stated in general or abstract or plural terms. With the main clause stated, the forward movement of the sentence stops, the writer shifts down to a lower level of generality or abstraction or to singular terms, and goes back over the same ground at this lower level.[1] "He has just bought a new car, a 1963½ Ford, a Galaxie, a fastback hardtop with four-on-the-floor shift." There is no theoretical limit to the number of structural layers or levels, each at a lower level of generality, any or all of them compounded, that a speaker or writer may use. For a speaker, listen to Lowell Thomas; for a writer, study William Faulkner. To a single independent clause he may append a page of additions, but usually all clear, all grammatical, once we have learned how to read him. Or, if you prefer, study Hemingway, the master of the simple sentence: "George was coming down in the telemark position, kneeling, one leg forward and bent, the other trailing, his sticks hanging like some insect's thin legs, kicking up puffs of snow, and finally the whole kneeling, trailing figure coming around in a beautiful right curve, crouching, the legs shot forward and back, the body leaning out against the swing, the sticks accenting the curve like points of light, all in a wild cloud of snow."

This brings me to the fourth, and last, principle, that of texture. *Texture* provides a descriptive or evaluative term. If a writer adds to few of his nouns or verbs or main clauses and adds little, the texture may be said to be thin. The style will be plain or bare. The writing of most of our students is thin—even threadbare. But if he adds frequently or much or both, then the texture may be said to be dense or rich. One of the marks of an effective style, especially in narrative, is variety in the texture, the texture varying with the change in pace, the variation in texture producing the change in pace. It is not true, as I have seen it asserted, that fast action calls for short sentences; the action is fast in the sentence by Hemingway above. In our classes, we have to work for greater density and variety in texture and greater concreteness and particularity in what is added.

I have been operating at a fairly high level of generality. Now I must downshift and go over the same points with examples. The most graphic way to exhibit the layers of structure is to indent the word groups of a sentence and to number the levels. Since in the narrow columns of this journal indentation is possible only with short sentences whose additions are short, I have used it with only the first three sentences; the reader is urged to copy out the others for himself. I have added symbols to mark the grammatical character of the additions: SC, subordinate clause; RC, relative clause; NC, noun cluster; VC, verb cluster; AC, adjective cluster; Abs, absolute (i.e., a VC with a subject of its own); PP, prepositional phrase. With only a few exceptions (in some the punctuation may be questioned) the elements set off as on a lower level are marked by junctures or punctuation. The examples have been chosen to illustrate the range of constructions used in the lower levels; after the first few they are arranged by the number of levels. The examples could have been drawn from poetry as well as from prose. Those not attributed are by students.

1

1 He shook his hands,
   2 a quick shake, (NC)
      3 fingers down, (Abs)
         4 like a pianist. (PP)—Sinclair Lewis

2

   2 Calico-coated, (AC)
   2 small bodied, (AC)
   2 with delicate legs and pink faces (PP)
      3 in which their mismatched eyes rolled wild and subdued, (RC)
1 they huddled,
   2 gaudy motionless and alert, (AC)
   2 wild as deer, (AC)
   2 deadly as rattlesnakes, (AC)
   2 quiet as doves. (AC)—William Faulkner

3

1 The bird's eye, / , remained fixed upon him;
  2 bright and silly as a sequin (AC)
1 its little bones, / , seemed swooning in his hand. —Stella Benson
  2 wrapped . . . in a warm padding of feathers (VC)

4

(1) The jockeys sat bowed and relaxed, moving a little at the waist with the movement of their horses$^{2\text{-VC}}$. —Katherine Anne Porter

5

(1) The flame sidled up the match, driving a film of moisture and a thin strip of darker grey before it$^{2\text{-VC}}$.

6

(1) She came among them behind the man, gaunt in the gray shapeless garment and the sunbonnet$^{2\text{-AC}}$, wearing stained canvas gymnasium shoes$^{2\text{-VC}}$. —Faulkner

7

(1) The Texan turned to the nearest gatepost and climbed to the top of it, his alternate thighs thick and bulging in the tight jeans$^{2\text{-Abs}}$, the butt of his pistol catching and losing the sun in pearly gleams$^{2\text{-Abs}}$. —Faulkner

8

(1) He could sail for hours, searching the blanched grasses below him with his telescopic eyes$^{2\text{-VC}}$, gaining height against the wind$^{2\text{-VC}}$, descending in mile-long, gently declining swoops when he curved and rode back$^{2\text{-VC}}$, never beating a wing$^{2\text{-VC}}$. —Walter Van Tilburg Clark

9

(1) The gay-sweatered skaters are quick-silvering around the frosty rink, the girls gliding and spinning$^{2\text{-Abs}}$, the boys swooping and darting$^{2\text{-Abs}}$, their arms flailing like wings$^{3\text{-Abs}}$.

10

(1) He stood at the top of the stairs and watched me, I waiting for him to call me up$^{2\text{-Abs}}$, he hesitating to come down$^{2\text{-Abs}}$, his lips nervous with the suggestion of a smile$^{3\text{-Abs}}$, mine asking whether the smile meant come, or go away$^{3\text{-Abs}}$.

11

(1) Joad's lips stretched tight over his long teeth for a moment, and (1) he licked his lips, like a dog$^{2\text{-PP}}$, two licks$^{3\text{-NC}}$, one in each direction from the middle$^{4\text{-NC}}$. —Steinbeck

12

(1) We all live in two realities: one of seeming fixity$^{2\text{-NC}}$, with institutions, dogmas, rules of punctuation, and routines$^{3\text{-PP}}$, the calendared and clockwise world of all but futile round on round$^{4\text{-NC}}$; and one of

whirling and flying electrons, dreams, and possibilities[2-NC], behind the clock[3-PP].—Sidney Cox

13

(1) It was as though someone, somewhere, had touched a lever and shifted gears, and (1) the hospital was set for night running, smooth and silent[2-AC], its normal clatter and hum muffled[2-Abs], the only sounds heard in the whitewalled room distant and unreal[2-Abs]: a low hum of voices from the nurse's desk[3-NC], quickly stifled[4-VC], the soft squish of rubber-soled shoes on the tiled corridors[3-NC], starched white cloth rustling against itself[3-NC], and outside, the lonesome whine of wind in the country nights[3-NC], and the Kansas dust beating against the windows[3-NC].

14

(1) The beach sounds are jazzy, percussion fixing the mode[2-Abs]—the surf cracking and booming in the distance[3-Abs], a little nearer dropped bar-bells clanking[3-Abs], steel gym rings, flung together[4-VC], ringing[3-Abs], palm fronds rustling above me[3-Abs], like steel brushes washing over a snare drum[4-PP], troupes of sandals splatting and shuffling on the sandy cement[3-Abs], their beat varying[4-Abs], syncopation emerging and disappearing with changing paces[5-Abs].

15

(1) A small negro girl develops from the sheet of glare-frosted walk, walking barefooted[2-VC], her bare legs striking and coiling from the hot cement[3-Abs], her feet curling in[4-Abs], only the outer edges touching[5-Abs].

16

(1) The swells moved rhythmically toward us irregularly faceted[2-VC], sparkling[2-VC], growing taller and more powerful[2-VC], until the shining crest bursts[3-SC], a transparent sheet of pale green water spilling over the top[4-Abs], breaking into blue-white foam as it cascades down the front of the wave[5-VC], piling up in a frothy mound that the diminishing wave pushes up against the pilings[5-VC], with a swishmash[6-PP], the foam drifting back[5-Abs], like a lace fan opened over the shimmering water as the spent wave returns whispering to the sea[6-PP].

The best starting point for a composition unit based on these four principles is with two-level narrative sentences, first with one second-level addition (sentences 4, 5), then with two or more parallel ones (6, 7, 8). Anyone sitting in his room with his eyes closed could write the main clause of most of the examples; the discipline comes with the additions, provided they are based at first on immediate observation, requiring the student to phrase an exact observation in exact language. This can hardly fail to be exciting to a class: it is life, with the variety and complexity of life; the workbook exercise is death. The situation is ideal also for teaching diction—abstract-concrete, general-specific, literal-metaphorical, denotative-connotative. When the sentences begin to come out right, it is time to examine the additions for their grammatical character. From then on the grammar comes to the aid of the writing and the writing reinforces the grammar. One can soon go on to multi-level narrative sentences (1, 3, 9–11, 15, 16) and then to brief narratives of three to six or seven sentences on actions that can be observed over and over again—beating eggs, making a cut with a power saw, or following a record changer's cycle or a wave's flow and ebb. Bring the record changer to class. Description, by contrast, is static, picturing appearance rather than behavior. The constructions to master are the noun and adjective clusters and the absolute (13, 14). Then the descriptive noun cluster must be taught to ride piggy-back on the narrative sentence, so that description and narration are interleaved: "In the morning we went out into a new world, a glistening crystal and white world, each skeleton tree, each leafless bush, even the heavy, drooping power lines sheathed in icy crystal." The next step is to develop the sense for variety in texture and change in pace that all good narrative demands.

In the next unit, the same four principles can be applied to the expository paragraph. But this is a subject for another paper.

I want to anticipate two possible objections. One is that the sentences are long. By freshman English standards they are long, but I could have produced far longer ones from works freshmen are expected to read. Of the sentences by students, most were written as finger exercises in the first few weeks of the course. I try in narrative sentences to push to level after level, not just two or three, but four, five, or six, even more, as far as the students' powers of observation will take them. I want them to become sentence acrobats, to dazzle by their syntactic dexterity. I'd rather have to deal with hyperemia than anemia. I want to add my voice to that of James Coleman (*CCC*, December 1962) deploring our concentration on the plain style.

The other objection is that my examples are mainly descriptive and narrative—and today in freshman English we teach only exposition. I deplore this limitation as much as I deplore our limitation to the plain style. Both are a sign that we have sold our proper heritage for a pot of message. In permitting them, the English department undercuts its own discipline. Even if our goal is only utilitarian prose, we can teach diction and sentence structure far more effectively through a few controlled exercises in description and narration than we can by starting right off with exposition (Theme One, 500 words, precipitates *all* the problems of writing). The student has something to communicate—his immediate sense impressions, which can stand a bit of exercising. The material is not already verbalized—he has to match language to sense impressions. His acuteness in observation and in choice of words can be judged by fairly objective standards—is the sound of a bottle of milk being set down on a concrete step suggested better by *clink* or *clank*? In the examples, study the diction for its accuracy, rising at times to the truly imaginative. Study the use of metaphor, of comparison. This verbal virtuosity and syntactical ingenuity can be made to carry over into expository writing.

But this is still utilitarian. What I am proposing carries over of itself into the study of literature. It makes the student a better reader of literature. It helps him thread the syntactical mazes of much mature writing, and it gives him insight into that elusive thing we call style. Last year a student told of re-reading a book by her favorite author, Willa Cather, and of realizing for the first time *why* she liked reading her: she could understand and appreciate the style. For some students, moreover, such writing makes life more interesting as well as giving them a way to share their interest with others. When they learn how to put concrete details into a sentence, they begin to look at life with more alertness. If it is liberal education we are concerned with, it is just possible that these things are more important than anything we can achieve when we set our sights on the plain style in expository prose.

I want to conclude with a historical note. My thesis in this paragraph is that modern prose like modern poetry has more in common with the seventeenth than with the eighteenth century and that we fail largely because we are operating from an eighteenth-century base. The shift from the complex to the cumulative sentence is more profound than it seems. It goes deep in grammar, requiring a shift from the subordinate clause (the staple of our trade) to the cluster (so little understood as to go almost unnoticed in our textbooks). And I have only lately come to see that this shift has historical implications. The cumulative sentence is the modern form of the loose sentence that characterized the anti-Ciceronian movement in the seventeenth century. This movement, according to Morris W. Croll,[2] began with Montaigne and Bacon and continued with such men as Donne, Brown, Taylor, Pascal. Croll calls their prose baroque. To Montaigne, its art was the art of being natural; to Pascal, its eloquence was the eloquence that mocks formal eloquence; to Bacon, it presented knowledge so that it could be examined, not so that it must be accepted.

But the Senecan amble was banished from England when "the direct sensuous apprehension of thought" (T. S. Eliot's words) gave way to Cartesian reason or intellect. The consequences of this shift in sensibility are well summarized by Croll:

> To this mode of thought we are to trace almost all the features of modern literary education and criticism, or at least of what we should have called modern a generation ago: the study of the precise meaning of words; the reference to dictionaries as literary authorities; the study of the sentence as a logical unit alone; the careful circumscription of its limits and the gradual reduction of its length; . . .[3] the attempt to reduce grammar to an exact science; the idea that forms of speech are always either correct or incorrect; the complete subjection of the laws of motion and expression in style to the laws of logic and standardization—in short, the triumph, during two centuries, of grammatical over rhetorical ideas. (p. 1077)

Here is a seven-point scale any teacher of composition can use to take stock. He can find whether he is based in the eighteenth century or in the twentieth and whether he is consistent—completely either an ancient or a modern—or is just a crazy mixed-up kid.

NOTES

1. Cf. Leo Rockas, "Abstract and Concrete Sentences," *CCC*, May 1963. Rockas describes sentences as abstract or concrete, the abstract implying the concrete, and vice versa. Readers and writers, he says, must have the knack of apprehending the concrete in the abstract and the abstract in the concrete. This is true and valuable. I am saying that within a single sentence the writer may present more than one level of generality, translating the abstract into the more concrete in added levels.

2. "The Baroque Style in Prose," *Studies in English Philology: A Miscellany in Honor of Frederick Klaeber* (1929), reprinted in A. M. Witherspoon and F. J. Warnke, eds. *Seventeenth-Century Prose and Poetry*, 2nd ed. New York: Harcourt, Brace & World, 1963. I have used the latter, and I have borrowed from Croll in my description of the cumulative sentence.

3. The omitted item concerns punctuation and is not relevant here. In using this scale, note the phrase "what we should have called modern a generation ago," and remember that Croll was writing in 1929.

9 *The Relation of Grammar to Style*

VIRGINIA TUFTE

The goal of this book is to explain its title. The task is quite ambitious enough, for *Grammar as Style* is not just a topic, or two topics. It is a thesis. It does not merely advertise that the book it names will discuss the paired subjects of grammar and style, but it presumes that grammar and style can be thought of in some way as a single subject.

There are those who would at once take objection. To view grammar as style blurs the traditional distinction between the grammarian and the critic of style, and it threatens another time-honored division of labor, the separate teaching of grammar, composition, and literature. As a thesis, then, the title must be defended, and it must seem to deserve a book to explain and justify it. Its proponents must show what its claim for the merger of grammar and style can conceivably teach the amateur writer and the student of literature. Once the writer has ceased committing dramatic, showstopping blunders, once he has mastered the notions that a sentence needs a subject and predicate, that a plural subject needs a plural verb, that a pronoun usually needs a referent, and all such matters, how much further can grammar possibly take him toward improving his style? "A very long way indeed" is the answer upon which these first pages will enlarge, and which the coming chapters will exemplify. And what of the student of literature? Can viewing grammar as style add anything to his appreciation of a play, or a novel, or a poem? These chapters will suggest that it can, and that details of technique, illustrated here in samples from twentieth-century prose, can be helpful in studying the prose and poetry of any era.

This set forth, there is no escaping that ubiquitous requirement to define one's terms. Grammar? It is an account of the formation of words and of the structures for putting them together in sentences. Words and compounds must of course come to be; the investigation of this process is morphology, but it is only occasionally relevant to style. A single word may well catch our attention in continuous prose, but nearly always for reasons of diction rather

---

From *Grammar as Style* (New York: Holt, Rinehart and Winston, 1971), 1–12.

than morphology. It is when words are hooked together and made to work as a unit, when *syntax* is involved, that grammar makes its main contribution to style. Grammar, then, for purposes of this book, is narrowed to syntax: it is mainly as syntax that we can know grammar as style.

What of the remaining term in our quasi-equation of grammar (as syntax) as style? When we come to think of grammar as style, what in fact are we thinking of grammar *as*? What is style? Its Latin ancestor, *stilus*, was a writing tool, but the term has wandered into modern English to mean roughly "a way of writing." If we were asked to describe someone's "way of writing," would we not be fair in choosing our answer from among such different ones as "by fits and starts" or "in French" or "sitting at the beach" or "for money" or "with a mechanical pencil" or "gracelessly"? If the poser of such a question were annoyed with any of these answers, it would serve him right. The case, of course, is fanciful, for anyone wishing to know about another's style would be likely to ask about it directly, and not about his "way of writing." He would rely on common assumptions about the meaning of "style," which he would probably have trouble articulating, and he would expect an answer like "graceless" rather than any of those above. The point is simply that both questions and answers about style are likely to be ambiguous and to produce very little objective information.

Most talk about style, by professional critics as well as amateurs, leaves much to be desired: it is often subjective, impressionistic, unhelpful, sometimes misleading. The natural way to react to a piece of writing is to take it personally, to perform private acts of association, without worry over precision. But we need only see how vague, how various, even how contradictory these intuitive, untutored reactions to language can be to appreciate the need for a more certain vocabulary in discussing style, to wish that something at least resembling the clear categories of syntax might be available to stylistic analysis.

In the summer of 1966, I conducted an experiment at the NDEA Institute at the University of California, Los Angeles, asking forty-four college and high school English teachers to jot down a half-dozen words or phrases they would use to describe the style and tone of thirty sentences, the opening of Truman Capote's *In Cold Blood*. Their lists included 222 different adjectives, and there was only one adjective that was used by as many as twelve of the teachers. These are some of the words they used: *plain, elaborate, formal, informal, detailed, general, specific, objective, matter-of-fact, stylized, literary, poetic, conversational, pedestrian, taut, over-drawn, visual, direct, lucid, dramatic, dispassionate, forceful, harsh, suspenseful, brisk, meditative, mysterious, polished, graceful, precise, blunt, symbolic, omniscient, prosaic, conventional, unconventional, clear, crisp, cadenced, colorful, drab, graphic, photographic, concise, verbose, wordy, moving, uninvolved, detached, balanced, discerning, alliterative, well-developed, orderly, impressionistic, rhythmic, ominous, reportorial, natural, artificial, easy, pretentious, methodical, rambling, compact, vivid, thoughtful, imagistic, sensitive, incisive, clinical, chiseled,* and *sterile.*

The reports of professional critics on a given style betray as much seeming confusion and difference of opinion. Louis T. Milic gives evidence of this when he points to some of the adjectives other critics have applied to the prose style of Jonathan Swift, among them *civilized, clear, common, concise, correct, direct, elaborate, elegant, energetic, graceful, hard-round-crystalline, homely, lucid, manly, masculine, masterly, muscular, nervous, ornamented, perfect, perspicuous, plain, poor, proper, pure, salty, simple, sinewy, sonorous, strong, vigorous.*[1]

The classification of different types of prose style has evoked a similar variety of labels, with commentators naming one type by analogy with another, or describing it, as if definitively, with submerged metaphors of no exact application. These tendencies characterize five centuries of talk about English prose style. In the late sixteenth century and early seventeenth, descriptions such as *Ciceronian, anti-Ciceronian, Attic, Senecan, Stoic,* and *Tacitean* linked certain English styles to classical rhetoric. Adjectives like *baroque, curt, libertine, loose, plain, courtly,* and *grand* carried aesthetic, cultural, and even moral overtones. Others like *trailing, rambling, circuitous, hopping, tumbling,* and *jog-trotting* suggested affinities of language with motion, exercise, even acrobatics. Sir Francis Bacon, in contrasting what he called *magistral* or *peremptory* prose with *probative,* associated prose techniques with those of law and science. Critics later than Bacon, with labels such as *metaphysical, prophetic, romantic,* and *democratic,* brought into the description of prose an aura of religion, sentiment, and politics. A recent classification of prose styles distinguishes five primary types: the *deliberative style* of persuasive prose; the *expository,* that of the treatise, the lesson, and the sermon; the *prophetic* style, of biblical prophecy, of Stoic philosophy, and of the essay (all of these styles with counterparts in narrative writing); the *tumbling* style, itself a narrative style of energy and heavy accent; and the *indenture* style of legal documents and private formal messages.[2] The twentieth century has made frequent use of the label *colloquial* to align written prose with the speaking voice. And Walker Gibson's book *Tough, Sweet & Stuffy* uses a kind of colloquial language itself to designate in the title what its author believes to be the three reigning styles in American English today.[3] Professor Gibson, unlike many critics, offers some precise and observable characteristics to identify the three categories.

With a few exceptions, however, most efforts to divide and classify style do not succeed in telling us very much more than do impressionistic definitions of style, of the sort collected by Professor Milic: *"Le style, c'est l'homme même"* (Buffon). "Proper words in proper places make the true definition of a style" (Swift). "Style is the ultimate morality of mind" (Alfred North Whitehead). "Style is not a dance, it is an overture" (Jean Cocteau). Or "In stating as fully as I could how things really were, it was often very difficult and I wrote awkwardly and the awkwardness is what they called my style" (Hemingway).[4]

The welter of impressions summoned up by the very idea of style, like the many reactions a single piece of writing can awake in us and the parade of labels we muster to approximate our feelings—all this merely attests to the richness of language, and should not in itself hinder our appreciation of it. The beginning writer, however, like the critic, needs a more accurate and consistent method, and a more concrete vocabulary, for examining the work of others and for making and remaking his own. The emotive and the metaphoric should not be lost to the study of language—and could never be to reading itself—but should be accompanied by and grounded in some more careful and specific observations. The intuitive approach must not be cured, it must be educated. To this end it is a premise of *Grammar as Style* that an understanding of syntax can be most instructive.

This confidence rests on another premise, namely that style can be found to depend closely on grammar and can be thought of in this way at no cost to the subtlety and strength and emotional variety of its effects. To defend this assumption we must now brave the crossfire of the debate about the nature of style and its relation to meaning. A stand must necessarily be taken on this issue before style's relation to grammar can be adequately decided.

A position must be secured somewhere between the opposing forces of the *ornamental* and the *organic* schools, between those who think that meaning precedes and is then decorated by style, and those who feel that meaning and style are simultaneous because the same. If style is purely ornamental, if it only adorns written ideas, it can hardly be possible to consider grammar as style. Grammar is itself the carrier of ideas, syntax no accessory but the very means of meaning. This fact seems also at first to exile grammar-as-style from the opposing organic view, in that the same grammatical form must carry many different meanings. Thus, if style is meaning, grammar can claim only small and unconvincing credit for the full impact of any piece of prose. The grammar-as-style idea could, of course, reconcile itself to this organic theory, which is certainly much sounder and more useful than thinking of style as ornament. Grammar could, if it had to, live with the rudimentary role thus assigned it in comprising the whole meaning that is style. But the title-thesis of this book would welcome a more complete marriage of grammar and style, performed with benefit of theory, and it is worth contending briefly with the organicists in order to have this.

They have almost won the day. Their position is established as a kind of orthodoxy, and they defend their truth against all heretical comers. Richard Ohmann observes that their cause, which champions the union of form and content, "has nearly attained the status of dogma, of an official motto, voiced in the triumphant tones of reason annihilating error."[5] We can catch these tones in William Wimsatt's rendition of the ornamental view he is opposing: "It is as if, when all is said for meaning, there remains an irreducible something that is superficial, a kind of scum—which they call style."[6] But is there not in fact something left to talk about, after all is said for meaning—not a "scum" to be sure—but some essential quality that gets slighted if only meaning is considered?

Perhaps we can call forth an example that will help settle this, at least for all practical purposes. The example comes from C. S. Lewis, from the famous conclusion to his chapter on "Courtly Love" where he summarizes the retractions of medieval writers with an implied metaphor of truancy:

> In the last stanzas of the book of Troilus, in the harsher recantation that closes the life and work of Chaucer as a whole, in the noble close of Malory, it is the same. We hear the bell clang; and the children, suddenly hushed and grave, and a little frightened, troop back to their master.[7]

There is some controversy about Lewis's ideas here, his reading of Medieval literature, but it would widely be agreed that his last sentence, say, is quite well done. Subscribers to the organic theory, where style and meaning are inseparable, if they happened to disagree with Lewis's attitude toward Chaucer and Malory, would be forced to say something like: "This has a fine meaning, but it is false." Yet doesn't this kind of example begin to show what we can obviously say about style apart from meaning? Lewis might have written "We hear the bell sound; and the children, suddenly taciturn and solemn, and somewhat alarmed, return to their master." He did not, and he has our gratitude. The organicist might rightly insist that, if he had, he would have *meant* something different from what his actual sentence managed to say. We can object that changes in diction have made the sentence flaccid and lifeless, but we should also notice that they have caused it to say something not quite the same as the original. Changes in syntax, however, alter meaning, if at all, much less obviously. Endure one more revision as example: "We hear the bell clang, and the children are suddenly hushed, grave, and a little frightened, and they troop back to their master." Again great damage has been done, but it is hard to see how meaning itself has suffered any change. One may surely say that more is lost to our enjoyment in reading the idea than is lost to our understanding of it. There may be an enlightened sense in which meaning and emphasis have been minutely altered, but to nothing like the extent to which rhythm and impact have been violated. Our first revision suggests that diction, a major element in what is usually called style, is so much allied with the specific meaning of words, as well as with levels of usage, that it lends itself easily to the organicist position. It is in the area of syntax, as seen by comparing Lewis's original with the second revision, where style can best be recognized as something not exactly like meaning, and where one feels justified in talking at some length about grammar as style.

When the example from Lewis was brought to the rescue, it was said to be recruited "for all practical purposes." This can now be read "for all pedagogical purposes." Indeed, a very large objection to the organic theory of style's oneness with meaning is the difficulty in finding the idea at all useful when trying to write better sentences, or when helping others to write them. It is all very well for teachers to ask their students to improve their thinking, to refine their powers of meaning, until their new brand of thought warrants nice, stylish sentences, but this is almost certain to produce no results. Better to instruct them, with practice and example, in the many possibilities of English prose—and, importantly, of English syntax—so that they can make anything they might have to say clearer, more assured, more attractive. With this new access to the countless effective ways of putting ideas down on paper, writers may well become eager to make use of appositives, say, or of nominative absolutes, of devices learned for subordinating ideas, of right-branching sentences maybe, or of the previously undreamed-of benefits of parallelism. Doing this, writers are likely to think through their ideas, elaborate and sharpen them, until they deserve such professional treatment. When this becomes habitual, the actual teaching of style is over.

One last excursion into theoretical waters, however, may yet be worthwhile, to find out a bit more exactly what those qualities of style are that we enjoy in a sentence of C. S. Lewis, for instance, and how those qualities owe, for a large measure of their success, a discoverable debt to the nature of English syntax. Venturing once more into theory, we again need to adopt a compromise position. It profits us to consider Richard Ohmann's modest but important one, in the essay already cited. He divides style into "epistemic choice" and "emotional form." By the first he means the selections and decisions a writer must always make with respect to his materials and their arrangement, as he sorts out his experience of the world. Grammar figures importantly in this phase of "style."

> A heavy dependence on abstraction, a peculiar use of the present tense, a habitual evocation of parallel structure, a tendency to place feelings in syntactic positions of agency, a trick of underplaying causal words: any of these patterns of expression, when repeated with unusual frequency, is the sign of a habit of meaning, and thus of a persistent way of sorting out the phenomena of experience.[8]

Ohmann admits, as he must, that this does not amount to much of a departure from the conventional organic view. He is talking about a writer's persistent manner, not about particular sentences in isolation. Stylistic tendencies thus accompany tendencies in meaning, and style as a "habit of meaning" is little more than a generalization, for a particular writer, about style as meaning, and grammar as its carrier.

Syntax begins to separate from meaning, as style, only in the second stage of Ohmann's classification, in the area of feeling rather than of choice. Traditional rhetoric tells us about the emotion involved in *persuasion*, and Ohmann adds the feeling of personal *expression*, the recorded emotion of a private speaking voice. "Emotion enters prose not only as disguises for slipping into the reader's confidence, but as sheer expression of self."[9] But beyond persuasion and self-expression, emotion makes a third entrance into prose, in a way that Ohmann finds "almost beyond the power of language to describe."[10] His is a very good try, nonetheless. He suggests that a sentence begins by raising rather than answering questions, and that the incomplete utterance sets up demands for completion.

> These demands for completion of a sequence are of course subverbal; they are the vaguest sort of dissatisfaction with suspended thought, with a rational process not properly concluded. As the sentence progresses,

> some of its demands are satisfied, others deferred, others complicated, and meanwhile new ones are created. But with the end of the sentence comes a kind of balance which results from something having been *said*.[11]

Ohmann speaks here in "the vaguest sort of" terms, making his way toward a feeling for style as itself a matter of feeling, and, consequently, as a matter hard to be exact about.

But is this quality of style really so much a "subverbal" phenomenon, really so elusive as to tax description "almost beyond the power of language"? Is it not, rather, a very sensitive way to appreciate, apart from meaning, and with a real sense of its nature and function, the role of syntax itself at that final level of reading that goes beyond the reception of ideas to the emotional response we have, and the pleasure we take, in the way we are allowed to receive them? Take as examples Ohmann's last two sentences from the passage just quoted. In the first, a parallel syntax, tightened by ellipsis, itself complicates the sentence, and defers its conclusion. Meanwhile, Ohmann adds mention of new created demands by adding a new clause to tell about them. The unmistakable rhythm of his sentence is an effort to give us in his own prose some feeling for what he is saying about sentences at large, and his means are neither mysterious nor subverbal. They are syntactic. Grammatical patterns establish the "demands for completion" and move us along until they are satisfied. So too with his last sentence, which might have run: "But a kind of balance which results from something having been *said* comes with the end of the sentence." Instead, his inversion of normal syntax imparts a quality of anticipation to the prose, holding appropriately till the end the grammatical subject and the idea of balanced completion, and thus balancing his own sentence with a sense of something awaited finally "having been *said*." Ohmann has succeeded here with a rhythm, an "emotional form," that is obviously syntactic. It should be clear, too, that his larger theoretical understanding of a sentence's felt movements rests on the very nature of syntax—on its rhythm as a series of relationships unfolded in time.

A dictionary records that syntax is "the arrangement of words as elements in a sentence to show their relationship." The key to this definition is the phrase "to show." It names the real action of syntax, which should be thought of as a disclosure made piece by piece, not as a revealed frame or pattern to be seen and comprehended at once. Syntax has direction, not just structure. It starts, and goes forward, and concludes. It is an order of grammar experienced *in* a certain order, not a system or arrangement so much as a succession—*syntax as sequence*. As a stretch of verbal space, a sentence has an entrance and an exit and a terrain we cross and track—and all this over a stretch of time. As an emotional span, uniting its movement in space and time, a sentence seems to generate its own dynamics of feeling, ushering us into its meaning and escorting us across it, anticipating, deflecting, suspending, and finally going to a satisfactory close. As a verbal terrain, as a series of encounters across it, or as the emotional curve that follows them through, the sentence—as a unit of style—is being defined by its syntax. It is often said of prose, as of poetry, that it must be read aloud to be really known. The indispensable quality of prose that is met by the ear in reading, that must be heard as passing sounds and stresses and ideas, that must be listened to as much as understood, followed through as a sequence rather than grasped whole as a structure: it is this quality that brings style and syntax closest together. For it is the effect of syntax on style. It is *grammar as style*. . . .

Even *kernel sentences*, the spare source from which other structures and sentences are generated, work as a sequence, however compact. They set up a basic pattern of expected order, and are expanded with this in mind. There must be something to talk about, the *noun phrase*, and once the subject has been selected, something must be said about it in a predication, a *verb phrase*. *Adjectives* and *adverbs* help to fill out the patterns, and they do not merely specify or qualify or complicate. They have a place as well as a meaning. They come before or after the word with which they are associated, to anticipate or complete its meaning, sometimes piled around it in groups of two or three, or more, to dramatize what they do. Prepositional phrases, too, expand the patterns. More than just signaling a new relationship, a *preposition* that starts a phrase makes an independent grammatical move, briefly channeling the sentence away from its main course in some new syntactic direction. Simple *conjunctions* and *correlatives* are readily available for compounding, and thus enlarging the parts of a basic sentence, or for hooking two sentences together. They are less important to the drift of a sentence because they weigh the elements they join and tell us they are equal, however, than because they reveal a decision to give us one before the other, to move us along in a determined order. *Coordination* itself is a logical relation, but in syntax it is also a sequence.

Kernels are expanded with *dependent clauses*, for a remarkable variety of effects. The way we leave such clauses and move into the main one, or encounter them in the middle of a main clause, or come to them later, the whole strategy of sequence and transition accounts for the chief effects of relative and subordinate expansions. Neither is the *sentence opener* a static factor, a grammatical fixed point to which the elements that follow are attached. On the contrary, the opener can be a crucial first move, overcoming inertia, ushering us into a thought, or nudging us backward for an instant, before activating necessary grammatical momentum to send us off in one syntactical direction or another. *Inversions* other than those necessary for questions and exclamations also have an important stylistic role. They can manipulate the order in which we reach certain parts of a sentence. Varying the way we normally receive information, their effects, successful or not, may shift the focus, may alter the linkage of one sentence to another.

In addition to the familiar means of expanding kernel structures, and of opening all kinds of sentences, a whole class of nonrestrictive modifiers, well-named *free modifiers* by Francis Christensen, also depends on syntactic movement for its effects. When free or even bound modifiers come together in such numbers or are so extensive themselves as to define the overall shape of a sentence, when they accumulate before the subject, or between it and the verb, for instance, or after the predicate of the base clause, their weight and placement are so important to the sentence that we are warranted in using directional labels: *left-branching*, *mid-branching*, and *right-branching sentences*. Professor Christensen's title for the last, the cumulative sentence, also captures that interest in one-thing-after-another that is at issue here. Often the cumulative sentence makes use of the *nominative absolute construction*. It creates a grammatical subplot quite distinct from the main action of a sentence, and one sequence must be held loosely in mind while the other is assimilated.

Perhaps the most useful of all free modifiers, and one of the easiest to master, is the *appositive*. It renames smoothly without requiring any change in syntactic plan. It simply appears after (sometimes before) the word or phrase it restates, and we are involved as much in the feeling of afterthought, or of arriving clarification, as we ever are in a sense of alternate and equal possibilities. It really matters what comes first, what is named, and how it is then amplified. With appositives as with all free modifiers, and indeed with syntactic expansion in general, order and movement are more important than structure and logical relationship.

The process of transformation is able not only to enlarge the basic patterns with added or embedded materials, but also to deform certain kernels themselves into new arrangements, and these may stay short or themselves receive new material. *Interrogative, imperative,* and *exclamatory* transforms are examples, with distinct emotional patterns of emphasis and expectation set up by their syntax.

With the *passive transformation*, minor changes in meaning and emphasis may occur, sometimes with deadening results. But when passives are cleverly used, it is often their syntactic features on which a writer is capitalizing. The passive can serve as a kind of tactical inversion. It can be used to arrange ideas for a special stress, or to move them into positions from which they can be more easily modified.

Within a single sentence or across wider verbal spaces, syntax also has an important part to play in the experience of *parallelism* and *cohesion*. It is a role that assumes an audience reading one thing after another and feeling how things begin to take shape as they have done before, or how one idea grows out of another comfortably, coherently. The dramatic analogy here, of a role played to a reading audience, is deliberate. It is meant to suggest again what the recent discussion has said about syntax as sequence, with every sentence performing its own separate drama and involving the emotions of its readers in the way it develops syntactically and is worked out. The main grammatical action of a sentence and its subplots should never be at odds with meaning, of course, but they have a motion and a rhythm all their own. Yet when the rhythm and sequence of syntax begins to act out the meaning itself, when the drama of meaning and the drama of syntax coincide perfectly, when syntax as action becomes syntax as enactment, this last refinement of style is called *syntactic symbolism*. Beginning with a thesis that allows us to talk separately about style and meaning, we naturally work toward the organicist's equation of the two, the fusion of form and content, not as the inevitable condition of language, but as a very special achievement.

NOTES

1. Louis Tonko Milic, *A Quantitative Approach to the Style of Jonathan Swift* (The Hague: Mouton, 1967), pp. 15–39.

2. Huntington Brown, *Prose Styles: Five Primary Types* (Minneapolis: U of Minnesota P, 1966).

3. Walker Gibson, *Tough, Sweet & Stuffy: An Essay on Modern American Prose Styles* (Bloomington: Indiana UP, 1966).

4. Louis Tonko Milic, "Metaphysics in the Criticism of Style," *College Composition and Communication* (October 1966): 124.

5. Richard Ohmann, "Prolegomena to the Analysis of Prose Style," in *Essays on the Language of Literature,* ed. Seymour Chatman and Samuel R. Levin (Boston: Houghton Mifflin, 1967), p. 398.

6. William K. Wimsatt Jr., "Introduction: Style as Meaning," *The Prose Style of Samuel Johnson* (New Haven, CT: Yale UP, 1941), p. 1.

7. C. S. Lewis, *The Allegory of Love* (London: Oxford UP, 1936), p. 43.

8. Ohmann, p. 405.

9. Ohmann, p. 409.

10. Ohmann, p. 410.

11. Ohmann, p. 410.

10   *Closing the Books on Alchemy*

MARTHA KOLLN

In 1963 two publications appeared, one from NCTE, the other from the NEA, both summarizing the state of the art, or science, of composition research. One of them created a wave so big that even after seventeen years its ripples continue to wash the shores of the English curriculum; the other, unfortunately, sank without a trace.

The authors of the NCTE report, *Research in Written Composition*—Richard Braddock, Richard Lloyd-Jones, and Lowell Schoer—recognized that such research was not highly developed; in fact, they compared research in composition "to chemical research as it emerged from the period of alchemy" (p. 5). We've come a long way since then. Recent work in such areas as invention, error analysis, the process of writing, holistic scoring, and sentence combining testifies to the progress we have made as researchers; the variety of program topics at CCCC demonstrates how far we have come and how much we have learned since 1963. That NCTE report, in fact, with its detailed accounts of empirical studies and scientific research methods, probably had a great deal to do with bringing us out of the dark ages.

Yet the biggest wave that report made had just the opposite effect: it encouraged the alchemists. The most quotable statement in all of its pages effectively turned back the clock on grammar research; it is still causing ripples:

> In view of the widespread agreement of research studies based upon many types of students and teachers, the conclusion can be stated in strong and unqualified terms: the teaching of formal grammar has a negligible or, because it usually displaces some instruction and practice in actual composition, even a harmful effect on the improvement of writing. (pp. 37–38)

I suspect that the authors were surprised at the press coverage that statement received. Perhaps if they had anticipated such attention, they would have been more careful in applying their criteria for good research to themselves; they might have defined their terms. What do they mean by "formal

From *College Composition and Communication* 32 (1981): 139–51.

grammar"? Do they mean memorizing rules and definitions? Diagramming and parsing sentences? Or does "formal grammar" simply refer to an organized subject in the curriculum? And certainly they would have asked another, related question: If formal grammar has a negative effect, is there an alternative that might have a positive one?

That's one of my criticisms of that quotable line: its undefined terms. The other is its "strong and unqualified" language. The authors' conclusions in every other area of composition, without exception, are couched in tentative language, as well they should be: "with these cautions" (p. 30); "some of his procedures . . . seem very questionable, and some of his conclusions seem to leap beyond the reasonable distance" (p. 31); "it is not clear yet" (p. 35); "certainly it has not been proved" (p. 36). Such qualifications concern the methodology as well as the interpretation of data in every area except the teaching of grammar. The authors do admit that much of the research on instruction in grammar is based on objective tests rather than actual writing; and they concede that "carefully conducted research which studies the effect of formal grammar on actual composition over an extended period of time" is uncommon (p. 37). Yet they still summarize the research on the teaching of grammar with that "harmful effects" statement in "strong and unqualified terms"— clearly, the last word in grammar research.

That highly-quotable, 56-word statement has appeared over and over again these seventeen years, in books and articles and convention papers and classrooms and casual conversations. As recently as December 1979, in fact, it turned up yet again in the pages of *College English*.[1] Alchemy persists.

But what of the other 1963 report? In "Research on Teaching Composition and Literature," his contribution to the 1,200-page *Handbook of Research on Teaching* (N. L. Gage, editor [Chicago: Rand McNally and Company]), Henry C. Meckel describes many of the same research studies that Braddock et al. looked at, but he reaches far different conclusions. (I quote his summary in full);

1. There is no research evidence that grammar as traditionally taught in the schools has any appreciable effect on the improvement of writing skill.

2. The training periods involved in transfer studies have been comparatively short, and the amount of grammar instruction has frequently been small.

3. There is no conclusive research evidence, however, that grammar has *no* transfer value in developing composition skill.

4. More research is needed on the kind of grammatical knowledge that may reasonably be expected to transfer to writing. For example, commonly accepted principles of transfer of training would not lead an experimenter to expect much transfer value from knowledge of grammar which has not included the knowledge and ability to apply grammatical principles to the construction of the pupil's own sentences. [See J. M. Stephens, "Transfer of Learning," in C. W. Harris, ed., *Encyclopedia of Educational Research* (3rd edition. New York: Macmillan Company, 1960), pp. 1535–1543.]

5. Research does not justify the conclusion that grammar should not be taught systematically. In some appraisals of research there has been a confusion be-

tween the term *formal grammar* as used to denote systematic study and mastery and the term as used to mean grammar taught without application to writing and speaking. Systematic study does not preclude application.

6. There are more efficient methods of securing *immediate* improvement in the writing of pupils, both in sentence structure and usage, than systematic grammatical instruction.

7. Improvement of usage appears to be more effectively achieved through practice of desirable forms than through memorization of rules.

8. The items of usage selected for inclusion in the curriculum should be determined not only by "errors" made in students' papers but also by descriptive studies of national usage by linguistic experts.

9. In determining what grammar is functional and what is not, teachers cannot safely rely on textbooks used in schools but must depend on the expert opinion of linguists based on modern studies of the usage and structure of the language. (pp. 981–982)

Meckel also suggests that "much of the earlier research on teaching grammar must be regarded as no longer of significance outside the period in educational history which it represents" (p. 982).

Unfortunately, Meckel's advice was lost in the wake of the strong and unqualified language of the Braddock report. As a result, no one heard his call for a definition of "formal grammar" or his conclusion, in paragraph five, that the "systematic study (of formal grammar) does not preclude application." Not only can we teach grammar—the internalized system of rules that the speakers of a language share—we can do so in a functional way, in connection with composition. When we teach our students to understand and label the various structures of the system, when we bring to conscious awareness those subconscious rules, we are, in fact, teaching grammar.

But Meckel's advice went unheard. As a result, instead of determining what grammar is functional, instead of discovering what aspects of grammar study would be the most helpful for our students, we continue to cite those early studies, which Meckel judged "no longer of significance," to justify excluding grammar study of any kind from the curriculum.

To mention only one example of the alchemists' continuing influence, Dean Memering has recently asserted that "the evidence is incontestable that grammar teaching achieves nothing useful in composition":

> There is no way to teach students grammatical terminology and a set of rules for describing the language that will have any effect on writing. No amount of practice in analyzing, dissecting, or diagramming sentences will change student performance in composition. It makes no difference whether we teach Latin, structural, transformational, stratificational, tagmemic, or any other brand of grammar: endless efforts to show that grammar does too affect writing have repeatedly come up with the same weary finding—no significant difference. This finding has been advertised since 1906 when Hoyt concluded that there was "an absence of relationship between a knowledge of technical grammar and the ability to

use and interpret language." The same results or worse have been noted more or less consistently by researchers since that time: Rapeer, 1913; Asker, 1923; Segal and Barr, 1926; Symonds, 1931; Frogner, 1939; Harris, 1962. If we know anything at all about composition, we know that students can't be "grammared" into better writers.[2]

With seven reports to back him up, we're not surprised that Memering states his opinions in such strong and unqualified terms. But perhaps we should give those reports a closer look to see if they justify his conclusions.

In 1906 Hoyt questioned the place that formal grammar study occupied in the elementary school curriculum, mainly because of what we know about children's psychological development.[3] He described grammar study, from the child's point of view, as consisting, "very largely of generalizations to be memorized and applied to the classification and parsing of words and combinations of words by a kind of mental assortment of them into given groups . . . tagged with technical names, usually meaningless to the child" (p. 475). Influenced by Thorndike's research into learning, Hoyt considered this kind of mental exercise "ill-adapted to immature pupils." However, he did believe that for students beyond elementary school, "the study of formal grammar may be pursued entirely in accordance with psychological principles" (p. 476).

With his research Hoyt hoped to disprove two of the arguments commonly advanced for teaching grammar to young children: "that a knowledge of grammar leads to the use of better English in oral and written expression," and "that a knowledge of grammar is a considerable aid in the interpretation of language" (p. 478). For the experiment, ninth-graders in Indianapolis wrote 40-minute essays, restated in prose four stanzas of Gray's "Elegy Written in a Country Churchyard," and answered ten grammar questions about four other stanzas of the same poem. He found the correlations between scores on the three subtests—composition, interpretation, and grammar—low, but nonetheless positive, ranging from .30 between grammar and composition to .41 between interpretation and composition. But on the basis of these results Hoyt concluded, as Memering quotes, that there was no relationship between grammar and the other skills. He also concluded, after correlating grammar scores and marks in other subjects, such as arithmetic and geography, that the mental processes involved in grammar study contribute little to general mental training.

In light of Hoyt's concerns about the content of the elementary school grammar curriculum and its appropriateness for children, we can understand his eagerness to present conclusive findings. But certainly questions remain. First, the tests were scored subjectively by two raters, who, as far as we know, were given no specific training. Hoyt briefly mentions inter-rater reliabilities, giving them as percentages rather than correlations: 86 percent on the grammar test, 83 percent on interpretation, and, not surprisingly, only 58 percent on composition. Perhaps even more questionable are the tests themselves. For instance, had the essay topic been tested? We know from our own experiences, as well as from reports of ETS, what a difference the topic itself makes both to the writer and the reader. And what exactly was he measuring? Were the tests valid? Was the level of difficulty on the grammar and interpretation tests appropriate for first-term ninth graders? One grammar question asked students to identify the part of speech of the first word in stanzas like this one:

> Save that, from yonder ivy-mantled tower,
> The moping owl does to the moon complain
> Of such as, wandering near her secret bower,
> Molest her ancient solitary reign.

Other questions asked them to name the adjectives in this stanza, explaining their use in the sentence, and to give the voice, mode, tense, and number of the verbs, telling whether they are transitive or intransitive and why.

But questions of reliability and validity aside, let's look at Hoyt's own conclusions. He clearly does not advocate the banishment of grammar, as Memering would have us to believe. His criticisms were directed at the place it occupied in the elementary curriculum. He suggested two possible solutions to the problem of grammar study: either postpone it until high school or change the character of instruction "so that its study may be more fruitful." He urged that grammar study in elementary school be taught "in connection with the language work . . . to become an effective tool in the work in composition and interpretation" (p. 490).

Rapeer (1913), in a replication of Hoyt's study, concurs with these conclusions, suggesting that only those grammatical terms that are actually necessary be taught in the elementary grades and that formal grammar instruction be postponed to the last half of the eighth year.[4] Both Hoyt and Rapeer emphasized the need to evaluate the amount of time devoted to formal grammar study in an overcrowded curriculum when the schools had to provide "the whole range of vocational, hygenic, and socializing training needed by our 'nation of sixth graders'" (p. 131). We should also emphasize that in these studies Hoyt and Rapeer did not compare students who studied grammar with others who did not, nor did they compare methods of teaching grammar; they simply correlated scores on a three-part test.

In comparison with the next three studies on the Memering list, even Hoyt's research design looks meticulous. None of the other early studies include actual composition. Asker (1923) did nothing but compare scores on grammar tests with grades in college freshman composition courses.[5] The erroneous assumption that writing ability alone determines course grades is a problem that Braddock et al. cite in their discussion of research design, and they list eight other factors that commonly raise or lower composition grades (p. 22). Yet on the basis of such a comparison, Asker jumps to the conclusion that "time spent on formal grammar in the elementary school is wasted as far as the majority of students is concerned" (p. 111).

The Segal and Barr report (1926) makes no such unsupported claims, but Memering errs in thinking that it supports his bias against grammar study.[6] On the contrary, in comparing results of a "formal-grammar test" with an "applied-grammar test," Segal and Barr conclude that "there may be a decided transfer value" for "specialists in English speech in particular and college students in general" (p. 402). They base this conclusion on the finding that even though "formal grammar" scores of juniors were lower than those of sophomores, the "applied grammar" scores were higher. "Evidently," they report, "formal grammar is forgotten but language usage improved" (p. 402). Segal and Barr's only negative finding was based on the correlation of .48 between the two grammar tests, which was no higher than the correlation between marks in any two subjects in high school. On that evidence they conclude that formal grammar has no immediate transfer value to applied English grammar. This experiment included no actual writing, however; what they refer to as "practice" or "applied grammar" is nothing more than a series of workbook exercises on usage ("I [can't, can] hardly see it"; "James [done, did] his work yesterday"). So whatever the outcome, we can certainly draw no valid conclusions about the students' writing ability.

The other two studies from the 1930s that Memering cites compare teaching methods by means of objective tests. The purpose of the Symonds experiment (1931) was to discover what influence learning grammar has on usage.[7] In what he calls a test-teach-test experiment, Symonds administered a pre-test to six groups of sixth graders in New York City, using a 40-item usage test in which students rewrote sentences containing errors, such as these:

Are you most ready to go?

He said that I was most there.

He then subjected each group to one of six different experimental procedures—methods of teaching that were suspect even while he was using them. Some were the very methods of teaching grammar that twenty-five years earlier Hoyt had recommended be abandoned. And Symonds himself reports in his summary that "time and again during the course of the work reported in this article, principals and teachers would complain that the methods . . . were too formal and dry to be practically used" (p. 95).

But Symonds persevered. For example, one group did nothing but memorize definitions, rules, and principles, with teachers being explicitly cautioned about letting the students stray from the method being tested:

Do *not* ask the pupils to make up examples of their own illustrating the rules.

Do *not* give the pupils additional examples of the rules.

Do *not* ask pupils to analyze the rules.

Do *not* give the pupils practice in applying any of the rules. (p. 84)

Then there were the repetition groups who studied no rules or definitions; they simply read aloud, in unison, one or three or five or ten times a list of forty correct sentences like these:

The boy was almost killed by an automobile.

My baby brother is almost two years old. (p. 83)

Still another recitation group chanted both right and wrong sentences aloud, in unison:

> "The boy was most killed by an automobile" is wrong;
>
> "The boy was almost killed by an automobile" is right.
>
> "My baby brother is most two years old" is wrong;
>
> "My baby brother is almost two years old" is right. (p. 84)

Another group practiced correct constructions by filling in blanks; two others used combinations of all of the above. To evaluate these so-called "teaching methods," Symonds administered the same forty-item test at the end of the experiment. We surely aren't surprised at his conclusion:

> In the writer's opinion it is relatively unprofitable for the average child either to study grammar as a means for learning correct usage (because there are more direct, simpler, and easier means for learning usage) or as a means of summarizing the correct usage which one has learned (because there are other things more worthwhile in the curriculum). (p. 94)

What does surprise us is that Memering and others can seriously consider such research as proof that grammar study has no positive effect on composition.

Some of the studies designed to demonstrate that traditional grammar study is ineffective have shown that other methods of teaching grammar do, in fact, work. Frogner (1939) compared two teaching methods, the "grammar" approach and the "thought" approach, neither of which included the obvious weaknesses of Symonds' methods.[8] Frogner describes her grammar group as going somewhat beyond what she considered "typical of grammar teaching today." For example, in studying the subordination of ideas in phrases, the grammar group did more than simply learn to recognize prepositional, appositive, participle, gerund, and infinitive phrases and to differentiate their kind and use in the sentence; they applied the principles they learned by effectively combining short, choppy sentences and then "proceeded to the discussion and correction of errors in the use of phrases, such as the misplaced prepositional phrase or the dangling participle" (p. 521). The thought group, on the other hand, began their study of phrases not by learning to identify types and labeling them but "by noticing the various ways of subordinating ideas" (p. 521). They discussed examples written on the board and combined ideas in as many ways as possible. Here is Frogner's illustration of one such lesson:

> "Mr. White is our class advisor. He grasped the seriousness of the situation. He immediately called a meeting of the officers." How could the ideas be combined to avoid the monotonous childish sentences? Several possibilities were suggested, one of which was: "Having grasped the seriousness of the situation, Mr. White, our class advisor, immediately called a meeting of the officers." Pupils improved the expression of thought by means of subordinating ideas in a participial and an appositive phrase; yet they were not drilled in the recognition of the grammatical construction. (pp. 521–522)

It is clear even from her brief description of this and other lessons that what the "thought" group thought about was, of course, grammar. They thought about and discussed coordination and subordination of ideas, parallel structure, and the relationship of punctuation to meaning. Apparently what they did not do was the drilling and memorizing of labels and definitions that in 1939 was synonymous with the study of grammar.

Unfortunately, Frogner's conclusions were based on objective tests rather than actual writing, and although she claims significant differences in favor of the thought group, she fails to report either the nature of the tests or the exact levels of confidence of her findings. But the more important issue in Frogner's study has been ignored: What is the "thought" approach, the one that worked? Both Frogner and, two decades later, Harris set out to prove that writing can be taught without teaching grammar. But what both studies actually bring to light are alternative methods that do seem to work. Frogner's thought approach, in fact, looks very much like sentence combining. But unfortunately, only the negative results of the study have received any attention.

In the case of the Harris study, too, only the negative aspects have been reported.[9] In fact, it is this study, which Braddock et al. considered the "most soundly based" of all the research on the teaching of grammar they examined, that supplied them with the phrase "harmful effects." Working with junior-high-level classes in five London schools in 1960, Harris "investigated the relative teaching usefulness of what might be loosely referred to in the United States as 'formal grammar' and a 'direct method' of instruction" (Braddock et al., p. 70).

All of the classes in the experiment met five times a week; four of the five periods were the same. The difference between the two methods

> ... came in the fifth period, when one group emphasized formal grammar and the other focused on direct methods of instruction ... Some of the time released by omitting study of the terminology of formal grammar could be devoted to writing activity projects and to drawing illustrative sentences, points of usage, and paragraphs from the stories to teach the improvement of writing. A piece of continuous writing was also attempted in the Formal Grammar classes, but not much time was available for the project inasmuch as these classes were carefully following the integrated grammar and composition lessons in their textbooks. (p. 78)[10]

A sample lesson included in the Braddock report shows the direct-method teacher leading the students to an understanding of subject-verb agreement through inductive reasoning, by plumbing their own linguistic resources, using examples from their own compositions ("Me and Jim was going into the cave"):

> Would you say "We was going into the cave"? [negative reply]
>
> What would you say? ("We were ...")
>
> How many is "we"? ["More than one ..."]
>
> Well, "Jim and me" is more than one. (p. 71)

The formal grammar students tackled such errors using traditional terminology. To do so, as Harris points out, they had already learned such concepts as agreement and case.

At the end of two years, Harris analyzed compositions written at the beginning and at the end of the experiment, using eleven different measures, including sentence length, frequency of subordinate clauses and compound sentences, sentence variety, and the like. All of the results that were statistically significant (the majority of the measures, incidentally, were not) favored the direct-method group. However, for each of the eleven measures, the grammar group came out on top in at least one of the five schools; for two of the measures, results in three of the five schools favored the grammar group. Nevertheless Harris claims to have discovered what he set out to discover: the "functions and value of formal traditional grammar in the teaching of English"—or, as it turned out, the lack thereof.

Harris concludes his study in these words: "It seems safe to infer that the study of English grammatical terminology had a negligible or even a relatively harmful effect upon the correctness of children's writing in the early part of the five Secondary schools" (p. 83). And while the Braddock report does put this conclusion in some sort of perspective with the qualification "because it usually displaces practice in actual composition," it remains a misleading and simplistic conclusion. A positive—and more accurate—version of that conclusion might read like this: "The student who spends an extra period every week for two years on actual composition will show more improvement in certain aspects of writing than the student who does not." Harris, after all, did not simply test the effect of studying formal grammar on writing ability; rather, he tested the effect of replacing writing practice with something else—in this case with formal grammar study and, we assume, the traditional memorizing and drilling associated with it. The only surprise in his outcome is that no significant difference showed up after the first year.

In all fairness I must add that Braddock et al. conclude their summary of the Harris study with a parenthetical disclaimer: "Based as it was on the use of traditional grammar, the Harris study does not necessarily prove, of course, the ineffectiveness of instruction based on structural or generative grammar" (p. 83). Unfortunately that qualification appears forty pages away from their well-known "harmful effects" quotation with its "strong and unqualified" finality.

That famous statement has probably had a more harmful effect on our students these past seventeen years than all the time spent memorizing rules and diagramming sentences ever had. The babies born in 1963 are babies no longer; they are juniors and seniors in high school. That 1963 report has probably affected the education of every one of them. Shortly after its appearance, textbooks on teaching methods began quoting its memorable line. And before long our elementary and secondary English classes were staffed by eager young teachers who believed that teaching grammar was a waste of time—even worse, it was downright harmful. In her 1965 text, for example, Fowler quotes that sentence along with other findings and then summarizes: "Despite the overwhelming and incontrovertible evidence, large amounts of class time are still being spent on the study of grammar to the neglect of practice in writing and reading.[11] In 1969 Loban, Ryan, and Squire follow the "harmful effects" statement with the concession that knowledge of grammar is valuable for its own sake.[12] Then they explain that while the study of usage has a place in the curriculum, it must be taught without recourse to grammar terminology. Stephen Judy offers a chapter entitled "Twenty Alternatives to the Study of Grammar."[13]

While these authors do offer sensible instruction on teaching composition, such strong and unqualified positions on grammar are hard for impressionable students to dispute—and to forget. No doubt countless English Education majors have left their methods courses convinced that they needn't concern themselves with grammar, that no one teaches grammar anymore. Often, in fact, their own experiences as high school and junior high students confirm these beliefs. Their college curriculum may confirm them as well, with perhaps only one required course in grammar or linguistics to prepare them as teachers. For years my students, in describing their own secondary school experiences, have told me they studied no grammar at all, often because their English teachers didn't like it; they stuck to literature. The Braddock report certainly justifies that position. So instead of trying to discover what does work—for example, what is Frogner's "thought" approach? what is Harris's "direct method"?—instead of seeking ways to use what the linguists have pointed out about the rules we have within us, to help our students better understand their own linguistic resources, we have quoted over and over again that unqualified and misleading statement about the harmful effects of teaching formal grammar. And we have bent over backwards to avoid spending classroom time on anything that smacks of grammar, old or new.

Is there room in the language arts curriculum or in the freshman composition class for grammar study? Certainly. In some classrooms it never left; many teachers have never stopped believing that the teaching of composition and literature can be more effective when they are able to discuss details of syntax with their students. In other classrooms grammar actually slipped in quite some time ago under the guise of sentence combining. Frank O'Hare, who introduced many of us to sentence combining some years ago, might disagree with such a notion; after all, he introduced his well-known study, *Sentence Combining: Improving Student Writing without Formal Grammar Instruction*,[14] quoting the "harmful effects" statement on page one. In fact, he explicitly denies any connection between sentence combining and grammar:

> The greatest attraction for both teacher and pupils of the system of sentence-combining practice described here is, of course, that it does not necessitate the study of a grammar, traditional or transformational. The English teacher who simply "doesn't like grammar" can use this system. (p. 30)

But even though O'Hare perpetuates the myth, his experimental students, like Frogner's "thought" group back in 1939 and Harris's "direct method" group, actually did study grammar. They didn't memorize Mellon's transformational formulas, it's true, but they did study the system underlying their own language ability; they learned to manipulate sentences in a conscious way.[15] That they labeled clause modifiers as "who statements" rather than "relative clauses" doesn't mean they didn't study grammar. Among the recent versions of sentence combining is at least one that includes traditional terminology without apology. Students using *The Writer's Options: College Sentence Combining* by Daiker, Kerek, and Morenberg learn about—and learn to control—relative clauses in Chapter One, participles in Chapter Two, appositives in Chapter Three, and absolutes in Chapter Four.[16] If sentence combining does indeed have transfer value—that is, if it improves the writing that students do beyond the sentence-combining lesson—then surely a conscious understanding of such structures, along with the labels that help them think about the structures and remember them, can only add to that value.

Perhaps Hoyt was right in 1906 to believe as he did that young children did not profit from studying abstract concepts of grammar; perhaps grammar classes of old were too prescriptive, too bound up with drilling and memorizing, too nonfunctional in their methods. But even very young writers can come to understand consciously the structures they use in their writing and can profit by that understanding. "Sesame Street" watchers, including preschoolers, easily learn the ways of words, from principles underlying the "silent e" to the meaning of prepositions and the importance of word order. Elementary language arts teachers can capitalize on that beginning, not by routinely drilling year after year the traditional sequence of topics that begins with the parts of speech and ends with complex sentences, but by helping the students discover and understand and appreciate their innate language abilities.

"Grammar" need not be synonymous with diagramming or drillwork or memorizing rules; studying grammar can also mean thoughtful discussion of choices in generating and combining and manipulating sentences—at every level of the curriculum. O'Hare asserts that "most teachers of writing either ignore or neglect the importance of syntactic manipulative ability" (p. 75). Surely he is wrong. We do understand its importance. But we have been misled into thinking we should somehow be able to teach such skills without giving our students a conscious understanding of grammar, the system of syntax, in any systematic way. We have been warned so often against teaching grammar for its own sake, we are even wary about asking our students to learn basic terminology. We haven't learned, as Jim Corder puts it, "to use grammar as a sprightly instrument in composition."[17] Nor have we been encouraged to do so.

Is there room in the composition class for that "sprightly instrument"? Of course. Grammar is there whether we like it or not. The question is, do we acknowledge its presence and its importance to our teaching? The alchemists have been in charge long enough. Nothing is more important to our students than an understanding of language, the mark of their humanity, which they use every hour of every day—if not in reading and writing, then in speaking and listening and thinking. Our goal should be to help them understand consciously the system they know subconsciously as native speakers, to teach them the necessary categories and labels that will enable them to think about and talk about their language, so that when they use it consciously, as they do in writing, they will do so with control and grace and enthusiasm.

NOTES

1. Julia S. Falk, "Language Acquisition and the Teaching and Learning of Writing," *College English*, 41 (December, 1979), 446.

2. Dean Memering, "Forward to the Basics," *College English*, 39 (January, 1978), 559. Most of what Memering has to say about going forward, not backwards, to the basics makes good sense. He believes in the sentence as the basic unit of composition; he extols the merits of sentence combining and sentence generating; he urges us "to go *forward* to a literary and rhetorical appreciation of the sentence" (p. 561).

3. Franklyn S. Hoyt, "Grammar in the Elementary Curriculum." *Teachers College Record*, 7 (November, 1906), 473–494.

4. Louis W. Rapeer, "The Problem of Formal Grammar in Elementary Education," *The Journal of Educational Psychology*, 4 (March, 1913), 124–317.

5. William Asker, "Does Knowledge of Formal Grammar Function?" *School and Society* (January 27, 1923), 109–111.

6. D. Segal and N. R. Barr, "Relation of Achievement in Formal Grammar to Achievement in Applied Grammar," *Journal of Educational Research*, 12 (December, 1926), 401–402.

7. Percival M. Symonds, "Practice versus Grammar in Learning of Correct English Usage," *Journal of Educational Psychology*, 22 (February, 1931), 81–95.

8. Ellen Frogner, "Grammar Approach versus Thought Approach in Teaching Sentence Structure," *English Journal*, 28 (September, 1939), 518–526.

9. Roland J. Harris, "An Experimental Inquiry into the Functions and Value of Formal Grammar in the Teaching of Written English to Children Aged Twelve to Fourteen." Unpublished Ph.D. dissertation, University of London, 1962. (Summarized in Richard Braddock, Richard Lloyd-Jones, and Lowell Schoer, *Research in Written Composition* [Champaign, Ill.: National Council of Teachers of English, 1963], pp. 70–83.)

10. The textbooks were published in 1939.

11. Mary Elizabeth Fowler, *Teaching Language, Composition, and Literature* (New York: McGraw-Hill Book Company, 1965), p. 131.

12. Walter Loban, Margaret Ryan, and James R. Squire, *Teaching Language and Literature, Grades Seven–Twelve*, 2nd edition (New York: Harcourt Brace and World, 1969).

13. Stephen N. Judy, *Explorations in the Teaching of Secondary English* (New York: Dodd, Mead & Company, 1974).

14. Urbana, Ill.: National Council of Teachers of English, 1973.

15. Donald A. Daiker, Andrew Kerek, and Max Morenberg, *The Writer's Options* (New York: Harper & Row, 1979).

16. The O'Hare experiment was a replication of an earlier sentence-combining study by John Mellon that required students to learn certain transformational formulas. O'Hare's version eliminated that aspect of the experiment.

17. Jim W. Corder, "Outhouses, Weather Changes, and the Return to Basics in English Education," *College English*, 38 (January, 1977), 480.

11   *Use Definite, Specific, Concrete Language*

RICHARD OHMANN

My title is Rule 12 from Strunk and White's *The Elements of Style,* and it probably comes as close as any precept to claiming the unanimous endorsement of writing teachers. After E. D. Hirsch Jr., in *The Philosophy of Composition,* develops his principle of "relative readability," grounding it in historical and psychological evidence, he turns for support to "the accumulated wisdom of the handbooks." (The ones he chooses are Strunk and White, Crews, McCrimmon, Lucas, Gowers.) He reduces their wisdom to ten or a dozen maxims each: there is much overlap from book to book, but only two maxims appear in nearly the same form in all five books, and my title is also one of those two.[1]

Does anyone besides me feel uneasy when Strunk and White begin exemplifying this reasonable advice? For "A period of unfavorable weather set in," they substitute "It rained every day for a week." The rewrite is indeed more definite, specific, and concrete, and less pompous to boot. But it doesn't say the same thing, and in that difference there is a loss as well as a gain, especially if the writer means to relate the weather to some undertaking rather than just describing it. The original conveys—however inadequately—a more complex idea. The same is true when "He showed satisfaction as he took possession of his well-earned reward" becomes for Strunk and White "He grinned as he pocketed the coin."

In this essay I want to look at the way some authors of textbooks show students how to be definite, specific, and concrete. The questions I have in mind as I do so are whether in teaching a skill like this we may inadvertently suggest to students that they be less inquiring and less intelligent than they are capable of being, and whether the teaching of basic skills is an ideological activity. To bring suspense down to a tolerable level, let me reveal now that my answer to both questions is yes.

I will examine just three textbooks, chosen not as bad examples—they seem to me lively, serious, and honest—but for these reasons: They are current

From *College English* 41 (1979): 390–97.

(1978). They are second editions, an indication of acceptance in the market. Their authors teach in a large city university, a community college in a large northern city, and two community colleges in a southern town and a southern city; such institutions are close to the center of the freshmen composition industry. All three textbooks give unusually ample attention to style, and in particular to the matters I am concerned with here.

I will look first at the recently published second edition of David Skwire and Frances Chitwood, *Student's Book of College English* (Glencoe Press), and refer to a section in it on "Specific Details" (pp. 347–49). Skwire and Chitwood introduce the section by saying "The use of specific details is the most direct way to avoid abstract writing." (And students *should* avoid it, since "abstract writing is the main cause of bored readers" [p. 346].) Detail is a plus. In fact, "within reason, the more specific the details, the better the writing." "Within reason" means that the detail must be relevant and neither obvious nor trivial. To illustrate, they offer three passages, labeled "Abstract (weak)," "More Specific (better)," and "Still More Specific (much better)." Here are the first and third.

1. Abstract (weak)

    The telephone is a great scientific achievement, but it can also be a great inconvenience. Who could begin to count the number of times that phone calls have come from unwelcome people or on unwelcome occasions? Telephones make me nervous.

3. Still More Specific (much better)

    The telephone is a great scientific achievement, but it can also be a great big headache. More often than not, that cheery ringing in my ear brings messages from the Ace Bill Collecting Agency, my mother (who is feeling snubbed for the fourth time that week), salesmen of encyclopedias and magazines, solicitors for the Policemen's Ball and Disease of the Month Foundation, and neighbors complaining about my dog. That's not to mention frequent wrong numbers— usually for someone named "Arnie." The calls always seem to come at the worst times, too. They've interrupted steak dinners, hot tubs, Friday night parties, and Saturday morning sleep-ins. There's no escape. Sometimes I wonder if there are any telephones in padded cells. (pp. 348–49)

Consider now how revision has transformed the style of the first passage. Most obviously, one generalization—"unwelcome people"—disappears entirely, to be replaced by a list of eight people or types of people the writer doesn't want to hear from; and another generalization—"unwelcome occasions"—is changed to "worst times," then amplified in another list. Seriation has become the main principle of structure. When items are placed in a series, the writer implies that they are alike in some respect. But in what respect? Here the angry neighbors and possessive mother are placed on par with salesmen and others connected to the writer only through the cash nexus. Are the callers unwelcome because the writer does not get along with his or her family and neighbors, or for a less personal reason: that businesses and other organizations in pursuit of money use the phone as a means of access to it? The answer may be both, of course, but in expanding the idea of "unwelcome people," Skwire and Chitwood add no insight to it. The specific details close off analysis.

The same holds for their treatment of "unwelcome occasions." An occasion is a time that is socially defined and structured: a party or a steak dinner, yes, but sleep and a bath are more private activities, hardly occasions. Of course a phone call is usually as unwelcome in the middle of a bath as during a party. My point is that in changing "occasions" to "times" and letting detail do the work, the germ of an idea has been lost: the idea that we like to control our own social time, and that the telephone allows other people to intervene and impose *their* structure. What the details communicate instead is a loose feeling of harassment—easier to visualize, more specific, but certainly not more precise in thought.

Other changes have a similar effect. "Headache" is more sensory than "inconvenience," but less exact, and personal rather than social. The phrase, "cheery ringing in my ear," is a distraction, from the perspective of developing an idea: the point is not the sound, but the fact, of the intrusions and their content, the social relations they put the writer into or take him or her out of. And where the final sentence of the original implicitly raised a fruitful question (why "nervous"?), the new conclusion—"Sometimes I wonder if there are any telephones in padded cells"—closes off inquiry with a joke and points up the writer's idiosyncrasy rather than the social matter that is under discussion.

On the level of speech acts, too, the rewrite personalizes, moves away from social analysis. In the first passage, emphasis falls on the general claims made about phones and the people who use them and are used by them. The rewrite buries those claims in a heap of reports of "my" experience, reports for which only the writer need vouch. The speaker of an assertion must be in a position to make it, or it isn't "felicitous," in Austin's terms. (I cannot felicitously assert that there is life in the next galaxy.) The writer of the second passage *risks* less by moving quickly from generalizations that require support from history and social analysis, to those that stand on private terrain. This reduction in scope accords well with the impression given by the rewrite of a person incapable of coping with events, victimized by others, fragmented, distracted—a kind of likable schlemiel. He or she may be a less "boring" writer, but also a less venturesome and more isolated person, the sort who chatters on in a harmless, gossipy way without much purpose or consequence: a *character*.

If a student showed me the first passage (as the outline of a composition or the beginning of a draft), I would want to say that it expresses an interesting idea, inadequately handled to be sure, but begging for a kind of development that amplification by detail, alone, can never supply. The contradiction with which it begins is familiar but perplexing: How is it that so many of our scientists' "achievements," with all their promise of efficiency and ease, turn out to be inconvenient or worse in the long run? Why does an invention designed to give people control over their lives make many of us feel so often in the control of others? Why does a device for bringing people together (as its proprietors are constantly telling us in commercials) in fact so often serve as the carrier of frictions and antagonisms?

To make any headway with such questions it is necessary to stay with the abstractions awhile, penetrate them, get at the center of the contradictions they express, not throw them out in favor of lists of details. "Achievement": By whom? Who calls "science" into being and engineers its discoveries into commodities? The telephone as we have it is a hundred-year-long achievement of patent lawyers and corporate planners more than of Alexander Graham Bell. "Inconvenience": For whom? Not for the salesmen and bill collectors, presumably. And certainly not for executives barricaded behind secretaries making sure the boss talks only with people he wants to talk with, and at a time of his choosing. The telephone represents a network of social relations embedded in history. In order to gain any leverage on the badly expressed contradiction of the first passage, it is necessary to unpack some of those relations. Piling on the details, as in the rewrite, may create a kind of superficial interest, but no gain in insight. The strategy, as exemplified here, is a strategy for sacrificing thought to feckless merriment.

Skwire and Chitwood are concerned with adding detail. In the section I wish to consider from Winston Weathers and Otis Winchester's *The New Strategy of Style* (McGraw-Hill), the authors show how to make detail more specific. They do this under the heading of "Texture" (pp. 135–44), explaining that different subjects call for different textures: the simpler the subject, the more elaborate the texture. The maxim begs the question to an extent, since whether or not a given subject is simple or complex depends partly upon the diction used in exploring it. But apparently the first passage below is about a simple subject, since as the authors take it through four revisions their instructions all advise elaboration of texture. (*"Make your nouns more specific."* *"Make your adjectives more specific."*) Passage 2 is the second of the rewrites.

1. The country store was an interesting place to visit. In the very heart of the city, it had the air of a small-town grocery store combined with a feed and hardware supply house. There were flower seeds and milk churns, coal buckets and saddle blankets, all mixed together. Walking down the crowded aisles, you felt you had gone back to the past—to the time of pot-belly stoves and kerosene lamps and giant pickle jars. You could smell the grain, you could touch the harnesses, you could even sit down in the old wooden chair. When you finally left the store and were once more in the activity of the city, you felt as you sometimes do when you come out of an old movie into the bright light of reality.

2. Charlie's Country Store was a *spell-binding* emporium. In the very heart of Minneapolis, Charlie's had the *dubious* charm of a small town grocery combined with a feed and hardware supply house. There were *zinnia* seeds and milk churns, *shiny* coal buckets and *garish* saddle blankets, all mixed together. Walking down its *quaint*

passageways—*narrow, poorly lighted, but nevertheless immaculate*—you felt you had gone back to nineteenth-century America—to the lost years, the *faintly remembered* days of *squat* pot-belly stoves and *sturdy* kerosene lamps and *rotund, ceramic* crocks—meant for pickles or pastries. You could smell the cornmeal, you could touch the *leather* harnesses, you could even sit in the *stern* wooden rocker. And when you finally left this anachronism—and were once more in the bustle of the city—you felt as you sometimes do when you come out of an old cinema into the *blinding* glare of a *rocket-age* reality. (pp. 135–38; emphasis in original)

Passage 2 is the result of making nouns and adjectives more specific and also (though Weathers and Winchester don't say so) of adding adjectives. Setting aside some words that might be criticized as elegant variations (e.g., "emporium," which suggests a grander establishment than is implied by the rest of the passage), consider the ways the description has become more specific.

1) The scene is particularized. The store is now Charlie's; the city, Minneapolis; the past, nineteenth-century America. Note that this change blurs the two main contrasts in which the description is grounded, country versus city and present versus past. For the sharpening of these contrasts, it does not matter whose store it is or in what city, or whether the visitor travels back in imagination to America or England. Some of the other specifics are equally irrelevant: zinnia seeds, pastries, cornmeal. The point, I take it, is not the kind of flowers people used to grow, but that they had gardens; not what kind of grain they used, but that they did more of the work of preparing their own food, and that the arts of preserving, packaging, and marketing were in a primitive state of development compared to our present attainments as represented by freezers full of TV dinners and by the Golden Arches.

2) The writer's own impressions and values are foregrounded, most often adjectivally. The store is now *spell-binding*, its passageways *quaint*, and so on through "dubious charm," "faintly remembered," "stern," and "blinding." The writer has become much more of a presence, reacting, exercising taste, judging. These responses seem to issue from no particular perspective; for instance, what's "dubious" about the store's charm? They scarcely relate to the content of the original passage, certainly not to the ideas latent in it. They seem like the reflexes of a dilettantish tourist whose fugitive sensations and values clutter the picture and block analysis.

3) Similarly, the adjectives highlight the thinginess of things, their physical appearance, rather than what they are, what they meant, how life might have been organized around them. "Shiny," "garish," "poorly lighted," "squat," "sturdy," "rotund," "ceramic." The picture turns into a kind of still life, crowded with visual detail apparently valuable in itself. Such emphasis on visible surfaces, along with the esthetic perspective, draws attention to a detached present experience, dissipating the image of an earlier kind of civilization in which most people lived on farms, the family was the main productive unit, few of people's needs were commercialized, and technology was manageable and local.

Like the telephone, the objects in the country store embody social relations. And even more clearly than the initial passage about telephones, Weathers and Winchester's original version supports a sense of history, of a society that has been utterly transformed so that most of the things in the store have lost their usefulness. The society these artifacts imply—in which local people grew the grain, harvested it, ground it into flour, and baked it into bread—has given way to one in which almost all of our labor is sold in the market and controlled by employers rather than expended at our own pace and to our own plans; and almost all of our consumption takes place through markets organized not by a village merchant but by distant corporations.

Of course the first passage doesn't say what I have just said, even by implication. But in the way it sets up contrasts and in the details it presents, it provides the ground and even the need for such analysis. The student who takes Weathers and Winchester's guidance in making the passage "richer," more "vivid," and more "intense" will lose the thread of *any* analysis in a barrage of sensory impressions, irrelevant details, and personalized or random responses. Once again, the rhetorical strategy scatters thought.

With my final example I turn to the injunction to use concrete language. The textbook is the second edition of *Composition: Skills and Models*, by Sidney T. Stovall, Virginia B. Mathis, Linda C. Elliot, G. Mitchell Hagler Jr., and Mary A. Poole (Houghton Mifflin). Here are two of the passages they present for comparison in their chapter on forming a style, the first from Fielding's *Tom Jones*, and the second from Nevil Shute's *On the Beach*:

1. The charms of Sophia had not made the least impression on Blifil; not that his heart was pre-engaged, neither was he totally insensible of beauty, or had any aversion to women; but his appetites were by nature so moderate that he was easily able by philosophy, or by study, or by some other method to subdue them; and as to that passion which we have treated of in the first chapter of this book, he had not the least tincture of it in his whole composition.

But though he was so entirely free from that mixed passion of which we there treated, and of which the virtues and beauty of Sophia formed so notable an object, yet was he altogether as well furnished with some other passions that promised themselves very full gratification in the young lady's fortune. Such were avarice and ambition, which divided the dominion of his mind between them. He had more than once considered the possession of this fortune as a very desirable thing, and had entertained some distant views concerning it, but his own youth and that of the young lady, and indeed, principally a reflection that Mr. Weston might marry again and have more children, had restrained him from too hasty or too eager a pursuit.

2. He went back to bed. Tomorrow would be an anxious, trying day; he must get his sleep. In the privacy of his little curtained cabin he unlocked the safe that held the confidential books and took out the bracelet; it glowed in the synthetic light. She would love it. He put it carefully in the

breast pocket of his uniform suit. Then he went to bed again, his hand upon the fishing rod, and slept.

They surfaced again at four in the morning, just before dawn, a little to the north of Gray Harbor. No lights were visible on the shore, but as there were no towns and few roads in the district that evidence was inconclusive. They went down to periscope depth and carried on. When Dwight came to the control room at six o'clock the day was bright through the periscope and the crew off duty were taking turns to look at the desolate shore. He went to breakfast and then stood smoking at the chart table, studying the minefield chart that he already knew so well, and the well-remembered entrance to the Juan de Fuca Strait. (p. 390)

The authors have couched their discussion of style in historically relative terms. Styles change, and students will want to choose from among styles suited to contemporary life. Eighteenth-century readers could "idle" over "long sentences"; "leisure is at a premium" now. Stovall and his colleagues do not absolutely value Shute's style over Fielding's, but since they say that the earlier style would strike the modern reader as awkward, stilted, colorless, complex, plodding, tedious, and wordy, their counsel to the student is reasonably plain.

They direct their judgment partly against Fielding's long and complex sentences, partly against the quality of his diction. The latter is my concern. Stovall et al. object to phrases like "entertained some distant view" and "had not the least tincture," and especially to Fielding's dependence on the big abstractions, "passion," "virtues," "avarice," "ambition," words which "elicit no emotional response from the reader." They praise Shute for "concrete words" that give life to the passage, citing "curtained cabin," "glowed in the synthetic light," "surfaced," and "desolate shore." Later in the chapter they urge the student to "Strive for the concrete word" (pp. 390–91).

Abstract nouns refer to the world in a way quite different from concrete nouns. They do not point to a set of particulars—all curtained cabins—or to any one cabin. They are relational. For instance, in speaking of Blifil's "avarice," Fielding calls up at least the relation of a series of acts to one another (a single act of acquiring or hoarding is not enough); of Blifil's feelings to these actions and to the wealth that is their goal; of those acts and feelings to a scale of values that is socially established (avarice is a sin, and so related to salvation and damnation); and of Blifil to other people who make such judgments, as well as to people whose wealth he might covet and who would become poorer were he to become richer. The term also evokes a temporal relationship: an avaricious person like Blifil seeks to become wealthy over time, and it is this future goal that informs his conduct. Abstract nouns that characterize people do so through bundles of relationships like these.

In short, one need not adopt an eighteenth-century faculty psychology, or expect Nevil Shute to adopt it, to see that Fielding's abstract nouns give a rich social setting to Blifil's sordid intentions. This setting is made more rich as, in context, Fielding humorously brings avarice into parity with love, under the higher level abstraction of passion. (Herein another relationship, that of the narrator to his subject and his reader.) Abstractions are for Fielding a speculative and interpretive grid against which he can examine the events of the novel, and which themselves are constantly tested and modified by those events.

Shute's language in this passage, by contrast, sets his hero's actions against a background mainly of objects and of other people treated more or less as objects. The moral implications of the passage will have to be supplied by the reader. And there is no way for the narrator, given his style, to place that moral content in a dynamic relationship with social values, at least within the passage cited. This may be appropriate enough in a story from which society has literally disappeared; I do not mean to disparage Shute's diction, only to question the wisdom of commending it to students as plainly superior (for the twentieth-century reader) to Fielding's. Some important kinds of thinking can be done only with the help of abstractions.

In sum, as this textbook teaches the skill of using definite, specific, concrete language, it joins the other two in preferring realia to more abstract inquiry about realia, and to the effort to connect them. In doing so, it seems to me, the authors convey a fairly well-defined ideological picture to students. I would characterize this picture in these terms:

1. Ahistoricism. The preferred style focuses on a truncated present moment. Things and events are frozen in an image, or they pass on the wing, coming from nowhere.

2. Empiricism. The style favors sensory news, from the surfaces of things.

3. Fragmentation. An object is just what it is, disconnected from the rest of the world. The style obscures the social relations and the relations of people to nature that are embedded in all things.

4. Solipsism. The style foregrounds the writer's own perceptions: This is what I saw and felt.

5. Denial of conflict. The style typically pictures a world in which the telephone has the same meaning for all classes of people, a world whose "rocket-age reality" is just mysteriously *there*, outside the country store, a world where avarice is a superfluous and tedious concept.

Furthermore—and I think this, too, a matter of the ideology of style— the injunctions to use detail, be specific, be concrete, as applied in these books, push the student writer always toward the language that most nearly reproduces the immediate experience and away from the language that might be used to understand it, transform it, and relate it to everything else. The authors privilege a kind of revising and expanding that leaves the words themselves unexamined and untransformed. Susan Wells has suggested that Christensen's rhetoric does not open "to investigation the relations among language, vision, and their objects,"[2] but takes those relations for granted. Her comment applies well to the use of detail recommended in these textbooks.

In an epoch when so much of the language students hear or read comes from distant sources, via the media, and when so much of it is shaped by advertisers and other corporate experts to channel their thoughts and feelings and needs, I think it a special pity if English teachers are turning students away from critical scrutiny of the words in their heads, especially from those that are most heavily laden with ideology. When in the cause of clarity or liveliness we urge them toward detail, surfaces, the sensory, as mere *expansion* of ideas or even as a *substitute* for abstraction, we encourage them to accept the empirical fragmentation of consciousness that passes for common sense in our society, and hence to accept the society itself as just what it most superficially seems to be.

Yes, it is good to keep readers interested, bad to bore them. Like Hirsch's principle of readability, the injunction to be interesting is on one level a bit of self-evident practical wisdom, not to mention kindness. Whatever you are trying to accomplish through a piece of writing, you won't achieve it if the reader quits on you, or plods on in resentful tedium. But mechanically applied, the principles of interest and readability entail accepting the reader exactly as he or she is. The reader's most casual values, interests, and capacities become an inflexible measure of what to write and how to write it, a Nielsen rating for prose. What happens to the possibility of challenging or even changing the reader? If keeping readers' attention is elevated to the prime goal of our teaching, the strategies we teach may well lead toward triviality and evasion.

Yes, I also realize that most students don't handle abstractions and generalizations well. I know that they often write badly when they try, and how depressing an experience it can be to read a batch of compositions on free will or alienation or capital punishment. And I am aware of the pressure many English teachers now feel to teach basic skills, whatever they are, rather than critical inquiry.[3] But I can't believe that the best response to this pressure is valorizing the concrete, fragmented, and inconsistent worldviews that many of our students bring to college with them. Jeffrey Youdelman refers to colleagues he has heard say, "They can't handle abstraction . . . and therefore I always give them topics like 'describe your favorite room.'" Youdelman continues: "Already stuck in a world of daily detail, with limited horizons and stunted consciousness, students are forced deeper into their solipsistic prison."[4] Like him, I am concerned that in the cause of improving their skills, we may end up increasing their powerlessness.

NOTES

1. The other is, avoid padding. *The Philosophy of Composition* (Chicago: University of Chicago Press, 1977), 148–49.

2. "Classroom Heuristics and Empiricism," *College English* 39 (1977): 471.

3. Obviously critical inquiry requires both abstractions and details, and a fluid exchange between them. I hope not to be taken as merely inverting the values I have criticized and recommending the abstract and general over the concrete.

4. "Limiting Students: Remedial Writing and the Death of Open Admissions," *College English* 39 (1978): 563–64. Anyone interested in the politics of rhetoric and composition should read this excellent article and that of Susan Wells, cited earlier. I consider the present essay a supplement to theirs.

12   *Defining Complexity*

JOSEPH M. WILLIAMS

The first problem we have to resolve when we want to define what we mean by mature and complex is not so much how we define those words but why we want to define them in the first place. I assume that as teachers, we want to explain something about mature and complex styles so that we can use those terms when we teach our students how to write effectively. If so, we can exclude purely theoretical or speculative reasons, reasons that are remote—or seemingly remote—from what we want to do with those words.

One thing we want to do is establish values for simple and complex styles. We want to know when simple is too simple or not simple enough, when complex is too complex or not complex enough, whether mature means complex, and vice versa. How we define those words would establish the values we would use when we decide what to teach our students and how to evaluate them. And since we need some means to evaluate whether anything we are doing leads our students to do what we want them to do, we need a way to describe simple and complex styles in quantitative terms. We need some way to measure simple and complex styles.

Now in some ways, all this is self-evident, indeed. But we ought to be very certain that when we use these terms, we use them in ways that let us address specific and final goals. Whatever we ask of our students while they are in our classrooms, we want them eventually to become adults who communicate easily and clearly to readers who do not have to struggle to understand what those writers mean. This may seem even more self-evident than what I said before, but in light of some recent data that have been offered as evidence of improved, i.e., more complex and therefore more mature prose styles, I don't think that it is at all a simple matter to relate to that goal the unexamined ways that many of us have been using the terms simple and complex.

There are one or two more preliminary issues here. We have to be aware that what we measure in a prose style we can find in at least three places. First, we can find it entirely in the text. That is, we can look for features that

From *College English* 40 (1979): 595–609.

we can count entirely in what is there on the page. This is the way most of those who analyze sentences into their T-units seem to measure styles and how they grow.[1] But it strikes me as not a very useful way for us to measure simple and complex styles because it does not obviously bear on our final goal. Those numbers they accumulate do not tell us whether a writer has written clearly something that his or her readers can understand easily. It is a matter I will return to.

The most salient place we can look to understand what complex and simple styles do is in the ways we experience a text, how easy or how difficult it is to process the text. We would look into the way we behave when we read—it is the objective of many who do psycholinguistics. Just as obviously, once we discover those features of style that determine whether we process a text more or less easily, then we can turn back to the text and count what we find there. But we have to begin with how readers experience a text—not with arbitrary numbers.

Perhaps a less obvious place we can look for the ways in which simple and complex styles relate to how we behave is in the way the writer writes. A very large literature exists on how readers read, on how they respond to, store, memorize, and process different syntactic structures. But so far as I know, nothing has been written on how difficult it is for us to write in a difficult, that is, in a complex style. Intuitively, I think that we write in excessively complex styles much more naturally and unself-consciously than we write in simple styles. Nothing else would explain why so many adults write so badly. This would seem to be a matter we ought to think about when we try to define complex and mature or simple and immature styles. If the task we set for our students requires that they behave in complex ways in order to write in complex ways, then it is something we ought to anticipate. And if we find that they write in complex ways because they are behaving in simple ways, then it is something we ought to wonder about.

One more preliminary point. It is easy for us to pick out syntactic structures that are obviously complex in that they are difficult to process—self-embedded relative clauses, for example:

The man the woman the dog bit married left.

But we have very little occasion to teach students how to avoid patterns like that because they never use them in the first place. What we ought to attend to are those patterns that occur often enough in adult prose to constitute serious problems in adult prose. We ought to be very careful to select those patterns that occur frequently enough to repay us if we concentrate on them.

Now, given all this, I would like to discuss the ways in which some among us have recently described complex and mature styles and identify those ways to describe them that would most repay our efforts if we concentrated on them.

Traditional grammars define complex and simple in ways that we all understand, but we also know that given a specific semantic structure, we can process that structure more easily as a series of clauses constituting a complex or compound-complex sentence than as a series of phrases constituting a simple sentence, even when the sentence elements are ordered in the same relative way:

> The government's investigation into the shipment of the wheat by the exporter was met by his refusal in regard to an examination of his method of payments for its domestic transportation.

> The government investigated how the wheat was shipped by the exporter, but he refused to let the government examine how he paid to have the wheat transported domestically.

In the past, we have implicitly equated complex sentences with mature sentences because we have assumed that the more ideas we express in a sentence, the more semantically complex a sentence must be and the more subordinate clauses it is likely to contain. But if we begin with a single semantic structure (no matter how complex) and encode that structure in clauses or in phrases, in complex or in simple sentences, then we ought to recognize that the simple sentence is more cognitively complex than the complex sentence.

So if we try to measure a complex style by the number of dependent clauses in a sentence, then we have a paradoxical situation in which the more complex the style is, the more easily we process it; and the simpler the style, the less easily we process it. (There is a point where this is not quite true, but in most cases it is.)

On the other hand, we find it very difficult to express every idea in its full clausal form rather than its more abstract phrasal form. Indeed, I required a good deal of effort to write this paper in the way I have written it. Some of you may have tumbled to what I am attempting to do here. You will discover how difficult it is if you try it. In any event, given the problems with the traditional ways we define simple and complex, we would do well to ignore them when we try to define simple and complex for our purposes.

An even less clearly relevant way we can try to measure complex styles is by means of the T-unit criteria I referred to earlier. It is clear that as writers mature, they write longer T-units, particularly longer clauses. But however these numbers change, we have no direct way to relate any of them to any threshholds we might have in the way we respond to sentences composed of more or less complex T-units. (I am, of course, measuring simple and complex styles here only in terms of larger and smaller numbers.)

Most of those who measure how well they have taught their students to create big sentences out of little sentences have simply assumed that bigger is better. But we have no idea at all whether the numbers they report relate to anything we might be interested in: whether adults will be better writers if they make lots of long sentences out of lots and lots of small ones. We have just seen how we can increase the number of words in a clause if we reduce the number of clauses. But if we do, we only make the sentence more difficult to process. So T-units provide no straightforward way to understand how we respond to these numbers, much less how difficult it is for a writer to achieve them.

And under any circumstances, if we encourage the idea that longer is better, then we tacitly encourage a more rather than less cognitively complex style. But what we need least of all in the style of adults who have to write in order to hold a job is a more rather than less complex style. Every program that attempts to teach adults how to write, adults who have graduated from college and hold even modestly responsible positions, every one of these programs concentrates on the ways that those adults can write less complex, simpler clauses; not longer, but shorter sentences. Every such program attempts specifically to undo what sentence combiners specifically want to do.

This is a case where we have not only failed to relate numbers to anything except other numbers, but we may even be inviting trouble if we do not stop to think about the way these increasing numbers may result in exactly the opposite style we want: not clear, easily understood prose, but the confused and prolix sentences that too many adult writers already write.

A way to measure complex styles not too different from one that counts clauses and measures T-units is that devised by Rudolf Flesch.[2] He offers a scale of simple to complex styles that depends on a formula that factors X-number of words per sentence with Y-number of syllables per word to produce a scale that will tell us how readable a text is. Of course, we ought not overlook the fact that what the sentence combiners strive to teach their students to do — produce longer and more complex sentences — Flesch views as an unqualified bane of clear prose.

In fact, Flesch has identified a characteristic of prose that is too complex to read easily — long sentences and long words. But these are only the symptoms of an unclear style; they do not cause a style to be unclear and difficult to process. If we merely tell our students to use short words in short sentences, we will not get at those underlying reasons and our students will only restrict their vocabulary and limit what they will be able to express. And, under any circumstances, if we really took Flesch seriously, our students would spend more time counting than they would writing. So if Flesch has identified a symptom of a style that can become too complex for us to process easily, it is not a metric that provides us with a way to *teach* a clear style.

I mention a fourth way to measure complex styles because it was for a time used extensively as a way to inquire into the matter of cognitively complex syntax. In the last several years, though, it has been generally rejected as a criterion by which to measure styles. And that is a metric that merely counts the number of times a base structure has been transformed before it becomes a surface structure.[3]

For example, these two sentences seem to have identical surface structures, but to get to that surface structure, the second requires us to transform its remote structure one more time than the first:

(1) John is eager (John pleases someone)
 → John is eager   to please someone
 → John is eager   to please.

(2) (For someone to please John) is easy.
 → It   is easy (for someone to please John)
 → It   is easy   to please John
 → John   is easy   to please.

In fact, some who have researched this problem reported that the second *was* in fact more difficult to process. But as we shall see, it was probably not for the reason they thought. It is now generally accepted that rules such as these, the kind proposed by Chomsky and others of that school, relate not at all to the way the mind actually processes language.

Surface-structures, however, do seem to determine more strongly how we process sentences. And one very widely discussed and tested criterion is the degree to which a tree-structure branches to the left or to the right. It has been generally assumed in this area that as we process sentences, we have to store in our short-term memories the fact that we must anticipate structures to come, those parts of a sentence that will close a grammatical structure that we are at any moment processing, and that the more we have to store and the longer we have to store it, the more difficult it is for us to process a sentence. It is the theory first proposed by Victor Yngve, a theory which he named the "depth hypothesis."[4]

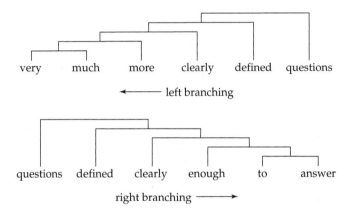

In the first, each successive word requires that we continue to store the fact that we must subsequently close the whole phrase. Each word postpones the moment when that will happen, and so we are required to hold in our short-term memory an increasing number of grammatical bits. The other does not require us to anticipate and store nearly as many grammatical bits and, to that degree, it is claimed, is easier for us to process.

But two reasons argue against the position that we ought to take any of this seriously when we teach our students how to write. First, few of our students have any serious problems with sentences that branch too extensively to the left. If anything, they string their sentences out too much to the right. The pattern that comes closest to a left-branching structure is an excessively long subject, somewhat less frequently a modifier that intervenes between a subject and verb:

> The inability of college students to write clearly and directly in their tests and term papers, as reported in recent newspaper stories, is serious.

But that is a problem easy to correct and not a serious one in the first place.

The other fact that argues against the hypothesis about left-branching patterns is that the evidence that supports it is at best ambiguous. A number of researchers have recently argued that it is not significantly more difficult for us to process structures that branch to the left rather than structures that branch to the right.[5]

A considerably more interesting index to a complex style correlates semantic, syntactic, and what are currently known as functional components of sentence structure. A growing body of evidence suggests that readers of English typically process a sentence assuming that the subject of the sentence coincides with the agent or source of what the verb (or verb plus what completes it) refers to. It has been more recently suggested that we even metaphorically transform instruments into agents in sentences such as[6]

Williams' argument does not persuade me he is right.

An agent-subject sentence that would correspond to this is

Williams does not persuade me with his argument that he is right.

I do not have the space here to explore this general position in detail, but one or two examples might illustrate my point. We seem to process in different ways passive sentences that can and cannot be reversed. A sentence such as

The boy was hit by his sister.

can be reversed in an active sentence:

The boy hit his sister.

A sentence such as

The cake was cut by the boy.

cannot be reversed in an active sentence:

The cake cut the boy.

The passive sentence that we *can* reverse (The boy was hit by his sister) is more difficult to process, retain, memorize, whatever, than passive sentences that we *cannot* reverse (The cake was cut by the boy). The reason for this seems to be that we tentatively assume that all subjects are agents, unless some aspect of semantic or syntactic structure signals otherwise. If the agent or source of what is happening in a sentence immediately precedes the verb, then that coincides with what the reader tacitly searches for. If a different grammatical-semantic pattern occurs, the reader must call on a second tactic to process the sentence.

And this way we process sentences would explain why we process

John is eager to please.

more easily than we process

John is easy to please.

In the first, *John* is the agent of both *eager* and *please*. The grammatical structure corresponds to the semantic structure. But in the second, *John* is not the agent of *please* but its goal: some unspecified person pleases him. And what is easy is not John but the phrase *To please John*:

> To please John   is easy.

In this sentence, the grammatical structure contradicts the semantic structure at every point.

On these grounds, we might then want to define as complex those styles that regularly require of us this secondary tactic, because this secondary tactic requires of us a more cognitively complex way to process the sentence.

There is also some evidence that speaks to the corresponding matter of verbs and what they refer to. A very common pattern in mature prose, i.e., the prose written by adults, is for some word other than the verb to refer to what the agent or source does or is. The most common pattern that reflects this is the noun derived from a verb, a noun we create when we "nominalize" a verb. We can recall the pair of sentences I used to illustrate the different ways traditional grammars distinguish simple and complex sentences:

> The government's attempt at an investigation into the corporation's handling of the contract was met by its refusal to allow an examination of its assignment of costs. [one clause = simple sentence]

> The government attempted to investigate how the corporation handled the contract, but it refused to allow the government to examine the way it assigned costs. [((one main clause + one subordinate clause) + (one main clause + one subordinate clause)) = one compound-complex sentence]

Perhaps we can illustrate how these semantic and grammatical structures may deviate from one another with a pair of shorter sentences more schematically arranged:

NOUN SUBJECT AGENT₁	VERB ACTION₁	PRONOUN SUBJECT AGENT₂	VERB ACTION₂	NOUN SUBJECT/ OBJECT GOAL₂/ AGENT₃	VERB ACTION₃
The scientists	analyzed	what	caused	the genes	to mutate

The causes	of the mutation	of the genes	received	analysis	from the scientists
SUBJECT ACTION₂ NOUN	OBJECT ACTION₃ NOUN	OBJECT GOAL₂/ AGENT₃ NOUN	OBJECT ACTION₁ NOUN	OBJECT AGENT₁ NOUN	

When the subject does not express the agent and the verb does not express what that agent does, then the syntactic and semantic structures of a sentence become to that degree even more complex, if, again, we define complex as "more difficult to process." When subjects and verbs consistently fail to coincide with what those agents do, then the sentences become significantly more difficult for us to process.

In the middle 1960s, E. B. Coleman researched the problem a bit and demonstrated that sentences with frequent nouns derived from verbs were significantly more difficult for a reader to process than sentences which expressed the same ideas with verbs.[7] My colleague, Rosemary Hake, of Chicago State University, and I have investigated the problem from a somewhat different perspective. We have created papers in which we systematically displaced agents from the subject position and what those agents do from the verb position. They differed in roughly the same way that the sentences [just discussed] differed. We gave these passages on different days to about seventy typists of different levels of skill and background. They typed the versions in which the semantic agents and grammatical subjects coincided about 15 percent faster than the versions in which they did not and made about 25 percent fewer errors (evidence, we might note, for an economic as well as aesthetic basis for a clear and concise style).

If we reflect on these patterns a moment, we can understand why a reader will more easily read a style in which agents and subjects, verbs and what those agents do, coincide, than a style in which they do not.

First, since subjects and agents tend to coincide in the vast number of languages in the world, we might assume that their nexus is one of the "natural ways" that reinforce what the sentence is about to express.[8] The particular semantic structures that regularly coincide with subjects and verbs are, of course, language-specific. What one language expresses as a noun, another may express as a verb. But it is still a very regular pattern for the *perceived* semantic agency to be signalled by the subject position.

In English, the way that the agent relates to what it does is most directly and immediately reflected in the way the verb immediately and directly follows the subject-agent. The semantic structure is further reinforced by the fact that the agent is expressed by a particular form class, a noun, and what the agent does is expressed by a different form class, a verb. Thus the way an agent and what it does semantically relate to one another is redundantly signalled by at least three grammatical structures:

(1) by the grammatically defined roles of subject and what is predicated of it;

(2) in English, by the sequence of subject-agent first and what it does second;

(3) by form class: the subject/agent is a noun and what it does is a verb.

As I said, the same semantic import may be differently encoded from language to language, but speakers of particular languages must develop—or at least they seem to develop—habitual ways, particular tactics which they use to process sentences most efficiently.[9]

In short, the clearest style is one in which the grammatical structures of a sentence most redundantly support the perceived semantic structure. The more consistently the grammatical structure reinforces—or reflects—the semantic structure, the more easily a reader takes up that semantic structure.

It is not always possible—as demonstrated by the way in which this sentence opens—for us to write sentences in which every agent occurs in the subject position and precedes what it does, in which what that agent does is expressed in a verb directly following a subject/agent. We cannot write effectively about some abstract topics if we can never use an abstract noun derived from a verb to express what that verb expresses. We have to write some sentences in the passive voice in order to create a coherent sequence of sentences.

But it is possible for us to come far closer to this kind of maximally redundant pattern than most writers in fact do. In what you have read so far, I have come very close, and I intend to continue in this pattern until I reach the last few pages of what I have to say, when I will change my style so that I can make a different point.

I do not doubt at all that this kind of style is easier to read and understand than styles in which the agents consistently do not correlate with subjects, and verbs consistently do not correlate with what those agents do. I know for a fact that this structurally redundant style is a style that we can teach and that students who are not beyond the stage of freshman English can profit greatly if they concentrate on these matters. I know for a fact that we find the worst kind of public prose unintelligible largely because its grammatical and semantic structures do not correlate in the ways I have described. I know for a fact that adult writers understand most clearly of all how these patterns work in what they write, and that once they understand the principles behind what I have been describing here, they can change how they write so that they can make those grammatical and semantic structures coincide, and thereby write in a way that they instantly perceive to be much clearer.[10]

So this last point—the way semantic and grammatical structures do or do not coincide—would appear to be a very salient metric of a complex style, if we agree to define complex in a special way—as the style in which grammatical structures systematically fail to support semantic structures and thereby make sentences relatively more difficult for us to read. The features that create this kind of style are very frequent in modern prose; they are crucial to the way we process sentences; they are structures that we can teach our students to avoid; and we can demonstrate what happens when they do not. So as a metric of complex and simple styles, it meets every one of our criteria.

Unfortunately, this still means that we must pejoratively equate a complex style with a mature style, because most mature writers write in this way. On the other hand, I think that what I am doing right now is also extremely complex. I have deliberately shaped my grammatical and semantic structures so that they coincide in the ways that I have described to a very high degree—over 99 percent (excluding agentive nouns such as *writer*, *student*, *researcher*, *reader*, and so on). I have squirmed at an occasional awkward phrase. But I think I have demonstrated my point: It is possible to communicate fairly complex ideas in a style that is, from the point of view of the reader, easy to read, but which from the point of view of the writer is, I can assure you, extremely complex to write.

I have specifically avoided all nouns derived from verbs or adjectives. Indeed, this is the first academic discourse in the history of perhaps any language that has ever done so. I have used many abstract words, some of which ultimately derive from Latin verbs. But in English, they relate very remotely to those verbs. If pressed, I could rephrase the semantic structure in a way that would avoid these nouns.[11]

It is true that not all genres of discourse allow this degree of what I will call an agent-action style. Many writers believe that scientific journals demand that we write in an objective, third-person, abstract-noun sort of style. It is to some degree true. But it is a greatly exaggerated notion, if we believe what editors have to say, for few editors of scientific journals have ever claimed that contributors may not write in the first person, a style that ordinarily does not encourage lots of abstract nouns. Bad scientific prose is bad to the degree that it departs from an agent-action style, and most editors recognize that fact.

But regardless of whether anyone believes that this kind of straightforward prose is or is not favored by such journals, it is the kind of prose that our students should begin with, the kind of prose they should become most sensitive to in order for us to encourage them to write in the clearest and most direct way possible when the occasion demands and for them to learn to protect themselves from all the bad prose they will have to read when they become adults. They do not have to be taught to write long, complex sentences. They will, willy-nilly.

I want to mention one more point where structures must coincide in order to create a maximally efficient style. I could have devoted this entire paper to the subject. And that is the way in which those structures that have come to be known as rheme-theme or topic-comment sequences coincide with subjects and noun/agents and the verb phrases that follow. The topic is that element in the sentence from which the rest of the sentence flows. The topic ordinarily communicates the most familiar, the previously mentioned, the implied ideas. In most languages, the topic regularly coincides with the subject.[12] But even in English, it need not:

In regard to style, there are still many unknowns.

The topic is *style* but *style* is not the subject. The topic is regularly the first noun in the sentence, but again, it need not be:

In this paper, style has been the main subject.

Style is not the first noun, but it is still the topic.

The comment expresses the new ideas, ordinarily that which cannot be deduced from what is assumed or already mentioned. And the end of the comment, the end of the clause, emphasizes that new information most strongly. So in one way, the first part of a sentence is least important because it is most familiar, and the last part is most important because it is most heavily stressed.

On the basis of some preliminary evidence collected by one of my graduate students, it appears that a series of consistent topics is judged to be more clearly written than a series of sentences in which the topic is not consistently selected. And when we reinforce a consistent topic with a consistent nexus between subject and agent, with a consistent nexus between verbs and what the agents do, then the style appears to become the clearest and most efficient of all.

I should point out that by consistent topic, I do not mean simply the same or repeated topic. The matter is consistently more complicated than that, but not so complicated that we cannot teach it and our students cannot learn it. Here is an example of what I mean. The second paragraph maintains a consistent topic in the form of a largely repeated topic:

(a) An awareness of transient angle-closure glaucoma in central retinal vein occlusion is of obvious importance and must be suspected if no iris bombé is present and if the uninvolved eye has a normal angle. Visualization of the fundus is indicated using topical glycerin and dilating agents if necessary. Once the diagnosis is made, treatment with cyclopegics and carbonic anhydrase inhibitors is warranted. Surgical intervention is not indicated unless medical management is unsuccessful.

(b) If iris bombé is not present and the uninvolved eye has a normal angle, the physician must be aware of transient angle-closure glaucoma. If necessary, he should use topical glycerin and dilating agents in order to visualize the fundus. Once he diagnoses this condition, he should treat it with cyclopegics and carbonic anhydrase inhibitors. Only if he cannot manage it through medication should he consider surgery.

Here is an example where the consistent topics in (b) belong to the same set of agents. (Because this is excerpted from an actual case, I delete some words.)

(a) In carrying out the sale, the normal invitation for bids procedure was followed on the part of X. However, we found a lack of policy coordination among the agencies of the Department responsible for sales and a lack of documentation showing methods used to determine acceptable sales prices or policy considerations which might have influenced sales determinations. Attempts were being made by several agencies and officials to find outlets for all or most of the stock through different channels, including donations and sales. However, these attempts were not coordinated, resulting in issuance of conflicting information on the agencies' and X's intentions.

(b) When it carried out the sale, X followed its normal procedure of inviting bids. However, we found that the agencies of the Department responsible for sales did not coordinate their actions or document what they did to show how they determined prices or set policies that might have influenced their sales. Several different agencies and officials tried to find outlets for all or most of the stock through dif-

ferent channels, including donations and sales. However, they did
not coordinate these attempts. As a result, X and the other agencies
issued conflicting information on what they intended to do.

There are, of course, a great many more ways in which styles can be made
unnecessarily complex: exceptionally long sentences, lots of deadwood, obscure words. One place where syntax and narrative intersect is in the way in
which we order events. Compare these two:

Visualization of the fundus is indicated using topical glycerin and dilating agents if necessary.

If necessary, the physician should use topical glycerin and dilating
agents in order to visualize the fundus.

Disregarding the *visualize* meaning "look at," we can see that the second sentence follows the logical sequence of what happens: *the physician needs . . . , he
uses . . . , he looks at. . . .* In the first, the order is precisely reversed.

But if we are concerned with the most general problems, problems that
let us give students rules of style that are as general as the problems they
will confront once they become functioning adults, then what I have described here in regard to subjects and agents, etc., is entirely pertinent, more
pertinent, I would argue, than any other index to complex and simple styles.
As criteria, clauses-per-T-unit, words-per-clause, left-branching or right-
branching syntactic trees, self-embedded clauses, and so on are either irrelevant, misconceived, or only the symptoms of the more crucial matters I have
been discussing here.

Now what I have been discussing here is the plainest of the plain styles,
discussed in just about the plainest possible of the plainest styles. But if we
equate complexity with maturity, and if mature writing communicates not
just clearly but with some minimal degree of clarity and grace, then our definition of complexity will have to be more subtle than what I have so far offered. One of the consequences of that style I was demonstrating, but am no
longer, was clarity, except where in order to make a point I had to be unnecessarily awkward in avoiding a nominalization like *action* or *writing*.

But even when it is always clear, that plain style finally wears just a bit
thin. It lacks the kind of texture that we associate with appropriately mature
writing, writing that is not just clear but vigorous, not just direct but forceful.
We have to be able to write in a way that lets us communicate clearly but still
sound as if what we have to say is invested with a sense of significance. I am
tempted to suggest here the term *significant style*, but I have already multiplied terms beyond our immediate needs, and I have more to come.

There is yet another whole paper that could be offered here, for example,
on how clauses end. In a study too long to be included here, I have analyzed
the last several words of every sentence in a rather well-written article by Lee
Edson, "The Advent of the Laser Age," that appeared in the *New York Times
Magazine,* March 26, 1978, pp. 34 ff. It illustrates the following claim: It is the
end of the clause, the last part of the comment, where the texture that I have

mentioned manifests itself with the greatest salience.[13] (The same point is made in the sentences you are reading.) Clauses written in an emphatic and confident style end about two times out of every three with one of the following three structures, or with some combination of them. (And that sentence illustrates all three.)

(1) A coordinate structure either within the last phrase or as the last phrase;
(2) A nominalization (a noun derived from a verb or an adjective, including gerunds);
(3) A prepositional phrase introduced by *of*.

A very big generalization about one kind of style: Sentences that are both clear and strong are predominantly agent-action sentences, sentences that move briskly through relatively short subjects and verbs into a comment that climaxes with one of those three structures. (Narrative sentences do not reflect these distributions.)

A good way to demonstrate the effect of these patterns is to contrast pairs of sentences that end in different ways. Here are a few from W. Somerset Maugham. I do not think I have to indicate which was the original:

I have never had much patience with the writers who claim from the reader an effort to understand their meaning.

I have never had much patience with the writers who claim from the reader an effort to understand what they mean.

Few people have written English with more grace than Berkeley.

Few people have written English more gracefully than Berkeley.

You would have thought that men who passed their lives in the study of the great masters of literature would be sufficiently sensitive to the beauty of language to write if not beautifully at least with perspecuity.

You would have thought that men who passed their lives in the study of the great masters of literature would be sufficiently sensitive to the beauty of language to write if not beautifully at least perspicuously.

. . . it is natural enough that he should not find a precise expression for a confused idea.

. . . it is natural enough that he should not be able to express a confused idea precisely.

And from Churchill's "Finest Hour" speech:

. . . until in God's good time, the New World, with all its power and might, steps forth to the rescue and the liberation of the Old.

. . . until in God's good time, the New World, with all its power, steps forth to liberate the Old.

Now we can scarcely do less than to call this kind of style complex. It is surely a mature style because it requires considerable practice and experience to achieve. And it is certainly complex in its effect. On the other hand, it is by no means difficult to process.

We are obviously caught in a web of ambiguities and apparent contradictions, so let me try to cut through this web by stipulating some more definitions.

From the point of view of the reader, the pejorative sense of *complex* means unnecessary syntactic dislocation from an underlying semantic structure. If I could wave my hand and substitute another word for this pejorative meaning of complex, I think I would suggest *perplexed*, from the Latin *perplexus*, meaning thoroughly intertwined, hence involved or confused. (Incidentally, I have no illusions that any of the definitions I suggest here will ever again be used in the history of the English language.)

But using *perplexed* for this sense would leave only a positive sense of *complex*. I would use this now restricted, ameliorative sense of complex to cover two kinds of complex styles. I think I would call the plainest of the plain style complex, but more specifically, *efficient*. And I would also call complex the kind of writing that goes beyond the simplest communication of the simplest ideas but still, where possible, coincides with the underlying semantic structure. More specifically, though, I think I would call it *textured*, the kind of style that I have tried to demonstrate in the last few pages.

We could then use *mature* to mean only complex styles, either the plainest of the plain, which is by no means easy to create; or a textured style in which the syntactic complexity invests the sentence with some special sense of distinctive force. Neither is a style we can expect of young and inexperienced writers. This definition would then allow us to distinguish the complex writer from the perplexed writer, and so allow us to avoid equating perplexity with maturity. Correspondingly, immature writing would be the sort of simple writing of the kind the sentence combiners seem most concerned with, the kind of writing that few educated adults write.

Having said all this, I think we could now argue that sentence combining is not the malignant influence I may have suggested. Many high school and college students do write one ten-word sentence after another. They would undoubtedly profit from making longer sentences out of shorter ones, so long as those who direct them in this exercise make it utterly clear that length is not the *sine qua non* of good writing, that every sentence those students create must be clear and direct according to principles that everyone understands. Above all that their growth is *not* to be measured in terms of words-per-clause.

For good measure, let me suggest a couple of patterns that the sentence combiners might want to include in their exercises. Both are a bit like the sort of free modifiers described by Christensen:

He walked down the street,
> swinging his arms,
> worried about his job,
>> but
> certain he would handle his life. . . .

Unfortunately, patterns of this particular kind occur in expository prose with no great frequency. What sentence combiners seem not to have attended to are those cumulative patterns that *do* characterize mature (in our special definition) expository prose. Two of them I have used in the last few pages. I call them *resumptive* and *summative* modifiers.

A resumptive modifier is a structure that occurs at the potential end of a clause. The modifier begins after a comma, repeating a word either at the end of the clause or close to the end, then continues with a relative clause:

> I would call the kind of *writing* that I've tried to develop
> during the last pages textured,
> > *writing* that goes beyond the simplest
> communication of the simplest ideas, beyond the plainest of the plain
> styles.

It is a structure that allows the writer to break the flow of clause, a structure that lets the reader take a mental breath, and then sustain the syntactic line for several more words. Like that.

A summative modifier has somewhat the same effect. It begins with a word that sums up a preceding clause, then continues with a relative clause:

> The plain style is by no means difficult to process,
> *a claim* which I hope this paper has demonstrated.

And again, it lets the reader take a mental breath, something an unbroken string of phrases and clauses prevents. These two modifiers occur much more frequently in the expository styles of mature writers than do the kind of postposed modifiers described by Christensen.[14]

Needless to say, and yet I say it anyway, I do not believe that we have even begun to understand the notion of complexity and maturity in any but the most primitive ways. If nothing else, though, I hope that we can now get away from the kind of counting of features that have no evident relevance to how we experience good and bad prose. Writing has consequences. Whatever does not bear on those consequences is irrelevant to our task—to help our students become what they want to be.

NOTES

1. Kellogg Hunt. *Grammatical Structures Written at Three Grade Levels*, Research Report no. 3 (Urbana, Ill.: NCTE, 1965).

2. *The Art of Plain Talk* (New York: Harper & Row, 1962); *The Art of Readable Writing* (New York: Harper & Row, 1962).

3. J. Mehler, "Some Effects of Grammatical Transformations on the Recall of English Sentences," *Journal of Verbal Learning and Verbal Behavior* 2 (1963): 346–51. J. A. Fodor, T. G. Bever, and M. F. Garrett, *The Psychology of Language* (New York: McGraw-Hill, 1974), 323 ff.

4. "A Model and an Hypothesis for Language Structure," *Proceedings of the American Philosophical Society* 104 (1960): 444–66.

5. Judith Greene, *Psycholinguistics* (Harmondsworth, England: Penguin, 1972), 144–74, particularly 171–73. Fodor et al., 268–73.

6. I. M. Schlesinger, *Production and Comprehension of Utterances* (Hillsdale, N.J.: Lawrence Erlbaum, 1977), 24–32.

7. "The Comprehensibility of Several Grammatical Transformations," *Journal of Applied Psychology* 48 (1964): 186–90; "Learning of Prose Written in Four Grammatical Transformations." *Journal of Applied Psychology* 49 (1965): 332–41.

8. Charles Fillmore, "The Case for Case," in E. Bach and R. Harms. eds., *Universals in Linguistic Theory* (New York: Holt, Rinehart, and Winston, 1968); H. H. Clark, "Some Structural Properties of Simple Active and Passive Sentences," *Journal of Verbal Learning and Verbal Behavior* 4 (1965): 365–70; M. G. Johnson, "Syntactic Position and Rated Meaning," *Journal of Verbal Learning and Verbal Behavior* 6 (1967): 240–46; Fodor et al., 221–372, particularly 244–45.

9. *Papers on Functional Sentence Perspective*, F. Danes, ed. (The Hague: Mouton, 1974); *Symposium on Subject and Topic*, Charles Li, ed. (New York: Academic Press. 1976).

10. Since it is important that I appear credible when I say these things, I feel I must state how I learned them. For a year I have been a consultant to the United States Department of Agriculture. I have taught auditors how to write in the ways I have described. On the basis of this, I have been asked to create a program that would be used nation-wide. I have edited and written materials for a very large corporation in the Chicago area, explicitly observing the principles I have described here. On the basis of this, I have been asked to undertake a number of larger projects. I have revised a rule governing how trains are operated for a major railroad system whose headquarters is in the Chicago area. I have taught a course in how to write for medical journals to physicians on the staff of a very large medical school. In every case, I have explicitly laid out the principles I have described here, and, in every case, they have been immediately perceived as speaking to the problems that adult writers must deal with.

11. Until I change my style, I will use 98 different abstract words: Those a bit like verbs are these: *evidence, effort, import, notion, position, purpose, occasion, reason,* and *version*. Should anyone object that these are derived from verbs, I could find other ways to express what these words mean. Some of the other nouns that are not quite so close to verbs are these: *basis, aspect, circumstances, case, degree, discourse, element, event, example, error, fact, hypothesis, idea, means, metric, memory, nexus, perspective, principle, problem, pattern, rule, sequence, system, subject, structure, source, term, trouble, theory, tactic, value.* Some examples of others are these: *body, area, criteria, data, element, goal, form, index, job, kind, light, matter, number, prose, role, series, task, topic, way.* Many of these may be related to verbs; but I do not think we could argue that any are rhetorically derived from verbs in the way imagination derives from *imagine* or the noun *control* derives from the verb *control*. Because they were technical terms and I could not avoid them, I exclude from this list *depth* in *depth hypothesis* and *comment* in *topic-comment*.

12. *Parasession on Functionalism*, R. Grossman, L. San, and T. Vance, eds. (Chicago: Chicago Linguistic Society, 1975).

13. Some subtotals: the number of sentences in Edson's article that end in comments with:

of:	22	15.6%	
nominalizations:	22	15.6%	
coordination:	17	12.1%	
of + nomin.:	14	9.9%	70.2%
of + coord.:	5	3.5%	
nomin. + coord.:	7	5%	
all three:	12	8.5%	
none:	43	29.8%	
total *of*:	53		
total nomin.:	55		
total coord.:	41		

14. Since writing this, I have had an opportunity to see Donald Daiker, Andrew Kerek, and Max Morenberg's *The Writer's Options: College Sentence Combining* (New York: Harper and Row, 1979), certainly the best of the recent textbooks that use sentence combining as a device for teaching composition. It includes under "appositives" these patterns and others that are appropriate to expository prose.

PART THREE

Style and Pedagogy

Introduction to Part Three

The study of style has had a long association with pedagogy, beginning with schools established by ancient rhetors in both Greece and Rome where style constituted an essential part of rhetorical education. In composition studies, the connections between style and pedagogy have become more attenuated, especially with the virtual disappearance of style from composition theory and teaching in the mid-1980s, part of an overall diminution in the focus on the sentence, according to Robert Connors. Despite this recent development, there is an abundance of scholarship that reflects the varied ways in which style has been linked to pedagogical goals through the years. From traditional pedagogies that involve imitation, sentence combining, and analyzing prose passages to those that employ postmodern or other critical approaches, teaching style has emphasized the strategies of reading and writing to achieve specific effects in varied contexts. While stylistic pedagogy is deployed in the writing classroom as a way to improve writing among students, it is also a vital reading strategy, as it is used to achieve rhetorical effects or to elicit specific responses from readers. Pedagogical strategies for teaching style are generally not included in first-year composition textbooks today; however, they have been used in various ways through the years, and they have included, for example, Francis Christensen's generative rhetoric exercises (see Part Two) as well as sentence-combining practice and imitation strategies. This section collects articles that reprise some of the techniques available to teachers interested in teaching style in the classroom. Though classroom discussions of style today tend to be reserved for the end of the composing process—often as a function of revision—the essays here suggest how stylistic resources can be used throughout the writing process.

In "Teaching Style," Edward P. J. Corbett, with a nod to the classical curriculum of the Renaissance schoolboy, provides a primer for the study of style, incorporating elements not only to develop a writer's style but to analyze the recurring stylistic elements in other writers. According to Corbett, a broad range of stylistic resources converges to enrich a student's education. He shows, for example, the often fluent range of connections between grammar and style, connections that do not require formal knowledge of grammar but anticipate, to a large extent, a student's rhetorical familiarity with aspects of diction, sentence patterns, figures of speech, and paragraphing. Corbett focuses on imitation in many different contexts, from verbatim copying to transforming model sentences through variation or sentence combining. Throughout his piece, Corbett makes the case for teaching style as an integral part of composition pedagogy and argues that stylistic study has the secondary benefit of helping teachers learn to improve their own writing styles. Corbett's article is important in showing how stylistic analysis works as a process of critical interpretation; thus in his pedagogy he asks students to connect the stylistic data they gather (such as sentence length or the frequency of interrogative sentences) to the rhetorical situation, thereby leading them to question, for instance, how an author's purpose or subject matter leads him or her to make certain stylistic choices. When students apply that analysis, in turn, to their own prose, they can exploit these stylistic discoveries to become more effective writers.

In "Grammars of Style: New Options in Composition," Winston Weathers offers an alternative way of looking at style that he names Grammar B, the opposite of Grammar A, his term for the traditional grammar of style that includes the structure, organization, diction, vocabulary, usage, and general stylistic conventions in composition. In an article that inspired the book *Elements of Alternate Style*, Weathers proposes a unique approach to style pedagogy, identifying elements of style that reflect more closely the pluralism and diversity he sees as important to the composition classroom. Hence, Weathers directly confronts what he calls "the beast sniffing outside the door"—or Grammar B—a way of writing that offers new options, including "variegation, synchronicity, discontinuity, ambiguity," among others. Weathers's stylistic invention is ahead of its time in encouraging writers to consider unusual juxtapositions (e.g., fragments and labyrinthine sentences), to think about form without hierarchical or cause-and-effect relationships (e.g., the list), and to avoid the use of traditional transitional or spatial devices (e.g., the "crot"). His support for collage- or montage-based multigenre styles in composition pedagogy anticipates a time when such stylistic blending has become far more commonplace in the field. His is thus a prescient viewpoint that may explain the decision of the *Alternate Style* editors to organize an entire collection around his ideas.

Just as Weathers offers unusual pedagogical insights about alternate style, Elizabeth Rankin, in "Revitalizing Style: Toward a New Theory and Pedagogy," proposes a new way of thinking about stylistic theory and pedagogy. Citing Corbett, Weathers, Christensen, and Williams for the proposition that "style is a teachable art," Rankin argues that these scholars devise innovative heuristics that help students learn and eventually internalize stylistic techniques. What is particularly noteworthy about Rankin's piece is her discussion of how style is both *consciously* learned and *unconsciously* acquired, an insight that acknowledges the difficulty of determining what ultimately makes up a writer's style, how much of it can actually be learned (or taught), and whether, given that uncertainty, the dualistic theory of teaching style makes sense (see Milic in Part Two). Drawing on what is known, and not known, from language acquisition theory, Rankin contends that the unconscious acquisition of style—especially as embodied in the concept of "voice"—is probably relied on too much as a pedagogical principle. In the end, however, she cites the study of voice as one area that not only calls for a new theory of style but a new pedagogy as well. Furthermore, she suggests that a new pedagogy of style might allow teachers to tap students' unconscious processes more effectively in helping them develop their style. Rankin adds that redefining style might also guide us in rethinking when it is most beneficial to teach style during the writing process.

In "Making a Case for Rhetorical Grammar," Laura Micciche argues that teaching grammar rhetorically, mindful of audience, purpose, subject, and context, is central to teaching thinking, and, by extension, to critical pedagogy and the goals of emancipatory teaching. Micciche distinguishes grammar—which she calls the "ordinary" use of language—from style, which she names the "extraordinary" use of language, though, in an endnote, she acknowledges that a course she taught integrating issues of rhetorical grammar and style "reflects the frequent blurring of distinctions between grammar and style in composition scholarship." Micciche's goal is to show the highly relational nature of rhetorical grammar, which, she argues, ultimately encourages choices that implicate "relations between writers and the world they live in." Micciche, however, has broader goals for her pedagogy: she wants students to use rhetorical grammar to understand the "living quality" of language as well as its transformative capacity, and, owing to the choices inherent in grammar, to do the political work of cultural critique. Rhetorical grammar also plays a role in critical pedagogy, exposing language that "reproduces oppressive cultural discourses." Micciche's pedagogical project, in this light, is aimed at using rhetorical grammar to analyze cultural inequalities, including those reinforced by certain institutional and societal assumptions about the nature of grammatical competency itself.

In the same way that Micciche's article draws upon pedagogical concepts relevant to both grammar and style, Shirley Rose's "Down from the Haymow: One Hundred Years of Sentence-Combining" examines the use of grammar and style involved in sentence combining, a pedagogical practice that at its most basic level involves combining (or embedding within each other) two or more sentences to help writers develop greater syntactic maturity. Rose discovers that some of the early sentence-combining exercises that date back more than 100 years—before the practice was even called sentence combining—are similar to more recent versions. She cites what she considers the extraordinary importance of Noam Chomsky's generative-transformational grammar for sentence combining, especially his distinction between competence and performance and his work in transforming sentences from deep structures (relational patterns), to one or more surface structures (understandable statements). Despite Rose's discussion of Chomsky's influence, however, Frank O'Hare, in a 1973 NCTE monograph, challenges the idea that Chomsky's grammar—or any grammar, for that matter—is necessary for students to make gains in sentence combining. He suggests, on the contrary, that the same results are possible without any explicit grammatical knowledge. Rose, after reviewing the early sentence exercises and discussing them with her grandfather—a former schoolteacher who taught them—arrives at the same conclusion, which seems to have carried the day. While critics have questioned the long-term benefits of sentence combining, no one, as Connors points out (see Part One), has ever proved sentence combining ineffective in improving stylistic maturity.

13   *Teaching Style*

EDWARD P. J. CORBETT

I f your educational experience in any way resembled mine, you have been uncertain about what style is. *Style* was a familiar enough word for you, but your concept of style was probably vague. You sensed that certain authors had a distinctive style, but you were not quite sure what it meant to say that an author "has style" and even less sure about what made a style distinctive. In reading a piece of prose, you experienced an undeniable effect, but you could not designate just what it was in that collection of sentences that caused that effect. Consequently, you still may not know how to analyze style or how to talk about it in any meaningful way.

Style may be a vague concept to us because our own teachers spent little or no time talking about style. They may have used such general terms as "lucid," "elegant," "labored," "Latinate," "turgid," or "flowing" in commenting on an author's style, but they never bothered to analyze the features or the constituents of the styles that bore those epithets. Those were largely impressionistic labels, and if we too regarded a certain author's style as, say, "turgid" — whatever *that* was — then we agreed with our teacher's classification of the style. But if we felt that this same author had a "lilting style," we knew no way of describing a "lilting style" or no way of refuting our teacher's judgment. So we dutifully copied down in our notebooks the appropriate epithets for each author we read and discussed in class, and we delighted in moving on to talk about more determinable matters, like the content or the structure of the piece of literature. If we listed ourselves as members of that post–World War II generation of students who regularly practiced the Brooks-and-Warren method of close analysis, we could talk about the linguistic features of a poem with great specificity. Yet we may well have been stymied when we wanted to talk about the linguistic features of a prose text.

If you could put these questions concerning style (What is it? What effects does it produce in a reader? What does one look for in studying it?) to a Renaissance schoolboy, he could give you satisfactory answers. His education

From *The Territory of Language: Linguistics, Stylistics, and the Teaching of Composition,* ed. Donald McQuade (Carbondale: Southern Illinois University Press, 1986), 23–33.

was predominatly language-oriented. From the beginning to the end of the school day, he was steeped in words—English words, Latin words, sometimes even Greek words. He had to recite the grammatical rules that he had memorized the night before; he had to parse sentences; he had to translate Latin sentences into English sentences or English sentences into Latin sentences; he had to be able to write original sentences according to a prescribed pattern; he had to paraphrase sentences in a variety of ways; he had to be able to recognize, classify, and define the schemes and tropes in a passage being studied (and there were more than a hundred of those listed in the Renaissance rhetoric texts). T. W. Baldwin's *William Shakspere's Small Latine & Lesse Greeke*, or Sister Miriam Joseph's *Shakespeare's Use of the Arts of Language*, or Donald L. Clark's *John Milton at St. Paul's School* will give you a generous sense of the language-arts regimen that the Tudor school boy was subjected to in the grammar schools.[1] If we required of our students what Renaissance schoolmasters demanded of theirs, we would no doubt face a general revolt.

This rigorous regimen, however, produced students who really learned grammar and rhetoric and who knew not only the meaning of style but also the procedures for analyzing someone else's style and improving their own. They could tell you that style represented the choices that an author made from the lexical and syntactical resources of the language. Style represented a curious blend of the idiosyncratic and the conventional. The more idiosyncratic a style, the more distinctive it became; the more conventional, the more bland it likely became—although not necessarily less serviceable for being bland. In one sense, then, "Style was the man," because it represented the characteristic way in which a person expressed his or her thoughts and feelings.

For that reason, everyone can be said to "have a style." But some styles are more pleasing, more distinctive, more effective than others. Some writers can command several styles—a range of styles into which they can readily shift as the subject-matter, the occasion, or the audience necessitates. There are high styles and low styles and middle styles. In his book *The Five Clocks*, Martin Joos compares these various styles to what he calls the five registers— the frozen, the formal, the consultative, the casual, and the intimate.[2] Joos also notes that sophisticated language-users can shift into and out of these registers as the occasion demands. Some people do not command the full range of styles or registers, simply because they have not yet acquired the full repertory of diction and syntax needed for stylistic versatility. As the philosophers would say, they have the command *potentially* but not *actually*. Our task as teachers is to turn the *potency* into *act*.

If we as teachers want to engage our students in the study of style, the first point that needs to be made is that the circumstances in which we teach may not allow us to deal with style at all. Many of us teach in a curriculum so crowded that there simply is not enough time to deal adequately with style. And the study of style does take time. The Renaissance schoolmaster had the same group of pupils for the full academic year, often had them six days a week for six to eight hours a day. That generous allotment of time allowed for relentless recitation, rigorous drill, and reinforcing repetition. And the curriculum then was not as cluttered as it is now. If you cannot devote at least two weeks to the study of style, either in a concentrated period or in scattered sessions throughout the semester, you had better not deal with style at all.

The relative sophistication of your students in language matters may also determine whether you can deal with style in the classroom. I can imagine some teachers saying, "Good heavens, I have all I can do just to get my students to the point where they can consistently write sentences that parse. My students have to learn how to walk before I can teach them how to run." There is no question that a minimal grammatical competence is a *sine qua non* for stylistic studies. If style represents the choices one makes from the available grammatical options, then students must have at least a basic awareness of what the grammatical options are if they are to profit from stylistic studies. But a deficiency in conscious knowledge of grammar is not an insuperable disqualification for studying style. Many students can learn their grammar while studying style. I have found that students are invariably fascinated by style—not only because it offers something new and different but also because it provides an element of fun in changing words and shifting parts. And in such a positive and creative atmosphere, students may well be more inclined to develop an interest in grammar or at least to absorb grammar subconsciously.

Studying style in English courses can have two focuses or objectives: to learn either how to analyze someone else's style or how to improve our own. These two objectives are ancillary rather than countervailing. As teachers, we can pursue either or both, but we should determine our main objective for the course at the outset. Learning how to analyze someone else's style belongs primarily to the literature class; learning how to improve one's own style belongs primarily to the composition class. But there is no reason why both kinds of learning cannot take place in both classes. In fact, learning how to analyze someone else's style in the composition class is almost a necessary prelude for learning how to improve one's own style. By analyzing an accomplished writer's style, we can recognize the marks of effective style, and then we can begin, either consciously or unconsciously, to incorporate some of those features into our own style. The process works in reverse too. By deliberately working on our own style to refine it, we learn what to look for in analyzing someone else's style.

Studying style begins with some awareness of what we should look at or look for. In the chapter on style in my *Classical Rhetoric for the Modern Student* and in my "A Method of Analyzing Prose Style, with a Demonstration Analysis of Swift's *A Modest Proposal*," I outline the features that can be observed and analyzed.[3] I divide these features into four main categories: diction, sentence patterns, figures of speech, and paragraphing. But my designating those main categories may not be very helpful to you. What about diction? What about sentence patterns? Just what aspects of diction and sentence patterns are significant?

Let me be a little more specific here. A writer's choice of words contributes to the effects that style has on readers. If we think about it for a moment, we must acknowledge that choosing a big word or a little word, a general word or a specific word, an abstract word or a concrete word does make a difference in what the text conveys to us either explicitly or implicitly. And when we observe that certain kinds of words are recurrent, when we observe that sets of words exemplify certain motifs, these words become even more significant because of what they tell us about an author's characteristic way of saying things. A writer's working vocabulary—the stock of words that a writer actually uses in a piece of writing rather than the words that he or she can recognize in someone else's writing—reflects the range of a writer's knowledge and interests. The larger one's working vocabulary, the more likely it is that one can choose precise diction. Shakespeare's working vocabulary of over 21,000 words was an extraordinary lexicon—and not only for his time.

The study of the lexical element of style involves fewer objectively observable items than the study of any other stylistic element. By the term "objectively observable item," I mean an item which can be definitely classified by observation rather than by judgment. For instance, one can decide whether a particular word is monosyllabic or polysyllabic by simply looking at the word. The decision, however, about whether a word is abstract or concrete, general or specific, often involves a judgment, because those dichotomies are more relative than absolute. Consider, for example, a sentence like "The wealthy Texan owned huge herds of cattle." Is the word *cattle* general or specific? It is more specific than *livestock* but less specific than *steers*. Because of the relativity of the general-specific dichotomy, the classifier has to make an arbitrary judgment about the word *cattle* in this particular context. In this respect, it is worth remembering that any tabulating of percentages of words in a text according to whether the words are abstract or concrete, general or specific, formal or informal, denotative or connotative is likely to be somewhat less than precise, simply because in many instances the yes-no decision represents someone's arbitrary judgment.

When we move on to study collocations of words in sentences, we find not only more objectively observable items but more significant features of writing habits. Most of the stylistic features of sentences are objectively observable items: length of sentences (in number of words); grammatical types of sentences (simple, compound, complex, compound-complex); rhetorical types of sentences (loose, periodic, balanced, antithetical); functional types of sentences (statement, question, command, exclamation); types and frequency of sentence-openers; methods and location of expansions in sentences; amount of embedding. Analysis and classification of features like those tell us a great deal about the level of a writer's "syntactic fluency."

Syntactic patterns also tell us something about the way a writer structures his or her thoughts, about a writer's "epistemic orientation," to use Richard Ohmann's term.[4] The frequent occurrence, for instance, of balanced or antithetical patterns in Dr. Johnson's sentences suggests that he tended to structure his thinking in terms of parallel or opposing dichotomies. The many levels of subordination in John Henry Newman's prose suggest that he tended to see things in terms of hierarchies. The stringing together of independent clauses in Hemingway's prose, often with redundant use of coordinating con-junctions, indicates that Hemingway tended to view the phenomenal world as a flux of discrete, coordinate elements. Henry James's heavy use of paren-thetical elements reflects a mind disposed to meticulous qualifications. And so on.

The gathering of data about syntactic patterns involves a lot of tedious counting and tabulating. Data of that sort were not previously available be-cause the counting and measuring had to be done by hand and took hours and weeks. When Edwin Lewis and L. A. Sherman did their studies in the 1890s of sentence and paragraph length in the works of several British writ-ers, they did all their counting by hand.[5] Today, the computer facilitates such tedious data-gathering, and as a result, stylistic studies of large corpuses of prose and poetry have proliferated.

Collecting data—once tedious and time-consuming—still must be done. We are much more impressed when someone pronounces that a certain writer strings together unusually long sentences and supports that claim with the empirically derived evidence that the writer's average sentence length is 37.8 words. And we are further impressed by the disclosure that 18 percent of that writer's sentences are ten or more words longer than that average.

How much of a corpus has to be studied before valid generalizations can be made about someone's style? I have told undergraduate students studying style—either their own or some professional writer's—that they must ana-lyze somewhere between 1,000 and 1,500 words of a piece of prose. That is not very much really—at most four double-spaced typescript pages, maybe two pages of printed text. But it is substantial enough to allow for some valid in-ferences to be drawn. Students writing a dissertation or a scholarly article on someone's prose style should be reminded not only that they would have to study a much larger corpus but also that they would have to study several specimens of a writer's prose, pieces written at different periods and on dif-ferent subject matters for different audiences. As in any inductive study, the larger and the more representative the sampling, the safer the conclusions will be.

The gathering of data is a necessary stage but should not be the stopping point. Necessary as the gathering of the data is, what one does with the data matters more. Data—even raw statistical data—can convey some illuminat-ing information. But often the full or the most salient significance of the data depends upon interpretation. The act of interpretation calls upon all of one's intellectual and imaginative powers; it requires that one shift from the role of a mere counter to the role of a critic.

Critical interpretation demands that one be able to detect the relevance or the relationship of the data to the exigencies of the rhetorical situation—to the occasion, purpose, subject matter, audience, or author of the discourse. We may find, for instance, that in a particular discourse, the author used an unusually high percentage of interrogative sentences—let us say 18 percent, almost one out of every five sentences. Why? A question like that poses a real challenge for the critic. The critic may find the answer by relating the statistical fact to the nature of the subject matter that the author addressed. The writer may have been writing on a subject about which he was uncertain. He was exploring the subject, probing for answers. So he frequently resorted to questions, knowing that sometimes asking the right questions can be as illuminating as proposing hesitant answers. Or the critic might relate the statistical fact to the disposition of the audience for this piece of discourse. The author, let us say, knew that his audience harbored a certain hostility to the position he was espousing. He knew that he could exacerbate that hostility if he were dogmatic in his pronouncements. So he decided that it would be a prudent strategy to soften his assertiveness by frequently resorting to the tentativeness of questions. But looking closely at his questions might reveal, for example, that many of them are framed as rhetorical questions in which the writer has subtly implied the answers he wants to elicit from his audience.

That kind of interpretation, that kind of relating of fact to function, may be beyond the capacity of some students in basic writing courses. After all, that kind of interpretation requires a great deal of linguistic and rhetorical sophistication. Some students may not be mature enough to make such connections and to come forth with anything more than the most superficial interpretation. But the present incapacity of some students for such critical insights is not the issue. They have learned something valuable about the text simply from gathering the data. They have learned something too from the mere *attempt* to interpret the data. Inadequate as their interpretation may be, they have grown a few inches in the attempt.

In addition to diction and syntax, there are other aspects of style that we might have our students look at: the incidence of figures of speech, the rhythms of sentences, the manner of paragraphing.

A figure of speech may be defined as any artful deviation from the ordinary way of speaking or writing. The classical rhetoricians commonly divided the *figura* into two main groups: schemes and tropes. A scheme involves a deliberate deviation from the ordinary pattern or arrangement of words. In addition to common patterns like parallelism and antithesis, schemes include such artistic patterns as the inversion of the natural or normal word order (*anastrophe*), deliberate omission of the normally expected conjunctions in a series of related words, phrases, or clauses (*asyndeton*), repetition of the same word or group of words at the beginning of successive clauses (*anaphora*), repetition of initial consonants in two or more adjacent words (*alliteration*), and reversal of the grammatical structures in successive clauses (*chiasmus* or *cross-cross*). Tropes, the second main kind of figurative language, are deliberate deviations from the ordinary *meaning* of words and include such familiar figures as metaphor, simile, hyperbole, synecdoche, metonymy, oxymoron, and irony.

In the schools of rhetoric, pupils were expected to be able to identify, define, and illustrate the figures they encountered in the texts they read and to be able to invent similar figures. Their task was complicated by the fact that the number of schemes and tropes had proliferated enormously. *Rhetorica ad Herennium*, an influential Roman rhetoric text, listed 65 figures; the 1577 edition of Henry Peacham's *The Garden of Eloquence* identified 184. Undoubtedly, the proliferation of the figures resulted from overly subtle anatomizing, but amazingly, once students were made aware of the many kinds of artful deviations from the normal meanings or arrangements or words, they readily found the figures in the prose and poetry they read. In the second edition of my *Classical Rhetoric for the Modern Student*, more than half of the schemes and tropes illustrated there were supplied to me by two classes of freshman students who, over a six-week period, searched for examples in their reading. They found a surprising number of examples in magazine advertisements and television commercials. Once students become familiar with a wide range of schemes and tropes, they find them everywhere, even where authors were not conscious that they were creating figures.

What should teachers encourage students to look for when studying the figures, and what does the occurrence of figures tell them about an author's style? First of all, we ought to ask them simply to look for the schemes and tropes. When they find them, they ought to identify and tabulate them and perhaps draw up some statistical information about them. If there are many schemes and tropes, they can begin to classify them into groups or clusters. A particular author, let us say, uses mainly schemes of repetition. Most of this author's metaphors are based on agricultural analogies. Certain patterns or motifs begin to emerge that tell students something about a particular author's mind-set. The presence—or the absence—of figures tells students something about the texture and flavor of an author's prose.

In the modern classroom, teachers rarely, if ever, consider prose rhythms, but our forebears in Greek and Latin schools regularly engaged their pupils in analyzing and composing various prose rhythms. The Greeks and the Romans, of course, had developed elaborate prosodies for their synthetic languages, and since a good deal of their formal communication took place in the oral medium, they were much more conscious than we of the sounds and rhythms of words when they composed their orations. We have only to read sections of Cicero's rhetoric texts or his orations to find out the careful attention this rhetorician gave to the composition of euphonious prose.

English-speaking people probably lost their ear for verbal rhythms when written or printed documents superseded oral discourse as the primary mode of communication. In the late eighteenth century, the elocutionary movement in England, fostered by former actors like Thomas Sheridan, tried to revive interest in the sounds of prose.[6] Although English teachers continued to teach students how to scan lines of poetry, they began to lose all interest in the aural dimensions of prose early in the twentieth century, along about 1915, when teachers of speech formally divorced themselves from the National Council of Teachers of English and formed their own speech association.

But at a time when the aural element has become dominant again and music is the favorite medium of young people, perhaps we should revive the study of prose rhythms in the classroom. Litterateurs like George Saintsbury have shown us that there is an elaborate prosody for scanning prose rhythms,[7] but I would not recommend that we spend valuable time in the classroom exploring the technicalities of that system. If we would revive the practice of reading prose aloud, we might be able to cultivate our students' ears for the harmonies of prose. In the February 1977 issue of *College Composition and Communication*, Thomas Kane published an engaging article about what teachers might do in the classroom to cultivate a sense for the ring and rhythm of well-constructed sentences.[8] Prose, of course, is most often read silently, but curiously enough, euphonious sentences somehow disclose their meanings more easily than awkwardly constructed sentences do, even when read silently. Rhythm is a neglected area of stylistic study, but the classical rhetoricians were right when they preached that the harmonies of prose did make a positive contribution to the conveyance of a message.

For the classical rhetoricians, stylistic study rarely extended beyond the limits of the sentence. Maybe the reason for that neglect was that the concept of paragraphing had not yet developed, even in their writing system. The typographical device of paragraphing was largely the invention of printers, and it was not until the late nineteenth century that a systematic rhetoric of the paragraph was developed by Alexander Bain.[9] Recently, however, such rhetoricians as Francis Christensen, Alton Becker, Paul C. Rodgers, and Frank D'Angelo have convinced us that there is such a thing as a "style" of paragraphing.[10]

What should teachers and students look for in studying the "style" of paragraphing? They can, for example, examine the length of paragraphs, measured in number of words or sentences per paragraph. Information about the average length of paragraphs reveals whether an author tends to break up the discourse into small units or into large units and whether an author tends to develop topics elaborately or minimally. Teachers and students can also note whether an author uses explicit topic sentences and where those topic sentences are placed in the paragraph. Moreover, they can observe the coherence devices that an author uses to articulate sequences of sentences within and between paragraphs. Using Francis Christensen's system, they can diagram the levels of coordination and subordination in paragraphs. They can also catalogue the methods of development that an author uses. Indeed, the kinds of choices that an author makes in composing a paragraph are comparable to, if not identical with, the kinds of choices an author makes in composing a sentence. There is, then, a style of paragraphing.

Each aspect that teachers and students can look at when studying someone else's style can be applied to studying specimens of their own prose. And I would strongly urge teachers to analyze their own style. They can take a paper of 1,000 to 15,000 words that they wrote for one of their college classes or a paper that they have published and subject it to some of the kinds of counting and measuring that I outlined. They will find the investigation fascinating, and they will discover some surprising features about their style—some felicitous characteristics and some regrettable mannerisms.

Improving our students' analytical skills is a proper concern of English teachers, but improving our students' synthetical skills should be our main concern as teachers of composition. And let me suggest, although in the broadest terms, the kinds of exercises that can help our students refine their style and enhance their stylistic virtuosity.

In my own rhetoric texts, I have suggested a number of imitative exercises that have proven fruitful for me and for my students. Let me just mention those exercises, without elaborating on them. (1) Simply copying verbatim admired passages of prose. (2) Copying a passage but changing one element in it—for instance, changing all the past-tense verbs to present-tense verbs. (3) Composing a sentence on the pattern of a sentence written by some admired author. (4) Taking a sentence that someone else has written and seeing in how many different ways one can say essentially what the model sentence says. (5) Taking a group of isolated kernel sentences and combining them into a single sentence.

You can get more details about these exercises by consulting the chapters on style in my two rhetoric texts, in Francis Christensen's article "A Generative Rhetoric of the Sentence," in the two NCTE monographs on sentence-combining by John Mellon and Frank O'Hare, in Walker Gibson's *Tough, Sweet, and Stuffy*, in Winston Weathers and Otis Winchester's *Copy and Compose*, in Joseph Williams's *Style: Ten Lessons in Clarity and Grace*, or in Thomas Whissen's *A Way with Words*.[11]

Perhaps the classroom practices I have suggested here are wholly impracticable for your situation. With all the requirements—and time constraints—of a composition course, the study of style may be more than you can handle. Or some of your students may be so minimally literate that engaging them in any of the analyses or exercises I have proposed would prove futile. But even if your students are not ready to engage in stylistic studies, you can do so yourself. Such a regimen promises to help you grow immeasurably in your awareness of the remarkable richness and variety of our language and in your resourcefulness as a teacher of language, literature, and composition.

NOTES

1. T. W. Baldwin, *William Shakspere's Small Latine & Lesse Greeke*, 2 vols. (Urbana, IL: Univ. of Illinois Pr., 1944); Sister Miriam Joseph, *Shakespeare's Use of the Arts of Language* (New York: Columbia Univ. Pr., 1947); Donald L. Clark, *John Milton at St. Paul's School: A Study of Ancient Rhetoric in English Renaissance Education* (New York: Columbia Univ. Pr., 1948).

2. Martin Joos, *The Five Clocks* (New York: Harcourt, Brace, and World, Harbinger Books, 1962), p. 11.

3. Edward P. J. Corbett, "Style," in *Classical Rhetoric for the Modern Student*, 2d ed. (New York: Oxford Univ. Pr., 1971), pp. 414–593; Edward P. J. Corbett, "A Method of Analyzing Prose Style, with a Demonstration Analysis of Swift's *A Modest Proposal*," in *The Writing Teacher's Sourcebook*, ed. Gary Tate and Edward P. J. Corbett (New York: Oxford Univ. Pr., 1981), pp. 333–52.

4. Richard Ohmann, *Shaw, the Style and the Man* (Middletown, CT: Wesleyan Univ. Pr., 1962).

5. Edwin H. Lewis, *History of the English Paragraph* (Chicago: Univ. of Chicago Pr., 1894); L. A. Sherman, *Some Observations upon the Sentence-Length in English Prose* (Lincoln, NB: Univ. of Nebraska Pr., 1892).

6. See Wilbur Samuel Howell, "The British Elocutionary Movement," in his *Eighteenth-Century British Logic and Rhetoric* (Princeton, NJ: Princeton Univ. Pr., 1971), pp. 145–256.

7. George Saintsbury, *A History of Prose Rhythm* (London, 1912; reissued Bloomington, IN: Indiana Univ. Pr., 1965).

8. Thomas S. Kane, " 'The Shape and Ring of Sentences,' *College Composition and Communication*, 28 (February 1977), 38–42.

9. Paul C. Rodgers Jr., "Alexander Bain and the Rise of the Organic Paragraph," *Quarterly Journal of Speech*, 50 (December 1965), 399–408.

10. Francis Christensen, "A Generative Rhetoric of the Paragraph," in his *Notes Toward a New Rhetoric* (New York: Harper and Row, 1967), pp. 74–103; Alton L. Becker, "A Tagmemic Approach to Paragraph Analysis," *College Composition and Communication*, 16 (December 1965), 237–42; Paul C. Rodgers Jr., "A Discourse-Centered Rhetoric of the Paragraph," *College Composition and Communication*, 17 (February 1966), 2–11; Frank D'Angelo, "Style as Structure," *Style*, 8 (Spring 1974), 322–64.

11. Edward P. J. Corbett, "Style," in *Classical Rhetoric*, pp. 414–593; Edward P. J. Corbett, "Expressing What You Have Discovered, Selected, and Arranged," in *The Little Rhetoric and Handbook*, 2d ed. (Glenview, IL: Scott, Foresman, 1982), pp. 70–120; Francis Christensen, "A Generative Rhetoric of the Sentence," in his *Notes Toward a New Rhetoric*, pp. 23–44; John C. Mellon, *Transformational Sentence-Combining: A Method for Enhancing the Development of Syntactic Fluency* (Urbana, IL: National Council of Teachers of English, 1969); Frank O'Hare, *Sentence-Combining: Improving Student Writing without Formal Grammar Instruction* (Urbana, IL: National Council of Teachers of English, 1973); Walker Gibson, *Tough, Sweet, and Stuffy* (Bloomington, IN: Indiana Univ. Pr., 1966); Winston Weathers and Otis Winchester, *Copy and Compose: A Guide to Prose Style* (Englewood Cliffs, NJ: Prentice Hall, 1969); Joseph Williams, *Style: Ten Lessons in Clarity and Grace*, 2d ed. (Glenview, IL: Scott, Foresman, 1984); Thomas Whissen, *A Way with Words: A Guide for Writers* (New York: Oxford Univ. Pr., 1982).

ADDITIONAL READINGS

Those interested in pursuing the study of style may consult the following selected readings, as well as the books and articles cited in the notes.

Bennett, James R., et al. "The Paragraph: An Annotated Bibliography." *Style*, 2 (Spring 1972), 107–18.

Corbett, Edward P. J. "Approaches to the Study of Style." *Teaching Composition: 10 Bibliographical Essays*. Ed. Gary Tate. Fort Worth: Texas Christian University Press, 1976, pp. 73–109.

Corbett, Edward P. J. "Ventures in Style." *Reinventing the Rhetorical Tradition*. Ed. Aviva Freedman and Ian Pringle. Ottawa, Ontario: Canadian Council of Teachers of English, 1980, pp. 79–87.

Davidson, Donald. "Grammar and Rhetoric: The Teacher's Problem." *Quarterly Journal of Speech*, 39 (December 1953), 425–36.

Fleishauer, John. "Teaching Prose Style Analysis: One Method." *Style*, 9 (Winter 1975), 92–102.

Graves, Richard. "A Primer for Teaching Style." *College Composition and Communication*, 25 (May 1974), 186–90.

Love, Glen A., and Michael Payne, eds. *Contemporary Essays on Style: Rhetoric, Linguistics, and Criticism*. Glenview, IL: Scott, Foresman, 1969.

Milic, Louis T. "Theories of Style and Their Implications for the Teaching of Composition." *College Composition and Communication*, 16 (May 1965), 66–69, 126.

Milic, Louis T. *Style and Stylistics: An Analytical Bibliography*. New York: Free Press, 1967. Since 1967, the journal *Style* has been publishing the annual bibliographies on style and also several special bibliographies on style.

Price, Marian. "Recent Work in Paragraph Analysis: A Bibliography." *Rhetoric Society Quarterly*, 12 (Spring 1982), 127–31.

Secor, Marie J. "The Legacy of Nineteenth-Century Style Theory." *Rhetoric Society Quarterly*, 12 (Spring 1982), 76–94.

Vitanza, Victor J. "A Comprehensive Survey of Course Offerings in the Study of Literary Style in American Colleges and Universities." *Style*, 12 (Fall 1978), 342–82.

Weathers, Winston. "Teaching Style: A Possible Anatomy." *College Composition and Communication*, 21 (May 1970), 144–49.

Weaver, Richard M. "Some Rhetorical Aspects of Grammatical Categories." In his *The Ethics of Rhetoric*. Chicago: Henry Regnery, 1953, pp. 115–27.

14 Grammars of Style: New Options in Composition*

WINSTON WEATHERS

2.

One of our major tasks as teachers of composition is to identify compositional options and teach students the mastery of the options and the liberating use of them. We must identify options in all areas—in vocabulary, usage, sentence forms, dictional levels, paragraph types, ways of organizing material into whole compositions: options in all that we mean by style. Without options, there can be no rhetoric for there can be no adjustment to the diversity of communication occasions that confront us in our various lives.

To identify options we must not only know about those already established in the language but we must also be alert to emerging ones, and in some cases we must even participate in creating options that do not yet exist but which would be beneficial if they did. We must never suppose that the options in front of us represent the complete and final range of possibilities and that now we can relax: that because we have options enough to avoid rigidity and totalitarianism that we have thus fulfilled our obligations to do all we can to free the human mind and the communication issuing from it.

Most of us do, of course, make options available to our students. Most of us have long shucked off the prescriptions and strictures of an earlier day that gave us "no choice" in how to write but insisted only upon the "one good way." Most of us who teach writing attempt to provide our students with a repertoire of writing styles—from the plain to the elegant, from the tough to the sweet, from the colloquial to the formal, from the simple to the complex— in order that our students may make more refined stylistic decisions in consideration of subject matter, audience, occasion, and so forth. Many of us have argued for many years now that our task is to reveal to our students a full range of styles and to provide our students with a rationale for making appropriate selections from that range.

---

*Ed. note: Parts 2–5 are excerpted here; remaining sections omitted for length.
From *Freshman English News* 4.3 (1976): 1–4, 12–18.

Yet even in our acceptance and inculcation of pluralism and diversity, we stay—if we stop and think about it—within the safe confines of a general "grammar of style," a grammar within which our options are related one to another, all basically kin, none of which takes us outside a certain approved and established area.

By "grammar of style" I mean the "set of conventions governing the construction of a whole composition; the criteria by which a writer selects the stylistic materials, method of organization and development, compositional pattern and structure he is to use in preparing any particular composition." This "grammar" defines and establishes the boundaries in which a composition must take place and defines the communication goals to which a composition is committed.

Any number of such "grammars" may theoretically exist and be available to a writer at any one time. Yet on a practical level, in today's classroom we keep all our stylistic options within the confines of one grammar only—a grammar that has no particular name (we can call it the "traditional" grammar of style/or maybe even call it Grammar A) but has the characteristics of continuity, order, reasonable progression and sequence, consistency, unity, etc. We are all familiar with these characteristics for they are promoted in early every freshman English textbook and taught by nearly every English teacher.

Our assumption—regardless of liberality so far as diversity of styles is concerned—is that every composition must be well-organized and unified, must demonstrate logic, must contain well-developed paragraphs; that its structure will manifest a beginning, middle, and end; that the composition will reveal identifiable types of order; that so far as the composition deals with time it will reveal a general diachronicity; etc. Our teaching and texts will be concerned, almost without exception, with "subject and thesis," "classification and order," "beginning and ending," "expansion," "continuity," "emphasis," and the like. All remains, in other words, within a particular grammar of style that leads to compositions that "make sense": it is a grammar that cannot tolerate a mixed metaphor because a mixed metaphor is not "reasonable," and cannot tolerate a mixture of the impersonal third-person "one" and the impersonal "you" because that would be "inconsistent" and contrary to "unity."

We allow options "within reason." We allow options, but only those that fit within a particular box.

In our charity, we allow our students to write in one style or another—

Arriving in London in the spring of 1960, when crocuses were first blooming in Regency Park, I went directly to the Mount Royal Hotel (the hostelry that many an American tourist knows very well, located as it is on Oxford Street, near the Marble Arch and Hyde Park and conveniently located near everything the American tourist wants to see) where I registered for a room and indicated my intention to stay for seven or eight weeks at least.

I arrived in London in the spring of 1960. Crocuses were blooming in Regency Park. I went directly to the Mount Royal Hotel. It's located on Ox-

ford Street, near Marble Arch and Hyde Park, and it's convenient to a lot
of things the American tourist wants to see. I checked in at the hotel and
told the clerk I was going to stay in London seven or eight weeks at least.

but both must do just about the same thing. You can try to write like Henry
James or you can try to write like Ernest Hemingway, but you must not forget
that both James and Hemingway, quite different in their literary styles, wrote
within the same "grammar of style"; neither of them went beyond the para-
meters that Grammar A provides.

It is as though we told a card-player that his deck of fifty-two cards (equal
let's say to the "things we can do with language, our stylistic materials") is
good only for playing the game of bridge. As good teachers, we explain the
rules of bridge and at the same time point out to the student/player his options within bridge: he can play the Culbertson system or the Goren system or
the Jacoby system. And indeed he can play his bridge hands even contrary to
best advice if he himself so decides, though tradition and good sense usually
suggest that he draw trumps early in the hand and play second hand low. We
teach him to play bridge, to practice a certain freedom within it (he can conceivably play "high style" or "low style" or "middle style") but there is no
way under the sun that he can, in playing bridge, meld a pinochle or "shoot
the moon."

Not that anyone really argues that while playing bridge one should not
play bridge. But our fault is that we teach students to play bridge only and
to have access only to the options that bridge provides. We teach only one
"grammar" and we only provide square/rectangular boxes. We don't teach
students other games with other options. And in our teaching, when someone
does "meld a pinochle" at the bridge table, all we know to do is to mark it in
red ink and say "wrong," without ever suggesting to the student that if he
wants to meld pinochle he might like to know about *another game* where it
would be very "right."

We identify our favored "grammar of style," our favored game and box,
as the "good" grammar of style, and we identify what it produces as "good
writing." And anything that looms upon the horizon as a distinctly different
possibility we generally attack as "bad writing," or identify as "creative writing which we don't teach in this class" or ignore altogether, claiming it is a
possibility that only rare persons (like James Joyce or Gertrude Stein) could
do anything with and that ordinary mortals should scrupulously avoid.

Yet there it is. The beast sniffing outside the door. And ultimately we
must deal with it.

It is, of course, *another* grammar of style, another set of conventions and
criteria, another way of writing that offers yet more options and offers us
yet further possibilities for rhetorical adaptations and adjustments. It is not
just another "style"—way out on the periphery of our concerns—but is an
altogether different "grammar" of style, an alternate grammar, Grammar B,
with characteristics of variegation, synchronicity, discontinuity, ambiguity,
and the like. It is an alternate grammar, no longer an experiment, but a mature

grammar used by competent writers and offering students of writing a well-tested "set of options" that, added to the traditional grammar of style, will give them a much more flexible voice, a much greater communication capacity, a much greater opportunity to put into effective language all the things they have to say.

And be assured: Grammar B in no way threatens Grammar A. It uses the same stylistic "deck of fifty-two cards" and embraces the same English language with which we are familiar. Acknowledging its existence and discovering how it works and including it in our writing expertise, we simply become better teachers of writing, making a better contribution to the intellectual and emotional lives of our students.

3.

An alternate "grammar of style" actually has been present in Anglo-American writing for quite some time now, at least since the end of the eighteenth century, though its presence has generally been obscured by the simple relegation of it to fiction and poetry. Until recent times, it has never been tolerated outside "imaginative writing" and even within "imaginative writing" it has been considered simply an eccentricity by a "few crazy writers," not to be taken seriously by anyone else. Laurence Sterne's violation of narrative in *Tristram Shandy* provides great fun, but surely no one would suggest that some of Sterne's tricks and his overall manner might be considered a useful part of every writer's stylistic know-how—would they?

Relegation of Grammar B to fiction and poetry did not mean, however, that Grammar B was never used as an acceptable alternative in prose nonfiction. There are instances where writers did dare to use Grammar B in lieu of A, even in Grammar A's supposedly sacrosanct territories. Such writers in the nineteenth century as William Blake (in the prefatory remarks to each book of *Jerusalem*, for instance) and Walt Whitman (in the 1855 Preface to *Leaves of Grass* and in *An American Primer*) and such writers as D. H. Lawrence (certainly in *Studies in Classic American Literature*) and Gertrude Stein (in such essays as *Reflection on the Atomic Bomb, Descriptions of Literature, et alia*) in the twentieth century demonstrated the use of Grammar B in prose nonfiction efforts. (Interestingly enough, Lawrence's statement in "The Spirit of the Place," the first chapter in *Studies in Classic American Literature*, is, though dealing with American literary content, very *à propos* to the grammar of style in which he is writing: "It is hard," he says, "to hear a new voice, as hard as it is to listen to an unknown language. . . . Why?—Out of fear. The world fears a new experience more than it fears anything. Because a new experience displaces so many old experiences. And it is like trying to use muscles that have perhaps never been used, or that have been going stiff for ages. It hurts horribly.")

The efforts of such earlier prose practitioners gave the necessary precedent for bringing Grammar B out of the closet of fiction/poetry and making of it a viable contemporary prose—especially when the innovative fiction writers in the post–World War II period, writers like Barth, Barthelme, Brautigan, Burroughs, and others, developed Grammar B into a full-fledged and enduring kind of writing, with a full display of its capacities and possibilities in a remarkable number of stories, novels, plays, and even poetry.

The precedent of using Grammar B in prose and the grand demonstrations of Grammar B in latter-day fiction/poetry coalesced in the emergence of the "new journalism," and if any single event can be identified as establishing Grammar B as a truly significant alternative in our times it is Tom Wolfe's writing his now-famous essay, "The Kandy-Kolored Tangerine-Flake Streamline Baby" for *Esquire* magazine in 1963. According to Wolfe's own account, he went to California for *Esquire* to do a story on custom cars; having studied the California car-culture, he returned to New York and sat down to write his copy. He "had a lot of trouble analyzing exactly what I had on my hands." (Note the key word "analyzing" which has to do with the traditional grammar of style.) Finally up against a deadline, the only thing Wolfe could do was to "type up my notes" with the understanding that the *Esquire* editor "will get somebody else to write" the story. About eight in the evening, Wolf started typing his notes in the form of a memorandum; "I just started recording it all, and inside a couple of hours, typing along like a madman, I could tell that something was beginning to happen. By midnight this memorandum was . . . twenty pages long and I was still typing like a maniac. About 2 a.m. . . . I turned on WABC, a radio station that plays rock and roll music all night, and got a little more manic. I wrapped up the memorandum about 6:15 am and by this time it was 49 pages long. I took it over to *Esquire* as soon as they opened about 9:30 a.m." (Note Wolfe's "madman" and "maniac" and "manic" references—words that should not be read pejoratively at all but as attempts simply to describe something contrary to analysis and order.)

Esquire published it "as written" and thus "new journalism" was introduced into contemporary culture and thus, too, Grammar B made its most dramatic appearance in contemporary prose style: a grammar that could tolerate the quasi-amorphousness of a memo, the ongoing chain effect of thought-association, the incorporation of "notes" directly into a text.

Listening to Wolfe's account, we have to take notice, of course, of the part that twentieth-century electronic media have played in bringing the alternate grammar on stage. Wolfe's listening to rock and roll music on the radio was but a minor incident so far as his own composition was concerned, yet the influence of radio, television, and the movies on the evolution of Grammar B is tremendously important. Many of the stylistic devices that finally became a part of Grammar B are based upon cinematic techniques as well as upon the audio techniques found in radio and stereo systems. More important, it was the electronic media that used an alternate grammar of style so frequently and so powerfully that the grammar could no longer be ignored; especially the movie—emerging as the most exciting art form of the century—revealed the alternate grammar in such spectacular and acceptable ways to such sizeable audiences that Anglo-American culture in the sixties and seventies was prepared to be hospitable when the same grammar of style flowered in written composition.

The alternate grammar of style has received a certain amount of describing and evaluating in recent times, mainly by literary critics, though no real codification of the style has taken place. (You can't buy a textbook anywhere that will show you how to write a theme in Grammar B.) Most discussions are still tentative attempts to define the "grammar," to indicate the general boundaries of it, to suggest its general characteristics. Only recently in the *New York Times Book Review*, Roger Shattuck discussed, in his review of Donald Barthelme's *The Dead Father* (November 9, 1975), the characteristics of a certain way of writing that he acknowledges runs all the way from Sterne's *Tristram Shandy*, through Baudelaire's prose poems, to such recent novels as Paul Metcalf's *Genoa*, Guy Davenport's *Tatlin!*, Alain Robbe-Grillet's *In the Labyrinth*, and Thomas Pynchon's *Gravity's Rainbow*. Though Shattuck, rather typically of current commentators, limited his discussion to works of fiction, he nevertheless was dealing with the alternate grammar of style which, according to his analysis, is characterized by four basic techniques: montage, pastiche, linguistic generation (that is, one supposes, a great deal of word play and linguistic manipulation) and supersaturation (that is, one supposes, a great amount of verbosity, repetition, restatement).

Shattuck's very brief and limited list of characteristics is, nevertheless, a sign of a growing attempt in American literature/writing to codify the alternate grammar, to say just exactly how it does work. And behind the attempt at codification is perhaps the recognition of the alternate grammar as having validity as an equal partner in composition in general. Admittedly, Shattuck asks the questions, "Who let all these winds of change out of the bag? . . . Can he so easily jettison the myth of organic unity?" And the questions imply skepticism and some anxiety. Yet behind the questions is perhaps the recognition that the alternate grammar is not going away.

And why won't it go away? There are two major justifications for the alternate grammar, justifications for its emergence and endurance over the past century or two, and for its particular validity here in the final decades of the twentieth century. First of all, there is a general cultural value, so we increasingly realize, in having access to "both sides of the coin" in all our affairs, to having access—in lifestyles or literary styles—to what William Blake labelled the "contraries." The "contrary" or "alternate" completes a picture, saves us from the absoluteness of one single style, provides us with the stimulating, illuminating, and refreshing *opposite* that makes the traditional grammar of style even more meaningful and useful: as the alternate grammar of style more and more takes on strong and viable identity, so the traditional grammar is lifted from the lethargy/monotony of its solitude. There is, indeed, a certain "through the looking glass" quality to the alternate grammar but that very quality reminds us, in composition as in life, that wholeness must embrace all possibilities; that true expertise in writing must always be able to evaluate one writing procedure in the context provided by a totally different writing procedure.

Second, the alternate grammar is "justified" today because it is seen by many writers as a more appropriate grammar so far as the communication of certain realities is concerned. Many writers believe that there are "things to say," not only in fiction but in nonfiction as well, that simply cannot be effectively communicated via a traditional grammar; that there are "things to say" in a highly technological, electronic, socially complex, politically and spiritually confused era that simply cannot be reflected in language if language is limited to the traditional grammar; that the "conventions" of language in the traditional grammar are so much a product of certain thought processes, certain worldviews, certain notions about the nature of man and society that the conventions force upon much of our content a compromise, a qualification, an unwanted prevarication. Whether or not "style" can ever "match" reality is a debatable question, of course; but if the illusion can be maintained by rhetoricians and stylists that the traditional grammar somehow matches and corresponds to an orderly universe or an orderly mentality, then surely a similar illusion can be posited that a variegated, discontinuous, fragmented grammar of style corresponds to an amorphous and inexplicable universe and mentality. More important than whether such a correspondence is "true" is the fact that it can be taught and maintained as a writing convention; a mixed metaphor may not really correspond to a mixed world, but if we agree upon it then it does: the mixed metaphor becomes a "word" in our stylistic vocabulary the definition of which is "mixed-upness" — mixed-up societies, personalities, cultures, and what have you.

(One of the most vigorous justifications of the alternate grammar of style on grounds of better correspondence with reality is that given by Jerome Klinkowitz and John Somer in their introduction to *Innovative Fiction* [New York: Dell, 1972]. Though talking only about fiction, their argument applies finally to all kinds of writing: "The reorganization of values in the twentieth century has displaced man from his traditional notion of self. To regain any notion of the self at all, new writers . . . have placed themselves at the fore of movements to understand and artistically interpret the Einsteinian, relativistic, fourth-dimensional world, and the quality of man's life in it.")

Other justifications for the alternate grammar can perhaps be found. (Perhaps it is justifiable on the grounds of "novelty" or "welcome relief" if nothing else.) But the justification of "wholeness through inclusion of the alternate" and "better correspondence with certain aspects of reality" have been enough to support the alternate grammar and give writers reason to push the grammar beyond experimentation and give it the status of utility.

4.

The writer who wishes to practice the alternate grammar — for whatever reasons — will want to master a number of stylistic maneuvers and conventions from which he may select, just as he does in the traditional grammar, the particular devices/schemes/techniques that seem useful in a particular communication/rhetorical situation and that he can combine into the "style" appropriate, as he so judges, to the composition he is writing. The following presentation of such maneuvers/conventions/devices is not complete, of course, but is representative of the sort of writing practices found in the alternate grammar and does provide a writer with a basic and beginning set of "things to do":

The *Crot.* A crot (crots, plural) is an obsolete word meaning "bit" or "fragment." The term was given new life by Tom Wolfe in his "Introduction" to a collection of *Esquire* magazine fiction, *The Secret Life of Our Times*, edited by Gordon Lish (New York: Doubleday, 1973). A basic element in the alternate grammar of style, and comparable somewhat to the "stanza" in poetry, the crot may range in length from one sentence to twenty or thirty sentences. It is fundamentally an autonomous unit, characterized by the absence of any transitional devices that might relate it to preceding or subsequent crots and because of this independent and discrete nature of crots, they create a general effect of metastasis—using that term from classical rhetoric to label, as Fritz Senn recently suggested in the *James Joyce Quarterly* (Summer, 1975), any "rapid transition from one point of view to another." In its most intense form, the crot is characterized by a certain abruptness in its termination: "As each crot breaks off," Tom Wolfe says, "it tends to make one's mind search for some point that must have just been made—*presque vu!*—almost seen! In the hands of a writer who really understands the device, it will have you making crazy leaps of logic, leaps you never dreamed of before."

The provenance of the crot may well be in the writer's "note" itself—in the research note, in the sentence or two one jots down to record a moment or an idea or to describe a person or place. The crot is essentially the "note" left free of verbal ties with other surrounding notes.

Very brief crots have the quality of an aphorism or proverb, while longer crots may have the quality of descriptive or narrative passages found in the traditional grammar of style. The crots, of whatever kind, may be presented in nearly random sequence or in sequences that finally suggest circularity. Rarely is any stronger sense of order (such as would be characteristic of traditional grammar) imposed upon them—though the absence of traditional order is far more pronounced when the grammar is used in fiction and poetry. The general idea of unrelatedness present in crot writing suggests correspondence—for those who seek it—with the fragmentation and even egalitarianism of contemporary experience, wherein the events, personalities, places of life have no particular superior or inferior status to dictate priorities of presentation.

Nearly always crots are separated one from the other by white space, and at times each crot is given a number or, upon rare occasion, a title. That little spectrum—white space only, white space plus a numbering, white space plus a titling—provides a writer with a way of indicating an increase in separation, discreteness, isolation. Occasionally, but rarely, crots are not separated one from the other typographically but the reader is left to discover the "separation" while he seems to be reading a linear, continuous text; jamming crots against each other becomes a fourth option in presentation, one that provides a greater sense of surprise (or perhaps bewilderment) for the reader.

The effect of writing in crots is intensified, of course, as the number increases. Since each crot is not unlike a "snapshot" or a color slide, the overall composition, using crots, is similar to a "slide" show, especially if the slides have not been arranged into any neat and tidy sequence. "My Trip to New Orleans" written in traditional grammar will have some sort of orderly quality to it; the trip will be presented chronologically, spatially, or what have you. But "My Trip to New Orleans" written in the alternate grammar will depend, not upon the order in which the "slides" appear, but upon the sharp, exceptional quality of each crot or "slide" and upon the "crazy leaps of logic" that Wolfe mentioned, with the reader jolted from one snapshot to the next, frequently surprised to be given an "aerial view of New Orleans as the plane begins its descent to the airport" and immediately after that "a close-up of an antique candelabrum used in a Louisiana antebellum mansion and now on sale in a New Orleans antique store" followed by "a broad shot of Canal Street" followed by a picture of "Marge and Myrtle getting into the taxicab at the airport to come into the city."

Crots at their best will not be all that banal of course in content, but will have some sharp, arresting, or provocative quality to them. Even if they are unable to stand alone as mini-compositions (sometimes they actually are capable of that) and gain their full effect in association with others, each one should have a certain integrity and interestingness about it. Crots may be written in any dictional style deemed appropriate to the communication occasion, with a single dictional style prevailing, usually, throughout an entire composition. On rare occasions, dictional level may shift from one crot to another, but usually the level of diction is a constant.

Crots are akin, obviously, to a more general kind of "block" writing—the kind of writing found, for instance, in E. M. Forster's *Two Cheers for Democracy* and in Katherine Anne Porter's essay "Audubon's Happy Land." In such block writing, the authors have strung together short, fairly discrete units of composition to make whole compositions. Likewise, a series of crots is not unlike a collection of aphorisms—say those of Eric Hoffer who, in a book like *The Passionate State of Mind and Other Aphorisms*, has brought together brief compositional units, some a sentence long, some several paragraphs long, each quite distinct from the other, yet grouped into a whole composition on the basis of a certain attitude and view of life common to them all. These compositions of "blocks" or "aphorisms" are so much in the spirit of crot writing that they may be considered a part of its development out of a traditional grammar of style into the alternate grammar. The writing of Forster, Porter, and Hoffer—in fiction *and* nonfiction—gives evidence of the usefulness of something other than the ordered, liner procedure of traditional grammar even to writers who would not be identified as especially experimental or stylistically daring.

The *Labyrinthine Sentence* and the *Sentence Fragment*. Though the alternate grammar of style uses the ordinary range of sentence types, it makes use also, and more frequently, of two radical sentence types: the labyrinthine sentence and the sentence fragment. And it tolerates a certain mixture of sentence types that would not be found in the traditional grammar of style. The alternate grammar tolerates great leaps from the long, labyrinthine sentence to the short fragmentary sentence, creating a sharp, startling effect at times. Yet it is not committed entirely to the startling juxtaposing: often enough a composition in the alternate style will be wholly labyrinthine or wholly fragmentary. Or at times, a most ordinary traditional sentence "style" will prevail. Usually, if traditional sentence types are to be mixed with the more radical forms, the mix will involve only traditional types and sentence fragments. Rarely do the traditional sentences and labyrinthine sentences mix successfully.

The labyrinthine sentence is a long, complex sentence, with a certain "endless" quality to it, full of convolutions, marked by appositives, parentheses, digressions. A parody through exaggeration of the highly structured Johnsonian sentence of the eighteenth century, the labyrinthine has immediate ancestry in the long, radical sentences of twentieth-century fiction—such as the famous Molly Bloom one-sentence soliloquy that ends Joyce's *Ulysses*. The current master of the labyrinthine sentence is John Barth—but there are numerous other practitioners: one interesting (and perhaps unlikely) example that comes to mind is the opening sentence of *Rousseau and Revolution* by Will and Ariel Durant.

This long, almost picaresque sentence—through which an author rides picaro like—works for many writers as a correspondence to the complexity, confusion, even sheer talkativeness of modern society. When a writer talks about Walt Whitman this way—

> Walt Whitman, born on Paumanok (that is: Long Island), saw in that island's shape (understandably, when you look at the map) the fish that, in the context of Western-Christian iconography, equals Christ equals rebirth equals, especially for Whitman, messianic connotations and (given Whitman's translation of biographical events and conditions into transcendental mythological patterns) therefore portends for "I, Walt Whitman" (to be born later, again, with the writing of *Leaves of Grass*) a divine dimension and a capacity for illuminating the masses who, though they never read him, remained always his projected audience, and revealing, to the enslaved (more than "the slaves," of course; all of us at one time or another) a certain kind of liberation, freedom, escape from the prison.

he is suggesting, via style, the entangling environment in which the masses and the enslaved live and are living and from which Whitman sought to rescue.

In contrast with this kind of labyrinthine sentence but often its companion (à la Quixote and Panza), the sentence fragment—frequently a single word or a very short phrase of only two or three words—suggests a far greater awareness of separation and fragmentation: not entanglement but isolation. It is also a highly emphatic kind of sentence and, in conjunction with other sentence types, creates a variegated, more sharply pointed kind of reading line. Gertrude Stein was a great pioneer in the use of the single word/word phrase/sentence fragment unit: as Robert Bartlett Haas says in an introductory note to Stein's essay on "Grant or Rutherford B. Hayes": "During the late 1920s and early 1930s, Gertrude Stein seems to have been dealing with . . . what the sentence was . . . as seen from the standpoint of an American syntax. Another concern was the description of events by portraying movement so intense as to be a thing in itself, not a thing in relation to something else.

"'Grant or Rutherford B. Hayes' attempts to do this by replacing the noun and the adjective and emphasizing the more active parts of speech. Here a driving pulse is created by syncopating the sentence. The thrust comes from a concentrated use of verbs and verb phrases" (Gertrude Stein, *How Writing Is Written*, ed. R. B. Haas; Los Angeles: Black Sparrow Press, 1974, p. 12).

Only a few words from Stein's essay are needed to indicate her method:

Grant or Rutherford B. Hayes.
Jump. Once for all. With the praising of. Once for all.
As a chance. To win.
Once for all. With a. Chance. To win.

The farther reach of sentence types in the alternate grammar of style provides the writer with a much greater number of options. He can write the crots of the alternate grammar (a) in the traditional sentence types, (b) in the labyrinthine sentence, (c) in sentence fragments, or (d) in combinations of (i.) traditional sentences and sentence fragments or (ii.) labyrinthine sentences and sentence fragments.

The *List*. To create a list, a writer presents a series of items, usually removed from sentence structure or at least very independent of such structure. Usually a list contains a minimum of five items, the items being related in subject matter but presented in list form to avoid indicating any other relationship among the items than that they are *all there at once*, that they are parts of the whole. Presenting a list of items is comparable to presenting a "still life" of objects without indication of foreground or background, without any indication of relative importance, without any suggestion at all of cause-effect, this-before-that, rank, or the like. Obviously the items on the list must be presented one first, one second, one third—but the sequence is generally arbitrary and meaningless.

Adapted from the plethora series found in the traditional grammar of style, and antedated by "catalogues" such as appear in Whitman's poetry, the list stands in stark simplicity—a list of objects, observations, or what have you—to give a quick representation of a character, a situation, a place by the simple device of selecting items to represent the subject under discussion. Donald Barthelme, a frequent user of lists, can range—as he does in a short story "City Life"—from a list dealing with television viewing ("On 7 there's 'Johnny Allegro' with George Raft and Nina Foch. On 9 'Johnny Angel' with George Raft and Claire Trevor," all the way through a total of eight variations to the final "On 31 is 'Johnny Trouble' with Stuart Whitman and Ethel Barrymore") to a "list" description of a wedding with such items as "Elsa and Jacques bombarded with flowers" to "The minister raises his hand" to such a simple item as "Champagne."

Though lists may be presented in a straight reading line, they are usually presented in columnar form, the items arranged typographically one beneath the other just as one writes a grocery list.

One of the attractions of the list to the contemporary writer is that—disregarding the fact that bias may have entered into the selection of the items in the first place—the list is basically a presentation of items without commentary, seeming to say, "Consider these items without any help from the writer. The writer is keeping his mouth shut. He is simply giving you the data, the evidence, the facts, the objects. You, the reader, must add them up and evaluate them." Or there is the suggestion that there are no "values" at all that can be imposed upon the list, that reality stands before us neutral, amoral, and that if we do impose values upon a list it is an arbitrary act upon our part.

Whereas in the traditional grammar of style, one might write —

Whitman grew up as a boy on Long Island, absorbing all the images of sea and sky and shore, all the images of the pastoral world that were always to be a part of his poetry even as he later celebrated the urban glories of Manhattan.

in the alternate grammar one might well write —

Whitman grew up as a boy on Long Island.
   Sea.
   Gulls.
   Sky.
   Shore.
   Stones.
   Roses.
   Salt air.
   Tides.
   Farms.
   Dusty Roads.
   Mockingbirds.
   Horses.
   Summer Clouds.
Later: Brooklyn. Later: Manhattan. But always: Sea. Stones. Cattle. Birds. Lilacs. Even as the metropolis paved its way toward mercantile grandeur and urban glory.

The difference between the two is not a matter of "quality," but is a matter of differing effects, differing reader involvement, differing authorial voice. One is no more creative than the other; one is no more fictional than the other.

Double-Voice. Even in nonfiction, as in fiction, a writer speaks with a "voice" — if not always the same voice in all his writing, certainly a given voice in a given composition. Indeed, the creation of "voice" is one of the tasks of "style," and the traditional grammar of style has always been used for that purpose among others. In the alternate grammar, however, voice is not always considered a singular characteristic, but often enough a plural characteristic — not a surprising consideration in an age of stereophonics and multimedia dispositions in general.

Writers use double-voice many times when they feel that they could say this *or* that about a subject; when they feel that two attitudes toward a subject are equally valid; when they wish to suggest that there are two sides to the story (whatever the story may be); when they wish to distinguish between their roles as (a) provider of information and data, and (b) commentator upon information and data; or when they wish to effect a style "corresponding" to ambiguous realities.

The double-voice may be presented in straight-line form —

Whitman was born on Long Island in 1819. Are island children marked for a certain sense of individuality, or separation? He was the Whitmans' second child. Do "second" children make a greater struggle for identity than the oldest or the youngest? Whitman moved with his parents to Brooklyn when he was four years old. Have children, by the age of four, absorbed most of their primary images, established their essential attitudes and feelings toward life regardless where they move?

Straight-line presentation of double-voice is what John Barth uses, for instance, in "Lost in the Funhouse": one example occurs in the opening paragraph of the story:

> For Ambrose it is *a place of fear and confusion*. He has come to the seashore with his family for the holiday, *the occasion of their visit is Independence Day, the most important secular holiday of the United States of America*. A single straight underline is the manuscript mark for italics *which in turn* is the printed equivalent to. . . .

The shift of voice that comes with the words "A single straight underline" provides Barth with a way of writing both as storyteller and as "observer" of the storyteller.

Obviously, one effective way for writers to present double-voice is to present parallel passages in column form, simply running two tracks of composition down the page, side by side. John Cage does this often enough, notably in his essay on "Erik Satie," in *Silence* (Wesleyan University Press, 1961; M.I.T. Press, 1966). In this essay, Cage alternates two voices, one indicated by italics to the left of the page, the other by Roman type to the right of the page. In another essay, "Where Are We Going? And What Are We Doing?" Cage sets up double-voice, at times even triple-voice, by writing this way —

The candles at the Candlelight Concert are

One New Year's Eve I had too
electric. It was found dangerous

many invitations. I decided to
for them to be wax. It has not yet

and so forth.

By far, though, the standard way of presenting double-voice is simply to present the columns without any further complications:

Whitman was born in 1819 on Long Island. When he was four, his parents moved to Brooklyn where Whitman grew up and went to school. All his youth he spent, one place or another, in town or in country, betwixt East River and the Atlantic Ocean.	We are born by accident in a certain location, yet the location impinges upon our soul and psyche, and we absorb the shapes and sounds and sights peculiar to that location and our view of reality is constructed from this primary, childhood material.

And obviously, two *lists* can run parallel to each other—doing all that lists themselves do and at the same time creating the double-voice:

Sea	Atlantic/Womb & Tomb/Such Mystery
Gulls	Arcs of whiteness/plaintive screams
Sky	Endless/one should not stare into space too long a time
Shore	Boundaries/the line between
Stones	Foundation & Crushing Force
Roses	Perfume & Thorn
Salt Air	Wake me up! Sting against my face!
Tides	Of blood
Farms	Pastoral themes/dirty labor in barns
Country Roads	Delicate tracks/muddy ruts
Mockingbirds	Music & Irony
Horses	I stare into their eyes & wonder about the universe.
Summer Clouds	Like every child, I Walt Whitman, lie & stare into their magic shapes, their shifting forms, and see men and beasts.

(Double-voice embraces, actually, what might be called double-perception or double-thought, and it is sometimes difficult to distinguish between a dual vision and a dual sound. Many times the writer, in juxtaposing two statements, gives less attention to distinguishing his "voices" and concentrates upon the fact that he is seeing two scenes at once or is approaching a subject from two different angles at once.)

Repetitions/Repetends/Refrains. Repetitions play a more important part in the alternate grammar than they do in the traditional; repetitions are used to achieve a kind of momentum in composition when traditional continuity has been suppressed, eliminated, or handled with such subtlety that it scarcely seems present at all. The repetitions come in all forms: simple *repetitions* of individual words; phrases and sentences used as *refrains*; words, phrases, or sentences used as *repetends*. The repetitions are mostly devoted to binding and holding together, creating even at times a certain rhythm that carries a reader through disjointed sentences and passages. Perhaps the concern with repetitions in the alternate grammar is compensatory for a pervasive acceptance of fragmentation and discontinuity.

In the recent volume, *Style and Text* (ed. Hakan Ringbom, issued by the Abo Akademie, Finland), Irma Ranavaara notes, in her essay on Virginia Woolf's style, that Woolf makes great use of repetition, a use that ranges through all parts of speech. Some examples given by Professor Ranavaara are these, taken from Woolf's last novel, *Between the Acts*:

She had come into the stable yard where the dogs were chained; where the buckets stood; where the great pear tree spread its ladder of branches against the wall.

what a cackle, what a raggle, what a yaffle—as they call the woodpecker, the laughing bird that flits from tree to tree.

Faster, faster, faster, it whizzed, whirred, buzzed.

The cook's hands cut, cut, cut.

Woolf was concerned in all her writing, of course, with answering the question, "How can we combine the old words in new orders so they survive, so that they create beauty, so that they tell the truth?" And she foraged into the alternate grammar of style, trying this and trying that, with repetition being one of the stylistic devices she used heavily to escape the very economy of the traditional grammar and all the implications of that economy.

Woolf's repetitions, though of high incidence, are essentially limited to an easily achieved epizeuxis. Gertrude Stein, in such an essay as "American Food and American Houses" (1938), uses a slightly more subtle kind of repetition and in ways more typical of the alternate grammar. Stein writes such sentences as "salads fruit salads have immensely taken their place," with the "salad" repetition being quite different from ordinary epizeuxis. Likewise, her repetition of the word "pancake" in this sentence—

> Then there used to be so many kinds of pancakes, every kind of pancake, that too has disappeared the pancake has pretty well disappeared and I imagine that there are lots of little Americans who have never even heard of them never even heard of the word pancakes. (Haas, ed., Gertrude Stein, *op. cit.*)

The efforts of a Stein or a Woolf are simply preludes to the full use of repetition that we find in full-blown examples of the alternate grammar. When we come to Tom Wolfe's essay "Las Vegas (What?) Las Vegas (Can't Hear you! Too Noisy!) Las Vegas!!!" we find him opening with a tremendously exaggerated super-epizeuxis, repeating the word "hernia" thirty times in a row; then—after a slight interruption for the phrase "eight is the point, the point is eight"—repeating the word "hernia" another seven times, pausing for the phrase "hard eight," then finishing out the opening paragraph with another sixteen "hernia" 's.

Wolfe's repetition in this case suggests movement and energy, and probably most repetitions, when presented in tightly concentrated form this way, are "corresponding" to a certain "throb of life." Sometimes, though, repetitions are less concentrated, more scattered—as in this passage from John Dos Passos' *U.S.A.*—

> Thomas A. Edison at eighty-two worked sixteen hours a day; he never worried about mathematics or the social system or generalized philosophical concepts; in collaboration with Henry Ford and Harvey Firestone who never worried about mathematics or the social system or generalized philosophical concepts.
>
> He worked sixteen hours a day trying to find a substitute for rubber; whenever he read about anything he tried it out; whenever he got a hunch he went to the laboratory and tried it out.

In such repetition the correspondence is probably more with the idea of inevitable recurrence of experience, the "sameness" and "inevitability" of reality, a recognition that in reality there are both stabilizing "things we count on" and boring things that never go away. Different writers will find different values in the repetition, some writers using it sparingly but some writers creating, with it, a great sense of saturation and density. Once again, the writer has options.

Given such stylistic maneuvers and devices as these (there are many more of course—including the many that are shared with traditional grammar and including more exceptional devices absolutely beyond the pale of traditional grammar, e.g., the non-sequitur and the mixed metaphor) the contemporary writer can mix and match as his own compositional inclinations and rhetorical commitments determine. He may, in his use of such maneuvers and devices, achieve, as he often does, two stylistic effects quite characteristic of compositions in the alternate grammar. They are the effects of (a) synchronicity and (b) collage-montage.

Synchronicity. In the traditional grammar of style all "time" considerations are diachronic or chronological. Even the devices of "foreshadowing" and "flashback" are still part of a diachronic conceptualization. In the alternate grammar, however, there is an acceptance of "all things present in the present moment" with many of the devices already mentioned implying this effect: double-voice implies a certain simultaneity in reality: two things going on at once. Repetitions/repetends/refrains also imply recurrence: certain material occurs in the composition; one reads it and passes on, assuming *those words* to be in the "past" of the composition; but no—we meet the material again; it was not a prisoner of the "past" but is present now, the same as it was, transcending a past/present/future sequence.

If the desire of the writer is to suggest synchronicity, he can indeed make use of double-voice and repetition. He can make use of the double-column list. He can make use of the labyrinthine sentence, especially when it emphasizes circularity (borrowing epanalepsis from the traditional grammar and making heavy, exaggerated use of it).

Much use is made also of the present tense to achieve synchronicity since the present tense can equal both the real present and the historical present; without moving from one verb to another, synchronicity can be created—as in such a passage as this—

Whitman is crossing East River on the Brooklyn Ferry. A woman is giving birth on a farm on Long Island on the thirty-first of May. He observes the reflections in the water. Whitman is dying in Camden. Peter Doyle conducts the trolley through the broad streets of Washington and the old man stares out the window, stares at the American people. The woman calls her second child Walter. And crossing on the ferry with him are all types of people, all the diverse faces, all the diverse parts of the American whole. So he walks through Camden. So he walks through Washington, D.C. He climbs up on the trolley and visits with Peter Doyle. He shortens his name to Walt. He tells his mother he is going to cross on the ferry, make his way to Manhattan, he has things to say. Thus Whitman is born on Paumanok, 1819. Thus he is dying, carefully, in the spring of 1892. He is making a kind of journey through the flow of people and across the broad river.

(Note: In synchronicity, use is often made of transitional and relating words—such as "so," "therefore," "thus," "then"—in a kind of "binding of time," parodying the traditional grammar of style wherein transition/relationship is accepted and expected. The resulting non-sequiturs are a by-product, yet become an important characteristic of the alternate grammar, since the non-sequiturs cut through old logical patterns and question the validity of old connections.)

Synchronicity is often achieved simply through the scrambling of sentences or paragraphs or crots, scrambling them out of ordinary time sequences, so that one keeps encountering them again and again in a certain time period. For instance, if one had crots dealing with (a) one's arrival in New Orleans, (b) one's visit to the French Quarter, (c) in particular one's dining at Antoine's, and (d) one's departure from New Orleans, synchronicity would be achieved by scrambling the crots to present now one from group b, now one from group c, now one from group a, now one from group b, now one from group d, now one from group c, now one from group d, etc. Even if the individual crots use appropriate verb tenses (past tense primarily, with some past perfect) still the effect of the scrambling would be synchronic—all events indistinguishable within one large time frame.

Synchronicity is, of course, a stylistic effect used to support a writer's concern with the "here and now," the contemporary. Synchronicity also allows the writer to concentrate upon the immediate moment and yet include matter from the past without having to compromise the discussion of the present. If, in the opinion of the writer, the only reality is what stands in front of him here and now, then his knowledge of the past is best presented in present terms. With appreciative nods toward such a history theorist as R. G. Collingwood, the writer conceives his very "knowledge of the past" as a current knowledge: knowledge *in* the present *of* the past is a synchronous situation. All in all, synchronicity provides stylistic correspondence to the "timelessness of events."

Collage/Montage. Another frequent effect of the alternate grammar is collage/montage in which diverse elements are patched together to make the whole composition. Easily achieved with crots and the other stylistic devices so far identified, collage/montage reacts against the "categorizing" of traditional grammar and insists on packaging together into a heterogenous community all those matters that in traditional grammar would be grouped into homogenous units. Quite compatible with and similar to synchronicity, the collage/montage effect (which in traditional grammar would be considered random, hodge-podge, patchwork) is a stylistic effort at synthesis, distinguishable from traditional grammar's effort, nearly always, at analysis.

In extreme form, collage/montage can mean something as radical as William Burroughs's famous cut-up method, whereby texts written in traditional grammar are arbitrarily cut up, horizontally and vertically, and converted into near-unintelligible scraps of text. The scraps are then shuffled (or folded in) and joined randomly Sometimes Burroughs carries his cut-up method so far as to cut up individual sentences into fragments, then paste the fragments back into new sentences. He does this for instance in *A Distant Hand Lifted*, wherein a typical sequence reads: ". . . remember/my/messages between remote posts of/exploded star/fold in/distant sky/example agent K9 types out a/distant hand lifted. . . ." Burroughs says this collage "method can approximate walky talky immediacy."

Less radical, and more useable, are methods of collage that use larger and more intelligible units of composition, each unit—like the crot—communicative within itself simply being joined in the collage to other communication units, perhaps from different time periods, perhaps dealing with different subject matter, perhaps even containing different sentence/dictional style, texture, tone. Collage at its best actually countermands much of the discontinuity and fragmentation of the alternate style by revealing, by the time a composition ends, a synthesis and a wholeness that might not have been suspected at any station along the way.

As the compositional units to be "synthesized" become larger, more substantial, and more complete within themselves, we come to the sense of montage—a presentation in sequence, side by side, of compositional units less fragmental, yet fairly disparate so far as form or content are concerned. Frequently the disparate units are actually examples of various established compositional forms—e.g., poem, aphorism, letter, description, narration, anecdote, interview, questionnaire, etc. William Blake achieved such a montage effect in the prefaces to the various chapters of *Jerusalem*: In the preface to the first chapter, for instance, he presents (a) a prose apologia for the writing of *Jerusalem*, (b) a verse apologia and address to readers, (c) a verse quatrain, (d) a brief prose theological essay, (e) a thirty-five line poem in a rough kind of iambic pentameter, (f) a three-stanza hymn-like poem made up of four-lined stanzas in generally rhymed tetrameters.

In current montage effects, writers create multigenre compositions, using as Dylan Thomas does, for instance, in his essay "Reminiscences of Childhood," a sequence of (a) description, (b) an original poem, (c) more prose description containing (d) passages of dialogue, and ending with (e) an aphoristic-like statement, "The memories of childhood have no order, and no end."

This kind of multigenre montage effect in the alternate grammar replaces, somewhat, the more traditional method of citation and quotation, though quotations themselves—in isolated forms—are often used in montage.

The use of various genres within the prose nonfiction composition— (e.g., the "mimeographed schedule" in Terry Southern's "Twirling at Ole Miss"; the dramatic "scene" complete with dialogue, along with song lyrics and individual "testimonial" statements by Frank Sinatra's family in Gay Talese's "Frank Sinatra Has a Cold"; tape transcripts of earth-to-moon conversations in Norman Mailer's *Of a Fire on the Moon*)—is valued by contemporary writers because it suggests that there is little difference between genres, between fiction/nonfiction in the verbal response to reality, that the category lines separating "literary forms" in the traditional areas do not really make sense if we begin to perceive reality and the verbal response to that reality in new and different ways. Hence: Norman Mailer's *The Armies of the Night*: History as a Novel, The Novel as History; Truman Capote's nonfiction novel *In Cold Blood*.

5.

Other devices/maneuvers are available in the alternate grammar, of course, but these are the most frequently encountered, I believe. The manipulation of these devices/maneuvers ranges from high/ornate styles to low/plain styles, and writers working in the alternate grammar have as great a range of options as do writers working within the traditional grammar. Obviously, writers working *both* grammars have the greatest range of all.

Compositions achieved through the alternate grammar—with its devices/maneuvers and effects—will obviously be fairly open-ended in structure. That is, they will have less well-defined beginnings and endings, the composition being, to quote Baudelaire, "a work of which one could not say without injustice that it has neither head nor tail, for, on the contrary, everything in it is both head and tail, alternately and reciprocally." Compositions in the alternate grammar more frequently open "in medias res" and more frequently come to an abrupt stop without any well-controlled closure. The endings also have a tendency to refer back to the beginning, à la the opening and closing sentences of Joyce's *Finnegans Wake*, creating the circularity that often accompanies synchronicity and montage/collage.

Compositions in the alternate grammar may be of any length, of course, but there is greater tolerance for the short piece, since the "grammar" is not as committed to the traditional forms of development. The whole composition can be, in effect, a single statement, a single observation—and can be made rather quickly. Large, full-length works—such as complete books—that are written in the alternate grammar have a tendency to "break down" into parts, each chapter having its own compositional quality, with some chapters even being written in traditional grammar, other chapters being very noticeably in the alternate grammar: e.g., Robert M. Pirsig's autobiographical work, *Zen and the Art of Motorcycle Maintenance: An Inquiry into Values*.

Within the alternate grammar, writers adhere, of course, to certain basic principles of composition: (1) A writer commits himself to one grammar or the other early in a composition, and once he has asked his reader to accept one grammar or the other, the writer must not "switch" on the reader; (2) Even though a writer is working within a grammar of discontinuity and fragmentation and even randomness, he must still be concerned with a rationale for his composition, a rationale that informs the composition, if not with "order and sense," then certainly with "interest and effectiveness" in a kind of drama imperative; no composition in any grammar should exist for "no reason" even if "reason" is not part of the grammar; (3) A writer in the alternate grammar of style must be especially concerned not to bore his reader, and therefore he—far more than the writer in traditional grammar—must be concerned with variation, variegation; (4) A writer in the alternate grammar must always distinguish between those devices/maneuvers that have already achieved the status of convention and those that are yet experimental; even in the alternate grammar, a writer needs to have "agreement" with his audiences about devices/maneuvers; indeed, one of the main points to be made is that the devices/maneuvers we have just cited have left the realm of experimentation and now exist as viable conventions, with a sizeable enough audience prepared to read them and understand them.

15 Revitalizing Style: Toward a New Theory and Pedagogy

ELIZABETH D. RANKIN

In the past several years, we have seen various attempts to define and explain the dramatic changes occurring in the field of composition studies. In particular, Richard Young, James Berlin and Robert Inkster, and Maxine Hairston have spoken of a "paradigm shift," a change in the basic assumptions and attitudes that underlie all our theory and pedagogy.[1] One result of this paradigm shift has been a noticeable decline in the status of style as a pedagogical concept. By this I mean that the teaching of style no longer enjoys a prominent place in our discipline.

Some see this as a change for the good. For too long, they argue, style dominated our pedagogy—almost to the exclusion of other concerns. And of course they are right. But what I fear may be happening now is an over-correction of sorts. Style hasn't just stepped back to take a less dominant role in our teaching—style is out of style.

Before I go any further, it is probably wise to stop and explain what I mean by style in this context. To do so is no easy task, for style has had a protean identity over the years. "Historically," says Linda Woodson, "style has been interpreted both narrowly, as referring only to those figures that ornament discourse, and broadly, as representing a manifestation of the person speaking."[2] Most often, however, those who write about style in texts and in journals define style, implicitly or explicitly, in terms such as these:

> The style of a piece of writing is the pattern of choices the writer makes in developing his or her purpose. If the choices are consistent, they create a harmony of tone and language that constitutes the style of the work. A description of the style of any piece of writing is therefore an explanation of the means by which the writer achieved his or her purpose.[3]

In practice, discussions of style nearly all deal with particular linguistic choices: with diction, syntax, and tone. So I'll start out my own discussion with this definition in mind, though the definition itself, if regarded narrowly, may well be a factor in style's decline.

From *Freshman English News* 14 (1985): 8–13.

What, then, are the reasons for that decline? I think there are two. One has to do with the claims of competing concerns. As modern composition studies rediscovered its roots in classical rhetoric, it discovered whole areas of study that had been neglected for years. One of these areas, invention, has attracted much attention of late, and as rhetoricians rush in to fill the gap in research, interest in style has declined. The same could be said for other new areas of interest, such as the composing process. Although there is really no need to see these new fields as competing with the old, the politics of our profession and the rhetoric that it gives rise to have created such an effect.

Of course this is not to say that no one is interested in style these days. Style does have a place in the New Rhetoric—or rather, it has a place in both branches of the New Rhetoric that Richard Young has identified.[4] And this is the second reason for style's decline. For so far, neither branch of the New Rhetoric has offered us a sound, complete, and adequate theory of style. Until such a theory is formulated—or at least until such a formulation seems *possible*—we are left with a good deal of skepticism and confusion.

Is such confusion resolvable? Is there any way to reclaim for style the respect which it has lost? I believe there is, and a little later in this essay I will make some preliminary suggestions toward that end. But first, I must go back and fill in the substance of the argument I have just outlined.

A good place to begin, I think, is with the whole notion of a "paradigm shift," or, more specifically, with the concept of competing paradigms. When we look at the work of the scholars I mentioned earlier—Young, Berlin and Inkster, and Hairston—one thing we see them all doing is trying to define the characteristics of the old paradigm, the "current-traditional" paradigm, as it has come to be called. In doing so, all take note of the prominence given to style. Here is what Richard Young has observed:

> The overt features [of the current-traditional paradigm] are obvious enough: the emphasis on the composed product rather than the composing process, the analysis of discourse into words, sentences, and paragraphs, the classification of discourse into description, narration, exposition, and argument; *the strong concern with usage* (syntax, spelling, punctuation) *and with style* (economy, clarity, emphasis); the preoccupation with the informal essay and the research paper; and so on (Paradigms, 31; emphasis mine).

Picking up where Young left off, Berlin and Inkster trace the rhetorical history of the old paradigm, exposing the philosophical and epistemological assumptions on which it is based. As they do so, they also note the importance of style in the paradigm. The most salient assumption of current-traditional rhetoric, say Berlin and Inkster, is the notion that reality is fixed, knowable, and rational, and that discourse, to be valid, need only conform to that reality:

> One may ask how one piece of discourse is to be distinctive from any other discourse, given the powerful impetus for conformity that grows from the epistemology of the current-traditional paradigm. The answer

lies in the concern for style, for here is the one avenue by which one may write distinctive prose, given the assumptions behind the paradigm. Hence, the elevation of style in the texts (5).

What Young and Berlin and Inkster have said here is most assuredly true: we need only look at the more traditional handbooks and texts in our field to see how important the concept of style has been for teachers of composition. And I must point out that nowhere do these authors suggest that style is an inappropriate concern. If they see a problem with the old paradigm, the problem isn't with style per se, but with an overemphasis on style. Maxine Hairston is particularly careful in this regard. She closes her essay with the caution that "it is important for us to preserve the best parts of earlier methods for teaching writing: the concern for style and the preservation of high standards for the written product" (88).

Alas, though, intentions are sometimes beside the point, and in this case I fear that the otherwise useful concept of competing paradigms has had some unfortunate side effects. For one thing, it sets up false dichotomies. The process/product opposition is one that many have been uncomfortable with. Less noticed, but just as unfortunate, is a similar implied opposition between invention and style. For instance, consider this prominent item in Hairston's proposed "new paradigm," a list of twelve tenets of current composition theory: "It teaches strategies for invention and discovery; instructors help students to generate content and discover purpose" (86). Here invention, the first of the five canons of classical rhetoric, gets mentioned by name; in contrast, neither style nor arrangement appears on the twelve-item list. Earlier in Hairston's essay, however, style was twice mentioned explicitly in association with the old paradigm. Thus, though no opposition between style and invention is stated, one does get conveyed in subtle ways nonetheless.

In Berlin and Inkster, too, invention seems to get counterpoised with style. Recounting the factors that led Hugh Blair "to reject the heuristic procedures of classical invention as mechanical algorithms," the authors go on to say, "One need not search far in modern texts to find that this legacy is still with us: 'The stylistic side of writing is, in fact, the only side that can be analyzed and learned'" (3). The point that Berlin and Inkster make is a valid one: for modern rhetoricians and textbook authors since Blair, invention has not until recently been regarded as a teachable art. But to go on and quote an author who says that only style can be taught is a little misleading. After all, arrangement—that second canon of classical rhetoric—has also been a concern of the current-traditionalists. When it is left out of discussions like these, a false opposition of style and invention inadvertently gets implied.

Just as damaging to style's reputation as this implied opposition is the power of connotation. Let us look once again at Richard Young's definition of the old paradigm. Certain features he mentions are connotatively neutral, including "the strong concern . . . with style." Others, however, are negative, and they have a kind of rub-off effect on their less judgmental neighbors. Take, for example, "the emphasis on the composed product rather than the composing process." It's hard to say at this point when "composed product" acquired the negative connotations it holds for us today, but I would argue that the term itself gave us very little choice. Given our characteristic humanist antipathy toward the marketplace, "product" will generally always have negative associations. (If you don't agree, try substituting a term like "finished discourse" and compare the effect. The latter term is more neutral, but it doesn't have that alliterative antithesis that "product/process" has.) The last item in Young's definition has an even stronger negative bias. Current-traditionalists, says Young, have a "preoccupation with the informal essay and the research paper." Here the negative associations of "preoccupation" are obvious. (For an interesting contrast, compare this item in Hairston's proposed new paradigm: "It includes a variety of writing modes, expressive as well as expository.") Finally, consider the rhetorical effect of mentioning style in the same breath with usage. Usage has fallen on bad times of late—largely because it has become the domain of prescriptive grammarians and linguistic reactionaries like Edwin Newman and William Safire. What this casual yoking of terms may suggest is that style belongs in that same domain—a suggestion which produces the effect of guilt by association.

If the rhetoric of competing paradigms has had, in certain respects, a chilling effect on our attitudes towards style, so has the rhetoric of the composing process. In the past few years, considerable research has been devoted to investigating that process (or those processes, to be more accurate). Much of it remains descriptive, while some results in the formulation of models. Probably the most well-known and comprehensive model is the cognitive process model constructed by Linda Flower and John Hayes. In this model, "a writer uses a goal to generate ideas, then consolidates those ideas and uses them to revise or regenerate new, more complex goals."[5] As the examples that Flower and Hayes use indicate, many of the goals that writers set and revise are stylistic goals, having to do with such matters as word choice, syntax, and tone. Thus, their model could well be used to explore the complexities of style. But in actuality, the work that derives from the cognitive process model rarely pertains to style. Why is this? I suspect its because of the rhetoric of the model itself.

One salient feature of the Flower-Hayes model is its hierarchical structure. Writing processes are "hierarchically organized" and writers "create a hierarchical network of goals." Within this hierarchical structure, "low-level goals" (such as stylistic goals) are embedded within or subsumed to "higher-level" goals involving, for instance, content, organization, or audience adaptation. As writers work, they "not only create a hierarchical network of guiding goals, but, as they compose, they continually return or 'pop' back up to their high-level goals. And these higher-level goals give direction and coherence to their next move" (379).

What Flower and Hayes say here makes perfect sense and rings true to our intuitive notion of how writers work. But almost inevitably, its effect has been to focus our interest—as teachers and researchers—on the "top-level" or "middle-range" goals of the writer. Partially, this is because those "higher-level" goals are so crucial. They do "give breadth and coherence to local decisions about what to say next" (379). But consider the connotations involved. When "narrow," "local," stylistic decisions occupy a "low-level" position in the "hierarchy," it's hard to see them as very important. Thus, though the Flower-Hayes model is broad and inclusive enough to account for stylistic decisions at all levels and stages in the writing process, the rhetoric of the model—like the rhetoric of competing paradigms—to some extent undermines the significance of style.

This same effect can be seen in some of the recent work on revision, particularly that of Donald Murray and Nancy Sommers. In a 1978 essay entitled "Internal Revision: A Process of Discovery," Murray divides the revision process into "two principal and quite separate editorial acts": internal and external revision. In setting up this division, Murray is not attempting to be rigorously scientific, as later researchers have been. Rather, he has a rhetorical purpose in mind. He wants us to see that revision includes not only matters of "form and language, mechanics and style" (external revision), but "everything writers do to discover and develop what they have to say, beginning with the reading of a completed first draft" (internal revision). It is this latter kind of revision that Murray is most interested in and goes on to discuss in his essay.[6]

If we look at the essay closely, we see that Murray clearly intends no denigration of style. For one thing, he concedes that "external revision has not been explored adequately or imaginatively." For another, as he goes on to discuss "internal revision," he is in fact discussing matters of style:

> . . . language itself leads writers to meaning. During the process of internal revision [writers] reject words, choose new words, bring words together, switch their order around to discover what they are saying. "I work with language," says Bernard Malamud, "I love the flowers of afterthought."
>
> Finally, I believe there is [another] area, quite separate from content, form, or language, which is harder to define but may be as important as the other sources of discovery. That is what we call *voice*. I think voice, the way in which writers hear what they have to say, hear their point of view toward the subject, their authority, their distance from the subject, is an extremely significant form of internal revision (93–94).

What Murray is saying here is important, and I will return to it later. For now, though, I will only point out one thing. Although Murray is clearly discussing style as an aspect of internal revision, he never actually uses the word there. He does mention style, however, when discussing external revision, and when he does, he inadvertently packs it with all the slightly disparaging connotations of words like "conventions" and "mechanics." Here again, as in delineations of the old paradigm, we have the effect of guilt by association. Very subtly, the pedagogy of style gets devalued.

A similar phenomenon occurs, I think, in the work of Nancy Sommers. In "Revision Strategies of Student Writers and Experienced Adult Writers," Sommers writes:

> Experienced writers see their revision process as a recursive process—
> a process with significant recurring activities—with different levels of
> attention and different agenda for each cycle. During the first revision
> cycle their attention is primarily directed towards narrowing the topic
> and delimiting their ideas. At this point, they are not as concerned as
> they are later about vocabulary and style. [However,] during the later
> cycles, . . . the experienced writers' primary attention is focused upon
> stylistic concerns.[7]

Throughout this section of her essay, Sommers speaks of ideas, form, and
style as separate "objectives." Because these objectives cannot be attended to
all at once, she says, the writer must prioritize one or two. In her research,
Sommers found that experienced writers tend to prioritize idea and form,
leaving "stylistic concerns" for the later cycles of the process. Student writers,
on the other hand, seem to get hung up on lexical concerns, perhaps because
they "do not have strategies for handling the whole essay" (383).

The problem with Sommers' rhetoric here is that, as Murray has suggested, style and stylistic concerns are often tied in with other aspects of
writing. It's true that narrow stylistic concerns can and do impede the composing process for many of our students; but likewise narrow ideas or narrow notions of form can impede the process. Although Sommers' research has
broadened (and thereby strengthened) our concept of revision, she is still employing a fairly traditional and limited concept of style—and this in itself is
part of a larger problem.

The problem, ultimately, has to do with our failure, as a profession, to
come up with a unified theory of style. In his essay, "Theories of Style and
Their Implications for the Teaching of Composition," Louis Milic distinguishes three different philosophies of style: 1) rhetorical dualism, which sees
language and thought as separate entities, with style being the "dress" of
ideas; 2) aesthetic monism, which sees style (and form) as an inevitable consequence of content; and 3) psychological monism, which regards style as the
expression of a unique personality ("Style is the man").[8] In Milic's terms,
Sommers would be a dualist. For her, by implication at least, style can be separated from idea and form, and when it is, it can be attended to in meaningful
ways. In this, Sommers resembles a wide range of modern composition theorists and pedagogues, a heterogeneous group that Richard Young has labeled
the "new classicists."

For the new classicists—including such people as Edward Corbett, Winston Weathers, Francis Christensen, and Joseph Williams—style is a teachable art. It is taught by first determining what expert stylists do, then
constructing heuristics that will help beginners master—and eventually internalize—their techniques (Young, Arts, 57–58). On the one hand, this view
of style is liberating. It takes style out of the domain of the handbook rhetoricians and makes it a serious object of research and investigation. It encourages
computer-based stylistic analysis and results in the formulation of such innovative heuristics as sentence-combining and generative sentence-building, as
well as in the revitalization of classical concepts like imitation. On the other

hand, though, the new classicists' pedagogy of style is problematic. Despite protests to the contrary, it often tends to be prescriptive. (One thinks immediately of people like Williams here, but Christensen too was accused of promoting a particular kind of style.)[9] In addition, the heuristics proposed by the new classicists are often hard to implement. Imitation exercises, sentence-combining, stylistic analysis—all of these take enormous amounts of time. For teachers committed to a process-centered approach to composition, such time takes away from the already limited time their students have for drafting and revising, and in their view the benefits may not be worth the costs.

More problematic than practical limitations, however, is one shaky assumption that underlies new classical pedagogy. This is the assumption that most stylistic decisions are conscious decisions—or can be made conscious with careful attention to the revision process. Ian Pringle has already raised objections to this assumption, in a review of Joseph Williams' text *Style: Ten Lessons in Clarity and Grace*. Calling attention to the work of second language researcher Stephen Krashen, which makes a distinction between conscious *learning* of language and unconscious *acquisition*, Pringle argues the following:

> If students are to produce literate writing, they will do so primarily on the basis of what is acquired, and what they acquire will come to them not through the explicit study of style (or for that matter grammar), but from "comprehensible input," from reading good, relevant models . . .[10]

Of course Pringle's point of view is also problematic. In the first place, it assumes that the model implies that stylistic decisions are "primarily" acquired, not learned. At this point, though, Krashen's model is purely hypothetical. It may *suggest* directions for further research, but as yet it can tell us little about what specific aspects of language may be consciously learned and which must be unconsciously acquired. And secondly, we must remember that Krashen's model is not only a construct, it's a construct that may be more field-specific than we realize. Its adequacy as a descriptive model of the acquisition of *written* language has yet to be fully explored.

Nevertheless, what Pringle is voicing here is a reservation that many would share. It's the same reservation implied by Milic in his essay "Rhetorical Choice and Stylistic Options." In that essay, Milic considers the very question that Pringle (via Krashen) has raised: To what extent are stylistic decisions *conscious* decisions? Citing personal experience, observations, and anecdotes about professional writers, Milic concludes the following:

> Without for a moment denying the possibility that some part of a writer's style is conscious artistry or craftsmanship, I am convinced that most writers, even some of the greatest, knew very little about what they were doing when they wrote and had much less conscious control over the final product than is commonly supposed.[11]

With some exceptions, he seems to corroborate Krashen.

What all this suggests is that there are complex aspects of style that the dualist theory of the new classicists is ill-equipped to deal with. These aspects, the unconscious aspects of style, are of interest to the "new romantics."

The new romantics, says Richard Young, are committed to the notion that creativity is a mysterious process—a process that is ultimately unavailable to conscious, rational analysis and control. Thus, the creative process (which includes the composing process) cannot be taught in the conventional sense— but it can be facilitated by a teacher who acts as helper or guide (Young, Arts, 55). For new romantics like William Coles, Peter Elbow, James Miller, Gordon Rohman, and others, style is also a matter cloaked in mystery. But what the romantics mean by style is radically different from what new classicists or current-traditionalists mean. Take Peter Elbow, for instance. For Elbow, style is virtually synonymous with voice. Thus, it isn't so much a skill to be learned as a capacity to be realized. Style is something the writer discovers within him or herself, and the teacher's role is not to teach it but to encourage and facilitate its expression.

Like the new classicists' approach, this new romantic attitude has had a mixed effect on the status of style in our pedagogy. On the one hand, it inflates the concept's importance. For Elbow, it is voice more than anything that gives writing *power*. On the other hand, though, just because voice is so important, the concept becomes all-pervasive and tends to diffuse. As it does so, it carries off with it the language we need to describe it, and what we are left with is just the kind of vague, subjective abstraction that Louis Milic has decried in traditional studies of style.[12] Here, for example, is Elbow's reaction to a sample student passage:

> This writing has the lively sound of speech. It has good timing. The words seem to issue naturally from a stance and personality. But what strikes me is how little I can feel the reality of any person in these words. I experience this as a lack of any deeper resonance. These words don't give off a solid thump that I can trust.[13]

If style as a pedagogical concept has suffered at the hands of the new romantics, it may be because of the necessary subjectivity of their approach.

At this point it becomes clear that the problematic assumptions underlying the new romantics' approach to style are in fact the opposite of equally problematic assumptions held by the new classicists. If the classicists embrace an essentially dualistic notion of style, the romantics are committed to the view that says "Style is the man." If the classicists view style as a conscious art to be mastered, the romantics see it as an unconscious voice to be discovered. The question is this: To what extent are these two theories of style mutually exclusive? Is there any way of reconciling them, and in doing so revitalizing the teaching of style?

For Louis Milic, the theories *are* reconcilable. He has no problem seeing that real writers "write in a certain way because they select the most effective artifices of expression, but also because they are unconsciously bound to the requirements of individual personality." Still, Milic thinks that "For teaching, a dualistic theory seems to be essential, at least in the early stages." He has no faith in new romantic approaches to teaching style (Theories, 126). In part, Richard Young shares Milic's view: "The durability of these two fundamental conceptions of rhetorical art and the effectiveness of the pedagogical methods based on them suggest that in some sense both are true—in spite of the fact that they seem incompatible." Though he doesn't propose it himself, Young believes that "there may be a more adequate conception of rhetorical art that does not lead us to affirm the importance of certain psychological powers at the cost of denying the importance of others" (Arts, 60).

From what Young and Milic say, it is clear that they see the essential differences in theories of style as psychological differences. It could be, though, that the conflict goes even deeper. According to John Gage, for instance, different theories of style are manifestations of more deeply rooted philosophical assumptions about the nature of language and reality.[14] If these assumptions can be reconciled in a theory of hermeneutics—and Gage's remarks about rhetorical communities suggest that they can—then we may not have to wait long for a unified, comprehensive theory of style. What such a theory will look like we do not yet know. But in light of what I've been saying here, I would expect it to meet the following criteria:

1. *A new theory of style would offer a broad yet workable definition of style.* This definition would be specific enough to distinguish stylistic considerations from other concerns of the writing process, such as content and formal matters. At the same time, it would be broad and inclusive enough to account for overlap between style and invention, say, or stylistic decisions and audience adaptive techniques.

If we look once again at the textbook definition of style given earlier, we see that it contains the seeds of such a definition. On the one hand, it describes style as a "pattern," a "harmony," a set of consistent choices. On the other hand, it also sees style as "a means by which the writer achieve[s] his or her purpose." What the definition implies is that style is both "product" and "process," both a set of observable features of a finished text and a way of discovering what that text will become. Such a flexible definition is crucial if we are to develop style's full potential as a rhetorical and pedagogical concept.

2. *A new theory of style would take into account the wide range of psychological operations that go into the making of stylistic decisions.* That is, it would account for not only the conscious, rational decisions that Milic calls "rhetorical choices," but for the murkier matter of the formation of stores of unconscious "stylistic options" as well. In particular, it would provide some means of distinguishing when such operations are *acquired*, when they are *learned*, and if/when they might be effectively taught.

This is not to say, of course, that there is a clear line of demarcation between conscious and unconscious choices. Still, a complete definition of style will recognize that some of those choices are more indirect than others: they are influenced by social background, by linguistic experience, and by intellectual capacity; by deep psychological factors and momentary situational constraints. In short, they are complex and fascinating—a fertile subject for further research.

3. *A new theory of style would be grounded in sound and consistent philosophical/ epistemological assumptions about the nature of language and reality.* Ideally, such a theory would mediate between those who see language (and style) as representative of a fixed, orderly reality, and those who see it instead, in John Gage's terms, as "a useful but imperfect . . . manifestation of a reality maybe orderly, maybe

not" (617). As I mentioned earlier, Gage himself has laid the foundation for such a theory. What it relies on ultimately is the concept of the rhetorical community, a community within which linguistic positivists and relativists can meet and, to some extent, coexist. In this community, which Stanley Fish has called the interpretive community, the essentially arbitrary and self-referential nature of language is acknowledged, yet a flexible set of acceptable meanings and standards is agreed upon. The fact that these meanings and standards change is not taken as cause for concern but as natural and expected—the result of a continuous dialogue in which meaning is negotiated.

In terms of style, such a concept *seems* to undercut monistic theories because it regards both the self (the individual personality) and meaning as relativistic constructs—entities that are themselves created by language (style). But if these constructs are seen as existing within a rhetorical (or interpretive) community, they can be provisionally regarded as determinant, even while their relativistic nature is acknowledged. Thus, the theory accommodates both dualistic and monistic concepts of style.

Richard Lanham outlines another way of resolving the problem of conflicting theories in his essay "*At* and *Through*: The Opaque Style and Its Uses." For Lanham, conflicting theories of art (and style) can be resolved if seen as points on a matrix constructed around a single variable: "degree of self-consciousness." Although he argues in different terms, Lanham seems to agree with Gage when he says that "each theory, if adequately rigorous and comprehensive, creates the object it criticizes."[15] In doing so, he implies, it also creates its audience, its rhetorical community, by whose standards and expectations its adequacy and rigor are judged.

In more practical terms, a new theory of style would have certain pedagogical consequences. By broadening our narrow definitions of style, it would force us to reconsider our notions of when, where, and how style can be taught in the process-centered classroom. Is it best to encourage students to prioritize content and form as they go through the writing process—or can style sometimes be profitably focused on even in earliest drafts? Is it enough to concentrate on those aspects of style that are most accessible to conscious control—or are there ways of reaching and shaping the less conscious processes too? And what about style as voice? Is it something the writer discovers within his or her unique individual self—or is it an interpretive construct the writer creates as he/she goes along?

All these are provocative questions, and they merit our serious attention. If we begin to address them in the context of a comprehensive theory—avoiding the negative rhetoric we hear in our discipline lately—we may be able to bring style back into style.

NOTES

1. Richard E. Young, "Paradigms and Problems: Needed Research in Rhetorical Invention," in *Research in Composing*, ed. Charles R. Cooper and Lee Odell (Urbana: NCTE, 1978), pp. 29–47; James A. Berlin and Robert P. Inkster, "Current-Traditional Rhetoric: Paradigm and Practice,"

Freshman English News, 8 (Winter 1980), pp. 1–4, 13–14; Maxine Hairston, "The Winds of Change: Thomas Kuhn and the Revolution in the Teaching of Writing," *CCC*, 33 (February 1982), pp. 76–88.

2. Linda Woodson, *A Handbook of Modern Rhetorical Terms* (Urbana: NCTE, 1979), p. 58.

3. James M. McCrimmon, *Writing With A Purpose* (Eighth Edition) (Boston: Houghton Mifflin, 1984), p. 311.

4. Richard Young, "Arts, Crafts, Gifts, and Knacks: Some Disharmonies in the New Rhetoric," in *Reinventing the Rhetorical Tradition*, ed. Aviva Freedman and Ian Pringle (Ottawa: CCTE, 1980), pp. 53–60.

5. Linda Flower and John R. Hayes, "A Cognitive Process Theory of Writing," *CCC*, 32 (December 1981), pp. 365–87.

6. Donald Murray, "Internal Revision: A Process of Discovery," in *Research in Composing*, ed. Charles R. Cooper and Lee Odell (Urbana: NCTE, 1978), pp. 85–103.

7. Nancy Sommers, "Revision Strategies of Student Writers and Experienced Adult Writers," *CCC*, 31 (December 1980), pp. 378–88.

8. Louis Milic, "Theories of Style and Their Implications for the Teaching of Composition," *CCC*, 16 (1965), pp. 66–69, 126.

9. Richard Lanham's "Paramedic Method," in *Revising Prose*, is also frankly prescriptive; however, his broader theory of style, which I will refer to later, is more complex and inclusive.

10. Ian Pringle, "Why Teach Style? A Review Essay," *CCC*, 34 (February 1983), p. 94. For an explication of Krashen's model, see "On the Acquisition of Planned Discourse: Written English as a Second Dialect," in *Proceedings of the Claremont Reading Conference* (1978), pp. 173–85.

11. Louis Milic, "Rhetorical Choice and Stylistic Options," in *Literary Style: A Symposium*, ed. Seymour Chatman (London: Oxford University Press, 1971), p. 87.

12. Louis Milic, "Metaphysics in the Criticism of Style," *CCC*, 17 (1966), pp. 124–29.

13. Peter Elbow, *Writing With Power* (New York: Oxford University Press, 1981), p. 292.

14. John T. Gage, "Philosophies of Style and Their Implications for Composition," *College English*, 41 (February 1980), pp. 615–22.

15. Richard Lanham, "*At* and *Through*: The Opaque Style and Its Uses," *Literacy and the Survival of Humanism* (New Haven: Yale University Press, 1983), pp. 58–86.

16 *Making a Case for Rhetorical Grammar*

LAURA R. MICCICHE

Grammar makes people anxious, even—perhaps especially—writing teachers. Just as writing teachers dread when, our identities discovered, strangers announce that they had better "watch their grammar," we also recoil at the idea of teaching grammar, often considered a mind-numbing pedagogical task that offends our rhetorical sensibilities. In composition studies, grammar instruction is unquestionably unfashionable. It is frequently associated with "low-skills" courses that stigmatize and alienate poor writers while reproducing their status as disenfranchised. This association emerges naturally from teaching methods that present grammar as a fix-it approach to weak writing rather than, as Martha Kolln describes, "a rhetorical tool that all writers should understand and control" (*Rhetorical Grammar* xi). As a result, students' understanding of the tight weave between what we say and how we say it often gets short shrift as we reserve instruction on grammar for the very final stage of drafting.

In composition's disciplinary discourse (and perhaps in practice, though it's hard to know), teaching grammar and teaching writing are separate enterprises. While teaching style, the "extraordinary" use of language, is a familiar enough focus in disciplinary scholarship, teaching the "ordinary" use of language—grammar—is often constructed as ineffective because, it is widely believed, grammar knowledge out of context doesn't translate to grammatical correctness in context.[1] Further complicating the problematic place of grammar in writing instruction is the matter of what *kind* of grammar we're talking about. Often *grammar* is used in a way that assumes we all understand and agree upon its meaning—and, in fact, grammar referred to loosely seems to signify traditional "school grammar" and its focus on repetitive, decontextualized, drill-and-kill exercises. However, grammar has a range of referents (i.e., prescriptive, descriptive, rhetorical) that describe very different kinds of intellectual activities, differences that matter tremendously. These differences evaporate, reducing the issue of grammar instruction to a rather simple rejec-

---

From *College Composition and Communication* 55 (2004): 716–37.

tion of a banal practice, when we fail to specify just what kind of grammar we're rejecting.

My aim in this paper is to establish grounds for teaching grammar rhetorically and for linking this pedagogical effort to larger goals of emancipatory teaching. Teaching grammar is not *necessarily* incompatible with liberatory principles; binaries that suggest otherwise constrain our teaching and our thinking, solidifying and casting as unquestionable rehearsed assumptions about writing. The absence of a sustained contemporary conversation about grammar instruction at the college level does not eclipse the practical reality that nearly every writing teacher struggles with at one time or another: how to teach students to communicate effectively. And effective communication, which entails grammar knowledge, is essential to achieving many of the goals regularly articulated in composition studies. Chief among them are teaching students to produce effective writing that has some relevancy to the world we live in, to see language as having an empowering and sometimes transformative potential, and to critique normalizing discourses that conceal oppressive functions.

Rhetorical grammar instruction, I argue here, is just as central to composition's driving commitment to teach critical thinking and cultural critique as is reading rhetorically, understanding the significance of cultural difference, and engaging in community work through service-learning initiatives. Yet, teaching students grammar skills is rarely associated with the political programs that characterize our disciplinary rhetoric and is seldom linked with rhetorical education or the practice of cultural critique. Grammar instruction, in short, is decidedly not sexy but school-marmish, not empowering but disempowering, not rhetorical but decontextualized, not progressive but remedial.

I hope this study of rhetorical grammar will contribute to our collective thinking about the work of rhetorical education, its possibility and its promise. Donald Bryant, in "Rhetoric: Its Functions and Its Scope," offers an instructive description of the need for rhetorical education:

> If enlightened and responsible leaders with rhetorical knowledge and skill are not trained and nurtured, irresponsible demagogues will monopolize their power of rhetoric, will have things to themselves. If talk rather than take is to settle the course of our society, if ballots instead of bullets are to effect our choice of governors, if discourse rather than coercion is to prevail in the conduct of human affairs, it would seem like arrant folly to trust to chance that the right people shall be equipped offensively and defensively with a sound rationale of informative and suasory discourse. (291)

The construction of "informative and suasory" discourse includes knowing one's audience, responding appropriately to a particular situation, and drawing on relevant examples and illustrations. As I suggest here, it also requires an ability to communicate effectively, using grammatical devices that enable us to respond appropriately and effectively to a situation. Like Bryant, I believe that rhetoric—including rhetorical grammar—should occupy a place of "uncommon importance" in general education (291). While this emphasis is consistent with that of some ancient rhetoricians,[2] contemporary rhetoricians, by omission rather than vocal opposition, tend to construct grammar as outside the realm of rhetoric.

We need a discourse about grammar that does not retreat from the realities we face in the classroom—a discourse that takes seriously the connection between writing and thinking, the interwoven relationship between what we say and how we say it. In addition, we need to ask questions about the enabling work of grammar instruction alongside composition's view of writing and its instruction as social practices that have the potential to both reproduce and challenge cultural values, truths, and assumptions. Can grammar knowledge be conceived as extending the work of cultural critique? How might we teach grammar in a way that supports rhetorical education? I believe that the examinations of language made possible through rhetorical grammar pedagogy encourage students to view writing as a material social practice in which meaning is actively made, rather than passively relayed or effortlessly produced. In this sense, rhetorical grammar instruction can demonstrate to students that language does purposeful, consequential work in the world—work that can be learned and applied.

RHETORICAL GRAMMAR AS A WAY OF THINKING

> Let no man, therefore, look down on the elements of grammar as small matters;
> not because it requires great labor to distinguish consonants from vowels, and to
> divide them into the proper number of semivowels and mutes, but because, to
> those entering the recesses, as it were, of this temple, there will appear much
> subtlety on points, which may not only sharpen the wits of boys, but may exercise
> even the deepest erudition and knowledge.

> —QUINTILIAN (IN MURPHY 29)

The chief reason for teaching rhetorical grammar in writing classes is that doing so is central to teaching thinking. The ability to develop sentences and form paragraphs that serve a particular purpose requires a conceptual ability to envision relationships between ideas. Such relationships involve processes of identification with an imagined or real reader and reflection on the way our language invites and/or alienates readers. The grammatical choices we make—including pronoun use, active or passive verb constructions, and sentence patterns—represent relations between writers and the world they live in. Word choice and sentence structure are an expression of the way we attend to the words of others, the way we position ourselves in relation to others. In this sense, writing involves cognitive skills at the level of idea development *and* at the sentence level. How we put our ideas into words and comprehensible forms is a dynamic process rather than one with clear boundaries between what we say and how we say it.

Of course, linking grammar and conceptual thinking is not the first thing that comes to mind when we think of teaching grammar. Usually, our minds go to those unending rules and exceptions, those repetitive drills and worksheets, perhaps even to diagramming sentences with a ruler, performing a quasiscientific operation on language (one that I found particularly satisfying while in middle school). These are the hallmarks of formal grammar instruction, the deadening effects of which are widely known. A familiar argument against teaching formal grammar, particularly forceful since the rise of process pedagogies, insists that integrating grammar instruction would dangerously reduce time spent on higher-order concerns like invention and arrangement. Another argument contends that if students can't articulate their ideas in a comprehensible form, correct grammar does nothing to improve their writing. Both lines of argument rely on the faulty assumption that grammar instruction means only *formal* grammar instruction, the deadly kind that teaches correctness divorced from content and situation. Both lines of argument keep intact the binary that defines grammar instruction in opposition to composing and thinking, a binary that reproduces the notion that grammar-talk is most appropriate for the end stage of drafting.

When grammar is reserved for end-stage drafting, it is most often a version of formal grammar or "school grammar." The following passage, excerpted from the *Instructor's Manual and Answer Key to Accompany The Writer's Harbrace Handbook*, provides a familiar, though not an isolated, example of just what generates fear and paranoia in students and teachers alike:

> Once we diagnose and show students how to correct errors, then they must correct them consistently. Making comments about errors on drafts and then requiring students to turn in revisions provide immediate practice. However, only through subsequent assignments, however [sic], can we assess students' mastery over errors. Therefore, instructors and students should record errors, and instructors should hold students accountable for correcting those errors. (Winchell 21)

The orientation to grammar here is error driven and disciplinary, as evidenced in the description of efforts to "diagnose," "record," and "correct" errors. The goal is student "mastery over errors," resulting in self-conscious correction. Intentionally or not, the framework is one of finding and fixing errors rather than of active choice making for a purpose. Rhetorical grammar instruction, in contrast, emphasizes grammar as a tool for articulating and expressing relationships among ideas. The purpose of learning rhetorical grammar is to learn how to generate persuasive, clear thinking that reflects on and responds to language as work, as *produced* rather than evacuated of imperfections.

How we think and give shape to ideas is intimately tied up with the forms, patterns, and rhythms of spoken and written language. Thus, writing is profoundly reflective of the deep grammars that we absorb as inhabitants of a particular place and time. For this reason, when we reserve grammar-talk for the end of the drafting stage, I think we miss opportunities to discuss with students how the particulars of language use show us something about the way we figure relationships among people, ideas, and texts. Writing teachers need to be able to talk about how a well-coordinated sentence can keep your reader breathlessly moving with you, how techniques that create rhythm and emphasis heighten the feeling being conveyed, how subordination expresses relationships among ideas, how someone like Eminem uses repetition and power words—or words of emphasis—to create culturally relevant and, for some people, resonant stories.

More than a systematic application of rules, Mina Shaughnessy reminds us, grammar involves "a way of thinking, a style of inquiry," as opposed to "a way of being right" (129). For instance, we learn through Quintilian's excerpt above that *men* and *boys* are the subjects of education; his word choice reveals his "way of thinking" about who is entitled to an education. His male referents point to the real exclusion—as opposed to functioning as convenient placeholders for all people—of women and girls from the educational enterprise in the eighteenth century. When we broaden the goals of rhetorical grammar, it's possible to see how the intimate study of language it encourages has enormous potential for studying language as central to constructions of identity and culture. Rhetorical grammar enables such readings because it is "grammar in the service of rhetoric," which means that grammar is never divorced from ideological functions (Kolln, "Rhetorical Grammar" 29).

I am talking about rhetorical grammar as an integral component of critical writing, writing that at minimum seeks to produce new knowledge and critique stale thinking. One of the key operations of critical writing is that it locates an object of discourse in space and time, thereby placing it in a system of relationships. Joan Didion, in "Why I Write," describes this function when commenting on grammar's "infinite power": "All I know about grammar is its infinite power. To shift the structure of a sentence alters the meaning of that sentence, as definitely and inflexibly as the position of a camera alters the meaning of the object photographed" (7). As Didion's comment suggests, grammar is a positioning tool, a way of framing and presenting ideas that influences how and what we see.

This shaping of meaning through writing is intimately connected with a writer's grammatical choices. Elizabeth Bruss illuminates this idea in her brilliant study of the discourse of literary theory, *Beautiful Theories*. She suggests that the rhetoric of grammar is an important factor in the construction and consumption of theoretical discourse, and it tells us something about the "mind" in the writing. She explains, "In reading theory, one often notes where the energy of the writing seems to have been expended—in lush diction or well-turned phrases, in the juxtaposition between sentences or organization of larger episodes. From this, one receives a first (if not always a lasting) impression of the power or delicacy of mind that informs the theory" (117). She notes that the "manipulation of syntax" in theoretical writing creates a "disturbing sense of disorientation," a point that nicely describes the way grammar and content work together in theoretical writing to disturb settled or "natural" ways of thinking (122).

Referring to language as "conceptual machinery," Bruss observes: "One comes to know the nature of this machinery through watching how it functions and using it for oneself, rather than by visualizing or possessing it as a set of properties" (131). Bruss's emphasis on *use* as a way to test and experiment with the possibilities of language informs my commonplace book assignment, designed for teaching rhetorical grammar. As demonstrated in the student writing samples in the next section, the study of rhetorical grammar encourages students to experiment with language and then to reflect on the interaction between content and grammatical form. While this approach entails study of sentence slots, structures like participial phrases and adverbials that add information to a sentence, and the difference between independent and dependent clauses, rhetorical grammar more generally requires students to think about the work these aspects of grammar achieve for a writer's message. In practical terms, as well as identifying a dependent clause, students are asked to construct a sentence with a dependent clause in it and to explain the discursive effects of subordinating one idea to another.

Among other things, I want students to consider how such a sentence-level choice might reflect configurations of power in a more general sense. Explaining how discursive practices signify more than technical skill, Michel Foucault writes, "Discursive practices are not purely and simply ways of producing discourse. They are embodied in technical processes, in institutions, in patterns for general behavior, in forms for transmission and diffusion, and in pedagogical forms which, at once, impose and maintain them" (128). To illustrate just how language practices are embodied in cultural institutions, I have asked students to read a variety of texts that bring this issue to life. Selections have included George Orwell's "Politics and the English Language," bell hooks's "Language," excerpts from Robin Lakoff's *Language and Woman's Place*, and James Baldwin's "If Black Language Isn't a Language, Then Tell Me, What Is?" In different ways, each reading offers students a framework for understanding how grammar and language practices are schooled and maintained in culture. In addition, we learn that grammar use can sometimes function as a form of resistance, a point that bell hooks discusses in relation to slave songs. She writes that the English in these songs "reflected the broken, ruptured world of the slave. When the slaves sang 'nobody knows de trouble I see—' their use of the word 'nobody' adds a richer meaning than if they had used the phrase 'no one,' for it was the slave's *body* that was the concrete site of suffering"(170). hooks argues that the syntax of the songs did not change over the years because "the incorrect usage of words" expressed "a spirit of rebellion that claimed language as a site of resistance" (170). hooks's essay, along with the readings named above, encourages my students to think about grammar as a crucial tool for both communication and the expression of identity. This way of thinking about grammar often challenges students' preconceptions about grammar as a rigid system for producing correctness, preparing them for the commonplace book assignment described below.

GETTING CLOSE TO LANGUAGE

I emphasize the rhetorical aspects of grammar by asking students to focus on connections between grammar and concepts such as audience and purpose, paying particular attention to grammar as an art of selection. I want students to consider how and why discourses take the form they do, seeing discourse as a production that involves work and intention and craft. In setting up a classroom study of grammar as rhetorically produced, I use Kolln's *Rhetorical Grammar* as the primary theoretical framework, supplemented by excerpts on figures of thought from Sharon Crowley's *Ancient Rhetorics for Contemporary Students*. My course[3] is based on the assumption that learning how to use grammar to best effect requires lots of practice and a good deal of exposure to varied writing styles. To this end, students maintain a commonplace book throughout the semester in which they imitate and record passages of their own choosing. In *Ancient Rhetorics*, Crowley explains the history of commonplace books as follows: "In pre-modern times, most rhetors kept written collections of copied passages; these were called *florilegia* (flowers of reading) in medieval times, and commonplace books during the Renaissance and into the eighteenth century" (250; emphasis in original). She defines such a book as "a notebook kept by a rhetor as a storehouse of materials to be remembered or quoted" (335).

As I have conceived the commonplace book, students follow each entry with at least one paragraph of analysis in which they identify the work achieved by specific grammatical techniques in the passage. I ask students to look critically at writing by analyzing passages from their favorite authors, literature and textbooks they are reading in other courses, syllabi, Web-based texts, television advertisements, segments from presidential debates — in short, any text that students find interesting. I have two goals for the commonplace books: first, to emphasize the always entangled relationship between *what* and *how* we say something; second, to designate a place where students document and comment on their evolving relationship to writing and grammatical concepts. Both goals circulate around the idea that learning how to recognize and reflect on language as *made* and *made to work* on people's lives is central to being able to use language strategically.

Commonplace books encourage students to read and analyze texts as skillfully crafted documents that convey and perform different kinds of meanings — among them, aesthetic, rhetorical, and political. Students are able to tinker with language, seeing how it is crafted and directed rather than as simply "correct" or "incorrect." Thinking of language as correct or incorrect distorts it into an objective medium consisting of ahistorical rules and truths, obscuring the living quality of language. This aliveness — the changing, transforming capacity of language — is what makes the study of rhetorical grammar especially relevant and necessary. Rhetorical grammar offers a perspective on the way people purposefully use language to describe problematic or possible new realities. It presents students with a framework and a vocabulary for examining how language affects and infects social reality, as it also provides them with tools for creating effective discourse.

Understanding how language is made and then deployed for varying effects has the potential to highlight the important work of language in our culture. This goal is especially important at the present time, as political dissent is increasingly under suspicion, and the USA Patriot Act of 2001 threatens speech acts both within and beyond the classroom. An ability to examine closely and carefully the work of language could influence discussions of political texts in the classroom. For instance, in my fall 2002 Functional Grammar class, students analyzed the grammar of President Bush's speech to the United Nations on 12 September 2002. The speech, printed in the *New York Times on the Web*, sought to present evidence to the U.N. that would make a case for moving "deliberately and decisively to hold Iraq to account" for its harboring of weapons of mass destruction. In a large-group discussion, my students analyzed Bush's use of hedging, or qualification of claims. They noted the following language choices: "U.N. inspectors *believe* Iraq has produced two to four times the amount of biological agents it declared"; "United Nations inspections also reveal that Iraq *likely* maintains stockpiles of VX, mustard, and other chemical agents . . ."; if not for the Gulf War, "the regime in Iraq would *likely* have possessed a nuclear weapon no later than 1993" ("Bush's Speech"; emphasis added).

The students' examination of hedging, demonstrated by Bush's word choice, evolved into a lively discussion about what counts as evidence in the context of declaring war; indeed, more recently, critics worldwide have begun asking questions about the "facts" regarding Iraq's weapons development program. This example is meant to suggest that rhetorical grammar analysis can form the basis for wider analyses of civic discourse, enabling students to hone in on the specific grammatical choices that give shape and meaning to content. While the following student applications of rhetorical grammar analysis do not take this sort of politicized focus, the close study of how grammar enhances and conceals meaning can certainly be applied in this way.

I ask students to make a variety of entries in their commonplace books. Recordings are entries that require students to record a passage of their own choosing and then analyze how grammar and content work together to convey meaning. In the following recording,[4] the student writer illustrates how language works on her as a reader. She records a passage from Washington Irving's "Rip Van Winkle." Rip comes down the mountain after being asleep for twenty years and is confused by the amount of time that has elapsed and by the figure, which turns out to be his son, who looks remarkably like Rip himself. " 'God knows,' exclaimed [Rip], at his wit's end; 'I'm not myself— I'm somebody else—I'm somebody else—that's me yonder—no—that's somebody else got into my shoes—I was myself last night, but I fell asleep on the mountain, and they've changed my gun and every thing's changed, and I'm changed, and I can't tell my name, or who I am!' " In her analysis, this student writes,

I think Irving does a great job of showing the puzzlement Rip Van Winkle feels when he comes down the mountain and doesn't know himself or anyone else. The use of dashes in this text is effective, which is sometimes hard to accomplish. If dashes are overused, the reader can get confused and have a hard time grasping the feeling the author is trying to convey. But in this passage, Irving uses dashes to help the reader understand how Rip is feeling. Rip is disoriented, confused, and he feels lost. The dashes break up his thoughts, and the reader can hear the panic he is feeling.

The structure of the sentence also conveys the alarm Rip feels. As I read the passage out loud, I found that my voice got higher and I read faster as I got toward the end. The emphasis is put on the end of the sentence, and this lets the reader know that Rip is getting more and more upset as his thoughts go on.

This analysis explains how grammatical techniques intertwine with meaning to convey Rip's confusion. When the writer points out that the dashes help the reader to experience Rip's fragmented sense of identity, she demonstrates her ability to see that meaning emerges from the very specific marks a writer chooses. The writer's analysis offers a reading of how feeling is suspended in this passage, which creates, to borrow from Bruss, an "impression of the power or delicacy of mind" that shapes the narrative (117).

Other commonplace entries include imitations of a writer's form—not, it should be noted, imitations of content.[5] In these entries, the student writer must not only mimic the writer's syntax, but must also identify the specific effects created by the syntax. In an example from Brian's commonplace book, he begins with a quotation from Harper Lee's *To Kill A Mockingbird*. In this scene, Atticus, a lawyer, is questioning Mr. Ewell to determine why he failed to retrieve a doctor to examine his daughter who was allegedly raped. " 'Mr. Ewell,' Atticus began, 'folks were doing a lot of running that night. Let's see, you say you ran to the house, you ran to the window, you ran inside, you ran to Mayella, you ran for Mr. Tate. Did you, during all this running, run for a doctor?' " In his analysis, Brian writes.

> Lee, through Atticus, uses parallelism to emphasize that Mr. Ewell seemed to be running everywhere. By beginning each clause with *you ran*, he adds emphasis each time as he builds to the final point. Lee uses an asyndeton series style sentence to add emphasis to the final point. By using this type of series, there is no *and* used between each item in the series. This absence says to the reader that I could go on and on. This type of series is important in the underlying motive of the statement. Atticus is trying to emphasize that Mr. Ewell should have run for a doctor. By using the asyndeton series, he is saying that you ran here, you ran there, and I could go on and on pointing out where you did run; but the most important thing is that you didn't run to the doctor.

Having decided that Lee's passage is similar to "the kinds of speeches a coach might give his team for motivation," Brian creates the following imitation: " 'Boys,' the coach began, 'this team has been doing a lot of scoring on us today. Let's see, they scored on a free kick, they scored on a header, they scored on a penalty kick, they scored on a cross, they scored on a nice shot. Did you, during all their scoring, score any of your own?' "

A similar attention to the grammatical work of a passage characterizes Chris's analysis of one passage in Kurt Vonnegut's *Breakfast of Champions*. Explaining Vonnegut's use of the word *charm* in a passage, Chris writes,

> In his definition, Vonnegut uses the word "charm" in one form or another six times within five sentences, and he uses the word "oodles" three times. He also uses the same basic sentence structure for the last three sentences. These repetitions convey the satirical nature of the explanation. That is, Vonnegut is mocking the word by over doing its definition. Rather than combining the subjects in the last three sentences and making one compound sentence, Vonnegut chooses to repeat the same sentence format three times in a row. This has the effect of enforcing each separate subjects place in the explanation. In this case the word comes out as being somewhat discredited. Vonnegut's point is that lots of people have charm and those who don't can usually fake it.

Drawing on descriptions of sentence structure and repetition that Kolln describes in *Rhetorical Grammar*, Chris shows us how Vonnegut reinforces the idea of the passage through grammatical techniques. He chose to examine Vonnegut's work because he had always admired it and wanted to get a better look at how Vonnegut creates such an effective tone. By requiring students to select texts to record or imitate in their commonplace books, this assignment can work well to get students to look closely at language that pleases or disturbs them. Students are pushed to think in unfamiliar ways about texts to which they have developed familiar responses. Or, in some cases, students analyzed texts that they come into contact with on a regular basis but never read attentively.

Getting close to a passage in order to reveal the technical processes that make it work forms the basis of another student's reading of Ambrose Bierce's story, "An Occurrence at Owl Creek Bridge." This excerpt, taken from a student's grammatical analysis paper,[6] was originally a recording in her commonplace book. In her discussion of Bierce's use of parallelism, she writes,

> Bierce masters this technique, and seems to understand the effects that it has on the rhythm: "The water, the banks, the forest, the now distant bridge, fort, and men—all were commingled and blurred" (86). To achieve parallelism, Bierce repeats "the," followed by a noun phrase, four times. He opts not to use it, though he has the opportunity, a fifth and sixth time—doing this may make the parallelism redundant or gratuitous. Bierce thoughtfully controls the rhythm of this sentence. The reader is made to slow down where the word "the" appears—it takes more time to say "the water" than to say "water." Furthermore, the sentence gets progressively slower as we push through "the now distant bridge" and then are set free by the sleek, and fast flow of "fort, and men." This control of rhythm relates to control of emphasis, and thus drama. We emphasize the words following "the" simply because we slow down and have more time to absorb the image. Correspondingly,

we pass over words without the "the" in front of them and do not have time to savor their meanings.

This writer's analysis highlights Bierce's use of momentum and rhythm to mirror the feeling of the passage. As I think her reading illustrates, the closeness to language encouraged by the commonplace book assignment requires students to dig around in the writing of others and really think about what makes it tick. This intimacy with the language of others can be an enormously powerful way to impress upon students that writing is made and that grammar has a role in that production. In addition, the commonplace book assignment offers a productive space where students document their sense of writing as reflecting intentional choices that have consequences.

While the examples I've included draw from literary texts, I want to note that my students have selected a variety of texts as the basis for commonplace book entries. These have included billing information accompanying phone bills and credit card bills, instruction manuals for appliances, text on food packaging, advertisements, textbooks, and syllabi. Whatever the textual source for entries, the model of rhetorical grammar pedagogy described here can be an asset to teaching practices that view analytical thinking as a necessary component of any socially engaged pedagogy.

RHETORICAL GRAMMAR AND EMPOWERING PEDAGOGIES

Composition scholars have yet to map out the potentially productive connections between rhetorical grammar and composition's disciplinary commitment to cultural difference and ethical rhetoric. What's notable about liberatory pedagogies of the 1980s and 1990s is not that they reject grammar instruction but that grammar is largely absent from their descriptions of critical education. The higher-level concerns of liberatory pedagogies focused on creating social change by teaching students skills with which to challenge cultural norms (Berlin; Fitts and France; Luke and Gore) and by articulating teaching and writing as cultural practices that transmit and produce cultural meanings (Giroux and McLaren; Sullivan and Qualley). Internal analyses of composition's identity as a discipline have revealed the troubling working conditions and wages of part-time teachers (Schell); the gender, race, and class politics of composition studies (Bullock and Trimbur; Jarratt and Worsham); and the relationship between pedagogy and diverse student populations (Ashton-Jones; Severino et al.).

This body of work has profoundly shaped my intellectual and political orientation in composition studies, and I believe that its politicized dimensions can provide insights about teaching grammar as a study of how language does work *in* (and sometimes *against*) the world. Gary Olson's "Encountering the Other" offers a framework for considering this claim. Olson notes that composition studies has increasingly come to focus on "issues of gender, race, or 'contact zones'" as an ethical commitment to foregrounding "interaction with an Other" (92). Ethics, for him, deals with "how we balance our own needs, desires, and obligations with those of the Other" (92). This balancing act, which requires careful consideration of self/other relations, is relevant to grammatical choices that writers make because it is part of the conceptual work that we do as writers. We envision and construct an audience through diction, tone, and the selection of examples; and as writers we seek to reach across the space that separates us from our audience, using techniques that engender trust, establish credibility, and sometimes build connection.

A student in my sophomore-level Writing with Style course demonstrates how attention to grammatical choices dovetails with an understanding of self/other relations in his analysis of the grammar and style that typifies Malcolm X's writing. He argues that Malcolm X's use of "you" in "Not Just an American Problem but a World Problem" involves his African American audience in an intimate way:

> Speaking in the second person helps urge audience members to personally take responsibility for creating a political change and becoming active participants in the revolt for racial equality. . . . By constantly using words and phrases that signify "togetherness" to refer to himself and his audience, Malcolm urges African-Americans to organize and unify.

Throughout his paper, this student examines how grammatical choices reinforce Malcolm X's emphasis on black unity as a necessary component of meaningful social change, a focus that centers on the relations between the speaker and conditions in the world. Like other forms of textual analysis, grammatical analysis can yield engaged political and cultural insights about language as "the carrier of culture, the facilitator of humanity, and the most powerful of the means of social control" (Sledd 62).

Such insights form the basis of critical pedagogy, which reveals how language constructs and reproduces oppressive cultural discourses that naturalize inequality. For instance, Ira Shor describes critical pedagogy as a teaching method that "questions the *status quo*," and is consistent with democratic values, political activism aimed at eliminating inequalities, and efforts toward "desocializing" (3). Critical pedagogy, for Shor, entails a questioning "posture towards the construction of the self in society" (16), a model of inquiry that is also key to Krista Ratcliffe's conceptualization of feminist composition pedagogy. This pedagogy "foregrounds the functions of gender as it intersects with other categories (e.g., race, class, sexual orientation, nationality); as such, it attempts to empower real historical students, particularly real historical women students, by helping them to recognize their own politics of location and negotiate such positions" (58). This kind of cultural work associated with liberatory pedagogical efforts is not incompatible with analyses that foreground rhetorical grammar analysis. In fact, such analysis can enrich our understanding of how writers use language to construct identity—both that of self and other—and to position themselves alongside or in opposition to the status quo.

In a large-group discussion of Gertrude Stein's grammatical inventions and subversions, for instance, my students commented on the way Stein uses language to deconstruct prescribed subject positions. Stein, the students argued, constructs something like a new language, using repetition and alliteration of words to do the work of punctuation. She constructs herself as a builder of meaning who uses the conventional tools of language in unconventional ways. My students were interested in how Stein, rather than duplicating moves that characterize "good writing," uses language to assert her identity as a different kind of writer; in addition, they made links between Stein's disruption of language conventions and her disruption of sexual categories and desires (portrayed especially in *Tender Buttons*).

As I'm suggesting, rhetorical grammar analysis promises to offer students more tools for analyzing culture. Cultural studies scholars, according to Pamela Caughie, make "the construction of the subject in cultural institutions and social discourses central to their investigations" (111–12). Interdisciplinary approaches to cultural studies share a common goal of investigating "the complex ways in which identity itself is articulated, experienced, deployed" (Nelson et al. qtd. in Caughie 112). By looking at practices of representation in various discursive forms, cultural studies methodologies tell us something about the way desires are fabricated and reproduced in order to construct certain kinds of subjects. Rhetorical grammar analysis can work in concert with these goals by making available to students a vocabulary for thinking through the specificity of words and grammatical choices, the work they do in the production of an idea of culture and an idea of a people.

This insight is revealed not only in studies of grammar use but also in studies that make visible the cultural attitudes and assumptions informing grammar instruction itself. Miriam Brody's *Manly Writing*, for instance, examines gendered metaphors in advice texts from the Enlightenment through the twentieth century that liken good writing to manliness and virility. Brody's study reveals what she calls the "hidden curriculum" of writing instruction—a curriculum that, mirroring the shift from a rural to an industrialized culture, ennobled masculine virtues and repelled feminine "vice," or the arts of deception, emotion, and flowery language. Brody discusses early grammar texts, in which a "fusion of patriotic, linguistic, and gendered issues forged an ideology for an age that frankly and reasonably imagined itself as perfectible, if only young boys learned their mother tongue well" (96). In this context, Brody argues writing was gendered as a male activity that signaled a boy's civility, intelligence, and cleanliness. In addition, grammar texts from the late 1700s and early 1800s compared writing to men's work, just as the increasing industrialization during the period was seen as male labor requiring strength, forcefulness, and muscular achievement. Brody contends that the grammar exercise was the method by which young boys learned their trade: "The grammatical exercise assumed that the student was like a master builder with words, which, like so many levers and bolts, became tools for production" (105). The simplicity and cleanliness of grammar exercises, while no longer gendered in the same way that Brody describes, continue to provide students with a sense of achievement and mastery and, perhaps most satisfying of all, finality. Yet, as many have noted, when correcting language outside a meaningful context, students and teachers alike are often frustrated by the lack of transfer from the exercise to the rhetorical situation (see note 1).

The point I want to emphasize is that grammar skill and instruction are linked to cultural attitudes, beliefs, and assumptions. But an absence of attention to grammar instruction prevents us from considering productive links. Instead, we adhere to a normalized reflex against teaching grammar in the context of writing instruction. David Lazere makes a similar point in "Back to Basics" when he questions leftists' automatic reflex against "basic skills" instruction. "Basic skills," for him, refers to a somewhat amorphous "factual knowledge" and to the more explicit "mechanical and analytic skills (including remedial instruction in reading and writing standard English)" (19). While he does not utter the *g*-word here, it seems that Lazere's focus on mechanical skills and Standard English is connected to teaching grammar. He finds that a lack of "basic skills and factual knowledge" among students and teachers creates obstacles "to autonomous critical thinking and to openness toward progressive politics," a point largely overlooked or simplified by leftist educators (9). By rejecting "basic skills" as dogmatically as conservatives endorse it, leftists err, Lazere contends, in failing to see that basic skills instruction "might be a force for liberation—not oppression—if administered with common sense, openness to cultural pluralism, and an application of basics toward critical thinking, particularly about sociopolitical issues, rather than rote memorizing" (9). Although the particulars of basic skills instruction are never made clear, Lazere poses a useful challenge to binaries that refuse to see skills instruction—including grammar instruction—as anything other than conservative and dehumanizing, a position that bespeaks the already achieved privileges of rhetorical skill and the cultural capital that accompanies it (see Delpit). The opposition between teaching grammar and teaching writing—which depends on an understanding of grammar instruction in the traditional, formal sense—limits and forecloses productive discussion about rhetorical grammar as a tool for supporting and extending cultural analysis.

Grammar competency has always been linked with social power or the lack thereof. As a component of written literacy, grammar knowledge often functions to "draw lines of social distinction, mark status, and rank students in meritocratic order" (Trimbur 279). In addition to its association with class markers that lock people into social place, grammar competency also raises difficult questions concerning second-language learners and the teaching of grammar as a skill (not a craft, an art, or a tool for cultural critique) that serves the dominant economic order (i.e., see Giroux). We can challenge these associations, exploring what it might mean to teach grammar in a way that promotes composition's goals to equip students to be active citizens of the worlds they inhabit. Rather than abandon grammar instruction, I'm suggesting that writing teachers seek avenues from which to revitalize practice, positioning rhetorical grammar as a necessary component of rhetorical education.

Acknowledgments: An earlier version of this paper was delivered at the 2000 NCTE Conference in Milwaukee. I want to thank Alice Gillam for introducing me to rhetorical grammar in her Teaching Composition seminar; thanks go also to Gary Weissman, Martha Kolln, and an anonymous reader for their generative feedback on earlier drafts. In addition, I want to acknowledge my graduate research assistant, Sean Memolo, who so carefully gathered and summarized research materials for this project. His assistantship was supported by the English Department at East Carolina University.

NOTES

1. A number of studies questioning how formal grammar instruction translates into writing improvement have been influential in composition studies (Braddock et al.; D'Eloia; Hartwell; Hillocks; Meckel; Sutton; Tabbert). For useful reviews of this work, see Bonnie Devet, Susan Hunter and Ray Wallace, and Rei Noguchi.

2. On ancient rhetoricians and grammar instruction, see Gina Claywell, Cheryl Glenn, or Jon Olson.

3. In this section, I describe and draw examples from two different courses in which I taught the same material. One is Writing with Style, a sophomore-level course that I taught in spring 1999 while a graduate student at the University of Wisconsin-Milwaukee. This course integrated rhetorical grammar study with issues of style, a pairing that reflects the frequent blurring of distinctions between grammar and style in composition scholarship (see Zemliansky).

The other course described in this section is a sophomore-level course entitled Functional Grammar, which I have taught during three noncontiguous semesters at East Carolina University since fall 2000. Like several of the linguists in my department, I teach the course as rhetorical grammar because this terminology highlights grammar as integral to persuasive speech acts. As an approach to studying language, however, rhetorical grammar shares several principles with functional grammar, including the idea that language *does* something, language use varies according to context, and learning grammar entails sentence-level and larger discursive-level knowledge. See Charles Meyer for a useful overview of functional grammar with specific attention to M. A. K. Halliday's functional theory of language.

4. I'd like to extend special thanks to those students who gave me permission to quote from their commonplace books; those whose names are not given wished to remain anonymous. All student writing appears here exactly as it was written.

5. Resources on using imitation exercises in the writing classroom are plentiful. For a sampling, see Robert Connors on rhetoric and imitation, Frank D'Angelo on "strict" and "loose" imitations, and Winston Weathers on "creative imitation."

6. Students wrote an eight-page analysis of the grammar of any text of their choosing. For more information on this and other assignments, visit the following links on my Web site: http://personal.ecu.edu/miccichel/grammar02.htm and http://personal.ecu.edu/miccichel/2730.htm and http://personal.ecu.edu/miccichel/style.htm. Send me an e-mail at miccichel@mailecu.edu regarding suggestions and/or comments about the ideas discussed in this article.

WORKS CITED

Ashton-Jones, Evelyn. "Collaboration, Conversation, and the Politics of Gender." *Feminine Principles and Women's Experience in American Composition and Rhetoric.* Ed. Louise Wetherbee Phelps and Janet Emig. Pittsburgh: U of Pittsburgh P, 1995. 5–26.

Baldwin, James. "If Black English Isn't a Language, Then Tell Me, What Is?" *Ten on Ten: Major Essayists on Recurring Themes.* Ed. Robert Atwan. Boston: Bedford, 1992. 321–24.

Berlin, James A. "Rhetoric and Ideology in the Writing Class." *College English* 50.5 (1988): 477–94.

Braddock, Richard, Richard Lloyd-Jones, and Lowell Schoer. *Research in Written Composition.* Champaign, IL: NCTE, 1963.

Brody, Miriam. *Manly Writing: Gender, Rhetoric, and the Rise of Composition.* Carbondale, IL: SIUP, 1993.

Bruss, Elizabeth W. *Beautiful Theories: The Spectacle of Discourse in Contemporary Criticism.* Baltimore: Johns Hopkins UP, 1982.

Bryant, Donald C. "Rhetoric: Its Functions and Its Scope." *Professing the New Rhetorics: A Source-book*. Ed. Theresa Enos and Stuart C. Brown. Englewood Cliffs, NJ: Prentice Hall, 1994. 267–97.

Bullock, Richard, and John Trimbur, eds. *The Politics of Writing Instruction: Postsecondary*. Portsmouth, NH: Boynton/Cook, 1991.

"Bush's Speech to U.N. on Iraq." *New York Times on the Web* 12 Sept. 2002. 12 Sept. 2002. www .nytimes.com/2002/09/12/politics/12AP-PTEX.html.

Caughie, Pamela L. "Let It Pass: Changing the Subject, Once Again." *Feminism and Composition: In Other Words*. Ed. Susan C. Jarratt and Lynn Worsham. New York: MLA, 1998. 111–31.

Claywell, Gina. "Reasserting Grammar's Position in the Trivium in American College Composition." Hunter and Wallace 43–53.

Connors, Robert J. "The Erasure of the Sentence." *College Composition and Communication* 52.1 (2000): 96–128.

Crowley, Sharon. *Ancient Rhetorics for Contemporary Students*. New York: Macmillan, 1994.

D'Angelo, Frank. "Imitation and Style." *The Writing Teacher's Sourcebook*. 2nd ed. Ed. Gary Tate and Edward P. J. Corbett. New York: Oxford UP, 1988. 199–207.

D'Eloia, Sarah. "The Uses—and Limits—of Grammar." *Journal of Basic Writing* 1.3 (1977): 1–20.

Delpit, Lisa. *Other People's Children: Cultural Conflict in the Classroom*. New York: The New P, 1995.

Devet, Bonnie, "Welcoming Grammar Back into the Writing Classroom." *Teaching English in the Two-Year College* 30.1 (2002): 8–17.

Didion, Joan. "Why I Write." *Joan Didion: Essays and Conversations*. Ed. Ellen G. Friedman. Princeton, NJ: Ontario Review P, 1984. 5–10.

Fitts, Karen, and Alan W. France, eds. *Left Margins: Cultural Studies and Composition Pedagogy*. Albany: SUNY P, 1995.

Foucault, Michel. *Language, Counter-Memory, Practice*. Ed. Donald F. Bouchard. Ithaca: Cornell UP, 1980.

Giroux, Henry A. *Teachers as Intellectuals: Toward a Critical Pedagogy of Learning*. Granby, MA: Bergin and Garvey, 1988.

Giroux, Henry A., and Peter McLaren, eds. *Critical Pedagogy, the State, and Cultural Struggle*. Albany: SUNY P, 1989.

Glenn, Cheryl. "When Grammar Was a Language Art." Hunter and Wallace 9–29.

Hartwell, Patrick. "Grammar, Grammars, and the Teaching of Grammar." *College English* 47.2 (1985): 105–27.

Hillocks, George, Jr. *Research on Written Composition: New Directions for Teaching*. Urbana, IL: NCRE/ERIC, 1986.

hooks, bell, "Language." *Teaching to Transgress: Education as the Practice of Freedom*. New York: Routledge, 1994. 167–75.

Hunter, Susan, and Ray Wallace, eds. *The Place of Grammar in Writing Instruction: Past, Present, Future*. Portsmouth, NH: Boynton/Cook, 1995.

Jarratt, Susan C., and Lynn Worsham, eds. *Feminism and Composition Studies: In Other Words*. New York: MLA, 1998.

Kolln, Martha. "Rhetorical Grammar: A Modification Lesson." *English Journal* 85.7 (1996): 25–31.

———. *Rhetorical Grammar: Grammatical Choices, Rhetorical Effects*. 4th ed. New York: Longman, 2003.

Lakoff, Robin. *Language and Woman's Place*. New York: Harper & Row, 1975.

Lazere, David. "Back to Basics: A Force for Oppression or Liberation?" *College English* 54.1 (1992): 7–21.

Luke, Carmen, and Jennifer Gore, eds. *Feminisms and Critical Pedagogies*. New York: Routledge, 1992.

Meckel, Henry C. "Research on Teaching Composition and Literature." *Handbook of Educational Research*. Ed. N. L. Gage. Chicago: Rand McNally, 1963. 966–1006.

Meyer, Charles F. "Functional Grammar and Discourse Studies." *Discourse Studies in Composition*. Ed. Ellen Barton and Gail Stygall. Cresskill, NJ: Hampton P, 2002. 71–89.

Murphy, James J., ed. *Quintilian on the Teaching of Speaking and Writing*. Carbondale, IL: SIUP, 1987.

Noguchi, Rei R. *Grammar and the Teaching of Writing: Limits and Possibilities*. Urbana, IL: NCTE, 1991.

Olson, Gary A. "Encountering the Other: Postcolonial Theory and Composition Scholarship." *Ethical Issues in College Writing*. Ed. Fredric G. Gale, Phillip Sipiora, and James L. Kinneavy. New York: Peter Lang, 1999. 91–105.

Olson, Jon. "A Question of Power: Why Fredrick Douglass Stole Grammar." Hunter and Wallace 30–42.

Orwell, George, "Politics and the English Language." *Ten on Ten: Major Essayists on Recurring Themes.* Ed. Robert Atwan. Boston: Bedford, 1992. 309–20.

Ratcliffe, Krista. *Anglo-American Feminist Challenges to the Rhetorical Traditions: Virginia Woolf, Mary Daly, Adrienne Rich.* Carbondale, IL: SIUP, 1996.

Schell, Eileen E. *Gypsy Academics and Mother-Teachers: Gender, Contingent Labor, and Writing Instruction.* Portsmouth, NH: Boynton/Cook, 1998.

Severino, Carol, Juan C. Guerra, and Johnnella E. Butler, eds. *Writing in Multicultural Settings.* New York: MLA, 1997.

Shaughnessy, Mina P. *Errors and Expectations: A Guide for the Teacher of Basic Writing.* New York: Oxford UP, 1977.

Shor, Ira. *Empowering Education: Critical Teaching for Social Change.* Chicago: U of Chicago P, 1992.

Sledd, James. "Grammar for Social Awareness in Time of Class Warfare." *English Journal* 85.7 (1996): 59–63.

Sullivan, Patricia A., and Donna J. Qualley. eds. *Pedagogy in the Age of Politics: Writing and Reading (in) the Academy.* Urbana, IL: NCTE, 1994.

Sutton, Gary A. "Do We Need to Teach a Grammar Terminology?" *English Journal* 65.9 (1976): 37–40.

Tabbert, Russell. "Parsing the Question 'Why Teach Grammar?'" *English Journal* 73.8 (1984): 38–42.

Trimbur, John. "Literacy and the Discourse of Crisis." *The Politics of Writing Instruction: Postsecondary.* Ed. Richard Bullock and John Trimbur. Portsmouth, NH: Boynton/Cook, 1991. 277–95.

Weathers, Winston. "Teaching Style: A Possible Anatomy." *The Writing Teachers Sourcebook.* 2nd ed. Ed. Gary Tate and Edward P. J. Corbett. New York: Oxford UP, 1988. 187–92.

Winchell, Donna A. "Teaching the Rhetoric of Grammar and Style." *Instructors Manual and Answer Key to Accompany The Writers Harbrace Handbook.* Ed. Robert K. Miller, Suzanne S. Webb, and Winifred B. Horner. New York: Harcourt College Publishers, 2001. 16–58.

Zemliansky, Pavel. "Mechanical Correctness." *Composition Forum* 10.2 (2000): 1–19.

17

Down from the Haymow: One Hundred Years of Sentence-Combining

SHIRLEY K. ROSE

1. Her eyes are grey.
2. *Her eyes reveal her character.*
3. Her eyes are fearless.

This incomplete exercise, which follows the model used in William Strong's textbook, *Sentence Combining: A Composing Book* (New York: Random House, 1973), probably looks familiar to anyone who has worked with sentence-combining exercises in the past five to ten years. Few composition teachers haven't at least examined one or another of the sentence-combining textbooks such as Strong's, or Frank O'Hare's *Sentencecraft* (Lexington, Mass.: Ginn [Xerox], 1975), or *The Writer's Options* by Donald A. Daiker, Andrew Kerek, and Max Morenberg (New York: Harper and Row, 1979). The last decade has been a time of great interest in sentence-combining, as evidenced by the appearance of these and a number of other sentence-combining textbooks. Sentence-combining exercises are now also almost obligatory in the most recent handbooks or general composition texts, and our knowledge of it and its uses is further enlarged by several research studies into its effectiveness and a proliferation of articles arguing for or against or merely explaining sentence-combining in English curricula at all levels.

Because sentence-combining has received so much attention in the past few years, it is all too easy to believe that this classroom practice is only as old as its recent popularity. But the example which opens this essay was taken from a text first published in 1906 by Henry Holt: Alfred E. Hitchcock's *Composition and Rhetoric* (1917 edition). Sentence-combining has in its twentieth-century history fit into at least three different paradigms of grammar instruction—the traditional schoolbook grammar, structural grammar, and transformational grammar.

From *College English* 45 (1983): 483–91.

The significant differences in early and current sentence-combining practice are not differences in the exercises themselves but differences in explanations of how and why the exercises work. In order to show just what is and isn't new in sentence-combining instruction, I will briefly compare current sentence-combining exercises with one another and with exercises from textbooks published over the past one hundred years. Sentence-combining exercises could probably be traced as far back as Quintilian, but I will concentrate on this last century.

To begin, let's look at some early sentence-combining exercises. In Hitchcock's text I found this exercise:

EXERCISES IN SENTENCE MUTATION

Exercise 6

Combine each of the following groups of related assertions into a single sentence. Try to make the sentence either simple or complex.

1. Harry has been invited. Mary has been invited. Ellen has been invited.
2. A nobleman was to marry a princess. His servants were busy. They were preparing a wedding feast.
3. My den is in the attic. It is a large, airy room. There is little furniture in it. The walls are bare.
4. The boys had selected a site for the camp. This they had done before I had arrived. It was in a grove of pines. The pines bordered a beautiful sheet of water. This sheet of water is about three miles in circumference.
5. He gave her a ring. This, he said, the King had given him for saving his life.
6. The skipper was an old man. He liked to spin yarns. His face was brown and wrinkled.
7. John Bright became an excellent speaker. He also became an excellent writer. This he accomplished by studying the best English authors.
8. The Richard had forty guns. Six of them were eighteen-pounders. The rest were twelve-, nine-, and six-pounders.
9. Her eyes are gray. They reveal her character. They are fearless.
10. Morning came. John arose early. He breakfasted hastily. He did not stop to light the fire. He paddled across the lake. He hoped to find his companion. This companion he had lost the day before.

From Fred Newton Scott's and Joseph Villiers Denney's text, *Elementary English Composition* (Boston: Allyn and Bacon, 1900, revised edition 1908), I have copied these exercises:

WRITING OF SENTENCES

B. Write a news item of one sentence embodying the following facts: A boy was hurt this morning. He was ten years old. His name is Arthur Smith. He is the son of Amos Smith, the well-known merchant. He was not fatally hurt, but was very seriously hurt. He fell from an apple tree in his father's yard. The Smiths live at 246 Washington Street.—What kind of sentence have you made,—simple, complex, or compound?

C. Put into two sentences, as if for a news item, the following facts: There will be no school Friday afternoon. The School Board decided this at its last meeting, which occurred Monday evening. The reason is that the President of the United States will pass through the town on Friday afternoon. The President's train will stop ten minutes at the station and the President will speak from the rear platform of his car to the school children.—What kinds of sentences have you used?

Here is a representative sentence-combining exercise from John F. Genung's *Outline of Rhetoric* (Boston: Ginn, 1894):

> Combine the following isolated assertions into sentences, supplying proper connectives, or cutting down clauses as needed, and giving a reason, founded on Rules 74 to 76, for each combination.
>
> Balthazar Gérard was the murderer of Prince William of Orange. William was surnamed William the Silent. Gérard had dropped his pistols. He dropped them on the spot. The spot was where he had committed the crime. Upon his person were found two bladders. These bladders were provided with a piece of pipe. With these bladders he had intended to assist himself across the moat. Beyond this moat a horse was waiting for him.
>
> Of two old men, the one who is not your father speaks to you with the more sensible authority. For in the paternal relation the oldest have lively interests and remain still young. Thus I have known two young men great friends. Each swore by the other's father. The father of each swore by the other lad. And yet each pair of parent and child were perpetually by the ears. This is typical. It reads like the germ of some kindly comedy.

Though these early exercises look, at first glance, very different from the more current sentence-combining exercises of Strong, O'Hare, or Daiker, Kerek, and Morenberg, they share the same essential features. For example, here is a typical exercise from Frank O'Hare's *Sentencecraft*:

PROBLEMS

Combine each of the following sets of sentences according to the instructions in parentheses.

1. Ryan was surprised to learn SOMETHING.
   No one understood SOMETHING. (THAT)
   His paintings represented something. (WHAT)

This exercise is from William Strong's *Sentence-Combining: A Composing Book*:

STREET SCENE

1. A dude swaggers down the sidewalk.

2. He clicks his fingers to the beat.

3. He is tuned in to music.

4. He is tuned in to verbal hysteria.

5. These come from his radio.

6. The sound jerks ahead of him.

7. It bounces ahead of him.

8. It announces his arrival to the shoppers.

9. It announces his arrival to the storekeepers.

10. It announces his arrival to the girls in the cafe.

11. One girl giggles.

12. She blushes.

13. She tries to look bored.

14. She tries to look very cool.

15. The scene is tense.

16. The scene is clicking.

This last sample exercise is taken from *The Writer's Options*:

BASIC PATTERN EXERCISE

Combine each of the groups of sentences below into a single sentence containing at least one absolute.

Example
　　1. When I walked in, Grandpa was sitting at the kitchen table.
　　2. The newspaper was spread before him.
　　　　　　　↓
When I walked in, Grandpa was sitting at the kitchen table, *the newspaper spread before him.*
A.　1. Jimmy walked slowly to the corner of the playground.
　　2. His face was streaked with tears.
B.　1. The station wagon sped away.
　　2. The taillights disappeared into the distance.

The important similarities and differences among these exercises are described by John Mellon in his definitive paper, "Issues in the Theory and Practice of Sentence Combining: A Twenty-Year Perspective" (introductory essay in *Sentence-Combining and the Teaching of Writing*, Daiker, Kerek, and Morenberg, eds. [Conway, Ark.: University of Central Arkansas, 1979]). Mellon first describes the difference between the exercises he used in his own study, reported in *Transformational Sentence Combining: A Method for Enhancing the Development of Syntactic Fluency in English Composition* (Research Report #10, NCTE Committee on Research), and the exercises in O'Hare's experiment, reported in *Sentence-Combining: Improving Student Writing without Formal Grammar Instruction* (Research Report #15, NCTE Committee on Research). While Mellon had given an operative grammatical term to cue the student to the structure of the target sentence for the exercise, O'Hare substituted the actual word to be used. While Mellon's exercises were included in grammar instruction in a three-part curriculum of grammar/composition/literature, O'Hare placed his exercises in the composition component of a two-part curriculum of composition/literature.

William Strong's contribution, according to Mellon, is his presentation of sentence-combining problems in "whole discourse sets" (groups of three to twelve sentence-combining problems which together form a complete discourse) and his introduction of "open format" — that is, elimination of cues. The most recent of the sentence-combining textbooks evaluated by Mellon is *The Writer's Options*, which contributes the concept of a regimen of sentence-combining to be followed over an entire school term.

The characteristics common to all of these more recent sentence-combining models are: The exercises 1) may or may not require a student's mastery of basic grammatical terms; 2) may or may not be put together in whole discourse sets; 3) may or may not have cueing systems; 4) may be a small or a large component of an entire composition course; 5) may be considered grammar exercises or may be considered composition exercises. The essential seems to be: the student is asked to combine two or more sentences into a single sentence.

If this is the only essential (iconographic similarity can hardly be required), then the exercises from the early textbooks should certainly qualify as sentence-combining problems. In fact, some of these older sentence-combining exercises have one attractive feature which will not be found in the recent exercises. The Scott and Denney exercises are designed so that the sentences are not only related to one another, but also are placed in a total rhetorical context — the writer, the reader, and the purpose are provided along with the message.

This identity then raises the question: If sentence-combining itself isn't new, what are the significant recent developments in instruction in syntactic fluency and what are the improvements and contributions offered by Mellon, O'Hare, and others?

One of the important recent developments in sentence-combining pedagogy is that it has been subjected to empirically based research. Mellon was not the first to guess the usefulness of sentence-combining exercises for developing syntactic fluency, but he was among the first to design, carry out, and publish the results of research attempting to verify and measure the effects of sentence-combining practice. At the close of his "Twenty-Year Perspective," Mellon identifies what he considers a cause of — but what a hundred-year perspective shows to be only a development in — sentence-combining pedagogy: the appearance of Chomskian linguistics. Mellon says that twenty years ago, when an older colleague of his showed him how to do sentence-combining, "it wasn't called that, was hardly used at all, anywhere, and loomed in the consciousness of no one. But Noam Chomsky's transformational grammar changed all that, just as it changed so many aspects of our understanding of language and mind" (p. 34).

Mellon's exercises and those of O'Hare, Strong, and Daiker, Kerek, and Morenberg are all supported by the paradigm of generative-transformational grammar in two important ways: the competence/performance relationship in language skill and use and the concept of transformations, which allow the embedding of one sentence within another.

The competence/performance concept distinguishes between utterances an individual speaker (or writer) is *theoretically* capable of constructing, given experience with the language, and utterances that speaker is *practically* capable of producing in an actual set of circumstances. For example, as I write this essay, my competence would be all the combinations of words I could possibly put together and still construct an essay following the outline I have before me as I write. My performance is all the combinations I have actually produced from the first draft through the final draft. My competence is theoretically unlimited. My performance is limited by time (whether a week, a month, a deadline), by my awareness of my options, and to some degree by my willingness to play with my words and sentences as I work.

This competence/performance distinction can justify use of sentence-combining exercises to increase syntactic fluency. If students can be made aware of their competence to create greater variety in their sentences by combining two or more propositions, and then be given practice which guides them in doing so, perhaps their actual performance or production of these sentences will be more fluent.

The second Chomskian concept, the transformation, can explain why one sentence can be combined with another. Chomsky's Standard Theory, or generative-transformational grammar, offers a model of the way sentence-combining works. In syntactic or structural terms, the idea of a transformation can account for the disappearance of parts of the original kernel sentences in the process of their combining with or becoming embedded within one another. The theory that a sentence undergoes structural changes or transforms between its original form (deep structure) and final form (surface structure) allows for all the parts of the two or more original sentences to exist in deep structure while some of these parts do not appear in surface structure.

Because transformational grammar so neatly explains how sentence-combining works and why the exercises appear to enhance the development of syntactic fluency, it is predictable that we would begin to think that without transformational grammar we would never have had sentence-combining. But as the exercises from the turn of the century through the 1940s indicate, sentence-combining has been around longer than Noam Chomsky. Knowing this we might, predictably, conclude that transformational sentence-combining is radically different from "old-fashioned sentence-combining." But as my earlier analysis of the newer exercises shows, this is not necessarily the case.

Why does sentence-combining predate the transformational grammar paradigm?

One answer I can offer is that sentence-combining is also compatible with other grammars which have served in composition pedagogy over the last century. This is true of the grammar Henry A. Gleason Jr. calls the "School Tradition"[1] and of structural grammar, or "structural linguistics."

According to Gleason, the school tradition grammar in the late nineteenth and early twentieth centuries is characterized by these features. First, the most important units are the word and sentence—a result of two competing instructional approaches of the nineteenth century, parsing individual words and analyzing whole sentences. Words are classified into parts of speech described in terms of their relationship to other words in the sentence; sentences are classified either as declarative, interrogative, exclamatory, and imperative or as simple, compound, and complex (pp. 74–75). I place Scott and Denney, Genung, and Hitchcock, the textbooks from which I took the early sentence-combining exercises, in the school tradition.

A book published at the turn of the century, *The Teaching of English Grammar: History and Method* by F. A. Barbour (Boston: Ginn, 1901), nicely explains the nineteenth-century rationale for sentence-combining pedagogy:

> In modern pedagogy there is a consensus of opinion as to [the] high educational value [of grammar] in three leading aspects: 1. It has no superior in the school curriculum, and no substitute in the school curriculum, as a discipline of the logical faculties. 2. In a marked degree, it increases the power of interpretation of thought in all subjects of study. 3. It has an indirect though important bearing upon expression of thought in two respects: (a) in all cases of careful revision and especially in the case of mature students, who through self-criticism need to correct bad habits of long standing; and (b) the establishment in the mind of a sort of rough-hewn model of thought form—a powerful, though it may be unconscious, aid, whenever the mind is seeking to shape its own ideas into similar concrete form . . . the analytic-synthetic process of mind. (p. 31)

Barbour's third reason seems to offer an especially strong explanation of why sentence-combining exercises were usually included in the schoolbooks. These exercises offered training to develop analytic-synthetic skills in construction of both thought and expression.

This emphasis on analytic skills is justified by Huber Gray Buehler in the preface to his text, *A Modern English Grammar* (New York: Newson, 1900):

> When a new language is to be learned, a synthetic treatment is natural and interesting. But when the mother tongue is the subject of critical study, the aim is, not to learn new forms of speech, but to investigate the nature of forms that are already familiar; therefore the treatment should be analytic. (pp. iii–iv)

Though Mellon maintains that the sentence-combining exercises in these textbooks are "incidental in the author's consciousness," it is difficult at this distance in time to determine exactly how great a part sentence-combining exercises played in classroom practice. To get a firsthand account, I visited my grandfather, William E. Rose, who attended school from 1901 to 1913 and taught all grades in country schools from 1915 to 1926. Most of my information about sentence-combining pedagogy is drawn from a two-hour interview with him. Many of the books from which I have taken excerpts are books he and my grandmother Carrie Melton Rose, also a country school teacher, used. (My father and I rescued them from a crate in our haymow where they had been moldering for at least thirty years.)

According to my grandfather, sentence-combining exercises were used often for the purpose of getting students to "do more than simple sentences." These exercises were used after a student had learned the essentials of grammar (from Hoenchel's *Grammar* in my grandfather's classroom) and had mastered the distinctions between simple, compound, and complex sentences. Students were encouraged to use as many complex sentences as possible because they created variety and reflected a writer's stylistic fluency. Students were expected to have mastered the essentials of grammar and to have developed their syntactic fluency to some extent by the time they finished the eighth grade, because this instruction would not be presented again in the high-school classroom.

When I asked my grandfather if his students could have done the sentence-combining exercises without knowing grammar, he said yes—that "you don't need grammar until you have trouble writing and want to work out a sentence so it's right."

I am assuming that my grandfather was typical of rural school students and teachers in training and outlook. And I assume that the textbooks he used and other textbooks from the turn of the century are indicative of a pedagogy and practice common at the time. Sentence-combining exercises were considered a logical and integral step in teaching composition, built as they were on a foundation of grammar study and foundational themselves to later work in paragraphs and essays.

At the same time my grandfather and others were learning and in turn teaching according to this school tradition, such grammarians and linguists as Henrik Poutsma, Itsko Kruisinga, Otto Jesperson, and Georg Curme were developing a quite different grammar, which Gleason calls the "European Scholarly Tradition" (p. 76). The scholarly grammar did not reach most public schools during the first part of the century, and by the time it might have, C. C. Fries and his structural grammar had appeared. Structural linguistics began to reach the schools in the mid-1950s with the publication of college textbooks such as Paul Roberts' *Patterns of English* (New York: Harcourt, Brace, and World, 1956). In a few years, high-school textbooks incorporating structural linguistics were developed, and in some schools structural linguistics began to filter down through English curricula at all levels.

Sentence-combining exercises appeared once again in composition teaching based on structural linguistics. Instead of learning a classification of the parts of speech, a student could learn a classification of words according to their function in a sentence. The emphasis in grammar instruction would be shifted from individual words to the structure of the whole sentence. Students would be taught to identify sentences according to the pattern they followed (Subject-Verb; Subject-Verb-Object; Subject-Verb-Complement; etc.).

Representative of the use to which the "new grammar" put sentence-combining is the following exercise from Enola M. Borgh's *Grammatical Pat-*

terns and Composition (Oshkosh: Wisconsin Council of Teachers of English, 1963). This is a book of suggestions for classroom techniques in teaching composition using structural linguistics.

Exercise 2

DIRECTIONS: This is an exercise in the use of specific grammatical structures to improve sentence structure. Read the following paragraphs and then combine the short, disconnected sentences according to the directions at the righthand side of the page. Make no changes in vocabulary except those necessitated by changes in structure and no unspecified changes in word order. Sentences to be combined into one sentence are separated from each other by slanted lines.

1. The frontier had always spelled hardship.	1. Combine sentences 1, 2, and 3 as follows:
2. It had also spelled danger.	A. Combine sentences 1 and 2 by compounding the direct objects.
3. The last frontier was no exception.	B. Add sentence 3 to the combined sentence to form a compound sentence.
4. Men and women left the towns or the wooded farms of the East.	2. Combine sentences 4, 5, 6, and 7 as follows:
5. They left to try their luck on the High Plains.	A. Change the subject of sentence 4 to a prepositional phrase and the predicate to a dependent clause modifying *men and women*.
6. It was always hard for them.	B. Change sentence 5 to an infinitive phrase.
7. It was often bitterly disappointing.	C. Combine sentences 6 and 7 by compounding the subjective complements.

In the structural grammar paradigm, sentence-combining exercises were seen as practice in manipulating the sentence pattern by expanding parts within the pattern and linking two separate patterns. The design of these exercises required the student to have mastered structural grammar well enough to be able to produce sentences by pattern and identify their parts by function. But it is only the design (for example, the wording of the instructions) that requires this mastery of grammar. Models or cueing devices which eliminated the need for familiarity with grammatical terminology could easily be devised.

In *Teaching English Grammar* (New York: Appleton-Century-Crofts, 1957), Robert C. Pooley gives this explanation of why structural grammar should be taught: "The thesis of this book is that the teaching of grammar in schools has this very purpose as its foundation: to show how the materials of English sentences are assembled to create a happy blend of clear meaning and interesting variety of structure" (p. 88). His reasons for teaching subordination (a common operation in sentence-combining) are explained in this statement: "A leading characteristic of modern English prose is the tendency to construct sentences in which several associated ideas are attached to or subordinated to a leading idea. It is not too great an exaggeration to say that skill in subordination is the first requisite of a successful writer of our times" (p. 100).

I should note that though sentence-combining has been used with structural grammar instruction, this grammar has never been universally adopted in the English curriculum at any level. Generative transformational grammar replaced it in scholarly circles, few teachers ever received adequate training in it, and few really good textbooks using it were developed.[2]

Though the theory of grammar explaining sentence-combining exercises has changed since the turn of the century, the underlying pedagogical apology and objectives have not. In the paradigm of the schoolbook tradition, sentence-combining exercises were placed after the "grammar" sections explaining the parts of the sentence and before the "composition" sections. In the structural grammar paradigm, sentence-combining exercises were taught after the basic sentence patterns had been learned and before the larger structural elements of paragraph and essay were introduced. The role of sentence-combining as a link between grammar and rhetoric in the current transformational grammar paradigm is apparent in the continuing controversy over whether sentence-combining exercises belong in the writing lab or the writing workshop. Sentence-combining has continued to serve as a bridge between grammar instruction and rhetorical instruction because it provides a way to move from manipulations of sentence structure as grammar exercise to manipulations of sentence structure as rhetorical choices.

It seems that though our explanations of why we do what we do in the composition classroom change, some of our methods have changed very little. The objectives of sentence-combining have remained the same—"to get students to do more than simple sentences." Perhaps the most productive direction for future sentence-combining research is not toward developing further theoretical explanations of the phenomenon of sentence-combining but toward a newly examined and articulated apology for sentence-combining pedagogy.

NOTES

1. *Linguistics and English Grammar* (New York: Holt, Rinehart and Winston, 1965), p. 70.
2. This point is developed in an unpublished paper by Nancy Rose MacKenzie, Structural Grammar in the High School English Curriculum" (Nov. 1980, Kansas State University).

PART FOUR

Style and Culture

Introduction to Part Four

While the historical, theoretical, and pedagogical issues surrounding stylistic study are widespread in rhetoric and composition, the cultural influences on style are equally ubiquitous in the discipline, related to the social, political, economic, and geographic realities of diverse groups in a changing global environment. If style's relationship to culture is thus immanent in the field, arguably its most pronounced effects exist in areas like African American Vernacular English (AAVE) or Ebonics (also known as African American Language) and Spanglish, in diverse linguistic traditions, registers, and dialects, and in interdisciplinary conversations on language. One of the earliest examples of composition studies' interest in the cultural aspects of style is the Committee on CCCC Language's 1974 document "Students' Right to Their Own Language," which argues that students' development of their own dialect and style is an essential part of their cultural heritage: "We affirm the students' right to their own patterns and varieties of language—the dialects of their nurture or whatever dialects in which they find their own identity and style." This document—controversial when it was enacted and still the subject of ongoing discussion in composition and rhetoric—makes style the catalyst for connecting language to culture through student writing. Yet its affirmation of stylistic difference does not exist in a cultural vacuum but rather has been buffeted by such controversies as the Oakland School Board's 1996 resolution to recognize Ebonics as the primary language (rather than dialect) and language of instruction of African American students. In addition, Conference on College Composition and Communication (CCCC) passed a National Language Policy in 1988, this time in response to the "English Only" movement and its attempt to make English the "official" language of the United States.

At times the intersection of style and culture may seem essentially to parallel societal upheavals related to group identity—for example, race and dialect, gender and feminism, the clash of representation in "contact zones"—yet its reach is indisputably broader, touching, for instance, upon institutional, disciplinary, rhetorical, and pedagogical fault lines that never lie far from the social milieu in which they are situated. Hence, in rhetoric and composition, style arguably serves as an instrument of *negotiation* (see Lu, "Professing Multiculturalism: The Politics of Style in the Contact Zone"), mediating contested cultural values and forces. How does such a cultural negotiation occur stylistically? Put simply, stylistic choices are *cultural* choices—the decision whether to follow or deviate from norms, for instance, made within a broader cultural context and a sphere of countervailing interests. As many of the articles in this book show, normative interests often try to prescribe choices, yet culture exerts a centrifugal counterforce, diffusing the unifying forces that may seem at first to be controlling. This tension is of particular concern in writing classrooms, where the competing interests of teaching students, for example, to use Standard English as well as to respect the linguistic differences of various language communities often result in conflicting curricular goals and pedagogies. At the confluence of all these disputes, as the selections here demonstrate, is the canon of style.

The contours of the often-competing interests in style are evident in the first selection by Geneva Smitherman, " 'How I Got Ovuh': African World View and Afro-American Oral Tradition," a chapter from *Talkin and Testifyin: The Language of Black America*. In arguing that the communication system of black America—based on its cultural roots in Africa—constitutes a vital *oral* tradition, Smitherman juxtaposes a community that "places high value on the spoken word" with its ostensible counterpart, print-oriented culture. In a work first published in 1977, before the explosion of rap and hip-hop as musical and scholarly genres (see Additional Readings for recent books in the field on hip-hop literacy and culture), Smitherman discusses the importance of verbal performance—especially the rap—as a teaching and socializing force within the African American community that paradoxically uses a lexicon of "White English words." Specifically, she illustrates how African Americans' sacred and secular oral traditions are often blended in contexts that range from the church to the street to black music and include stylistic qualities such as exaggerated language, mimicry, aphoristic phrasing, puns and plays on words, and various forms of indirection. Smitherman's work is significant in showing how the African oral tradition, often seen as the antithesis of the European written tradition, infuses language and culture with new styles that inform, in turn, the written word. For example, Smitherman not only mentions indirection and circumlocutory rhetoric as aspects of African discourse strategy but implements them in her own writing. She deploys indirection, for example, to emphasize the way African American congregations demand that preachers digress during their sermons. In this piece, then, Smitherman, an architect of the Students' Right resolution, introduces the value of orality as a stylistic resource for writing.

While Smitherman focuses on the cultural aspects of African Americans' oral styles, Min-Zhan Lu, in "Professing Multiculturalism: The Politics of Style in the Contact Zone," examines the question of multicultural deviation from normative styles as an expression of politics in the contact zone, a contested space, according to Mary Louise Pratt, where cultures clash. Dissatisfied with the way student writers are often ghettoized in relation to "real writers"—only the latter granted the right to experiment with style—Lu encourages her students not only to find deviations from the codes of Standard English in their reading but to negotiate and modify them in their own writing. Analyzing the work of one of her students, a native Chinese speaker, who initially chooses a nonstandard phrase, Lu argues that the student, rather than making an error, is actually negotiating a position related to competing American value systems (one, not surprisingly, vaunting the individual) and unequal power relationships. In an argument important to composition, Lu asserts that deviating from normative language is part of a negotiated process that encourages students to resist unifying codes as well as to deploy them in innovative ways, even while acknowledging Standard English's omnipresent power. Lu's article is thus a disciplinary call for experimenting with stylistic options within cultural contexts often at odds with hegemonic language conventions.

Reexamining the conventional wisdom about style and gender is the defining feature of Mary Hiatt's "The Feminine Style: Theory and Fact," a Braddock Award–winning article. Challenging the premise that the way men write is considered *the* way to write as well as the stereotype that women's writing is, among other things, emotional, illogical, and vapid, Hiatt concludes that women do write differently than men—confirming the existence of a "feminine style"—but not in expected ways. For example, after categorizing what she calls "logical-sequence indicators," Hiatt discovers, contrary to common belief, that women use them more frequently than men do, but women's logic, in contrast to men's, "depend[s] on reasons and extra information rather than on exemplifications and conclusions." Thus her findings, based on empirical evidence, that the feminine style is "conservative, structurally sound, logical in its own way, balanced in terms of emotionality and pace," demonstrate how stylistic analysis can reveal the inaccuracies behind culturally constructed beliefs. Hiatt's work is an example of the kind of stylistic inquiry advocated by Edward P. J. Corbett (see Part Three) and offers some surprising evidence of how cultural assumptions can be revised through research on style.

Just as Hiatt reexamines the apparent cultural divide between "feminine" and "masculine" styles, Peter Elbow articulates what he sees as a schism of a different kind, that is, the division between the cultures of literature and composition, particularly when it comes to style. In "The Cultures of Literature and Composition: What Could Each Learn from the Other?" Elbow argues, in the part of his discussion most relevant here, that literary studies is "a culture that considers the metaphorical and imaginative uses of language basic and primal," an approach to language that includes sophistication, artificiality, artifice, and mannerism—all essentially elements of style. According to Elbow, literature embraces playfulness, fun, pleasure, and humor, stylistic qualities he finds virtually absent in composition, which, he says, assumes that discursive language is the norm. While postulating a cultural divide between literature and composition, Elbow also calls for a rapprochement, asking composition—whose concern for students and teaching he considers laudatory—to have students employ stylistic and imaginative aspects of language, just as he calls on literature to develop more concern for students and teaching. "What would it look like," Elbow asks, "for the two cultures to learn from each other?" Elbow argues that just this type of integration is already beginning.

18

"How I Got Ovuh": African World View and Afro-American Oral Tradition

GENEVA SMITHERMAN

My soul look back and wonder
How I got over.

Both in the old-time black Gospel song and in black street vernacular, "gittin ovuh" has to do with surviving. While the religious usage of the phrase speaks to spiritual survival in a sinister world of sin, its secular usage speaks to material survival in a white world of oppression. Since men and women live neither by bread nor spirit alone, both vitally necessary acts of gittin ovuh challenge the human spirit to "keep on pushin" toward "higher ground." In Black America, the oral tradition has served as a fundamental vehicle for gittin ovuh. That tradition preserves the Afro-American heritage and reflects the collective spirit of the race. Through song, story, folk sayings, and rich verbal interplay among everyday people, lessons and precepts about life and survival are handed down from generation to generation. Until contemporary times, Black America relied on word-of-mouth for its rituals of cultural preservation. (For instance, it was not until the late nineteenth century that the Negro spirituals were written down, though they date well back to the beginnings of slavery.) But word-of-mouth is more than sufficient because the structural underpinnings of the oral tradition remain basically intact even as each new generation makes verbal adaptations within the tradition. Indeed the core strength of this tradition lies in its capacity to accommodate new situations and changing realities. If we are to understand the complexity and scope of black communication patterns, we must have a clear understanding of the oral tradition and the world view that undergirds that tradition.

• • •

From *Talkin and Testifyin: The Language of Black America* (Detroit, MI: Wayne State University Press, 1986), 73–100.

The Black communication system is actualized in different ways, dependent upon the sociocultural context—for instance, "street" versus "church"—but the basic underlying structures of this communication network are essentially similar because they are grounded in the traditional African world view. In brief, that view refers to underlying thought patterns, belief sets, values, ways of looking at the world, and the community of men and women that are shared by all traditional Africans (that is, those that haven't been westernized).

The mainstream tradition of European scholarship on Africa has rested on a conceptual framework relative to the so-called "diversity" of Africa. To be sure, there are differences in the many tribes, languages, customs, spirits, and deities that exist throughout the African continent, but these seeming diversities are merely surface variations on the basic "deep structure" themes of life acknowledged by traditional Africans. Focusing on such surface differences as tribal customs or politically defined African boundaries has only served to obscure that existence of the deep structure that is shared by all traditional African people. Robert F. Thompson conducted field studies of African art in nine different African cultures and was able to identify common canons of form pervading them all. Similarly, Daryll Forde's studies of African social values in various tribal cultures brought him to remark that: "One is impressed, not only by the great diversity of ritual forms and expressions of beliefs, but also by substantial underlying similarities in religious outlook and moral injunction." And the West African scholar Fela Sowande, as well as the East African scholar John S. Mbiti, present nearly identical descriptions of the African view of the universe and man's place in the scheme of things. To be sure, students of African culture have yet to detail *all* of the salient features that transcend tribal differences and constitute what is here being called the "traditional African world view." But recent findings and field studies, especially those of African scholars themselves, point to sufficient patterns of commonality to suggest an interlocking cultural and philosophical network throughout Africa. We can thus assert that similar underlying thought patterns do exist amid the unending diversity of African people, and therefore it is appropriate to speak of traditional African thought as a single entity—albeit with complex and diverse manifestations.

What is the traditional African world view? First, there is a fundamental unity between the spiritual and the material aspects of existence. Though both the material and the spiritual are necessary for existence, the spiritual domain assumes priority.

The universe is hierarchical in nature, with God at the head of the hierarchy, followed by lesser deities, the "living dead" (ancestral spirits), people, animals, and plants. Though the universe is hierarchical, all modes of existence are necessary for the sustenance of its balance and rhythm. Harmony in nature and the universe is provided by the complementary, interdependent, synergic interaction between the spiritual and the material. Thus we have a paradigm for the way in which "opposites" function. That is, "opposites" constitute interdependent, interacting forces which are necessary for producing a given reality.

Similarly, communities of people are modeled after the interdependent rhythms of the universe. Individual participation is necessary for community survival. Balance in the community, as in the universe, consists of maintaining these interdependent relationships.

The universe moves in a rhythmical and cyclical fashion as opposed to linear progression. "Progression," as such, occurs only into the past world of the spirit. Thus the "future" is the past. In the community, then, one's sense of "time" is based on participation in and observation of nature's rhythms and community events. (In the African conception of "time," the key is not to be "on time," but "in time.") And since participatory experiences are key to one's sense of "time," the fundamental pedagogy in the school of life becomes experience, and age serves as a prime basis for hierarchical social arrangements.

Community roles are equally governed by the hierarchical unity of the spiritual and material aspects of the universe. Since the spiritual realm is the ultimate existence of humankind, those closest to the spiritual realm assume priority in social relationships. Thus, elders are of great importance, and the spiritually developed people serve as rulers and doctors.

Naturally, Black Americans, having had to contend with slavery and Euro-American ways, have not been able to practice or manifest the traditional African world view in its totality. But, as we shall see in closely examining the many facets of the oral tradition, the residue of the African world view persists and serves to unify such seemingly disparate black groups as preachers and poets, bluesmen and Gospel-ettes, testifiers and toast-tellers, reverends and revolutionaries. Can I get a witness?

Both in slavery times and now, the black community places high value on the spoken word. That community supports a tradition that the anthropologists would call "preliterate." (Although the great Margaret Mead laid the classic bomb on the superiority complex of the Western world when she said that the "influence" of Western culture on non-Western peoples was to make the "preliterate illiterate." In fact, the black oral tradition links Black American culture with that of other oral "preliterate" people—such as Native Americans—for whom the spoken word is supreme.) The persistence of the African-based oral tradition is such that blacks tend to place only limited value on the written word, whereas verbal skills expressed orally rank in high esteem. This is not to say that Black Americans never read anything or that the total black community is functionally illiterate. The influence of White America and the demands of modern, so-called civilized living have been too strong for that. However, it is to say that from a black perspective, written documents are limited in what they can teach about life and survival in the world. Blacks are quick to ridicule "educated fools," people who done gone to school and read all dem books and still don't know nothin! They have "book learning" but no "mother wit," knowledge, but not wisdom. (Naturally, not *all* educated people are considered "educated fools," but if the shoe fits . . .) Furthermore, aside from athletes and entertainers, only those blacks who can perform stunning feats of oral gymnastics become culture heroes and leaders in the community. Such feats are the basic requirement of the trade among preachers, politicians, disc jockeys, hustlers, and lovers. Like the preacher who was exhorting his congregation to take care of themselves and their bodies:

PREACHER: How many of y'all wanna live to a old age?

CONGREGATION: Hallalujah!

PREACHER: Or is y'all ready to die and go to Heaven?

CONGREGATION: (uncomfortable; some self-conscious laughter) Well, no Lord, not yet, suh!

PREACHER: Y'all wanna stay here awhile?

CONGREGATION: Praise the Lord!

PREACHER: Well, y'all better quit all this drankin, smokin, and runnin 'round. Cause, see, for me, I got a home in Heaven, but I ain't homesick!

And check out this from a black disc jockey on a "soul" station. He is urging his audience to listen to his station because it's the best, and to call in to win the "top ten" album, therein making the winner eligible for the grand prize: "Super CHB . . . making the music work for you. When one quits, another hits . . . Looking for that seventh caller . . . Caller number seven, call, cop, and qualify."

In any culture, of course, language is a tool for ordering the chaos of human experience. We feel more comfortable when we have names for events and things. To know that "the earth is round and revolves around the sun" might not bring us any closer to solving the riddle of the universe, but at least it helps in imposing an orderly explanation upon a seemingly disorderly world. To use words to give shape and coherence to human existence is a universal human thing—a linguistic fact of life that transcends cultural boundaries. The crucial difference in American culture lies in the contrasting modes in which Black and White Americans have shaped that language—a written mode for whites, having come from a European, print-oriented culture; a spoken mode for blacks, having come from an African, orally-oriented background As black psychiatrist Frantz Fanon describes it, to "talk like a book" is to "talk like a white man."

The oral tradition, then, is part of the cultural baggage the African brought to America. The preslavery background was one in which the concept of Nommo, the magic power of the Word, was believed necessary to actualize life and give man mastery over things. "All activities of men, and all the movements in nature, rest on the word, on the productive power of the word, which is water and heat and seed and Nommo, that is, life force itself . . . The force, responsibility, and commitment of the word, and the awareness that the word alone alters the world . . ." In traditional African culture, a newborn child is a mere thing until his father gives and speaks his name. No medicine, potion, or magic of any sort is considered effective without accompanying words. So strong is the African belief in the power and absolute necessity of Nommo that all craftsmanship must be accompanied by speech. And it is not uncommon for a verbal battle to precede or accompany warfare.

In the African epic of Sundiata, a renowned king of ancient Mali, the exiled king must wage war to regain his throne, but, as the griot tells us, "those fighting must make a declaration of their grievances to being with":

"Stop, young man. Henceforth I am the king of Mali. If you want peace, return to where you came from," said Soumaoro.

"I am coming back, Soumaoro, to recapture my kingdom. If you want peace you will make amends to my allies and return to Sosso where you are the king."

"I am king of Mali by force of arms. My rights have been established by conquest."

"Then I will take Mali from you by force of arms and chase you from my kingdom."

"Know, then that I am the wild yam of the rocks; nothing will make me leave Mali."

"Know, also that I have in my camp seven master smiths who will shatter the rocks. Then, yam, I will eat you."

"I am the poisonous mushroom that makes the fearless vomit."

"As for me, I am the ravenous cock, the poison does not matter to me."

"Behave yourself, little boy, or you will burn your foot, for I am the red-hot cinder."

"But me, I am the rain that extinguishes the cinder; I am the boisterous torrent that will carry you off."

"I am the mighty silk-cotton tree that looks from on high on the tops of other trees."

"And I, I am the strangling creeper that climbs to the top of the forest giant."

"Enough of this argument. You shall not have Mali."

"Know that there is not room for two kings on the same skin, Soumaoro; you will let me have your place."

"Very well, since you want war I will wage war against you, but I would have you know that I have killed nine kings whose heads adorn my room. What a pity, indeed, that your head should take its place beside those of your fellow madcaps."

"Prepare yourself, Soumaoro, for it will be long before the calamity that is going to crash down upon you and yours comes to an end."

Thus Sundiata and Soumaoro spoke together. After the war of mouths, swords had to decide the issue.

The above exchange of word-arrows is not unlike that of two bloods squaring off on any street corner or in any cottonfield in the U.S.:

"If you don't quit messin wif me, uhma jump down your throat, tap dance on your liver, and make you wish you never been born."

"Yeah, you and how many armies? Nigger, don't you know uhm so bad I can step on a wad of gum and tell you what flavor it is."

Even though blacks have embraced English as their native tongue, still the African cultural set persists, that is, a predisposition to imbue the English word with the same sense of value and commitment—"propers," as we would say—accorded to Nommo in African culture. Hence Afro-America's emphasis on orality and belief in the power of the rap which has produced a style and idiom totally unlike that of whites, while paradoxically employing White English words. We're talking, then, about a tradition in the black experience in which verbal performance becomes both a way of establishing "yo rep" as well as a teaching and socializing force. This performance is exhibited in the narration of myths, folk stories, and the semiserious tradition of "lying" in general; in black sermons; in the telling of jokes; in proverbs and folk sayings; in street corner, barbershop, beauty shop, and other casual rap scenes; in "signifying," "capping," "testifying," "toasting," and other verbal arts. Through these raps of various kinds, black folk are acculturated—initiated— into the black value system. Not talking about speech for the sake of speech, for black talk is never simple cocktail chit-chat, but a functional dynamic that is simultaneously a mechanism for learning about life and the world and a vehicle for achieving group approval and recognition. Even in what appears to be only casual conversation, whoever speaks is highly conscious of the fact that his personality is on exhibit and his status at stake. Black raps ain bout talkin loud and saying nothin, for the speaker must be up on the subject of his rap, and his oral contribution must be presented in a dazzling, entertaining manner. Black speakers are flamboyant, flashy, and exaggerative; black raps are stylized, dramatic, and spectacular; speakers and raps become symbols of how to git ovuh.

In his autobiography *Black Boy*, Richard Wright excellently depicts the dynamics of a street corner rap in a Southern town:

> "You eat yet?" Uneasily trying to make conversation.
> "Yeah, man. I done really fed my face." Casually.
> "I had cabbage and potatoes." Confidently.
> "I had buttermilk and black-eyed peas." Meekly informational.
> "Hell, I ain't gonna stand near you, nigger." Pronouncement.
> "How come?" Feigned innocence.
> "Cause you gonna smell up this air in a minute!" A shouted accusation.
> Laughter runs through the crowd.
> "Nigger, your mind's in a ditch." Amusingly moralistic.
> "Ditch, nothing! Nigger, you going to break wind any minute now!" Triumphant pronouncement creating suspense.
> "Yeah, when them black-eyed peas tell that buttermilk to move over, that buttermilk ain't gonna wanna move and there's gonna be war in your guts and your stomach's gonna swell up and bust!" Climax.
> The crowd laughs loud and long.
> "Man, them white folks ought catch you and send you to the zoo and keep you for the next war!" Throwing the subject into a wider field.
> "Then when that fighting starts, they oughta feed you on buttermilk and black-eyed peas and let you break wind!" The subject is accepted and extended.

"You'd win the war with a new kind of poison gas!" A shouted climax.

There is high laughter that simmers down slowly.

"Maybe poison gas is something good to have." The subject of white folks is associationally swept into the orbit of talk.

"Man, you reckon these white folks is ever gonna change?" Timid, questioning hope.

"Hello, no! They just born that way." Rejecting hope for fear that it could never come true.

"Shucks, man. I'm going north when I get grown." Rebelling against futile hope and embracing flight.

"A colored man's all right up north." Justifying flight.

"They say a white man hit a colored man up north and that colored man hit that white man, knocked him cold, and nobody did a damn thing!" Urgent wish to believe in flight.

"Man for man up there." Begging to believe in justice.

Silence.

"Listen, you reckon them buildings up north is as tall as they say they is?" Leaping by association to something concrete and trying to make belief real.

"They say they gotta building in New York forty stories high!" A thing too incredible for belief.

"Man, I'd be scareda them buildings!" Ready to abandon the now suppressed idea of flight.

"You know, they say that them buildings sway and rock in the wind." Stating a miracle.

"Naw, nigger!" Utter astonishment and rejection.

"Yeah, they say they do." Insisting upon the miracle.

"You reckon that could be?" Questioning hope.

"Hell, naw! If a building swayed and rocked in the wind, hell, it'd fall! Any fool knows that! Don't let people maka fool outta you, telling you them things." Moving body agitatedly, stomping feet impatiently, and scurrying back to safe reality.

Silence. Somebody would pick up a stone and toss it across a field.

"Man, what makes white folks so mean?" Returning to grapple with the old problem.

"Whenever I see one I spit!" Emotional rejection of whites.

"Man, ain't they ugly?" Increased emotional rejection.

"Man, you ever get right close to a white man, close enough to smell 'im?" Anticipation of statement.

"They say we stink. But my ma says white folks smell like dead folks." Wishing the enemy was dead.

"Niggers smell from sweat. But white folks smell *all* the time." The enemy is an animal to be killed on sight.

And the talk would weave, roll, surge, spurt, veer, swell, having no specific aim or direction, touching vast areas of life, expressing the tentative impulses of childhood. Money, God, race, sex, color, war, planes, machines, trains, swimming, boxing, anything . . . The culture of one black household was thus transmitted to another black household, and folk tradition was handed from group to group. Our attitudes were made, defined, set, or corrected; our ideas were discovered, discarded, enlarged, torn apart, and accepted.

While some raps convey social and cultural information, others are used for conquering foes and women. Through signification, the Dozens,[1] and boastful talk, a dude can be properly put to rest with words. (Recall the verbal duel in the Sundiata epic.) Hubert "Rap" Brown, the controversial black leader of the 1960s, describes this cultural phenomenon in his autobiography, *Die Nigger Die!*:

> . . . what you try to do is totally destroy somebody else with words. It's that whole competition thing again, fighting each other. There'd be sometimes 40 or 50 dudes standing around and the winner was determined by the way they responded to what was said. If you fell all over each other laughing, then you knew you'd scored . . . The real aim of the Dozens was to get a dude so mad that he'd cry or get mad enough to fight . . . Signifying is more humane. Instead of coming down on somebody's mother, you come down on them . . . A session would start maybe by a brother saying, "Man, before you mess with me you'd rather run rabbits, eat shit, and bark at the moon." Then, if he was talking to me, I'd tell him:
> Man, you just don't know who I am.
> I'm sweet peeter jeeter the womb beater
> The baby maker the cradle shaker
> The deerslayer the buckbinder the women finder
> Known from the Gold Coast to the rocky shores of Maine
> Rap is my name and love is my game.

Since it is a socially approved verbal strategy for black rappers to talk about how bad they is, such bragging is taken at face value. While the speakers may or may not act out the implications of their words, the point is that the listeners do not necessarily *expect* any action to follow. As a matter of fact, skillful rappers can often avoid having to prove themselves through deeds if their rap is strong enough. The Black Idiom expression "selling woof [wolf] tickets" (also just plain "woofin") refers to any kind of strong language which is purely idle boasting. However, this bad talk is nearly always taken for the real thing by an outsider from another culture. Such cultural-linguistic misperception can lead to tragic consequences. Witness, for instance, the physical attacks and social repression suffered by black spokesmen of the 1960s, such as the Black Panthers. "Death to the racist exploiters!" "Off the pigs!" "Defend our communities by any means necessary!"—the white folks thought the bloods was not playin and launched an all-out military campaign. These aggressive moves resulted partly from White America's sense of fear that the radical rhetoric (much of which was really defensive, rather than offensive) constituted more than idle threats. The whites were not hip to braggadocio and woof tickets; at any rate, they wasn't buying none.

While boastful raps are used to devastate enemies, love raps help in gittin ovuh with women. Both, of course, require speakers with intellectual adroitness and a way with words. Since it is believed that the spoken word has power, it is only logical to employ it with what many regard as men's most formidable obstacle—women. Many black rappers specialize in the verbal art of romantic rappin. Like Hubert "Rap" Brown said, love is his game. Examples of such "game," dating from the nineteenth century, are provided in the folklore collection of Hampton Institute. Here is one such example which appeared in an 1895 edition of the *Southern Workman*, a journal published by the institute: "My dear kin' miss, has you any objections to me drawing my cher to yer side, and revolvin' de wheel of my conversation around de axle of your understandin'?" A contemporary example is provided in the novel *Snakes* by Al Young, in which Young depicts a heavy love rapper in his main character, Shakes (short for Shakespeare). Exemplifying the rich ability of black speechmakers, Shakes gives propers to another great rapper who taught him that "you can get away with anything if you talk up on it right."

> I just wanna knock out chicks and show these other dudes they aint hittin on doodleysquat when it come to talkin trash. I got it down, jim! You hip to Cyrano de Bergerac? . . . Talk about a joker could talk some trash! Cyrano got everybody told! Didn't nobody be messin with Cyrano, ugly as he was. Some silly stud get to cappin on Cyrano's nose and he dont flinch an inch. He get right up in the stud's face and vaporize him with several choice pronouncements, then he go and waste the cat in a suhword fight. Meantime, there's this little local lame that's tryna make it with Cyrano's cousin Roxanne, so old Cyrano and the lame get back up behind the bushes one night while the chick up there on the balcony. Cyrano whisperin all in the lame's ear what he spose to be sayin, but the lame messin up the lines so bad until Cyrano just sweep him on off to one side and stand up and make the speech his own self. He commence to messin up the broad's mind so bad she ready to out and out say I do. See, she don't know it's her own cousin that's been layin down that incredible rap. And now, to show you what kinda man Cyrano was, after that lady is on the verge of succumbing to the amorous design that his words had traced in the air of that night, so to speak, then he just step off to one side and let her old lame boyfriend move on into the picture and cop, like he the one been doin all that old freakish talk out there under the moonlight.

Contrary to popular stereotype, black men have never really regarded black women as sex objects, pure and simple, for the love rap, based on the African view of the reconciliation of opposites, is a synthesis of emotional and intellectual appeal and has as its ultimate objective the conquest not simply of the woman's body, but her mind as well. As one blood said, "Baby, I don't just want your behind, I want your mind." Romantic raps not only contain sweet and complimentary "nothings" that lovers like to hear, but they must demonstrate the rapper's power and ability of persuasive verbal logic. An excellent example of a unique rap is provided by Woodie King in "The Game," a description of his early life in the streets. In an effort to git ovuh with Edith, a very foxy but "religious broad," Sweet Mac introduces the Bible into the game—surely an unprecedented technique in this tradition:

. . . for the last couple of weeks I been quoting the Good Book and all that stuff to her; telling her I am now saved myself, you dig . . . I says to her, "Edith, baby, we can't go on like this. I dig you *but* . . . baby I'm one hundred percent man. And baby, from looking at you, you are one hundred percent woman (the broad went for this evaluation) . . . So . . . if that is the case, something or someone is trying to keep us—two pure American religious people of the same order—apart." At this point, I drop a quote or two from the Good Book on her; *"Thou shall not covet thy neighbor's wife;* and baby since you're not anybody's wife, I pleaded, *do unto others as you would have them do unto you* . . ." Next, I whispered to her secretly, doing the ear bit with the tongue, "Baby only something like that no-good Satan would want to stop something as mellow as laying naked in the Foggy Night with MJQ or Ravel on the hi-fi, me there playing with you, only Satan," I says. "He trying to put game on us, momma." The broad is looking dazed like she done seen the handwriting on the wall.

The existence of love rappin in the oral tradition allows a strange black man to approach a strange black woman without fear of strong reprisal. Black women are accustomed to—and many even expect—this kind of verbal aggressiveness from black men. Black culture thus provides a socially approved verbal mechanism with which the man can initiate conversation aimed at deepening the acquaintance. Rappin also accounts for what whites often label as "aggressive," "brash," "presumptive," or "disrespectful" behavior by black men toward black women. "Hey pretty momma, where you goin, wit you baaaad self? I know you a movie star or somebody important, but could I just have a minute of yo time?" If she's interested, he gets more than a minute, if not, she just smiles and keeps on steppin.

Though this approach was previously reserved for males, with the advent of feminist assertion black women are beginning to develop the art of romantic rappin. However, it is a strictly contemporary, slowly developing trend, and verbal aggressiveness from women is still not approved in any but the most sophisticated social sets.

Black sermons also form an important part of the oral tradition. By now the sermonizing style of traditional black clergy is perhaps rather widely known, especially given the preacher imitations done by popular black comedians Flip Wilson and Richard Pryor. What has not been too well publicized is the devastating raps black preachers run down before and after their sermons. Since the traditional black church service is an emotion-packed blend of sacred and secular concerns, informality is the order of the day. It is not a lax, anything-goes kind of informality, though, for there are traditional rituals to be performed, and codes of proper social conduct must be observed. For instance, if the Spirit moves you, it's acceptable to get up and testify even though that's not on the church program. On the other hand, when the preacher is "taking his text,"[2] a hushed silence falls over the whole congregation, and it is most out of order to get up, move around in your seat, talk, or do anything until he finishes this brief ritual in the traditional structure of the sermon.

Since the traditional black church is a social as well as a religious unit, the preacher's job as leader of his flock is to make churchgoers feel at home and to deal with the problems and realities confronting his people as they cope with the demands and stresses of daily living. Thus preachers are given wide latitude as to the topics they can discuss and the methods of presentation. Indeed, the congregation virtually demands digressive commentary and episodic rappin as a prelude to the big event. I mean, if you a preacher in a traditional black church you just don't be gittin up and going right into yo sermon like they does in them other churches. The best preachers use this time wisely as in the case of the big city "Reb" who was called on the carpet for healing and selling blessings over the radio:

PREACHER: I thank God for this radio station.

CONGREGATION: My Lord! Yes, Lord!

PREACHER: Y'all know you got some radio directors with two years of eduma-cation.

CONGREGATION: Look out, now! You on the case! Tell it! Tell it! Two years!

PREACHER: And they have decided that they know what you want to hear. Who ever head of a radio station licensed by the Federal Communications System that's gon tell *you* that you can't heal?!!

CONGREGATION: Right on, brother!

PREACHER: Gon tell you that you cain't read a Scripture.

CONGREGATION: Well, well!

PREACHER: You don't tell them white folks that.

CONGREGATION: Hallelujah!

PREACHER: So don't tell me that 'cause I don't wanna hear it!

CONGREGATION: No, Lord!

PREACHER: If Jesus hada healed all the rich folks, he wouldn'ta had no problems!

CONGREGATION: Amen! Speak on it!

The inclusion of church raps here in practically the same breath as street raps is to demonstrate the sacred-secular continuum in the oral tradition and to dramatize the importance of the black church in the culture and verbal style of black people. Very broadly speaking, and for purposes of illustration only, we can think of black language as having both a sacred and a secular style. The sacred style is rural and Southern. It is grounded in the black church tradition and black religious experience. It is revealed in the spirituals, the Moan, the Chant, the Gospel songs; it is testifyin, talkin in tongue, and bearin witness to the power of God and prayer. It tends to be more emotional and highly charged than the secular style. Though urban and Northern, the secular style also has its roots in the rural South. It is manifested in forms like the Dozens, the Toast, the blues, and folk tales, all of which were transformed to accommodate the urban experience. Within the secular style is the street culture style, the style commonly associated with, but not exclusive to, barbershops, pool halls, and street corners in black communities. More cool, more emotionally restrained than the sacred style, newer and younger in time, the secular style only fully evolved as a distinct style with the massive wave of black migration to the cities.

Sacred style is an important force in black culture because the traditional black church is the oldest and perhaps still the most powerful and influential black institution. To speak of the "traditional" black church is to speak of the holy-rolling, bench-walking, spirit-getting, tongue-speaking, vision-receiving, intuitive-directing, Amen-saying, sing-song preaching, holy-dancing, and God-sending church. Put another way, this church may be defined as that in which the content and religious substance has been borrowed from Western Judaeo-Christian tradition, but the communication of that content—the process—has remained essentially African. The specific convergence of Judaeo-Christian content and African process is found in Protestant denominations, such as Baptist, Methodist, Holiness, and Sanctified, where the worship patterns are characterized by spontaneous preacher-congregation calls-and-responses, hollers and shouts, intensely emotional singing, spirit possession, and extemporaneous testimonials to the power of the Holy Spirit.

The traditional black church is peopled by working-class blacks—domestics, factory workers, janitors, unskilled laborers. While today there is an ever-increasing number of high school graduates and college-educated members, most "pillars of the church" have less than a high school education. The preacher of such a church may or may not be university-educated, but he must be able to "talk that talk" (preach in Black English style and lingo). It is within the traditional black church that traditional black folk (blacks who haven't been assimilated into the elusive American mainstream) create much of their reality, which includes the preservation and passing on of Africanized idioms, proverbs, customs, and attitudes. During slavery, the church was the one place Ole Massa allowed the slaves to congregate unsupervised and do pretty nearly as they pleased. Not surprisingly, a number of slave rebellions and revolutionary leaders (such as preacher Nat Turner) were spawned in the church. In addition to serving as a buffer and source of release against white oppression, the traditional black church functions as an important social unit where the rich and needy are helped, community news is exchanged, and black men gain opportunities (as deacons, trustees, officers) to play leadership roles. Speaking to the importance of the church, C. Eric Lincoln, the noted black historian, put it this way:

> The black man's pilgrimage in America was made less onerous because of his religion. His religion was the organizing principle around which his life was structured. His church was his school, his forum, his political arena, his social club, his art gallery, his conservatory of music. It was lyceum and gymnasium as well as sanctum sanctorum. His religion was his fellowship with man, his audience with God. It was the peculiar sustaining force which gave him the strength to endure when endurance gave no promise, and the courage to be creative in the face of his own dehumanization.

Viewing it from this perspective, we can see how the traditional black church became paramount in the history of Black America. But more than that, the embracing of a white God was a natural, cultural response based on the African way of life. Recall that in traditional African society it is believed that there is a unity between the spiritual and material selves, but the prime force behind the movements of man and the universe is spiritual. This conception of a "spiritual universe" means that man's ultimate destiny is to move on to the "higher ground" of the spiritual world. Concomitant with the African's emphasis on spirituality, "religion" (in the sense in which Westerners use the term) becomes a pervasive dominating force in the society. Throughout Africa, there is no dichotomy between sacred and secular life, and there are no "irreligious people" in traditional African society, for to be "without religion amounts to a self-excommunication from the entire life of society . . . African people do not know how to exist without religion." As "common as daily bread, religion is not a sometime affair. It is a daily, minute involvement of the total person in a community and its concerns. Indeed, the spirit will not come forth with power apart from the community emptying itself (and thus the priest), so that the power can reign without interference . . . The heart of traditional African religions is the emotional experience of being filled with the power of the spiritual." In the traditional black church, and in Black American culture generally, this aspect of the traditional African world view strongly continues in the emphasis on spirituality ("soul") rather than materiality. Black Americans believe the soul, feeling, emotion, and spirit serve as guides to understanding life and their fellows. All people are moved by spirit-forces, and there is no attempt to deny or intellectualize away that fact.

However, while blacks realize that people cannot live by bread alone, they believe that God helps those who help themselves. As the church folk say, "don't move the mountain, Lord, just give me strength to climb." Thus the traditional black church's other-worldly orientation is balanced by coping strategies for *this* world. And, like the traditional African God, the Black American God is viewed not only as Someone Who dwells on High but as One Who also inhabits this mundane earthly world of ours. As such, He too balances His other-worldly concerns with those of this world. Black American men and women, like traditional African men and women, are daily "living witnesses" to God's Supreme Power; thus they look up to God while simultaneously being on regular speaking terms with Him. As comedian Richard Pryor says, in talking about how a black preacher would function as an "exorcist": "Now, I knows you's busy, Lord—I done check yo schedule—but there's a person here who is PO-sessed."

Given the unity of the spiritual and the material, the sacred and the profane, in traditional African culture, it is not surprising to find the "circle unbroken" in Black America. None of this is to say that *all* black people go to and support the church. On the contrary, the stomp-down shonuff church-goers are in the minority in the community. What we are stressing here is the heavy preservation of Africanisms in the church which have had an impact on Black American culture at large. For instance, when a soulful black singer or musician of secular music is really gittin down, members of the audience unconsciously respond by "shouting," (also referred to as "gittin happy"), that is, they show signs of being moved by the musical spirit—hollering, clapping hands, stomping feet, frenzied dancing, and other kinds of emotional responses. In other words, here is a secular audience gittin the Spirit! That very African tradition—belief in and expression of spirit possession—was retained in the traditional black church. ("If you got religion, show some sign.") Here we are in contemporary times finding this behavior being exhibited by blacks who don't even set foot inside the church door!

Thus while the secular style might be considered the primary domain of the street, and the sacred that of the church, no sharp dichotomy exists, but a kind of sacred-secular circular continuum. As we have said, the black preacher's rap and traditional black church service tend to be highly informal and both abound in secularisms. For example, it is considered entirely appropriate for a preacher to get up in the pulpit and, say, show off what he's wearing: "Y'all didn notice the new suit I got on today, did y'all? Ain the Lord good to us?" Similarly, there is very often a sacred quality surrounding the verbal rituals of the secular style, with all gathered about the rapper, listening attentively, looking idolizingly and lingering on his or her every word, mystically engrossed in the rap. This is the effect achieved, for instance, by a black-culture poet such as Haki Madhubuti (Don Lee) or Imamu Baraka (LeRoi Jones) verbally performing ("reading") before a black audience. The most striking example of this merging of sacred and secular styles is in the area of black music, where lyrics, musical scores, and singers themselves easily float in and out of both worlds. Black blues and soul artists who came out of the church include the Staple Singers, Sam Cooke, Lou Rawls, Dionne Warwick, Dinah Washington, Nina Simone, Sly Stone—the list goes on and on. One of the deepest of this group is Aretha Franklin, who started singing and playing piano in her father's church at a very young age, went on to make record hits in the secular world, and then "returned" to the church to record the hit album *Amazing Grace* with the Reverend James Cleveland. (White America might have just "discovered" Gospel singers and Gospel rock, but they been there all the time in the traditional black church.) Another fantastic move was made by James Brown when he appropriated the preacher's concluding ritual for his secular performances. "Soul Brother Number One" has a classic number that climaxes each performance: he goes offstage and returns wearing a black cape, reminiscent of the preacher's robe, then he proceeds to do his soulful thing until he gits the Spirit; he keeps on "shoutin" until he has to be pulled away from the mike, fanned, his perspiration toweled down, and his spirit brought back under "normal" control. Can I get a witness?

• • •

The language and style that comprise the sacred-secular oral tradition can be characterized in a number of ways . . . we might speak in terms of the rhetorical qualities of smaller, individual units of expression. The qualities are: exaggerated language (unusual words, High Talk); mimicry; proverbial statement and aphoristic phrasing; punning and plays on words; spontaneity and improvisation; image-making and metaphor; braggadocio; indirection (circumlocution, suggestiveness); and tonal semantics. A black rap can have one, all, or any combination of these. Rappers must be skillful in reading the vibrations of their audience and situation, for the precise wording depends on what is said to whom under what conditions. We shall briefly illustrate each.

Exaggerated language. Rappers sprinkle their talk with uncommon words and rarely used expressions. Recall Shakes's lady "succumbing to the amorous design his words had traced in the air of the night." Martin Luther King Jr., once referred to a matter as being "incandescently clear." A lesser-known preacher said emphatically in his sermon: "When Jesus walked the face of the earth, you know it upset the high ES-U-LAUNCE [echelon]." Sometimes the whole syntax of a sentence may be expressed in an elevated, formal manner, as in this invitation from a working-class black male: "My dear, would you care to dine with me tonight on some delectable red beans and rice?"

Mimicry. A deliberate imitation of the speech and mannerisms of someone else may be used for authenticity, ridicule, or rhetorical effect. For instance, whenever rappers quote somebody, they attempt to quote in the tone of voice, gestures, and particular idiom and language characteristic of that person. A black female complains to a friend about her man, for instance: "Like he come tellin me this old mess bout [speaker shifts to restatin and imitatin] 'Well, baby, if you just give me a chance, Ima have it together pretty soon.' That's his word, you know, always talkin bout having something 'together.' " Occasionally, the mimicking takes the form of a title or line from a song: "Told you she wasn't none of yo friend; [singing] 'smiling faces' . . ."

Proverbial statement. The rapper sprinkles his or her talk with familiar black proverbs and drives home the points with short, succinct statements which have the sound of wisdom and power. While proverbs have been around for ages, we are here referring to the black rapper's tendency to encapsulate and in a sense "freeze" experience through his or her own aphoristic phrasing. "It ain no big thang" originated in this manner; it was followed up by the aphoristic repartee: "But it's growing." Two well-known examples of proverbial-sounding statements often used by churchgoers are: "I been born again" and "My name is written on High."

Many old black proverbs become titles or lines in hit songs—for instance, Aretha Franklin's "Still Water Runs Deep" and Undisputed Truth's "Smiling Faces Sometimes Tell Lies." Many proverbs are quoted by mothers to their children and serve as child-rearing devices to teach rapidly and in no uncertain terms about life and living. "A hard head make a soft behind," "If you make yo bed hard, you gon have to lie in it," and "God don't like ugly" are three such frequently used proverbs. Proverbs and proverbial expressions are significant in the oral tradition because they hark back to an African cultural-linguistic pattern that was retained and adapted to the conditions of the New World. Among the Ibo people of West Africa, according to the African writer Chinua Achebe, "the art of conversation is regarded very highly, and proverbs are the palm-oil with which words are eaten."

Punning. While many verbal wits employ this rhetorical strategy, punning in the black heavily depends on the threads of the black experience common to all, and knowledge of black speech. For example, it is commonly believed that black people are adept with knives and razors as weapons, thus James Brown's "I don't know Karate but I know Karazor." Another such example depends on one's knowledge of how Black English is pronounced. It goes as follows:

> Knock, knock.
> Who's there?
> Joe.
> Joe who?
> Joe Momma.

This is a good example of playing the Dozens by punning on the similarity in sound between *yo* (not *your*) and *Joe.*

Spontaneity. Though black raps have an overall formulaic structure, the specifics remain to be filled in. The rapper is free to improvise by taking advantage of anything that comes into the situation—the listener's response, the entry of other persons to the group, spur-of-the-moment ideas that occur to the rapper. For example, the preacher will say, "Y'all don wont to hear dat, so I'm gon leave it lone," but if the congregation shouts, "Naw, tell it, Reb! Tell it!," he will. Rarely does the rapper have a completely finished speech, even in more structured "formal" kinds of speech-making, such as sermons or political speeches. (Many a would-be romantic rapper has been known to blow his thang with a canned rap.) By taking advantage of process, movement, and creativity of the moment, one's rap seems always fresh and immediately personalized for any given situation. For instance, before Malcolm X's prison background became widespread knowledge, he mentioned to an audience the fact that he had once been in prison. He read the vibrations of the audience, sensing their surprise, and quickly reacted. Noting that all black people in this country were, in a sense, imprisoned, he capped: "That's what America means: prison."

Image-making. An important criterion of black talk is this use of images, metaphors, and other kinds of imaginative language. The metaphorical constructs are what give black raps a poetic quality. Ideas, trivial or small though they may be, must be expressed in creative ways. Preachers especially must be good at image-making. The Reverend Jesse Jackson refers to the plight of black people as analogous to being on the expressway with all the entrances and exits closed off. Another Baptist preacher compared Christ's work to a "mission: impossible." The figures of speech created in black linguistic imagery tend to be earthy, gutsy, and rooted in plain, everyday reality. One blood's distaste for wig-wearing females was expressed as: "They look like nine miles of bad road with a detour at the end."

Braggadocio. The rapper boasts a good deal, as we have seen in earlier examples. The bragging is of various kinds and dimensions. Instead of saying something limp like "If you so bad, gon and start something," one potential fighter boldly rapped: "If you feel froggy, leap!" Of course the badness of heroes must be celebrated, as for instance Stag-O-Lee, who was so bad "flies wouldn't fly around him in the summertime, and even white folks was scared of him." Whether referring to physical badness, fighting ability, lovemanship, coolness (that is, "grace under pressure"), the aim is to convey the image of an omnipotent fearless being, capable of doing the undoable. Consider two contrasting love raps using braggadocio. Smokey Robinson confidently croons:

> I'll take the stars and count them
> and move the mountains
> And if that won't do
> I'll try something new.

But the Temptations, with all their badness, have run into some hard times:

> I can change a river into a burning sand
> I can make a ship sail on dry land
> All these things I'm able to do
> But I can't get next to you.

Indirection. The rapper makes his or her points by the power of suggestion and innuendo. It is left to the listener to decipher and explicate the totality of meaning. Much signifyin works through indirection. For instance, Malcolm X once began a speech in this way: "Mr. Moderator, Brother Lomax, brothers and sisters, friends and enemies: I just can't believe everyone in here is a friend and I don't want to leave anybody out." Not only is Malcolm neatly putting down his enemies in the audience without a direct frontal attack, he is also sending a hidden message (to those hip enough to dig it). Since it is an all-black audience, Malcolm is slyly alluding to the all-too-familiar historical and contemporary pattern of blacks being betrayed by other blacks; traitors in their midst who ran and told the white folks everything they knew. (A number of slave uprisings were foiled because of these "black Judases," and there is a saying that surely dates back to the slave experience: when a blood does something, however small or innocuous, maybe something not even having to do with white folks, he or she will typically say, "Now, run and tell that!")

Indirection gives longer black raps their convoluted style, that is, the rapper will start with a point, then proceed to meander all around it; he may return, circular fashion, to the point, but he typically does not proceed in a straight, linear, point-by-point progression. Unless you are good at circumlocution, it is difficult to win an argument with a rapper skilled in this device. For one thing, such rappers will refuse to confront head-on any contradictory points raised. When dealing with such rappers, it is best to remember that they depend on psychological and experiential logic, rather than some abstract system of logic that maybe exists nowhere but in somebody's head. As an example, Jesse B. Simple is trying to prove he is part Indian, but his friend says he is just plain "colored," and besides, "Jesse is not even an Indian name." Simple counters this with the fact that he had a Hiawatha in his family "but she died," whereupon he is promptly contradicted and threatens to be caught in his lie: "*She*? Hiawatha was no *she*." Not at all undaunted by this correction of facts, Simple reasons that the sex of Hiawatha neither proves nor disproves that he has Indian blood. His experience has taught him that a lot of black people are part Indian. At any rate, he has to win the argument, so he refuses to even deal with the implications of the rebuttal, and in a smooth psych-out move, he promptly proceeds to change the subject: "She was a *she* in our family. And she had long coal-black hair just like a Creole. You know, I started to marry a Creole one time when I was coach-boy on the L & N down to New Orleans. Them Louisiana girls are bee-oou-te-ful! Man, I mean!"

Such indirection and circumlocutory rhetoric are also a part of African discourse strategy, and Afro-Americans have simply transformed this art to accommodate the English language. As an example of this technique in West Africa, Chinua Achebe, in his first novel *Things Fall Apart*, depicts the example of Unoka from the Ibo village of what is now Biafra. Supposedly, Unoka, father of the main character, Okonkwo, is a failure by village social standards; people laugh at him, and they "swore never to lend him any more money because he never paid back." However, "Unoka was such a man that he always succeeded in borrowing more, and piling up his debts." Surely part of his success must be attributable to the fact that Unoka can skillfully employ circumlocutory reasoning in his discourse, as Okoye found out when he came to collect the two hundred cowries that Unoka had been owing him for more than two years.

> As soon as Unoka understood what his friend was driving at, he burst out laughing. He laughed loud and long and his voice rang out clear as the *ogene*, and tears stood in his eyes. His visitor was amazed, and sat speechless. At the end, Unoka was able to give an answer between fresh outbursts of mirth.
>
> "Look at that wall," he said, pointing at the far wall of his hut, which was rubbed with red earth so that it shone. "Look at those lines of chalk"; and Okoye saw groups of short perpendicular lines drawn on chalk. There were five groups, and the smallest group had ten lines. Unoka had a sense of the dramatic and so he allowed a pause, in which he took a pinch of snuff and sneezed noisily, and then he continued: "Each group there represents a debt to someone, and each stroke is one hundred cowries. You see, I owe that man a thousand cowries. But he has not come to wake me up in the morning for it. I shall pay you, but not today. Our elders say that the sun will shine on those who stand before it shines on those who kneel under them. I shall pay my big debts first." And he took another pinch of snuff, as if that was paying the big debts first. Okoye rolled his goatskin and departed.

Tonal semantics. Verbal power can be achieved through the use of words and phrases carefully chosen for sound effects. (Since this can be either a line or a pervasive structure in a total rap, it is briefly mentioned here.) In employing tonal semantics, the rapper gets meaning and rhetorical mileage by triggering a familiar sound chord in the listener's ear. The words may or may not make sense; what is crucial is the rapper's ability to make the words *sound* good. They will use rhyme, voice rhythm, repetition of key sounds and letters. Fighter-poet Muhammad Ali was working right in this tradition with his taunting rhymes predicting his opponents' defeats: "They all must fall/in the round I call" and "If he mess wif me, I'll drop him in three." Most Toast-tellers rely on tonal semantics, their verbal ingenuity taxed to the limit in trying to sustain the melodic structure. "I'm Peter Wheatstraw, the Devil's son-in-law," or "I'm sweet peeter jeeter, the womb beater." Obviously, preachers rely on tonal semantics. For example, my father, Reverend Napoleon, once expressed the following theme in a sermon: "I am nobody talking to Somebody Who can help anybody." Other deep-down church folks use tonal semantics too; for instance, they will use the Moan to trigger a responsive chord, establishing a kind of psycho-cognitive reality of one who knows the Lord: "Hmmmmmmmmmmmmmmmmm," or "HHHHHHHHHHHHHHHHHmmmmmmmmmmmm."

NOTES

The material from Thompson (1974) is found on pp. 5–45; that from Forde (1954) on p. x. Sowande (1974) and Mbiti (1969) are other excellent sources of information on the cosmology of traditional Africa. Jahn (1961), a useful study of African orality, provided the quote on Nommo, pp. 125–33. A *griot* (pronounced *greeo*) is one who, by memory alone, preserves and teaches the tradition and history of the tribe. In some traditional African societies, this master of "historical oratory" is an important sacred figure—akin to a storyteller, minstrel, jester, herald, annalist, troubadour, gleeman, and poet all rolled into one. The legend of Sundiata was told to D. T. Niane by an "obscure griot" from a village in Guinea and was translated by Pickett (1965). Mitchell (1970) presents a thorough analysis of black preaching style. Mitchell (1975) explores the relationship between the black church, black values, and African heritage. Daniel and Smitherman (1976) is a more concise treatment of the same. Washington (1973) is good on background and description of black religious cults. The quote from C. Eric Lincoln is from the Foreword in Barrett (1974), p. viii. On August 21, 1831, preacher Nat Turner led the greatest slave rebellion in history, killing some sixty whites in Southampton County, Virginia, and sending the entire South into a state of panic. He was captured on October 30 and hanged in Jerusalem, the county seat, twelve days later. For more rhymes, toasts, and choice quotes from Muhammad Ali, see Cottrell (1967) and Olson (1967).

  1. *Signification* refers to the act of talking negatively about somebody through stunning and clever verbal put-downs. In the black vernacular, it is more commonly referred to as *sigging* or *signifyin*. The *Dozens* is a verbal game based on negative talk about somebody's mother.

  2. Also referred to as "announcing" his text, this involves a fairly consistent three-part structure: 1) the act of citing the Scriptural reference from which the message of the sermon is to be taken, followed by 2) the reading of the passage, and concluding with 3) a usually cleverly worded statement articulating the "theme" (message) of the sermon.

WORKS CITED

Achebe, Chinua. *Things Fall Apart*. New York: Fawcett, 1959.
Baraka, Imamu. *Blues People*. New York: William Morrow, 1963.
Barrett, Leonard E. *Soul-Force*. New York: Anchor Books, 1974.
Brown, Hubert Rap. *"Die Nigger Die!"* New York: Dial Press, 1969.
Cottrell, John. *Muhammad Ali: The Man of Destiny, Formerly Cassius Clay*. New York: Muller, 1967.
Daniel, Jack L., and Smitherman, Geneva. " 'How I Got Over': Communication Dynamics in the Black Community." *Quarterly Journal of Speech*, February 1976, pp. 26–39.
Fanon, Frantz. "The Negro and Language." *Black Skin, White Masks*. New York: Grove Press, 1967.
Forde, Daryll, ed. *African Worlds: Studies in the Cosmological Ideas and Social Values of African Peoples*. New York: Oxford University Press, 1954.
Jahn, Janheinz. *Muntu*. London: Faber and Faber, 1961.
King, Woodie Jr., comp. "The Game." *Black Short Story Anthology*. New York: Columbia UP, 1972, pp. 301–10.
Lincoln, C. Eric. Foreword. *Soul-Force*. By Leonard E. Barrett. New York: Anchor, 1974, p. viii.

Madhubuti, Haki (Don Lee). "Directions for Black Writers." *Black Scholar,* December 1969, pp. 53–57.

Malcolm X. *Malcolm X Speaks.* New York: Grove Press, 1965.

———. *The Autobiography of Malcolm X.* New York: Grove Press, 1965.

Mbiti, John S. *African Religions and Philosophies.* New York: Doubleday, 1969.

Mead, Margaret. *Coming of Age in Samoa: A Psychological Study in Primitive Youth for Western Civilization.* New York: W. Morrow, 1928.

Mitchell, Henry. *Black Belief.* New York: Harper and Row, 1975.

———. *Black Preaching.* Philadelphia: J. B. Lippincott, 1970.

Olson, Jack. *Black Is Best.* New York: Putnam, 1967.

Pickett, G. D., ed. and trans. *Sundiata: An Epic of Old Mali.* London: Longman Group, Ltd. Edition, 1965.

Sowande, Fela. "The Quest of an African World View: The Utilization of African Discourse," in Jack L. Daniel, ed., *Black Communication: Dimensions of Research and Instruction.* New York: Speech Communication Association, 1974.

Washington, Joseph R. *Black Sects and Cults.* New York: Doubleday, 1973.

Wright, Richard. *Black Boy.* New York: Harper & Row, 1966.

Young, Al. *Snakes: A Novel.* New York: Holt, Rinehart and Winston, 1970.

19

Professing Multiculturalism: The Politics of Style in the Contact Zone

MIN-ZHAN LU

In her 1991 "Arts of the Contact Zone," Mary Louise Pratt points out that while colleges and universities have increasingly deployed a rhetoric of diversity in response to the insistence of non-mainstream groups for fuller participation, the "import" of "multiculturalism" remains "up for grabs across the ideological spectrum" (39). I begin with Pratt's reminder because I want to call attention to the images of "grabbing" and "import." These depict "multiculturalism" as a construct whose "import"—meanings, implications, and consequences—is available only to those willing to expend the energy to "grab" it: to search, envision, grasp, articulate, and enact it. And these images conjure up the act of importing—of bringing in—perspectives and methods formerly excluded by dominant institutions. I want to articulate one "import" of multiculturalism here by exploring the question of how to conceive and practice teaching methods which invite a multicultural approach to style, particularly those styles of student writing which appear to be ridden with "errors." And I situate this question in the context of English Studies, a discipline which, on the one hand, has often proclaimed its concern to profess multiculturalism but, on the other hand, has done little to combat the ghettoization of two of its own cultures, namely composition teaching and student writing.

My inquiry is motivated by two concerns which I believe I share with a significant number of composition teachers. The first results from a sense of division between the ways in which many of us approach style in theory and in our teaching practices. I have in mind teachers who are aligned in theory with a view of composition which contests the separation of form and meaning and which also argues against a conception of "academic discourse" as discrete, fixed, and unified. This alignment, while generating a critical perspective towards traditional methods of teaching style through drills in "correct usage," does not always result in any immediate revision of such methods in classroom practice. Some of us tend to resolve this gap between theory and

From *College Composition and Communication* 45 (1994): 442–58.

practice in one of two ways: (1) We set aside a few weeks to teach "usage" or "copyediting" in the traditional way while spending the rest of the term helping students to revise their work on a more conceptual level; or (2) we send students who have "problems" with "usage" to the writing center. Such "resolutions" often leave the teacher frustrated. Because she recognizes the burden on those at the fringe of having to "prove" themselves to those at the center by meeting the standards set by the latter, she cannot but take seriously students' anxiety to master "correct" usage. Nevertheless, she is aware that instead of helping them to overcome such an anxiety, her teaching strategies risk increasing it, as they may reinforce students' sense of the discrepancy between their inability to produce "error-free" prose and their ability to come up with "good ideas," and they may confirm these students' impression that only those who make "errors" need to worry about issues of usage and editing. My second concern has to do with a division many of us feel between our role as composition teachers and the role we play as students, teachers, or scholars in other, supposedly more central areas of English Studies. As our interest in composition teaching, theory, and research evolves, we are increasingly interested in contesting the second-class status of work in composition. At the same time, we are often all too aware that we ourselves are guilty of perpetuating the divisions between composition and other areas of English Studies by approaching the writings of "beginners" or "outsiders" in a manner different from the approach we take to the writings of "experts."

Two stories, both of which took place around the turn of this century, illustrate part of the historical power of that kind of division. The first story comes from Gertrude Stein's *The Autobiography of Alice B. Toklas*. According to Stein, right after she had made arrangements to have her book *Three Lives* printed by Grafton Press of New York, "a very nice American young man" was sent by the press to Paris to check on her:

> You see, [the young man] said slightly hesitant, the director of the Grafton Press is under the impression that perhaps your knowledge of english. But I am an american, said Gertrude Stein indignantly. Yes yes I understand that perfectly now, he said, but perhaps you have not had much experience in writing. I suppose, said [Stein] laughing, you were under the impression that I was imperfectly educated. He blushed, why no, he said, but you might not have had much experience in writing. Oh yes, she said, oh yes. . . . and you might as well tell [the director] . . . that everything that is written in the manuscript is written with the intention of its being so written and all he has to do is to print it and I will take the responsibility. The young man bowed himself out. (68)

This exchange between an indignant Stein and an embarrassed "young man" reveals some of the criteria used by "educated america" when dealing with an idiosyncratic style. These criteria are (a) the writer's "knowledge of english," which is seen as somehow dependent on whether she is a native speaker, and (b) the writer's "experience in writing," which is seen as related to whether she has been "[im]perfectly educated." Stein, an "American" bearing certification of a "perfect" education from Radcliffe and Johns Hopkins Medical School, knew she had the authority to maintain that everything in her manuscript was "written with the intention of its being so written." Stein's indignation and the embarrassment she elicited from the "young man" suggest that in the early 1900s, ethnic and educational backgrounds were two common denominators for determining whether style represented self-conscious and innovative experimentation or blundering "errors."

The second story took place a few years prior to the Stein event, when the style of another writer, Theodore Dreiser, was also questioned by a publisher to whom he had submitted his first novel, *Sister Carrie*. The rejection letter from Harper faults Dreiser for his "uneven" style which, according the editors, was "disfigured by . . . colloquialisms" (*Sister Carrie* 519). Existing manuscripts of the book's revision indicate that Dreiser did not defend his style with the kind of authority Stein exhibited. Instead he sought editorial help from his wife Jug and friend Henry because he deemed both to have been better educated than himself. There is evidence in the revised manuscript that Dreiser adopted nearly all of Jug's corrections of grammar and Henry's rewording of his Germanic rhythms and cumulative sentence structures (*Sister Carrie* 580–81). Read in the context of Stein's story, Dreiser's willingness to have all aspects of his style "corrected" might be attributed in part to his acute awareness of the criteria used by "educated america" when dealing with the writing of the son of an impoverished German immigrant with extremely sporadic formal education. The early reception of *Sister Carrie* proves the validity of Dreiser's concern, as even its defenders attributed its "crude" style to his ethnic background and lack of formal education.[1]

Almost a century after these events, more and more English courses are now informed by a view of language as a site of struggle among conflicting discourses with unequal socio-political power. Students in these courses are beginning to approach the style of what they call "real" writers like Stein and Dreiser very differently. Interest in multiculturalism has also shifted the attention of some teachers to writers' success at what Bakhtin calls "dialogically coordinating" a varied and profound "heteroglossia" (295–96). Analysis of style in these classrooms often centers on the politics of the writer's stylistic decisions: (a) mapping the "heteroglossia" on the internal and external scenes of writing, (b) attending to the writer's effort to look at one discourse through the eyes of another, and (c) considering the writer's willingness to resist the centripetal forces of "official" discourses. Viewed from this multicultural perspective on style, the writings of both Dreiser and Stein could be considered in terms of the efforts of each to dialogically coordinate the profound heteroglossia within and outside official "educated" discourses. For readers adopting this perspective, neither Dreiser's ethnic background nor his "imperfect" educational background would be used to dismiss his "uneven" style solely as evidence of "error" — that is, to conclude that his style merely reflects his lack of knowledge or experience in writing. In fact, given the frequency with which writings from what Gloria Anzaldua has called the "borderlands" are being currently assigned in some English courses and the praise this type of writing receives for its hybridization of "official" discourses, Dreiser's readiness to yield to the authority of the "better educated" now appears conservative—indicating a passive stance towards the hegemony of ethnocentrism and linguistic imperialism. In fact, the publication of the Pennsylvania edition of *Sister Carrie* in 1987 indicates that such a critical view privileging resistance was in operation when the editors decided to delete many of the changes made by the "better educated" Jug and Henry in the hope of preserving the "power and forcefulness" of Dreiser's original prose (*Sister Carrie* 581).

However, Dreiser's reaction still haunts me, especially when I move from teaching students to analyze the idiosyncratic style of "real" writers to helping them to work on their own styles. In my "literature" courses for junior- or senior-level college students or "writing" courses for first-year students, students learn to talk with considerable eloquence about the politics of stylistic decisions made by "real" writers, especially those writing from the borderlands by choice or necessity. Most of the readings I assign for these classes call attention to writers' need and right to contest the unifying force of hegemonic discourses, and thus make Dreiser's submission to the authority of the "better educated" appear dated and passive. Yet the meaning of Dreiser's submissiveness changes for me and most of my students as soon as we move to work on the style of a student writer, especially when we tinker with what we call the writer's "discursive voice"—that is, when dealing with deviations in diction, tone, voice, structure, and so on (which we loosely call the "rhetorical register"), or with punctuation, syntax, sentence structure, and so on (which we refer to as the "grammatical register"). On those occasions, how to sound "right" suddenly becomes a "real" concern for my students: pervasive, immediate, and difficult for me to dismiss. My students' apparent anxiety to reproduce the conventions of "educated" English poses a challenge for my teaching and research. Why is it that in spite of our developing ability to acknowledge the political need and right of "real" writers to experiment with "style," we continue to cling to the belief that such a need and right does not belong to "student writers"? Another way of putting the question would be, why do we assume—as Dreiser did—that until one can prove one's ability to produce "error-free" prose, one has not earned the right to innovative "style"?

Again, I believe Dreiser's account of his own educational experience might shed some light on the question. In *Dawn*, Dreiser writes about his opportunity to attend the University of Indiana, Bloomington for two short terms. A former teacher made arrangements to exempt Dreiser from the preliminary examinations because, Dreiser points out, these exams would have quickly "debarred" him (342). Life as what we might today call an open admissions student at Indiana made Dreiser feel "reduced." He "grieved" at his "inability to grasp . . . such a commonplace as grammar" (378). Even though he knew he was able to apprehend many things and to demonstrate his apprehensions "quite satisfactorily" to himself, he found the curriculum "oppressive," leaving him "mute" with "a feeling of inadequacy" (425). The events surrounding the efforts of Dreiser and Stein to publish their first books indicate that the common approach of the editors, publishers, and critics to their idiosyncratic styles was not coincidental. Dreiser's experience at Indiana, his willingness to have his "uneven" style "corrected," and Stein's quick rebuttal to the "young man" all point to the institutional source of this approach. A common view of "style" as belonging only to those who are beyond "error," and a certain type of college curriculum treating matters of grammar or usage as the prerequisites to higher education, seem mutually reinforcing. It is this belief that pushes students identified as having "problems" to meet such "prerequisites" and assigns teachers trained to deal with such "problems" to the periphery or borderlands of higher education.

Dreiser's memories of Indiana seem symptomatic of the feelings of a significant number of college students I encounter. I have in mind particularly students who seem quick to admit that they are "not good" at writing because they have been identified at some point in their education as needing special—remedial, laboratory, or intensive—instruction in the "basics." Like Dreiser, they are frustrated at their inability to grasp "grammar" because they have been encouraged to view it as "such a commonplace"—something everyone who aspires to become anyone ought to be able to master. And they feel muted and reduced by the curriculum because it does not seem to recognize that they are quite able to grasp subjects other than "grammar" and demonstrate their understanding of such subjects satisfactorily to themselves, if perhaps not in writing to others. It seems to me that one way of helping students to deal with this frustration would be to connect their "difficulties" with the refusal of "real" writers to reproduce the hegemonic conventions of written English. And it seems to me that this will not take place until teachers like myself contest the distinction between "real" and "student" writers and stop treating the idiosyncratic style of the not yet "perfectly educated" solely in terms of "error." One form of contestation could be to apply to student writing the same multicultural approach we have been promoting when analyzing the work of "real" writers. Susan Miller has argued in *Textual Carnivals* that the tendency to treat student writers as "emerging, or as failed, but never as actually responsible 'authors'" has served to maintain the low status of composition studies in its relations to those "outside it, and its self-images and ways of working out its new professionalization" (195–96). An approach to student writing that treats students as real writers would undo such binaries and thus assert the right and ability of writing teachers and students to fully participate in a truly multicultural curriculum.

My aim here is to discuss a teaching method formulated out of my attempt to apply a multicultural approach to student writing: an approach which views the classroom as a potential "contact zone"—which Pratt describes as a space where various cultures "clash, and grapple with each other, often in contexts of highly asymmetrical relations of power" (34). In arguing for a multicultural approach to styles traditionally displaced to the realm of "error," I align my teaching with a tradition in "error" analysis which views even "error-ridden" student writings as texts relevant to critical approaches available to English Studies. I am particularly interested in explicitly foregrounding the category of "resistance" and "change" when helping students to conceptualize the processes of producing and interpreting an idiosyncratic style in students' own writings. In the classroom I envision, the notion of "intention" is presented as the decision of a writer who understands not only the "central role of human agency" but also that such agency is often "enacted under circumstances not of one's choosing" (West 31). I define the writer's attempt to "reproduce" the norms of academic discourses as necessarily involving the re-production—approximating, negotiating, and revising—of these norms. And I do so by asking students to explore the full range of choices and options, including those excluded by the conventions of academic discourses.

These aspects in the classroom I envision inevitably distance it from classrooms influenced by one belief prevalent in ESL courses or courses in "Basic Writing": namely, that a monolingual environment is the most conducive to the learning of "beginners" or "outsiders." This belief overlooks the dialogical nature of students' "inner voices" as well as the multicultural context of students' lives. The classroom I envision also differs from approaches to students' ambivalence towards the effects of education exemplified by Mina Shaughnessy's *Errors and Expectations*. Shaughnessy convincingly shows the relevance to error analysis of a range of feelings common to students likely to be identified as basic writers: their anxiety to "sound academic" and to self-consciously emulate the formal style (194), their low self-esteem as learners and writers, and their sense of ambivalence towards academic discourse. But as I have argued in "Conflict and Struggle," Shaughnessy's goal in acknowledging students' ambivalence is only to help them dissolve it (904–06). Because this ambivalence arises from sources well beyond the classroom— coming from the unequal power relationships pervading the history, culture, and society my students live in—not all students can or even want to get rid of all types of ambivalence. On the contrary, the experiences of writers like Gloria Anzaldua, bell hooks, and Mike Rose suggest that, appropriately mobilized, a sense of ambivalence might be put to constructive uses in writing.

To foreground the concepts of "resistance" and "change" when analyzing the styles of a student or "real" writer, I ask students to read deviations from the official codes of academic discourses not only in relation to the writer's knowledge of these codes but also in terms of her efforts to negotiate and modify them. Aside from increasing the student's knowledge of and experience in reproducing these official forms, I am most interested in doing three things: (1) enabling students to hear discursive voices which conflict with and struggle against the voices of academic authority; (2) urging them to negotiate a position in response to these colliding voices; and (3) asking them to consider their choice of position in the context of the socio-political power relationships within and among diverse discourses and in the context of their personal life, history, culture, and society.

Because of the tendency in English Studies to ghettoize the culture of composition, I will use some student writing produced in writing courses for first-year students to illustrate how I would actually go about teaching a multicultural approach to style. And I am going to focus on features of writing styles which are commonly displaced to the realm of "error" and thus viewed as peripheral to college English teaching. In using these rather than other types of examples, I hope to illustrate as well the need to view composition as a site which might inform as well as be informed by our effort to profess multiculturalism in other, supposedly more "advanced" and "central" areas of English Studies. David Bartholomae has recently reminded us that there is no need "to import 'multiple cultures' [into the classroom, via anthologies]. They are there, in the classroom, once the institution becomes willing to pay that kind of attention to student writing" (14–15). Such attention, he explains, could produce composition courses in multiculturalism "that worked with the various cultures represented in the practice of its students" (14). My second reason for using these examples is related to the ways in which conflict and struggle have been perceived by teachers specializing in error analysis. These teachers tend to hear arguments foregrounding conflict and struggle in the classroom as sloganeering "the students' right to their own language" in order to eliminate attention to error, or as evidence of a "PC" attack on the "back to basics" movement (see, for example, Traub). The examples I use here, I hope, will demonstrate a way of teaching which neither overlooks the students' potential lack of knowledge and experience in reproducing the dominant codes of academic discourses *nor* dismisses the writer's potential social, political, and linguistic interest in modifying these codes, with emphasis on the word "potential."

When teaching first-year writing classes, I usually introduce the multicultural approach to student writing style around the mid-point of the term, when I feel that students are beginning to apply to their actual practices a view of writing as a process of re-seeing. To present the writer's experimentation with style (including what is generally called "copyediting" or the "correction of error") as an integral part of the revision process, I look for sample student writings with two characteristics. First, I am interested in writings with the kinds of "error" a majority of the class would feel they can easily "spot" and "fix." This type of writing allows me to acknowledge some potential causes of non-conventional styles and effective methods of revising them which are more widely disseminated in traditional writing classrooms and familiar to most students. Second, I look for styles which are also more conducive to my attempt to help the writer to negotiate a new position in relation to the colliding voices active in the scenes of writing.[2]

Following is a handout I have used when teaching first-year composition classes. The two segments on the handout are from the papers one student wrote in response to two assignments, one asking her to discuss an essay, "From a Native Daughter," by Haunani-Kay Trask, and another asking her to comment on the kind of "critical thinking" defined in the "Introduction" to an anthology called *Rereading America*. For the convenience of discussion in this essay, I have added emphasis to the handout:

Segment One:

As a Hawaiian native historian, Trask *can able to* argue for her people. As a Hawaiian native, she was exposed to two totally different viewpoints about her people. She was brought up in Hawaii. During this time, she heard the stories about her people from her parents. Later on she was send to America mainland to pursue higher education, in which she learnt a different stories about her people. Therefore, she understood that the interpretation of land was different between the "haole" and the native. To prove that the "haole" were wrong, she went back to Hawaii and work on the land with other native, so she *can* feel the strong bond with land her people have which the "haole" *could* not feel. The "haole" historians never bother to do so as they were more interested in looking for written evidence. That was why Trask, as a native Hawaiian historian, argued that these "haole" historians were being ignorant and ethnocentric. That is also why Trask suggested the "haole" historians learn the native tongue.

***

Segment Two:

Elements like perceiving things from different perspective, finding and validating each alternative solutions, questioning the unknown and breaking the nutshell of cultural norms are important for developing the ability of "critical thinking." . . . Most of the new universities' students are facing new challenges like staying away from family, peer pressure, culture shock, heavy college work etc. I *can* say that these are the "obstacles" to success. If a student *can able to* approach each situation with different perspectives than the one he brought from high school, I *may* conclude that this particular student has climbed his first step to become a "critical thinker." . . . However, there is one particular obstacle that is really difficult for almost everyone to overcome, that is the cultural rules. From the textbook, I found that cultural rules are deep rooted in our mind and cause us to view things from our respective cultural viewpoint. Even though cultural values lead the way of life of a particular group of people, they blind us as well. I relate to this because I truly believe that the cultural rules of my country, Malaysia, make my life here difficult. In order to achieve a "critical mind," one should try to break from his own cultural rules.

***

"can," verb:

1. to be able to; have the ability, power, or skill to. 2. to know how to. 3. to have the power or means to. 4. to have the right or qualifications to. 5. *may; have permission to. (The Random House Dictionary)*

"able," adjective:

1. having necessary power, skill, resources, or qualifications; qualified; able to lift a trunk; . . . able to vote (*The Random House Dictionary*).

When using this handout, I usually begin by asking students what particularly about the two segments might be said to make the voice of the writer idiosyncratic. My students in both writing and literature classes have been fairly quick in tracing it to the "can able to" structure in the two segments. Then I ask the class to speculate on potential causes of that idiosyncrasy. Students' responses to this question usually go something like this: Here is a "foreign" speaker, a student from Malaysia, trying to use the English idiom "to be able to" and ending up with an "error." So we usually talk a little bit about the difference in grammatical function between the verb "can" and the verb "to be" in relation to the adjective "able." And I describe the writer's own initial interpretation of the cause of this "error": her native language is Chinese. With the help of a tutor, she had realized that the Chinese translation for both "can" and "be able to" is the same. When using the expression "be able to," she would be thinking in Chinese. As a result, she often ended up writing "can able to." I would refer to her own initial reading because I am interested in complicating but not denying the relationship between style and the writer's knowledge of and experience with the conventions of written English. So I try to acknowledge first that exposure to and practice in reproducing the "be able to" structure could be one of the ways to revise these segments.

I then go on to complicate this approach by also calling attention to the relationship between form and meaning. What might be the difference in meaning between "can," "be able to," and "can able to"? Most of the students I have encountered tend to see "can" as interchangeable with "be able to." To them, "can able to" appears redundant, like a double negative. To problematize this reading, I usually call attention to the two dictionary entries included in the handout, especially to definition 5 under "can." Definition 5 opens up a new reading by presenting the word "can" as having one more meaning than "to be able to." Rather than approaching the issue of ability from the perspective of what an individual possesses, definition 5 approaches it from the perspective of the external forces *permitting* something, as in the verb "may."

Most native English speakers among my students tend to argue that in actual usage, only grandmas and schoolteachers make the distinction between "can" and "may." *Everyone* uses "can" and "be able to" interchangeably nowadays. In response, I tell them the writer's position on the issue. She was aware of the distinction—she was the one who first called my attention to definition 5. At this point, a "contact zone" would begin to take shape with three conflicting positions on the meanings of "can" and "able to": the position of a speaker of idiomatic English, the position of the dictionary, and the position of a "foreign" student writer. Since the "foreign" student writer is here being cast as that of someone lacking knowledge and expertise in formal and idiomatic English and thus the least powerful of the three, I am most interested in furthering the students' existing construction of that position so it is not so easily silenced.

To that end, I pose the question of whether, read in the context of the two segments in the handout, one might argue that the "can" in the two "can able to" structures does not take on the same meaning as the other uses of "can" in the rest of the segments. This line of inquiry usually leads us to compare the meaning of the "can" in the first sentence in Segment One to the two "can's" in the seventh sentence and to the meaning of the "can" in the "can able to" in Segment Two as well as the "can" in the previous sentence or the "may" in the second half of the same sentence. My aim here is to get students to reconstruct the voice of the writer by focusing on the various uses of the word "can" in the two segments. When exploring the question, I also try to direct attention to the passive voice (Trask was "brought up in Hawaii" and "send to America mainland to pursue higher education") in the sentences following the statement "Trask can able to argue for her people." I explore with the class how and why this passive voice might be read as indicating that the student writer is approaching Trask's ability from the perspective of the external circumstances of Trask's life—using "can" in the sense of her having the "permission to" become a native Hawaiian historian—as well as from the perspective of her having the qualifications to argue as an historian. The two uses of "can" in sentence seven, however, present Trask's and the "haole" historians' (in)ability to "feel" the Hawaiian's bond with the land as more related to a person's will and attitude rather than to whether each "may"—has the permission to—learn the Hawaiian language or work with the people. ("The 'haole' historians never bother to do so.") Similarly, in the second segment, the "can" in "a student can able to adopt different perspectives," when read in the context of the writer's discussion of the difficulties for "everyone to overcome" the "obstacle" of cultural rules and of her own experience of that difficulty, again foregrounds the role of external conditions and their effect on one's ability to do something. In that sense, this "can" is closer in meaning to the "may" in "I may conclude," a conclusion presented as depending more on the action of someone else than on the ability of the "I" drawing the conclusion. At the same time, this "can" is different from the "can" in the "I can say . . ." since the latter seems to depend on the ability of the speaker to name the situations as "obstacles" rather than on whether or not the speaker has permission to so name them.

In getting the class to enact a "close reading" of the two segments, I aim to shift attention to the relationship between a discursive form, "can able to," and the particular meanings it might be said to create in particular contexts. As a result, a new question often surfaces: What kind of approach to "ability" is enacted by a speaker of idiomatic English who sees "can" and "be able to" as completely interchangeable in meaning? In exploring this question, students have mentioned popular sayings such as "if there is a will, there is a way"; TV shows such as *Mr. Rogers' Neighborhood* which teach viewers to believe "everyone is special," possessing unique qualities; and various discourses promoting the power of positive thinking. Students begin to perceive the way in which a common treatment of "can" and "to be able to" as interchangeable in meaning might be seen as contributing to a popular American attitude towards the transcendental power of the individual. Once we locate these conflicting approaches to the notion of ability, it becomes clear that the revision or "correction" of the "can able to" in these two segments can no longer take place simply at the level of linguistic form. It must also involve a writer's negotiating a position in relation to value systems with unequal social power in the U.S.: one "popular" and the others "alien," "dated," or "formal" but critical. Once this structural "error" is contextualized in conflicting attitudes towards a belief in the transcendental power of the individual, the issue can no longer be merely one's knowledge of or respect for the authorities of a dictionary English versus colloquial English, or one's competency in a particular language, but also one's alignment with competing discursive positions.

At this point, we will have mapped a contact zone with a range of choices and options both among linguistic forms and discursive alignments. As we move on to the question of how each of us might revise these two segments, I would make sure that each student further enlarges this contact zone by taking into consideration the specific conditions of her or his life. I would have already introduced my definition of the "conditions of life" in previous assignments and class discussions, a definition that includes a whole range of discursive sites, including that of race, ethnicity, gender, sex, economic class, education, religion, region, recreation, and work. I also encourage each student to think about "life" in terms of the life she has lived in the past, is living in the present, and envisions for the future. Furthermore, I stress that decisions on how to revise should also be related to each student's interpretation(s) of the two texts discussed in the segments. To summarize, the contact zone in which the revision takes place would encompass the collision of at least the following voices: the voice of a "foreign" student writer (as constructed by the class at the beginning of the discussion), the voice(s) of the writer of the two segments (as constructed by the class discussion resulting from a "close reading" of the various uses of "can"), the voice of a dictionary, of a speaker of idiomatic English, the voices important to the specific conditions of each student's life, the voice of a teacher, and the voice emerging from each student's interpretation of the two texts discussed in the two segments.

Since decisions on how to revise the "can able to" structure depend on who is present, the particular ways in which the discussion unfolds, and who is doing the revision, such decisions vary from class to class and student to student. To illustrate the unpredictability of the outcome, let me use two decisions made in two different courses, one by the original writer of the two segments and one by another student whose native language is also Chinese. Like all other students in my class, during the process of a "close reading" of the uses of "can" in these two segments, the original writer encountered a construction of her "voices" which she may not have fully considered before the discussion. Therefore, when revising the two segments, she too had to negotiate with these forms of reading and constructions of voices. Upon reflecting on the conditions of her life, she reviewed the attitude towards "ability" promoted in the particular neighborhood in Malaysia where she grew up. In view of that as well as of her own experience as a daughter (especially her difficulties persuading her parents to let her rather than only their sons go abroad for college), her current difficulty in adjusting to the kind of "critical thinking" promoted in my classroom (which she felt was the direct opposite of what she was told to do in her schooling back home), and her admiration of Trask's courage to "argue for her people," the writer decided to foreground the relationship between individual ability and the conditions in which that ability "may" be realized. With the help of her classmates, she came up with several options. One was to add an "if" clause to a sentence using "be able to." Another was to change "can able to" to "may be able to." One student suggested that she use "can able to" and then tag a sentence to explain her reasoning—her view of "ability." Among the suggestions, the writer picked "may be able to" because, as she put it, it was clearly "grammatically correct" and "says what I want to say." As the term progressed, one of the students in the class used "can able to" playfully in a class discussion, and others caught on. It became a newly coined phrase we shared throughout the term.

However, a Vietnamese-American student whose home language is also Chinese took a very different stance towards the hegemonic attitude toward "ability" and for a quite different reason from what led some of my American-born students to identify with the voice of an idiomatic speaker. Using examples from his immigrant community, he argued for the importance of believing in the capacity of the individual. He pointed out that the emphasis on external conditions had made some people in his community fatalistic and afraid to take up the responsibility to make changes. According to him, there is a saying in classic Chinese similar to "if there is a will, there is a way." His parents used it repeatedly when lecturing him. So he was all for using "can" and "be able to" interchangeably to foreground the power of the individual. He hoped more people in his community would adopt this outlook. Accordingly, his revision changed "can able to" to "be able to." At the same time, he also changed the passive voice in the sentences referring to Trask's childhood and education in the first segment to the active voice, arguing that there is enough basis in the essays to sustain that reading.

Given the frequency with which students opt for the voices of academic authority, I used to wonder if this kind of teaching is driven more by my view of language as a site of struggle than by the needs of students eager to internalize and reproduce the conventions of academic discourse. My conclusion is: No, this process of negotiation is particularly meaningful for students anxious to master the codes of academic discourse, especially because their discursive practices are most likely to have to take place in the kind of postmodern capitalist world critics such as Fredric Jameson have characterized. Although the product, their decision to reproduce the code, might remain the same whether it is made with or without a process of negotiation, the activities leading to that decision, and thus its significance, are completely different. Without the negotiation, their choice would be resulting from an attempt to passively absorb and automatically reproduce a predetermined form. In such cases, the student would perceive different discourses, to borrow from Bakhtin, as belonging to different, fixed, and indisputable "chambers" in her consciousness and in society. And she would evaluate her progress by the automatism with which she was able to move in and out of these "chambers." If and when this student experienced some difficulty mastering a particular code, she would view it as a sign of her failure as a learner and writer.

On the other hand, if the student's decision to reproduce a code results from a process of negotiation, then she would have examined the conflict between the codes of Standard English and other discourses. And she would have deliberated not only on the social power of these colliding discourses but also on who she was, is, and aspires to be when making this decision. If the occasion arises in the future when she experiences difficulty in reproducing a particular code, as it very likely will, her reaction may be much more positive and constructive. Learning to work on style in the contact zone is also useful for those students interested in exploring ways of resisting the unifying force of "official" discourse. First, it can help students hear a range of choices and options beyond the confines of their immediate life. Second, negotiating as a group gives them the distance they need but might not have when dealing with their own writing in isolation. Therefore, devoting a few class periods to familiarizing students with this approach to style can be fruitful, especially if students are asked to theorize their action afterwards by reflecting on its strengths and limitations.

Obviously, one of the challenges for such a teaching method is that one can only project but not predict a class discussion on the basis of the chosen sample. In fact, life in the contact zone is by definition dynamic, heterogeneous, and volatile. Bewilderment and suffering as well as revelation and exhilaration are experienced by everyone, teacher and students, at different moments. No one is excluded, no one is safe (Pratt 39). Therefore, learning to become comfortable in making blunders is central to this type of teaching. In fact, there is no better way to teach students the importance of negotiation than by allowing them the opportunity to watch a teacher work her way through a chancy and volatile dialogue. Seemingly simple markers such as skin color, native tongue, ethnic heritage, or nationality can neither prescribe nor pre-script the range of voices likely to surface. How to voice and talk to rather than speaking for or about the voices of the "other" within and among cultures is thus not a question which can be resolved prior to or outside of the process of negotiation. Rather, it must remain a concern guiding our action as we take part in it.

Needless to say, this type of teaching would work better when students are also asked to try the same method when analyzing the style of "real" writers so they understand that the "problems" they have with style are shared by all writers. For example, when students in a first-year writing course were reading Trask's essay "From a Native Daughter," I asked them to discuss or write about aspects of her style which seemed to deviate from the style of other historians they had encountered. Several students observed that the paragraphs in Trask's essay are shorter, including a series of one-sentence paragraphs with parallel structures of "And when they wrote . . . they meant . . ." (123–24). Others were struck by the opening of Trask's essay, where she addresses her audience directly and asks that they "greet each other in friendship and love." She tells many more personal stories and uses fewer references for support, and she uses the imagery of a lover to depict the role of language. I urged them to examine these stylistic features in relation to the particular stance Trask seems to have taken towards the conflict between "haole" (white) culture and the native Hawaiian culture. Having approached the writing of a "real" writer from the perspective of the relationship between meaning, form, and social identifications, students are likely to be more motivated in applying this perspective to their own style and its revision.

At the same time, using a student paper to enact a negotiation in the contact zone can create a sense of immediacy and a new level of meaningfulness about abstract concepts discussed or enacted in the assigned readings for students in "literature" and "critical theory" classes. For example, I have used the handout with the "can able to" construction in senior-level critical theory courses when discussing Bakhtin's notion of "internal dialogism," Raymond Williams' concept of "structures of feeling," Cornel West's "prophetic critics and artists of color," and "dense" critiques of colonial discourse by such writers as Edward Said or Homi K. Bhabha. In the process of revising the "can able to" structure in the handout, in actively negotiating conflict in a contact zone, students in literature and cultural critical theory courses can gain a concrete opportunity to test the theories of various critics against their own practice. This type of activity reduces the "alienation" students often experience when asked to "do" theory. Testing theories against their own writing practices can also enable students to become more aware of the specific challenges such theories pose as well as the possibilities they open up for the individual writers committed to practicing these viewpoints. And I have used this method in upper-level literature courses when teaching such "borderland" literature as Sandra Cisneros's short story "Little Miracle, Kept Promises" or *Breaking Bread* by Cornel West and bell hooks. Reading and revising a student text, students can become more sensitive to the ways in which a "real" writer negotiates her way through contending discourses. At the same time, such reading and revision of their own writing allows students to enter into dialogue with "real" writers as "fellow travellers," active learners eager to compare and contrast one another's trials and triumphs.

One reaction to teaching style on the contact zone is fear that it will keep students from wanting to learn the conventions of academic discourse. My experience so far suggests that the unequal socio-political power of diverse discourses exerts real pressures on students' stylistic choices. After all, students choose to come to college, the choice of which speaks volumes on that power. The need to write for professors who grade with red pens circling all "errors" is also real for a majority of our students in most classrooms outside English departments. Therefore, although the process of negotiation encourages students to struggle with such unifying forces, it does not and cannot lead them to ignore and forget them. It acknowledges the writer's right and ability to experiment with innovative ways of deploying the codes taught in the classroom. It broadens students' sense of the range of options and choices facing a writer. But it does not choose for the students. Rather, it leaves them to choose in the context of the history, culture, and society in which they live.

Acknowledgments: Earlier versions of this paper were delivered at the 1993 CCCC and at the University of Washington. My thanks go to the respondents in the audiences at both occasions. I am also grateful for comments on drafts of this piece from Elizabeth Robertson, Ira Shor, Anne Herrington, and James Seitz. Work on this essay was supported by a grant from the Drake University Center for the Humanities. And I offer special thanks to Bruce Horner for his contributions to the conception and revisions of this essay.

NOTES

1. See Anderson, "An Apology for Crudity"; Kazin, *On Native Grounds*; and Mencken, "The Dreiser Bugaboo."

2. For an extended discussion of teaching editing that informs my own, see Horner, "Rethinking," especially pages 188–96.

WORKS CITED

Anderson, Sherwood. "An Apology for Crudity." *The Stature of Theodore Dreiser: A Critical Survey of the Man and His Work.* Ed. Alfred Kazin and Charles Shapiro. Bloomington: Indiana UP, 1965. 81–84.

Anzaldua, Gloria. *Borderlands/La Frontera: The New Mestiza.* San Francisco: aunt lute, 1987.

Bakhtin, Mikhail. *The Dialogic Imagination.* Ed. Michael Holquist. Trans. Caryl Emerson and Michael Holquist. Austin: U of Texas P, 1981.

Bartholomae, David. "The Tidy House: Basic Writing in the American Curriculum." *Journal of Basic Writing* 12 (1993): 4–21.

Dreiser, Theodore. *Dawn.* New York: Fawcett, 1931.

———. *Sister Carrie: The Pennsylvania Edition.* Philadelphia: U of Pennsylvania P, 1981.

Horner, Bruce. "Mapping Errors and Expectations for Basic Writing: From the 'Frontier Field' to 'Border Country.' " *English Education* 26 (1994): 29–51.

———. "Rethinking the 'Sociality' of Error: Teaching Editing as Negotiation." *Rhetoric Review* 11 (1992): 172–99.

Kazin, Alfred. *On Native Grounds: An Interpretation of Modern American Prose Literature.* New York: Harcourt, 1942.

Lu, Min-Zhan. "Conflict and Struggle: The Enemies or Preconditions of Basic Writing?" *College English* 54 (1992): 887–913.

Mencken, H. L. "The Dreiser Bugaboo." *Seven Arts* 2 (1917): 507–17.

Miller, Susan. *Textual Carnivals: The Politics of Composition.* Carbondale: Southern Illinois UP, 1991.

Pratt, Mary Louise. "Arts of the Contact Zone." *Profession* 91 (1991): 33–40.

Shaughnessy, Mina. *Errors and Expectations: A Guide for the Teacher of Basic Writing.* New York: Oxford UP, 1977.

Stein, Gertrude. *The Autobiography of Alice B. Toklas.* New York: Vintage, 1933.

Trask, Haunani-Kay. "From a Native Daughter." *Rereading America: Cultural Contexts for Critical Thinking and Writing.* 2nd ed. Ed. Gary Colombo, Robert Cullen, and Bonnie Lisle. Boston: Bedford, 1989. 118–27.

Traub, James. "P.C. vs. English: Back to Basic." *The New Republic* Feb. 8, 1993: 18–19.

West, Cornel. "The New Cultural Politics of Difference." *Out There: Marginalization and Contemporary Cultures.* Ed. Russel Ferguson, Martha Gever, Trinh T. Minh-Ha, and Cornel West. Cambridge, MA: MIT P, 1990. 19–36.

20 *The Feminine Style: Theory and Fact*

MARY P. HIATT

Critics often have trouble dealing with style, probably for two reasons. In the first place, stylistic theory itself ranges widely. Some stylisticians hold that style is totally a matter of one individual's writing—that, in effect, there is no such thing as a group or mass style. Others take an opposing view and maintain that it is possible to describe the characteristics of a group of writers or of writers of a certain era. Stylisticians further differ on whether style is the sum total of the characteristics of the writing or whether it describes in what way the writing departs from a norm, roughly defined as a standard or commonplace manner of writing. Some theorists also hold that any style can only be adequately described in the context of another style, whether individual or group. The state of the theory itself is therefore conflicting and confusing.

In the second place, the metalanguage of style often relies on inadequate descriptors. Thus, in considering an individual's writing style, impressionistic adjectives abound: "muscular," "manly," "clear," "hothouse," "lush," "lean," etc. And in considering group style—or types of style—we are confronted with the traditional adjectives such as "plain," "high," and "grand," as well as "Baroque," "Ciceronian," "Attic," "Augustan," and so on. Few of these descriptors, whether of individual or group styles, have been objectively assayed, for upon close evaluation, they might vanish, leaving the critic at an unendurable loss for words.

Castigation of the manifold efforts at stylistic description serves little purpose. Nonetheless, an awareness of some of the pitfalls and complexities involved in the task of such description is essential to any adequate consideration of written style. To some degree, the critic of style is faced with choosing or developing a theory.

As mentioned above, a theory has persisted over the years that common characteristics in the writing of certain groups, perhaps during certain eras, do exist, despite the abjurations of those theorists who claim that style can only be an individual matter. This group-style theory is reflected in the de-

From *College Composition and Communication* 27 (1978): 222–26.

scriptors, "masculine" style and "feminine" style. Men and women, it is commonly believed, write differently. The conviction has run strong. Notably absent are any data to support the conviction.

But whereas data are missing, we generally find, once again, a plethora of adjectives being flung about. The "masculine" style is held to be terse, strong, rational, convincing, formidable, and logical. The "feminine" style is thought to be emotional, illogical, hysterical, shrill, sentimental, silly, and vapid. The "masculine" style seems to be described in terms of a male view of *men*—not necessarily of men's style. And the "feminine" style is described in terms, often pejorative, of a male view of *women*—not of women's style. Whether or not the difference exists at all is important to establish, but most certainly the stereotyped descriptors are impressionistic, biased, and consequently less than useful.

Opting for the theory, however, that style need not always be an individual matter and that there do exist types of style consisting of linguistic features shared by groups of writers at particular times, I have studied a large sample of contemporary American prose to see, first, whether there are discernible differences between the way men write and the way women write, and, second, if there are differences, what these differences are.[1] One hundred books, 50 by women and 50 by men, were objectively selected for the study. Objectivity was maintained by *not* choosing books on the basis of literary "merit," for merit is a subjective matter. To have selected books because anyone in particular—I, my friends, critics in general—liked them would have seriously prejudiced the study. In the study, therefore, the books include non-fiction by Albert Ellis, Telford Taylor, Marjorie Holmes, and Frances Fitzgerald and fiction by Charles Simmons, Bernard Malamud, Andrea Newman, and Joyce Carol Oates.

The two categories (women's books and men's books) were subdivided equally into fiction and non-fiction. From each of the 100 books, four 500-word selections of running text were randomly chosen. Each book, therefore, contributes a 2000-word sample to the study, which finally consists of 200,000 words of contemporary prose.

If one is attempting to discern stylistic differences between two sets of 100,000 words each, one can, of course, try to read all these words and note the occurrence of such stylistic matters as sentence-length and complexity, inserts, types of modification, and so on. One can try to do this, but no one should. The human mind is often an inaccurate perceiver, and errors inevitably occur. A mechanical mind is not inaccurate. Hence, the only objective and accurate way to deal with such a vast amount of text is to use a computer.

The 200,000 words of prose were therefore keypunched onto IBM cards. Each of the 100 samples was scanned by computer for such major aspects of style as sentence-length and complexity, logical sequence of ideas, similes, *-ly* adverbs, parenthetical expressions, structural parallelism, and rhetorical devices.

The findings indicate that contemporary male and female authors do write differently. I can report, with a fair degree of confidence, that there is a feminine style that is not the same as a masculine style. I definitely do not postulate, however, that either style is a "norm," from which the other style varies, although the way men are thought to write tends to be considered the way *to* write, probably because there are so many more male authors and critics than female authors and critics. The emergence of specific differences between the two groups of writers does, however, lend valid support to the theory that types of styles or styles characteristic of groups of writers do exist.

Of greater interest, perhaps, is the discovery that the masculine style and the feminine style do not always differ in the commonly perceived or described ways. A consideration of some specific results bears out this conclusion.

For example, close study of sentence-lengths[2] and average sentence-lengths of all the authors reveals that the men are not terse and that the women are not verbose. Of the non-fiction authors, the men's average sentence-length is 23 words; the women's, 21 words. The gross averages are not significantly different. All that can be said is that the women do not go on and on— if anything, their thoughts are phrased in shorter units. But if the sentences of all the non-fiction authors are divided into two groups, those of twenty words or fewer ("short" sentences) and those of more than twenty words ("long" sentences), a statistical analysis indicates that the women use significantly more short sentences—58 percent, versus 48 percent of the men's sentences.

Generally speaking, the longer the sentence, the more likely it is to be structurally complex. And, in the non-fiction studied, both the men's and the women's long sentences are certainly complex. But they are complex in different ways. The structure of the long sentences of *each author* in the men's non-fiction exhibits specific, often repeated aspects of style. Norman Mailer's long sentences, for example, are highly complicated, involving lengthy seriation, many parenthetical phrases and clauses, and many self-interrupters; Frank Mankiewicz uses many introductory and inserted adverbial phrases and clauses and many appositives; Frederick Cartwright often uses right-branching sentences; Rudolf Bing employs many complicated series, all in perfectly parallel constructions. In other words, the long sentences of each male non-fiction author usually offer readily identifiable types of complexity that are characteristic of that author.

With the exception of two women non-fiction authors, the long sentences of the women do not generally display individual patterns of complexity. The exceptions are Eda LeShan and Joyce Maynard, both of whom use dashes and parentheses in their long sentences. The constructions delineated by dashes and parentheses, however, could just as well have been delineated by periods. In other words, their long sentences do not display the subordinate constructions that are the hallmark of complexity. Their long sentences thus are not so complex as those of the men. Among the other women writers, the long sentences are carefully organized syntactically but cover a range of types of complexity. It is difficult to discern any one constructional characteristic for any one of these writers. The complexity of their sentences therefore is not so individually delineated as the complexity of the men's sentences.

As for the fiction writers, the average sentence-length for men is 17 words; for women, 16 words per sentence—again not really a significant difference. But the men tend to write longer sentences than the women and *more* longer sentences than the women. Nine men produce fourteen sentences of over 80 words, whereas only five women write even one sentence of more than 80 words, none of them longer than 90 words.

The *range* of sentence-lengths in fiction is also quite different between the two groups. Using as examples the two writers of the longest sentences in each group, we find that John O'Hara's longest sentence is 116 words, his shortest is two, and his range is 114 words; Tom Wicker's longest sentence is 104 words, his shortest is two, presenting a range of 102 words. On the other hand, Ruth Macdowell's longest sentence is 90 words, her shortest is two, and her range is 88; Daphne DuMaurier's longest sentence is 86 words, her shortest is three, and her range is 83 words. The foregoing are only examples, but the relatively narrow range of sentence-lengths is a repetitive feature of the women writers of fiction.

In fiction, sentence complexity is not a particularly cogent parameter of style, because fiction is so studded with dialogue. But in sentence-length, it does not seem that the women writers vary as widely as do the men. In this respect, their writing is perhaps less daring, more conservative.

Another aspect of style is the logical development of ideas. Examination of this feature was confined to non-fiction writers and carried out by studying the occurrence of certain words or phrases that often indicate a particular kind of logical sequence. There are, of course, many ways of indicating a particular logical process without the use of specific words. Instead of the word "because," for example, indicating that a reason is being offered, a writer may simply choose to say, "Another reason is that . . ." The existence of a logical sequence without the use of specific "signaling" words cannot be gainsaid. However, a search for what may be called "signals of logic," occurring at the beginning or within the sentence, reveals a difference in the writing of the men and the women.

Logical-sequence indicators (or the particular group of words or phrases signaling a particular process of logic) may be divided into five types:[3] (1) Illustratives ("for example," "that is," "for instance"); (2) Illatives ("therefore," "(and) so," "thus," "hence"); (3) Adversatives ("however," "but," "yet," "nevertheless," "on the other hand"); (4) Causatives ("because," "for," "since"); and (5) Additives ("and," "so . . . did").

The women use 190 of these logical-sequence indicators, whereas the men use 160. On the basis of the indicators, therefore, the women cannot be said to write illogically. But there is a difference in the type of logic used by the women writers. The men and the women use approximately the same number of Adversatives, but the women employ 50 percent fewer Illustratives and Illatives and 50 percent more Causatives and Additives. The logic of the feminine style would thus seem to depend on reasons and extra information rather than on exemplifications and conclusions. In terms of the low ratio of Illatives—those words indicating conclusions—the logic of the women is less definitive than that of the men. In terms of the high ratio of Causatives, their logic is more self-justifying. Neither the men's nor the women's style is, however, "illogical." Both are logical in different ways.

The occurrence of -ly adverbs offers another measure of style. Women's speech has been reported to contain many more adverbs ending in -ly than that of men, with high use of such words as "simply," "utterly," and "awfully" as modifiers of adjectives. The unadorned adjective is presumably the province of men.

Such may indeed be the case in women's speech, but in this study, it does not carry over into their writing. There is no significant difference between the men's and the women's writing in either the total number of -ly adverbs used or in the number of different adverbs, and the type-token ratio for both groups is almost exactly the same in fiction and in non-fiction. But the adverb "simply" is used more often by the men than by the women; the adverb "utterly" is rarely used by either group; and the adverb "awfully" is used only by the men.

In the interest of discovering whether women writers are, as frequently claimed, "hyperemotional," adverbs of emotion (such as "amiably," "abjectly," "coldly," "angrily," etc.) were studied. That emotion is often expressed verbally or nominally is true; the expression of emotion via adverbs is only one means. Nonetheless, the two groups' use of adverbs of emotion is startlingly different in fiction and scarcely different at all in non-fiction. In fiction, the women use twice as many adverbs of emotion as do the men, a finding that probably is the basis for calling women writers "hyperemotional."

But if another type of adverb is examined, the adverb of pace (such as "gradually," "hastily," "slowly," etc.), a reverse trend is seen. The men's fiction contains twice as many of these adverbs as the women's, and again there is no difference in the non-fiction of the two groups. The men's fiction style thus seems to be "hyperactive" as compared to the women's.

If both types of adverbs are considered together, however, a more accurate evaluation of the two fiction styles is possible. In all, the women fiction writers use approximately the same number of adverbs of emotion and adverbs of pace, whereas the men fiction writers use four times as many adverbs of pace as adverbs of emotion. Thus, in fiction, where the major differences occur, there is evidence that the feminine style balances pace of action and expression of emotionality. The women writers are not hyperemotional, except in terms of the men writers. There seems to be far less basis for labeling the feminine styles as hyperemotional than for labeling the masculine style as hypo-emotional.

The adverb really deserves special mention. The women writers use the word two and a half times more often than the men writers in non-fiction, and one and a half times as often in fiction. One male novelist (Anthony Burgess) accounts for the lessening of the difference in fiction by using that particular adverb more often than any woman writer. If his sample is disregarded, the same high proportion of really's exists in the women's fiction as in their non-fiction. The relatively high occurrence as characteristic of the feminine style is probably at least unconsciously and generally recognized. It actually is very consciously recognized in the words of one male character in a woman writer's novel when he says to a woman character, " 'Really,' 'really,' 'really'! That's all you can say!" Its use probably reflects women's feelings that they will not be believed, that they are not being taken seriously or "really." These feelings would quite naturally lead women to claim sincerity and validity more frequently than do men.

To recapitulate, in those areas of style discussed here, the way the women write emerges as distinct from the way the men write. This distinction is consistently borne out in the study of other areas of style, such as the use of similes, certain adjectives and verbs, parallel structures, and various aspects of rhetoric. There is, in other words, clear evidence of a feminine style and sound justification for the theory of group style.

But the feminine style is in fact rather different from the common assumptions about it. Solely on the basis of just those aspects discussed in this paper, it can be claimed that the feminine style is conservative, structurally sound, logical in its own way, balanced in terms of emotionality and pace. There are no excesses of length or complexity or emotion. Its only excess lies perhaps in the protesting use of *really*, an understandable protest against being disbelieved.

NOTES

1. See Mary P. Hiatt, *The Way Women Write: Sex and Style in Contemporary Prose* (New York: Teachers College Press, Columbia University, 1977), for the complete report, including the list of the 100 authors forming the basis of the study.

2. A sentence is defined as any word or words beginning with a capital letter and ending with end punctuation. This is not a grammatical definition but one that accommodates the vagaries of dialogue and speech patterns.

3. The logical-sequence indicators were suggested by a system of eight logical relationships posited by Louis T. Milic, *Stylists on Style* (New York: Scribners, 1969), p. 21.

21

The Cultures of Literature and Composition: What Could Each Learn from the Other?

PETER ELBOW

The history of relations between composition and literature has involved a vexed tangle of misunderstanding and hurt. Both fields would benefit if we could think through some of the vexations. That's what I'm trying to do here.

But I won't talk about the most obvious problems: political and material issues of power, money, and prestige. These matters cannot be ignored, but I will mention them quickly and pass on. Composition has been the weak spouse, the new kid, the cash cow, the oppressed majority. When writing programs are housed in English departments, as they so often are, teachers of writing are usually paid less to teach more under poorer working conditions—in order to help support literature professors to be paid more to teach less under better working conditions. I'm hoping that these material vexations might be starting to recede just a bit now—as composition gets stronger and more secure, as writing programs find they can prosper outside English departments, and as literature itself struggles because of weak support for the humanities (not to mention frequent attacks on "professors" and all of higher education). Even the virus of relying on part-timers and adjuncts is increasing in mainstream literature too. I ask only that we not forget how hard it will be to get past the deep legacy of anger, hurt, and guilt.

I won't even address the much-discussed question of whether writing and literature should marry, stay married, or divorce. My essay could be read as an argument for maintaining the marriage; and I certainly admire the situation in many high schools and a few smaller liberal arts colleges where members don't actually feel a tension between literature and composition. But I hope my thoughts will be of use, whatever the contractual or sleeping arrangements are between literature and composition.

I turn away here from those issues and seek instead to explore what might be called—very loosely—the *cultures* or *traditions* or *identities* of literature and composition. I'm interested in the intellectual and psychological traditions of these fields—not just practices but what I sense still lurks in our

From *College English* 64 (2002): 533–46.

minds and in the air when we experience ourselves as "literature persons" and/or "composition persons." My ultimate goal is to answer some practical professional questions: What does the tradition or culture of literature have that composition needs? What does composition have that literature needs? How could each learn from the other?

I must confess at once that I am writing from a personal and subjective point of view. Worse yet, this essay is an exercise in large arguable generalizations (one reviewer called them "too easy") based on my "feel" or "sense" of things over the years — rather than on scholarship and research in the manner of Graff and Scholes. I present no proof; only a pudding. If my generalizations don't ring usefully true to many members of both communities, I've simply failed. Still, my subjectivity is based on forty years' teaching at six colleges or universities — and consultations, talks, and workshops at countless others.

I started full-time college teaching in 1960 and, having made it to age sixty-six, I've retired from full-time university employment. I'm continuing busy in my professional career, but this new step makes me look back. One thing I notice is my recurring sense of being torn between my identities as a literature person and as a composition person. I've long been seen as a composition person, and I've been a writing program director at two universities. But all my training was in literature, my first book was about Chaucer, and I didn't experience myself as a member of the "field of composition" till at least twenty of these past forty years had passed.

I.

I start with a sentence that makes me nervous (although I enjoy how it links the personal and professional): "I miss literature." What do I mean? First, it's just literal: I miss having works of literature central in some of my teaching. Why should I be nervous to say this? The problem is not so much sounding disloyal as being actually misleading. For when I say "I miss literature," it will sound to many as though I am voicing a whole complex of other thoughts that people in composition so often hear from people in literature: "I can't stand reading student writing." "Students have nothing of significance to write about." "No one could really get intellectually interested in student writing." "We can't teach students to write unless we give them models of good writing by good authors to imitate." How do I say, "I miss literature," without saying any of these other things that seem toxically false?

I miss the comfort and pleasure of planning a whole class around a literary text and preparing for class by simply immersing myself in it as deeply and carefully as I can and preparing generative questions (assuming that I already possess enough background secondary knowledge). The goal in preparing is the same as the goal for the class: not just to understand but to try to get inside of and be stretched or even transformed by a text that is miraculously good.

As a teacher of writing, I focus on texts in class that are fruitful and interesting (student writing and published essays about writing and other topics), and they can stretch us—not the least, student writing. But these texts are seldom transcendent or magical the way so many works of literature are. They seldom make me choke up.

Yet since I've become a composition person, I've come to use a richer process for class planning. I plan by devising *workshop activities* designed to create *experiences*: all kinds of writing exercises, out-loud readings, and various kinds of work in peer groups or pairs. Class planning feels more like trying to manage complex activities than quiet immersion in an amazing text. This approach to teaching that I learned as a teacher of writing tends to result in classes that are more lively and active than my old literature classes: fewer dead spells, less tooth pulling, less talk from me, more learning. I know now, of course, that this difference is a historical accident. I can now teach a "product" of literature by using active, experiential workshop activities I learned as a teacher of writing—and thereby increase the chances of students' actually *experiencing* the literary work and the critical concepts we are studying. A fair number of literature teachers have learned to do the same, but I think the field of composition gets some of the credit for this. (See *When Writing Teachers Teach Literature* [Young and Fulwiler], which contains my "Breathing Life into the Text.")

Process and Product. People in composition have taken to using rubber gloves for the word "process" ("Oh, we're *way* beyond the 'process approach'!"), but an emphasis on process is ineluctably in the bloodstream of composition. (Similarly, no one in literature would be caught dead identifying as a New Critic, but the profession has permanently digested that essential methodological contribution of close reading for the sake of focusing on the usually complicated relationship between what's stated and what's implied. New Criticism and the focus on writing process were surely the founding—and I daresay defining—events of the two professions as they presently exist.) Almost every literature class is about a "product," a text, and the literature teacher usually wants the students to carry away a product too—some summarizable knowledge about that text. Almost every writing class is about a process, and the writing teacher usually wants the students to carry away some increased skill in that process. Of course literature teachers seek to teach the process of reading, but I think my rough contrast is supported by a glance at two characteristic teaching practices in the two fields. In literature classes, lecturing is extremely common. It's rare or absent from writing classes. Literature exams rarely ask students to read a new text; they usually focus on works the students have already studied—and heard the teacher's conclusions about. Writing exams (if used at all) ask students to write a new text.

Still, "I miss literature" in another sense. I miss living in a culture that considers the metaphorical and imaginative uses of language basic or primal. Owen Barfield wrote a useful essay about the "invention" of literal language, arguing that metaphor came first as the default, and literal language was a late development achieved only through a complex process of mental and linguistic differentiation. I'm not saying that the culture of composition *ignores* metaphor and imaginative language altogether. People in the field usually acknowledge that such language helps essays do their discursive work; and some teachers invite students to write a story at the start of the semester. But I'm sad that the composition tradition seems to assume discursive language as the norm and imaginative, metaphorical language as somehow special or marked or additional. I'd argue that we can't harness students' strongest linguistic and even cognitive powers unless we see imaginative and metaphorical language as the norm—basic or primal.

Yet I found I was pleased and proud when I was drawn *away* from literature by my growing interest in writing. When I finally came to see myself as a composition person, I felt an enormous relief at finally feeling *useful*—as though I could make an actual difference for people. I'd never felt solidly useful trying to teach and write about literature. I'm proud that composition is the only discipline I know, outside of schools of education, where members feel their field has a built-in relationship to teaching and to students.

I fear, in fact, that the culture of literary studies still carries a bit of that traditional implication that there is something "lower" about teaching than scholarship; that the tone of a scholarly essay is reduced if there is talk about teaching; and that teaching issues are for the less able. People in literature are more likely than those in composition to make a distinction between teaching and their "real work."[1] George Levine, introducing the new journal *Pedagogy*, meditates at length on the phrase "my work," and how people in literary studies tend to use it to mean research rather than teaching—in explicit contrast to people in composition (10). David Bartholomae points out tellingly that at the beginning of the twentieth century, when the profession of "English" was still primarily philological and not yet "literary," the teaching of writing was taken very seriously at the highest levels. But then, "Composition fell out of sight of the MLA and most of the other significant venues of professional discussion" ("Composition" 1952).

The culture of composition carries a concern not just for teaching but also for students: attention, interest, and care for them, their lives, and what's on their minds. The core activity in teaching composition is the act of reading what's on students' minds; the core activity in teaching literature is reading the literary text. ("[T]he writing of my students and the problematic relationship between their work and the work of the academy[:] these seemed to hold all of the material I needed to make a career" [Bartholomae "Freshman" 39].) Composition teachers are more likely, when asked what they teach, to give that ornery answer: "I teach students." I'm proud that we can be a rich scholarly field and still keep these ties to teaching and students. The culture has somehow managed to build a felt value in *identifying with* students—or at least refusing to see them as "other." Writing is more of a leveler than reading: in writing more than reading, teachers and students tend to feel the same anxieties (see my "War between Reading and Writing").

And yet I seem to be praising composition for being more "real" and practical, and for dealing more directly with the genuine needs of students (and also, by the way, with concerns felt by the public). I am. Yet I must turn again and choose a different lens for a different view. For in a genuine sense, the most real and practical use of language is for making stories, images, and even poems. Mark Turner, in *The Literary Mind*, talks of story as the primary mode of language that organizes our very minds. When we dream, we may sometimes explain or argue, but the basic language of our nightly dreams is images and stories. Imaginative language touches people most deeply; sometimes it's the only language use that gets through. When people feel the tug of wanting to write (it's too little recognized in both traditions that *most* people actually feel such a tug)—what most often tugs at them is the call to render experience in narratives, images, or poems. (On the burgeoning research on "everyday writing," see Barton, Bloome, Sheridan, and Street; Barton and Ivanic; Hamilton, Barton, and Ivanic.)

So literature is no less "real" or "useful" than composition. And yet sadly I feel that the culture of literature misses the boat here. Most teachers of literature neglect the task of teaching students how to *use* language imaginatively—how to write stories and poems. The tradition in literature seems to declare: "Imaginative writing can't be taught—it's too mysterious," or "Only artists or geniuses create art," or "We must try to staunch the hemorrhage of second-rate writing into the world." (I sometimes sense teachers of literature trying to stamp out "bad" amateur poetry. But it's a futile effort. Huge numbers of people write it, although they usually fear to show it to most of their teachers—whether literature or composition.)

But imaginative writing *can* be taught—and taught well, even to rank novices. I'm not, by the way, thinking of the teaching in MFA programs—where faculty assume that their students have no trouble producing imaginative writing, and therefore see their task as providing "workshops" to help students "critique" better. No, I'm thinking about a small but powerful stream of teachers in the schools (and in a few undergraduate writing courses) who are helping their students in a more generative fashion to write stories and poems and other imaginative and personal pieces. This interesting tradition has many sources. I am proud of its roots in the early days of composition—back when folks were not so nervous to talk about "creativity" or "invention." But I want to pay special homage to a crucial bridge that has carried this fragile tradition of teaching imaginative writing from the early days of composition to these important school classrooms: the so-called "area writing projects" scattered all around the country that grew from the original Bay Area Writing Project. There are now some 165 National Writing Project sites every summer, and they maintain a sturdy tradition of inviting teachers themselves to do imaginative writing of their own. (Of course they sponsor academic and critical writing, too.) This tradition of imaginative writing in the schools derives in addition from some crucially generative poets like Kenneth Koch—and from some small, powerful organizations like Teachers and Writers Collaborative and Poets in the Schools.

Not only does the literary tradition neglect the teaching of imaginative *writing*, it also neglects teaching us to *read* in such a way as to help bring powerful imaginative texts most palpably into our lives. The problem I'm speaking of could be called the "distancing mode"—the tradition of "critical reading." In the tradition of New Criticism, students are urged to look at literary works as complex artifacts rather than as devices for making sense of their lives and feelings. In addition, postmodernist and deconstructive practices also function as ways to distance oneself from the text as a kind of *intellectualized* aesthetic object. In contrast, teachers in the newer and powerful tradition of cultural studies usually *do* try to help students use texts for making sense of their lives (and often seek texts that students feel as part of their lives already—such as popular music or TV). But even here, I often sense the tradition of distancing. The goal in cultural studies tends to be to help students read with more critical detachment—to separate themselves from felt involvement in these texts.

Thus, the culture of literary studies feels to me to work against students' impulses to involve themselves personally with literature and feel they are making personal connections with characters and authors—to feel a genuine relationship with Chaucer or Iago. I'd argue that most good readers actually *do* this—and that even good critics do it and take it for granted before they go on to their critical practices. But most students need *help* achieving this kind of personal entanglement with texts.

I imagine readers of *College English* resisting me here and arguing that the problem with students is that they *already* identify too much—that they lack the ability to question and to achieve critical distance—to read against the grain. But the validity of this objection papers over a crucial distinction. Yes, students often don't read against the grain; but that doesn't mean they are good at reading *with* the grain. Lack of critical distance is *not* the same as full, rich involvement. For all too many students, the text is a pretty "nothing" experience. Why should they be interested in learning to question or see contrary depths in a "nothing" experience? I'm not making an either-or argument against critical detachment; I'm arguing that most students need help learning how to enter into mentalities and experience points of view different from their own (see Nemerov; see also my essays about "the believing game" or "methodological belief").

We can better notice the distancing dimension in the culture of literary studies if we compare it to the work of Robert Coles. A psychoanalyst and scholar in many fields, he describes in *The Call of Stories* how he teaches literature to Harvard undergraduates and medical and business students as ways to help them work through larger ethical questions of life and work (see also O'Connor's "Words and the World at a New York Public School: Can Writing Really Matter to Inner City Children?"). I'm not suggesting that teachers of literature abandon the use of all distancing techniques; I'm suggesting the need for what is almost entirely neglected, namely "involving" techniques (as in much of Young and Fulwiler).

Speaking of distance, let me stand back now and meditate for a moment on the two essential dimensions of language use that I have been implying here: rhetoric and poetics. In one sense, *all* language is rhetorical; Wayne Booth made it clear that even literature has designs on readers—argues, does business. But the tradition from Nietzsche and I. A. Richards provides the opposite lens to help us nevertheless see that all language use is also an instance of poetics: a figurative or metaphorical structure that characteristically yields up more meaning or pleasure when we see it as a self-contained or intertextual structure—one that always means more than it purports to mean. (Deconstructive critics—wisely or perversely?—define rhetoric itself as figurative language or poetics.) Once we stand back this way, it's obvious that neither rhetoric nor poetics is better. What's sad is that a discipline devoted to understanding language use should tend to restrict itself to one lens.

I'll end Section I by summarizing what I wish the cultures of literature and composition might learn from each other:

- I wish the culture of composition would learn to give an equally central place to the imaginative and metaphorical dimensions of language. And I don't want my emphasis on stories and poems to obscure my larger emphasis on *all* language—even if the only goal is teaching essays. Surely many of the best and most effective essays don't just make good *use* of metaphors and images; rather, they grow out of imaginative metaphorical *thinking*—out of the imagination itself. But we won't understand the craft of such essays unless we feel their roots in the imagination rather than only in clear logical thinking and language.

- I wish the culture of literature would learn more inherent attention and concern for students—their lives and what's on their minds. If it did, I think teachers of literature would give more attention to helping students read with involvement and *write* imaginative pieces. Even if our only goal is to get students to understand a work of literature, nothing works better than inviting students to write stories or poems that are structurally, thematically, or rhetorically related to it (see my "Breathing Life into the Text").

II.

I fear I sound hopelessly corny and naive. I hear a contrary voice even in my own mind: "But your only use for literature is in fact to *use* it—for personal therapy. You want everything to be utilitarian and pragmatic. You're just a cornball—blind to all the sophistication in the literary tradition."

Sophistication. Yes. Just as I started off saying I miss literature, so too I miss sophistication. I miss elegance and irony and indirection—qualities that composition has sometimes reacted against. My dissertation and first book were about complex or double irony in Geoffrey Chaucer. What I love about Virginia Woolf is not just that she finds words for the felt texture of human experience but that she somehow embodies mental rawness in such elegance and sophistication.

But just as loving literature has gotten itself all tangled up with a noxious tradition of failing to value students and their writing and thinking, so, too, loving sophistication is all tangled up with an equally noxious tradition of condescension, snobbery, and elitism. Let me explain.

When I was trained in literature, both as an undergraduate and as a graduate student, I felt a subtle but insidious pressure: if I wanted to be good in this field, I had to learn somehow to be a slightly different kind of person from who I was—somehow "not ordinary." I happened to have had the right gender, race, sexual orientation, and a more or less acceptable accent, but I still felt I was supposed to learn to be in some subtle internal sense *different*—somehow "higher" or "finer."

That was a long time ago. Perhaps I can be convinced that this aura is no longer in the air, but I still feel in many departments and seminar rooms today that old feeling: that training in literary study is not just learning knowledge and skills but learning to stop being "ordinary" or "regular" and instead be more sophisticated and even oblique. Close reading, highly refined perception, and fine-tuned awareness of nuance: these usually involve the ability to process texts and ideas not just with your intellect or thinking but with your self or sensibility. All this often shades over into a value system that asks aspiring graduate students to have a better sensibility or self. "Better" sometimes connotes "more cultured," slightly "higher class"—even more conservative. Sometimes it connotes something leftist or politically correct. Political correctness is strong in composition too, but somehow I don't feel in this culture the same faint pressure to *be* different or feel different as *people*—somehow faintly to improve or abandon *who* we are.

I've always sensed that this training in sensibility or taste that we get in literary studies explains why people with literary training take everything so personally—and why English departments are so remarkably rancorous: if you disagree with my reading of a text or my judgment about a theory, you aren't just criticizing my thinking, you are impugning my very self-assensibility. (Cathy Davidson, having moved from being a chair to being a vice provost, writes: "From conversations I've had with administrators across the country, I know that, relative to other departments, English departments are frequently embattled" [102].) If you fail to appreciate what's good or if you like what's bad, there is something wrong with *you*—not just your opinions. Taste is feeling and sensibility, not just thinking. What does it mean to have better taste if not to have your teeth set on edge by more things than the other person? (Is there any other discipline than English that has cast off so many sub-groups that used to be integrally part of it? Speech, communication, theater, film, ethnic studies, women's studies—not to mention a professional or technical interest in the nature of language?[2] Interestingly, literary studies now hankers for a piece of theater's turf: performance studies.)

And yet I have to turn again. I love it that I got training in a culture that asked me to develop not just my thinking skills but my ability to attune my every fiber to the text or the idea at hand. It's a common failure of rationality or intelligence to restrict the definition of rationality to the exercise of conventional reasoning. Frankly, I credit widespread literary training with the fact that so many people in composition take emotion so seriously and insist on links between feelings and cognition—and haven't allowed the powerful war against the personal dimension in writing to be won. And there's no doubt that my literary training gave rise to one of my main preoccupations and areas of research in composition: "voice" in writing. (Interestingly, I've found in linguistics the most compelling empirical evidence that humans tend to put their individual stamp on the language they use. I'm thinking of a remarkable book, *The Linguistic Individual: Self-Expression in Language and Linguistics*, by Barbara Johnstone.)

Let me briefly focus my attention on a particular thread in the larger weave of sophistication: *high*. What better word than "high" to connote all the condescension people in composition often feel from literary folk—and to connote the elitism and snobbery that so many people at large have felt in the culture of literary studies. From on high, we can look down. Yet again I turn. I can't throw away "high." I want to value it and keep it—yet peel away what's noxious. Is there not something valuable that follows from revering and even trying to live with things one experiences as "above" one—Milton? Woolf? Morrison?—from trying to get our minds around things that are miraculously good? Edward Said, no conservative, insists baldly that the word "exalted" has "a particular resonance for me"—and quotes Michael Fried on the "unshakeable conviction in the supreme achievement and absolute importance of certain works of art" (7). When we try to give full attention to such works, I think we are likely to feel the need to "give in" to them, to submit, to play the believing game. So even though I fight elitism, I still want to value "high." The problem is the temptation to feel "higher than others" if one appreciates high and subtle things they don't appreciate—whereas true awareness of the high ought to make us feel low.

Let me pull a different thread from the weave of sophistication: style. And with it, artificiality, artifice, mannerism. The culture of literary studies puts a high value on style and on not being like everyone else. I think I see more mannerism, artifice, and self-consciousness in bearing (sometimes even slightly self-conscious speech production) among literary folk than composition folk. Occasionally I resist, yet I *value* style and artifice. What could be more wonderful than the pleasure of creating or appreciating forms that are different, amazing, outlandish, useless—the opposite of ordinary, everyday, pragmatic? Every child is blessed with an effortless ability to do this: it's called play.

So I miss sophistication; and yet I fight back when people in literature condescend to composition as unsophisticated. I am proud of what I sense as a kind of *resistance* to sophistication—a kind of allergy—that I feel in the culture of composition. (The last chapter of my Chaucer book is about how he *relinquishes* irony.)

Uh oh. Does it sound as though I'm painting composition as a culture of innocent, childlike naiveté? I don't mean that; it has its share of skepticism and even corruption. Still, I'd insist that there *is* a genuine naiveté, corniness, or innocence in the world of composition, and I value it and wish more literature people could learn it. Is it not naive in the best sense to think we can truly identify with our students? Is it not corny to think we can be or can strive to be "like everyone else" or "regular"? That we can transmit the power of literacy to *everyone*? That we can be a democratic or egalitarian force to change society? These are values deep in the culture of composition.

Let me move toward my ending with another tiny meditation. Just as rhetoric and poetic are two essential dimensions of language, so sophistication and naiveté (or refusing sophistication) are two ways of being in the world: we can be complex, sophisticated, ironic, and adorn ourselves with style and artifice; or we can be naked, naive, and direct. Here again I'm trying to escape either-or thinking—escape the tired habits in which the sophisticated look down on the naive, while the naive look back down just as haughtily. There's no need for higher or lower, better or worse, with these two ways of being. We can have sophistication without snobbery, elitism, or condescension; we can have naive and open identification with everyone else, and yet not neglect intelligence, complexity, and careful thinking. And it is perfectly feasible for *both* cultures, literature and composition, to help both styles to flourish.[3]

So I wish more people in literature could learn less pretension and more acknowledgment that, really, we *are* all like one another—driven by the same basic need to be loved and heard. I wish the culture of literary studies gave more honor to the courage of just sitting with, attending to, or contemplating a text—or enacting or performing it without any striving for an interpretation. And I see signs for hope that more people in literary studies are on their way to giving more honor to being pragmatically useful in the world—for example, with the recently awakened interest in the training of teachers of English.

And what do I wish people in composition could learn from the culture of literature? More honoring of style, playfulness, fun, pleasure, humor. Better writing—and a more pervasive assumption that even in academic writing, even in prose, we can have playfulness, style, pleasure—even adornment and artifice—without being elitist snobs.

There's also a piece of *scholarly* sophistication I wish composition could learn from literary scholarship. I've noticed in composition scholarship a tacit acceptance of reductive oversimplifications about historical periods and movements (for example, claims that take the form of "Romanticism meant . . ." or "Romantics believed . . .")—and readings of important historical figures (claims that "Plato said . . ." or "Aristotle said . . .") based only on quotations from a reductive secondary source. It's almost as though people in composition insist on more care and respect for student texts than for texts from large figures from distant historical eras.

Finally, I think both cultures can learn from each other with respect to their *status as disciplines*. I have a vision of composition and literature passing each other on opposite escalators at Macy's. Just as composition is achieving disciplinary strength, literary studies is relinquishing whatever pretensions it had for disciplinary coherence—and sometimes seems in fact to be disintegrating as a discipline. Literary studies has become more and more a motley crew thrown together by history and change.

Composition, on the other hand, started out as nothing *but* a motley collection of people historically thrown together (mostly by teaching exigencies) who even now continue to call on an amazing array of disciplines: rhetoric (classical and modern), linguistics, literary studies, history, philosophy, psychology, education, and others. There is still no preferred methodology, paradigm, or point of view. Different members use historical investigation, quantitative research, qualitative/ethnographic research, and textual studies (hermeneutic and theoretical) of the sort traditionally practiced in English and philosophy. For this reason—or perhaps because the field is so tainted by its commitment to teaching—the National Endowment for the Humanities won't recognize composition as a field of scholarship: no one can take part in NEH activities or get any NEH support for scholarly work in the field of composition. When the *Chronicle of Higher Education* lists "New Scholarly Books" every week, it doesn't include books in composition. None of this goes for *rhetoric*, of course, which is old enough to see English as a recent upstart. Rhetoric is seen as coherent and untainted by teaching and is thus recognized by both the NEH and the *Chronicle*.

Composition is just as polyglot as it's always been, but its on the up escalator. It's become ever more vigorous and impressive as a scholarly field in the last couple of decades and developed an amazingly coherent energy and esprit de corps—a sense of itself as a healthy undertaking marching down the road as a single enterprise. The contrast with literary and cultural studies couldn't be more striking. I admire how this has happened without composition closing ranks around a dominant vision or discipline or methodology. But I fear the hunger to be more impressive by becoming a "real discipline" in the old-fashioned sense of *having* a dominant vision and methodology.[4] I sense the scholarly discourse having sometimes become more competitive and divisive—as though we can't be a real discipline unless some vision or methodology or paradigm "wins"—as though one paradigm can't be right unless the others are wrong. I fear the culture of composition losing its venerable tradition of "big tent" tolerant pluralism and mutual respect toward all stances. Even in 1989, David Bartholomae saw the danger of coherence-yearning: "I am suspicious of calls for coherence. I suspect that most of the problems in academic life—problems of teaching, problems of thinking—come from disciplinary boundaries and disciplinary habits [. . . .] The charge to this generation and the next is to keep the field open, not to close it" ("Freshman" 49).

Interestingly, I see people in literary studies beginning to develop a genuine if grudging tolerance and even respect for the deep differences that have been increasing in recent decades—learning to live productively with a wildly diverse plurality of outlooks and critical and methodological practices. People in composition have always been good at this in the past but have sometimes felt it as an accidental function of oppressed status. So I wish *both* cultures could fully accept that a discipline can be even richer and healthier if it lacks a single-vision center. A discipline based on this multiplex model can better avoid either-or thinking and better foster a spirit of productive catholic pluralism.

What would it look like, then, for the two cultures to learn from each other? Obviously—and very hopefully—it's been starting to happen. I can't do better than to quote, with deep gratitude, from Jane Danielewicz's response to an earlier draft:

Literature and composition people need to get off those diverging escalators and join forces. Not just learn from each other but live with each other—go for integration rather than separate but equal accommodations. There's lots of movement in this direction already. Interestingly, there are a number of comp people turning up as chairs of English departments. [The field of composition often attracts community-minded "good citizens," and writing program administration has given lots of them good experience in tricky administration. PE] We see composition and literature people team teaching; some literature professors are retooling to teach composition while comp professors are teaching lit courses. If we consider the texts people are producing, there has been an explosion in both fields of mixed genres of writing, as well as the introduction of creative nonfiction in both fields, renewed interest in the personal and in the personal essay, and attention to writing as a force (as in feminist manifestos, regional and ethnic texts such as Caribbean and Latino literatures, cultural literatures such as gay and lesbian studies, and so on). We have a chance now and ought to run with the momentum generated by current circumstances (even negative ones such as budget cuts in the humanities) to find ways of working together.[5]

NOTES

1. Thanks to Elizabeth Sargent for this point.
2. Thanks to Charlie Moran for this perspectival point.
3. Of course these are slippery matters. One of the guises of sophistication is naiveté (nakedness as high artifice), as in the genre of the pastoral. True enough; a special case, but not the whole story of plainness. I can't resist citing a piece of work that admirably defies these two categories. It's a literary essay that stakes out a stance called and even claimed as naive (insisting on treating "the speaker" in a poem as "the author"), but that enacts far more grace, sophistication, and learning than most writers who might charge it with naiveté: Clara Claiborne Park's "Talking Back to the Speaker."
4. A large coalition of writing program administrators from across the country has pulled off an impressive job of collaboration in producing a single "outcomes statement" for first-year writing courses. Of course first-year writing is *not* the same as the large field of composition, and the administrators are *not* trying to produce a uniform curriculum. Their goal is only to clarify thinking (and I've written "A Friendly Challenge to Push the Outcomes Statement Further" for their planned book about it), but I fear the pressure of orthodoxy that such impressive unity might engender. For the outcomes statement, see the Works Cited.
5. My deep thanks go especially to Jane Danielewicz, but also to Sheridan Blau, Joe Harris, Charlie Moran, Jean Nienkamp, Irene Papoulis, Elizabeth Sargent, and *College English* readers—and others—for helpful responses to drafts.

WORKS CITED

Barfield, Owen. "The Meaning of the Word 'Literal'." *Metaphor and Symbol.* Ed. L. C. Knights and Basil Cottle. London: Butterworths, 1960.
Bartholomae, David. "Composition, 1900–2000." *PMLA* 115 (2000): 1950–54.
———. "Freshman English, Composition, and CCCC." *CCC* 40 (1989): 38–50.
Barton, D., David Bloome, D. Sheridan, and Brian Street. *Ordinary People Writing: The Lancaster and Sussex Writing Research Projects.* Working Paper Ser. 51. Lancaster, England: Center for Language in Social Life, Dept. of Linguistics and Modern English Language, Lancaster U, 1993.
Barton, David, and Roz Ivanic. *Writing in the Community.* Newbury Park: Sage, 1991.
Coles, Robert. *The Call of Stories: Teaching and the Moral Imagination.* Boston: Houghton, 1989.
Davidson, Cathy N. "Them versus Us (and Which One of 'Them' Is Me?)." *Profession 2000*: 97–108.
Elbow, Peter. "Breathing Life into the Text." *When Writing Teachers Teach Literature.* Ed. Art Young and Toby Fulwiler. Portsmouth: Heinemann Boynton, 1995. 193–205. Rpt. in *Everyone Can Write: Essays Toward a Hopeful Theory of Writing and Teaching Writing.* Ed. Peter Elbow. New York: Oxford UP, 2000. 360–71.

————. "The Doubting Game and the Believing Game." Appendix. *Writing without Teachers*. New York: Oxford UP, 1973. 147–91.

————. "Methodological Doubting and Believing: Contraries in Inquiry." *Embracing Contraries: Explorations in Learning and Teaching*. New York: Oxford UP, 1986. 254–300.

————. "The War between Reading and Writing—and How to End It." *Rhetoric Review* 12 (Fall 1993): 5–24. Rpt. in *Everyone Can Write: Essays Toward a Hopeful Theory of Writing and Teaching Writing*. Ed. Peter Elbow. New York: Oxford UP, 2000. 281–99.

Graff, Gerald. *Professing Literature: An Institutional History*. Chicago: U of Chicago P, 1987.

Hamilton, Mary, David Barton, and Roz Ivanic. *Worlds of Literacy*. Toronto: Ontario Institute for Studies in Education, 1994.

Johnstone, Barbara. *The Linguistic Individual: Self-Expression in Language and Linguistics*. New York: Oxford UP, 1996.

Levine, George. "The Two Nations." *Pedagogy: Critical Approaches to Teaching Literature, Language, Composition, and Culture* 1 (Winter 2001): 7–19.

Nemerov, Howard. "Speaking Silence." *New and Selected Essays*. Carbondale: Southern Illinois UP, 1985. 49–55.

O'Connor, Stephen. "Words and the World at a New York Public School: Can Writing Really Matter to Inner-City Children?" *Teachers and Writers* 32.2 (Nov.–Dec. 2000): 1–8.

"Outcomes Statement." *WPA: Writing Program Administration* 23 (1999): 59–70.

Park, Clara Claiborne. "Talking Back to the Speaker." *Hudson Review* 42.1 (1989): 21–44. Rpt. in *Landmark Essays on Voice and Writing*. Ed. Peter Elbow. Hermagoras, 1994. 139–56.

Said, Edward. "Scholarship and Commitment: Introduction." *Profession 2000*: 6–11.

Scholes, Robert E. *The Rise and Fall of English: Reconstructing English as a Discipline*. New Haven: Yale UP, 1998.

Turner, Mark. *The Literary Mind*. New York: Oxford UP, 1996.

Young, Art, and Toby Fulwiler. *When Writing Teachers Teach Literature: Bringing Writing to Reading*. Portsmouth: Heinemann Boynton, 1995.

PART FIVE

Style and the Future

Introduction to Part Five

Despite the relative disciplinary invisibility in which it dwelled for the better part of two decades, style has arguably undergone a renaissance in rhetoric and composition in the twenty-first century. From critical examinations of the reasons for its disappearance to revisionist histories of its usefulness in the field, past and present, scholars in composition studies have begun to set the groundwork for its reemergence as an indispensable canon in the future. In that light, they have connected style to such representative areas as visual rhetoric, digital literacies, the public sphere, educational policy, and composition pedagogies; additionally, they have reimagined its innovative ties to other canons of rhetoric, new genres, and interdisciplinary sites of investigation. These collective associations point to a fundamental shift in disciplinary attitudes, recognizing that style is not a hermetically sealed phenomenon of rhetorical history but, rather, a productive site of new knowledge and approaches to writing and composition instruction.

In the chapters collected in this part, each author explores style from an original vantage point, including, for example, the critical rereading of past scholarship, applications to new media, and calls for political rethinking and cultural recalibration. In this way, then, the chapters form a guide to the areas where style is migrating in the field, whether redeployed from past iterations or reconceived in light of changes in the field — taking into account such developments as the visual turn, the digital turn, the cultural turn, and the public turn in composition. If style has been a vital, if recently forgotten, part of the field's past, then how can it be recovered as an indispensable aspect of its future as well? The authors suggest that the potential answer lies in a combination of what style has done — how it has functioned traditionally — and its recent reinventions. Therefore, the canon of style is perhaps most productively seen as a hybrid form, forged in the interstices of past and current variations of language, rhetoric, culture, and identity. Such hybridity contemplates, in Richard Lanham's formulation, for instance, that style and substance have essentially been reversed, with style a new cultural phenomenon of economic attention, or, in T. R. Johnson's rendering, that style should be reconsidered through a new concept of voice, based on the rhythms of sound. Given all these possibilities, the future of style seems, above all, omnipresent, part and parcel of a new *stylistic* turn in composition that stands, Janus-like, between past and future fructifications.

In "Ancient and Contemporary Compositions That 'Come Alive': Clarity as Pleasure, Sound as Magic," T. R. Johnson articulates a new kind of style that approaches the concept of "voice" neither as a key component of expressivist pedagogy nor as a form of discourse. Arguing instead for what he calls a "renegade rhetoric" that redeploys stylistic figures, schemes, and tropes as part of the composing process, Johnson suggests that the best way to teach prose style is to ask students to think about it as voice redirected toward how their writing *sounds*. This sound sensation, Johnson argues, is based on a spontaneous, ongoing dialogue that he sees as transformative because, drawing on rhythmic figures of speech, it resists prescriptive forms, and, in a far more intuitive move, it allows the sound of language to "override my will." In so describing the impact of hearing on him, Johnson suggests that sound has a dynamic and captive quality that defies human dominion—unlike sight, for example, where one can simply choose to close one's eyes. Johnson's piece is helpful in showing how the rhythms of music and other aural forms generally accessible to students can be used to make language a form of play and to inspire students to write. He draws on ideas by Joseph Williams such as putting the old information in a sentence before the new (a form of cohesion) to illustrate how style makes connections with audiences. By facilitating an understanding of how readers experience prose, Johnson says, writers can cultivate Sondra Perl's notion of the "other within." Johnson's return to the pleasure inherent in the aural qualities of style is reminiscent of Richard Lanham's work as well as the sophistic tendency to combine various sensory impressions to enrich the experience of texts.

If Johnson's chapter extends Lanham's work in significant ways, then Kathryn Flannery, in "The National Prose Problem," a chapter from her book *The Emperor's New Clothes*, urges us to reconsider the limiting conceptions of style that she sees in Lanham as well as E. D. Hirsch, whose work, she asserts, ultimately ignores style's ideological and culturally normalizing influences. While giving Hirsch credit for recognizing the importance of cultural influences on style (his prescriptive "lexicon of cultural literacy" comes in his later work) and the need for teaching writing differently to diverse populations, she critiques what she considers one of his fundamental failures: after discovering that style does not help the ease of reading as readers encounter unfamiliar material, Hirsch did not use those findings as the basis for a new pedagogy that could help students learn. Flannery's critique is not reserved for Hirsch alone, however, as she finds Lanham's call for an opaque or ornamental style, despite its commendable playfulness, divorced from the material realities of a multicultural society (economic circumstance, social class and uneven access to literacy, political realities about who gets to speak, what they can say, etc.). In a reading of Lanham that diverges significantly from his own, she argues that his critique of C-B-S style (clarity, brevity, sincerity) is, in reality, diametrically opposed to what she sees as his call for linguistic control by protectionist decorum and a common language—essentially, Lanham's middle style. Like Min-Zhan Lu, Flannery brings attention to the inherent ideology of style, and her piece prompts a rereading of two composition scholars whose contributions, she suggests, paradoxically undermine the very complexity they call for. Flannery's work is a warning to those who teach style to look behind the curtain: we are always already interpellated by ideological influences attempting to prescribe our stylistic choices.

While Flannery proposes a fundamental revaluation of style as an ideological part of cultural politics, my article "Style and the Public Intellectual: Rethinking Composition in the Public Sphere" argues for a different kind of politics in which composition scholars respond publicly to mischaracterizations of language issues—especially stylistic ones—by public intellectuals from outside the field. In urging a revitalization of composition studies in the public sphere, I suggest that the discipline's tendency to retreat from style and associate it with formalism and current-traditional rhetoric is misguided, especially when, in reality, the canon enjoys a long history complicated by issues of difference and variation. This article contributes a unique argument to disciplinary discussions in calling for a renaissance of stylistic discourse by composition-trained public intellectuals and proposing a new kind of activism on the part of the field, mediated by its expertise in style and other language-related matters. In keeping with composition's public turn, I suggest in this essay, the field must reinvent itself by addressing the issues those outside the field care most about, especially style, and clearly distinguishing its dynamic qualities from grammar, usage, and literacy, with which it is often conflated.

Given the way my article rethinks composition in the public sphere, it is instructive to consider Frank Farmer's rereading of imitation through a Bakhtinian lens in a chapter from *Saying and Silence*, "Sounding the Other Who Speaks in Me: Toward a Dialogic Understanding of Imitation." Arguing that traditional representations of imitation as mechanical replication (what several critics have called "servile copying") fall outside the purview of Bakhtin, Farmer suggests instead that imitation must "give voice to other voices," even going so far as to "talk back" to the author. Locating his proposal in Bakhtin's view of double-voiced discourse, which the Russian theorist defines as speech "with an orientation toward someone else's discourse," Farmer calls for a "dialogic imitation," characterized by prose that is, he says, "engaged, worked over, disputed, confirmed—in a word, *answered*." In thus advocating a dynamic view of imitation that excludes monologic, or single-voiced, discourse and invests itself instead in such techniques as stylization, parody, and paraphrase, Farmer effectively advocates a new understanding of imitation in composition based on utterance rather than on sentences. Farmer's piece is significant in explaining that Bakhtin's view of imitation rejects the formalist or mechanical approach so often critiqued in composition studies. His selection also anticipates the field's concern for socially relevant rhetoric by cultivating a dialogic imitation that is positional (i.e., students must assume a stance toward what is being imitated), revisable (from the inside out, according to Farmer), and rhetorical, having and desiring effects in and upon the world.

In "Style/Substance Matrix," a chapter in his book *The Economics of Attention: Style and Substance in the Age of Information*, Richard Lanham offers the most developed presentation to date of an idea that runs throughout his work: that we miss out on a great deal by simply looking *through* style to a fictive reality beneath rather than *at* its surface, where its ornate and affected features must be confronted—the latter the equivalent, he says, of play (rather than game), toys (rather than seriousness), and fluff (rather than stuff). Lanham asserts that "the love of form for its own sake" exists throughout Western culture and recently has brought about a fundamental reversal in style and substance, with style rather than substance taking center stage. However, like sins of excess in diet or behavior, style is still seen as a sin of *self-consciousness* that must be eliminated from our Spartan tastes. Lanham's piece thus shows the cultural relevance of what he calls a style/substance matrix and the often-changing vantage points from which we approach both ideals on a daily basis. His chapter, tied to other imperatives he enumerates based on motive and purpose, implicitly argues for restoring style to composition studies by documenting its broader cultural importance and its connections to other disciplines—a true economy of style that demonstrates how its place in writing pedagogy and culture, historically as well as recently, has been vastly underestimated.

22 Ancient and Contemporary Compositions That "Come Alive": Clarity as Pleasure, Sound as Magic*

T. R. JOHNSON

> I am driven to write, compelled by a constant longing to choreograph, to bring words together in patterns and configurations that move the spirit. As a writer, I seek that moment of ecstasy when I am dancing with words . . . toward the infinite.
> —BELL HOOKS, 2000

> If clarity indicates a successful relationship between reader and writer, pleasure makes part of that success.
> —RICHARD LANHAM, 1974

[S]tudents do not *always* stagger hurriedly through the composing process in deep dread and anxiety. Sometimes, something enables students to bring real enthusiasm to their assignments. Their intervals of inspiration, of pleasure, no matter what else we might profess to value, charm many of us and make us feel as though our teaching has at least partially succeeded. How we precipitate this pleasure in our students, however, resists formulation in a foolproof recipe, for just as these experiences are far too particularized, far too keenly rooted in immediate contexts to allow for an all-encompassing theory or general description, so too do they resist a fully guaranteed, rote method. Nonetheless, this chapter's epigraphs by bell hooks and Richard Lanham offer important clues to the theoretical question of how, in general, pleasure can blossom in the act of writing, as well as to the more practical question of how we can, without reducing our students to mere masochists, help them enjoy the work of producing clear, even powerful, prose.

"Clarity," of course, is a well-worn, but rather misleading metaphor: language is never a transparent window into some extra-linguistic reality. Rather, clarity, as Lanham suggests, really refers to an experience of connection

---

*Ed Note: Minor deletions have been made to the original due to length.
From *A Rhetoric of Pleasure: Prose Style and Today's Composition Classroom* (Portsmouth, NH: Heinemann Boynton/Cook, 2003), 23–56.

between author and audience, an experience of the transpersonal dimension of language, something like the experience, as bell hooks notes, of becoming swept up in dance. In fact, when hooks compares writing to choreography, she reminds me of that important breakthrough in my teaching—classroom exercises with poetic language.

I hardly intend to advocate any sort of empty, lockstep formalism, in which students march through fill-in-the-blanks drillwork, nor do I push my students to produce language unduly weighted with stylistic ornaments. Rather, I've simply decided to introduce my students to a set of stylistic devices and principles as a kind of interim measure toward getting them to listen to language more carefully. I hope that, as my students develop an increasingly "objective" relation to language, perhaps they will eventually learn to make words dance and dance well enough ultimately to approach that circle of belief in which reader and writer, self and other, are drawn so tightly together that it feels as if the thoughts of one person are becoming the thoughts of the other, an experience in which any delimiting boundary between reader and writer seems, at least for a fleeting instant, altogether impossible. This experience is the opposite of the masochism—not a locking down and staving off of the Otherness-within that sparks change and growth, but its cultivation. This, I think, is what bell hooks calls an experience of "the infinite."

Some might suggest that I'm being awfully grandiose, given that what I'm calling "the infinite," we have traditionally referred to as mere "clarity." But I like hooks' term. It underlines and lays bare the very real profundity of the phenomenon we want students to be able to precipitate and, too, it helps me to think about what Richard Lanham points to as its principal feature: that is, pleasure. I should hasten to add that what I'm proposing is hardly any sort of holy grail that will end once and for all the search for a perfect pedagogy, one that students will instantly love and that will permanently assuage the age-old concerns of teachers and administrators. Instead, what I offer here will, I hope, help us move beyond, in a partial and limited way, the impasse in which our impulses to inspire students and help them enjoy writing would seem to run counter to the goal of acquainting them with the conventions that enable them to write effective prose. More particularly, I've chosen to explore a way to teach renegade rhetoric—that highly pleasurable practice in which selves, texts, and worlds are experienced as dynamic, interanimating processes—in a way that honors the need for certain structuring, teachable, concrete strategies.

Neither Voice Nor Discourse: Sophistry and the Power of Sound

I'd like to begin, however, by specifying what a pedagogy that would aim in this direction is *not*. First, I am not simply advocating a so-called free or open classroom, nor a pedagogy that emphasizes revision as a potentially endless or infinite process. In that sort of utopian classroom, particular drafts become unimportant, or, at least, have no more social footing than random watercolor doodles done by blindfolded students, for, no matter what a student writes in such a context, it can always be rewritten again and again. While I remain very much interested in reviving the notion that writing is a process I want to link, rather than oppose, this idea to the obvious fact that writing is also a product. I think we have limited our understanding of how to teach the writing process by defining it, as we have ever since Donald Murray's 1972 manifesto "Teach Writing as a Process, Not a Product," as the opposite of studying literary models and learning to appropriate their formal devices. Instead, I would like to define in this chapter a pedagogy that collapses this binary, one that advocates multiple drafts, and, at the same time, considers the ways the formal features of finished products—stylistic figures, schemes, tropes—can actually play a powerful role in the drafting and revising process. These stylistic devices can help the student string together sequences of moments in their texts, help them choreograph these moments toward an increasingly grand moment of powerful connection between reader and writer.

Another qualification: this pedagogy by no means seeks to distinguish the domain of feeling from that of thinking, learning, and knowing, for, as recent generations of feminists have taught us, such binaries are logically untenable and usually only serve to mask highly asymmetrical gender relations (i.e., masculinity equals rationality or The Good; femininity equals mere feeling or The Bad). Instead, this pedagogy explicitly operates from a middle ground where the two domains of thinking and feeling are indistinguishable. Similarly, this pedagogy does not seek to goad students into a purely histrionic, confessional mode, for, as valuable as such personal writing can be, it doesn't necessarily, by itself, acquaint students with the sorts of rhetorical tools they need for generating power in the world. Moreover, the connection between reader and writer that I want students to learn how to build is not to be confused with the sort of passion that Jane Gallop describes (1997) and that may have made her vulnerable to charges of sexual harassment. While strong emotions and personal experiences can play a key role in good writing, the focus of the writing classroom I'll describe here is always on writing itself—that is, on writing, in a highly technical sense, *as writing*.

Moreover, this pedagogy does not foreground emotion itself as an isolated object of inquiry. Despite the considerable value, for example, of historical research into the ways that different rules for the experience of pleasure have been enforced by different power structures and applied in varying ways to subjects with different race and class affiliations and different sexual identities, this inquiry into what Raymond Williams calls historical structures of feeling (1977, 128–31) offers no particular pedagogic method that applies directly to the specific challenges faced by writing teachers. Similarly, this pedagogy does not provide instruction in what Megan Boler describes as "emotional literacy" (1999), in which students are taught to be more sensitive to each other, to resolve conflict, to subdue their emotions, and to develop a more expansive and nuanced vocabulary to describe emotion. On the contrary, my classroom seeks not simply to enable students to "express" their emotions or "resolve" their conflicts, but rather to refine, communicate, and negotiate their differences more pointedly by uniting the cultivation of inward feeling as a moral register with an immersion in certain technical aspects of prose. In other words, the emotion this classroom would seek to cultivate, over all the others, is the pleasure of connection between reader and writer, a connection that doesn't exclude but rather rests upon a rich capacity for debate and a rigorously practical sort of critical reflection about language.

What I propose is a pedagogy that differs significantly from the transcendentalism of the expressivist approach to writing pedagogy and its highly individualistic pleasures of "voice" that, through the late 1980s, were heavily attacked and largely discredited. Of course, many might assume that any pedagogy interested in pleasure is necessarily expressivist, so I'd like to linger a moment over the differences between the goals attributed to expressivism and what I'm advocating here. Expressivists allegedly believe that no one can really teach anyone else how to write, for good writing originates in the innermost depths of the private individual; instead, the expressivist strives to create a classroom atmosphere in which the student is free to access his or her own, individual "true voice." Expressivism's underlying metaphor, as Peter Elbow puts it, "is that we all have a chest cavity unique in size and shape so that each of us naturally resonates to one pitch alone" (*Writing with Power*, 1981, 281–82). What expressivists value most is this sense of voice, for it distinguishes a piece of writing as coming from a particular author, and, as such, is closely related to the idea of *ethos* or personae. At the same time, as Joseph Harris suggests, voice in the expressivist view is also, importantly, a kind of prized quality, for the more a writer has a sense of her own voice, the more "voice" she'll get into her text, and the more successful that text will be, for voice is what gives the text what Elbow calls "juice" and "electricity," and makes it more and more "real." This way of thinking about voice is tied with our field's interest in the growth of the "whole person" (1996, 25), for the more we can help students find their voices, in this sense, the more we enable them to use language as a tool for authentic self-discovery and self-expression, to access a self that transcends the deadening constraints of school and the wider culture, even the constraints that accompany the goal of communicating with others.

Many have condemned pedagogies that emphasize the expressivist version of voice, for, as Harris points out, expressivists are more interested in rendering experience than analyzing it, and, as such, they tend to sidestep the broad intellectual project of developing shared understandings. Instead, the detractors of expressivism favor a way of thinking about voice that at first seems rather awkward or counterintuitive, and that, as I'll argue here, is just as limited, though in a different way, as the one attributed to expressivism.

For expressivism's critics, voice should be understood as discourse. "Instead of starting with the idea of a personal voice that comes from within, from a 'chest cavity unique in size and shape,'" argues Harris, "we need to begin with the idea that our culture speaks to us through many competing voices" (34). Harris offers as examples of what he is talking about the voices of home, school, neighborhood, work, leisure, childhood, parenting, youth, age, friendship "as well as the various fields and methods that make up our ways of knowing" (34). He adds, "a voice [is] a way of speaking that lies *outside* a writer, and which she must struggle to appropriate or control." Harris explains that not only is voice *not* an extension of the self, but that the self, too, is *not* some sort of mysterious, primordial essence that transcends the social sphere and gives rise to voice as a spirit-like quality that makes writing more "real." Rather, those who criticize this expressivist notion argue that the self exists only as a set of perspectives on or relationships with other entities. Thus many of them advocate the sort of pedagogy associated with David Bartholomae and Anthony Petrosky, in which the student doesn't seek to escape conventions or liberate a transcendent self and its "true" voice but rather to try on the particular, conventional voices/discourses of the university and use them as tools to reconsider, in turn, the stock notions of common sense, the naïve routines, stereotypes, and all-too-"clear" discourses that govern our experience of the everyday world. Harris suggests that this way of thinking about voice (as discourse) allows for far more rigorous teaching and learning; where the expressivist classroom favored an uncritical rendering of experience, this one urges us to explore our experiences critically, testing the discourses we might use to describe them and the nature of the events themselves in a general project of acquiring more skeptical and sophisticated habits of thinking.

This more complex understanding of voice (as discourse) has surely made a great many of us far more effective teachers than we could hope to be in the earlier, more naïve paradigm. But I fear that this view, representative as it is of the now-dominant view in composition theory, has left certain loose ends dangling and obscured certain useful dimensions of the expressivist version. More specifically, while I very much like the practice of having students read an assemblage of essays on some particular theme (home, work, friendships, and so on) and then sort out a position vis-à-vis the tensions or gaps among the readings, a position that says something more or less original about the readings and about the students' own lives, I worry that to discuss voices/discourses in such general terms obscures crucial details in the ways we encounter and learn to use them. Though a thoroughly appropriate theoretical description of the goals of our teaching, it explains very little about what actually happens at the level of lived experience and daily practice as students develop the abilities we want them to have. In short, I find nothing in this theory that accounts for how we encounter these voices in a direct, material way as different *styles*; in simplest terms, it neglects an experience that is vital to the developing writer, the experience of how a particular piece of writing sounds.

When Harris writes about the voices of home, of work, of friendship, and so on, I can't help but wonder what they sound like, how they compete for the trust that sooner or later I have to give to some of them over others, what role the winning of this trust plays in the larger project of persuasion, and how I can best attune my students to the sound of this all-important credibility to help them gain a share of it. In other words, I've never been certain of what exactly Harris means by voice: for him, disciplinary methods are a kind of voice, and so is the voice of "the neighborhood." I understand the connection, of course, but only in a highly generalized, abstract way, and I worry that, in this significant departure from the stream of spontaneous, sensory experience, certain powerful tools for teaching, learning, and writing are being left behind.

And so, I decided to revive aspects of the earlier concept of voice, but to deliver them from the naïve expressivist school as well as from the overly abstract concept of mere "discourse." That is, I decided to explore ways to teach students about voice in terms of how their writing sounds. While the domain of sound might seem awfully nebulous, I've taught this powerful dimension of our experience of writing very concretely through a practical, even quasi-formulaic interest in prose style, and I've tried to push questions of prose style constantly toward questions of ethics.

That earlier, expressivist model of voice obliquely touches on the power of sound as I intend to delineate it here. Unfortunately, as Harris and many others would surely point out, that version of voice usually miscasts the power of sound as the driving force in an apotheosis of purely individualistic personality. More specifically, when Elbow speaks of how each of us "resonates to one pitch alone," I think he's quite right to talk about a deep sense of how we want our texts, quite literally, to sound, but the idea that each person has his or her own particular pitch wholly reverses the important truth that Elbow's comment is on the verge of articulating. That is, when he talks about writing that has "juice" and "electricity," writing that we experience as "real" or "meaningful," he is not pointing, as so many claim he is, to an apotheosis of individual personality, but of the opposite: an apotheosis of the transpersonal. The writer, in such passages, connects with readers because he or she has tapped into that which exceeds the author as an individuated source of meaning. In short, the writer has tapped into the power of sound. When writers access the profoundly social force that is sound, they create as well a vital opportunity for critical reflection: in simplest terms, stylistic choices are also ethical choices.

Much this same implication arises in Elbow's award-winning but too-seldom-cited essay from the mid-1980s, "The Shifting Relationships Between Speech and Writing" (1985, 1999). What he says about speech opens the way for how I've come to think about sound as a broad category that involves timing and tone (or ethos, and, in turn, ethics) and, most concretely, stylistic devices and principles. Instead of addressing the rhetorical value of sheer personality, Elbow traces in this essay certain "speech-like" qualities that we would do well to cultivate in our students' composing processes: speech is spontaneous, prompted by immediate contexts, usually as an explicit reply to something else that has been said, and it proceeds with a distinct rhythm, asking the listener to engage the words closely, filling in and following implications as needed, participating in the dance of the speaker's mental events. Elbow adds that the best teachers know how to prompt their students to capitalize on the oral language skills they already possess (179). That is, good teachers know that when they're working with a student whose prose is so badly scrambled as to be more or less impenetrable, they need only "ask the student to *say* what she was getting at," and then the student will almost always articulate her point in ways that are "perfectly clear and lively" (180). The clearer, spoken version need only be transcribed, and the paper is then well on its way to considerable improvement.

This talk-based technique works quite well in many of the tutoring sessions in the writing center that I run, for it exploits a skill all native speakers have acquired long before they've reached college, a skill for managing language *not* as an objective entity resting statically in space (or the sort Harris implies when he lists the monolithic "voices of . . . work and leisure, childhood and parenting," and so on) but as a dynamic event that unfolds in and through time. As Elbow notes, we can take in only a few words at a time, never a whole document at once, and therefore the rhetorical skills of style and arrangement involve leading the reader/listener on a journey through time, using language to record a parade of "live mental events" in such a way that they'll live again, parade again, in the minds of readers.

The transformative powers of time are inherent in speech, for speech, as Elbow notes, is spontaneous, rhythmic, and rooted in the immediate, ongoing context of dialogue. Although these seem like relatively ordinary features of the temporal quality of speech, they come to inhabit our writing only during "magical" intervals of inspiration, which are, for most of us, all too rare. More specifically, when our writing proceeds fluently rather than in tortured fits and starts, with rhythmic thrust rather than in diffuse, undisciplined clumps, and with the feeling of a reply to an interlocutor who is immediately present rather than with a hazy sense of there being little possibility of ever actually being read, when all of these conditions apply, we are inhabiting a mysterious, highly pleasurable territory that all successful writers have learned to cultivate and, when they sit down to write, to summon with some fair degree of consistency.

By deliberately imagining this experience of dialogue as we compose and thus stylizing our sentences with distinctly rhythmic figures of various kinds, we can begin to lay claim to a sort of temporal power, a momentum, something like the sheer spontaneity of thought, that our readers can perceive and experience as well. In fact, this curious power and pleasure, this "inspiration" is purely an affair of carefully stylized language. This point was made quite succinctly by one of my students, Tharon McDowell, who, a few weeks after I introduced the class to stylistic figures of various kinds, said, "These stylistic devices help me incorporate the way I talk into my writing." And another, Brad Monnet, said, "These devices make an ordinary, dry sentence come alive," which, he added, "keeps the reader more interested." When my students say that their writing is better when it incorporates aspects of their speech, I don't think they are simply suggesting that their writing is better when it slips into the vernacular and drifts away from academic rigor. I think, instead, that they're referring ultimately to their experience of sound, for sound has a unique power to override the individual will, to promote experiences of connection between people, to keep "the reader more interested."

I can best explain what I mean by contrasting the experience of hearing to that of eyesight, for eyesight far more thoroughly undergirds the will than does hearing, and it therefore lends itself more readily to the phenomena of individuation. For example, I can turn to look to the left or I can turn to look to the right or I can choose to close my eyes to stop looking altogether. Sounds, on the other hand, override my will, for if a jet passes overhead right now, I will hear it whether I choose to or not—but I will only see it if I deliberately get up, go to the window, and search the sky. This binary, of course, is by no means absolute: musicians will surely tell us that hearing can involve an enormous intensity of the will, and visual artists, conversely, will likely describe all sorts of experiences of surrendering to the pleasures afforded by their eyes. Nonetheless, sounds, much more than sights, have a dynamic, event-like power, a power to undermine the structures that individuate the subject, a power that is manifest much more rarely in visual material. To put it in simplest terms, we can willfully close our eyes anytime we wish, but we can never really close our ears. Sounds capture our attention; they have the power, moment to moment, to change us. Sound, in this sense, is something like a distillation of time itself. This, I think, is what my students are talking about when they say they are bringing their writing closer to speech through the use of stylistic devices: not the dubious rhetorical value of sheer personality or "true voice," but the opposite, the transpersonal, transformative force of sound.

To attune my students to this force, I decided to teach them to attend closely to the process of generating sentences, something most teachers of writing no longer do. Though our field had, in the late 1970s, a richly developed rhetoric and pedagogy of the sentence—the generative sentence-rhetoric of Christensen, imitation exercises, and, of course, sentence combining—our field increasingly moved away from this approach in the early 1980s. As Robert Connors argues, these pedagogic techniques seemed to improve student writing, and no research ever proved otherwise; what's more, students seemed to show great enthusiasm for them. The only problem with them, as Connors argues, was in the way this material was presented—that is, in the exercises themselves (2000, 115). Connors quotes James Moffett, who says, "For the learner, basics are not the small-focus technical things but broad things like meaning and motivation, purpose and point, which are precisely what are missing from exercises" (110). What Connors doesn't mention, however, strikes me as precisely what's most curious about the exercise-oriented version of sentence-level pedagogy: that is, sentence-level pedagogy reached its zenith of popularity in the late '70s and early '80s, the moment that was also nearly the height of the process movement.

Why can't we link the two great passions of that era and thereby revive them? Why reduce an interest in style to mere exercises when these devices have such generative power, can so readily focus revision, and thus so easily play a role in process-based pedagogy? Why *not* teach these stylistic devices explicitly as tools for invention and revision, as a means to create and craft sentences and paragraphs, to choreograph writing so that it can participate in the flight of time the way speech does, so that it can resonate with that same fullness of spontaneity, contextual immediacy, and distinct rhythms? Indeed, when writing is most successful, it passes through time, as bell hooks says, to yield an experience of the infinite, the dimension in which the boundaries that delimit and differentiate writer and reader, self and other dissolve. After all, to write so engagingly, as Lanham (1974) puts it, is simply to write "clearly."

Therefore, rather than focus students on style through a series of exercises, my pedagogy explicitly presents the work of practicing these techniques as a form of play. I try to emphasize play not simply as something children do, but also as something that musicians, actors, and athletes do, something they do with utmost discipline. Though each of these people might seem to "play" very differently, for all three of them playing implies a performance that unfolds *in and with time*. In fact, a spirit of play, argues John Dewey, characterizes the best classrooms—not simply as an expedient, temporary reprieve from the tedium of real schoolwork, not just as an aimless amusement for the immature, but rather as a process of serious absorption in an activity that, in its purest form, takes as its primary goal only the endless continuation of the activity itself. In other words, while play might yield tangible results, these are not really the purpose of the activity but something more like incidental souvenirs or toys that serve only to spur yet further, more pleasurable continuation of the activity, openings by which the activity accesses an ever-greater experience of eternity or the infinite.

The best teachers, Dewey suggests, ultimately want the attitude of play to permeate the students' concept of work, for "Work which remains permeated with the play attitude is art" (1994, 194–206); and art, for Dewey, is that which constantly nourishes and renews the imagination, and, in turn, the entire culture. As a writing teacher, then, my goal has become not simply to avoid turning students into masochists, but to turn them into artists by teaching them how to play with prose style.

These stylistic principles and devices, while often described as the tools that oralist rhetors of old might have used to make their texts more easy to memorize, can also be used to generate a dynamic experience of time or timing that is highly pleasurable, even "magical" for both reader and writer. Again, this particular interest in timing is as old as rhetoric itself, for, as James Kinneavy and Charles Bazerman both note, the ancient concept of *kairos* imbued nearly all early thinking about rhetoric. This concept translates roughly as a sense of temporal appropriateness, of the opportune or fortuitous moment, a sense not simply of saying the right thing but specifically the right thing *at the right time*. Although *kairos* is most often used to refer to rhetorical situations as located in time, the concept clearly has implications for making local decisions within a particular text, how to sequence, arrange, and *time* the specific effects one seeks to achieve, to make them, as my students put it, do what speech does: that is, "come alive."

To clarify how and why I've begun to foreground matters of style in my writing classes, I want to begin by linking it to what is perhaps the oldest method for teaching composition, the very first insight of the sophists, the one from which their writing pedagogy sprang. As Jacqueline De Romilly tells it in the opening chapter of *The Great Sophists of Periclean Athens*, the sophists were "a handful of men active for the span of roughly one generation" (1992, 2) who appeared in Athens in the middle of the fifth century with a bold promise. They would provide to anyone with the means to pay for it an education that would enable that student to play a distinguished part in the life of the city (4). They were, in a sense, composition's first professionals, but the understanding of writing-as-a-process that interested them was not stuck in binary opposition to the experience of literary models, but instead was explicitly based, as I'll show, on the temporal or kairotic experience of the poetry of the rhapsodes. As such, the sophists offer a powerful resource for the contemporary discipline of composition as it struggles to define itself as a profession without losing the renegade powers that have always been its heart and soul. What I'm suggesting, on one hand, is hardly new: in fact, figures as diverse as Susan Jarratt, Jasper Neel, and Victor Vitanza, all prominent voices in our discipline, have identified themselves one way or another with the sophists. A full generation ago, Edward P. J. Corbett and Richard Lanham made much the same move I'm making here when they published lists of rhetorical terms, tropes, and stylistic devices, all of which they borrowed directly from the sophistic tradition. More recently, Arthur Quinn published *Figures of Speech: Sixty Ways to Turn a Phrase*, Sharon Crowley and Debra Hawhee wrote a textbook called *Ancient Rhetorics for Contemporary Students*, and Robert Harris published *Writing with Clarity and Style*, each of which features page after page of sheer verbal technique.

These formal devices are the very things the sophists sold to their students: techniques for speaking in public, for defending and advancing one's interests in courts or civic assemblies (De Romilly 1992, 6), for organizing language dynamically as a sequence of moments that, if choreographed well, will open that powerful, transpersonal force of clarity that, at its strongest, has been associated with inspiration, magic, and the infinite.

The sophists quickly extended their interest in verbal techniques to political philosophy and from there to modes of human behavior. Eventually, they began to "note down and classify a whole mass of data relating to all areas of life" (8), so much so that, for example, when one of them, Thrasymachus, was passing away, he composed for his tomb an epitaph that ran "Chalcedon was my country, knowledge my profession" (1). Sophists, De Romilly explains, explicitly distinguished themselves from sages and philosophers, for these terms imply, respectively, a state of being and the patient, disinterested search for truth, whereas the sophists cast aside both in favor of cultivating the magic-like power to manipulate social reality and achieve certain effects in their immediate surroundings (1). For the sophist, De Romilly points out, knowledge "was their specialty, just as the piano is the pianist's" (1).

The analogy of sophistic knowledge to musical knowledge couldn't be more appropriate, for, as Stephen Katz (1996) argues, at the core of the sophistic practice of knowing was a preoccupation with the sound of language. More specifically, the sophists led a sweeping dismissal of the gods and a powerful critique of all forms of transcendental philosophy, following instead the assertion of Protagoras that "Man is the measure of all things"; but they went even further to doubt the power of the human senses to discern reality and truth. Given the absence of any reliable cognitive anchors—no gods, no transcendent ideals, not even any reliable sensory faculties—what leads men and women to construct and live in their world one way rather than another, according to the sophists, is the sheer magic of the *sound* of how they speak to each other. The pleasures of verbal style, as Katz writes, were seen as far more than just "irrational sensations"; they were "fundamental to knowing" (89). The sophists, says Katz, felt that knowledge could not be developed by rational inquiry but rather "was created in and (through response to) poetic arrangement and style" (88). The power of language, he adds, is rooted in the "musical property of words," and this power always takes a sensuous form that creates feeling, thought, and reality by evoking sensory action. For this reason, rhetoric as the study of style is the primary focus of education, culture, and even humanity. It is the root of all knowledge (93).

My students intuitively seem to understand this idea without having it explained to them, and, too, many of them find this "musical property" to be a sharp spur to critical thought. For example, toward the end of a class period early one semester, I asked my students to freewrite for a few minutes about what they took to be the most important ideas to have emerged during class discussion. Then, after I stopped them, I told them to look back through what they had written and craft some particular moment of it into a syncresis— that is, a comparison-contrast that proceeds in parallel clauses, such as "Cowards die a thousand deaths—heroes die but once." Within a few moments, several of them were ready to share their attempts. Some, as it turned out, were perfect, and others needed to be tweaked slightly to fit the form. After hearing a few of them, a particularly earnest student, Charlie O'Connor, raised his hand rather tentatively with a perplexed look on his face. "You know," he began, "I'm not so sure about this. When I hear these sentences, they really sound good—they've got that feeling, that literary feeling, so I just know they gotta be true." I replied, "But there's a problem, isn't there?" And Charlie quickly shot back, "Well, yeah. Anytime anything sounds that good, I get suspicious and can't help but question it. With some of these sentences, I agree, but others I'm really not sure about."

I told Charlie how pleased I was to see him engaging in this kind of critical reflection and that I hoped he would keep cultivating that capacity all semester. Our purpose, I said, was not simply to surrender to the pleasures of that "literary feeling" but to develop an increasingly refined sense of what that "literary feeling" might have the power to conceal. And I added that a moving piece of language, when we're learning how to write, should move us at least partly to question where that moving feeling comes from and how it works. And, as easy as it is to let these sorts of figures pass without thinking critically about them when they appear in isolation, they prove even more slippery when many of them are embedded together in a larger swatch of prose.

In fact, when a good many sentences are stylized rhythmically, they can really carry us off our feet or at least lull us into nodding agreement. After all, that's what they were originally designed to do. These rhythmic techniques, as Eric Havelock explains, originally served the rhapsodes in ancient Greece, in the era before the advent of writing and the rise of the sophists, as tools for memorizing the vast cultural encyclopedia that they were required to recite, and through which they exercised enormous power (1963, 145). These techniques allowed the rhapsode to weave and reweave the vast repository of cultural memory into a heavily stylized, easily remembered tapestry; in short, they enabled the past to "come alive" and persist into the future, and this highly pleasurable re-creation engendered something like what Emile Durkheim calls the *mana*-feeling, a communal feeling of collective self-knowledge (O'Keefe 1982, 166).

This feeling, according to Daniel O'Keefe, first occurs during dramatic group activities, a feeling that the group then symbolizes with *mana*-objects which gradually come to constitute the sacred sphere; around these objects, certain beliefs and rites take root, which, once organized, become religion (187). Once a religion becomes formalized, fragments of the *mana*-system can be broken off, isolated, and reorganized to antagonize or at least dialogue with the larger *mana*-system, and this activity, according to O'Keefe, is what we traditionally identify as the practice of magic. Examples might include the Black Mass, voodoo, tarot cards, the Ouija board, and so on.

This process by which religion is created and then fragmented to give rise to magic explains, too, how the rhapsodes made possible the careers of the sophists. The fragments that the sophists appropriated from the rhapsodes were, of course, the stylistic devices. These units of musical technique in language could be used in dialogue with the collective and precipitate such extraordinary experiences of pleasure as to seem magical. The stylistic devices still seem to have a magical quality, for they strike students as part of an ancient, esoteric knowledge system, one that can provide them with considerable power. In fact, when I first introduced my students to concepts like syncresis and zeugma and so on, they nearly unanimously responded with comments like, "I've always heard and read sentences that were set up this way, but I had no idea there were names for these patterns, much less that anyone could actually plan to use them."

When my students asked me how and why these techniques manage to stir such strong feeling, I suggested that all of them are essentially ways of creating and manipulating the experience of rhythm. I draw on Havelock's work to say that by encoding certain repetitive patterns into our discourse, we allow for a wide variety of oral utterances that repeat the same structure of movement between the lungs, throat, tongue, and teeth, and, even when we're silently reading, our vocal cords register regular patterns of movement (Katz 1996, 137). Perhaps we feel these rhythms spreading, sending scarcely perceptible signals to related parts of the body as an essential element in processing abstract chains of symbols. These patterns of repetition might organize various complex motor reflexes to such a degree that they operate without any need on the part of the subject to think about them; that is, the act of communicating proceeds in ways roughly analogous to "similar reflexes of the sexual or digestive apparatus" which are "highly sensual and closely linked with physical pleasures" (Havelock 1963, 149). For example, mechanisms in the inner ear give us our sense of balance and therefore undoubtedly play a role in our broader experience of symmetry and, in turn, rhythm—that is, of meanings suspended in equilibrium to create yet greater meanings.

Rhythm, as Katz points out, functions as a tacit, physical form of knowledge (107–08). In short, what Cicero, Isocrates, and others understood is that these stylistic devices are not merely *fun*, not just toys for writers, but tools by which writers can create certain effects on readers, physical feelings of comprehension and power, knowledge and connection. Careful rhythms and repetitions create, in a text, a latticework of interconnected moments, and this burgeoning bubble of "now" can, when one inhabits it, give rise to parallel experiences of connection between reader and writer and spark powerful acts of intuition that feel like the substance of knowledge itself. This intersubjective experience, which teachers call clarity, connects the writer's self with the Other, with that which, as such, has no clearly defined, easily controlled boundaries. In its profoundest instances, these are experiences of the infinite.

Unfortunately, this experience is often cast in naïve, popular discussions as liberation or, more vulgarly, self-indulgence. Or, just as bad, we strive to safeguard against these pleasures by reducing the whole domain of style to a set of tedious little exercises. Historically, however, the dominant metaphor for authorial pleasure is magic. Even today, when writers feel that their work is proceeding smoothly and spontaneously and in a way that feels readily readable, many of them will refer lightheartedly to the occult power of "the muse." Such remarks, though seemingly quite casual, actually embed a profound assertion about authorial pleasure. For example, in a chapter of *Writing with Power* called "Writing and Magic," Elbow notes that when your writing lacks magic, this absence is manifest in "little tell-tale movements in the body that somehow manifest discomfort" and "there are comparable micro-fidgets in our syntax and diction" (366–67). In other words, if the absence of "magic" leads to a flustered, uncomfortable experience of the composing process and a composition that is itself characterized by "micro-fidgets," then magic connotes the opposite: a pleasurable experience of composing and a composition that is comparatively more pleasurable (less "fidgety") for the reader. The experience of "magic" is the experience of pleasure in composing, but not just the pleasure of the writer alone: somehow, it is the pleasure of sharing pleasure with the Other, a quasi-erotic contact with that which is beyond the author. And, importantly, it registers in the text as the absence of "micro-fidgets in our syntax and diction." In short, it registers as highly disciplined style. Indeed, stylistic techniques provide the conduit between self and other. They create and sustain the moment of contact, of connection, of "clarity," in which the remarks of the author are renewed, made to "come alive" once again for the reader. This is the magical appearance of the muse as a textual bridge between author and audience and between past and future, a dissolution of the boundaries between them, an apotheosis of what hooks calls "the infinite."

While issues of the magical and the infinite might seem awfully exotic from the perspective of the workaday realities of the contemporary composition classroom, and while the preceding discussion might seem, theoretically, too abstract and, historically, too remote to have any meaningful bearing on practical matters of how we teach, I've developed some quite simple strategies for bringing my students to share in these considerable powers.

But How Do You Teach This Stuff?

On the first day of class, I distribute to my students a handout with the heading "Stylistic Devices" that begins this way:

> What follows is a list of verbal patterns for forms or "tricks" that you can use to make your prose more graceful, more powerful, and more memorable. Think of them, on one hand, as ornaments, as means to take what you've said and recast it in ways that your readers will enjoy. On the other hand, working with these forms can also stimulate your imagination—that is, as you work to reshape certain moments in your paper to fit these formulae, you may find all sorts of new ideas popping up.
>
> These devices are quite powerful. They were first organized more than two thousand years ago in ancient Greece, and they have had an overwhelming influence on the ways we've used language ever since. I've taken most of the information that follows from Richard Lanham's book *A Handlist of Rhetorical Terms*, where you'll find dozens upon dozens more such devices.
>
> Don't be intimidated or put off by the exotic names for these devices. Whether you learn to pronounce or spell these names correctly is not what's important. Also, don't feel as though you have to memorize them: at no point in the semester will you take a quiz or an exam in which you have to define each of these terms. Instead, simply try to become comfortable with these devices as tools that can give you more and more control over your prose, and, in turn, more and more success communicating with your readers. Remember, you should try to use at least two of these when you write your short homework papers, and, what's more, you will be required to use eight of them in your longer essay assignments.
>
> One last point by way of introduction, one that's *very, very important*: don't get hung up trying to fulfill these formulae before you know what you want to say! Rather, after you've done some brainstorming and have a general sense of the ideas and details you want to engage in your paper, then—and only then—should you start trying to make certain moments in your paper fulfill some of these formulae. On the other hand, you might find that if you can't come up with ideas that you need for your paper, playing around with some of these devices can help generate ideas for writing. But only think of them this way when the brainstorming process feels genuinely stuck or blocked.

What follows is a list of some thirty terms. The first one is *accumulatio*, and I present it this way:

ACCUMULATIO (ak kyu myoo la TEE o): The heaping up of terms of praise or condemnation to summarize the points you've made. It works especially well in the conclusion of your paper. Example: "Thus, we see that Mayor Smith has been arrogant, uninformed, disloyal, greedy, deceitful, unreliable, and destructive."

The thirty or so terms end up with *zeugma*; I define and illustrate each one in a few short sentences. Initially, these terms were a little intimidating to students, and many of them felt, at the outset, that my requiring them to use these devices seemed incredibly difficult, even "a real pain in the neck."

To rescue my students from what they might otherwise view as an arduous, alienating, even pointless set of requirements, I began by explaining that what I want them to learn is something that, historically, has been thought of as magic. By using such a frankly silly-seeming term in the otherwise solemn context of the academy, I manage to lessen my students' feelings of intimidation and quicken their interest. I tell my students that I'm *not* talking about magic in the literal sense of ESP or levitating objects or rain dances. Rather, I'm talking about using symbols, not to fly in the face of the laws of nature and rationality but rather to produce dramatic effects in the people around us. In this sense, the concept of magic applies to stunning works of art that change the way people think about their lives, deeply moving sermons or political speeches that prompt people to action, even great athletic performances that bring fans together and alter the ways people imagine the human body and its potentials.

I draw on William Covino (1994) and Kenneth Burke (1945) to say that what I'm interested in here is *generative magic* rather than *arresting magic*. The latter is a kind of lockstep incantation that is the opposite of critical and creative thinking. An example of arresting magic in the classroom would be the widespread belief of many students that fully formed texts simply spring forth from writers, effortlessly and inexplicably, like rabbits out of hats (see Young 1982). This arresting magic, too, is what Paulo Freire has in mind when he describes the mesmerized passivity and abject resignation of illiterate peasants, for arresting magic is employed by those at the center of mass culture to dazzle and coerce yet further those whom they dominate: it diminishes the masses' sense of choices and options, and, in turn, any experience of their own power and knowledge. Examples of arresting magic can be culled, as Covino points out, from the headlines of any of the supermarket tabloids: *Amazing New UFO Diet—Shed Pounds While You Sleep; Ten Steps to a Hotter Marriage; Get Rich the Easy Way with Trump's Simple Plan*. This sort of magic, as I said, is the opposite of the generative magic that, I hope, comes to permeate my classroom.

Magic in the generative sense is the mysterious power that drives the play of language. Generative magic can be cultivated by writers who, as Covino puts it, learn to serve as "assistants to the [generative] magic of words causing words," (1994, 92) who learn how, as Kenneth Burke puts it, to use those moments when "the act of writing brings up problems and discoveries intrinsic to the act, leading to developments . . . purely from the foregoing aspects of the act itself" (1945, 67). This mysterious playfulness that inheres in strings of words and causes them to yield more words, as Covino argues, "enlarges the grounds for action by the creation of choices"; because it creates choices, it in turn gives way to inward dialogue and reflection and then precipitates critique and judgement, which, as decisions are made, yield creative synthesis and commitment (1994, 26).

To cultivate generative magic, writers must learn techniques and principles that, rather than arrest the play of critical thought, stimulate it, structures that liberate rather than merely limit the composing imagination. These techniques allow the writer to cultivate that mysterious playfulness by which writing begets more writing and summons with keen temporal immediacy — just as speech does — responses from audiences.

When I introduce my students to these stylistic devices, I explain that my goal is not simply to get them to produce heavily stylized language, such as we might find in the Bible or Shakespeare, but rather to practice these devices as a kind of interim measure toward listening to and thinking about their prose more carefully. I think these devices achieve this end quite well. For example, one of my recent students, Elizabeth Sosa, told me that her previous schooling had instilled in her the habit of approaching writing assignments recklessly: "I would just put down any words that came to me without thinking about them at all till my paper was as long as it needed to be." But after just a few weeks of engaging these stylistic devices, she said, "I've changed. These devices force me to actually think about what I'm saying, rather than just putting down whatever." What I think is happening in Elizabeth's case, and in the case of many of my students, is that making use of these stylistic devices leads them to write with a greater degree of inward reflection, a heightened interaction with what Sondra Perl calls "the felt sense" (1980).

As my students struggle to use the stylistic devices, they constantly must ask themselves if a particular phrasing makes sense, if it feels right, or whether perhaps it feels like a problem, a snag in their attempts to communicate. Over the course of the semester, my students become increasingly familiar with the felt sense of communicative effectiveness, increasingly able to draw upon this "soft underbelly of thought . . . [this] bodily awareness" (Perl 1980, 363). The felt sense, they come to see, is a crucial tool for all writers. As Perl writes, "When we write and the writing is going well, we can tell by how we feel. This is not a purely mental or logical knowing but a bodily one." And she adds, "At such times we may feel a quickening and a sense of expansion or relief. But the reverse is also true. When the writing is not going well, we know it. We don't like how the words sound" (1994, 81). My students' use of these stylistic devices led them to interact with and learn to use the felt sense to increasing degrees over the course of the semester, and, as they did, they seemed to feel less alienated from the scene of writing, more happy to meet the challenges I set before them. They discovered the felt sense, in fact, as if it were something quite new, quite exciting, something they could cultivate and renew on an ongoing basis.

Given that Perl first introduced this concept of the felt sense in 1980, many teachers of writing have probably associated it with the expressivist idea of the authentic, personal voice, and, as such, it very likely ran afoul of the social-constructionist trend then beginning to move toward ascendance. The felt sense, however, despite its obvious resonance with popular concepts of so-called gut instinct, also can be thought of as something like an "audience-within," a receptor or interlocutor we carry in our musculature and that tells us if we're writing well or not. The felt sense also functions much the same way that the collective encyclopedia functioned in the ancient rhapsodes. "The felt sense," as Perl quotes Eugene Gendlin, "encompasses everything you feel and know about a given subject at given time" (1980, 365). It is not therefore a private space, a space of purest subjectivity or self-expression, not the "real me" or "my true voice," but just the opposite: the felt sense is the domain of the transpersonal, the point of contact with the Other. In this light, learning to "get in touch" with the felt sense means learning to connect with the surrounding community, learning to overcome alienation and master strategies for meeting audiences. When students play around with ways of patterning sentences in a given passage, this activity not only triggers new ideas for writing, but, at the same time, it also enables them to get a feel for what sounds best in a given moment in their prose and a feel for the generative magic by which words beget more words. Their pleasure, I believe, is a residue of the ecstasy of the ancient rhapsodes.

In fact, my students manifest a quite stunning sort of energy when I link these stylistic devices, explicitly, to exercises with the felt sense. Early in the semester, as was the case with Elizabeth, they wanted to "hurry up and get it over with," putting down words fairly thoughtlessly to bring the anxious experience of the composing process to a quick, sloppy end. And so, they initially resisted these devices. In order to diminish their sense of the sheer hassle of dealing with language as carefully as I required, I devoted a class meeting to helping them rethink, through the felt sense and through a stylistic device known as *chiasmus,* their recently completed rough drafts. I had assigned my students a topic that required them to synthesize ideas in essays by Alice Walker and Nancy Mairs on the dynamics of body image and the practice of writing and to use this connection as the springboard for their own thoughts on what role writing can play in the struggle to cultivate what the students had come to call, through our class discussions, "inner beauty." We had had several great discussions, most of which I had ended by asking my students to freewrite, so they would have plenty of raw material from which to create a draft. On the day the first drafts were due, I told them that today there would be no discussion, that instead, I wanted to ask them a series of questions about their drafts and that they should write the answers out in their notebooks.

I told them first to read through their drafts once, straight through, without pausing to make any changes. Once they had finished, I asked each of them to write a paragraph on how they felt about the draft. I gave them a few minutes, and then asked a question that probed a little more deeply: "What moment in your essay is the smartest, the most impressive? Why?" I then asked a couple of questions designed to promote a certain kind of free-association that would lead to the felt sense. "Can you," I asked, "link this moment to a particular person or place or event? If you already have made a connection to one of these in your paper, try to link it to one of the others, to something that is not, at present, in your paper." I then asked them, "What emotions do you associate with this connection?" And then, after a minute or two, "Suppose, for the time being, that an emotion is really something like a half-formed thought, an incomplete thought, something you know but that you don't realize that you know—yet. What message or information might be hiding inside the emotion that you've mentioned?" I then told them to freewrite and develop this idea for five minutes.

Next, I said, "Now, read back over what you just wrote. Can you boil it down to a sort of basic opposition, something like X *versus* Y?" I gave them some time to think, and then I said, "Now, try putting the two terms of this conflict together under a single label, a label that pins down not their opposition, but the connection between them, the thing they share." Again, I gave them some time to think and said, "Now that you've got this term that binds them together, jot down what you think might be the opposite of this term." I then asked them to retrace these steps and come up with a sentence in which the two key terms of the first half of the sentence were repeated in reverse order in the second half. That is, I asked them to create a chiasmus, something like "Ask not what your country can do for you, but what you can do for your country." The steps I had just led them through by no means could automatically yield a chiasmus, but I hoped that, by helping them to think in terms of oppositions and multiple levels of generalization, I could get them moving toward one.

Needless to say, they struggled. After a few minutes, though, several of them were ready to share their attempts, and, as we jostled these examples to fit the form, more of the students began to catch on. The students soon began to bring an extraordinary energy to this task, and this energy accumulated in intensity as they competed with each other to engineer a chiasmus. One student, Jessi Courville, said that working on her chiasmus was triggering so many new ideas and possibilities for her paper that she felt as if her mind was about to "boil over." As she said this, she was beaming. Nearly everyone in the class became increasingly animated as we worked on shaping their assertions into a chiasmus: hardly the ecstasy of the ancient rhapsodes, but certainly something bordering on its elusive descendant, that strange sensation that we've traditionally called inspiration or magic.

One student raised his hand and read his sentence: "The question, ultimately, is this: Does having a keen sense of your own inner beauty turn you into a writer, or does writing on a regular basis give you a keen sense of your own inner beauty? In other words, the question of beauty and becoming a writer is just like the question of the chicken and the egg. It's impossible to say which comes first and causes the other." Another student wrote, "If you can master your feelings about the issue of external beauty, you will be beautiful, but if questions about external beauty master you, you will be ugly. Writing can help the inner defeat the outer, but advertising and the media can help the outer defeat the inner."

Most of the others weren't quite as good, but my students found that, in spite of the difficulty of creating a chiasmus, the struggle itself was producing lots of new ideas and details that they could include in their essays. What's more, the students seemed to be having fun, and the work they produced was certainly fun to read: when I looked at their next drafts, the writing was indeed richer and more complex than most freshman writing I'm used to seeing.

The chief flaw in my students' drafts at this stage was that they often dropped the stylistic figures into their papers pretty much at random. Those examples of chiasmus, above, might appear virtually anywhere in the essay, and, as I discussed the students' drafts with them, nearly all of them reported that, despite the power of the stylistic devices to generate ideas, the devices' placement in the finished product was not so much due to careful reflection but rather to chance or random opportunity. The figures could just as easily appear in the middle of a paragraph somewhere toward the middle of the essay as in the introduction or conclusion, and they could be used to express minor details or major themes. In other words, the devices seemed to destabilize, sometimes quite drastically, their experience of the overall structure of the essay.

After looking at their drafts and considering the problem, I decided to help them situate this sense of the architecture of individual sentences within the larger architecture of the entire essay. Borrowing from Joseph Williams (1981), I introduced them to four stylistic principles that the class came to identify, respectively, as "focus," "flow," "story," and "rhythmic emphasis."

In short, "focus" is the idea that, within each paragraph, each sentence should begin with a topic that fits with the other topics of the other sentences in that paragraph. If these topics, together, form a consistent string, then the paragraph is well focused; that is, if the topic of several sentences in a row is "I" but then a fifth sentence in the paragraph sets forth, as its topic, the words *pickup truck*, then, right there, at *pickup truck*, the focus has begun to blur. The same principle that can help writers focus individual paragraphs can be used to focus an entire essay: that is, if the topic of each paragraph throughout the essay makes a consistent set, then the paper is well focused, but if one paragraph suddenly begins with a reference that seems unrelated to the openings of the other paragraphs that precede and that follow it, then the essay's focus, at exactly that moment, has temporarily wobbled or even gone entirely off track.

Much like the principle of "focus," I explained to them that the principle of "flow" allows writers to reflect in fairly objective ways on how readers will experience their prose. Very simply, if each sentence begins with a word, phrase, or concept that, within the immediate context, is familiar to the reader, and if the sentence then ends with material that is not familiar, then readers will find that the sentence flows smoothly and will proceed along to the next sentence without stumbling.

I then told my students about a principle that is closely related to these concepts, an idea we came to call, in shorthand, the idea of "story." I suggested that the human mind seems to have a relatively easy time engaging information when that information is organized at least in part as a story. That is, we like to organize information in terms of characters and the actions they perform. This dynamic of character and action (that is, story) accounts for why our sentences usually must have a subject (character) and a verb (action) in order to really engage the reader. Moreover, the sooner within the sentence that writers deliver what readers most want—a subject followed very closely by a verb—the more readily will those readers engage the writer's sentences.

I was careful not to overwhelm the students by introducing them to these ideas all at once. Rather, I took up only one per class meeting, provided many examples, and gave the students time in class to tinker with moments in their drafts according to these ideas. I constantly reminded them that they should always have these principles in mind when they were revising their work, especially when they were working with a stylistic device.

This concept of "story" connects well with another concept for revising their essays and connecting with readers, the idea of rhythmic emphasis. This, I told them, is one of the most important features of successful prose. Of course, prose style is way too complicated a subject to allow for any sort of simplistic definition of its rhythm. Nonetheless, I drew again from Joseph Williams a way of tinkering with individual sentences to give them rhythmic emphasis, and this idea, especially when coupled with the previous idea of story, can make sentences more engaging for readers. Consider the fact, I told them, that when a reader reads a sentence out loud, his or her voice nearly always rises and falls toward the ends of sentences. "Try it yourself," I said, "you can hear your voice naturally rise and fall on the last word or two of a sentence as you stress one syllable more strongly than you do the others, like this—listen—'more strongly than you do the OTH-ers.'" I told them that same thing happens even when one is reading silently—that is, the rhythmic rise and fall is registered in the felt sense. And therefore, given that the ends of sentences are always places where we naturally expect to hear a certain dramatic rise and fall, we should only put words at the end of our sentences that are quite important—that is, words or phrases that are worthy of this special, rhythmic thrust.

I remind my students, again and again, that this principle of rhythmic emphasis should be exercised in a delicate balance with the idea of story. That is, the character and action of a sentence/story are certainly important, even essential, but so much so that they are often understood by readers, sentence by sentence, as a kind of "given," and what's most important of all, where the real drama of a sentence/story lurks is in the effect or result of the character's action, and that's why that material should come in the place of greatest rhythmic emphasis, the sentence's end. This formula is hardly as tired and lockstep as the five-paragraph theme and is, in fact, flexible enough to keep the students from falling into a rote method. Above all, it gives them a larger framework within which to imagine using particular stylistic devices, preventing them from suffering the completely open-ended sense that these devices can be randomly dropped into the text anywhere without careful attention to context or timing.

In the broadest sense, these devices and principles sensitize my students to how their readers experience their prose. In addition to structuring the work of revision and lending that potentially open-ended process a comforting set of priorities and a "to-do list," it awakens my students to the fact that reading too is, for readers, always a process, a sequence of moments that good writers know how to choreograph. In short, these devices allow my students to start playing around with the experience of time: if the principle of flow, for example, is observed rigorously, the essay will seem to move forward very quickly, but if it is troubled slightly, the essay will slow down, and certain dramatic, abrupt figures like the chiasmus can draw enough attention to themselves to stop, temporarily, the forward movement of the essay altogether. This power to manipulate time can feel magical and it derives directly from a keen, imaginative interaction with the reader.

Scarcely more than a month into the semester, my students began to report that working with the stylistic devices was getting easier and even downright fun, like playing a game. And so I thought about trying to cultivate this energy, to sensitize them yet further to style as a tool for the pleasurable experience of connecting with others. More and more often, I would ask students to read out loud so they could come to see the way patterns of stress interact with patterns of meaning (see Katz 1996). Whenever I did, I thought about Richard Lanham's idea (1983) that when we read out loud, we instantly radicalize the latent, social dimension of the text in ways that silent reading suppresses: that is, we evince an attitude toward it, and, beyond it, we set forth a web of emotionally nuanced relationships between ourselves, our immediate surroundings, the people who can hear us, and the text. I encouraged my students to note the ways reading out loud makes us take a stand and put ourselves on the line, activating the relations between self, text, and world in ways that are quite energizing (1983, 105). In the terms I've been using, this energizing effect—this pleasure—stems from the experience of reimmersion in community, in the realm of lived connections and consequences. Indeed, when called upon to read aloud, students often initially resist, for it throws into play all sorts of processes that they are programmed to lock down or sidestep.

In addition to thinking about reading out loud, I began to think about a technique I heard about several years ago in which students memorize and recite randomly chosen paragraphs from their papers. We always find it nearly impossible to memorize something that we don't find particularly meaningful or involving, but the opposite sort of language is quite easy to memorize. Should I, I asked myself, revive that old "memorization test"? Rather than actually assign it, I mentioned it, as a possibility, to my students, something I might offer to them as a chance for extra credit or as one aspect of a revision project. . . .

THE WRITER'S DOUBLE

Teaching students to play with stylistic devices and encouraging them to read out loud are part of the broad project of helping them to develop a sense of audience and engage in inward dialogue, critical reflection, and generative "magic." In other words, the trick of writing well has a great deal to do, as Walter Ong notes in "The Writer's Audience Is Always a Fiction" (1975, 1997), with one's ability to create and manage not just certain local effects on the audience but also a kind of consistent, global *role* for that audience. One can then put one's self in the position of that audience and reread one's work to look for moments when that audience might stumble. Much the same point occasions Joseph Williams' practical book on style (2000), which is organized around a list of ten highly flexible principles for considering one's prose from a reader's point of view and for revising it to ensure as much as possible that one's readers will have the experience one wants them to have.

All writers, Ong suggests, instinctively try to do this whenever they write. For example, when a student is faced with the problem of writing a paper for a teacher, he or she will likely muddle around trying to get a draft going, but no draft will begin to emerge until the student discovers how he or she wants to sound. Suppose the student has read *The Adventures of Tom Sawyer*. The student, says Ong, "knows what this book felt like, how the voice in it addressed its readers." And so the student supposes, "Why not pick up that voice and, with it, its audience? Why not make like Samuel Clemens and write for whomever Samuel Clemens was writing for?" (1975, 59). The student is instinctively playing on a particular strand in her partial version of the collective encyclopedia, her felt sense, one roughly labeled "Clemens," in the hopes that the patterns of that particular strand will serve to engage the reader the same way it so memorably did for her when she read Clemens' work. The student intuitively understands that if she does a fairly good job of imitating Clemens and if the teacher has no great problem playing the role of the Clemens-reader, then the paper is likely to be thought of as very "clear" and to earn a good grade. But what if the teacher finds such a voice either corny or stilted or arcane—what then? The student will have to redraft and, this time, she will have to adopt some other writer's methods for constructing the reader's role. What makes this task of inward dialogue so difficult is that there are no hard-and-fast rules or directives that one can memorize and repeat to govern what is, after all, an endlessly nuanced, almost molecular sort of connection between reader and writer.

A point like Ong's was made some two decades ago by Donald Murray. "The act of writing," he says, "might be described as a conversation between two workmen, muttering to each other at the workbench." He explains, "The self speaks, the other self listens and responds. The self proposes, the other self evaluates. The two selves collaborate" (1982, 140). What these two workmen mutter about is words and how it feels to use one rather than another, as well as phrases and their arrangement, and how one sequence rather than an alternate might sound better, might more fully connect with a particular audience. This second self, this internalized or imagined audience, is very much akin to what Havelock would call, in the context of the ancient rhapsodes, the collective, Homeric encyclopedia. To define it phenomenologically, I think we might characterize this special zone or force as something that writers can cultivate in much the same way that Elbow asks us to cultivate "speech." Like speech, like Perl's felt sense, it is dialogic, full of spontaneity, contextual immediacy, and rhythmic thrust. Whether we call it by any of these names or by *kairos* or timing or sound, we must surely agree that increasing sensitivity to it plays an invaluable role in the development of the student writer.

And, regrettably, this Other-within, as some have pointed out, is becoming more and more elusive, more and more difficult to contact. As Lynn Worsham puts it, this Other-within can harden into the sort of authority that blocks expression. That is, it can become "disembodied and abstract," but, once the student embraces it, she says, it can form the necessary rallying point for critical reflection (1993, 142). I think precisely this sort of block characterizes many students: they have, as Mike Rose might put it, internalized a conglomeration of half-understood but wholly inflexible rules, ideals, and goals that form a kind of buttress against the lived experience of the processes of thinking, writing, and learning, a firewall against the very inspiring, even bodily experience of awakening literacy (1980).

At the risk of waxing nostalgic for a Golden Age that most likely never was, my dream is [to] help students dismantle this modern firewall, to become what Jean Baudrillard (1993) calls "primitives." The primitive subject, according to Baudrillard, differs from the modern subject, first, because the primitive is suffused with pleasure, whereas the modern is fundamentally alienated and anxiety-stricken. The primitives experience pleasure because they have a relationship with a "double," whereas the anxiety-stricken moderns have internalized an abstract agency or idealized some dogmatic code that alienates them from their doubles. Between the primitive and the double, says Baudrillard, "there is neither a mirror relation nor one of abstraction, as there is between the subject and its spiritual principle, the soul, or between the subject and its moral or psychological principle, consciousness" (141). What, then, is this double? The double is not simply a repetition of one's self, not the "true self" of so-called expressivism nor a mirror image of one's ego, but simply an Other-within, one of a potentially vast horde of such doubles that one can conjure into dialogue. According to Baudrillard, the double is "an invisible part" of the self, a "partner with whom the primitive . . . has a certain type of visible exchange" via words, symbols, or gestures (141). This relation with the double, though "sometimes happy, sometimes not," is implicitly pleasurable, says Baudrillard, for its failure produces a profound anxiety. The double's erosion or complete disappearance occurs when one "internalizes an abstract agency . . . to which everything else is subordinated" (142). This is the advent of the "soul" or of "consciousness" (142), and with it the subject undergoes a very real confinement and separation, the worst sort of submission to mechanisms of social control. In short, one becomes "modern."

The modern is a masochistic subject, one who has internalized and fetishized some ideal, a representation of the Law, before which one must grovel and quake in the hope of appeasement, or still worse, sit frozen in fear of its power to harm. Indeed, to the degree that we forfeit our relationship with our double, to the degree that we become "modern," we are plunged into profound anxiety and alienation. "[T]he things closest to us," Baudrillard writes, "such as our own bodies, the body itself, our voice and our appearance, are separated from us to the precise extent that we internalize the soul (or any other equivalent agency or abstraction)." To do so, adds Baudrillard, "kills off the proliferation of doubles and spirits, consigning them once again to the spectral, embryonic corridors of unconscious folklore, like the ancient gods that Christianity . . . transformed into demons" (142).

The modern world, argues Baudrillard, "is haunted by the spectres of these alienated doubles, creating anxiety that wells up around the most familiar things" (142). Surely, this anxiety imbues the situation of sitting down to write, for, when we must imagine an audience to address, we are trying to interact with a double whom we have lost. Re-accessing one's double— or, rather, doubles—means conjuring them from the "spectral embryonic corridors of unconscious folklore," where they have been consigned as "demons." . . . [T]he "demon" whom the modern conjures is that idealized vision of perfection, the humiliating dominatrix who binds and secures us against any arcs of becoming, who sows doubt and defeatism in us, and who compels us to refuse challenges and turn away from growth.

How do we recreate the primitive experience of the double? I think that the kinds of ideas I've offered in this chapter might point in the right direction, for Baudrillard says that to interact with doubles is "to speak to one's body and to speak to language" (141). In the more familiar words of composition theory, I think we might translate this as a suggestion that we can help students return to the more pleasurable, primitive position by constantly asking them to reflect on their prose style from the standpoint of their felt sense.

Many might object that the emphasis on prose style I've delineated in this chapter can lead—no matter how much I invoke the felt sense—only to an empty and deadening formalism that our students will find an absolute bore. Surely they'll find no pleasure in writing unless the topic they're writing about has something to do with their own lives, their own ideas.

For example, when we were discussing their drafts for the essay in which students had to analyze the stylistic features of the concluding paragraphs of some of the essays we had been reading, the first question everyone wanted to raise was whether or not they could write about the tone of those endings by referring to their own personal experience of the ending. They kept asking, "Are we allowed to say, 'I feel that . . .' or 'My experience of this ending is . . .'"

Of course, my answer was yes. I was intrigued by their desire to take control over this daunting topic by connecting it to their own experience, so much so that I asked them how they might like to make more room in the next assignment topic for discussing their own experience. They responded in a general way by saying they didn't much care about how the assignment made this possibility available to them, just so long as the possibility was there. "All semester long," one of them said, "we've been writing about other writers," and, as the rest of the class nodded in agreement, the student went on, "so before the semester ends, can we please, please just write about ourselves." Many of those who had been nodding in agreement began to speak up: "Yeah, yeah, that would be good. We've done enough with the readings—let's just write about ourselves for once."

"All right," I said, "the last paper—which, as you know, has to be written in class—will be just about you."

They cheered.

And so, just before the last day of the semester, I gave them the following topic and told them they would have a little less than an hour to write, and added that they could not bring notes or outlines to class that day. Normally, my students dread this particular requirement of my department's composition curriculum, but this time they seemed excited. I began the topic with two quotes from their fellow students that had appeared during a self-reflexive journal assignment I had given them a few weeks prior. . . . Here's the topic:

"Okay, this is going to sound like I'm a nerd, but I already think this class is fun."

—STARR MOFFETT

"I actually enjoyed linking the stylistic devices into my paper."
—BRADLEY YEE

On Tuesday, April 30th, you will write a short paper in class. The paper should be roughly 500 words. Do not, however, waste valuable time counting the words—instead, before class that day, count how many words written in your own handwriting fill up a page and, from there, figure out how many pages you need to fill to create a long enough essay. Also, be sure to leave time at the end of the class period to proofread your work so no misspellings or grammatical errors disrupt the reader's experience of your paper.

As these two quotes from Starr and Bradley suggest, some people think that writing can be fun. What do you suppose are the crucial ingredients that make writing a pleasurable experience? If your experience this semester has differed significantly from that of Starr and Bradley, then attack their position: analyze how and why your own experience is so different, why their claims don't ring true. On the other hand, if you feel as though you can relate to their experience, then analyze this experience and explain what makes writing fun.

WORKS CITED

Baudrillard, Jean. 1993. *Symbolic Exchange and Death.* Trans. Iain Hamilton Grant. Thousand Oaks, CA: Sage.

Bazerman, Charles. 1992. "Theories That Help Us Write Better." In *A Rhetoric of Doing: Essays on Written Discourse in Honor of James L. Kinneavy,* eds. Stephen Witte, Neil Nakadate, and Roger Cherry. Carbondale: Southern Illinois University Press.

Boler, Megan. 1999. *Feeling Power: Emotions and Education.* New York: Routledge.

Burke, Kenneth. 1945. *A Grammar of Motives*. Berkeley: University of California Press.

Connors, Robert. 2000. "The Erasure of the Sentence." *College Composition and Communication* 52 (1): 96–128.

Covino, William. 1994. *Magic, Literacy, Rhetoric: An Eccentric History of the Composing Imagination*. Albany: State University of New York Press.

Crowley, Sharon, and Debra Hawhee. 1999. *Ancient Rhetorics for Contemporary Students*. New York: Longman.

De Romilly, Jacqueline. 1992. *The Great Sophists of Periclean Athens*. Trans. Janet Lloyd. Oxford: Oxford University Press.

Dewey, John. 1994. *Democracy in Education*. New York: The Free Press.

Elbow, Peter. 1981. *Writing with Power: Techniques for Mastering the Writing Process*. New York: Oxford University Press.

———. 1985/1999. "The Shifting Relationships Between Speech and Writing." In *The Braddock Essays, 1975–1998*, ed. Lisa Ede. Boston: Bedford/St. Martin's Press.

Gallop, Jane. 1997. *Feminist Accused of Sexual Harrassment*. Durham, NC: Duke University Press.

Harris, Joseph. 1996. *A Teaching Subject: Composition Since 1966*. Upper Saddle River, NJ: Prentice Hall.

Harris, Robert. 2003. *Writing with Clarity and Style*. Los Angeles: Pyrczak Publishing.

Havelock, Eric. 1963. *Preface to Plato*. Oxford: Blackwell.

hooks, bell. 2000. "Rhapsody Remembered: Dancing with Words." *Journal of Advanced Composition* 20 (1): 1–8.

Jarratt, Susan. 1998. *Rereading the Sophists: Classical Rhetoric Refigured*. Carbondale: Southern Illinois University Press.

Katz, Stephen. 1996. *The Epistemic Music of Rhetoric*. Carbondale: Southern Illinois University Press.

Kinneavy, James. 1986. "Kairos: A Neglected Concept in Classical Rhetoric." In *Rhetoric and Praxis*, ed. Jean Dietz Moss. Washington, DC: Catholic University of America Press.

Lanham, Richard. 1974. *Style: An Anti-Textbook*. New Haven, CT: Yale University Press.

———. 1983. *Analyzing Prose*. New York: Scribner's.

———. 1991. *A Handlist of Rhetorical Terms*. Berkeley: University of California Press.

Murray, Donald. 1972/1997. "Teach Writing as a Process, Not a Product." In *Cross-Talk in Comp Theory*, ed. Victor Villanueva. Urbana, IL: National Council of Teachers of English.

———. 1982. "Teaching the Other Self: The Writer's First Reader." *College Composition and Communication* 23 (2): 140–46.

Neel, Jasper. 1988. *Plato, Derrida, and Writing*. Carbondale: Southern Illinois University Press.

O'Keefe, Daniel Lawrence. 1982. *Stolen Lightning: The Social Theory of Magic*. New York: Continuum.

Ong, Walter. 1975/1997. "The Writer's Audience Is Always a Fiction." In *Cross-Talk in Comp Theory*, ed. Victor Villanueva. Urbana, IL: National Council of Teachers of English.

Perl, Sondra. 1980. "Understanding Composing." *College Composition and Communication* 31 (4): 363–69.

———. 1994. "A Writer's Way of Knowing: Guidelines for Composing." In *Presence of Mind: Writing and the Domain Beyond the Cognitive*, eds. Alice Glarden Brand and Richard Graves, 77–88. Portsmouth, NH: Boynton/Cook.

Rose, Mike. 1980. "Rigid Rules, Inflexible Plans, and the Stifling of Language: A Cognitivist Analysis of Writer's Block." *College Composition and Communication* 31 (4): 389–400.

Vitanza, Victor. 1997. *Negation, Subjectivity, and the History of Rhetoric*. Albany: State University of New York Press.

Williams, Joseph. 1981. "The Phenomenology of Error." *College Composition and Communication* 32 (2): 152–68.

———. 2000. *Style: Ten Lessons in Clarity and Grace*. New York: Longman.

Williams, Raymond. 1977. *Marxism and Literature*. New York: Oxford University Press.

Worsham, Lynn. 1991. "Writing Against Writing: The Predicament of Écriture Feminine in Composition Studies." In *Contending with Words: Composition and Rhetoric in a Postmodern Age*, eds. Patricia Harkin and John Schilb, 82–104. New York: Modern Language Association.

———. 1993. "Emotion and Pedagogic Violence" *Discourse* 15 (2): 119–49.

Young, Richard. 1982. "Concepts of Art and the Teaching of Writing." In *The Rhetorical Tradition in Modern Writing*, ed. James J. Murphy. New York: Modern Language Association.

23   *The National Prose Problem*

KATHRYN FLANNERY

I have been led from basic writing to Shakespeare by what seems to me an unbroken chain of implication.

—E. D. Hirsch, "Culture and Literacy"

All of us who teach about words find ourselves, nowadays, caught up in three overlapping perplexities: a literacy crisis so widespread it has shaken our national self-esteem as an educated democracy; a school and college curriculum that no longer knows what subjects should be studied or when; and a humanism so directionless, unreasoned, and sentimental that it seems almost to quest for Senator Proxmire's Golden Fleece.

—Richard Lanham, *Literacy and the Survival of Humanism*

The independence of liberal arts education from establishment values is an illusion.

—Anthony Grafton and Lisa Jardine,
From *Humanism to the Humanities*

Almost daily, news reports remind us that we are in the midst of a "literacy crisis." Literacy makes the headlines with warnings about how little young people know, how little they read, how little they write (and when they do write, how abysmal are the results). As the historian Carl Kaestle notes, "in the past few years measurement experts have documented low functional-literacy skills among young adults, educators have decried falling test scores, humanists have argued about the need for more 'cultural literacy,' books by reformers have warned us of an 'illiterate America,' and legislators have submitted bills to 'eliminate illiteracy.' Television networks, newspaper chains, business councils, and prominent political figures have joined the campaign" (xiii). Underlying the often heightened rhetoric is the assumption

From *The Emperor's New Clothes: Literature, Literacy, and the Ideology of Style* (Pittsburgh: University of Pittsburgh Press, 1995), 174–98.

that somehow things have gotten worse. Students somehow cannot read or write as students once could. The average citizen appears less able to handle written language than citizens in the past. While social historians in the last twenty-five years—Kaestle among them—have challenged any simple picture of a golden age of literacy, documenting, for example, an expansion rather than a decline in literacy and in access to literacy education since the turn of the century, educators and politicians continue nonetheless to write and lecture and legislate as if that national literate culture we were supposed to have enjoyed in the past was seriously threatened.

One could argue about definitions of literacy, about how the ante has been upped, about how what counts as literate behavior now is something more or at least other than it was at the turn of the century. One could consider how the United States has been "welcoming" new immigrants in increasing numbers, an estimated 562,000 people in 1985 (excluding refugees and illegal aliens)—less than the high in 1910 of 1,041,570, but more than at any other time in this century—and how such an increase in primarily non-English-speaking residents strains an already overburdened and undersupported educational system (Melville 14). One could consider the changing nature of the workplace and changing requirements for educating an employable citizenry (Sarmiento and Kay). The social, political, and economic factors that intersect with literacy, shaping in fact what it is and what it is good for, are numerous and complex. But few of the most public discussions of the so-called literacy crisis deal with that complexity and, in fact, cannot deal with it and still maintain a crisis rhetoric. It is crisis rhetoric that, while presumed to generate federal and state support, obscures the extent to which literacy campaigns can be both well-meaning and in the service of hegemonic structures.

. . . E. D. Hirsch . . . and . . . Richard Lanham [are] two influential writers who have attempted to confront the literacy question in some of its complexity as it impacts specifically on higher education. For both Hirsch and Lanham, literacy is situated in the American context in relation to particular social, economic, and political forces. Hirsch, for example, begins *Cultural Literacy: What Every American Needs to Know* with the assertion that the sort of literacy he advocates is the "only reliable way of combating the social determinism that now condemns [disadvantaged children] to remain in the same social and educational condition as their parents" (xiii). Hirsch explicitly connects literacy learning with social goals, with racial equality, with economic advantage. Similarly, in *Literacy and the Survival of Humanism*, Lanham places literacy in the midst of the changing needs of a "multiracial and multilingual America" (115). He ties literacy to the changing cultural character of America and to the needs of a democracy.

Each writer sees before him a literacy crisis, and each believes that to address that crisis is also to address other social ills. What they do not do, however, is interrogate that causal equation; they do not explore the extent to which literacy may not be the primary causal factor in bettering the human condition; they presume that literacy (as they define it) is good for you, will lead to better jobs, greater self-esteem, greater capacity to live in a complex world, and more active involvement in the democratic process, despite considerable and readily available evidence to the contrary.[1] Ultimately, each acknowledges something of the complexity of the literacy question in late twentieth-century America only to shut down the question, to put the complexity out of play. And (significantly) for each writer, style operates as a detour around that complexity.

For Hirsch, style is initially the primary site for solving the literacy crisis, but in later work it becomes the sign of the "doctrine of educational formalism" that he condemns. Educational formalism is, in his terms, an attempt to evade the interestedness of educational decisions: a "spirit of neutrality" misleads us into thinking that literacy is mere skill rather than "political decision" ("Cultural Literacy" 161–62). But Hirsch does not mean "political" (or "cultural," for that matter) in a contestatory or fluid sense of negotiated meanings, and he certainly does not mean that the classroom itself is one of the places where political decisions are constantly being negotiated (Hirsch says very little about pedagogy, in fact). Rather, he means that schools have to decide what will count as requisite cultural knowledge—not once and for all and not exclusively as the province of the schools, but largely as within teachers' control as culture makers ("Cultural Literacy" 166) and with relative stability because cultural knowledge rests primarily on traditional materials (*Cultural Literacy* 137). What might have served as a needed critique of the ideology of style (and through it, a critique of English studies), ends up being (despite Hirsch's disclaimers) fodder for a reactionary turn in American educational debate.

Richard Lanham also yokes style to literacy, beginning as does Hirsch with the problem of teaching composition at the university level and moving to the larger issues of educating citizens in a democracy. His first target and, to some extent, his perpetual nemesis is C B S style—a normative style promoting the three god terms, Clarity, Brevity, and Sincerity, at the expense of play. "America's current epidemic verbal ineptitude comes on two levels," he argues in *Revising Prose* (1987). There is the rudimentary level and that is a matter of "simply functional literacy" ("students on this level make mistakes from ignorance . . . they don't know the rules") and there is the stylistic level and that is a matter of having available a greater range of stylistic options ("you are not so much making 'writing errors' as trying . . . to imitate a predominant [normative] style") (vii). Someone else will have to be responsible for functional literacy (elementary and high school teachers presumably). Lanham concentrates instead on promoting a greater stylistic range by teaching us how to bring to wholeness the two halves of human nature, *Homo sapiens* (the Platonic principle) joined to *Homo ludens* (the Ovidian principle)—uniting, one might say, both Hirsch's "communicative efficiency" and Bakhtin's "*carnivale*."

This binary system evolves through the course of Lanham's writing to encompass a rather remarkable range of activity. In an address to the 1988 conference, Liberal Arts Education in the Late Twentieth Century: Emerging Conditions, Responsive Practices—a conference that received rather unusual media coverage because of its purportedly radical agenda—Lanham shifts from his earlier "motives of eloquence" to an "essential bistable alternation between the contingent and the absolute." It was precisely this bistable alternation, Lanham argues, upon which "the educational system that was invented to sustain democracy" was built in the first place—a base we need to return to if the humanities are to survive.

> If you want to teach citizenship in American democracy, you don't build your educational system on Hirsch's collection of canonical facts, or [William] Bennett's collection of canonical texts—or on Allan Bloom's collection of rancid Platonic pieties either. You build it . . . upon this essential bistable alternation between the contingent and the absolute. The only true absolute, in such a secular democratic education, is the obligation to keep that oscillation going, preserving a bistable core for the Western tradition which is not timeless but forever in time. The ways to do this are as infinite as the particular courses such a curriculum would create, but the center remains the same. ("Extraordinary Convergence" 51)

Although Lanham clearly distinguishes his notion of oscillation from Hirsch's infamous list, there are nonetheless rather striking similarities in their projects. Lanham, like Hirsch, understands the educational crisis in terms of binaries, and like Hirsch he argues for favoring one member of the binary pair over the other in order to right what is perceived to be the present imbalance. Each looks for a core, a center that will keep in check the centrifugal forces that threaten the liberal arts. Lanham's core is a return to rhetoric as the mother system, as the integrative heart, the common language of a liberal arts education, giving back to the lower-division courses the breadth that he believes has been eroded by increased pressure to specialize coming from the upper-division tendency toward "reductive specialized inquiry" ("Extraordinary Convergence" 49, 53). That common language is not so far removed from (though perhaps less literal-minded than) Hirsch's notion of cultural literacy as a national vocabulary or lexicon. Both men say that they are *not* proposing a static curriculum but rather a kind of antidote to perceived chaos. Like the post-Restoration move to find stability after the English civil wars and the nineteenth-century efforts to both accommodate and contain reform, Lanham and Hirsch represent a liberal desire to make room for learning by checking a cultural decentering whose most immediate origins might be located in the sixties but whose roots might be seen as planted more deeply in the promise of radical democracy.

Paul Feyerabend has argued that "liberal intellectuals are also 'rationalists.' And they regard rationalism (which for them coincides with science) not just as one view among many, but as a basis for society. The freedom they defend is therefore granted under conditions that they are no longer subjected to. It is granted only to those who have already accepted part of the rationalist (i.e., scientific) ideology" (77). This has meant *"equality of access to one particular tradition"* (77). While Lanham in particular wants to make room for the ludic, for what might be viewed as other than scientific, he (like Hirsch and Fred Newton Scott before him) nonetheless remains a rationalist, wary of extremes, wanting to admit more learners to a single tradition, rather than altering the fundamental grounding ideology. While both Lanham and Hirsch say they want to protect democracy, they register in their very concern for core/center/stability a fear of the consequences of a democracy unchecked. They embody, therefore, many of the conflicts I have traced and help to make visible what is at stake in the convergence of literature, literacy, and the ideology of style.

Hirsch and Lanham in their professional careers have straddled the institutional divide between literary study and the teaching of composition. Both have written about literature and both have directed composition programs—the institutionalized home for literacy instruction at the post-secondary level. In the not too distant past, this was not an unusual pattern. In fact, the Conference on College Composition and Communication (CCCC), the primary professional organization in composition studies, was founded in 1949 by men whose scholarly training was in literature but whose teaching and service obligations led them to reflect on the rather daunting task of managing often large freshman English programs.[2] Rather than keeping tidy and separate the two spheres of their professional lives—the scholarly and the service sectors—Hirsch and Lanham have drawn from the scholarly, from their literary study in their efforts to develop composition programs and, conversely, have found in composition a key to the salvation of the humanities. For Hirsch, this means drawing on the philosophy of language that underpins his literary theory (which hinges on the notion that the same thing can be said in different ways) and on a history of prose style (which he reads as revealing the progressive tendency toward ever greater communicative efficiency), to posit first a program for teaching writing and more recently a program for reforming all of education from elementary to post-secondary. Lanham also draws on a philosophy of language (more Wittgenstein, Kenneth Burke, and I. A. Richards than Hirsch's dyadic linguistics) and a history of prose from which he builds a theory of complex human motive (an explicitly Burkean term) to argue first for a composition program and more recently for a program by which composition can save English studies.

E. D. Hirsch had already published *Wordsworth and Schelling, Innocence and Experience*, and *Validity in Interpretation* when he stepped down from the departmental chairmanship at the University of Virginia in 1970 to direct composition. He refers to this move as a "conversion experience": "I write as one converted from aestheticism to the more practical side of an English teacher's responsibilities" (*The Philosophy of Composition* xii). Starting from the presumption of a divided field (theory as opposed to practice, literature as opposed to composition, the aesthetic as opposed to the practical), and having engaged in "an intensive study" of research in composition, Hirsch concludes that his previous literary studies had very little to do with this "more practical side." Hirsch's confession makes sense historically: nineteenth-century aestheticism arose in part in opposition to a rhetorical understanding of how texts work in the world; and, certainly, the ties that bound composition and literature together earlier in this century have been largely severed through increasing specialization, greater emphasis placed on graduate education and educating majors rather than on general education, and a devaluing of teaching more generally. But his confession also makes sense in terms of his own theory. His earlier work may not have appeared to him to have much to do with "practical" composition, but his philosophy of language and his theory of interpretation lead directly to his philosophy of composition and its later revision into cultural literacy.

In *The Philosophy of Composition* (1977), Hirsch argues for a particular kind of literacy on the basis of his construction of a history of prose style. The history of prose as he sees it reveals an "irresistible tendency" toward ever greater "communicative functionality" (*Philosophy* 52–53); and to resist such "progressive" tendencies, he warns, would lead not only to "logical and practical incoherence" but to (an unnamed) "social harm as well" (4). One could deconstruct Hirsch's argument to show that the concept *communicative functionality*—or what he calls later "intrinsic communicative effectiveness" ("Measuring" 196)—at the heart of his theory operates as an ahistorical term and thus cancels out his claim to be making a historical argument. Or, one could charge him with stacking the deck, with having premised an historical imperative, chosen his facts such that his history would support his pedagogy, thereby leaving no room but for the teacher to accept as inevitable that pedagogy. But Hirsch is too visible both within the academy and without to be dismissed so easily at the textual level.

Hirsch had committed himself to developing a theory that would make it possible to argue for validity in interpretation. His desire for certainty in the face of modern tendencies toward relativism is evident in his several articles on literary theory in *Critical Inquiry* and in his books *The Aims of Interpretation* and *Validity in Interpretation*. But that desire is evident as well in *The Philosophy of Composition* and in the subsequent series of revisionary articles in which Hirsh modifies his style-centered philosophy of composition to incorporate a cultural content. Certainty, for Hirsch, pivots on the principle that "meaning is unchanging" (*Validity* 214), which is an attempt, as David Hoy rightly observes, to counter what Hirsch considers "radical historicism" (Hoy 13–14). Thus for Hirsch, the reader can understand the (unchanging) meaning of the text independent of the interpretive context in which understanding takes place. The importance of a work may vary over time, in different contexts, but the meaning of the text remains the same, available to any reader.

In Hirsch's writings on literary theory, this theoretically determinate meaning is tied to a concept of author intentionality; put simply, the text's meaning is that meaning intended by the author (Literary Criticism Conference [Georgetown] 1985). In his work on composition, the principle of unchanging meaning is incorporated into the history of language and prose as underpinning the possibility of establishing a progressive history: if the meanings of texts stay the same, as Hirsch posits, we can then place them with certainty in relation to one another and evaluate their communicative functionality relative to other fixed texts. Unchanging meaning is further augmented in this argument by the corollary principle that the same meaning can be communicated through different combinations of words. It is just that some combinations are more efficient than others. Thus, in his early work, Hirsch could argue that not only can we place texts in a *certain* (in the sense of established) order, but we can evaluate the efficacy of each text against an ahistorical, acultural standard of relative readability.

Hirsch's theory of certainty in composition and literature generated ample opposition within the academy (cf. Hoy, Doherty, Douglas). But there is a very real sense in which none of the critiques seems to account for the strength or persistence of Hirsch's agenda. A clue to that strength is not to be found so much in theoretical consistency but in relation to an ideological climate in which what Hirsch argued—first with author intentionality and stability of meaning and later with the importance of cultural knowledge—appears to any reasonable man (to borrow the lawyer's phrase) as common sense. I would argue that Hirsch has given theoretical voice to what many of our students believe about reading, writing, language, and meaning; what their parents (and our parents) believe; what writing teachers in their gut understand when they ask students to "say the same thing, but in different words," and what literature teachers mean when they "get" students to "see" the text (or say to colleagues, "But *Antigone* is not about civil disobedience; it is about . . ."). Hirsch has given voice to the fundamental theoretical ground for what common law honors in the concept of the objective standard; what strict constructionist jurists such as former Attorney General Edmund Meese or Chief Justice William Rehnquist assert; what much of Protestant exegesis rests on; what William Bennett had striven for in his call for a national education policy. Even though Hirsch personally distances himself from the political Right, his philosophy of language and of meaning, in so markedly opposing "historical relativism" (which in Hirsch is equated with Marxism), lends itself to rightist readings.

Hirsch is neither villain nor hero in this piece. But he has been a remarkably vocal and public player whose ideas are embedded in the common life of most people inside and outside the academy. The fact, however, that one needs to argue for common sense, to build bulkheads around it against the rising tide of historical relativism, suggests that there is something more at stake here than the simple, innocent (however ironic) "desire to be right," as Hirsch has put it. It does have to do with an "ideology of truth"—again, his language—but not in the neutral, nonideological sense in which Hirsch attempts to use that phrase ("Politics of Theories of Interpretation" 235–36). Like the nineteenth-century advocates for the teaching of English before him, Hirsch has offered, in *The Philosophy of Composition* and more recently in *Cultural Literacy*, a version of literacy that aims to increase access, a laudable goal, at the same time that it staves off more radical cultural critique, a critique that may be necessary before larger cultural structures are changed to make other than token access a reality. I am thinking here, for example, of Anthony Sarmiento's call for changes in the workplace that would create a more hospitable, more democratic home for the exercise of more complex literacies.

If *The Philosophy of Composition* is the product of one conversion experience, *Cultural Literacy* is the product of another. After spending some time researching the "actual effects of a piece of prose as compared to its potential optimal effects on a competent audience" in order to determine "intrinsic communicative effectiveness" (see, for example, "Measuring the Communicative Effectiveness of Prose"), Hirsch in 1980 reported his "shock of revelation" in discovering that what he calls the "craft of writing," coherence, organization, syntax, and so on, is not all there is to writing. Style is not everything. It is only half the story. The other half of the story is the "cultural aspect of writing." But it is apparent that that "cultural aspect" becomes visible only when composition—the "practical side"—threatens the humanist heart of English studies.

In a telling move, Hirsch ties his revelation to the job market and to funding:

> I hope you will be tolerant if, still reeling from my newest conversion, I speak with some of the one-sidedness that new converts are all too apt to exhibit. Such one-sidedness may be just what is needed at the moment, since the craft approach to writing is so powerfully in the ascendant. Specialists in the craft of composition are in great demand for teaching posts. Money for composition research is easy to come by. And even now, as I write, Yale University is pondering ways of spending a grant of 1.25 million dollars to improve the writing abilities of Yale undergraduates. ("Culture and Literacy" 27–28)

As long as the heart of English studies remains unthreatened, composition can be treated as the teaching of craft—in fact, it would appear the less threatening as long as it is just the teaching of craft (important but not prestigious in the way teaching art would be, in this dichotomized discursive arena). Hirsch gallantly can offer to straighten out the compositionists' ideological muddle, to "uncover ever more efficient ways to teach [writing as craft]." But when real money and real jobs seem to validate the practical side of what we do in such a way that the practical side threatens the heart, it appears to be time to reconsider. Humanist values have to be brought back into view as the controlling center of the enterprise.

The problem here is not with Hirsch's claim that there is more to writing than craft. A number of critics of Hirsch have granted him the importance of knowledge, of *knowing about* (cf. Bartholomae, "Released into Language" 87). Indeed one might make a far more radical argument than has Hirsch about the capacity of composition, because of its apparent contentlessness (its very uncenteredness), to more readily make space for previously subjugated knowledges. But Hirsch's is no radical project. He does not construct a pedagogy that concerns itself with working on or producing knowledges—either of which might allow him to reconceptualize the relationships between writing and reading, between composition and literature. Instead, in commenting on the institutional allocation of resources he makes clear what is at stake: his dichotomized view of the field requires a practical side to be responsible for basic literacy, in contradistinction to the more highly valued, theoretically and aesthetically privileged domain of cultural content. It is particularly troubling to have the positivist-convert Hirsch claim that all work in composition has been as narrowly conceived as his own in order to disclaim such work so that the cultural-literacy-convert Hirsch can reclaim space for an embattled humanism.

Hirsch came across the importance of "extra-linguistic knowledge of the subject matter" while conducting a series of experiments measuring reading comprehension. Subjects were given both a well-written essay and the "same" essay "stylistically degraded." Hirsch expected that the "stylistically degraded" version would pose more difficulties for readers (assuming that clarity is exclusively a stylistic feature). But this turned out not to be the case. Hirsch found instead that style alone did not determine reading ease ("Culture and Literacy" 38). As he reports in a later article, "good style contributes little to our reading of unfamiliar material because we must continually backtrack to test out different hypotheses about what is being meant or referred to. . . . Style begins to lose its importance as a factor in reading unfamiliar material" ("Cultural Literacy" 163). This, it should be noted, is something that critics of readability have been saying for some time, but Hirsch is really not interested in abandoning altogether the formulaicism that informed his earlier work.

One may still refer to a text as having a "good style," but familiarity with the topic seemed to be the stronger determiner of reading ease. Hirsch deduced from this finding that there is "an unbroken continuum from cultural literacy, to literacy in reading, and thence to competence in writing." How could anyone write better than they read, he asks. If there is such a strong connection between reading and writing, it is reasonable to assume that training in writing skill alone will not lead to "advancement in general literacy." Indeed, Hirsch extends his argument to say that not only will training in basic skills alone not advance general literacy, but training in the writing process by itself is also inadequate: "This (for me) newly-won insight fosters a certain skepticism about the practical importance of new researches into the writing process. I am strongly in favor of this research. We can never learn too much about the most efficient and successful methods of teaching the skills of writing. On the other hand, we also need a reminder that even in the domain of writing skill per se, the cultural element always obtrudes" ("Culture and Literacy" 38–43).

In this early article, Hirsch ties his new insight to the Ann Arbor court case in which African American parents argued that white teachers should learn the language conventions of the African American community. Hirsch reads this case ("behind the ideological rhetoric") as confirming his sense that standardized methods of teaching writing cannot meet the diverse needs of diverse populations, an insight that seems to get lost in his later work, *Cultural Literacy: What Every American Needs to Know*, and that has certainly been lost on readers who have found in Hirsch support for the imposition of a national curriculum ("Culture and Literacy" 43–44). As long as culture is a content and writing is a skill, the possibility of thinking of language as always already cultural stays safely out of play. To really think of culture as fundamentally informing would mean that one could not simply add cultural content to the pedagogical pot without also changing the pot.

But culture as content preserves a place for the liberal arts, for a humanism that is threatened by a technological (practical) world. This is not a new story, as the history of nineteenth-century practice makes clear. The question, as Hirsch puts it, has been how to negotiate between "two equally American traditions of unity and diversity" ("Cultural Literacy" 161) or, put more politically explicitly, how to negotiate between cultural difference and cultural protectionism. In a 1983 essay in *The American Scholar*, Hirsch offers a brief history of the problem. The schools have been the place where the American culture was shaped by trying to "harmonize the various traditions of the parent cultures" but also by attempting to create what was uniquely American. The former celebrates pluralism; the latter, unity. We have resisted "narrow uniformity," Hirsch suggests, at the same time that we have striven for a "national culture." But now, in the late twentieth century, the balance has been tipped: in English courses—along with history, the subject closest to "culture making"—"diversity and pluralism now reign without challenge." Hirsch believes that such extreme diversity and pluralism threaten efforts to achieve a more literate culture. To correct the imbalance "we shall need to restore certain common contents to the humanistic side of the school curriculum" ("Cultural Literacy" 160–61).

Proposing something between the hyperbolic extremes of "lockstep, Napoleonic prescription of texts on the one side, and extreme laissez-faire pluralism on the other," Hirsch suggests that it would be useful to have "a lexicon of cultural literacy" available as a "guide to objects of instruction" ("Cultural Literacy" 166, 168). The choice of what should be this shared information is, he grants, a political one—not to be decided by "educational technicians" (an undefined phrase) but perhaps by a National Board of Education on the model of the New York State Board of Regents, "an imposing body of practical idealists" or, short of that, given our national suspicion of anything resembling a "ministry of culture," perhaps a consortium of universities or foundations or associations ("Cultural Literacy" 167–68). *Political* thus does not mean anything approximating democratic or even representative. And given recent controversies over such national ministries of culture as NEA and NEH and their political vulnerability, Hirsch now might modify his stance. The point, however, is to note how balance between unity and diversity in educational policy making is to be achieved through central control that on the face of it, tips the balance rather heavily toward unity (or order).

Unfortunately, what gets lost in all the talk about a national lexicon (the list) and a centralized board of education is any consideration of pedagogy, by which I mean not Hirsch's diminished sense of process or method but a reflective praxis that is itself a refusal of the theory/practice dichotomy (a dichotomy sustained as much by composition teachers as literature teachers).

Given Hirsch's dichotomized view of things, he has to think either form or content, process or product, writing or reading, craft or art.[3] And such dichotomized thinking allows pedagogy to be trivialized into mere method. One might grant Hirsch his point that too much of schooling is so frightened of offending *somebody* that curricula has been constructed (and the passive construction is appropriate here) as if it were culturally neutral ("Cultural Literacy" 169), as if we could achieve that Royal Society ideal of pure knowledge. But to think differently about literacy, and schooling more generally, requires that we read the politics even of what purports to be politically neutral, not by maintaining the binaries that sustain such ideological disingenuousness but by deconstructing them. Because Hirsch is so invested in one half of the binary equation, however, even when he has the insight to see the limitation of such bifurcation, he has to reinscribe it in order to maintain his own privileged position. The answer, as he poses it—and Hirsch is hardly unique here—is to alter instrumentalist pedagogies by simply inserting a controlled content, rather than reimagining the classroom, reimagining the relationship between content and form, ideology and style. When Hirsch discovered that readers had to backtrack in order to make sense of unfamiliar material, he might have reimagined writing/reading pedagogy as providing the occasion for students to take such backtracking as the opportunity to learn. Instead of preteaching, to call up James Moffett's insightful term, instead of, that is, prereading texts for students so that they learn a lexicon *in order to* read or write, one might approach backtracking as precisely that process by which all of us learn to teach ourselves how to make sense of a text, generating questions that lead us to read more, to talk with others, to write it out, to *make* it make sense.[4]

The lack of any real attention to the classroom might alert us to the extent to which Hirsch is not really interested in changing very much. Neither laboratory experiments with cooked texts nor a canned lexicon gets us very far toward understanding the complex arena of the classroom. Changing what we teach without theorizing more fully a pedagogical dialogics—how the way we teach has the potential to reshape the content and how the content pressures how we teach—changes very little. To theorize a pedagogical dialogics, however, would require that one abandon the philosophy of language on which Hirsch's project works—one *cannot* in fact say the *same* thing in different words—and that one deconstruct the dichotomies that keep literacy and literature institutionally separate.

Richard Lanham's work rests on a more explicitly playful sense of language and of style, leading him to try to reshape more than just content. From *Style: An Anti-Textbook* (1974) to his more recent work on the relationship of technology to the humanities, Lanham has offered not so much blueprints for change as sometimes gleeful inspiration for rearranging everything from academic structures to the very heart of civilization. But even in the midst of his talk of "oscillation" and playfulness and a homo ludens that can counter the stuffed shirts in and outside the academy, Lanham looks for a controlling center, less narrowly conceived than Hirsch but still protectionist in its desires. In

Literacy and the Survival of Humanism (1983), Lanham suggests the need for "homeostatic social regulators which will allow us, with our vast numbers and our lethal new toys, to survive." Such social regulation will have to come not from Marx or Mao—or even from Sir Thomas More and his utopian vision—but from something more like Castiglione's sense of *sprezzatura*: "the spontaneous affectation that self-consciously chooses to harmonize the various parts of our human nature and then pretends that this harmony is as natural as breathing." Human nature is prone to artifice, Lanham believes, and that artifice is the "generative concept of civility, of sociality itself" (12–13).

The old humanism, "which tried to repudiate stylistic motive," will not work anymore. For a uniquely American context—"America is the only country in the world rich enough to have the leisure, and democratic enough to have the inclination, to teach its whole citizenry not merely to write, but to write well" (*Style* ix)—and coming to the end of the culture of the book ("From Book to Screen"), a new (electronically informed) humanism that restores balance to human motive is needed. In a 1992 review of several books addressing the impact of electronic technology on the liberal arts, Lanham posits a rhetorical *paideia* or enculturation that might help accommodate (center) pedagogically and administratively a "non-hierarchical, non-canonical, interactive, unstable medium" such as the electronic text ("From Book to Screen" 206). Rhetoric—and more recently, the machine together with rhetoric—stand for order, not the stiffly serious order that Lanham describes variously as Newtonian, utopian, Edenic, Ramist, or Socratic, or the bureaucratic order represented in the C B S style, but a dynamic order more akin to the stylistic decorum of the early Renaissance as he reconstructs it but brought into a new electronic age. "Stylistic decorum measures how we look alternately at and through a text" and should stand at the center of the composition course and at the center of the liberal arts "more largely conceived" ("Extraordinary Convergence" 50).

Lanham had already written on Sidney's *Arcadia* (1965), *Tristram Shandy* (1973), and Renaissance rhetoric before turning in 1974 to a series of books on prose style intended for student and teacher use—all of which address what he sees as a "national prose problem." He has remarked that some of his friends thought that in this move he was "deserting" literature for composition—"as if a moderately well-established orthopedic surgeon had decided to abandon his practice and open an inner-city clinic in chiropractic acupuncture" (*Literacy* 2). Despite his friends' fears that his turn toward composition was akin to academic slumming, he saw his combined interests as making perfect sense. After all, the current literacy crisis as he read it paralleled in important features that of the Renaissance: "When the first humanist revival came to Europe in the Renaissance, it came as a result not only of a scholarly revolution—the rediscovery of classical texts—but also from a crisis of public literacy as hydra-headed as our own, one that comprehended the unsettling dangers of a Bible in English, the decay of church education following the Reformation, and an unprecedented social need for effective vernacular communication which would serve a plethora of new social, political, and economic purposes" (*Literacy* 177). The worldly and the scholarly came together in "a study of the word, a study of style." The present literacy crisis has the potential to become similarly centered.

In his version of the development of English as a discipline, Lanham explains the irony that we are now, after nearly a hundred years of practice, in a rather fine position to educate that society—"white, literate, and at least middle-class"—that was there at the founding of the Oxford English School in 1894:

> [The] process of disciplinary growth has now reached full self-conscious maturity: practitioners in the field are reflecting self-consciously on the boundary conditions of their own activity, anatomizing it into its careerist, gamelike, and creative aspects. The maturation was accelerated by the two go-go decades of academic prosperity from 1955 to 1975, a flood of students and money that released English studies not only from composition instruction, until then its historic base in America, but also from routine instruction in the lower division. The discipline was thus freed to draw in upon itself, become graduate- and professional-centered, and sponsor meta-level reflections upon literary texts and inquiry—upon, that is, itself. ("One, Two, Three" 15–16)

Despite brief distractions from the social upheaval of those years, Lanham contends that English studies developed in self-enclosed fashion. This allowed for a theoretical blossoming, but without much attention to the "social base": the "society in which English studies must function, in America at least, is no longer predominantly middle and upper middle class, nor is the dwindling white segment of it any longer reliably literate." Thus, "English studies, like so many armies in the past, now stands superbly equipped to fight the last war" ("One, Two, Three" 16). In this version of history, the foot soldiers—the composition teachers—may not know much theory, but they have a better sense than the generals of the enemy they face. They can see more clearly from the trenches the "enormous social need for instruction in language" ("One, Two, Three" 16).

Given the fact that graduate students and part-timers make up the bulk of composition teachers and that, in some institutions, few faculty see their students or their students' writing up close, Lanham can be said to register a disturbing truth. One might object that he oversimplifies institutional history—some theorists have been paying rather extraordinary attention to sociopolitical dimensions of English studies (if not until lately and with rather minimal impact on pedagogy), and composition has hardly been a theoretically virgin field (even if its tendency toward eclecticism may disturb theoretical purists). But Lanham is not so much interested in offering a messy materialist history of current practice as he is in constructing a fable with a particular moral. He makes a point of tweaking the theorists' noses for spending too much time examining their disciplinary navels, and yet he does not give over the hero's place to the composition Marthas set on theory-free foot washing. Instead, this fable requires a new — or, more accurately, a newly reformed — hero who will give social meaning and coherence to English studies. Lanham proposes that we bring back to center stage the liberal humanist, newly *pixilated*.

By rethinking what is at the center of both literature and composition study and teaching, Lanham hopes to preserve not only English studies as a discipline but the humanities more generally. "The literacy crisis presents literary studies with an enormous problem. We can of course ignore it, draw our wagons into a circle, and hope for the best. But if we do this, I think that sooner or later the problem will kill us. If we try instead to solve the crisis, dangerous as the trying will be, we may find that the crisis has redeemed us, both our teaching and our research — put literary study back in the center of modern humanism where in our hearts we know it belongs" ("One, Two, Three" 29). Having a big problem to solve — Lanham compares the literacy crisis to the problem faced by atomic physics during World War II — would give life to an English studies that may be at the end of an "exhausted paradigm." Literature faculty interesting themselves in composition might force a return to an earlier way of conceiving of the humanities — the Renaissance play of mixed motives with literature at the heart.

Some idea of what this might look like can be found in Lanham's *The Motives of Eloquence* (1976). Lanham "synthesizes a generic portrait" of "homo rhetoricus," one member of a binary opposition that Lanham constructs to characterize "Western man," the other member being "homo seriosus." The "Western self," Lanham posits, is a constantly shifting combination of these two members.[5] The function of literature is "to keep man in the rich central confusion of the mixed self . . . in the mixed middle, a self by turns central and social." That literature is best which neither veers too far toward seriousness nor too far toward play (32). Western man might wish to take himself seriously but, Lanham argues, "actual Western practice" suggests the extent to which Western man has trained himself rhetorically. Lanham does not cite "actual practice" but offers, instead, instructions for creating the rhetorical man: teach him young "a minute concentration on the word, how to write it, speak it, remember it. . . . Teach a taxonomy of impersonation. Drill the student incessantly on correspondences between verbal style and personality type, life style" . . . and so on. The student is urged to be forever "rehearsing," trying on different arguments, different stances, different selves. Rhetorical man is thus always an actor, "his reality public, dramatic" (2–4).

Our present literacy crisis is at least in part caused by our collective abandonment of such a (playful) rhetorical education, and that abandonment, Lanham argues, is sustained by a deep-seated suspicion of style: "The way we have trivialized the teaching of composition is exactly the way we have trivialized the liberal arts themselves. We teach comp only as the art of transparent expression of pure, apolitical, extrahuman truth. We remove the rhetoric, the human interest, from it." We have aspired to a pure utopian language; the "basic rhetorical impulses of competition and play are outlawed in favor of plain Edenic purpose." In such an Eden, style must give way to "an insub-stantial something we have learned to call 'substance'" ("Extraordinary Con-vergence" 49–50). Lanham blames this turn from style and rhetorical richness variously on Newtonian seriousness ("From Book to Screen" 202), Ramus's sense that "moral and formal judgments can never mix" ("Extraordinary Convergence" 47), and American pragmatism and American Puritanism (*Style* 10). Again, the rhetorical weight (whatever the historical slipperiness) of such shifting blame is to suggest how science, Puritanism, and pragmatism converge to push style, play, and ultimately humanism off center stage.

To restore humanism, and with it style and play, to their rightful position promises, in Lanham's fable, benefits for everyone from the individual stu-dent to the whole of western civilization. To the extent that "writing is a way to clarify, strengthen, and energize the self, to render individuality rich, full and social," a modern redeployment or appropriation of the Renaissance ideal of mixed motive has a kind of moral imperative: "What the act of writ-ing prose involves for the writer is an integration of his self, a deliberate act of balancing its two component parts. It represents an act of socialization, and it is by repeated acts of such socialization that we become sociable beings, that we grow up. Thus the act of writing models the presentation of self in society, constitutes a rehearsal for a social reality" (*Revising Prose* 105). The moral in-gredient, as Lanham poses it, works not on the message but on the sender. One should write well, then, "to invigorate and enrich [one's] selfhood, to in-crease, in the most literal sense, [one's] self-consciousness. . . . It makes [one] more alive" (*Revising Prose* 106). The style is thus the man himself, but "some-times as he is, sometimes as he wants to be, sometimes as he is palpably pretending to be, sometimes, as in comedy, both as he pretends to be and as he is" (*Style* 124). Not the Emersonian ideal, Lanham instead offers the self-fashioned courtier (or the Horatio Alger), the man of his own making, not class-marked, social but not socially or politically situated. A man, in other words, who does not live in this world.

This style-centered pedagogy, having its origins in the education of an elite, is stripped of its sociopolitical situatedness and offered up as an answer to American (classless) education. Despite his acknowledging the importance of political truth, Lanham's work rests on the assumption that transculturally, transhistorically, human motive is bistable. He does not look to see how social situation defines the nature of linguistic choosing. He stays, if not in the land of Clarity-Brevity-Sincerity, nonetheless in a land of ahistorical human nature. Lanham's playfulness, though appearing more flexible (and frankly more fun) than Hirsch's list making, cannot seem to acknowledge what Hirsch notes (if fails to fully understand): the determinative relationship between language and social status, the relationship between what jobs beckon what workers with what linguistic skills, the relationship between the kinds of literacies available to what students, and the relationship between what we know and what we can say. Who is deemed ready to play with language, after all? Who has the social right or luxury and the leisure to play? And why don't all kinds of language play count?

Too much of writing pedagogy, Lanham argues, has attempted to ban the expression of personality and social relationship through the imposition of an Official Style, with its moralizing, rule-centered pedagogy and its "simplistic static conception of self and society" (*Revising Prose* 115). The Renaissance ideal, however, is not without its own version of order. If we choose to resist the Official Style, Lanham makes clear, we will have to make room for expressions of personality and social relationships, but we will also have to *"try to control them"* (emphasis added; *Revising Prose* 113). Without control, we become a mob, represented most vividly for Lanham in the "tantrum prose" of political extremism (*Style* 126). One might hear in this an echo of Fred Newton Scott's fear of the Billy Sundays, earlier nineteenth-century fears of the illiterate rabble, and the Restoration fear of enthusiasm.

Stylistic decorum supplies the needed control. In describing the UCLA Writing Programs, Lanham suggests that because the "At/Through oscillation" is a natural outcome of a polyglot, multilingual university, teachers do not need to ask students to try on various styles as suggested in *Style: An Anti-Textbook*; rather, they have attempted to "reinvent a Drydenian middle style" (*Literacy* 175). Students, thus, do not in fact play with multiple styles, as Lanham earlier proposed, but work toward developing a "common language" to counter the centrifugal forces operating in the modern university. Leavis rather archly tagged Dryden with wanting to establish what was "correct" ("and what does 'correct' mean?" 95), but Lanham sees in the middle style hope for a common language. For all the celebration of oscillation, of stylistic play, when it comes down to conceptualizing a large writing program, Lanham opts for common language. Oscillation and play must be checked by commonality in terms remarkably like Hirsch's.

In much of his work, Lanham argues for a new pedagogy that is a return to a Renaissance model, modernized through technology and controlled so that it does not get out of hand. In its liberal lines, in its desire to control, it is in the direct line of descent from the nineteenth-century pedagogues. In a 1976 review of *Style*, Patrick Strong reads Lanham as a high Victorian liberal humanist "a la Mathew Arnold." Certainly Lanham is writing out of a tradition familiar to John Churton Collins, a pedagogy that situates itself in relation to some conception of an ideal past and sees itself as rescuing a version of liberal education that is perceived to be in peril. In Lanham's case, as in Leavis's and Eliot's, the ideal past is the style-conscious Renaissance (colored, in the case of the plan for the writing program, by a post-Restoration ethic). In order to oppose the utilitarians, foes we inherit from the nineteenth century (and before, if as Lanham views it they are aligned with Puritans [*Style* 10]), Lanham returns to the Renaissance to find a model for a "richer and more humane" pedagogy. At the same time, this more humane pedagogy has, as at least part of its aim, an opposition to what is read as extremism in terms similar to those used in the post-Restoration reaction to radical Puritanism.

Brian Doyle has remarked that "English and education both tend to carry the sense of an unproblematic national cultural heritage" (18). "Style" seems to operate in much the same way for Lanham, Hirsch, and the nineteenth-century pedagogues. But it is as evident in "disinterested" twentieth-century accounts of "style" as in earlier readings of "style" that (again to use Doyle's language) "style," like "English" and like "literature," represents a "ratification of a selective sense of culture and history" (18). The move that many academics make to try to clear themselves of the charge of bias (or, in its strongest form, the charge of cultural imperialism) is to argue in terms of a literary history that is simply factually there. As Lanham uses them, historical styles are simply there, already described for us like recipes to follow to produce new prose. Even when there is apparently some awareness of interconnections between "style" and "snob values" (*Motives* 3), such awareness does not serve to complicate the general presentation of "style" as classless. Neither Hirsch nor Lanham shies from the necessity of disseminating cultural value, but neither examines critically whose interest such values serve, assuming in fact that such values will serve all equally well.

The issue here, it should be stressed, is not that disseminating cultural values is necessarily bad, or that one could in fact teach in such a way that a course would be value-free. Rather, the problem is the refusal (perhaps the inability) to acknowledge the level to which any language learning is necessarily ideologically laden, and the reluctance to make that an explicit part of teaching (not by simply *telling* students how particular language forms are ideologically laden—not, that is, by playing the theoretical snake in the garden—but by engaging them in the question of how language in various forms works and has worked in the world).[6]

Indeed, the ideology of style—like the ideology of formalism more generally—directs us away from history and politics and complexity. The centripetal tendency to construct normalizing discourse inevitably involves constructing a vision of extremism, disorder, and mobbishness as the rhetorical counterweight to commonality, harmony, and rationality. I have been suggesting that we need to critically reread those terms in their material context in order to see how other cultural values—such as democracy and difference—may be lost in the recentering of normative discourse.

A study of style needs to pay attention to what has been and what continues to be at stake in struggles for cultural authority. This would mean . . . not simply adding names to the roster, or deleting canonical figures, or playing with styles supplied by the teacher but rereading and rewriting the collective cultural heritage with our students. In the present circumstance, the purported literacy crisis or the national prose problem tends to define the terms under which those of us who teach English operate. And those terms tend to derive from fairly unproblematized notions of reading, writing, and texts and generally unexamined notions of cultural heritage—much of which we inherit from the beginnings of the academic study of English in the nineteenth century. *Style* as used by Hirsch or Lanham offers no possibility for rethinking literacy, operating as it does as a detour to direct attention away from political or social issues. The study of style suggested here is not a solution to the so-called literacy crisis. But such studies of the implicatedness of language learning should lead us to question the ostensibly depoliticized discourse that dominates the present debate.

NOTES

1. Work in literacy studies since the 1970s has complicated our understanding of literacy. Earlier research had started from the premise that literacy represented a cognitive and cultural break from an oral (and savage) past: educational (and missionary) work concentrated on eliminating "illiteracy" locally and internationally; histories of the book and of printing presumed a Gutenberg revolution; and anthropological studies investigated what they took to be a radical break from "oral" to "literate" cultures. Thanks to the work of Harvey Graff, Natalie Zeman Davis, Brian Street, John Ogbu, Shirley Brice Heath, Sylvia Scribner and Michael Cole, and others who draw from crossdisciplinary (anthropological, educational, literary, linguistic, historical) culture studies, the literacy/illiteracy, civilized/savage sorts of dichotomies have been deconstructed— at least theoretically. But for various reasons that have not been adequately explored, such deconstruction has had relatively little impact on public policy makers, literacy workers (who must appeal for funds to the policy makers who do not do well with complex arguments), or the general public that supports (or fails to support) the policies and programs proposed and implemented by those policy makers and literacy workers.

2. A critical history of CCCC has yet to be written. The National Council of Teachers of English (NCTE) archives are underutilized, and Nancy Bird's dissertation, "The Conference on College Composition and Communication: A Historical Study of Its Continuing Education and Professionalization Activities, 1949–1975," while quite useful, focuses on organizational processes rather than institutional practices.

3. Gail Hawisher has critiqued Hirsch's content/process split, pointing out how disciplinary divisions exaggerate a false divide. But Hawisher, like Hirsch and Lanham, concludes that we should be seeking a balanced perspective—"a perspective that seeks not only to unite binary oppositions into productive synthesis but also seeks to preserve the rich diversity of knowledge among us" (16).

4. Mariolina Salvatori addresses the problem of a diminished sense of pedagogy in "Pedagogy: From the Periphery to the Center" and also the limitations of Hirsch's hermeneutic for the classroom in " 'Cultural Literacy': Critical Reading" and "Reading and Writing a Text."

5. Jonathan Crewe offers cogent criticism of Lanham's approach to the "problem of rhetoric," which he calls a "short cut": "Lanham's solution is to settle all the outstanding questions by begging them. Within an idealized Western order of things, the two principles oscillate without apparent cause or consequence, except that in doing so they maintain an exemplary balance" (5).

6. What is needed is the articulation of a postmodern rhetoric not as a globalizing pedagogy but as contingent, various, and local interventions, something Terry Eagleton hints at in the last pages of his *Literary Theory: An Introduction* and which I find versions of in Donahue and Quandahl's *Reclaiming Pedagogy*; in Paul Bové's "Theory as Practice, or, How One Studies Literature and Culture"; in Jerry Harste and colleagues' *Creating Classrooms for Authors* (aimed at teachers of young children but of potential interest to any teacher); and in Bartholomae and Petrosky's *Facts, Artifacts, and Counterfacts*.

WORKS CITED

Bartholomae, David. "Released into Language: Errors, Expectations, and the Legacy of Mina Shaughnessy." *The Territory of Language: Linguistics, Stylistics, and the Teaching of Composition.* Ed. Donald McQuade. Carbondale: Southern Illinois UP, 1986. 65–88.

Bartholomae, David, and Anthony Petrosky. *Facts, Artifacts, and Counterfacts: Theory and Method for a Reading and Writing Course.* Upper Montclair, NJ: Boynton, 1986.

Bird, Nancy. "The Conference on College Composition and Communication: A Historical Study of Its Continuing Education and Professionalization Activities, 1949–1975." Diss. Virginia Polytechnic and State U, 1977.

Bové, Paul. "Theory as Practice, or, How One Studies Literature and Culture." *Works and Days* 8 (1990): 11–28.

Collins, John Churton. *The Study of English Literature: A Plea for Its Recognition and Organization at the Universities.* New York: Macmillan, 1891.

Crewe, Jonathan V. *Unredeemed Rhetoric: Thomas Nashe and the Scandal of Authorship.* Baltimore: Johns Hopkins UP, 1982.

Davis, Natalie Zemon. *Society and Culture in Early Modern France: Eight Essays.* Stanford: Stanford UP, 1975.

Doherty, Paul C. "Hirsch's *Philosophy of Composition*: An Evaluation of the Argument." *College Composition and Communication* 33 (1982): 184–95.

Donahue, Patricia, and Ellen Quandahl, eds. *Reclaiming Pedagogy: The Rhetoric of the Classroom.* Carbondale: Southern Illinois UP, 1989.

Douglas, Wallace W. Rev. of *The Philosophy of Composition*, by E. D. Hirsch Jr. *College English* 40 (1978): 90–99.

Dowden, Edward. *New Studies in Literature.* London: Kegan Paul [1895].

Doyle, Brian. "The Hidden History of English Studies." *Re-Reading English.* Ed. Peter Widdowson. London: Methuen, 1982. 10–42.

Eagleton, Terry. *Literary Theory: An Introduction.* Oxford: Blackwell, 1983.

Feyerabend, Paul. *Science in a Free Society.* London: New Left Books, 1978.

Graff, Harvey Jr., ed. *Literacy and Social Development in the West: A Reader.* New York: Cambridge UP, 1981.

———. *Literacy in History: An Interdisciplinary Research Bibliography.* New York: Garland, 1981.

Grafton, Anthony, and Lisa Jardine. *From Humanism to the Humanities: Education and the Liberal Arts in Fifteenth- and Sixteenth-Century Europe.* Cambridge: Harvard UP, 1986.

Harste, Jerome, Kathy Short, and Carolyn Burke. *Creating Classrooms for Authors: The Reading-Writing Connection.* Portsmouth: Heinemann, 1988.

Hawisher, Gail. "Content Knowledge versus Process Knowledge: A False Dichotomy." *On Literacy and Its Teaching.* Ed. Gail Hawisher and Anna Soter. Albany: State U of New York P, 1990. 1–18.

Heath, Shirley Brice. *Ways With Words.* New York: Cambridge UP, 1983.

Hirsch, E. D., Jr. *Wordsworth and Schelling: A Typological Study of Romanticism.* New Haven: Yale UP, 1960.

———. *Innocence and Experience: An Introduction to Blake.* New Haven: Yale UP, 1964.

———. *The Aims of Interpretation.* Chicago: Chicago UP, 1976.

———. "Cultural Literacy." *The American Scholar* 52 (1983): 159–69.

———. *Cultural Literacy: What Every American Needs to Know.* Boston: Houghton, 1987.

———. "Culture and Literacy." *Journal of Basic Writing* 3 (1980): 27–47.

———. Literary Criticism Conference. Georgetown University, June 1985.

———. "Measuring the Communicative Effectiveness of Prose." *Writing: The Nature, Development, and Teaching of Written Communication.* Ed. Carl Fredriksen and Joseph Dominic. Vol. 2. Hillsdale: Erlbaum, 1981. 189–208.

———. *The Philosophy of Composition.* Chicago: U of Chicago P, 1977.

———. "The Politics of Theories of Interpretation." *Critical Inquiry* 9 (1982): 235–47.

———. *Validity in Interpretation.* New Haven: Yale UP, 1967.

Hoy, David Couzens. *The Critical Circle: Literature, History, and Philosophical Hermeneutics.* Berkeley: U of California P, 1982.

Kaestle, Carl F. *Literacy in the United States: Readers and Reading since 1880.* New Haven: Yale UP, 1991.

Lanham, Richard A. "The Extraordinary Convergence: Democracy, Technology, Theory, and the University Curriculum." *The Politics of Liberal Education.* Ed. Darryl J. Gless and Barbara Herrnstein Smith. Durham: Duke UP, 1992. 33–56.

———. "From Book to Screen: Four Recent Studies." *College English* 54 (1992): 199–206.

———. *Literacy and the Survival of Humanism.* New Haven: Yale UP, 1983.

———. *The Motives of Eloquence: Literary Rhetoric in the Renaissance.* New Haven: Yale UP, 1976.

———. "One, Two, Three." *Composition and Literature: Bridging the Gap.* Ed. Winifred Bryan Horner. Chicago: U of Chicago P, 1983. 14–29.

———. *Revising Prose.* 2nd ed. New York: Macmillan, 1987.

———. *Style: An Anti-Textbook.* 1974. New Haven: Yale UP, 1978.

Leavis, F. R. *English Literature in Our Time and the University: The Clark Lectures, 1967.* London: Chatto and Windus, 1969.

Melville, Keith. *Immigration: What We Promised, Where To Draw the Line.* National Issues Forums. Dubuque: Kendall/Hunt, 1987.

Ogbu, John. "Literacy and Schooling in Subordinate Cultures: The Case of Black Americans." *Perspectives on Literacy.* Ed. Eugene Kintgen, Barry Kroll, and Mike Rose. Carbondale: Southern Illinois UP, 1988. 227–42.

Richards, I. A. *Practical Criticism: A Study in Literary Judgment*. New York: Harcourt, 1929.

Salvatori, Mariolina. " 'Cultural Literacy': Critical Reading." *Correspondences Seven: Broadside Opinions and Conversations al Fresco*. Ed. Ann Berthoff. Upper Montclair: Boynton/Cook, n.d. n.p.

———. "Pedagogy: From the Periphery to the Center." *Reclaiming Pedagogy: The Rhetoric of the Classroom*. Ed. Patricia Donahue and Ellen Quandahl. Carbondale: Southern Illinois UP, 1989. 17–34.

———. "Reading and Writing a Text: Correlations between Reading and Writing Patterns." *College English* 45 (83): 657–66.

Sarmiento, Anthony, and Ann Kay. *Worker-Centered Learning: A Union Guide to Workplace Literacy*. Washington: AFL-CIO Human Resources Development Institute, 1990.

Scott, Fred Newton. "The Standard of American Speech." *English Journal* 6 (1917): 1–11.

Scribner, Sylvia, and Michael Cole. "Unpackaging Literacy." *Perspectives on Literacy*. Ed. Eugene Kintgen, Barry Kroll, and Mike Rose. Carbondale: Southern Illinois UP, 1988. 57–70.

Street, Brian. *Literacy in Theory and Practice*. Cambridge Studies in Oral and Literate Culture. Cambridge: Cambridge UP, 1984.

24

Style and the Public Intellectual: Rethinking Composition in the Public Sphere

PAUL BUTLER

In 2005, contributors to the Writing Program Administration Listserv (WPA-L) responded angrily when Stanley Fish, in a *New York Times* op-ed piece, derided decades of composition scholarship by stating that "content is a lure and a delusion and should be banished from the classroom." In its place, Fish advocates "form," his term for the grammar he asks students to use as they construct a new language. In his column, "Devoid of Content," the renowned literary scholar laments the emphasis on content in composition courses because of what he argues is the field's mistaken belief that "if you chew over big ideas long enough, the ability to write about them will (mysteriously) follow" (Fish 2005). He thus exorcises intellectual concepts, anthologized readings, controversy, and everything else except "how prepositions or participles or relative pronouns function." While compositionists' opposition to Fish's critique of "so-called courses in writing" is to be expected—in a letter to the *Times*, Deborah Brandt (2005) states that "what Stanley Fish teaches isn't writing"—their reaction is surprising in one respect: Fish (2002) had made almost the same claim three years earlier in *The Chronicle of Higher Education*, where he writes that content, useful *initially* to illustrate syntactical or rhetorical points, should then be "avoided like the plague." If Fish is merely rehashing an old argument, what accounts for the outcry over his later column only? On the WPA list, one contributor suggested that the problem was its public circulation: "Because it went to the *New York Times*, it circumvents the entire academic community and speaks directly to an audience that already believes that academics don't know what they are doing, especially when it comes to writing" (Galin 2005).

Unfortunately, Fish's commentary on the discipline is far from an isolated occurrence. In what seems at first to be nothing more than a relatively short *New Yorker* book review of a "throwback" style guide for college students, former CUNY English professor Louis Menand (2000), now at Harvard, ends up

---

From *Out of Style: Reanimating Stylistic Study in Composition and Rhetoric* (Logan: Utah State University Press, 2008), 114–41.

defining rhetoric and composition for readers—and his account is anything but flattering. Menand's review of literature professor David Williams's (2000) how-to text, *Sin Boldly! Dr. Dave's Guide to Writing the College Paper* is, simply put, a critique of composition studies, and what is particularly distressing is the way in which the staff writer for the *New Yorker* uses the piece to introduce the field in ways that are reductive, outdated, and unsupported by disciplinary scholarship. Take, for example, this early paragraph in Menand's article, "Comp Time: Is College Too Late to Learn How to Write?":

> Rhet Comp specialists have their own nomenclature: they talk about things like "sentence boundaries," and they design instructional units around concepts like "Division and Classification" and "Definition and Process." These are trained discipline professionals. They understand writing for what it is, a technology, and they have the patience and expertise to take on the combination of psychotherapy and social work that teaching people how to write basically boils down to. (Menand 2000, 92)

Even though Robert Connors countered the assumption that composition uses a modal (e.g., "division and classification") and, by extension, current-traditional, approach to writing instruction in an award-winning essay published in 1981, Menand nonetheless makes that implicit claim with impunity on the pages of the *New Yorker*—not to mention reducing writing, without complicating the notion, to merely "a technology" (see Ong 1982, 81–83). The staff writer then goes on to devalue the writing process: "Students are often told, for example, to write many drafts. . . . Here is a scandalous thing to say, but it's true: you are reading the first draft of this review" (94). In this statement, Menand contradicts a common practice—revision—that not only compositionists, but most professional writers, generally take as a given. He further misses the point of revision when he asks, "Would you tell a builder to get the skyscraper up any way he or she could, and then go back and start working on the foundations?" (93), thereby eschewing the more fitting comparison of a writer to an architect who may produce a number of preliminary designs before deciding on a "final" one that might be subject to additional changes. Menand's somewhat flippant charge that writing instruction combines "psychotherapy and social work" is exacerbated when he equates practices like free writing ("the whole 'get your thoughts down on paper' routine") with "the psychotherapeutic side of writing instruction"; attributes difficulties in invention to "subconscious phobia"; and suggests that composition's efforts to improve the "flow" of writing will allow student writers to "conquer their self-loathing and turn into happy and well-adjusted little graphomaniacs" (94).

While Fish and Menand's negative portrayals of composition studies are admittedly tongue-in-cheek at times—Menand even suggests that Williams's book "will be helpful mainly as a guide to writing college papers for Dr. Dave" (94)—no such mitigating factor is at work in Heather Mac Donald's (1995) *Public Interest* article[1] "Why Johnny Can't Write," which plays off *Newsweek*'s 1975 cover story with the same title announcing the nation's so-called literacy crisis. Mac Donald quickly reveals her ostensible purpose: to condemn composition studies for what she suggests are college students' declining literacy skills: "In the field of writing, today's education is not just an irrelevance, it is positively detrimental to a student's development." In her polemic against composition's supposed role in the decline of literacy, Mac Donald—trained in law and now a fellow at the Manhattan Institute—critiques the outcomes of the Dartmouth Conference and the process movement as a whole: "Dartmouth proponents claimed that improvement in students' linguistic skills need not come through direct training in grammar and style but, rather, would flow incidentally as students experiment with personal and expressive forms of talk and writing." Hence, Mac Donald obviously attributes the decline in literacy to process movement practices like free writing and the emphasis on "growth" in student writing.

Despite Mac Donald's apparent interest in student literacy, however, a close reading of her article reveals her real intention: exposing what she calls the disappearance of "objective measure[s] of coherence and correctness" in writing instruction. In other words, when Mac Donald suggests that "elevating process has driven out standards," by "standards" she means a current-traditional view of grammar, style, and correctness. Thus, when Mac Donald, in an attack on multicultural classrooms and difference, writes, "Every writing theory of the past thirty years has come up with reasons why it's not necessary to teach grammar and style" she is suggesting that composition has abandoned correctness because "grammatical errors signify the author is politically engaged." In asserting that the omission of "correctness" in composition curricula is a function of political decisions on the part of the field, she clarifies her real interest in literacy: a desire for a return to grammar-based instruction and a point of view that sees grammar and usage, style, and correctness as essentially the same—and as part of the same prescriptive instructional method.

The excerpts from Mac Donald, Fish, and Menand point to a common problem in composition studies: Topics about writing, rhetoric, and literacy are often brought up in the public sphere, where they are discussed authoritatively by "experts" outside the field of composition. Without an answering word from scholars within the field, however, compositionists are left out in the cold. How is it possible that Fish and Menand—in remarks about composition that generally go against the theoretical underpinnings of an entire field—are able to claim *the* authoritative word on these topics for an important part of the reading public? How can Mac Donald, in words reminiscent of Fish and Menand, resurrect a current-traditional view of style and grammar under the mistaken guise of "literacy" as well as the process movement? "In a process classroom," she writes, "content eclipses form. The college essay and an eighteen-year-old's personality become one and the same." How are these inaccurate characterizations possible when, according to Paula Mathieu, composition has made a "public turn," with an abundance of scholarship, theory, and writing by teachers and students that addresses, in her words, " 'real world' texts, events, or exigencies" (Mathieu 2005, 1)? If composition has, as

Mathieu claims, made a public turn (see also Weisser 2002, 43), with topics that hold interest for a broad range of individuals, why have writers like Fish, Menand, and Mac Donald—and *not* composition scholars—become the only ones to speak for the field in the public sphere?

COMPOSITION'S DISPLACED PUBLIC INTELLECTUALS

The answer, I suggest, involves one of the chief dilemmas facing composition studies today—the field's lack of public intellectuals, which Fish (1995), in a different forum, defines as "someone who takes as his or her subject matters of public concern, and *has the public's attention*" (118). A crucial question, then, is, where are composition's public intellectuals, and why does the field need them so urgently today? I am not the first person to pose this question about the dearth of public intellectuals in composition. In a *College English* review essay, Frank Farmer (2002) asks how composition can reconstitute the concept of the public intellectual to achieve its own goals: "How can we define—perhaps more accurately redefine—the public intellectual to meet *our* needs and purposes in *our* moment" (202)? Christian Weisser (2002), whose work on public intellectuals makes up part of Farmer's review, calls on compositionists "to rethink what it means to be an intellectual working in the public sphere today" (121) and suggests that one place to look is in "sites outside the classroom in which this discourse is generated and used" (42). Weisser hypothesizes that in composition, the sites of "public writing" and "service-learning," in his estimation, "might very well become the next dominant focal point around which the teaching of college writing is theorized and imagined" (42).

While Weisser's (2002) observations are promising, he bases his thinking in part on one of Fish's highly problematic claims, that is, "academics, by definition, are not candidates for the role of the public intellectual" (Fish 1995, 118)—an assertion that Fish, by virtue of his public work alone, clearly refutes. In a different context, Richard Posner also counters Fish's contention. In his book *Public Intellectuals: A Study of Decline*, Posner (2001) states, "Being an academic public intellectual is a career, albeit a part-time and loosely structured one" (41), and he goes on to suggest that academics are needed most as public intellectuals in areas that require expertise "beyond the capacity of the journalist or other specialist in communication to supply" (45). Within the context of composition studies, public intellectuals can accurately convey the field's theoretical knowledge about writing to the general public. For instance, when the widely circulated editorial by Fish appeared, it prompted one *New York Times* reader to write and advocate resurrecting the anachronistic practice of "teaching sentence diagramming as a prerequisite to proper writing" (Fahy 2005). Compositionists are ideally situated to counter just this type of public representation. As Weisser suggests, "Public writing consists of more than expressing your opinion about a current topic; it entails being able to make your voice heard on an issue that directly confronts or influences you" (Weisser 2002, 94). Applying this idea to public discourse would certainly answer Farmer's call for composition to recreate the public intellectual to fit its disciplinary needs, and, one might add, the needs of the public.

Given the field's lack of public intellectuals, what might account for the apparent disconnect between the discipline and public discourse? Clearly, the history of composition studies itself, including its gendered beginnings, offers a place to begin to answer that question. As Susan Miller (1991) asserts in *Textual Carnivals*, the field's identity is "deeply embedded in traditional views of women's roles," a fact Miller says has led the field to try to "overcome this ancillary status" and to redefine itself "in more crisply masculine, scientific, terms" (122). In tracing the tendency to identify composition with these qualities, Miller suggests that "like women in early communities that depended on their production of live births, composition teachers were at first necessarily placed where they would accrue subordinate associations that were no less binding than those still imposed on women" (127). Miller's connection of composition teachers to a subordinate status resonates with Michael Warner's notion of a "counterpublic." In his work *Publics and Counterpublics* (2002), Warner, borrowing from Habermas's analysis of the public sphere, suggests that "some publics are defined by their tension with a larger public" and argues that "this type of public is—in effect—a counterpublic." He goes on to state that a counterpublic "maintains, at some level, conscious or not, an awareness of its subordinate status." In addition to sexual minorities, Warner cites "the media of women's culture" (56) as one example of such a counterpublic. For his part, Posner indicates that a gendered divide similar to that postulated by Miller and Warner exists in the realm of public intellectuals as a whole, with women constituting just 15.8 percent of the total number Posner studied (2001, 207). Indeed, if we can extrapolate Posner's statistics to what Miller calls the "female coding" of composition (123), it may help explain the lack of public intellectuals in the profession at large and the predominately male pool of non-composition-trained public intellectuals who seem to "speak for" the field.

In addition to disciplinary associations based on gender—and what Warner might deem composition's status as a counterpublic—composition's sometimes contentious relationship with literary studies, the field to which Fish and Menand belong, may account for what often appears to be the absence of recognition for composition's independent disciplinary expertise. Thus, for example, in explaining the field to the public, Menand, a literary scholar who has taught composition, reveals his lack of knowledge of composition's theoretical underpinnings. Worse yet, he depicts the profession as one without any theory to be taken seriously. Fish (2005), meanwhile, in addition to attempting a kind of one-upmanship of composition studies through his "form is the way" approach, implies that composition is not doing its pedagogical job: "Students can't write clean English sentences because they are not being taught what sentences are." While compositionists may be tempted to discount these characterizations from those whose scholarship falls outside the field, Menand's critique nonetheless gains the patina of legitimacy by virtue of his role as a respected Pulitzer Prize-winning author and *New Yorker* writer, while Fish's proposal, as reflected in responses from readers, seems to be enthusiastically embraced. It's evident that a well-educated audience is hearing Fish's and Menand's views with no comparable response from composition professionals. This public discourse shows what happens to disciplinary ethos when compositionists become merely "these new writing clinicians" (Menand 2000, 92) under the acerbic pen of public intellectuals with an attentive audience.

THE ROLE OF STYLE

What has brought about this state of affairs? Why as a profession are we still searching for a valid *public* forum in which to express our views? If we accept Fish's definition of the public intellectual as someone who takes up matters "of public concern," the issue seems clear: As a field, we have not addressed those topics the public cares most deeply about and, as a result, to use Fish's corollary, we do not have the public's ear. What are the topics that most concern a public audience? Even a cursory analysis of Menand's review, Fish's editorial, Mac Donald's *Public Interest* piece, and regular public pronouncements on the decline of reading and writing offers a plausible answer: the areas that seem to be of chief concern outside the field are literacy, style, and grammar and usage. While much of the outcry over reading and writing issues seems to fall under the province of literacy, I argue that style, often viewed through the lens of literacy or grammar and usage, is of paramount importance. Mac Donald's article, for instance, suggests her interest—albeit a narrow, reductive one—in style. Menand (2000) seems to care most about the grammatical aspects of writing when he suggests that using red ink or lowering a grade for confusing "it's" as the possessive of "it" amounts to "using a flyswatter on an ox" (92). Yet, his deft use of metaphor here actually shows his reliance on style. Similarly, Menand approaches the topics of "voice" and imitation (aspects of style) when he critiques "Dr. Dave's" preference for "voices that are out there," like Camille Paglia's: "It is not completely settled that even Camille Paglia should write like Camille Paglia; what can be said with confidence is that she is not a writer whom college students would be prudent to imitate" (94).

The problem of style and the public intellectual is thus paradoxical: the very areas that seem to be of chief concern outside the field are generally disdained or ignored inside it. Our disciplinary abandonment of style in particular, I argue, has precipitated the incursion of the public intellectual into composition studies. Put differently, in its neglect of style as a topic of serious scholarly inquiry (as well as grammar and literacy, to varying degrees), the discipline of composition and rhetoric has ceded the discussion to others outside the field—generally to self-described public intellectuals like Menand, Fish, Mac Donald, and others. Hence, by adopting a hands-off approach to the study of style—and without putting forth our own group of public intellectuals to articulate composition's theories and practices—the field is left with popular, and often erroneous, views that have displaced our own. This situation is part of a scenario that has led composition studies itself to adopt a reductive characterization of style, that is, as merely equivalent to certain current-traditional conceptions of grammar, usage, or punctuation (similar to Mac Donald's, for instance). While compositionists do resist such portrayals — especially in light of our broader rhetorical knowledge of stylistic practices and recent scholarship on style (see, for example, Connors 1981, 2000; Johnson 2003; Micciche 2004; Johnson and Pace 2005; Duncan 2007) — the field is, at the same time, paralyzed by it, powerless to refute popular, often reductive characterizations for which there is no public counterargument.

In light of this impasse, I propose that it is time for composition and rhetoric to take back the study of style — to redefine the way the conversation is being framed and to rethink that concept in the public sphere. The urgency of this "call to style" goes beyond a desire to reanimate stylistic practices in composition. Indeed, it implicates the politics of the entire field. I contend that one reason composition has been unable to make its case publicly in virtually *any* arena of scholarship or practice, including literacy, is that it has failed to address the study of style (or to articulate a clear position on the difficult-to-limit area of grammar). Regrettably, our neglect comes at our own peril. In failing to articulate ideas about those language topics in which the public seems most invested, the discipline is left without sufficient credibility to bring up other concerns it considers pressing. What's more, this lack of response from composition-trained public intellectuals makes it difficult to dispel pejorative constructions of the field — or downright neglect — from outsiders who treat composition as less than the transformative discipline it is. To reiterate, if one analyzes the nature of the public discourse on language issues, the majority of that discourse arguably concerns the study of style, often appearing in the form of grammar, punctuation, and literacy. When style is discussed, it is frequently associated with current-traditional approaches to the topic (e.g., see Mac Donald 1995). To counter this tendency, it is essential for the field to go public with a renewed emphasis on style and to employ its disciplinary expertise.

While composition as a discipline has recently expressed some renewed interest in the study of style, it seems safe to say that, since around 1985, the field as a whole has largely ignored stylistic theory and practice and rendered it invisible. In fact, even as the study of style multiplied during the Golden Age, some were already retrospectively labeling it a "static" practice or including it as part of "current-traditional rhetoric." Mac Donald's *Public Interest* article attempts to make just that association while advocating the superiority of a product-based approach. Yet, I contend that the association of style with current-traditional rhetoric is not historically accurate. This period of style's ascendancy also included the development of what Connors (2000) has called "sentence-based rhetorics" (98) or the practices of sentence combining, generative rhetoric, and rhetorical imitation, the first two largely concerned with syntax. Connors questions the disappearance of these stylistic practices from composition theory and pedagogy and begins the tangible reemergence of discussions about the role of style in the field. T. R Johnson's

(2003) *A Rhetoric of Pleasure: Prose Style and Today's Composition Classroom* and Johnson and Tom Pace's (2005) *Refiguring Prose Style: Possibilities for Writing Pedagogy* offer an eclectic approach to studying style, while Richard Lanham's (2006) *The Economics of Attention: Style and Substance in the Age of Information* makes the claim that style and substance have, in effect, been reversed as we vie for attention in a technologically oriented society. Lanham writes, "If attention is now at the center of the economy rather than fluff, then so is style. It moves from the periphery to the center" (xi–xii).

THE STATUS OF GRAMMAR IN COMPOSITION STUDIES

In 2006, the WPA listserv responded quickly when an article about grammar instruction appeared in the *Washington Post*. In "Clauses and Commas Make a Comeback: SAT Helps Return Grammar to Class," staff writer Daniel de Vise (2006) features a high-school English teacher in Virginia who has resurrected "direct grammar instruction"—in other words, noncontextual grammar drills—in his classes, apparently in response to the new writing section of the SAT that consists primarily of grammar questions. Perhaps the most controversial aspect of the article is an erroneous assertion de Vise makes about a supposed change in NCTE's policy on grammar: "The National Council of Teachers of English, whose directives shape curriculum decisions nationwide, has quietly reversed its long opposition to grammar drills, which the group had condemned in 1985 as 'a deterrent to the improvement of students' speaking and writing.'" As NCTE President Kathleen Blake Yancey (2006) wrote on WPA after the *Post* article appeared, "This claim—that NCTE has changed its stance on grammar—is false, and we've spent the better part of the day trying to get it corrected. . . . You spend hours and hours trying to get some attention paid to what you stand for, and this is what they pick up. And of course, it would be about grammar." While de Vise (2006) fails to cite specific authority for this claim, the article does quote Amy Benjamin of the Assembly for the Teaching of English Grammar, a group affiliated with NCTE, who tells de Vise that "our time has come." However, Benjamin's group—which de Vise says has evolved into "standard bearers" on language issues—does not speak for the national organization of NCTE and is clearly at odds with NCTE on this issue.

It is important to acknowledge the extent to which the so-called "grammar question" remains particularly vexed in a field that has approached the subject with ambivalence for some time. For years, the study of style has overlapped with the discourse of grammar in a number of crucial respects. What de Vise's *Post* article shows, however, is that the public discourse about grammar tends to revive and, indeed, promote a prescriptive approach that the field officially abandoned long ago. Yet, even Menand (2000) assumes grammar's centrality to the field when he tries to dispel some "grammatical superstitions" and then goes on to discuss the composition teacher's "almost hopeless task of undoing this tangle of hearsay and delusion [that grammar and usage involve]" (92). Ironically, Menand's review is concerned primarily with stylistic issues—not the grammatical ones with which they are often confused or conflated. Indeed, the continued misunderstanding of composition's position on grammar suggests that this is another area in which the field could profit by clearly articulating a public position. Any effort to do so, however, would require an examination of the history of composition's relationship with grammar, including the importance of Patrick Hartwell's (1985) article "Grammar, Grammars, and the Teaching of Grammar" in which the author suggests that there are five different definitions of grammar, succinctly summarized by David Blakesley (1995) as follows:

> (1) the set of formal patterns in which the words of a language are arranged in order to convey larger meanings; (2) linguistic grammar, which studies these formal patterns; (3) linguistic etiquette (usage . . . which is not grammar, per se); (4) school grammar (the grammar of textbooks); and (5) stylistic grammar (grammatical terms used to teach style). (195)

In his conclusion, which echoes some of the findings of a 1963 NCTE study by Richard Braddock, Richard Lloyd-Jones, and Lowell Schoer, Hartwell (1985) argues that teaching formal grammar out of context does not help and in fact can harm the teaching of writing. He states, "One learns to control the language of print by manipulating language in meaningful contexts, not by learning about language in isolation, as by the study of formal grammar" (125). That claim, it seems, has remained the field's leitmotif on the role of grammar in composition instruction, as NCTE's position statement affirms. Even though Hartwell's conclusion that both style and grammar are inherently rhetorical may be accepted by most compositionists, however, I contend that when the "grammar question" arises in the public arena, it is not enough simply to reiterate Hartwell's conclusions. Instead, I argue that the field must publicly articulate a view of grammar that others can better relate to and understand. Is it possible, as compositionist Janet Zepernick seems to imply on the WPA listserv, that our often visceral reactions to public assertions about grammar have contributed to our invisibility within the public sphere?

> One of the public relations problems we face as a discipline is that instead of responding to the pro-grammar movement among noncomps by saying, "Yes, we see what you want. We call it X, and here's how we do it and why it works so well when we do it this way," we've generally responded by circling the wagons and writing diatribes against the grammar police. (Zepernick 2005)

Zepernick's concerns seem precisely on point, especially in light of the regular recurrence of the topic in what might be called composition studies' "private" sphere, the WPA listserv. In addition to discussions of the recent article on teaching grammar in high schools, list members responded en masse in 2004 when David Mulroy (2003), in *The War against Grammar*, directly took on NCTE and what Mulroy considered the professional organization's position that "instruction in formal grammar did not accomplish any positive goals" (15). Mulroy is effectively attacking NCTE's official adoption of the Braddock, Lloyd-Jones, and Schoer (1963) position that "the teaching of formal grammar has a negligible, or, because it usually displaces some instruction and practice in composition, even a harmful effect on improvement in writing" (37–38). NCTE's position so incensed Mulroy that, according to a review of the book, the author "set aside his special interest, translating Latin and Greek poetry, and devoted several years to researching the history of the study of grammar" (Reedy 2003, 15). In his book, Mulroy argues that university professors have ignored grammar instruction for the past 75 years and that the United States should adopt a policy similar to England's National Literacy Strategy, which offers workshops for teachers "deficient" in their knowledge of grammar and punctuation. Nick Carbone's (2004) response to the discussion on WPA-L is representative of compositionists' position:

> There is no war against grammar. There is instead a struggle to teach writing. That's a different thing. In that struggle we've come to believe, based on sound evidence and experience, that grammar in isolation, rules-only, skill and drill as the best approach for learning the basics of writing doesn't work. So teaching grammar for grammar's sake in a course that's a writing course or meant to help students write better, we're not for. (Carbone 2004)

In the aftermath of the WPA listserv discussion of *The War against Grammar*, Joe Hardin summarized his view of the field's complicated position on questions of grammar and style. Hardin (2004) goes beyond Carbone's statement to express the centripetal effect of the term "grammar" as it draws a host of disparate ideas within its nomenclature, making it difficult for the field to articulate its position clearly:

> It's really a complex argument that is linked to the whole contemporary language theory. Many believe that it's an argument against standards. It's not. Many believe that it suggests that we abandon style and syntax and sentence-level work completely. It doesn't. It's mostly an argument against the traditional way of teaching "grammar" and the goals of that tradition. It's an argument for a correction of terms and what those terms imply—what traditional books teach is "usage," not grammar, for instance. It's an argument against the transferability of the rules-example-exercises approach to the production of good writing. (Hardin 2004)

As Hardin suggests, the study of style (including syntax and sentence-level work) often gets indiscriminately wrapped up in the field's general prohibition against formal noncontextualized grammar instruction. In other words, we have come to confuse style and grammar, conflating it in the same way that those without disciplinary training do. What's more, because the field has adopted various rhetorical approaches to grammar that fall more accurately under the rubric of style, my discussion of the field's response to grammar—to the extent I discuss it here—relates to the study of style. In his article, Hartwell himself treats style (what he calls "stylistic grammar" or

"Grammar 5") differently from his other four categories of grammar and makes it clear that style is useful in ways that grammar per se is not. In fact, in his discussion of stylistic grammar, Hartwell (1985) writes, "When we turn to Grammar 5 . . . we find that the grammar issue is simply beside the point" (124).

STYLE, GRAMMAR, LITERACY, AND STUDENTS' RIGHT TO THEIR OWN LANGUAGE

Part of the fate of style, grammar, and literacy in the field today originates in an important document promulgated by the Committee on CCCC Language in 1974, the "Students' Right to Their Own Language." The resolution on language begins: "We affirm the students' right to their own patterns and varieties of language—the dialects of their nurture or whatever dialects in which they find their own identity and style" (Committee on CCCC Language 1974, 2). CCCC's adoption of the Students' Right resolution, with its affirmation of the diversity of literacy, style, and grammar in a multicultural society, precedes by a year *Newsweek*'s "Why Johnny Can't Write" issue (1975), which has resonated in the public sphere for decades (see, for instance, Mac Donald's 1995 article with the same title). In short, the connection between writing and "non-standard" dialects that the "Students' Right to Their Own Language" resolution supports has dictated disciplinary policy and thinking ever since. Among the points made in the document is that content should be emphasized: "If we can convince our students that spelling, punctuation, and usage are less important than content, we have removed a major obstacle in their developing the ability to write" (Committee on CCCC Language 1974, 8). The statement about the importance of content is clearly at odds with Fish's (2005) statement about form's paramount place in composition classes and may explain compositionists' response to Fish's op-ed piece. What's more, the Students' Right document, with its emphasis on content, may also help explain the resistance to style within the field itself. Paradoxically, however, what perhaps no one has recognized up to this point is that the Students' Right document is fundamentally—and has been since its inception—an explicit and implicit call to style for the field.

In other words, the Students' Right resolution proposes an interpretation of dialect, variation, and other language matters that suggests, in short, not only an explicit view of style—that is, "students' right to their own patterns and varieties of language . . . in which they find their own identity and style"—but an innovative one as well. The authors write that "in every composition class there are examples of writing which is clear and vigorous despite the use of non-standard forms . . . and there are certainly many examples of limp, vapid writing in 'standard dialect' " (8). It seems evident, then, that if composition as a field embraces the idea of difference in various dialects, that idea is inextricably linked to the idea of variation as a fundamental aspect of style. Thus, it is crucial that compositionists rethink the idea of style in conjunction with "Students' Right to Their Own Language"—

rather than in opposition to it. Along the same lines, the authors of the Students' Right document are effectively making an argument for style (while not necessarily calling it that) when they discuss the importance of embracing difference in student writing. That admonition occurs when the document describes writing in nonuniform dialects:

> Many of us have taught as though the function of schools and colleges were to erase differences. Should we, on the one hand, urge creativity and individuality in the arts and the sciences, take pride in the diversity of our historical development, and, on the other hand, try to obliterate all the differences in the way Americans speak and write? Our major emphasis has been on uniformity, in both speech and writing; would we accomplish more, both educationally and ethically, if we shifted that emphasis to precise, effective, and appropriate communication in diverse ways, whatever the dialect? (2)

Indeed, as the Students' Right document suggests, the question of whether the form of a person's dialect or home language can be separated from its content—and content in this case implicates a person's very identity—continues to trouble composition as a discipline. Thus, "Students' Right to Their Own Language" reflects the continuing relevance of the most important issue in style theory.

As part of reanimating style in composition, then, the field ought to draw more on the "Students' Right to Their Own Language" and the guidance it offers. Now almost thirty-five years old, the document often seems to go unnoticed. In terms of its reception in the public sphere, it arguably serves as the basis of misconceptions about how the field treats writing and how it has construed the very nature of difference with respect to language, dialect, and style. Within composition studies itself, the document, unwittingly perhaps, has given impetus to a reductive view of style that is, ironically, just the opposite of what the document's authors envision. It has perhaps produced an internal tension within the field that would, if explored more fully, help composition and rhetoric articulate far more clearly a position that could reinvigorate interpretations of style—and of the field—in the public sphere.

COMPLICATING "CLARITY" IN THE PUBLIC SPHERE

As "Students' Right to Their Own Language" suggests, the field of composition has a number of innovative ideas with respect to language that should be introduced in the public sphere, if only because they challenge conventional wisdom. One example of this is the complication of the notion of "clarity," which is often taken as a given not only in public discourse, but in the field, as well. Consider, for instance, Mac Donald's (1995) *Public Interest* article, which begins with the assertion that "the only thing composition teachers are not talking and writing about these days is how to teach students to compose clear, logical prose." Mac Donald's emphasis on clarity in writing is echoed by Menand (2000), who gives a list of speech characteristics that writing teachers should help students eliminate from their writing "in the interest of clarity"; these include "repetition, contradiction, exaggeration, run-ons, fragments, and clichés, plus an array of tonal and physical inflections—drawls, grunts, shrugs, winks, hand gestures—unreproducible in written form" (94). Yet, the idea of clarity is, in fact, more problematic than Menand or Mac Donald allows. At least one composition scholar, Richard Lanham, began to question the common assumptions about clarity as early as 1974. Recognizing that the term "clarity" itself is impossible to define (because it is a rhetorical concept that shifts), Lanham (1974) writes, "Obviously, there can be no single verbal pattern that can be called 'clear.' All depends on context—social, historical, attitudinal" (33). Lanham reveals the chief principle he sees at work in most theories of clarity: the tendency to want to make writing transparent, or to have it seem invisible to those reading it, as if it points to some definitive underlying reality.

Thus, at least part of the problem in the disappearance of stylistic study, I argue, is that composition has essentially been interpellated by myths regarding clarity as well as other public myths about style. By "interpellation" I mean that there has been a tendency to accept prescriptive standards of grammar, punctuation, and style that support a reductive view of the canon. By "myths" I mean that frequent repetition makes the so-called "rules" take on a life of their own, raising them to the level of prescription. As an example, in opposition to what many claim as the inherent transparency of a clear style, Lanham proposes instead the idea of an opaque style that calls attention to itself. He states, "Either we notice an opaque style as a *style* (i.e., we look *at* it) or we do not (i.e., we look *through* it to a fictive reality beyond)" (Lanham 1983b, 58). Lanham recognizes that an opaque style is seen as "the enemy of clarity" and that a binary has developed favoring a clear or transparent style. "Transparent styles, because they go unnoticed, are good," he writes. "Opaque styles, which invite stylistic self-consciousness, are bad" (47, 59).

Lanham's theory thus complicates the notion of clarity in writing in important ways. He argues persuasively that the injunction to "be clear" refers "not to words on a page but to responses, yours or your reader's" (Lanham 1983a, 2). In another nod at the inherently rhetorical nature of the concept, he goes on to suggest that the idea of clarity indicates how successful a writer might be in getting his or her audience "to share our view of the world, a view we have composed by perceiving it" (3). In *Publics and Counterpublics*, Warner (2002) offers a similarly rhetorical view of clarity: "It could be argued that the imperative to write clearly is not the same as the need to write accessibly, that even difficult styles can have the clarity of precision" (139).[2] Warner and Lanham's highly contextual views of clarity, however, differ markedly from the normal "take" on the notion, especially in the public sphere, where many writers, like Menand and Mac Donald, accept as a given its relative merits. Lanham's view, on the other hand, reveals that the concept of clarity is not as simple as it generally seems, but is extremely complex and difficult to explain in a style manual or an easy-to-digest formula. If we take Lanham's argument seriously, then, the major proscriptions against "muddy" writing become mere shibboleths that displace more nuanced positions in composition studies about what it means to "be clear."

The reason it is important to articulate such a position is that the meaning of "good writing" in the field is ultimately at stake. As Warner points out, the common conception is that "writing that is unclear to nonspecialists is just 'bad writing'" (2002, 138). Yet if style is not opaque or "ornamental"—in other words, if it does not call attention to itself in any way—then all that is left for us to discuss regarding "good" writing are the prescriptive views of clarity (and other myths) regularly reproduced both outside and inside the field. Taken to its logical conclusion, then, this conception of clarity implies that a clear style *has* no style and serves only as a mirror to an underlying meaning. This unquestioned acceptance of a transparent style, as Lanham points out, has read out of the equation any potentially interesting notions of an opaque or self-conscious style. As the clarity discussion demonstrates, the perpetuation of popular myths about style has unwittingly held the field hostage, rendering it unable to move beyond certain public perceptions despite the efforts of scholars like Lanham to challenge their underlying rationale and use. Indeed, in the public sphere, the field of composition might point to writing styles that are complex, nuanced, and yet highly effective at complicating and enriching the discussion of difficult ideas. Composition scholars could use the public sphere as a forum in which to explain the value of styles that may not, at first glance, appear transparent or clear to most people.

One instance where the explanation of a complex, yet meaningful style would have been helpful is in a "Readings" section of *Harper's Magazine* (Vitanza 1994) that quickly betrays its real purpose: to make its subject, composition professor Victor Vitanza—and, in turn, the field itself—seem vain, inarticulate, and, in the form in which it's presented, unclear. In "Reading, Writing, Rambling On," the *Harper's* (1994) piece undermines Vitanza by taking excerpts from his larger interview in *Composition Studies* (1993) conducted by Cynthia Haynes-Burton, without giving the broader context for his ideas. When, for instance, Haynes-Burton asks, "Who do you think your audience is?" Vitanza's theoretical response, reprinted in *Harper's*, shows some of his conflicted sense of the field: "I am always giving writing lessons and taking writing lessons. I don't know, however, if I am Levi-Strauss or if I am that South-American Indian chief in *Tristes Tropiques* that Levi-Strauss indirectly gives writing lessons to. Perhaps I am both. Which can be confusing" (29). On the surface, of course, Vitanza's (1994) statements appear opaque, even comical, even though they are arguably a stylistic tour de force in which the author uses the rhetorical trope of *periphrasis* to show the difficulty of capturing the rhetorical situation of literacy, which he names "inappropriation" (1993, 52). Yet, the *Harper's* excerpt does not capture Vitanza's dilemma or his uncertain relationship with the very notion of "audience," which he examines at length in the *Composition Studies* piece. In a portion of that interview omitted in *Harper's*, Vitanza states, "I think that audiences are really overrated!" (1993, 51), and one solution, he explains, is to rethink the relationship between writers and audiences.

Later, after Vitanza expresses doubts about how he positions himself as a researcher in the field, Haynes-Burton asks him to "please start over," and Vitanza's conflicted reply includes the following paragraph reproduced in *Harper's* (1994):

> Okay, so what I have said so far: I very consciously do not follow the field's research protocols. And yet, of course, I do; most other times, however, I do not. And yet again! Do you feel the vertigo of this? I hope that my saying all this, however, does not come across as if I am disengaging into some form of "individualism," or "expressionism," for I do not believe in such a fatuous, dangerous concept as practiced in our field. (29)

In the context of the full interview in *Composition Studies*, Vitanza expresses the point of view that as a field, composition has always been positioned among research protocols borrowed from various disciplinary interests, and he is acknowledging how, as a scholar allied with postmodern theory, he is torn trying both to conform to and resist those protocols. Yet, by focusing on these contradictory positions without giving additional context, the magazine attempts to ridicule Vitanza's equivocation. Nonetheless, his words express brilliantly the lack of clarity he obviously feels on this subject. Likewise, the debate over expressionism in the field is complicated by years of disciplinary discussion, and while Vitanza is in a camp that might indeed label expressionism "fatuous," the *Harper's* excerpt provides none of the background necessary for readers to understand its historical complexity, making the scholar again seem out of touch with the field — and certainly with his audience.

ONGOING DISCIPLINARY DIVISION

While much of the misunderstanding about the role of style in composition comes from outside the field, the abandonment of the study of style has led to the perpetuation of certain preconceptions from within the discipline as well. In a *College English* opinion piece, for example, Peter Elbow (2002), one of composition's best-known scholars, suggests that style is now almost exclusively a part of the "culture" of literary studies. In "The Cultures of Literature and Composition: What Could Each Learn from the Other?" Elbow, calling for a kind of revival of style in composition, suggests that currently it is literature — and *not* composition — that has "a culture that considers the metaphorical and imaginative uses of language as basic or primal" (536). In other words, Elbow suggests, the discipline of literary studies has become in essence *the* province of style:

> The culture of literary studies puts a high value on style and on not being like everyone else. I think I see more mannerism, artifice, and self-consciousness in bearing . . . among literary folk than composition folk. Occasionally I resist, yet I value style and artifice. What could be more wonderful than the pleasure of creating or appreciating forms that are different, amazing, outlandish, useless — the opposite of ordinary, everyday, pragmatic? (542)

Granted, Elbow does not go so far as to dismiss the role composition plays in a so-called culture of style. However, his acknowledgment that the "culture of composition" does not ignore "metaphor and imaginative language *altogether*" is really so much damnation with faint praise (536; emphasis added). Echoing in important respects the same assumptions often made about the field in the public sphere, he says that composition generally adopts a "literal language . . . that seems to assume discursive language as the norm and imaginative, metaphorical language as somehow special or marked or additional" (536). Elbow's concept of style is, of course, somewhat circumscribed in this instance, even though he suggests, as Lanham does, that style has an opaque quality he considers desirable. It's clear that Elbow is advocating a revival of style, yet instead of looking at style's important roots in composition, the only model he considers is literature.

By locating stylistic studies almost exclusively within the domain of literature, however, and by dichotomizing "literary" and "discursive" language, Elbow effectively initiates a "divide" or schism between literature and composition that mimics the divide between popular and academic views of style in the public arena. In other words, Elbow seems to create a public within a public (see Warner's "counterpublic") in the academic realm itself. Like Fish, Menand, and Mac Donald, however—and indeed, as I have argued, like composition studies as a whole—Elbow is failing to account for the broad body of scholarship on style in the field. For example, as Lanham, Edward P. J. Corbett, and others have pointed out, a wide variety of rhetorical figures (e.g., tropes and schemes) has been used throughout the history of stylistic studies and in the teaching of writing. Furthermore, by dividing literary or poetic style from what he labels composition's supposed focus—which he regrettably calls an "orientation toward grammar"—Elbow clearly adopts a view challenged not only by many scholars in the field itself (see, for example, Hartwell 1985; Carbone 2004; Hardin 2004), but by linguist Mary Louise Pratt. In *Toward a Speech Act Theory of Literary Discourse*, Pratt (1977) critiques that very binary when she argues that the supposed division between "poetic" and "non-poetic" language is based on an unverifiable split between poetic language (the language of literature) and linguistics (everyday language, the so-called "discursive" language Elbow refers to as the province of composition).

According to Pratt, this "poetic language fallacy" is a false division because it presupposes certain elements unique to literary or poetic language and ostensibly nonexistent in nonpoetic language. Pratt essentially challenges the claims of the Prague Circle—a group of linguists and writers interested in language in Russia during the 1930s—that there is a metaphorical *langue/parole* relationship unique to literature: "The fact that . . . there is a real *langue* shared by literary and nonliterary utterances alike is quite overlooked and seems almost irrelevant" (10). She goes on to argue that the faulty analogy between *langue* (as literary) and *parole* (as nonliterary) has widespread implications for style and underlies "the overwhelming tendency to view style as an exclusively or predominantly literary phenomenon and *to equate style out-side literature with mere grammaticality and conventional appropriateness*" (15; emphasis added). Clearly, this is the very separation that Elbow makes when he writes about the difference between literary and conventional discourse (i.e., the discourse of composition).

Even though I obviously share Elbow's claim that there is a problematic absence of attention to style in composition, I do not see the stylistic schism he hypothesizes between composition and literary studies. Instead, I argue, the problem is the inability of compositionists to articulate a clear view of the value of stylistic study in the field. Elbow suggests that the existence of a gap in stylistic study is currently filled by literary studies. Yet, it is evident that public intellectuals outside the field—many of whom are not literary scholars—are filling this gap in their own way. Elbow, like Menand and others, simply represents a different instantiation of the same disciplinary problem: the inability of composition to use and articulate its long-standing knowledge base. The field clearly has a rich tradition in the study of style. By reclaiming it, composition studies has nothing to lose and much to gain, both immediately and over the long term, in asserting knowledge about practices of style that have a rich disciplinary history. Illuminating those stylistic traditions for the public would give the field a claim to the very expertise held by composition scholars. It would establish the importance of composition studies by reclaiming language concerns that are important both inside and outside the field. Compositionists would be seen as public intellectuals with valuable theoretical positions on an array of language matters, including stylistic ones.

RESPONDING IN THE PUBLIC SPHERE

If the field of composition is to write in the public sphere, it has to start somewhere. I begin that process here by responding to Fish, Menand, Mac Donald, and others who have represented the field—often inaccurately, in my view—in the public sphere. I aim to show the benefit of writing as a public intellectual in public discourse.

In making the argument that form in composition courses is more important than content, Fish is stating a notion that is far from new—yet incorrect. Why? For years, a form/content dichotomy has existed, with form considered by some—like Fish—as a container that can be filled with any content. The idea that form (which includes style, structure, grammar, and so forth) can thus be separated from content led composition scholar Louis Milic to propose a dualistic view in the 1960s that he called the "theory of ornate form." Milic (1965) states that form is separate from, and, he implies, more important than, content because "ideas exist wordlessly and can be dressed in a variety of outfits depending on the need or the occasion" (67). For Milic, then (and we can assume Fish agrees), the opposite idea, which states that form and content are inseparable because the two are an "organic" whole, is erroneous. If this organic theory, which he calls "Crocean aesthetic monism," were correct, writes

Milic, and there were, in fact, "no seam between meaning and style," then even a small change in form would necessarily mean a change in content—and that implies there *is* no form (or style) but only "meaning or intuition" (67). Milic claims that ornate form is the only theory that allows composition instructors to teach style by making it separate from content.

However, Milic's idea is mistaken: form (style) and content (meaning) are actually inextricably linked, and here is the reason why. While it's true that ideas can be put in any number of ways—indeed, this is the very notion of style—what Milic and Fish both overlook is that the form itself carries meaning. How so? When Fish dismisses content, he is assuming that words carry only a denotative (or explicit) meaning. This denotative meaning, like the form/content division itself, is based on a positivist assumption that sees language narrowly in terms of one possible transparent meaning. However, much of what we take to be meaning is not denotative at all. Rather, it is connotative (suggested or implied) and comes from various rhetorical elements—e.g., humor, irony or sarcasm, emphasis, and even ethos, or the credibility/character of the writer—as well as cultural and social understandings, and thus a great deal of connotative meaning is conveyed through *form*. Form itself, then, often expresses meaning above and beyond the denotative meaning. Take Fish, for example. His column for *The Chronicle of Higher Education*, written before his *Times* piece, is entitled "Say It Ain't So" (2002), an ironic title that in its lexical choice ("Ain't"), its register (colloquial), and its use of allusion (a kind of cultural "gotcha") conveys, through form, a great deal about his resistance to conventional wisdom. This is an instance, then, when form, which is clearly significant in and of itself, works in conjunction with meaning, including the prior meanings attached to this expression without which the title itself would have a different meaning. Indeed, if Fish were to teach his students the way form can be used to alter meaning, it seems that he might reach a different conclusion from his decision to banish content from his classroom teaching.

If one idea could be said to characterize Menand's ideas in his *New Yorker* review, it would likely be his reliance on psychoanalytical theory to describe the process of writing in composition classrooms. As a matter of fact, issues of writing have long been tied to psychology, especially in the study of the writing process. Yet, comparing writing to issues of psychotherapy is rare. It is true that in a special double issue of *College English* on psychoanalysis and pedagogy, guest editor Robert Con Davis (1987) concludes that "the problematics of psychoanalytic therapy (defined by 'resistance,' 'transference,' and 'repression') are the same as 'the problematics of teaching'" (622), and Menand's ideas seem informed by similar considerations. Yet, when he talks about writing pedagogy as a "combination of psychotherapy and social work" (92), Menand (2000) is actually more interested in portraying composition in one light—as influenced by the theory of expressivism, or a movement that focuses on the idea that writing involves exploring personal experience and voice. The expressivist movement has generated a great deal of debate even in composition, as Vitanza's repudiation of it indicates, but Menand, as well as Mac Donald, confuse readers with their insistence that expressivist rhetoric, not to mention process, are the enemies of grammar and style.

This is where an important explanation is useful: Menand's and Mac Donald's characterizations of the field assume a view of writing based on current-traditional rhetoric, which emphasizes product over process, as Fish (2005) does in his *New York Times* op-ed piece. Current-traditional rhetoric is concerned with, among other things, grammar, usage, and mechanics—essentially aspects of language affiliated with the textual product rather than with the process of producing it. Menand's critique of the so-called "psycho-therapeutic approaches" (voice, free writing, drafting, revision, etc.)—along with Mac Donald's criticism of the Dartmouth Conference—basically amount to the same thing: a desire to return to a strict emphasis on the textual product and to throw out the process writers use to achieve it. Why is that harmful? Research has shown that all of the techniques associated with "process" are useful to writers in accomplishing their writing goals. They are productive not only for student writers, but for professional writers as well. The process movement has never ignored the textual product, but has looked at the individual, social, cultural, and public considerations that make up the text. When they write about the field, however, Menand and Mac Donald do not take these considerations into account, and therefore they dismiss a great deal of useful knowledge that has been acquired by writers and teachers over time.

It is the job of composition studies to develop writing through many processes. In doing so, the field shares the same goals as Fish, Menand, Mac Donald, and others who have portrayed us in public: to produce excellence in writing. Like these public intellectuals, we want to help writers compose with attention to style and contextually appropriate grammar and vocabulary. However, we have discovered methods for achieving good writing that allow writers to take into account the way they arrive at their product. Along the way, both form and content—and everything that goes along with these concepts—are important to composition professionals and should be to all writers and readers everywhere.

NOTES

1. The journal *The Public Interest* ceased publication with its Spring 2005 issue, after 40 years. Founding editor Irving Kristol suggested that the journal did not have a particular ideology, but most would describe the journal as conservative or "neo-conservative," and it's clear that Mac Donald's article (1995) presents a view of composition studies that is far from balanced.

2. Warner's (2002) view of clarity is highly relevant to composition and rhetoric. He asks, for instance, "What kind of clarity is necessary in writing?" After stating the conventional wisdom that "writing that is unclear to nonspecialists is just 'bad writing,'" Warner goes on to make an argument relevant to compositionists writing in the public sphere: "People who share this view will be generally reluctant to concede that different kinds of writing suit different purposes, that what is clear in one reading community will be unclear in another, that clarity depends on shared conventions and common references, that one man's jargon is another's clarity, that perceptions of jargon or unclarity change over time" (138).

WORKS CITED

Blakesley, David. 1995. "Reconceptualizing Grammar as an Aspect of Rhetorical Invention." In *The Place of Grammar in Writing Instruction*, ed. Susan Hunter and Ray Wallace, 191–203. Portsmouth, NH: Boynton/Cook.

Braddock, Richard, Richard Lloyd-Jones, and Lowell Schoer. 1963. *Research in Written Composition*. Urbana, IL: NCTE.

Brandt, Deborah. Letter. 2005 (May 31). *New York Times*. http://www.nytimes.com/2005/06/03/opinion/103language.html, accessed June 17, 2008.

Carbone, Nick. 2004 (February 25). "War against Grammar." Online posting. WPA-L. http://www.WPA-L@asu.edu, accessed May 15, 2007.

Committee on CCCC Language. 1974. "Students' Right to Their Own Language." *College Composition and Communication* 25: 1–18.

Connors, Robert. 1981. "The Rise and Fall of the Modes of Discourse." *College Composition and Communication* 32: 444–63.

———. 2000. "The Erasure of the Sentence." *College Composition and Communication* 52: 96–128.

Corbett, Edward P. J. 1990. *Classical Rhetoric for the Modern Student*. 3rd ed. New York: Oxford University Press.

Davis, Robert Con. 1987. "Freud's Resistance to Reading and Teaching." Psychoanalysis and Pedagogy I. *College English* 49: 621–27.

De Vise, Daniel. 2006 (October 23). "Clauses and Commas Make a Comeback: SAT Helps Return Grammar to Class." *Washington Post*. http://www.Washingtonpost.com/wp-dyn/content/article/2006/10/22/AR2006102201135_p..., accessed May 30, 2008.

Duncan, Mike. 2007. "Whatever Happened to the Paragraph?" *College English* 69: 470–95.

Elbow, Peter. 2002. "The Cultures of Literature and Composition: What Could Each Learn from the Other?" *College English* 64: 533–46.

Fahy, Francis L. Letter. 2005 (June 3). *New York Times*. http://www.nytimes.com/2005/06/03/Opinion/103language.html?ex=1177300800&en=525f..., accessed April 21, 2007.

Farmer, Frank. 2002. "Review: Community Intellectuals." *College English* 65: 202–10.

Fish, Stanley. 1995. *Professional Correctness: Literary Studies and Political Change*. New York: Clarendon.

———. 2002 (June 21). "Say It Ain't So." *The Chronicle of Higher Education*. http://chronicle.com/jobs/2002/0612002062101c.htm, accessed June 12, 2007.

———. 2005 (May 31). "Devoid of Content." *The New York Times*, A17.

Galin, Jeff. 2005 (May 31). "NYTimes.com: Devoid of Content." Online posting. WPA-L. http://www.WPA-L@asu.edu, accessed July 7, 2007.

Hardin, Joe. 2004 (March 10). "Back to Grammar." Online posting. WPA-L. http://www.WPA-L@asu.edu, accessed July 7, 2007.

Hartwell, Patrick. 1985. "Grammar, Grammars, and the Teaching of Grammar." *College English* 47: 105–27.

Johnson, T. R. 2003. *A Rhetoric of Pleasure: Prose Style and Today's Composition Classroom*. Portsmouth, NH: Heinemann-Boynton/Cook.

Johnson, T. R., and Tom Pace. 2005. *Refiguring Prose Style: Possibilities for Writing Pedagogy*. Logan: Utah State University Press.

Lanham, Richard A. 1974. *Style: An Anti-Textbook*. New Haven, CT: Yale University Press.

———. 1983a. *Analyzing Prose*. New York: Charles Scribner's Sons.

———. 1983b. *Literacy and the Survival of Humanism*. New Haven, CT: Yale University Press.

———. 2006. *The Economics of Attention: Style and Substance in the Age of Information*. Chicago: University of Chicago Press.

Mac Donald, Heather. 1995. "Why Johnny Can't Write." *The Public Interest* 120: 3–13. http://www.Search.ebscohost.com/login.aspx?direct=true&db=aph&AN=9510086540&site=ehost-live, accessed June 12, 2007.

Mathieu, Paula. 2005. *Tactics of Hope: The Public Turn in English Composition*. Portsmouth, NH: Heinemann Boynton/Cook.

Menand, Louis. 2000 (September 11). "Comp Time: Is College Too Late to Learn How to Write?" *The New Yorker*, 92–94.

Micciche, Laura R. 2004. "Making the Case for Rhetorical Grammar." *CCC* 55: 716–37.

Milic, Louis T. 1965. "Theories of Style and Their Implications for the Teaching of Composition." *College Composition and Communication* 16: 66–69, 126.

Miller, Susan. 1991. *Textual Carnivals: The Politics of Composition*. Carbondale: Southern Illinois University Press.

Mulroy, David. 2003. *The War against Grammar.* Portsmouth, NH: Boynton/Cook.

Ong, Walter J. 1982. *Orality and Literacy: Technologizing the Word.* London: Methuen.

Posner, Richard A. 2001. *Public Intellectuals: A Study of Decline.* Cambridge, MA: Harvard University Press.

Pratt, Mary Louise. 1977. *Toward a Speech Act Theory of Literary Discourse.* Bloomington: Indiana University Press.

Reedy, Jeremiah. 2003. Rev. of *The War against Grammar,* by David Mulroy. *Bryn Mawr Classical Review* 12:15.

Sheils, Merrill. 1975. "Why Johnny Can't Write." *Newsweek* 92: 58–65.

Vitanza, Victor J. 1993. Interview with Cynthia Haynes-Burton. *Composition Studies* 21: 49–65.

———. 1994 (January). "Reading, Writing, Rambling On." Interview with Cynthia Haynes-Burton. *Harper's* 29. http://www.search.ebscohost.comllogin.aspx?direct=true&db=aph&AN=9404120662&site=ehost-live, accessed June 12, 2007.

Warner, Michael. 2002. *Publics and Counterpublics.* New York: Zone.

Weisser, Christian. 2002. *Moving beyond Academic Discourse: Composition Studies and the Public Sphere.* Carbondale: Southern Illinois University Press.

Williams, David R. 2000. *Sin Boldly!: Dr. Dave's Guide to Writing the College Paper.* New York: Perseus.

Yancey, Kathleen Blake. 2006 (October 24). "Grammar Drills Coming Back?" Online posting. WPA-L. http://www.WPA-L@asu.edu, accessed May 30, 2007.

Zepernick, Janet. 2005 (May 31). "NYTimes.com: Devoid of Content." Online posting. WPA-L. http://www.WPA-L@asu.edu, accessed July 7, 2007.

25 Sounding the Other Who Speaks in Me: Toward a Dialogic Understanding of Imitation

FRANK FARMER

> What is wanted . . . is a fundamental intersecting of languages in a single given consciousness, one that participates equally in several languages.
>
> —M. M. BAKHTIN

Among present-day compositionists, there seems to be little doubt that imitation has all but disappeared from serious consideration as a viable practice in writing instruction. Edward Corbett's claim that imitation has little chance of making a "comeback" seems as prescient now as it did when it was first made some thirty years ago (249). Indeed, it has been eloquently reiterated by Robert Connors, who, in a recent essay on the erasure of sentence rhetorics, sees imitation's demise as the result of our discipline's wholesale rejection of formalism, behaviorism, and empiricism in favor of attitudes toward texts more agreeable to English departments than to departments of speech, psychology, or education—the supposed originators of our prior fascination with the sentence (120–21). Regardless, for many teachers of writing, imitation has been so thoroughly discredited that it may now be looked upon as something of a quaint vestige of days gone by, an amusing holdover from far more benighted times than our own.

Yet there are formidable stumbling blocks that must be overcome in our attempts to eulogize imitation as a pedagogical practice. One of the more baffling difficulties to be met is that despite imitation's reported demise, there exists an abundant literature on its value to the writing classroom. From the very beginnings of the process movement, a fairly large number of scholars in rhetoric and composition have vigorously championed the usefulness of imitation in the teaching of writing. Indeed, a remarkably varied and rich literature on imitation emerged during a time when imitation's fortunes were, in the view of Corbett and many other informed observers, on the decline.[1]

From *Saying and Silence: Listening to Composition with Bakhtin* (Logan: Utah State University Press, 2001), 73–94.

How, then, to explain this paradox? A few years ago, Phillip Arrington and I conducted an extensive review of the ample literature on imitation. Our purpose was to give an account of imitation's vexed status within our discipline; our method was to regard the many articles, chapters, papers about imitation as utterances situated within a dialogic context. What we found is that, apart from how pedagogically specific any individual article (utterance) might be, the characteristic feature of nearly all writing about imitation was the need to *justify* its usage. We grouped all such justifications into what we thought were the four most likely and predominant categories: stylistic, inventional, interventional, and social. We then argued that the ubiquitous, overwhelming need to justify imitation was, in some considerable measure, evidence that imitation had been *tacitly* rejected by our community at large and that those who championed imitation knew this to be the case. Otherwise, we reasoned, the literature on imitation would not be so abundant; its proponents would be more centrally concerned with refinements for its use; and critics of imitation would feel the need to be explicit in their opposition. We thus concluded that, indeed, imitation was a largely discredited practice among current writing teachers and scholars.

We nonetheless elected to close our review by hinting that maybe it was premature to sound imitation's death-knell, that perhaps there were other ways to think about imitation that had not been previously considered. In keeping with the dialogic approach we chose for our literature review, we suggested that it might be possible to think about imitation dialogically and indicated that two likely sources for such an endeavor could be found in the writings of Lev Vygotsky and Mikhail Bakhtin, especially the latter.

Of course, others before us had noticed that certain aspects of Bakhtin's work seemed to warrant a rethinking of imitation. In the one essay most responsible for introducing Bakhtin to compositionists, Charles Schuster had already pointed out that imitation, as a pedagogical practice, becomes vastly more interesting and approachable when regarded from a Bakhtinian perspective:

> When we think of the kinds of accents and intonations that can enter into language from other speakers, heroes, listeners, and languages we begin to establish a perspective from which we can understand more sophisticated language use such as sarcasm, parody, and irony. We begin to see how style develops through the imitation of—and association with—other styles. (598)

But in a disciplinary milieu wherein questions pertaining to style received scant attention at best, Schuster's passing observation about imitation did not spark any particular interest in its rethinking.

Nor, for that matter, did the work of Jon Klancher. In "Bakhtin's Rhetoric," Klancher took a decidedly ideological approach in trying to determine what Bakhtin has to offer the writing classroom. Klancher argues that both paraphrase and parody, from a Bakhtinian view, are capable of suggesting a "pedagogy whose aim is to disengage student writers from crippling subservience to the received languages they grapple with" (89). Klancher proposes that writing assignments ask students to parody the languages of others, so long as parody entails "not the lesser exercise of imitation, but the frankly critical, dialogically informed encounter between social languages" (93). Klancher clearly hoped to draw a qualitative distinction between those kinds of imitation (e.g., paraphrase, parody) that are "critical, dialogically informed" and those, we are to assume, that constitute the more traditional brands aligned with the "servile copying" and "mindless aping" sorts of old.

More recently, Mary Minock has asked for a reconsideration of imitation in light of certain strands of postmodern theory, especially as such strands come to us through the work of Jacques Derrida, Jacques Lacan, and Mikhail Bakhtin. Of these thinkers, in fact, it is Bakhtin who figures most prominently in Minock's argument. Reiterating Bakhtin's point that, understood dialogically, the boundary line between one's own words and another's words is always malleable, always elastic, always permeable, Minock argues that the unconscious imitation of another's words is crucial to the continuance of any dialogue with those words. To maintain and to further dialogue, therefore, we must first know how to speak the words *of* another as a requisite for dialogue *with* the other (494–95). If I understand her correctly, Minock is not too far from the view that imitation, from a Bakhtinian perspective, is something of a condition of possibility for dialogue.

Along with Schuster, Klancher, and others, Minock points to the likelihood that Bakhtin's theory of dialogue ought, at the very least, to encourage us to take another look at imitation. In the following pages, I would like to do just that. I would like to sketch out the features of what I call a dialogic imitation, illuminating, among other things, where and how a dialogic approach to imitation would differ from our received understandings of the term. Before offering a model for what I propose, however, it will be useful to review exactly what Bakhtin has to say about imitation.[2]

BAKHTIN AND IMITATION

On the face of things, we might expect Bakhtin to have absolutely no interest whatsoever in imitation. After all, it is hard to imagine a more *antidialogic* concept—literary, rhetorical, pedagogical, or otherwise—than that of imitation. Indeed, . . . silence itself might seem more potentially dialogic than the rote duplication of another's words, if only because parroted words, unlike certain silences, are addressed to no one. As if to emphasize this point, when Bakhtin chooses a counter term for dialogue, he does not offer silence but rather monologue. And yet insofar as language learning is concerned, it would seem that, for many, these terms ultimately become identical, since efforts directed toward imitating another's word, for most of us, could only be interpreted as a wish to merge with that word in some sort of monologic unity, that is to say, in undifferentiated silence.[3]

Ought we to conclude, then, that Bakhtin discusses imitation only for the purpose of illuminating the salient features of what he means by dialogue, of highlighting his privileged term, dialogue, by contrasting it with an opposite term that he disparages? No, this does not seem to be the probable motive for Bakhtin's scattered remarks on imitation. Rather, Bakhtin's comments on imitation emerge within the varied contexts of his working through larger problems and concerns. Thus, if we are to glean something of what Bakhtin thought about imitation, we must return to those contexts to understand what Bakhtin is saying about imitation and then explore whether or not it is possible to formulate a coherent understanding of how Bakhtin regarded imitation.

Imitation and Novelistic Discourse

It is within his varied discussions of the novel where we find Bakhtin evince an interest in the relationship of imitation to dialogue. Bakhtin is fully aware that the kind of novel he describes is very much situated in the *mimetic* tradition. The distinguishing feature in Bakhtin's understanding of the novel, however, is not the imitation of "reality" as such, nor the Aristotelian imitation of dramatic action, but instead the representation of the human voice, which is always and everywhere for Bakhtin, the imitation of the multiple voices that constitute social existence (Bialostosky, "Booth's").

Now, in light of the centrality of "the speaking person and his discourse" to Bakhtin's definition of the novel, it should come as no great surprise to hear Bakhtin aver that any stylistics of the novel must begin with the problem of *"artistically representing language, the problem of representing the image of a language"* (DI 336). One might point out that every mimetic conception of the novel has understood this to be a problem, whether explicitly acknowledged or no. But where Bakhtin complicates matters is in his realization that a represented language is always a *representing* language, that a represented language gives voice to *other voices*, that a represented language may even "talk back" to the author whose utterances presumably determine the whole of the novelistic discourse. The complexities of mapping out the dialogic relationships in any novelistic discourse are abundant and complex, as is obvious in Bakhtin's chart of discourses available to the novelist.

In *Problems of Dostoevsky's Poetics*, Bakhtin offers such a schematic of available discourse types. Among single-voiced discourses, for example, Bakhtin first identifies what he calls *direct, unmediated discourse*, a single-voiced discourse that simply has no need of another voice. It is discourse, as Bakhtin explains, "directed exclusively toward its referential object" by a speaker whose "ultimate semantic authority" is sufficient and absolute (99). David Lodge points out that this discourse type corresponds to Plato's description of *diegesis*, the representation of reality in the voice of the poet (or narrator) (33). A second kind of single-voiced discourse is *objectified discourse*, words that attempt to represent the speech of a character "objectively." This type corresponds to Plato's mimesis and would obviously include direct quotation, but also, as Lodge reminds, various types of reported speech (33). More to my purposes here, though, are the varieties of *double-voiced discourse*—or, as Bakhtin says, speech "with an orientation toward someone else's discourse" (*PDP* 199). Bakhtin identifies three main types.

First, there is a passive type of double-voiced discourse that Bakhtin calls *unidirectional double-voiced discourse*. It includes stylization, *skaz* (narrator's narration), "the unobjectified discourse of a character" for authorial intentions, and forms of first-person narration. What these share, according to Bakhtin, "is an intention on the part of the author to make use of someone else's discourse in the direction of its own particular aspirations" (*PDP* 193). While two voices are present, only one referential direction may be perceived, that of the author. As Morson and Emerson point out, in passive discourse, the author "uses the other's discourse for his own purposes, and if he allows it to be heard and sensed, that is because his purposes require it to be" (*Prosaics* 150).

Vari-directional double-voiced discourse, too, is a passive type of double-voiced discourse, but one where the author's purposes are different from the purposes of the "hero" or "character" or generalized "other." This type is passive because, most often, the discourse of the other is at odds with the discourse of the author, who, in order to evaluate the other critically, parodies or ironizes his speech. The other is unwittingly at the mercy of the author; their purposes diverge, and the other is vulnerable to the author's subterfuge. Obviously, then, this type of discourse includes all forms of parody, including what Bakhtin calls "parodic skaz."

Finally, there is *active double-voiced discourse*. Here, Bakhtin observes, the discourse of the other resists the exclusive purposes of the author, enters into dialogue with the author's discourse, and is able to modify, persuade, affect the author's intentions. Bakhtin claims that in discourse of this type, "the other's words actively influence the author's speech, forcing it to alter itself accordingly" (*PDP* 197). This is the most authentically dialogic of all forms of double-voicing and is, for Bakhtin, best exemplified in the novels of Dostoevsky. Under this category, Bakhtin places such forms of discourse as "hidden polemic," "hidden dialogue," "rejoinder in a dialogue," the word with "a sideward glance," and certain forms of parody, so long as the parodied language "answers" the language of the parodist author.

Bakhtin is quick to point out that his schematic is at best extremely limited, since, as he admits, "we have far from exhausted all the possible examples of double-voiced discourse" (*PDP* 198). But the classification system above should offer some insight into the remarkably complex variations that occur not only within the novel itself, but also within the relationships that the novel establishes with other extant genres. We have already seen, for example, how parody figures prominently in the discourse that occurs between and among characters and authors within a novel. But the novel, as a genre, parodies other novels and other genres as well. One of the ways, for example, that the novel relativizes other genres is through its open contentiousness with those genres. As Bakhtin himself says of the novel: "throughout its entire history there is a consistent parodying or travestying of dominant or fashionable novels that attempt to become models for the genre" (*DI* 6).

Parody may also be heard in the novel's representation of those languages within a language that Bakhtin refers to as *heteroglossia*, where, for example, such carnivalized genres as "street songs, folk-sayings, anecdotes," and the "low" genres of laughter consciously parody the "official languages of [their] given time" (*DI* 273). It can also be witnessed in the myriad languages that accompany the realities of everyday life. Bakhtin asks us to consider an "illiterate peasant" who "prayed to God in one language . . . sang songs in another . . . spoke to his family in a third and . . . [petitioned] local authorities through a scribe" in yet a fourth (*DI* 296). So long as this peasant is able to compartmentalize these distinct languages, each will remain "indisputable," that is, the peasant will be unable "to regard one language (and the verbal world corresponding to it) through the eyes of another language" (*DI* 296–97). However, once the peasant experiences the "critical interanimation of languages" in his own consciousness, the nature of each is radically altered, the hegemony of each compromised, the authority of each eroded. What ensues, instead, is a dialogic awareness that no particular worldview is beyond challenge, that is to say, indisputable.

This newly acquired dialogic consciousness is precisely what the novel concerns itself with. The languages of heteroglossia that interanimate each other in an individual's consciousness find outward expression "on the plane of the novel," the one genre capable of adequately representing the stratification of languages in a given social milieu, as well as the dialogue that occurs between such languages. Moreover, once integrated into the novel, heteroglossia cannot help but be what Bakhtin calls "a special type of *double-voiced discourse*," since heteroglossia in the novel must necessarily represent "the direct intention of the character who is speaking, and the refracted intention of the author" (*DI* 324). As in all double-voiced discourse, "two voices, two meanings, and two expressions" may be discerned. Moreover, as Bakhtin suggests, the double-voicedness of heteroglossia is of the *active* sort, because the two voices involved "know about each other (just as two exchanges in a dialogue know of each other and are structured in this mutual knowledge of each other" (*DI* 324).

To demonstrate at least partially why this is so and, at the same time, to reveal something of how Bakhtin understood imitation, it will be useful to return to Bakhtin's observations on that particular type of double-voiced discourse that he calls stylization.

Recall that Bakhtin regards stylization to be a "unidirectional" type of passive double-voiced discourse. The stylizer, as Bakhtin says, "works with someone else's point of view," or perhaps more exactly, "with the other's speech as an expression of a particular point of view" (*PDP* 189). Because stylization is a double-voiced discourse, there can be no merging of author and character's voices or perspectives. For this reason, Bakhtin points out, stylized discourse is *conditional*, that is, the author, while retaining the style of the character speaking, has nonetheless penetrated that character's speech with his own attitude, his own voice. The "objectified" discourse of the character "now serves new purposes, which take possession of it from within" and remove from it the possibility of being a thoroughly "earnest" discourse, since the character's discourse must now accommodate the author's intentions (*PDP* 190). Bakhtin goes on to note that "conditional discourse is always double-voiced" and hints that the same discourse was once "unconditional, in earnest" (*PDP* 190).

Bakhtin's observations on the conditionality of double-voiced discourse are important for a number of reasons, one of which is to provide him with a criterion by which to distinguish stylization from imitation—imitation, that is, as traditionally (or narrowly) understood:

> Imitation does not render a form conditional, for it takes the imitated material seriously, makes it its own, directly appropriates to itself someone else's discourse. What happens in that case is a complete merging of voices, and if we do hear another's voice, then it is certainly not one that had figured into the author's plan. (*PDP* 190)

Bakhtin warns that the stylizer is susceptible to crossing over into imitation, "should the stylizer's enthusiasm for his model destroy the distance and weaken the deliberate sense of a reproduced style as *someone else's style*" (*PDP* 190). If and when that occurs, the possibility for dialogue vanishes, since author and character have become one, and dialogue, therefore, has become unnecessary. Essential, then, to stylization, to all forms of double-voiced discourse, and to all manifestations of dialogue is the clear perception of *someone else speaking*, the voice of a necessary other without whom dialogue is impossible.

These observations, as noted above, are made in the context of Bakhtin's discussion of the novel, in particular, the range of author-character ("hero") relationships available to novelistic discourse. As I will show later, it is possible to make certain inferences about imitation in writing pedagogy from Bakhtin's limited remarks on double-voiced discourse in the novel. But what, if anything, does Bakhtin have to say about the role of imitation in more prosaic contexts?

Imitation and Everyday Discourse

Given Bakhtin's understanding of the novel as outlined above, it should come as no great surprise that, for Bakhtin, no absolute division exists between novelistic and everyday discourses. Just as the novel is able to give free expression to the discourses of contemporary, everyday life, Bakhtin likewise seems to indicate that all of the forms of discourse available to the novelist are also available to the speaker of everyday discourse, that is, to oneself as the "author" of one's own utterance. In everyday discourse, Bakhtin argues, we constantly appropriate someone else's words for our own purposes; we constantly represent the speech of others. What determines our particular relationship to the languages we borrow are the "tasks" before us, the discursive intentions we wish to effect. Bakhtin elaborates upon this notion of the speaker as author:

During everyday verbal transmission of another's words, the entire complex of discourse . . . may be expressed and even played with (in the
form of an exact replication to a parodic ridiculing and exaggeration of
gestures and intonations). This representation is always subordinated to
the tasks of practical, engaged transmission and is wholly determined by
these tasks. This of course does not involve the artistic image of his discourse, and even less the image of a language. Nevertheless, everyday
episodes involving the same person, when they become linked, already
entail prose devices for the double-voiced and even double languaged
representation of another's words. (*DI* 341)

In everyday discourse, then, the range of options available for incorporating another's speech into our own include many of the same devices available
to the prose artist: imitation (as replication), stylization, skaz, parody, and so
on. As in novelistic discourse, our "practical, everyday speech" is capable of
merging with the speech of another, losing itself within the speech of another,
and thereby becoming a single voice unto itself. But, as Bakhtin suggests, this
fusion of voices is rather difficult to accomplish, since the introduction of
"someone else's words . . . into our own speech inevitably assume[s] a new
(our own) interpretation and become[s] subject to our evaluation of them; that
is they become double-voiced" (*PDP* 195). Bakhtin seems to imply that pure
imitation of another's speech is possible only if the speaker is *unaware* that she
is using the words of another, "forgetting whose they are" (*PDP* 195). Otherwise, a *conscious* use of speech cannot avoid the necessity of having to interpret that speech, cannot escape the exigencies of hermeneutic translation.

Further support for this view of imitation can be found in Bakhtin's theory of the utterance. If one characteristic of the utterance is its unrepeatability,
then the use of someone else's words can never be a mere duplication of those
words, since another's words will necessarily be recontextualized by the
"host" speaker. As Bakhtin explains, "the speech of another, once enclosed in
a context, is—no matter how accurately transmitted—always subject to certain semantic changes. The context embracing another's word is responsible
for its dialogizing background, whose influence can be very great" (*DI* 340).
The implicit suggestion here is that only sentences can be imitated, since only
sentences are repeatable phenomena, a fact that results from their exclusively
linguistic and, therefore, decontextualized nature. From this point of view, the
history of imitation in discourse pedagogy might best be understood as the
history of students imitating the sentences (not utterances) of chosen others,
regardless of whether these sentences were of the spoken or written variety.
Models for imitation, in this scheme of things, were never meant to be engaged, worked over, disputed, confirmed—in a word, *answered*. Rather, they
were presented as reified, abstracted objects of language, whose forms were
deemed worthy of replication.

However simplistic this account might be, it is important to note that
Bakhtin did, in fact, address the problem of imitation in school learning,
though somewhat obliquely. "When verbal disciplines are taught in school,"
Bakhtin observes, "two basic modes are recognized for the appropriation and

transmission—simultaneously—of another's words (a text, a rule, a model): 'reciting by heart' and 'retelling in one's own words'" (*DI* 341). The first is essentially a verbatim transcription from memory and corresponds with most traditional understandings of imitation in the classroom. The second is more akin to what is usually referred to as paraphrase and is of considerable interest to Bakhtin, since it represents "on a small scale the task implicit in all prose stylistics":

> retelling a text in one's own words is to a certain extent a double-voiced narration of another's words, for indeed "one's own words" must not completely dilute the quality that makes another's words unique; a retelling in one's own words should have a mixed character, able when necessary to reproduce the style and expressions of the transmitted text. It is this second mode . . . that includes within it an entire series of forms for the appropriation while transmitting of another's words. (*DI* 341–42)

But Bakhtin does not regard these operations to be exclusively pedagogical in interest or value; rather, each strategy corresponds to separate kinds of discourse. . . . "Reciting by heart" is representative of what Bakhtin calls authoritative discourse—that is, discourse "intended to be admired, venerated, nostalgically invoked. It imagines itself to be eternally repeatable, and thus its authority is catechistic in nature" (*DI* 342). As I also pointed out earlier, and in contrast to authoritative discourses, "retelling in one's own words" approximates what Bakhtin calls *internally persuasive discourse*, a discourse close at hand. It is one open to appropriation by other discourses and thus one thoroughly situated *in dialogue* with those words told and retold. Internally persuasive discourse is nothing less than momentous in human development:

> Such discourse is of decisive significance in the evolution of an individual consciousness; consciousness awakens to independent ideological life precisely in a world of alien discourses surrounding it, and from which it cannot initially separate itself; the process of distinguishing between one's own and another's discourse, between one's own and another's thought, is activated rather late in development. When thought begins to work in an independent, experimenting, and discriminating way, what first occurs is a separation between internally persuasive discourse and authoritarian enforced discourse, along with a rejection of those discourses that do not matter to us. (*DI* 345)

Bakhtin obviously understands the importance of a dialogic relationship with the language of the *other* to be essential to the development of individuated consciousness. Bakhtin's remarks on the nature of these relationships, moreover, suggest a resistance to those forms of imitation that exclude—or, more precisely, attempt to exclude—genuine dialogue, since such forms, by virtue of trying to fuse with another's language, exclude the possibility of relationship with that language and, hence, the full development of consciousness. This should not be understood to mean, however, that Bakhtin rejects all forms of imitation. Rather, he disparages only those that seek identity with the object of imitation, that seek a monologic unity, a merging with the language of the other. There are, of course, other kinds of imitation, many of which Bakhtin writes of approvingly.

As noted, Bakhtin is explicitly critical of those kinds of discourse that preclude dialogue, namely, authoritarian discourse, the sentence (as a purely linguistic phenomenon), and the single-voiced discourse that results from a merging of authorial and character voices. In each of these, imitation is conceived as a monologic phenomenon: it refuses the creative mingling of internally persuasive words, the answerability of utterances, the necessary distance between the languages of the stylizer and the languages stylized. Imitation, understood in its most ordinary and narrow sense, attempts to remove the voice of the other from any zone of dialogic contact, either by refusing to hear it or by becoming one with it.

But *must* imitation be a verbal strategy whose only purpose is to silence or ignore the voice of the other; must imitation, in other words, be an exclusively monologic phenomenon? The answer to this is yes, *if*—and only if— imitation is rigidly construed to be the mechanical replication (i.e., "servile copying") of another's words. As I have shown, Bakhtin has very little to say about imitation of this sort, other than to posit its existence in novelistic and everyday discourses. He is far more interested in those representations of another's language that require two or more voices, e.g., stylization, skaz, rejoinder, parody, and paraphrase. Central to my argument, of course, is the proposition that each of these may likewise be, and indeed have been, considered a *kind* of imitation; and, thus, to the extent that each is, as Bakhtin says, a form of double-voiced discourse, it is reasonable to entertain the possibility of a *dialogic imitation*. But what would be the characteristic features of such an imitation? And how might it appear in the writing classroom?

OUTLINE FOR A DIALOGIC IMITATION

In light of the discussion above, it seems possible to infer certain features of what I call here a dialogic imitation—at least enough to offer a preliminary sketch of what such an imitation might look like. Before I offer that sketch, however, I would remind that, with the possible exception of a few remarks on paraphrase, Bakhtin does not concern himself with the pedagogical implications of imitation. Though by all accounts a remarkable teacher himself, Bakhtin's scholarly interests seldom gravitated toward education and pedagogy. I also wish to point out that in calling upon Bakhtin here, my purpose in these final pages is not to propose any startling "new and improved" forms of imitation. I don't believe any such forms exist, at least none that I could hazard. But as my reconstruction of his scattered comments will show, I do believe that Bakhtin gives us some very different starting points—premises, if you like—by which to reconsider imitation.

This is a matter of some importance. As many have pointed out, there are at least two standard reasons why imitation finds little favor among compositionists. One is that imitation has been inextricably aligned with text-based rhetorics and is, therefore, bound to "product" understandings of how writing should be taught. The other is that imitation is considered unaccept-able because it did not comport with expressivist, post-romantic conceptions of selfhood, with notions of the "true self" and how best to address that self in writing pedagogies.[4] Put differently, imitation in our time has been largely discredited because its premises, its starting points, have been aligned with the formalism of traditional rhetorics and because, at a crucial moment in our discipline's history, it stood in opposition to the widely endorsed expressiv-ism of romantic and post-romantic rhetorics.

But to reject imitation according to certain assumed premises is not to re-ject imitation altogether. It may be that a different understanding of imitation is possible, one that derives from very different starting points, very different assumptions about knowledge, subjectivity, and language than those that au-thorize our current refusal to look upon imitation favorably. So then, given a specifically dialogic understanding of imitation, what are its key features?

Dialogic Imitation Is Positional

Whether in novelistic or everyday discourse, when we ask of all forms of double-voicing—parody, skaz, paraphrase, hidden polemic, stylization, het-eroglossia, and so on—what they have in common, the answer is that each reveals how one speaker's discourse *positions* itself toward the discourse of another, or others. In an ontological sense, for Bakhtin, the acts of positioning, orienting toward, having an attitude—these are not simple matters of choice. Even from his earliest writings, Bakhtin doubts whether it is possible to expe-rience the world and the word in a condition of sublime neutrality. In *Toward a Philosophy of the Act*, for example, Bakhtin will repeatedly point out that words are never exclusively used to refer to the objects of the world; rather, words always express "my valuative attitude toward the object, toward what is desirable or undesirable in it" (32). Indeed, Bakhtin hints that it may be oxy-moronic to talk of disinterested experience: "an object that is absolutely in-different, totally finished," according to Bakhtin "cannot be something one actually becomes conscious of" (32).

And yet, what informs most traditional approaches to imitation is the tacit requirement that students *assume no position whatsoever* toward the mod-eled language, that students voice no evaluative stance toward other people's words *as words actually addressed to someone*. Rather, in a classroom of this sort, students are typically asked to imitate the "word as object" (admittedly, sublime object) or rather, the word as linguistic "matter," say, introductory participial phrases, apposition structures, figures of speech, cumulative sen-tences, T-unit variations, etc. For what distinguishes traditional imitation from the kind I propose here is that imitation, as it has been conventionally approached, seeks identity not difference, one voice not two, no boundaries instead of the one that allows a student to take a position toward the language of the other.

Cast in a Bakhtinian light, and as I mentioned earlier, the long history of imitation can be understood as the history of imitating sentences, not utterances. Yet if this is so, there exists no real possibility for a dialogic relationship to the language imitated. In other words, the modeled language is neither answered nor addressed, and thus any resulting imitation of that language could similarly invite no answer and address no one. The conclusion to be drawn here is that because only utterances, not sentences, seek and indeed require the voice of another, then any dialogic imitation will necessarily involve two voices. As Bakhtin says, "any truly creative voice can only be the *second* voice in a discourse" (*SG* 110), and thus dialogic imitation will ultimately require some form of double-voicing, if for no other reason than that a single voice can take no position toward itself.

Dialogic Imitation Is Revisable

The process movement took as a cornerstone of its approach the notion that we cannot effectively teach writing if we attend only to the finished product, instead of to the struggles that writers experience in their working toward that finished product. Indeed, I think it safe to say our discipline was founded on the realization that there is little to teach at all if we merely evaluate written products and ignore how student writers develop and order their ideas, how they revise for their own satisfaction and for that of their audiences, how they might better proof, edit, and present their work, and so on. In more recent years, we have expanded this idea to include social and cultural processes larger than the solitary writer and her struggles, but perhaps, in some measure, determinant of each. We have also turned our attentions to the processes of texts as they make their way in a field of other texts and contexts, other writers and other readers.

In light of more recent understandings of process, then, it is not only the case that texts can be mistakenly looked upon as finished products. It is also possible to reify *attitudes toward texts*. In an odd sort of way, that is, we can make into products the very attitudes we invite our students to take toward models that we present them with. Just as product approaches to teaching composition seriously limit the likelihood of any authentic teaching at all, the same follows from any attempt to treat our students' positions toward texts as final, rigid, unchanging. Therefore, if our students have no opportunity to struggle with the language of the other, if they have no opportunity to develop new perspectives by entering into, trying on, the perspective of another, then, indeed, we have taught them little more than to be content with the immediate positions they assume, to be satisfied with their first impressions, initial reactions, and so on. It is hard to imagine this as a worthwhile pedagogical goal.

But as we have seen earlier, Bakhtin places an enormous amount of importance on the developmental value of struggle, of working through another's discourse, of "coming to terms" with the words of another, so as to assimilate those words and make them one's own. Clearly, Bakhtin understands this struggle diachronically, as a process occurring through time—in fact, one could even say through a lifetime. Yet a problem remains: How is it possible to assimilate the language or voices or perspective of another without becoming one with the other?

Again, such is possible only if we realize that developing a position toward another's words is as much a process as writing a paper in one's own words. We might be able to illuminate this point by extrapolating from Bakhtin's early work on ethics and aesthetics, where he examines the phenomenon of "live entering" and "return" and the possibility of "co-experiencing" the other from within. As always, Bakhtin is resistant to any merging of identities, to any fusion with the other. As a matter of fact, Bakhtin will claim that, despite our occasional desires for achieving such complete empathy, it is not possible to do so. "Strictly speaking," Bakhtin observes, "a pure projection of myself into the other, a move involving the loss of my own unique place outside the other is, on the whole, hardly possible; in any event, it is quite fruitless and senseless" (*AA* 26). And yet, this does not mean that there is no value whatsoever in projecting oneself into the "life-horizon" of another, the position occupied by another. How else, in fact, would understanding and empathy be possible?

In his discussion on the aesthetic relationships that obtain between authors and their "heroes," Bakhtin notes that a "first step" in aesthetic activity is one whereby an author enters into the perspective of another—a narrator, character, hero—for the purpose of understanding that other by "experiencing his life from within. . . . I must experience—come to see and know," Bakhtin says, "what *he* experiences; I must put myself in *his* place . . . I must appropriate to myself the concrete life horizon of this human being as he experiences it himself" (*AA* 25). And yet, Bakhtin hastens to remind, this is only a first step. Whether friend or character, neighbor or narrator, we must not reside within the perspective of another. Doing so is "pathological," Bakhtin adds, unless my entering into is followed by "a *return* to my own place outside . . . for only from this place can the material derived from projecting myself into the other be rendered meaningful ethically, cognitively, or aesthetically" (*AA* 25). It is only from that place we return to, from our position outside another, that we can have any meaning for another. Or, for that matter, for ourselves.[5]

It would seem, then, that discovering one's position toward another's word is a sequenced process, a journey of repeated phases of venturing forth and return. Bakhtin's own vocabulary would suggest as much, particularly when he attempts to describe this movement in terms such as "first steps," "followed by," "actually begins," and "return." But, in fact, Bakhtin sees these two "moments" as simultaneous, insisting that they "do not follow one another chronologically," but rather are always "intimately intertwined," coupled (*AA* 27). And importantly, this simultaneity applies not merely to the other but also to that which the other cannot be separated from, the uttered word.

> In a verbal work, every word keeps both moments in view: every word performs a twofold function insofar as it directs my projection of myself into the other as well as brings him to completion, except that one constitutive moment may prevail over the other. (*AA* 27)

Bakhtin's specific concern here is the aesthetic relationship between author and hero. But having already shown how Bakhtin rejects any absolute division between novelistic and everyday discourses, we can safely assume that Bakhtin's observations have implications beyond their more narrow formulations.

In fact, it seems to me that within our own disciplinary context, Bakhtin's ideas are echoed in the early work of Ann Berthoff, who, in calling our attention to I. A. Richards's "continuing audit of meaning," also tried to capture something of the back-and-forth simultaneity involved in meaning-making — or, translated to my purposes here, the process by which one assumes a position (however much it might be later revised) toward the discourse of another. David Bartholomae has also pointed to what Bakhtin is after, I think, when observing that, as our students struggle with the discourses of the university, "there are two gestures present . . . one imitative and one critical. The writer continually audits and pushes against a language that would render him 'like everyone else' and mimics the language and interpretive system of the privileged community" ("Inventing" 143). These "two gestures" are each crucial to the development of writers, each simultaneously present as writers struggle to negotiate a position within the discourses of the institution.

Thus, even though positionality is key to any understanding of a dialogic imitation, it is a positionality that is, in some sense, hard-earned, struggled for, as we appropriate and are appropriated by other people's words. In the process of this struggle, a paradox emerges: to achieve a position toward another's word, we must come to know that word, as it were, from the inside out — never completely of course, since, as Bakhtin reminds, no total merging with another's discourse is possible. But we must know the other's word enough to eventually take up a position outside and directed toward it. To know the other's word in this way, as Mary Minock suggests, may in fact be a condition for dialogue.

Dialogic Imitation Is Rhetorical

Even its staunchest defenders, of course, would say that traditional imitation had very clear, rhetorical purposes — among them, to acquaint students with models of writerly excellence, to develop within students an available repertoire of styles and forms, and so on. All such purposes, however, seemed to be limited to the strictly pedagogical. But by rhetorical, I mean something more than what any given teacher might hope to accomplish by having students imitate another's models. I mean that dialogic imitation occurs within the context of some larger intention, some desire to accomplish an effect upon the world in which one's word is uttered.

Imitation, from this point of view, is hardly a passive operation, a simple parroting of someone else's words. It is, rather, something more akin to a rhetorical appropriation of another's words for one's own purposes. What, in fact, makes this appropriation rhetorical is Bakhtin's view that any speaker or writer will have purposes distinct from those to be found in the appropriated language of another speaker or writer. The rote, mechanical act of duplication for no obvious or immediate goal, the lamentable "imitation for imitation's sake" approach would find little favor with Bakhtin, since such a technique requires neither *authentic* struggle with another's language, nor demands any apparent purpose—for the student at least—beyond the fact of imitation itself. Imitation, from a Bakhtinian perspective, must have some purpose beyond itself.

And how might it be possible to illustrate the rhetorical character of a dialogic imitation? One way would be to return to that most obvious of double-voiced discourse, parody. By its very nature, parody offers a way to raise two issues of enduring concern to rhetorical instruction, namely, the importance of situational context and the significance of audience. Indeed, the writing of parody can serve as a springboard for discussions that attempt to address the problems of contexts and readers.

Of the first of these, for example, Gary Saul Morson observes that it is impossible to parody linguistic matter—say, for example, the "unit" of linguistics, the sentence. This is due to the fact that parody is always parody of an utterance, of a speech act occurring within a situational context. According to Morson, "we cannot parody words, syntax, or any other element, whether 'formal' or 'material' out of which utterances are made, but only utterances themselves, since parody cannot avoid the recontextualization of one voice by another ("Parody" 73). Parody, then, is not a comment about the linguistic features of another's word; it is a comment on the situational context in which the original voice was heard. Thus parody directs our attention away from the text "to the *occasion* (more accurately, the parodist's version of the occasion) of its *uttering*" (71). Morson explains how this is possible:

> The parodist . . . aims to reveal the otherwise covert aspects of that occasion, including the unstated motives and assumptions of both the speaker and the assumed and presumably sympathetic audience. Unlike that audience, the audience of the parody is asked to consider why someone might make, and someone else entertain, the original utterance. By pointing to the unexamined presuppositions and unstated interests that conditioned the original exchange, the parodist accomplishes what Fielding calls "the discovery of affectation" . . . the divergence between professed and unacknowledged intentions—or the discovery of naiveté. (71–72)

Parody, then, is not so much linguistic play, but social commentary, an evaluation and critique of someone else's use of language in a prior situation. And as Morson also indicates, parody is thoroughly contingent on a developed sense of audience awareness.

Some of the complexities of this awareness can be apprehended through an examination of parody, because parody presumes secondary and tertiary audiences. That is, not only does the parodist address the one parodied in the parody itself, but every parody is, as Morson points out, "an interaction designed to be heard and interpreted by a third person (or second 'second' person), whose own process of active reception is anticipated and directed" (65). The parodist, to borrow Bakhtin's phrase, deploys the "word with a sidelong glance," forever conscious that his message is one addressed in at least two directions. Moreover, the parodist often invokes what is sometimes called a *conspiratorial audience*, one that is invited to something of a privileged view on a prior discourse—or even a prior audience. Indeed, in order to accomplish their intended effects, some parodies demand that the parodist's audience evaluate the audience addressed by the original.

Requiring students to write their own parodies, then, is important because, as a particularly dialogic form of imitation, it allows them the opportunity to have experience and practice in writing double-voiced discourse and, hence, an opportunity to exercise simultaneously the "two gestures" that Bartholomae refers to—one imitative, the other critical. It also (and typically) entails seeing through the eyes of another's language, and, thus, requires the kind of continual shifting in perspective that Bakhtin might applaud. But finally, as I have tried to show here, parody is useful because it offers an excellent way to broach some of the complexities of three enduring staples of rhetorical education: context, audience, and purpose.

IMITATION, IMAGINATION, AND DIALOGUE

While I have taken some pains to show how Bakhtin might ask us to rethink imitation, and while I have tried to enunciate some general features of what such an imitation would consist of, I have avoided offering classroom activities and exercises, assignments, guidelines, pointers, etc. In one sense, I doubt whether it is necessary to do so. Having co-authored an extensive review of the literature on imitation, I can attest to no shortage of imaginative approaches to imitative pedagogies. The only shortage I can discern is that few scholars in rhetoric and composition have seriously attempted to develop classroom pedagogies that understand imitation dialogically.[6]

This is unfortunate in my view. Bakhtin's theories of dialogue, I think, have the potential to free us of our conventional ideas about imitation—and conventional ideas about why it ought to be rejected. Bakhtin would remind us that our present certainties, even those regarding imitation, are likely to become canonized, routinized, and that we therefore might be wise to eschew any and all last word pronouncements about anything. "Nothing is absolutely dead," Bakhtin tells us, "every meaning will have its homecoming festival" (*SG* 170). Could this be true, even of imitation?

I do not know the answer to that question. Perhaps, despite the judgments of Corbett and Connors, imitation will someday make a comeback. Whether or not this comes to pass, I happen to believe that Bakhtin's ideas may already help us understand why imitation was a centerpiece of language instruction through centuries past. I also happen to believe that Bakhtin's ideas could possibly challenge us to develop pedagogies that find a place for imitation in the future, but only an imitation understood dialogically. I have tried to offer a few signposts along this pathway.

NOTES

1. Our count of publications about imitation differs considerably from Connors's. Though we do not know his particular methodology or exactly how he defined imitation, we surmise that our study is generally broader in scope and more inclusive of how imitation has been approached in fields adjacent to composition studies (e.g., English education, speech communication, etc.), but not strictly within our disciplinary boundaries proper. Of course, the inclusion of these related disciplines bears precisely upon his argument: when composition studies emerged out of these other disciplines, according to Connors, sentence rhetorics, such as imitation, experienced their greatest popularity. Our trends, for the most part, confirm his own, and we generally agree with his conclusions. Where we depart, however, is on the question of whether or not imitation must be considered exclusively within the province of the sentence.

2. In addition to those postmodern thinkers that Minock identifies as possible sources for a revivified understanding of imitation, the work of René Girard has garnered some recent attention as well. In a response to Richard Boyd's "Imitate Me; Don't Imitate Me," Robert Brooke has sought to understand the mutual resistances that occur between teachers and their students in the context of Girard's work on mimetic desire and its consequent rivalries. Brooke speculates, as well, that Girard may offer us a framework for understanding how both the freshman student and the freshman writing programs they inhabit can be understood as scapegoats for institutional versions of mimetic rivalry. Conversely, Brooke points out that composition teachers often exercise what Girard calls "renunciative identifications" with the victims of the scapegoating process as, say, when we ally with students and Freire against the structure of institutional oppressions. Brooke doesn't explore the pedagogical implications of Girard's work as much as he does the professional, but he does suggest a promising avenue of inquiry along mimetic lines.

3. Yet, the idea that there may be some affinity between these two terms is an old one indeed. In his *Handlist of Rhetorical Terms*, Richard Lanham identifies "dialogismus" as a cross-reference for "mimesis," noting the former to be defined as "speaking in another's character" (52). In some considerable measure, of course, it is precisely the complexities of "speaking in character" (broadly understood) that Bakhtin explores.

4. See especially Sullivan, who identifies three "aspects of the modern temper" that make it difficult, if not impossible, to "appreciate imitation" in the same way our ancestors could (15): "the myth of progress," "the romantic emphasis on genius," and "the technological mind-set." The second of these aspects, Sullivan argues, results from the Romantic substitution of "genius for invention" (16). Recent scholarship, however, has challenged this view of Romantic rhetoric and its putative manifestation in expressivist pedagogy. See Roskelly and Ronald; Gradin.

5. This feature of Bakhtinian subjectivity has recently been critiqued by Jeffrey Nealon. Linking the Bakhtinian subject to the "bourgeois, appropriative self" of Horkheimer and Adorno, Nealon contrasts the Bakhtinian subject with the version of subjectivity proposed by Emanuel Levinas. Bakhtin serves as a rather stark foil for Levinas in Nealon's comparison.

6. I admit to being one of those few. See my "A Language of One's Own."

WORKS CITED

Bakhtin, M. M. *Art and Answerability: Early Philosophical Essays by M. M. Bakhtin.* Trans. Vadim Liapunov. Supp. trans. Kenneth Brostrom. Ed. Michael Holquist and Vadim Liapunov. Austin: Univ. of Texas Press, 1981.

———. *The Dialogic Imagination: Four Essays.* Trans. Caryl Emerson and Michael Holquist. Austin: Univ. of Texas Press, 1981.

———. *Problems of Dostoevsky's Poetics.* Trans. and ed. Caryl Emerson. Theory and History of Literature 8. Minneapolis: Univ. of Minnesota Press, 1984.

———. *Speech Genres and Other Late Essays.* Trans. Vern W. McGee. Ed. Caryl Emerson and Michael Holquist. University of Texas Press Slavic Series, 8. Austin: Univ. of Texas Press, 1986.

———. *Toward a Philosophy of the Act.* Trans. Vadim Liapunov. Ed. Michael Holquist and Vadim Liapunov. University of Texas Press Slavic Series, 10. Austin: Univ. of Texas Press, 1993.

Bartholomae, David. "Inventing the University." In *When a Writer Can't Write,* ed. Mike Rose, 134–65. New York: Guilford Press, 1985.

Bialostosky, Don H. "Booth's Rhetoric, Bakhtin's Dialogics, and the Future of Novel Criticism." *Novel: A Forum on Fiction* 18 (spring 1985): 209–16.

Boyd, Richard. "Imitate Me; Don't Imitate Me: Mimeticism in David Bartholomae's 'Inventing the University.'" *JAC* 11 (1991): 335–45.

Brooke, Robert. "René Girard and the Dynamics of Imitation, Scapegoating, and Renunciative Identification: A Response to Richard Boyd." *JAC* 20 (2000): 167–76.

Connors, Robert. "The Erasure of the Sentence." *College Composition and Communication* 52 (September 2000): 96–128.

Corbett, Edward P. J. "The Theory and Practice of Imitation in Classical Rhetoric." *College Composition and Communication* 22 (1971): 243–50.

Farmer, Frank. " 'A Language of One's Own': A Stylistic Pedagogy for the Dialogic Classroom." *Freshman English News* 19 (fall 1990): 16–22.

Freire, Paulo. *Pedagogy of the Oppressed.* Trans. Myra Bergman Ramos. New York: Continuum, 1970.

Gradin, Sherrie. *Romancing Rhetorics: Social Expressivist Perspectives on the Teaching of Writing.* Portsmouth, NH: Boynton/Cook-Heinemann, 1995.

Klancher, Jon. "Bakhtin's Rhetoric." In *Reclaiming Pedagogy: The Rhetoric of the Classroom*, eds. Patricia Donahue and Ellen Quandahl, 83–96. Carbondale: Southern Illinois Univ. Press, 1989.

Lanham, Richard A. *A Handlist of Rhetorical Terms.* 2nd ed. Berkeley: Univ. of California Press, 1991.

Lodge, David. *After Bakhtin: Essays on Fiction and Criticism.* London: Routledge, 1990.

Minock, Mary. "Toward a Postmodern Pedagogy of Imitation." *JAC* 15 (1995): 489–509.

Morson, Gary Saul. "Parody, History, and Metaparody." In *Rethinking Bakhtin: Extensions and Challenges*, ed. Gary Saul Morson and Caryl Emerson, 63–86. Evanston, IL.: Northwestern Univ. Press, 1989.

Morson, Gary Saul, and Caryl Emerson. *Mikhail Bakhtin: Creation of a Prosaics.* Stanford: Stanford Univ. Press, 1990.

Nealon, Jeffrey T. "The Ethics of Dialogue: Bakhtin and Levinas." *College English* 59 (February 1997): 129–48.

Roskelly, Hephzibah, and Kate Ronald. *Reason to Believe: Romanticism, Pragmatism, and the Teaching of Writing.* Albany: SUNY Press, 1998.

Schuster, Charles. "Mikhail Bakhtin as Rhetorical Theorist." *College English* 47 (1985): 594–607.

Sullivan, Dale L. "Attitudes Toward Imitation: Classical Culture and Modern Temper." *Rhetoric Review* 8 (fall 1998): 5–21.

Vygotsky, Lev S. *Mind in Society: The Development of Higher Psychological Processes.* ed. Michael Cole, Vera John-Steiner, Sylvia Scribner, and Ellen Souberman. Cambridge: Harvard Univ. Press, 1978.

26   *Style/Substance Matrix*

RICHARD A. LANHAM

Rationality is only an instrumental concept: it refers to how people go about achieving their goals. Where do goals come from? In traditional "narrow economics" we do not ask this question.

—Jack Hirshleifer and David Hirshleifer,
Price Theory and Applications

In the inanimate action of matter upon matter, the motion produced can be but equal to the force of the moving power; but the operations of life, whether private or public, admit no such laws. The *caprices of voluntary agents laugh at calculation.*

—Samuel Johnson, *Thoughts on the Late Transactions respecting Falkland's Islands* (my emphasis)

Style and substance, fluff and stuff are loose and baggy categories but useful ones even so. Important versus peripheral, planned versus spontaneous, natural versus mannered, appearance versus reality, inside versus outside, why versus how, manner versus matter: we must make such distinctions every day. Confusingly enough, though, such pairings describe both the world and what we think is important in it, so the opposites in each pair can change places in a wink. If you are a car designer, for you the style of the car will be the substance. If you are a philosopher, "what you think about things" will be the "things" of your world.

Such loose but handy categories do not endear themselves to the scientific mind, either physical or social, and rightly so. What good are terms if they can change places with their opposites just by how you look at them? Worse still, if you can't define the one without the other, if you can't define "backstage" without defining "front stage." Such definition by oscillation causes the poets no problem. So Wallace Stevens:

From *The Economics of Attention: Style and Substance in the Age of Information* (Chicago, IL: University of Chicago Press, 2006), 157–81.

> Two things of opposite natures seem to depend
> On one another, as a man depends
> On a woman, day on night, the imagined
> On the real. This is the origin of change.

But origin of change though it may be, such bi-polarity will cause those driving without a poetic license some difficulty. Let me try now to define the style-substance pairing more richly. If you are to understand how it does originate change, you must show it in action. I've chosen to do so in a set of spectra that I call a matrix. I use the term not in the mathematical or modern movie sense but in a simple dictionary definition: "A place or enveloping element within which something originates, takes form, or develops." The "something" here is the style/substance judgment we make every day.

Let me put the matrix before you (Figure 26–1); then we'll examine it a spectrum at a time.

FIGURE 26–1   Style/Substance Matrix

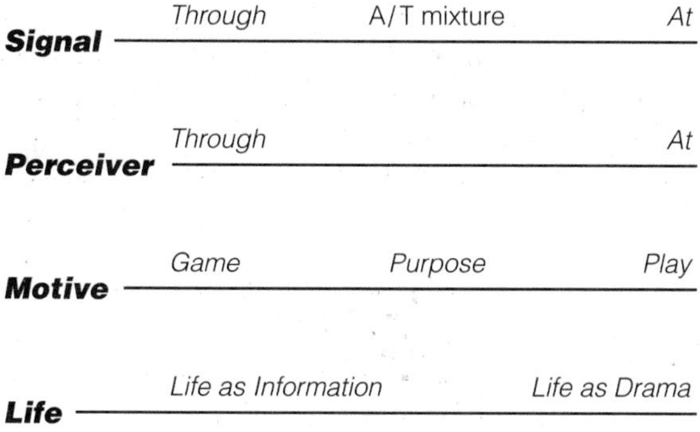

	Through	A/T mixture	At
Signal			

	Through		At
Perceiver			

	Game	Purpose	Play
Motive			

	Life as Information		Life as Drama
Life			

THE SIGNAL SPECTRUM

Let's start by considering the means of expression. I'm going to call it the signal and use it to refer to text, image, or sound. We first notice that it is a variable. Some signals are naturally more artful, more self-conscious than others. Some ask you to notice the magnificence of their going, others not. Some players only try to hit a home run; others point to center field first. We call a magnificent painting a "masterpiece," meaning a work of surpassing, but unassuming, genius. But a "masterpiece" originally meant a deliberate show-off piece, the piece of work every apprentice made to prove that he was a "master." It deliberately displayed all of the talents required for his craft. (Every scholar revising a Ph.D. dissertation into a first book is trying to move from a "masterpiece" in the original sense to one in the second.) Some movie celebrities are famous for their acting, others for being famous. A Honda sedan driven to work projects one kind of signal. A Honda coupe "slammed" by lowering the suspension, fitting a loud flow-through exhaust system, an even louder stereo system, and special wheels with inverted rims, projects quite another. You're reading these words in a transparent typeface but *suppose I change to a more ornate one?* Still easy to read but more attention is called to the form. We are asked to look at as well as through. And if I really want to show off? *How about this?*

How might we measure this variable without condemning any particular degree of it? Suppose we sought to plot expression on a spectrum that looked like this.

	Through	A/T mixture	*At*
Signal			

At one end, the *through* ideal. Minimal awareness of an expressive medium. At the other end, the *at* ideal. Maximal awareness of how we say what we do, or paint it, or sound it out. In the middle, all the daily mixtures. Please note: no point on the spectrum is intrinsically evil or virtuous; it seeks to describe rather than to proscribe, to analyze rather than to condemn. Our natural impulse is to condemn self-conscious form. Fonts made to be noticed are called display fonts. Hot-rodded cars are for "show" as often as for "go." Doctoral dissertations that parade your learning to prove you've done it are, often, a terrific soporific. But at that stage in the game you are obliged to display your learning. When you are an adolescent the temptation to display vehicular courtship splendor is irresistible. You want to celebrate the style of your going. Why, if all you need is American Typewriter, were the hundreds of other fonts invented? Why are there now Web sites devoted to inventing and selling, or giving away, new font designs? It is stylistic self-consciousness that drives much of human invention. We condemn it at our peril. Can't we bring to all these efforts a more capacious understanding? The human imagination wants to use the entire range of stylistic self-consciousness, not merely one point on it. And each point on it brings with it a characteristic mixture of powers.

Look . . . at the AB visual pun . . . (Figure 26–2). Here, the designer has deliberately invoked a particular kind of attention, one that oscillates between perception in two dimensions and perception in three, between letters as flat symbols and as three-dimensional objects. They are transparent as symbols, opaque as three-dimensional objects. The designer attempts to yoke together the two extremes of the signal spectrum, to bend it around into a circle. As with all puns, the aim is compression of meaning. Here again, the paradoxical connection is between stuff and what we think about stuff. Between two ways of thinking about (among other things) economics. To dismiss such an effort as "unclear" dismisses such an experiment before we can understand what it is trying to accomplish.

Designs, in the real world, are often more complex than they seem. Consider, for example, a famous architectural design, Mies van der Rohe's Farnsworth House (Figure 26–3). An example of *through* design if ever there was one—you can see straight through it into the garden beyond. Every detail has been pared away to reveal the genus "house" and nothing else: foundation,

FIGURE 26–2   Bart Overly, *Ligature* (1995). *By permission of the artist.*

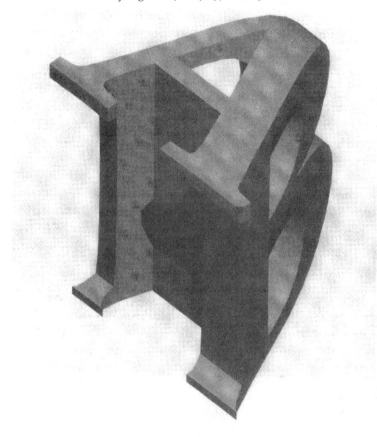

four walls, roof. Pure unornamented use. The glass walls provide a transparent window into a domestic dwelling space pared to its essentials.

When you walk around and in it, though, as you can now do since it has been opened to the public, you feel the spareness of it as you do, say, in Shaker designs. Mies's career was one long attempt to get rid of architectural decoration of every sort, but, as with Shaker design, the resulting aesthetic paradoxically brings formal self-consciousness, the basis of decoration, flooding in by the back door. Never has there been a structure more self-conscious about its form. Mies was compulsive about it, grinding the rough edges off the structural steel to make decoration out of its abolition, agonizing about what part of the utilities stack should show beneath the house, refusing to fit screens even though the mosquitoes in this river bottom land eat you alive in the summer.

The attention we bestow on the house is fundamentally paradoxical: our stuff/nonstuff paradox again. We feel its absence of ornamentation as intensely ornamental. It occupies, at the same time, the through and at extremes on our spectrum. The two ends of the spectrum seem to be pulled

FIGURE 26–3   Mies van der Rohe, Architect, Farnsworth House. *Photograph by author (1999).*

together into a style/substance pun. The house, in this way, seems almost a statement about the spectrum of design itself. The pun between the two kinds of vision makes us self-conscious about how we are seeing. This paradoxical placement at both extremes suggests a second spectrum, one that plots the same range of self-consciousness but in the beholder not in the signal.

THE PERCEIVER SPECTRUM

Signals of all sorts bring with them their own suggestions, then, about where they might be placed on a spectrum of formal self-consciousness. But we can choose, if we like, to ignore these indications and bring a different kind of attention to the experience. A simple example: an art gallery is a place to which we bring an *at* expectation. We expect to be looking at paintings as paintings. We don't usually look at a Brueghel harvest landscape as an agronomist might, trying to decipher what kind of grain is being cut and what the probable yield per acre might be. That's not what art galleries are for. Yet we could do this, if we happened to be an agronomist. We can for our own purposes bring a kind of attention that falls on the *through* side of the spectrum. Sailors do this when they look at a picture of sailboats at sea and check to make sure that wind and sails form a consistent and realistic relationship. I do exactly the opposite when the spirit moves me by going to granite yards to look at the stone. I'm not planning to build anything more from these huge sheets of polished stone. They simply embody beautiful patterns, these slices of geologic history. Masquerading as a customer, I visit these slabs of dirty rock exactly as I would go to an art gallery.

A literary critic does the same thing when she reads a work of literature. Ordinary readers read for pleasure, to "get lost in a book," live other lives and see through other eyes. Reading this way, we don't, as a critic does, chart, measure, analyze, count, because such murder by dissection spoils the fun. I'm an addicted reader of detective fiction, thrillers, war stories, and tales of the sea, and as I read I sometimes start locating them on an analytical grid of literary romance, starting with the Greek romances that come to us from several centuries before Christ. But when I do, I'm switching modes of attention, changing selves, working a different part of the brain. And the same thing happens when I notice Patrick O'Brian's prose style instead of wondering whether the ship will sink.

So here is a second spectrum, which plots the perceiver, not the signal perceived.

Perceiver — *Through* ———————————————— *At*

We can choose any point on this spectrum as a way to look at the world, to pay attention, to distinguish style from substance. Some people endure difficult lives by learning to look at them, consider them as dramas to which they have a free ticket. Jane Austen's Mr. Bennet, the father in *Pride and Prejudice*, learns to live this way as an alternative to strangling his wife and drowning one, or perhaps two, of his daughters. Other people come across as hysterical because they can never detach themselves from any scene, always seeking immersion in its drama. They live at the other end of the spectrum. Life is for them one emotional thunderstorm after another.

A great deal of money is spent in the business world on retreats and seminars of various sorts that aim to move the seminarians from the left side of the spectrum to the right, at least for a day or a week. People immersed in absorbing and demanding daily tasks are asked to step back and reflect on these tasks and on their place in the larger enterprise. They are being asked to look at the business as an art, to look *at* what they spend exhausting days working *through*. Because they have, mostly, had no training in throwing this switch, it is always hard for them to throw it. A consultant must be hired who specializes in this toggling. *At* vision looks impossibly theoretical and arty to someone hardened into one shape by daily tasks. Yet, obviously, employees who can range across the spectrum are the most adroit, in a larger sense the most efficient, employees. One might almost define managerial skill as the ability to understand and work at any point on the spectrum of perception. And the higher up you go on the management tree, the more this is so. The Japanese practice of rotating workers among the different jobs in a large corporation aims to cultivate just such awareness, as does the American military's conception of a tour of duty at a particular location for a definite time.

Human talents, these training procedures assume, are best cultivated by learning how to look at the world from many viewpoints on the perceiver's spectrum. This is the "practicality" that, in an economics of attention, replaces the "stick to your last," "keep your head down and work," and "don't go wandering off into academic theorizing," which defines "practicality" in a goods economy. You should certainly stick to your stuff, but the stuff you stick to is different, and always shifting. Style is always turning into substance and back again.

The same problem occurs in the world of university teaching and scholarship. People absorbed in a particular research agenda can teach that agenda quite well, sometimes at least, but find it awkward, or even repugnant, to step back and try to place it in the broader context of a survey course. And people good at teaching survey courses often don't triumph as researchers. The professional schizophrenia endemic in American higher education comes from its insistence that, at least in theory, professors successfully span the entire perceiver spectrum.

You can see this choice of an *at* perspective in all kinds of hobbies. A devotee of audio equipment will listen to music alert not to how well the Emerson String Quartet is playing Mozart but to how well they have been recorded, how clearly the separation of the instruments is rendered, how wide the soundstage is. A film director looking at Branagh's film of *Hamlet* will remark not on the quality of the acting but on how garishly the picture is lit. The experimental American composer John Cage made a career of asking us to listen *at* the sounds that surround us, rather than through them. If you notice ambient sounds as sounds, they become—at least to Cage—"musical" by that act of attention.

There is nothing wrong with any of this; you are free to choose what you pay attention to, and other people should be free to recommend one place on the perceiver spectrum rather than another. Sometimes, however, having chosen a particular way to look at the world, we cast a jaundiced eye on those who have chosen another way. There is a reason for this.

The great American rhetorician Kenneth Burke was fond of saying, "Every way of seeing is a way of not seeing." He meant that paying attention in one way means you cannot pay attention in another. And the manner of attention changes the object. A lawyer accustomed to reading legal prose will find there a transparent clarity that seems opaque to the lay reader. Translating the legal prose into plain English, as plain language laws now sometimes require, seems to many lawyers to be making it more obscure, not plainer. It undoes everything they were taught in law school.

The same rule governs moving from one sensory modality to another. Designers of multimedia texts, Web sites, for example, or educational texts that involve a real mixture of media, find that their first problem is getting the design team to see the problem in the same way. What is clear to one sense is opaque to another; what seems substance to one seems style to the other. Graphic designers construe the world differently from writers or musicians. One way to harmonize them might be along the perceiver spectrum. It provides a common ground on which to plot inevitable differences. It is thus the backbone, in the largest sense, of interdisciplinary effort of any sort. It provides a place to start useful conversations.

To bring this argument home, ask yourself, as an exercise, what part of your job requires *at* attention and what part requires *through* and which part you enjoy more and why. I asked the same question, although in a different way, when I recently visited a class in rhetoric at a large urban university. The class met at night, and the students all worked during the day in jobs involving, almost to a person, digital design work using words and images. I asked them to suppose that their company had given them six months off with full pay to study whatever it was they thought would help them do their jobs better. What would they study? Almost every reply fell on the right-hand side of the perceiver spectrum, involved a broader background, a more thorough theoretical grounding, training of all sorts that would allow them to look at their jobs rather than through them. Job training of the sort most companies provide falls emphatically on the left side of the spectrum. Practical training is required for jobs that need to be done. Maybe a broader definition of "practicality" might improve productivity fully as much. In a goods economy, the case is hard to make. If you have to run a lathe, you want to learn how to make it turn. In an attention economy, the case for the other side of the spectrum, for the "poetry" of work, may be a stronger one.

I've been developing a justification here for the utility of art. It is by no means an original one. To take only one example, a body of critical thinking in the twentieth century argued that art's job was to defamiliarize experience, to make it new by making us see it in a new way. The technique employed was to make us look at what we usually look through. The power resident in a polyvalent digital code may end up operating in precisely this way, allowing us to renew our experience and enrich it by displacing expression from one sensory mode into another, printing out a message in sound, say, rather than word, or "printing out" in real space the rapid prototype specified in a series of numbers. This defamiliarization has already happened across a broad range of scientific thinking through the visualization techniques developed by computer graphics. One striking example is the translation of mathematical formulas into their visual equivalents. To people like me, whose gift for mathematics must be reckoned in the minus numbers, such translation offers a miraculous democratization. Here's a window into a world that I otherwise simply could not see.

Surely this point is generalizable. Digital expression allows an ease of movement across the perceiver spectrum that was impossible in two-dimensional fixed media of expression. If it is important that we learn to see the world through others' eyes, digital expression offers powerful new tools to do so. The characteristic way to enter the digital expressive field is to fly over it. Here is defamiliarization with a vengeance. All of the now-myriad techniques for manipulating images and sounds fall into the same category. They allow us to work at various places along the perceiver spectrum in new ways. Doing so tells us a good deal about human motive.

THE MOTIVE SPECTRUM

Eric Hoffer, the American popular philosopher, once said that a vigorous society is a society that has set its heart on toys. What can he have meant by this? It contravenes all that we think about human seriousness. Toys are frivolous by definition. Fluff! A vigorous society is a society that has gone back to primitive and simple virtues, "russet yeas and honest kersey noes," seeks to live on Walden Pond, or at least join a volunteer simplicity group that reads Thoreau in the evening instead of going to the mall. No fluff! A vigorous society distinguishes genuine needs from "conspicuous consumption." Toys, except for children, are waste. Grownups should grow up out of them. Stop playing around. A people that has set its heart on toys, so conventional wisdom holds, is a corrupt people, in the last stage of cultural decline. Materialist! Consumerist! Style has replaced substance. The society has lost its moral center, a center that must reside in seriousness, restraint, good sense, and genuine need.

Toys are the behavioral equivalent of an ornate and affected prose style, of a fussy overdecorated Victorian parlor, of an SUV with rhinoceros-guard grille and backseat TV. And just as, when artistic and verbal styles become self-conscious and mannered, we know we have arrived at a "decadent" period, so we know that when toys begin to outnumber tools we have become a decadent people. Thus the formal judgments of art and the moral theories of behavior come together in the C-B-S theory of expression.

But, as we have seen, this theory excludes most of human expression and, in its moral branch, nine-tenths of human behavior as well. Leave out the toys and you leave out a lot. Let's try to recover them by building a third spectrum for our matrix, one on which we can plot human motive. It will allow us to think about style and substance in a more satisfactory way, to connect formal judgments about expression and moral judgments about behavior.

	Game	*Purpose*	*Play*
Motive			

This time let's start in the center and work outward to both sides. In the middle, we find the practical motives of daily life. Plain purpose, let's call it. Here in the middle we buy a car not to flaunt our income, or our good taste, but to get to work and to the grocery store. We buy a house not to feed a hunger for Mies-like simplicity or Victorian clutter, or to shoulder up to the curb a little larger than the house next door, but to give each of the kids a bedroom and mom and dad a little insulation from the rap music. We pay attention to things that architects ignore, like roofs that don't leak, floors that don't cup or squeak, and enough light so you can read a book. And we factor in our ability to pay the mortgage. Here reside good sensible people like us, and if the vigor of a society does not reside here, where are we to look for it?

At the left, or "game," extreme of our behavioral spectrum, we locate the competitive side of human nature. It is immense, if not always predominant. The struggle for dominance and reproductive advantage animates the animate world. We humans are hierarchical primates, concerned above everything else about where we stand on the social ladder. If we are born on the bottom, we fight our way to the top, or try to, thereby providing novelists with rich material. Or, if we are born at the top, we often lose our balance and fall off, thereby providing medieval storytellers with rich material about the wheel of fortune and the fall of kings. If we get to the top and stay there, we are likely to have a midlife crisis in which we feel sorry for ourselves because we did not spend more time sniffing the roses on the way up, providing yet more material for novelists and for social scientists who study the stages of life.

We dramatize this struggle in every way we know how because it is, after all, the fundamental human one, the struggle to survive and to prevail. The ancient Greeks calibrated it in fame, in the everlasting honor of always being first, *aien aristeuein*, as Homer puts it. We calibrate it in money, and business magazines obligingly provide rankings of the richest among us, so the next richest and next-next richest can eat their hearts out. The game is the best metaphor for this sort of human motive. We want to win the game. Which game is irrelevant. Winning is everything. The games themselves are like an expressive surface; you look through them to the vital struggle beneath. It doesn't matter whether you are a football captain, or an army captain, or a captain of industry, so long as you are a captain of something.

If this kind of motive stands at the bedrock of our nature — and human history seems to permit no other conclusion — it is often a pretty bleak rock. Ambition denatures experience, the day-to-day living of life, makes life so transparent that we no longer see it. We look through it to the vital scoring of points that lies beneath. We are held prisoner by our hierarchical hungers. (When Homer gives Achilles a choice of a short famous life or a long obscure one, he had in mind something deeper than death as the alternative. When you live the life of ambition, a part of you dies even if you live long.) Yet here, I think many people would agree, is where the real dynamic power, the true vigor, of a society resides. Ambition drives the intellectual as well as the economic engine. We must then reconsider our conclusion that social vigor, the real substance of life, lies in the careful center of practical purpose. Enterprises are not created by nine-to-fivers who go home and have dinner with their families, who work to live rather than live to work.

If we can all agree on anything, it seems to be that the other extreme of the motivational spectrum, which I have called play, saps social vigor rather than energizing it. Here clusters all the scorn contained in terms like "ornament" instead of "meaning," and "decoration" instead of "essence," "rhetoric" instead of "truth" — "style" instead of "substance." Fluff! Here we find the refined aesthetics of art rather than the firm realities of stuff. Here we find connoisseurs and students of the struggle rather than participants in it. Here we find scientists and scholars with paltry career skills who pursue inquiry for the pleasure of knowledge rather than the pursuit of a Nobel prize, a Barbara McClintock, for example, as against a James Watson. Here we find mountaineers who climb mountains simply because they are there to climb, as opposed to the rescue teams who climb them for the purpose of rescuing the climbers who climb them simply because they are there. In the valleys below, dedicated fishermen, having traveled far and expensively, take great pains to catch fish that they then release to bite again another day while, a pond away, naive natives catch the fish in order to eat them.

Kipling caught the essence of such motives in "When Earth's Last Picture Is Painted" (1892):

When Earth's last picture is painted and the tubes are twisted and dried,
When the oldest colors have faded, and the youngest critic has died,
We shall rest, and, faith, we shall need it — lie down for an aeon or two,
Till the Master of All Good Workmen shall put us to work anew.
And those that were good shall be happy: they shall sit in a golden chair;
They shall splash at a ten-league canvas with brushes of comets' hair.
They shall find real saints to draw from — Magdalene, Peter, and Paul;
They shall work for an age at a sitting and never be tired at all!
And only The Master shall praise us, and only The Master shall blame;
And no one shall work for money, and no one shall work for fame,
But each for the joy of the working, and each, in his separate star,
Shall draw the Thing as he sees It for the God of Things as They are!

"The joy of the working." Here we find the amateur as against the professional, the player who plays the game for the pleasure of the playing, not of the winning. Occasionally this contrast finds dramatic representation. In a recent Olympics, one of the ice-skaters, a young Japanese woman, gave a performance so tense and wound up, so concentrated on the technical acrobatics that she had to perform, that it was painful to watch. She was skating out the cold terrors of ambition before your very eyes. The skating was good enough, however, to win the competition and relieve her of the pressures of losing the game and, as she must have felt, disgracing her country. Afterward, the specter of shame banished, there was a skating exhibition by the medal winners, just for the pleasure of the skating. Here her performance was transformed into a beauty and grace and ease that brought tears to your eyes. Here, I said to myself, is what all the commentators were talking about when they talked about her transcendent talent. But it was allowed expression only when she moved from the game extreme of the spectrum to the play extreme.

If the game extreme has a biogrammatical underpinning in hierarchical primate hungers, so one occurs at the play extreme too. Konrad Lorenz, the great student of animal behavior, coined the term "vacuum behavior" for acts that a species just wants to do, has inherited a genetic hunger to perform. Performance brings its own satisfaction. It doesn't have to accomplish anything else. We are born, it seems, with hungers to behave in certain ways. Dancers are born wanting to dance, musicians to play, artists to draw. They do so because, in some deep way, they must. Something inside craves expression. The circuits want to fire. For the rest of us, although perhaps we feel such pressures, we don't find the opportunity (or, usually, the talent) to express them in practical daily life. From this genetic kernel springs one of the great, and greatly undervalued, domains of daily life, the world of hobbies.

Every activity on earth, it seems, can give pleasure in the enactment, from acting out deadly Civil War battles happily on a Saturday afternoon to jumping out of an airplane and doing group acrobatics before you open your parachute. This love of form for its own sake we see everywhere in Western culture, from Egyptian tomb decorations that would never be seen by the living, to gargoyles on Gothic cathedrals that the living could see only from airplanes not yet invented, to hot-rodders chrome-plating parts of the engine that no one will ever see. (But wait a minute; haven't style and substance changed places here, too? The tomb decorations were intended to serve a purpose in the afterlife; the gargoyles, as the art historian Ruth Mellinkoff has recently demonstrated in *Averting Demons*, were intended to scare away demons; chrome-plating, in its origins, was intended to preserve a metal surface.)

In play lie the pleasures of theater purely conceived, of amateur theater, whether it takes place on stage or in life. We might include here, for example, Louis XIV, who lived his life as a series of staged rituals, the *métier du roi*. Or closer to home, we might locate at this end of the spectrum people whose manners seem to us affected or needlessly refined, all the people who over-play their roles. All the behavior in life that is not sincere, and not likely to be brief or clear, either—"stylized" in fact.

We view this cluster of motives with an ambivalent and paradoxical eye. On the one hand, these are the motives that the clarity-brevity-sincerity theory of communication and behavior teaches us to despise. Behavior of this sort stands outside our normal range of causality and so, outside any productivity formula. It is a wild card, and bean counters don't like wild cards. Neither do scholars. If people often do things for the hell of it then much of intellectual history is devoted to finding motives and causes where there were none. If people write poetry or music simply because they were born to do so, then what becomes of copyright law, which argues that artistic creation must be motivated by profit or artists will down tools and sell insurance instead?

On the other hand, such motives seem to have an admirable purity. We admire the amateur playing the game for its own sake rather than the pampered shortstop whining because he makes a few million a year less than the man playing second base next to him. We admire a fisherman who will go to the antipodes to find rare fishing and then release the catch. A selfless dedication to what you do, a desire to do the best job you know how to do, whether it be restoring an old car or teaching a class or conducting a sales campaign or trying to find the answer to a scholarly question, brings out the best in us. We are not trying to serve ourselves and we are not trying to serve our fellows; we are serving a formal ideal. We act out of disinterested generosity of spirit, for the pure love of form. We pursue the goal for its own sake. We are drawing the Thing as we see it for the God of Things as They are.

Most of us act this way once in a while. Some people, however, characteristically act in this way. They are the pure researchers, the mechanics who love machinery, the workers who work for the joy of the working. They love their activity for its own sake, whether it is exploring the genetics of corn or the location of the magneto in a classic Isotta-Fraschini motor car. In a world of danger and chance, they find moral guidance in a loyalty to form. Hamlet says, of such guidance, "Rightly to be great is . . . to find quarrel in a straw, when honor's at the stake." They have chosen to live in the domain of pure play. They have "set their heart on toys." In more than a manner of speaking, style has become their substance.

Our paradoxical attitude toward this kind of motive has played itself out in contemporary society in two opposing directions. On the one hand, many of our basic activities have been displaced into the play sphere. Sex is for re-production only occasionally, the rest of the time for play. The cheaper food becomes, the more we flock to the gourmet club and the wine cellar. The cheaper computers become, the more popular the collection of antique foun-tain pens. We might consider the sixties one long displacement of human be-havior from competition to play. That is what "dropping out and turning on" meant, after all. Even the ultimate trips, the power trips, are moving in this direction. The more we write about the lives of tycoons of industry, the more we see the pattern coalesce into a genre (upward struggle hand-in-hand with partner no. 1, arrival and discontent with partner no. 1 as insufficient for pre-sent greatness, exchange for partner no. 2, high-maintenance but gorgeous, etc.), the more self-conscious we become about it, the more we see it as a role, as displaced to the right side of the spectrum from the left. "Oh, haven't had your midlife crisis *yet*?" And the richer we get, the more our behavior moves into the play sphere. We no longer have to work so hard for a living and we can play more.

At the same time, we intensify the competitive side of our lives at every stage of its living. Six-year-old children are put into football leagues, basket-ball and hockey and baseball leagues, with all the photo albums and awards and other panoply of the professionals. Executives become busier and busier, lawyers bill more and more hours. At every stage and in every occupation, the delights of the work for its own sake are eviscerated in the name of ambition. We become so accustomed to looking through life to the success that lies be-yond it that we forget how to look at it. We boast that we not only "work hard" but "play hard" as well.

A regular development flows in the opposite direction, too, from play to game. Poetry has from its earliest days in Greece moved from pure playful creation to struggle for first prize in that year's drama competition. Today there is something called a National Poetry Slam where poets come together to compete. Activities like drag racing, which began as pure play at making a car accelerate faster, immediately became a game and then moved back to the center of the motive spectrum as a big business. The most dramatic of these changes in motivational flow, in our time, has been in the invention of the computer. The early computer inventors, Zuse, Aiken, Atanasoff, Eckert, and Mauchly, all had practical purposes in mind; they lived in the middle of the motive spectrum. But the theoretical basis for their efforts had been laid by Alan Turing, working isolated in his own thoughts, and developed by John von Neumann, whose central intellectual focus began in game theory. The personal computer, by way of contrast, began in the domain of pure play, a product of the first generation of hackers. The continual dynamic interchange between play and game motives has characterized Western enterprise since World War II. Perhaps this continual flow and reflow characterizes dynamic societies of all sorts.

As in the signal spectrum, the opposites exhibit a strong attraction to one another. A newspaper article about the Tour de France offers a striking instance. "When Lance Armstrong was dropped to the pavement by the wayward handle of a fan's yellow bag, his closest pursuers, even Jan Ullrich, who had trailed Armstrong by only 15 seconds at the day's start, slowed to wait for Armstrong to pick himself up, dust himself off, and get back in the race." About this act of gentlemanly courtesy, so strange in today's world of athletic competition, Ullrich replied: "Of course, I would wait. If I would have won this race by taking advantage of someone's bad luck, then the race was not worth winning." Competition in the Tour de France is about as competitive as competition can be. Pure game. Yet insisting that the game be played in such a way that pure performance, not chance, determined the outcome showed an equal loyalty to pure form, the form of the game. Such behavior bends the two extremes of the spectrum back toward one another as if with a piece of spring steel. This tension, in the literature of chivalry, was called "honor." When you take the tension off the spring, disconnect "winning is everything" at one end of the spectrum from, at the other, the amateur's "it's not who wins but how you play the game," honor evaporates. The title of the article? "In Cycling, Winning with Honor Means Everything."

If there has been an intensification in American life of the middle position between these two extremes, however, I'm not aware of it. Play and game are self-motivating. They spring up spontaneously in human behavior. Not so with calm good sense in the center. Fondness for the ordinary moderate pleasures of ordinary moderate life, what the Greeks called *Sophrosyne*, has not threatened to run out of control. Why not? Isn't ordinary purpose where the generative force of human behavior originates? Doesn't human effort originate in the immediate purposes of ordinary life? Shelter, transportation, food? Shouldn't we, that is, chart the generative power of human behavior this way?

Motive   Game ⟵——————— Purpose ———————⟶ Play
                 _____

But suppose it works the other way, flows from the extremes inward rather than vice versa? Suppose it looks like this:

Motive   Game ———————⟶ Purpose ⟵——————— Play
                 _____

Practical purpose is driven and sustained, if not created, by the goadings of ambition on one side and play on the other. The economic history of the twentieth century would seem to bear this out. Economies driven by the collective dreams of practical purpose, economies where each gives what she can and takes what she needs, have proved gigantic failures. If you abolish hierarchies, they are either re-created or labor turns rancid. The dynamic of ordinary work vanishes. If you abolish nice clothes in favor of Peking uni-smocks or Fidel fatigues, if you outlaw cosmetics, if you proscribe the free play not only of ideas but of anything else, the joyful heart of human life—the joy of the working—shrivels up inside us. When we invert the common proverb by saying that "Invention is the mother of necessity" we try to describe this galvanizing of central ordinary purpose by game and play. Eric Hoffer was pointing to the same movement, but since the dynamics of ambition were so omnipresent, he wanted to stress the corresponding extreme.

But necessity does mother invention, too. A balanced chart of motivational dynamic would look like this:

Motive $Game \longleftrightarrow Purpose \longleftrightarrow Play$

We should bear this fundamental dynamic flow in mind for the other spectra on the matrix. It provides a fundamental, rather than simply a metaphorical, way to connect them. It shows how the style/substance pairing "originates, takes form, and develops."

Considered in this way, the motive spectrum might well be called the productivity spectrum. Whatever managers may think they are doing, they are trying to orchestrate these two flows. The dominant one seems at first to be from the center outward, but the larger lessons of collective versus free economies argue for the opposite flow. The inventor may work in the play sphere, and the entrepreneur in the game sphere, but the manager, who by definition works in the middle ground of practical purpose, finds his task in balancing the flow from the extremes without inhibiting it. No wonder good managing is such hard work.

We might for a moment reflect on markets in the light of this chart. We think of markets as created to exchange goods. And so they do, and in a goods economy that would seem to be the end of it. But in an economics of attention, markets trade motives rather than goods. Their great virtue is making human motive fungible. Motives can be mixed and traded. "Attention goods" carry a stylistic charge, and that charge can be competitive (putting down the Joneses) or playful (watching an Alexander Calder mobile detect the ambient air currents) or deceitful (selling a fake Calder as a real one). You can buy into a range of motives as wide as the range of goods. Imagine buying a new car: you don't want it to break down (Honda); you may want it to tell people where you are in the world (Mercedes, BMW, Ford Explorer, generic plain van); you may want it to be fun to drive (Miata). You buy a package of satisfied mixed motives. The attention economy that has always hovered over cars lets you pick and choose among motive packages.

Friedrich Hayek regarded this fungibility of motive as the purpose of money:

> ... the erroneous belief that there are purely economic ends separate from the other ends of life.
>
> Yet, apart from the pathological case of the miser, there is no such thing. The ultimate ends of the activities of reasonable beings are never economic. ... What in ordinary language is misleadingly called the "economic motive" means merely the desire for general opportunity, the desire for power to achieve unspecified ends. If we strive for money, it is because it offers us the widest choice in enjoying the fruits of our efforts. ... Money is one of the greatest instruments of freedom ever invented by man.

Here you can see the interface between the stuff economy and the attention economy.

If managing is an affair of motive mixing, then productivity is a matter of motive mixing, too, of encouraging the flow in both directions, from the extremes inward and from the center outward. To clarify the argument, let me cite two extreme examples from World War II, the Bletchley Park code-breaking establishment in England and the Manhattan Project, which made the atom bomb in the United States.

Work at Bletchley Park was exhausting, nonstop, and intellectually demanding to a surpassing degree. Both generative flows that we've been describing operated at full force. The practical purpose could hardly have been more exigent. Break the German codes and win the war; don't break them and lose it. Immense power flowed from the center outward. But code breaking depends on formal problem solving or playing with a code until it comes clear. The people good at it were people who liked to solve problems for their own sake: chess players, crossword puzzle players, scholars of dead languages, rarified mathematicians—people good at intellectual play. All the powers of play had to be invoked. And the struggle to win the game was equally strong. They had to come in first. Beat the Germans. Both motives operated equally strongly and in a rich roiling mixture. The people who worked there look back on it as the most exciting time of their lives, the time when they felt most engaged, most fulfilled, worked most to purpose.

The Manhattan Project evoked the same powerful mixture and the same sense of landmark labor, of productivity, but the management lesson played itself out more clearly. Physics was, and is, a discipline full of macho competition. A Nobel game. Ambition was the air universally breathed. Yet the play mentality was equally needed for the task in hand. And that task, the practical purpose, was momentous. Get the bomb before the Germans did or lose the war. A manager was needed who could orchestrate both directions of the flow. Normally, someone like General Leslie Groves would have been appointed. A creature of the center with the many talents of the center, he could understand neither the career game of physics nor the mentality of play. But, almost miraculously, Robert Oppenheimer was appointed, General Groves being added as business manager, as balancing liaison with the outside world. Oppenheimer understood both extremes and knew how to orchestrate them. That is what makes the Manhattan Project such a good lesson in management, in how to mix human motives for maximum yield.

I don't mean to suggest by these examples that such rich mixtures of motive occur only in war. Working at Apple Computer in the beginning, or at Microsoft, must have provided the same kind of intense mixture. And the world of ordinary work offers continual examples. But the crucible of war paints the mixture in exemplary colors.

If toys don't provide the sole dynamic, Hoffer was certainly right to single them out as the great neglected power. The play motive has from the beginnings of Western culture been denigrated. Its very name, like style and ornament, is tainted. Play is always opposed to purpose, just as style is always opposed to substance. Purpose is serious; play is not. The genre that has always stigmatized the play motive and despised toys is satire. The satirist's enemy is excess, excess in diet, behavior, clothes, pomp. But the common ground for all these kinds of sin is stylistic self-consciousness. Against the mountain of human folly created by stylistic hungers is juxtaposed good sense, plain purpose, useful clothes, pewter instead of gold. The locus classicus, the prime example, of this genre is Sir Thomas More's *Utopia*. There everything that More despised in the world around him, all the examples of excess, all the toys, all the style is abolished in favor of a regime of rigorous plain purpose and pure substance that has supplied both the model and the name for collective enterprise ever since. More's mantle has been worn most notably in our time by Thorstein Veblen, whose condemnation of "conspicuous consumption" has formed part of our guilt portfolio about stuff ever since. More taught us how and why to hate stuff and Veblen brought the argument up to date.

We might focus these three places on the motive spectrum by using the word "serious" to define them. What do we mean when we say someone is a serious person? Well, a serious doll collector is fully committed to the hobby of doll collecting, spending far too much time and money serving this enthusiasm. A serious lawyer is one who bills ninety hours a week. But if that lawyer should be elevated to the bench, the serious judge who results must consider the whole spectrum of motive in trying to adjudicate human behavior. Seriousness is to behavior as clarity is to writing. It sanctifies whatever position on the spectrum one wishes to make central.

THE REALITY SPECTRUM

The simplification of stylistic judgments is like the simplification of motivational judgments. If you are to give a rich description of style and substance, you must link these two kinds of judgment, consider style and behavior in the same universe. Plotting motive in the same matrix as signal and perceiver does just this. But we need one more spectrum to round out our periodic table for communication, our matrix for style and substance. We've created locations to plot the variables for signal, for perceiver, and for motive. But we need one more, one that plots the reality to which all the others refer. Much of Western intellectual history has been concerned with making reality an invariable. It is simply out there, the reference point for all we do and think. But the reference has varied. For Plato and the many philosophers who followed him, it was a world of ideal forms; for the Middle Ages, it was the mind of God; for Newtonian science, it was the laws of physics. In such worlds, we have felt equally rocklike about ourselves. They were actually there inside us, whether immortal souls or a confident if disbelieving me.

But from classical Greece onward, there has always been an alternative conception of human reality: *O kosmos skene*, the world as theater. The play of the world might be God's great play or humankind's smaller ones, but the dramatic metaphor was more than a metaphor. The world was an essentially theatrical one, essentially self-conscious. That is how we experienced it. Twentieth-century social science has elaborated subplots of the *kosmos skene*, talking about social roles, presentation of self, front stage and backstage, stages of life, and so on. Theatrical thinking is as much with us as ever, though it forms part of the insincere world of artifice that we ritually condemn. So we have now a spectrum with two extremes.

Life ──────────────────────────────────
        Life as Information   *Life as Drama*

At the left, extreme unself-consciousness, we might consider "life as information." Here information provides the stuff of life, not stuff. Plato's world of ideal forms has been reincarnated as a world of genes, of biological forms. It is the genes that provide the templates of life, not abstract forms of human invention. We might just as easily consider the genetic basis of life as the mind of God, manifesting itself in life. However we choose to construe it, though, it provides human life at its most unself-conscious. If we are only a gene machine, the device genes have created to replicate themselves, then the self has become an epiphenomenon, part of a much larger design with which it may have vague feelings of unity but from which it has not emerged as an independent consciousness. We border here on all the arguments from Eastern religions to Emersonian transcendentalism that think of us as all part of one vast oversoul, one great organism of life. Here, too, we might locate the world of dreams and the Freudian argument for human subconsciousness.

We have now to reckon with not only a genetic substrate but with a behavioral one as well. Behavioral biology has argued that behaviors form part of our evolutionary heritage as well as genes, that indeed the behavior is regulated by the genes. Both the genetic and the behavioral worlds preexist our social one and govern its development.

And so we have a full spectrum that looks like this:

Life ──────────────────────────────────
   Life as Information   *Life as Stuff*   *Life as Drama*

Both extremes have been focused and reinforced by digital technology. The left-hand extreme has been reinforced by the arguments of formal communications theory invented by Claude Shannon and by the metamorphic powers of a polyvalent digital code. There, as we have seen, the information precedes the printout we choose, the way we choose to incarnate the information in the world of stuff. The world as theater has intensified all the techniques of digital representation. Simulation, the conversion of conceptual thought into a theatrical equivalent, has become a dominant form of expression. Virtual reality, its real-time equivalent, imposes an omnipresent theatrical self-consciousness on the synthetic reality it creates. Perhaps the most revolutionary reinforcement of life as theater has come, however, from the new discipline of artificial life. Artificial life is the name given to the creation of new forms of life entirely within digital computers, life that evolves according to Darwinian principles but entirely within silicon, not in carbon-based matter, stuff. Life as purely information turns out to be essentially theatrical, radically self-conscious. Again, as with the Tour de France, the extremes attract one another.

Both of these extremes, then, are flooding the troubled middle ground of commonsense stuff-based reality with a confusing and disorienting self-consciousness. If we have to treat self-consciousness as a sin, in the way we have been accustomed to, there won't be much life left in which to be virtuous. Manifestly, our way of thinking about communication, and about how it works in human life, requires the expanded matrix we have constructed here.

OK. What have we constructed?

We started by redeeming the central villain in how we pay attention to the world: self-consciousness. In a textual signal, it need not be a sin. Objects in the world can be constructed to call attention to themselves in all kinds of ways, none intrinsically superior to the other. The long-established cliché that the best art is the art that conceals art is a half truth. It supplies no general rule because it omits much of what it claims to have generated the rule from. As with Mies van der Rohe's Farnsworth House, you do notice the art that is concealed. The better the art, the more it is concealed, the more you notice it. That's why we call it better.

But we can consider art not as objects but as ways of seeing objects. . . . If objects can invite us to look through them or at them, or alternate from at to through using a particular frequency of oscillation between them, then our attention can operate in the same way. Our attention is richest and most powerful when it oscillates between everything that *at* vision does and everything that *through* vision does. And this variation will operate concomitantly with the variation in the signal itself. A particular act of attention will connect a point on one spectrum with a point on another. Together they will constitute knowledge.

"Wisdom," Whitehead tells us in *The Aims of Education*, is "how knowledge is held." The central villainy in the diagram of attention constructed here is not self-consciousness but shutting the at/through oscillation down. When this fruitful oscillation, at a particular point on one spectrum or between spectra, shuts down, then atrophy begins. Francis Bacon saw this in the seventeenth century, when he was pondering how knowledge should be held: "Surely, like as many substances in nature that are solid do putrefy and corrupt into worms, so it is the property of good and sound knowledge to putrefy and dissolve into a number of subtle, idle, unwholesome, and (as I may term them) vermiculate questions, which have indeed a kind of quickness and life of spirit, but no soundness of matter or goodness of quality." Good and sound knowledge requires that questions be always submitted to testing in the world, that the play of theory be immersed in the game of practice. Good and sound knowledge requires, too, that soundness of matter and goodness of quality be continually leavened with the quickness and life of spirit. How we look, and how what we look at asks to be seen, exist in continually changing combinations. If we rule out our stylistic self-consciousness, we rule out the powers of mind that allow us to oscillate between the combinations.

We can, here, avail ourselves of an analogy from the world of electronic music. The Russian scientist and musician Lev Theremin invented a musical instrument that generated a sine wave between two electrical poles. The performer then made music by moving her hands between these two poles, thereby altering the frequency and amplitude of the audio signal. Exactly so do we act in the world, taking a basic oscillation in how we view the world and varying its frequency and amplitude in infinite ways. Game, play, and the central purpose created by their collaboration is always, as we make our way in the world, being mixed in different proportions. Energy flows only when we are waving our hands about!

By now we have moved to the bottom two spectrums of behavior. Let me here invoke an observation from Peter Drucker's first book, *The End of Economic Man.* "Economics as a social or 'moral' science dealing with the social behavior of man and with institutions devised by him, can only claim to be a science if the economic sphere is regarded as autonomous, if not as supreme, and economic aims as desirable over and above all others. Otherwise economics can offer only a historical or classifying description or technical rules for realizing certain economic intentions. But it can supply no 'laws' of economic cause and effect—the criterion of a science." I've been arguing that, in an economics of attention, the economic sphere is not autonomous. The "buying decision" that allocates the scarce commodity of attention is a complex one. It cannot be resolved into a simple choice between selfishness and altruism. The caprices of voluntary agents do indeed laugh at calculation. Information purchases must assess the informational signal, the category of information the perceiver is prepared to perceive, the motivational structure that animates the communication, and the global assumptions about the human world within which human communication takes place. In an economics of attention, we must ask not only how people go about achieving their goals but where the goals come from. Economics in an information economy is about how choices of attention are made and, thus, about human motive. That is what the matrix analyzes into its constituent parts.

To the degree that style and substance change places in an attention economy, it is vital that we be able to relate judgments of the one sort to judgments of the other, to put style and substance into relationships that are as complex as human reality. Only thus can we define either one. We can no longer afford to trivialize the one and reify the other by the words we use to describe them. If, as I've been arguing here, both can be plotted on a common matrix of self-consciousness, we have an integral, and not simply a metaphorical, way of relating them. Any time we discriminate between style and substance, we have made a fixation on all four spectra in the matrix. That self-consciousness should turn out to be a vital, perhaps the vital, variable, should not surprise us. Western culture has been confronting a crisis of self-consciousness ever since the Renaissance, doubly so since Darwin, and triply so since the invention of the new cultural notation, the new literacy, created by the digital expressive field. Coming to terms with self-consciousness means coming to terms with the kind of being we are. We have been sedulously dodging this audit since the Renaissance. The stigmatizing of stylistic self-consciousness is important not least because it points so directly to the similar and larger stigma attached to human motive and human reality. A single matrix, a "place or enveloping element," that aligns these similar variables will help us more candidly and capaciously to confront and understand them and, hence, ourselves.

I quoted Walter Wriston's plea for "a model of economics of information that will schematize its form and functions." The first step in schematizing the form and functions of an information economy is to establish what "style" and "substance" mean and how they are related. It is a complex and dynamic relationship, the one that the matrix of expression I've set forth aspires to model.

ADDITIONAL READINGS

THE RISE AND FALL OF THE STUDY OF STYLE

Brody, Sister Miriam. *Shakespeare's Use of the Arts of Language*. Philadelphia, PA: Paul Dry, 2005.

Butler, Paul. "Out of Style: Reclaiming an 'Inventional Style' in Composition." *Out of Style: Reanimating Stylistic Study in Composition and Rhetoric*, 56–85. Logan: Utah State University Press, 2008.

Cicero. *De Oratore*. Trans. E. W. Sutton. Vol. 1, Bks. 1, 2. Cambridge, MA: Harvard University Press, 1949.

———. Trans. H. Rackham. Vol. 2, Bk. 3. Cambridge, MA: Harvard University Press, 1960.

Crowley, Sharon. "The Current-Traditional Theory of Style: An Informal History." *Rhetoric Society Quarterly* 16 (1986): 233–50.

———. "Linguistics and Composition Instruction: 1950–1980. *Written Communication* 6 (1989): 480–505.

Demetrius. *A Greek Critic: Demetrius on Style*. Trans. G. M. A. Grube. Toronto: University of Toronto Press, 1961.

Fogarty, Daniel. *Roots for a New Rhetoric*. New York: Teachers College Press, 1959.

Fortune, Ron. "Style in Composition Research and Teaching." *Style* 23 (1989): 508–29.

Gorgias. "Encomium of Helen." In *The Older Sophists*, ed. Rosamund Kent Sprague, 50–63. Trans. George A. Kennedy. Columbia: University of South Carolina Press, 1972.

Howell, William Samuel. *Eighteenth-Century British Logic and Rhetoric*. Princeton, NJ: Princeton University Press, 1971.

————. *Logic and Rhetoric in England, 1500–1700.* New York: Russell & Russell/Atheneum, 1956.

Isocrates. "Against the Sophists." In *Isocrates,* vol. 2, trans. George Norlin, 162–77. Cambridge, MA: Harvard University Press, 1968.

Longinus. *On Great Writing (On the Sublime).* Trans. G. M. A. Grube. Indianapolis: Hackett, 1991.

Neel, Jasper. *Plato, Derrida, and Writing.* Carbondale: Southern Illinois University Press, 1988.

Pace, Tom. "Style and the Renaissance of Composition Studies." In *Refiguring Prose Style: Possibilities for Writing Pedagogy,* ed. Tom Pace and T. R. Johnson, 3–22. Logan: Utah State University Press, 2005.

Plato. "Gorgias." In *Plato,* vol. 5, trans. W. R. M. Lamb, 258–533. Cambridge, MA: Harvard University Press, 1925.

————. "Phaedrus." In *Plato,* vol. 1, trans. Harold North Fowler, 412–579. Cambridge, MA: Harvard University Press, 1914.

Rhetorica ad Herennium. Trans. Harry Caplan. Cambridge, MA: Harvard University Press, 1954.

STYLISTIC INFLUENCES AND DEBATES

Bartholomae, David. "Inventing the University." *Journal of Basic Writing* 5 (1986): 4–23.

Beardsley, Monroe E. "Style and Good Style." In *New Rhetorics,* ed. Martin Steinmann Jr., 192–213. New York: Charles Scribner's Sons, 1967.

Burke, Kenneth. *Counter-Statement.* 2nd ed. Berkeley: University of California Press, 1968.

Coe, Richard M. "An Apology for Form; or, Who Took the Form Out of the Process?" *College English* 49 (1987): 13–28.

D'Angelo, Frank. "Imitation and Style." *College Composition and Communication* 24 (1973): 283–90.

Enkvist, Nils Erik, John Spencer, and Michael J. Gregory, eds. *Linguistics and Style.* London: Oxford University Press, 1964.

Gage, John T. "Philosophies of Style and Their Implications for Composition." *College English* 41 (1980): 615–22.

Gibson, Walker. *Tough, Sweet and Stuffy: An Essay on Modern American Prose Styles.* Bloomington: Indiana University Press, 1966.

Hake, Rosemary L., and Joseph M. Williams. "Style and Its Consequences: Do as I Do, Not as I Say." *College English* 43 (1981): 433–51.

Hartwell, Patrick. "Grammar, Grammars, and the Teaching of Grammar." *College English* 47 (1985): 105–27.

Jakobson, Roman. "Concluding Statement: Linguistics and Poetics." In *Style in Language*, ed. Thomas Sebeok, 350–77. Cambridge, MA: MIT Press, 1960.

Joos, Martin. *The Five Clocks*. Bloomington: Indiana University Research Center in Anthropology, Folklore, and Linguistics, 1962.

Laib, Nevin. "Conciseness and Amplification." *College Composition and Communication* 41 (1990): 443–59.

Lanham, Richard A. *Style: An Anti-Textbook*. New Haven, CT: Yale University Press, 1974.

Love, Glen A., and Michael Payne, eds. *Contemporary Essays on Style: Rhetoric, Linguistics, and Criticism*. Glenview, IL: Scott, Foresman, 1969.

Martin, Harold C., ed. *Style in Prose Fiction: English Institute Essays*. New York: Columbia University Press, 1959.

Mellon, John C. "Issues in the Theory and Practice of Sentence Combining: A Twenty-Year Perspective." In *Sentence Combining and the Teaching of Writing*, ed. Donald A. Daiker, Andrew Kerek, and Max Morenberg, 1–38. Akron, OH: University of Akron Department of English, 1979.

Sebeok, Thomas, ed. *Style in Language*. Cambridge, MA: MIT Press, 1960.

Stull, William L. "Sentence Combining, Generative Rhetoric, and Concepts of Style." In *Sentence Combining: A Rhetorical Perspective*, ed. Donald A. Daiker, Andrew Kerek, and Max Morenberg, 76–85. Carbondale: Southern Illinois University Press, 1985.

Walpole, Jane R. "Style as Option." *College Composition and Communication* 31 (1980): 205–12.

Weaver, Richard. "Some Rhetorical Aspects of Grammatical Categories." *The Ethics of Rhetoric*. Chicago, IL: Henry Regnery, 1953.

Williams, Joseph M. "The Phenomenology of Error." *College Composition and Communication* 32 (1981): 152–68.

Winterowd, W. Ross. "Style: A Matter of Manner." *Quarterly Journal of Speech* 56 (1970): 161–67.

STYLE AND PEDAGOGY

Bazerman, Charles. "An Essay on Pedagogy by Mikhail Bakhtin." *Written Communication* 22 (2005): 333–38.

Berthoff, Ann E. *The Making of Meaning: Metaphors, Models, and Maxims for Writing Teachers*. Portsmouth, NH: Heinemann-Boynton/Cook, 1981.

Brooks, Phyllis. "Mimesis: Grammar and the Echoing Voice." *College English* 35 (1973): 161–68.

Christensen, Francis, and Bonnijean Christensen. *Notes toward a New Rhetoric: Nine Essays for Teachers.* 2nd ed. New York: Harper & Row, 1978.

Comprone, Joseph J. "Syntactic Play and Composing Theory: What Sentence Combining Has Done for Teachers of Writing." In *Sentence Combining: A Rhetorical Perspective,* ed. Donald A. Daiker, Andrew Kerek, and Max Morenberg, 219–31. Carbondale: Southern Illinois University Press, 1986.

Comprone, Joseph J., and Katherine J. Ronald. "Expressive Writing: Exercises in a New Progymnasmata." *Journal of Teaching Writing* 4.1 (1985): 31–53.

Corbett, Edward P. J., and Robert Connors. *Classical Rhetoric for the Modern Student.* 4th ed. New York: Oxford University Press, 2000.

Crowley, Sharon, and Debra Hawhee. *Ancient Rhetorics for Contemporary Students.* 3rd ed. New York: Pearson/Longman, 2004.

Daiker, Donald A., Andrew Kerek, and Max Morenberg, eds. *Sentence Combining and the Teaching of Writing.* Studies in Contemporary Language #3. Akron, OH, and Conway, AR: Published with the assistance of the Departments of English, University of Akron and University of Central Arkansas, 1979.

Daiker, Donald A., Andrew Kerek, Max Morenberg, and Jeffrey Sommers. *The Writer's Options: Combining to Composing.* 5th ed. New York: HarperCollins College, 1994.

Faigley, Lester. "Generative Rhetoric as a Way of Increasing Syntactic Fluency." *College Composition and Communication* 30 (1979): 176–81.

Farmer, Frank. "On Style and Other Unremarkable Things." *Written Communication* 22 (2005): 339–46.

Halasek, Kay. "An Enriching Methodology: Bakhtin's 'Dialogic Origin and Dialogic Pedagogy of Grammar' and the Teaching of Writing." *Written Communication* 22 (1985): 355–62.

Lanham, Richard A. *A Handlist of Rhetorical Terms.* Berkeley: University of California Press, 1991.

Mann, Nancy. "Point Counterpoint: Teaching Punctuation as Information Management." *College Composition and Communication* 54 (2003): 359–93.

McQuade, Donald A., ed. *The Territory of Language: Linguistics, Stylistics, and the Teaching of Composition.* Carbondale: Southern Illinois University Press, 1986.

Minock, Mary. "Toward a Postmodern Pedagogy of Imitation." *JAC: A Journal of Composition Theory* 15 (1995): 489–509.

O'Hare, Frank. *Sentence Combining: Improving Student Writing without Formal Grammar Instruction.* Urbana, IL: NCTE, 1973.

Pringle, Ian. "Why Teach Style? A Review-Essay." *College Composition and Communication* 34 (1983): 91–98.

Weathers, Winston. *An Alternative Style: Options in Composition.* Rochelle Park, NJ: Hayden, 1980.

———. "Teaching Style: A Possible Anatomy." In *The Writing Teacher's Sourcebook,* ed. Gary Tate and Edward P. J. Corbett, 325–32. New York: Oxford University Press, 1981.

Williams, Joseph M. "Bakhtin on Teaching Style." *Written Communication* 22 (2005): 348–54.

———. *Style: Ten Lessons in Clarity and Grace.* 8th ed. New York: Pearson, 2005.

Williams, Joseph M., and Rosemary Hake. "Non-Linguistics Linguistics and the Teaching of Style." In *The Territory of Language: Linguistics, Stylistics, and the Teaching of Composition,* ed. Donald A. McQuade, 174–91. Carbondale: Southern Illinois University Press, 1986.

Young, Richard E., Alton L. Becker, and Kenneth L. Pike. *Rhetoric: Discovery and Change.* New York: Harcourt, 1970.

STYLE AND CULTURE

Annas, Pamela J. "Style as Politics: A Feminist Approach to the Teaching of Writing." *College English* 47 (1985): 360–71.

Brummett, Barry. *A Rhetoric of Style.* Carbondale: Southern Illinois University Press, 2008.

Campbell, Kermit E. *"Getting' Our Groove On": Rhetoric, Language, and Literacy for the Hip-Hop Generation.* Detroit, MI: Wayne State University Press, 2005.

Cliett, Victoria. "The Expanding Frontier of World Englishes: A New Perspective for Teachers of English." In *Language Diversity in the Classroom: From Intention to Practice,* ed. Geneva Smitherman and Victor Villanueva, 67–75. Carbondale: Southern Illinois University Press, 2003.

Cmiel, Kenneth. "Refined and Colloquial, 1885–1900." In *Democratic Eloquence: The Fight over Popular Speech in Nineteenth-Century America,* 236–57. Berkeley: University of California Press, 1990.

Committee on CCCC Language. "Students' Right to Their Own Language." *College Composition and Communication* 25 (1974): 1–18.

Gilyard, Keith, and Vorris Nunley, eds. *Rhetoric and Ethnicity.* Portsmouth, NH: Heinemann-Boynton/Cook, 2004.

Gorrell, Donna. "Style and Identity: Students Writing Like the Professionals." *Teaching English in the Two-Year College* 32 (2005): 393–402.

Hebdige, Dick. *Subculture: The Meaning of Style.* London: Routledge, 1979.

Kells, Michelle Hall, Valerie Balestser, and Victor Villanueva. *Latino/a Discourses: On Language, Identity, and Literacy Education.* Portsmouth, NH: Heinemann-Boynton/Cook, 2004.

Labov, William. *Language in the Inner City.* Philadelphia: University of Pennsylvania Press, 1972.

Lanham, Richard A. *Analyzing Prose.* 2nd ed. London: Continuum, 2003.

Parks, Stephen. *Class Politics: The Movement for the Students' Right to Their Own Language.* Urbana, IL: NCTE, 2000.

Pratt, Mary Louise. "Arts of the Contact Zone." *Profession* 91 (1991): 33–40.

Redd, Teresa M., and Karen Schuster Webb. *A Teachers' Introduction to African American English: What a Writing Teacher Should Know.* Urbana, IL: NCTE, 2005.

Richardson, Elaine. *Hiphop Literacies.* New York: Routledge, 2006.

Smitherman, Geneva. *Talkin That Talk: Language, Culture, and Education in African America.* New York: Routledge, 2000.

———. *Word from the Mother: Language and African Americans.* New York: Routledge, 2006.

Smitherman, Geneva, and Victor Villanueva, eds. *Language Diversity in the Classroom: From Intention to Practice.* Carbondale: Southern Illinois University Press, 2003.

Syrquin, Anna. "Registers in the Academic Writing of African American College Students." *Written Communication* 23 (2006): 63–90.

Style and the Future

Bishop, Wendy, ed. *Elements of Alternate Style: Essays on Writing and Revision.* Portsmouth, NH: Heinemann-Boynton/Cook, 1997.

Brooke, Collin. *Lingua Fracta: Towards a Rhetoric of New Media.* New York: Hampton, 2008.

Butler, Paul. "Style in the Diaspora of Composition Studies." *Rhetoric Review* 26 (2007): 5–24.

Cope, Bill, and Mary Kalantzis, eds. *Multiliteracies: Literacy Learning and the Design of Social Futures.* London: Routledge/Taylor & Francis, 2000.

Holcomb, Chris. "Performative Stylistics and the Question of Academic Prose." *Rhetoric Review* 24 (2005): 188–206.

Lanham, Richard A. *The Electronic Word: Democracy, Technology, and the Arts.* Chicago, IL: University of Chicago Press, 1993.

McDonald, Susan Peck. "The Erasure of Language." *College Composition and Communication* 58 (2007): 585–625.

Myers, Sharon. "ReMembering the Sentence." *College Composition and Communication* 54 (2003): 610–28.

Schroeder, Christopher, Helen Fox, and Patricia Bizzell. *Alt Dis: Alternative Discourses and the Academy.* Portsmouth, NH: Heinemann-Boynton/Cook, 2002.

Steinberg, Erwin R., ed. *Plain Language: Principles and Practice.* Detroit, MI: Wayne State University Press, 1991.

Warner, Michael. "Styles of Intellectual Publics." In *Publics and Counterpublics,* 125–58. New York: Zone, 2002.

ABOUT THE EDITOR

Paul Butler is an assistant professor in the Department of English at the University of Houston, where he teaches undergraduate writing classes and graduate courses in a new PhD concentration, rhetoric, composition, and pedagogy. Butler's book, *Out of Style: Reanimating Stylistic Study in Composition and Rhetoric*, was published by Utah State University Press in 2008. His work also has appeared in several journals, including *JAC, Rhetoric Review, WPA*, and *Reflections*, and in an edited collection, *Authorship in Composition Studies*.

INDEX

abstract *vs.* concrete language. *See* concrete *vs.* abstract language

Achebe, Chinua, 297, 300

aesthetic monism. *See* organic theory of style

African American oral styles. *See* " 'How I Got Ovuh': African World View and Afro-American Oral Tradition" (Smitherman)

Aims of Education, The (Whitehead), 446

Aims of Interpretation, The (Hirsch), 374

"Alexander Bain and the Rise of the Organic Paragraph" (Rogers), 117

Ali, Muhammad, 301

allegory, 50

Alt Dis: Alternative Discourses and the Academy (Schroeder, Fox and Bizzell), 4

"An Alternate Style: Options in Composition" (Weathers), 86

Amazing Grace (record), 296

"American Food and American Houses" (Stein), 233

American Scholar, The (Hirsch), 378

amphibolies, 24

An American Primer (Whitman), 222

"Ancient and Contemporary Compositions That 'Come Alive': Clarity as Pleasure, Sound as Magic" (Johnson), 340, 343–68

    clarity, 343–44

    expressivist pedagogy, distinguished, 346–47

    felt sense, 358–60

    magic, writing and, 355–56, 357–58

    play attitude, 351

    rhapsodes, 354

    rhythm, 354–55

    sophists, 351–53, 354

    sound, teaching voice in terms of, 340, 348–56

    talk-based technique, 349

    teaching methods, 356–63

    voice as discourse, 346–48

    Williams's principles of focus, flow, story, and rhythmic emphasis, 361–62

    writer's double, 364–67

Ancient Rhetorics for Contemporary Students (Crowley and Hawhee), 256, 352

Angus, Joseph, 108, 111–12

anti-behaviorism criticism of sentence pedagogies, 16, 96–98

anti-empiricism criticism of sentence pedagogies, 16, 98–100

anti-formalism criticism of sentence pedagogies, 16, 93–96

antimetabole, 1, 5

antithesis, 29–30

Anzaldúa, Gloria, 5, 305, 308

"Apologies and Accommodations: Imitation and the Writing Process" (Farmer and Arrington), 15–16, 59–81

Applebee, Arthur, 67

appositives, 163
Aristophanes, 20–21
Aristotle, 13, 14, 15, 18–36, 50
Armies of the Night, The (Mailer), 237
arresting magic, 357
Arrington, Phillip, 15–16, 59–81, 411
"Arts of the Contact Zone" (Pratt), 303
Asiatic style, 2–3, 15
Asker, William, 169
"*At and Through*: The Opaque Style
        and Its Uses" (Lanham), 248
Attic style, 2–3, 14–15, 38–39, 47–49
"Audubon's Happy Land" (Porter),
        227
aural qualities of style. *See* "Ancient
        and Contemporary
        Compositions That 'Come
        Alive': Clarity as Pleasure,
        Sound as Magic" (Johnson)
Autobiography of Alice B. Toklas, The
        (Stein), 304
Averting Demons (Mellinkoff), 439

Babylonians (Aristophanes), 20–21
"Back to Basics" (Lazere), 263
Bacon, Sir Francis, 157, 447
Bain, Alexander, 108, 109, 110, 112–14,
        122, 123, 127, 216
Bakhtin, Mikhail, 16, 60, 73–75, 208,
        305, 314, 316, 411–19, 420,
        421–25
"Bakhtin's Rhetoric" (Klanchner),
        411–12
Baldwin, C. S., 83
Baldwin, James, 63
Baldwin, T. W., 210
Baraka, Imamu, 296
Barbour, F. A., 273
Barfield, Owen, 326
Barr, N. R., 169–70
Barth, John, 228, 231
Barthelme, Donald, 229
Bartholomae, David, 70, 309, 327, 334,
        347, 423, 425
Bateman, Donald, 87, 88, 89
Baudrillard, Jean, 365–66
Bazerman, Charles, 351
Beautiful Theories (Bruss), 254
Becker, Alton L., 3, 117, 118–19, 216

Benjamin, Amy, 396
Berlin, James, 72, 239, 240–41
Berthoff, Ann, 98, 423
Between the Acts (Woolf), 232–33
Bhabha, Homi K., 316
Bierce, Ambrose, 259–60
Bing, Rudolf, 320
Bishop, Wendy, 4
Bizzell, Patricia, 4, 98, 99
Black Boy (Wright), 288–90
Blair, Hugh, 110, 111, 125, 241
Blake, William, 222, 224, 236
boastful raps, 290
Boler, Megan, 345
Bond, Charles A., 84
Booth, Wayne, 329
Borgh, Enola M., 274–75
Braddock, Richard, 60, 98, 108, 119,
        123, 137, 165–66, 397
braggadocio, in African American
        oral tradition, 298–99
Brandt, Deborah, 389
Branson, Mark K., 112, 120, 121
Breakfast of Champions (Vonnegut), 259
Breaking Bread (West and hooks), 316
Brightland, John, 111
Britton, James, 97
Brody, Miriam, 262–63
Brooke, Robert, 68–69
Brooks, Cleanth, 116
Brooks, Phyllis, 63
Brown, Hubert, 290, 291
Brown, James, 296, 298
Bruss, Elizabeth, 254, 255
Brutus (Cicero), 37
Bryant, Donald, 251–52
Buehler, Huber Gray, 273
Burgess, Anthony, 322
Burke, Kenneth, 65, 74, 137, 357, 434
Burroughs, William, 235–36
Bush, George W., 257
Butler, Paul, 341, 389–409

Cage, John, 231
Call of Stories, The (Cole), 329
Campbell, George, 110, 111, 125
Capote, Truman, 237
Carbone, Nick, 398
Cartwright, Frederick, 320

catachresis, 50
Caughie, Pamela, 262
chiasmus, 360–61. *See* antimetabole
Chitwood, Frances, 178–80
Chomsky, Noam, 83, 87, 190, 207–8, 271–72
Christensen, Bonniejean, 94
Christensen, Francis, 16, 66, 88, 94–95, 108, 127, 135, 163, 199, 200, 216, 244
    "Generative Rhetoric of the Paragraph, A," 117
    "Generative Rhetoric of the Sentence, A" (*See* "Generative Rhetoric of the Sentence, A")
Christensen Rhetoric Program, 84–85, 94
Chronicle of Higher Education, The, 389, 406
church raps, 292–94
Cicero, 2–3, 13, 14–15, 28, 37–53, 62, 215, 355
Cisneros, Sandra, 316
"City Life" (Barthelme), 229
clarity, 14
    Aristotle on, 18–21
    Butler on, 400–3
    Johnson on, 343–44
Clark, Donald L., 210
classical rhetoric, style and, 5
Classical Rhetoric for the Modern Student (Corbett), 211, 215
clause endings, 197–200
"Clauses and Commas Make a Comeback: SAT Helps Return Grammar to Class" (De Vise), 396
Cleveland, James, 296
Clifford, John, 138
close imitation, 62
"Closing the Book on Alchemy" (Kolln), 136, 137–38, 165–76
Coban, Carol, 120
Coe, Richard, 61
cognitive approach to paragraph theory, 109, 122
cognitive-process model of composing process, 242–43
cola, style in, 28–30
Coleman, E. B., 193

Coleman, James, 152
Coles, Robert, 329
collage/montage, 235–37
College Composition and Communication, 216
College English, 17, 94, 96, 138, 392, 403, 406, 407
Collingwood, R. G., 235
Combs, Warren E., 90, 101
Committee on CCCC Language, 399
complex style, definition, 138–39, 186–201
    agent-action style, 194–95
    agents and subjects coincide, and verbs and agents actions coincide, styles where, 191–95
    clause endings, 197–200
    depth hypothesis, 190–91
    Flesch's scale of simple to complex styles, 189
    measuring simple and complex styles, 186–91
    resumptive modifiers, 200
    sentence-combining, 188–89, 199–200
    summative modifiers, 200
    textured style, 199
    topic selection and consistency, 195–97
composition, cultural divide between literature and. *See* "The Cultures of Literature and Composition: What Could Each Learn from the Other?" (Elbow)
Composition: Skills and Models (Stovall, Mathis, Elliot, Hagler and Poole), 182–84
Composition and Rhetoric (Hitchcock), 267, 268
"Comp Time: Is College Too Late to Learn How to Write" (Menand), 390
conciseness *(syntomia),* 24–25
concrete *vs.* abstract language, 138, 177–85
    concrete language, use of, 182–84
    details, adding, 178–80
    texture, use of, 180–82
connectives, 23–24

Connors, Robert, 5, 16–17, 82–107, 205, 208, 350, 390, 395, 410
contact zone, 7
    politics of style in (*See* "Professing Multiculturalism: The Politics of Style in the Contact Zone")
controlled composition exercises, 86
Copy and Compose (Weathers and Winchester), 86
Corbett, Edward P. J., 71, 85–86, 205–6, 209–18, 244, 281, 352, 410
Corder, Jim, 175
Covino, William, 357–58
"Craft of Writing, The" (Erskine), 147
Critical Inquiry (Hirsch), 374
Croce, Benedetto, 142, 143
Croll, Morris W., 153
crots, writing in, 226–27
Crowley, Sharon, 256, 352
cultural influences on style, 7, 279–82
    African American oral styles (*See* " 'How I Got Ovuh': African World View and Afro-American Oral Tradition")
    divisions between cultures of literature and composition (*See* "The Cultures of Literature and Composition: What Could Each Learn from the Other?")
    feminine style (*See* "Feminine Style: Theory and Fact, The")
    multicultural approach to style, teaching (*See* "Professing Multiculturalism: The Politics of Style in the Contact Zone")
    stylistic choices as cultural choices, 280
Cultural Literacy: What Every American Needs to Know (Hirsch), 370, 375, 376, 377
"The Cultures of Literature and Composition: What Could Each Learn from the Other?" (Elbow), 281–82, 324–36, 403–4
    class planning process, 325–26
    disciplines, status as, 333–34
    distancing techniques, 328–29
    metaphorical and imaginative language, 325–26
    process and product, 326
    sophistication of literary studies and naiveté of composition, 330–33
    teaching and students, differences in views on, 327–28
cumulative sentences, 84, 136, 147–48, 153
Curme, Georg, 274
current-traditional paradigm, 240–42

Daiker, Donald, 90, 102, 175, 267, 271
D'Angelo, Frank, 65, 86, 96–97, 108, 119, 121, 216
Danielewicz, Jane, 334–35
Davidson, Cathy, 331
Davis, Robert Con, 406
"Defining Complexity" (Williams), 138–39, 186–201
delivery and use of language, Cicero on, 43–44
Demetrius, 14, 25
Demosthenes, 26, 37–38
Denney, Joseph, 114–15, 268–69, 271, 273
depth hypothesis, 190–91
De Romilly, Jacqueline, 352
Derrida, Jacques, 412
Descriptions of Literature (Stein), 222
descriptive view, of paragraph theory, 108, 109, 114–16
deviation from normative styles. *See* "Professing Multiculturalism: The Politics of Style in the Contact Zone"
de Vise, Daniel, 396
"Devoid of Content" (Fish), 389
Dewey, John, 351
dialogic imitation, 410–27
    Bakhtin and imitation, 76, 341, 411–19
    double-voiced discourse, 341, 413–16
    everyday discourse and imitation, 416–19
    internally persuasive discourse, 418–19
    novelistic discourse and imitation, 413–16
    outline for, 419–25

paraphrasing, 417–18
parody, 415, 424–25
as positional, 341–42, 420–21
as revisable, 421–23
rhetorical purposes of, 423–25
single-voiced discourse, 413
stylization, 415–16
Vygotsky and, 76, 411
diction, study of, 211–12
Didion, Joan, 254
Die Nigger Die! (Brown), 290
diminutives, 20–21
Dionysius the Brazen, 20
discourse
dialogic imitation and (*See* dialogic
imitation)
oral discourse, 4
voice as, 346–48
discourse blocks, 119
"Discourse-Centered Rhetoric of the
Paragraph, A" (Rogers), 117
Distant Hand Lifted, A (Burroughs),
235–36
"Doctrine of the Paragraph, A"
(Whitmore), 116
double voice
dialogic imitation and, 413–16
Weathers on use of, 230–32
"Down from the Haymow: One
Hundred Years of Sentence-
Combining" (Rose), 87, 207–8,
267–76
characteristics common to recent
exercises, 271
Chomsky's generative-
transformational paradigm as
supporting exercises, 271–72
classroom practice, early 1900s,
273–74
comparison of early and recent
exercises, 268–71
school tradition grammar,
compatibility with, 272–73, 276
structural grammar paradigm,
exercises in, 274–76
Dowst, Kenneth, 99–100
Doyle, Brian, 384, 385
Dreiser, Theodore, 305–7
Drucker, Peter, 447
DuMaurier, Daphne, 321

Duncan, Mike, 17, 108–31
Durant, Will and Ariel, 228
Durkheim, Emile, 354

*The Economics of Attention: Style and
Substance in the Age of
Information* (Lanham), 395–96
Eden, Rick, 108, 120–21
Elbow, Peter, 95–96, 126, 246, 281–82,
324–36, 346, 348–49, 355, 403–4,
404, 405
Elegies (Dionysius the Brazen), 20
Elementary English Composition
(Newton and Denney), 115,
268–69
*Elements of Alternate Style: Essays on
Writing and Revision* (Bishop,
ed.), 4, 206
Elements of Style, The (Strunk and
White), 115, 138, 177
Elliot, Linda C., 182–84
Ellis, W. Geiger, 119
Emerson, Caryl, 414
Emotions and the Will, The (Bain), 122
Emperor's New Clothes, The (Perl), 340
empiricism
paragraph theory and, 119–21
sentence-based pedagogies and, 16,
98–100
"Encountering the Other" (Olsen),
260–61
End of Economic Man, The (Drucker),
447
English Composition and Rhetoric
(Bain), 108, 112, 122, 127
English Grammar (Murray), 110
English Journal, 116
English Sentences (Roberts), 148
epideictic oration, 40–41
"An Epistemic View of Sentence-
Combining: Practice and
Theories" (Dowst), 99–100
epithets, 20–22
"Erasure of the Sentence, The"
(Connors), 82–107
"Erik Satie" (Cage), 231
Errors and Expectations (Shaughnessy),
308
Erskine, John, 147

Eschholz, Paul, 66–67

Esquire, 223

exaggerated language, in African American oral tradition, 297

expansiveness *(onkos)*, 24–25

Expectations: Teaching Writing from the Reader's Perspective (Gopen), 126

expository prose, and generative rhetoric, 152–53

Faigley, Lester, 72, 85, 100–1

Falk, Julia, 63, 68

Fanon, Frantz, 286

Farmer, Frank, 392

"Apologies and Accommodations: Imitation and the Writing Process," 15–16, 59–81

"Sounding the Other Who Speaks in Me: Toward a Dialogic Understanding of Imitation," 340–42, 410–27

Faulkner, William, 148

felt sense, 358–60

"Feminine Style: Theory and Fact, The" (Hiatt), 281, 318–23

emotions, use of adverbs of, 322

group-style theory, 318–19

logical sequence indicators, use of, 321–22

-ly adverbs, use of, 322

pace, use of adverbs of, 322

"really," use of, 322–23

sentence length and complexity, 320–21

study of stylistic differences between male and female writers, 319–23

Ferrer, Daniel, 124–25

Feyerabend, Paul, 372

Fielding, Henry, 182–84

Figures of Speech: Sixty Ways to Turn a Phrase (Quinn), 352

figures of speech, study of, 214–15

Finnegan's Wake (Joyce), 237

Fish, Stanley, 389, 391, 392, 393–94, 405, 406

Five Clocks, The (Joos), 210

Flanigan, Michael, 66

Flannery, Kathryn, 340–41, 369–88

Flesch, Rudolph, 189

flow, 361

Flower, Linda, 72, 242–43

focus, 361

Fogarty, Daniel, 61

forceful style, 14

Forde, Daryll, 284

form-content split as condition for teaching of style, 62

form generating content, as justification for imitation, 65–66

Forster, E. M., 227

Foucault, Michel, 255

Fowler, Mary Elizabeth, 173–74

Fox, Helen, 4

Franklin, Aretha, 296

"Frank Sinatra Has a Cold" (Talese), 236

Freedman, Aviva, 101

free modifiers, 163

Freire, Paulo, 357

"Frequency and Placement of Topic Sentences in Expository Prose, The" (Braddock), 119, 123

Fried, Michael, 332

Fries, C. C., 274

frigidities as stylistic flaws, 14, 21–22

Frogner, Ellen, 171–72

"From a Native Daughter" (Trask), 315–16

Fulkerson, Richard, 110

functionalist view, of paragraph theory, 108, 109, 114–16

Gage, John, 61, 247–48

Gallop, Jane, 345

"Game, The" (King), 291–92

game motive, in style/substance matrix, 436–44

Garden of Eloquence, The (Peacham), 214

generative magic, 357–58

generative rhetoric, 83–85, 136–37, 146–54

See also sentence-based pedagogies composition as process of addition, 147, 148

criticisms of, 94–95, 98–99

cumulative sentences, 84, 136, 147–48, 153

direction of modification principle, 147, 148

expository prose and, 152–53

free modifiers, 163

layers of structure, examples of, 149–51

levels of generality, 148–49

paragraph theory and, 117

texture, 149

"Generative Rhetoric of the Paragraph, A" (Christensen), 117

"Generative Rhetoric of the Sentence, A" (Christensen), 83–85, 136–37, 146–54

Genetic Criticism (Ferrer and Rabaté), 124–25

genre models of imitation, 62–63

Genung, John, 113, 269, 273

Gernsbacher, Morton, 122–23

Gibson, Walker, 62, 157

Gildon, Charles, 111

Gleason, Henry A., Jr., 272–73, 274

Gopen, George, 126

Gorrell, Donna, 63

grammar
    Aristotle on grammatical correctness, 14, 23–24
    "Grammars of Style: New Options in Composition" (Weathers), 4, 206, 219–38
    pedagogy of (*See* pedagogy of grammar)
    style, relation to (*See* grammar, relation of style to)

"Grammar, Grammars, and the Teaching of Grammar" (Hartwell), 397

grammar, relation of style to, 137, 155–64
    classification of prose styles, 156–58
    control of syntax, 162–64
    emotional form, style as, 137, 160–61
    grammar as style, 162
    grammar as syntax, 155–56
    kernel structures, expanding, 162–63
    organic theory of style and, 158–60
    style, defined, 156
    syntactic symbolism, 163–64
    syntax, control of, 162–64
    syntax as sequence, 161–62

Grammar as Style (Tufte), 137

Grammar B. *See* "Grammars of Style: New Options in Composition" (Weathers)

Grammar of the English Tongue (Gildon and Brightland), 111

"Grammars of Style: New Options in Composition" (Weathers), 4, 206, 219–38
    characteristics of Grammar B, 224
    collage/montage, 235–37
    crots, writing in, 226–27
    devices/conventions/maneuvers for practicing Grammar B, 225–37
    double voice, use of, 230–32
    electronic media's influence on evolution of Grammar B, 223
    grammars of style, defined, 220
    justifications for Grammar B, 224–25
    labyrinthine sentences, 227–29
    lists, use of, 229–30
    practitioners of Grammar B, 222–23, 224
    principles of composition in Grammar B, 237–38
    repetition, use of, 232–34
    sentence fragments, 227–29
    synchronicity, 234–35
    traditional grammars of style (Grammar A), 220–21

grammatical correctness, 14, 23–24

Grammatical Patterns and Compositions (Borgh), 274–75

Grammatical Structures Written at Three Grade Levels (Hunt), 88

grand style, 14, 15, 37, 46, 50–51

"Grant or Rutherford B. Hayes" (Stein), 228–29

Graves, Richard, 62

Gray, James, 66

Great Sophists of Periclean Athens, The (De Romilly), 352

Greever, Garland, 115

Griffin, William, 88
Gruber, William, 86, 87, 97
Guth, Hans, 69

Haas, Robert Bartlett, 228
Hagler, G. Mitchell, Jr., 182–84
Hairston, Maxine, 61, 239, 240, 241
Hake, Rosemary, 86–87, 99, 193
Halloran, Michael, 3, 86
Hamilton, David, 70
Handbook of Research on Teaching
    (Gage, ed.), 166
Handbook of the English Tongue
    (Angus), 108, 111–12
Hardin, Joe, 398
Harper's Magazine, 402–3
Harris, Joseph, 346–48
Harris, Muriel, 67
Harris, Robert, 352
Harris, Roland J., 172–73
Hartwell, Patrick, 397, 398–99
Havelock, Eric, 354, 365
Hawhee, Debra, 352
Hayek, Friedrich, 443
Hayes, John, 242–43
Haynes-Burton, Cynthia, 402–3
Hemingway, Ernest, 148–49, 212–13
Hiatt, Mary, 281, 318–23
Hill, Adams Sherman, 83
Hillocks, George, 101
Hirsch, E. D., Jr., 177, 185
    Flannery's critique of, 340, 370, 371,
        372, 373–79
History of the English Paragraph, The
    (Lewis), 114
Hitchcock, Alfred E., 267, 268, 273
Hoffer, Eric, 227, 436, 442, 444
Holquist, Michael, 73
Holzman, Michael, 100
hooks, bell, 255–56, 308, 316, 343, 344,
    351
" 'How I Got Ovuh': African World
    View and Afro-American Oral
    Tradition" (Smitherman), 280,
    283–302
    black church, influence on cultural
        and verbal style of, 293–96
    boastful raps, 290
    braggadocio, 298–99

exaggerated language, 297
image-making, 298
indirection, 299–300
language and style of sacred-
    secular oral tradition, 296–301
love raps, 290–92
mimicry, 297
Nommo, concept of, 286–87
preliterate tradition, 285–86
proverbial statement, 297
punning, 298
rap, power and dynamics of, 287–92
sacred style, 293, 294, 296–301
secular style, 293–94, 296–301
sermons/church raps, 292–94
spontaneity, 298
tonal semantics, 300–1
traditional African worldview,
    284–85
Hoy, David, 374
Hoyt, Franklyn, 168–69, 175
Hunt, Kellogg, 88, 91
Hunt, Maurice, 71

image-making, in African American
    oral tradition, 298
imitation, 15–16, 59–81
    See also sentence-based pedagogies
    arguments for, 60–72
    Corbett's imitative exercises, 217
    criticisms of, 96–98
    definition of, 60
    dialogic imitation (*See* dialogic
        imitation)
    future of imitation in composition
        studies, 75–76
    imitation exercises, 85–87
    interventional justifications, 66–68
    inventional justifications, 64–66
    in Micciche's rhetorical grammar
        pedagogy, 258–59
    process approaches, justifying
        imitation according to norms
        and values of, 70–72
    Quintilian on, 5, 15, 54–58
    social justifications, 68–70
    stylistic justifications, 61–63
    utterances, imitation's relationship
        to, 73–75, 411, 417

In Cold Blood (Capote), 237
In Defence of Ctesiphon (Demosthenes), 38
indirection, in African American oral tradition, 299–300
Inkster, Robert, 239, 240–41
Innocence and Experience (Hirsch), 373
Innovative Fiction (introduction by Klinkowitz and Somer), 225
Institutio oratoria (Quintilian), 15, 54–58
Instructor's Manual and Answer Key to Accompany The Writer's Harbrace Handbook, 253
"Internal Revision: A Process of Discovery" (Murray), 243
interventional justifications for imitation, 66–68
inventional justifications for imitation, 64–66
"Inventive Modeling: *Rainy Mountain's* Way to Composition" (Roemer), 64
inversions, 162
Irving, Washington, 257–58
Isocrates, 26, 28, 40–41, 355
"Issues in the Theory and Practice of Sentence Combining: A Twenty-Year Perspective" (Mellon), 270–71

Jackson, Jesse, 298
James, Henry, 213
James Joyce Quarterly, 226
Jameson, Fredric, 314
Jarratt, Susan, 352
Jerusalem (Blake), 222, 236
Jesperson, Otto, 274
John Milton at St. Paul's School (Clark), 210
Johnson, Dr., 212
Johnson, Sabina Thorne, 94
Johnson, T. R., 4, 339–40, 343–68, 395–96
Johnstone, Barbara, 332
Jones, Easley S., 115
Joos, Martin, 210
Joseph, Sister Miriam, 210
Joyce, James, 228, 237
Judy, Stephen, 174

Kaestle, Karl, 369, 370
kairos, 351
"Kandy-Kolored Tangerine-Flake Streamline Baby" (Wolfe), 223
Kane, Thomas, 216
Karrafalt, David, 117
Katz, Stephen, 352–53, 355
Kehl, D. G., 69–70
Kennedy, George, 14
Kennedy, John F., 1, 4–5
Kerek, Andrew, 90, 102, 175, 267, 271
kernel structures, expanding, 162–63
King, Martin Luther, Jr., 5, 297
King, Woodie, 291–92
Kiniry, Malcolm, 62
Kinneavy, James, 99, 351
Kintsch, Walter, 122–23
Kipling, Rudyard, 438
Klanchner, Jon, 411–12
Klinkowitz, Jerome, 225
Koch, Kenneth, 328
Kolln, Martha, 4, 136, 137–38, 165–76, 207, 256
Krashen, Stephen, 245
Kruisinga, Itsko, 274

labyrinthine sentences, 227–29
Lacan, Jacques, 208
Langer, Judith, 67
"Language" (hooks), 255
Lanham, Richard, 3, 4, 69, 138, 248, 339–40, 342, 343, 351, 352, 363, 395–96, 401, 428–48
	Flannery's critique of, 340–41, 370, 371–73, 379–85
	style/substance matrix (*See* "Style/Substance Matrix")
Larmouth, Donald, 63
Larson, Richard, 67
"Las Vegas (What?) Las Vegas (Can't Hear You! Too Noisy!) Las Vegas!!!" (Wolfe), 233
Lauer, Janice, 98
Lawrence, D. H., 222
Lazere, David, 263
Le, Elizabeth, 122
Leatherdale, W. H., 65
Leaves of Grass (Whitman), 222
Lee, Harper, 258–59

LeShan, Eda, 320
levels of style, 2, 14–15
  forceful style, 14
  grand style, 14, 15, 37, 46, 50–51
  middle style, 14, 37, 46, 49–50
  plain style, 14–15, 37–39, 46, 47–49
Levine, George, 327
Lewis, C. S., 158–59
Lewis, Edwin Herbert, 111, 114, 213
Lincoln, Abraham, 5
Lincoln, C. Eric, 294
Lindemann, Erika, 67–68, 120
The Linguistic Individual: Self-
    Expression in Language and
    Linguistics (Johnstone), 332
lists, use of, 229–30
Literacy and the Survival of Humanism
    (Lanham), 370, 379–80
Literary Mind, The (Turner), 328
literature, cultural divide between
    composition and. See "The
    Cultures of Literature and
    Composition: What Could
    Each Learn from the Other?"
    (Elbow)
"Little Miracles, Kept Promises"
    (Cisneros), 316
Lloyd-Jones, Richard, 60, 98, 137,
    165–66, 397
Loban, Walter, 174
Lodge, David, 74, 413
Longinus, 14, 21
Lorenz, Konrad, 438
"Lost in the Funhouse" (Barth), 231
Loux, Ann, 63
Lu, Min-Zhan, 280–81, 303–17

Mac Donald, Heather, 390–91, 400–1,
    407
Macdowell, Ruth, 321
Madhubuti, Haki, 296
magic, writing and, 355–56, 357–58
Mailer, Norman, 236, 237, 320
Maimon, Elaine, 67
"Making a Case for Rhetorical
    Grammar" (Micciche), 207,
    250–66
Making of Knowledge in Composition,
    The (North), 100

Malcolm X, 261, 298, 299
male and female writers, stylistic
    differences between. See
    "Feminine Style: Theory and
    Fact, The" (Hiatt)
Mandel, Barrett, 66
Mankiewicz, Frank, 320
Manly, John Matthews, 115, 116
Manly Writing (Brody), 262–63
Mano, Sandra, 76
Markels, Robin, 120
Marzano, Robert, 100
Mathieu, Paula, 391–92
Mathis, Virginia B., 182–84
mature style, definition. See complex
    style, definition
Maynard, Joyce, 320
Mbiti, John S., 284
McCabe, Bernard, 68
McCrimmons, James M., 85
Mead, Margaret, 285
Meade, Richard, 119
meaning-style debate, 3
Meckel, Henry C., 166–67
Mellinkoff, Ruth, 439
Mellon, John, 89, 270–71, 273
Memering, Dean, 167–68
Menand, Louis, 389–90, 391, 393–94,
    396–97, 400–1, 406, 407
metaphors, 19–20, 21, 22–23
"A Method of Analyzing Prose Style,
    with a Demonstration Analysis
    of Swift's A Modest Proposal"
    (Corbett), 211
metonymy, 50
Micciche, Laura R., 207, 250–66
middle style, 14, 37, 46, 49–50
Milic, Louis, 62, 135–36, 140–45, 157,
    245, 246, 405–6
Miller, Edmund, 86
Miller, Susan, 307, 393
mimicry, in African American oral
    tradition, 297
Minock, Mary, 412, 423
Mitchell, Ruth, 108, 120–21
"Modeling: A Process Method of
    Teaching" (Harris), 67
"Modeling a Writer's Identity: Reading
    and Imitation in the Writing
    Classroom" (Brooke), 68–69

Modern English Grammar, A (Buehler), 273

Modern Rhetoric (Cleanth and Warren), 116

Moffett, James, 93–94, 95, 97–98, 350, 379

Momaday, N. Scott, 64–65

Mones, Leon, 116

montage, 235–37

Montaigne, Michel de, 141–42

More, Sir Thomas, 444

Morenberg, Max, 90, 102, 175, 267, 271

Morson, Gary Saul, 414, 424

Motives of Eloquence, The (Lanham), 382

motive spectrum of style/substance matrix, 436–44

Mulroy, David, 397–98

multicultural approach to style, teaching. *See* "Professing Multiculturalism: The Politics of Style in the Contact Zone"

Murray, Donald, 72, 95, 243, 345, 364

Murray, Lindley, 110, 111

"Music of Form, The" (Elbow), 126

Myers, Miles, 63

Napoleon, Reverend, 301

National Language Policy (CCCC), 279

"National Prose Problem, The" (Flannery), 340–41, 369–88
  Hirsch, critique of, 340, 370, 371, 372, 373–79
  Lanham, critique of, 340–41, 370, 371–73, 379–85

Neel, Jasper, 352

new classical pedagogy, 244–45, 246

Newman, Edwin, 242

Newman, John Henry, 212

new romantics pedagogy, 245–46

New Strategy of Style, The (Weathers and Winchester), 86, 180–82

Newsweek, 399

New Yorker, 389, 390, 393, 406

New York Times, 389, 407

New York Times Book Review, 224

Ney, James, 90

Norris, Raymond, 88

North, Stephen, 100

Notes toward a New Rhetoric (Christensen), 84, 85

"Not Just an American Problem but a World Problem" (Malcom X), 261

"An Occurrence at Owl Creek Bridge" (Bierce), 259–60

O'Donnell, Roy, 88

Of a Fire on the Moon (Mailer), 236

O'Hara, John, 321

O'Hare, Frank, 88, 89–90, 174, 207–8, 267, 269–71

Ohmann, Richard, 1, 135, 137, 138, 158, 160–61, 177–85, 212

O'Keefe, Daniel, 354

Olson, Gary, 260–61

Ong, Walter, 364

onkos (expansiveness), 24–25

On Lexis (Theophrastus), 18

On Prose Style (Aristotle), 18–36
  frigidities, 14, 21–22
  grammatical correctness, 14, 23–24
  onkos (expansiveness), 24–25
  periodic style, 27–30
  propriety, 14, 18–21, 25–26
  rhythm in prose, 26–27
  simile, 22–23
  syntomia (conciseness), 24–25
  virtues of style, 14, 18–21

On Style (Demetrius), 25

On Sublimity (Longinus), 21

On Teaching English (Bain), 112

On the Beach (Shute), 182–84

On the Sublime (Longinus), 14

oral discourse, 4

oral styles, African American. *See* " 'How I Got Ovuh': African World View and Afro-American Oral Tradition" (Smitherman)

Orator (Cicero), 14–15, 37–53
  delivery and use of language, 43–44
  elements of oratory, 42–43
  epideictic oration, 40–41
  grand style, 14, 15, 37, 46, 50–51
  middle style, 14, 37, 46, 49–50
  philosophers, style of, 45

Orator (Cicero) (*continued*)
  plain style, 14–15, 37–39, 46, 47–49
  poetic style, 45–46
  propriety, 14, 46–47
  sophist style, 45
organic theory of style, 244
  Milic on, 136, 142, 143–44, 405–6
  Tufte on, 158–60
"Originality and Imitation in the
    Work and Consciousness of an
    Adolescent Writer" (Phelps
    and Mano), 76
ornamentation, 14, 18–21
ornate form, theory of. *See* rhetorical
    dualism
Outline of Rhetoric (Genung), 269

Pace, Tom, 4, 395–96
paean, 27
Panegyric (Isocrates), 40
Panathenaicus (Isocrates), 40–41
"Paragraph Development in the
    Modern Age of Rhetoric"
    (Meade and Ellis), 119
"Paragraphing for the Reader" (Eden
    and Mitchell), 108, 120
paragraph theory, 17, 108–31
  in 18th and 19th century, 110–14
  argument for, 124–27
  Bain's contributions to, 108, 109,
    110, 112–14
  cognitive approach, 109, 122
  Corbett on, 216
  decline of, 109–10, 124
  descriptive view, 108, 109, 114–16
  empiricism and, 119–21
  functionalist view, 108, 109, 114–16
  in linguistics, 122–23
  in 1960s, 116–18
  in 1970s and 1980s, 119–21
  in other disciplines, 121–23
  prescriptive view, 108, 109, 112–14
  in psychology, 122
  in technical and professional
    writing, 122
Paragraph Writing (Newton and
    Denney), 114–15
paraphrasing, 417–18
Paris Review Interviews, 68

parody, 69–70, 415, 424–25
*Passionate State of Mind and Other
    Aphorisms, The* (Hoffer), 227
passive transformations, 163
Passos, John Dos, 233
Patterns of English (Roberts), 274
Peacham, Henry, 214
pedagogy
  of grammar (*See* pedagogy of
    grammar)
  of style (*See* pedagogy of style)
Pedagogy, 327
pedagogy of grammar, 136, 137–38,
    165–76
  Asker's study, 169
  Braddock, Lloyd-Jones and Schoer
    report, 165–66, 172, 173
  Frogner's study, 171–72
  Harris study, 172–73
  Hoyt's study, 168–69
  Meckel's report, 166–67
  Rapeer's study, 169
  rhetorical grammar pedagogy
    (*See* rhetorical grammar
    pedagogy)
  Segal and Barr report, 169–70
  sentence-combining and, 174–75
  Symonds experiment, 170–71
pedagogy of style, 6, 205–8
  Corbett on (*See* "Teaching Style")
  paragraph theory (*See* paragraph
    theory)
  "Revitalizing Style: Toward a New
    Theory and Pedagogy"
    (Rankin) (*See* "Revitalizing
    Style: Toward a New Theory
    and Pedagogy")
  rhetorical grammar pedagogy (*See*
    rhetorical grammar pedagogy)
  sentence-based pedagogies (*See*
    sentence-based pedagogies)
perceiver spectrum of style/substance
    matrix, 432–35
Perceptual and Motor Skills, 101
Perelman, Chaim, 71
periodic style, 27–30
Perl, Sondra, 340, 358, 359
Petrosky, Anthony, 347
Phaedrus (Socrates), 41
Phelps, Louise Wetherbee, 76

"Phenomenology of Error"
(Williams), 123
Philosophy of Composition, The (Hirsch),
177, 373, 374, 375, 376
Philosophy of Rhetoric (Campbell), 110
Pike, Kenneth L., 3
Pirsig, Robert M., 237
Pitkin, Willis, 119
plain style, 14–15, 37–39, 46, 47–49
Plato, 3, 23, 26, 41, 141, 142, 143, 413
play motive, in style/substance
matrix, 436–44
Poetics (Aristotle), 18, 19
Poole, Mary A., 182–84
Pooley, Robert C., 275–76
Popken, Randall, 108, 121
Porter, James, 70
Porter, Katherine Ann, 227
positional, dialogic imitation as,
420–21
Posner, Richard, 392
Poutsma, Henrik, 274
Pratt, Mary Louise, 7, 208, 280, 303,
307, 404
prescriptive view, of paragraph
theory, 108, 109, 112–14
Priestley, Joseph, 110
Pringle, Ian, 245
Problems of Dostoevsky's Poetics
(Bakhtin), 413
"Professing Multiculturalism: The
Politics of Style in the Contact
Zone" (Lu), 280–81, 303–17
analyzing style of real writers,
315–16
criteria used by mainstream in
dealing with idiosyncratic
styles, 304–5
dialogical coordination of
heteroglossia within and
outside of educated discourse,
305–6
handout used in classroom and
discussion thereof, 309–15
negotiation in student's choice of
code, 314–15
real *vs.* student writers, politics of
stylistic decisions by, 306–7
teaching method applying
multicultural approach, 307–16

propriety
Aristotle on, 14, 18–21, 25–26
Cicero on, 14, 46–47
prose rhythms, study of, 215–16
Protagoras, 23
proverbial statement, in Afro-
American oral tradition, 297
Pryor, Richard, 292, 295
psychological monism, 141–42, 143,
145, 244
Public Intellectuals: A Study of Decline
(Posner), 392
Public Interest, 390
Publics and Counterpublics (Warner),
393, 401, 402
public sphere, style in. *See* "Style and
the Public Intellectual:
Rethinking Composition in the
Public Sphere" (Butler)
punning, in Afro-American oral
tradition, 298
Purves, Alan C., 70
Purves, William C., 70
"Putting 'This and That Together' to
Question Sentence-Combining
Research" (Rosner), 101

Quinn, Arthur, 352
Quintilian, 5, 15, 54–58, 268

Rabaté, Jean-Michael, 124–25
Ramus, Peter, 3
Ranavaara, Irma, 232–33
Rankin, Elizabeth, 61, 206–7, 239–49
rap, power and dynamics of, 287–92
Rapeer, Louis, 169
Ratcliffe, Krista, 261
readability principle, 177, 185
"Reading, Writing, Rambling On"
(Harper's Magazine), 402–3
reality spectrum of style/substance
matrix, 444–48
*Refiguring Prose Style: Possibilities for
Writing Pedagogy* (Johnson,
Pace, eds.), 4, 395–96
Reflection on the Atom Bomb (Stein),
222
refrains, 232

"Relation of Grammar to Style, The" (Tufte), 137, 155–64
"Reminisces of Childhood" (Thomas), 236
repetends, 232
repetition, use of, 232–34
Republic (Plato), 23
Research in the Teaching of English, 92, 98
Research in Written Composition (Braddock, Lloyd-Jones and Schoer), 98, 165–66
"Research on Teaching Composition and Literature" (Meckel), 166–67
resumptive modifiers, 200
revisable, dialogic imitation as, 421–23
Revising Prose (Lanham), 4, 371
revision process, and style, 243–44
"Revision Strategies of Student Writers and Experienced Adult Writers" (Sommers), 243–44
"Revitalizing Style: Toward a New Theory and Pedagogy" (Rankin), 206–7, 239–49
  cognitive-process model of composing process, 242–43
  current-traditional paradigm, 240–42
  decline in pedagogy of style, 239–40
  new classical pedagogy, 244–45, 246
  new romantics pedagogy, 245–46
  new theory of style, criteria for, 247–48
  revision process, and style, 243–44
  style, defined, 239
  unconscious acquisition of style, 245–46
rhapsodes, 354
Rhetoric: Discovery and Change (Young, Becker and Pike), 3
"Rhetoric: Its Functions and Its Scope" (Bryant), 251–52
Rhetoric, The (Aristotle), 14, 18–36
Rhetorica ad Herennium, 214
"Rhetorical Choice and Stylistic Options" (Milic), 245
rhetorical dualism, 62, 136, 141, 142–43, 244
Rhetorical Grammar (Kolln), 4, 256

rhetorical grammar pedagogy, 207, 250–66
  commonplace book assignment, 256–60
  and critical pedagogy, 261
  cultural attitudes, beliefs and assumptions and, 262–63
  and empowering pedagogies, 260–64
  imitations of writers' form, 258–59
  need for rhetorical education, 251–52
  reason for, 252–53
  social power, grammar competency and, 263
  understanding how language is made and deployed for effect, 256–57
  as way of thinking, 252–56
Rhetorical Perspective (Daiker, Kerek and Morenberg), 102
Rhetoric for Writing Teachers, A (Lindemann), 120
Rhetoric of Pleasure, A: Prose Style and Today's Composition Classroom (Johnson), 4, 395–96
"Rhetoric of the Paragraph, The" (CCCC symposium), 116
rhythm
  Aristotle on, 26–27
  Corbett on study of prose rhythms, 215–16
  Johnson on, 354–55
rhythmic emphasis, 362
Richards, I. A., 423
Rickert, Edith, 115, 116
Ringbom, Hakan, 232
"Rip Van Winkle" (Irving), 257–58
Roberts, Paul, 148, 274
Robinson, Smokey, 299
Rodgers, Paul, 108, 114, 117–18, 123, 125, 216
Roemer, Kenneth, 64–65
Rohman, D. Gordon, 64
Romanticism, and imitation, 71–72
Rose, Bell, 308
Rose, Mike, 365
Rose, Shirley, 87, 92, 207–8, 267–76
Rose, William E., 273–74

Rosner, Mary, 101
Rousseau and Revolution (Durant and Durant), 228
Rudiments of English Grammar (Priestley), 110
Ruszkiewicz, John, 68
Ryan, Margaret, 174
Ryan, Sheila, 63

Safire, William, 242
Said, Edward, 316, 332
Saintsbury, George, 215
Sarmiento, Anthony, 375
satire, 444
Saying and Silence (Farmer), 340
"Say It Ain't So" (Fish), 406
schemes, 214
Schoer, Lowell, 60, 98, 137, 165–66, 397
Schroeder, Christopher, 4
Schuster, Charles, 411, 412
scientism, and imitation, 71–72
"Scientism and Sentence Combining" (Holzman), 100
Scott, Fred Newton, 114–15, 268–69, 271, 273
Secret Life of Our Times, The (Lish, ed.), 226
Segal, D., 169–70
Selzer, Jack, 68
Senn, Fritz, 226
Senses and the Intellect, The (Bain), 122
sentence-based pedagogies, 16–17
    anti-behaviorism criticism of, 16, 96–98
    anti-empiricism criticism of, 16, 98–100
    anti-formalism criticism of, 16, 93–94
    Christensen's generative rhetoric (See generative rhetoric)
    decline in, 91–103
    historical teaching of, 82–83
    imitation exercises, 85–87
    sentence-combining (See sentence-combining)
sentence-combining, 87–91
    See also sentence-based pedagogies
    criticisms of, 95–96, 99–101
    O'Hare's study of, 89–90, 174–75

Rose on (See "Down from the Haymow: One Hundred Years of Sentence-Combining")
teaching of grammar and, 174–75
Williams on, 188–89, 199–200
Sentence-Combining: A Composing Book (Strong), 90, 267
Sentence-Combining: A Rhetorical Perspective, 99
Sentence Combining: Improving Student Writing without Formal Grammar Instruction (O'Hare), 89–90, 174, 270
"Sentence Combining: Some Questions" (Freedman), 101
Sentencecraft (O'Hare), 90, 267, 269–70
sentence fragments, 227–29
sentence openers, 162
sentence rhetorics, 16
sermons/church raps, 292–94
" 'Servile Copying' and the Teaching of English" (Gruber), 97
Shakespeare's Use of the Arts of Language (Joseph), 210
Shannon, Claude, 446
Shattuck, Roger, 224
Shaughnessy, Mina, 254, 308
Sheridan, Thomas, 215
Sherman, L. A., 213
"Shifting Relationships Between Speech and Writing" (Elbow), 348
Shor, Ira, 261
Shute, Nevil, 182–84
signal spectrum of style/substance matrix, 429–32
simile, 22–23
Sin Boldly! Dr. Dave's Guide to Writing the College Paper (Williams), 390
Sister Carrie (Dreiser), 305, 306
Skwire, David, 178–80
Smith, William, 101
Smitherman, Geneva, 4, 280, 283–302
Snakes (Young), 291
social justifications for imitation, 68–70
Socrates, 41
solecism, 24
Somer, John, 225

"Some Tentative Strictures on
    Generative Rhetoric"
    (Johnson), 94
Sommers, Nancy, 243–44
sophists, 351–53, 354
sound, and style. *See* "Ancient and
    Contemporary Compositions
    That 'Come Alive': Clarity as
    Pleasure, Sound as Magic"
    (Johnson)
"Sounding the Other Who Speaks in
    Me: Toward a Dialogic
    Understanding of Imitation"
    (Farmer), 341–42, 410–427
Southern, Terry, 236
Southern Workman, 291
Sowande, Fela, 284
Spencer, Jacqueline, 63
spontaneity, in Afro-American oral
    tradition, 298
Squire, James R., 174
stadia, 118–19
"Stadium of Discourse, The" (Rogers),
    117, 118
Stark, Heather, 122
Starkey, Penelope, 71, 86
Stein, Gertrude, 222, 228–29, 233, 262,
    304–5, 306–7
Stern, Arthur, 119
Sterne, Laurence, 222
Stevens, Wallace, 428–29
story, 362
Stovall, Sidney T., 182–84
Strenski, Ellen, 62
Strong, Patrick, 384
Strong, William, 90, 267, 271
strung-on style, 28
Strunk, William, 115, 138, 177
Student's Book of College English
    (Skwire and Chitwood), 178–80
"Students' Right to Their Own
    Language" (Committee on
    CCCC Language), 279,
    399–400
Studies in Classic American Literature
    (Lawrence), 222
style
    in classical rhetoric, 5
    cultural influences on (*See* cultural
        influences on style)

defined, 1
formal *vs.* plain style, 2–3
future of, 7–8
grammar, relation to (*See* grammar,
    relation of style to)
importance in rhetoric and
    composition, 8
integration into composition
    classes, 4
levels of, 2
meaning-style debate, 3
pedagogy of (*See* pedagogy of style)
persuasive ability of, 5
possibilities and limitations of,
    5–6
study of style, rise and fall of
    (*See* stylistic studies, rise and
    fall of)
theories of (*See* theories of style)
types of, 2–3
Style: An Anti-Textbook (Lanham), 379,
    384
Style: Ten Lessons in Clarity and Grace
    (Williams), 4, 245
Style and Text (Ringbom, ed.), 232
"Style and the Public Intellectual:
    Rethinking Composition in
    the Public Sphere" (Butler),
    341, 389–409
    clarity, complication of notion of,
        400–3
    criticisms of composition studies,
        389–92
    disciplinary divisions, 403–5
    grammar, status of, 396–99
    public intellectuals for composition
        studies, lack of, 392–94
    "Students' Right to Their Own
        Language," implications and
        effect of, 399–400
    style, role of, 394–96
"Style/Substance Matrix" (Lanham),
    342, 428–48
    attention, 446–48
    bi-directional dynamic flow of
        motive spectrum, 441–43
    form for its own sake, 439–40
    game motive, 436–44
    motive spectrum of, 436–44
    perceiver spectrum of, 432–35

play motive, 436–44
  reality spectrum of, 444–48
  self consciousness, 446–48
  signal spectrum of, 429–32
stylistic justifications for imitation,
  61–63
stylistic studies, rise and fall of, 2, 3–4,
  5, 13–17
  "Apologies and Accommodations:
    Imitation and the Writing
    Process" (Farmer and
    Arrington), 15–16, 59–81
  "Erasure of the Sentence, The"
    (Connors), 82–107
  Orator (Cicero) (*See Orator*)
  On Prose Style (Aristotle) (*See On
    Prose Style*)
  Quintilian on imitation, 5, 15,
    54–58
  Rankin on, 239–40
  "Whatever Happened to the
    Paragraph" (Duncan),
    108–31
stylization, dialogic imitation and,
  415–16
Sullivan, Dale, 71–72
summative modifiers, 200
Symonds, Percival M., 170–71
synchronicity, 234–35
syntactic maturity, 88
syntactic patterns, study of, 211–14
Syntactic Structures (Chomsky), 87
syntactic symbolism, 163–64
syntax, grammar and. *See* grammar,
  relation of style to
syntomia (conciseness), 24–25

tagmemic approach, to paragraphs,
  117
Talese, Gay, 236
*Talkin and Testifyin: The Language of
  Black America*, 280
"Talk-Write: A Behavioral Pedagogy
  for Composition" (Zoellner), 96
Teaching English Grammar (Pooley),
  275–76
*Teaching of English Grammar: History
  and Method, The* (Barbour),
  273

"Teaching Style" (Corbett), 205–6,
  209–18
  diction, study of, 211–12
  features of style that are observable
    and analyzable, study of,
    211–16
  figures of speech, study of, 214–15
  grammatical competence and,
    210–11
  historically, in Renaissance era,
    209–10
  imitative exercises, 217
  objectives of, 211
  paragraphing, study of, 216
  prose rhythms, study of, 215–16
  syntactic patterns, study of,
    211–14
Teaching the Universe of Discourse
  (Moffett), 93–94
"Teach Writing as a Process, Not a
  Product" (Murray), 345
Temptations, 299
Textual Carnivals (Miller), 307, 393
textured style, 199
Theophrastus, 18
theories of style
  Milic on (*See* "Theories of Style and
    Their Implications for the
    Teaching of Composition")
  "Revitalizing Style: Toward a New
    Theory and Pedagogy"
    (Rankin) (*See* "Revitalizing
    Style: Toward a New Theory
    and Pedagogy")
  "Theories of Style and Their
    Implications for the Teaching
    of Composition" (Milic),
    135–36, 140–45, 244
  organic theory, 136, 142, 143–44,
    244, 405–6
  psychological monism, 141–42, 143,
    145, 244
  responding in public sphere, 405–7
  rhetorical dualism, 136, 141, 142–43,
    244
Theremin, Lev, 447
Things Fall Apart (Achebe), 300
Thomas, Dylan, 236
Thomas, Lowell, 148
Thompson, Robert F., 284

Tibbetts, A. M., 94–95
To Kill a Mockingbird (Lee), 258–59
Tom Jones (Fielding), 182–84
tonal semantics, in Afro-American oral tradition, 300–1
"Topic Sentence Revisited, The" (D'Angelo), 120
topic (subject) sentence, 112, 113, 114, 116, 120, 121, 126
Tough, Sweet & Stuffy (Gibson), 157
Tourney, Leonard, 71
Toward a Philosophy of the Act (Bakhtin), 420
Toward a Speech Act Theory of Literary Discourse (Pratt), 404
transformational-generative (TG) grammar, 87, 88, 89
Transformational Sentence Combining: A Method for Enhancing the Development of Syntactic Fluency in English Composition (Mellon), 89, 270
Trask, Haunani-Kay, 315–16
Tristram Shandy (Sterne), 222
tropes, 214
Tufte, Virginia, 135, 137, 155–64
turned-down style, 28
Turner, Mark, 328
"Twenty Alternatives to the Study of Grammar" (Judy), 174
"Twirling at Ole Miss" (Southern), 236
Two Cheers for Democracy (Forster), 227

Ulysses (Joyce), 228
unconscious acquisition of style, 245–46
U.S.A. (Passos), 233
"Use Definite, Specific, Concrete Language" (Ohmann), 138, 177–85
"Uses of Classical Rhetoric, The" (Corbett), 85
Utley, Thomas, 120
Utopia (More), 444
utterances, imitation's relationship to, 73–75

Validity in Interpretation (Hirsch), 373, 374
van Dijk, Teun, 122–23
Veblen, Thorstein, 444
vigorous style. *See* grand style
virtues of style, 14, 18–21
Vitanza, Victor, 352 402–3
voice as discourse, 346–48
Vonnegut, Kurt, 259
Vygotsky, L. S., 16, 76, 411

Walborn, Eric, 63
Walshe, R. D., 84–85
War Against Grammar, The (Mulroy), 397–98
Warner, Michael, 393, 401, 402
Warren, Robert Penn, 116
Washington Post, 396
Way to Rainy Mountain, The (Momaday), 64
Weathers, Winston, 4, 62, 244
   "Grammars of Style: New Options in Composition" (*See* "Grammars of Style: New Options in Composition")
   New Strategy of Style, The (Weathers and Winchester), 86, 180–82
Weisser, Christian, 392
Wells, Susan, 98–99, 184
Wendell, Barrett, 83, 113
West, Cornell, 316
"Whatever Happened to the Paragraph" (Duncan), 108–31
"When Earth's Last Picture is Painted" (Kipling), 438
"Where Are We Going? And What Are We Doing" (Cage), 231
Whitburn, Merrill, 3
White, E. B., 115, 138, 177
Whitehead, Alfred North, 446
Whitman, Walt, 222
Whitmore, Charles, 116
"Why I Write" (Didion), 254
"Why Johnny Can't Write" (Mac Donald), 390–91

"Why Johnny Can't Write" (*Newsweek* issue), 399

Wicker, Tom, 321

Williams, David, 390

Williams, Joseph, 4, 86–87, 99, 123, 135, 138–39, 186–201, 244, 245, 340, 361, 362, 364

Williams, Raymond, 316, 345

William Shakspere's Small Latine & Lesse Greeke (Baldwin), 210

Wilson, Flip, 292

Wimsatt, William, 157

Winchester, Otis, 86, 180–82

Winkler, Victoria, 65

Winterowd, W. Ross, 66, 95, 96, 99

Wolfe, Tom, 223, 226, 233

Woodson, Linda, 239

Woolf, Virginia, 5, 232–33

Wordsworth and Schelling (Hirsch), 373

Worsham, Lynn, 365

Wright, Richard, 288–90

Wriston, Walter, 448

"Writer's Audience Is Always a Fiction, The" (Ong), 364

The Writers Options: College Sentence Combining (Daiker, Kerek, and Morenberg), 175, 267, 270, 271

Writing and Sense of Self (Brooke), 69

Writing of English, The (Manly and Rickert), 115

Writing with a Purpose (McCrimmons), 85

Writing with Clarity and Style (Harris), 352

Writing with Power (Elbow), 355

Yancey, Kathleen Blake, 396

Yngve, Victor, 190

Youdelman, Jeffrey, 185

Young, Al, 291

Young, Richard E., 3, 61, 64, 239, 240, 241–42, 246–47

Zen and the Art of Motorcycle Maintenance (Pirsig), 237

Zepernick, Janet, 397

Zidonis, Frank, 87, 88, 89

Zoellner, Robert, 96